VICTORIA FORNER

PROSCRIBED HISTORY
The Role of Jewish Agents in Contemporary History

IV

THE HOLOCAUST, A NEW DOGMA OF FAITH FOR HUMANITY

VICTORIA FORNER

PROSCRIBED HISTORY
*The Role of Jewish Agents
in Contemporary History*
IV
THE HOLOCAUST, A NEW DOGMA OF FAITH FOR HUMANITY

Cover illustration:
Denkmal für die ermordeten Juden
(Memorial to the Murdered Jews of Europe) in Berlin

*HISTORIA PROSCRITA IV
La actuación de agentes judíos en la Hª Contemporánea
Holocausto judío, nuevo dogma de fe para la humanidad*
First published by Omnia Veritas in 2017

Translated from Spanish and published by
OMNIA VERITAS LTD

OMNIA VERITAS®
www.omnia-veritas.com

© Omnia Veritas Limited - Victoria Forner - 2025

All rights reserved. No part of this publication may be reproduced by any means without the prior permission of the publisher. The intellectual property code prohibits copies or reproductions for collective use. Any representation or reproduction in whole or in part by any means whatsoever, without the consent of the publisher, the author or their successors, is unlawful and constitutes an infringement punishable by articles of the Code of Intellectual Property.

CHAPTER XII 11

JEWISH HOLOCAUST, NEW DOGMA OF FAITH FOR HUMANITY 11

Part 1 Persecution and Deportation of European Jews................ 14

From emigration to deportation 15
Deportation of the Hungarian Jews.. 27

Part 2 About the camps in Germany 45

Buchenwald: the testimonies of Paul Rassinier and Eugen Kogon 47
Dachau 61
Bergen-Belsen 67

Part 3 Belzec, Treblinka and Sobibor, three "extermination camps 75

Belzec 76
Extermination by electrocution in Belzec 78
Other means of extermination in Belzec 85
From high voltage currents to tailpipes 89
The "Gerstein Report" on Belzec 93
Wilhelm Pfannenstiel, witness in Belzec 98
Archaeological investigations in Belzec 100
Belzec, transit camp 107
Treblinka 110
Confusion over method of extermination at Treblinka 113
Carbon monoxide is also a must for Treblinka 117
Treblinka, a fabled camp where anything is possible 120
John Demjanjuk's trial in Jerusalem 125
Treblinka investigation with GPR (Ground Penetrating Radar) 127
Sobibór 129

Part 4 Auschwitz 137

I. G. Farben 139
Propaganda by Jewish organisations in the USA 142
The War Refugee Board (WRB), at the origin of the Auschwitz fable 145
Rudolf Höss' confession, second pillar of the Auschwitz fable 148
On the crematorium ovens at Auschwitz-Birkenau 157
The high mortality rate in Birkenau 160
The *Leuchter Report* on Auschwitz-Birkenau and Majdanek 162
Short review of the *Leuchter Report* 164
David Cole, a Jewish revisionist, exposes Auschwitz fable 174
The *Rudolf Report* and the forensic investigation at Auschwitz 177

Part 5 The persecution of revisionists for thought crimes 183
1. Main victims of persecution in Germany: 185

Joseph Burg, a Jewish revisionist persecuted by Nazis and Zionists 185
Thies Christophersen convicted of "bringing the state into disrepute" 187
Wilhem Stäglich, the judge who demanded justice for Germany 190

Ernst Zündel, "Revisionist Dynamo", model of resistance 193
Germar Rudolf: persecution and destruction of an eminent scientist 209
Horst Mahler, from radical leftist to Holocaust denier 220
Sylvia Stolz, the uncompromising lawyer 228
Günter Deckert, a persistent symbol of freedom of expression 236
Udo Walendy, imprisoned for publishing revisionist texts 239
Ursula Haverbeck. The indecent condemnation of a venerable old woman 241
Reinhold Elstner, the revisionist who burned himself alive 246

2. Main victims of persecution in France: 250

François Duprat, murdered by Jewish terrorists 250
Roger Garaudy, the philosopher pilloried for denouncing Israel 251
Robert Faurisson, revisionism's essential alma mater 259
Vincent Reynouard, "Hearts go up!" 270

3. Main victims of persecution in Austria: 274

Gerd Honsik, victim of PSOE's surrender to Zionism 274
David Irving sentenced to three years in prison in Vienna 278
Wolfgang Fröhlich, the "canary" still singing in the cage 282

4. Main victims of persecution in Switzerland: 287

Jürgen Graf and Gerhard Förster sentenced for writing and publishing books .. 287
Gaston-Armand Amaudruz, one year in prison for an octogenarian 290

5. Main victims of persecution in Belgium and the Netherlands: ... 293

Siegfried Verbeke, stubborn fighter for freedom of expression 293

6. Main victims of persecution in Spain 298

Pedro Varela, an honest bookseller victim of hatred and sectarian intolerance .. 298
Post Scriptum 314
Other booksellers and publishers persecuted in Catalonia 316

7. Main victims of persecution in Sweden: 320

Ditlieb Felderer, the mocking Jew using corrosive satire 320
Ahmed Rahmi, the architect of *Radio Islam* and leading Muslim revisionist 322

8. Main victims of persecution in Australia: 327

Frederick Töben, imprisoned in Germany, England and Australia 327

9. Other victims of persecution for thought crimes: 335

All Against Catholic Bishop Richard Williamson 335
Haviv Schieber, the Jew who slashed his wrists to avoid deportation to Israel .. 338
Hans Schmidt, the American imprisoned for four words 339
Arthur Topham, convicted in Canada for "hatred" of Jews 340

10. Appendix on the ruthless persecution of nonagenarians 343

    Laszlo Csatary 344
    Samuel Kunz... 344
    Johan Breyer 345
    Oskar Gröning 345
    Reinhold Hanning 346
    Siert Bruins 346
    A 91-year-old woman 347

CHAPTER XIII 348

THE FIRST BIG LIE OF THE 21ST CENTURY: THE ATTACKS OF 11 SEPTEMBER 2001 348

    A new Pearl Harbour or the lie needed to start the war....................... 349
    Relevant events prior to the attacks 352
    The attacks 356
    Significant events after the attacks... 363
    On Osama bin Laden, Al Qaeda and the fake Arab-Muslim trail 366
    The truth is known, but all remain silent and obey. 369

BIBLIOGRAPHY 373
OTHER BOOKS 391

CHAPTER XII

THE JEWISH HOLOCAUST, NEW DOGMA OF FAITH FOR HUMANITY

Never in the history of mankind has there been a circumstance such as the one we will study in this chapter: a historical fact has become a dogma of faith and cannot be questioned by historians, scientists or researchers of any branch of knowledge. Two Jewish historians, Pierre Vidal-Naquet and Léon Poliakov, signed the declaration of faith that has become universally accepted. In it they said: "There is no need to ask how such a mass death was technically possible. It was possible because it took place. This is the obligatory starting point of any historical research on the subject. It is this truth that we simply have to remember. The existence of the gas chambers cannot be debated". Today, questioning all the paraphernalia surrounding the Holocaust myth is a thought crime and has become a criminal offence in the penal codes of many countries. Revisionists have been prosecuted and sentenced to years in prison for racial hatred or anti-Semitism. They are shunned by the media and their works do not deserve any attention, as they are considered to be of no interest and should not be disseminated.

Of course, if the arguments and theses of revisionism were pamphlets lacking the slightest rigour, one could accept the general disinterest in their approach; but this is not the case, quite the contrary. The works presented cover the different aspects of the alleged extermination of six million Jews and are extremely convincing. Any reader interested in discovering the historical truth will find in the works of the revisionists all that can be demanded of a rigorous researcher. Despite this, the number of supposedly democratic Western countries that enact laws infringing on freedom of thought and expression in relation to the Holocaust is increasing year by year. Today these countries are: Austria, Belgium, Bosnia-Herzegovina, Canada, Czech Republic, France, Germany, the Netherlands, Hungary, Liechtenstein, Luxembourg, Poland, Portugal, Romania, Spain and Switzerland.

At the Nuremberg trial, the victors accused the defeated Germany, specifically the Nazis, of having planned and ordered the physical extermination of Europe's Jews and of having used gas chambers as weapons of mass destruction to carry out this extermination. Since then, the Holocaust myth has been consolidated by massive media propaganda and the unconditional collaboration of Western leaders. On November 26, 1991, Ian J. Kagedan, Director of Government Relations for the B'nai B'rith Lodge of

Canada, told the *Toronto Star*, "the dogma of the Jewish Holocaust is the cornerstone of the New World Order arch, the fundamental tenet of the new age religion."

To achieve this goal, the "mass media" - television, agencies, newspapers, publishing houses and the film industry - are in complete control. The Hollywood production companies, the jewel in the crown of the all-encompassing Jewish propaganda empire, invest billions every year in the non-stop production of spectacular Holocaust propaganda and brainwashing films for people all over the world: 170 Holocaust films were released on the world market between 1989 and 2003 alone. With all these means, a fantasy world is created in the minds of the viewers, which makes it possible to falsify history. Not only the Holocaust doctrine is promoted, but any idea that is useful to realise the Jewish utopia of dominating the Earth. All nations and all races suffered enormously during the Second World War, but no race or nation has exploited their suffering as the Jews have done, and after the end of the war they emerged as the triumphant minority. This was acknowledged on 11 April 1953 by Dr. Max Nussbaum: "The position of the Jewish people in the world today," he declared, "is, in spite of our enormous losses, ten times stronger than it was twenty years ago".

In 1980, Professor Robert Faurisson summed up the conclusions of revisionist research in one sentence: "The alleged Hitlerite gas chambers and the alleged genocide of the Jews form a single historical lie, which has enabled a gigantic political-financial swindle, whose main beneficiaries are the state of Israel and Zionism and whose main victims are the German people - but not their leaders - and the Palestinian people as a whole". The Holocaust, then, is the focal point of a strategy put in place by international Jewish organisations; but it is, above all, a Zionist chimera, since it was conceived by the Zionists as a ruse to achieve their goals. Those who pushed hardest to get the Jews out of Europe were the Zionists, who had multiple organisations working to send them to Palestine. Faurisson, born in 1929 to a French father and a Scottish mother, a professor of Latin and Greek, a specialist in the analysis of modern and contemporary French literary texts, as well as in text and document criticism, taught at the Sorbonne and the University of Lyon until he was banned from teaching because of his revisionist positions. Physically assaulted ten times by Jewish fanatics, he has been banned from the French media: press, radio and television, and has been convicted on several times by the courts. He last appeared in court in Paris on 11 July 2006.

Holocaust museums, more than 250 around the world, have become the temples of a new religion taught in the schools of the Western world; not as a rudimentary doctrine, but as an incontrovertible historical fact turned into a dogma of faith. No religion today has the power to imprison apostates who do not believe in any of its dogmas, yet heretics of the religion of the

Jewish Holocaust are persecuted, arrested, tried, convicted and imprisoned. Why can there be no questioning of what really happened during World War II? Who are the revisionists and what are the main findings of their painstaking research? Why are prestigious scholars from various fields of knowledge and culture treated as criminals for bringing the results of their work to international public opinion? Why can one deny God, Christ, Mohammed, offend Christians and Muslims, despise the symbols of all religions, while, on the other hand, questioning the Holocaust is considered anti-Semitism and is punishable under criminal law? These and other questions will be the focus of our attention in the pages that make up this twelfth chapter.

PART 1
PERSECUTION AND DEPORTATION OF EUROPEAN JEWS

The fact that Jews backed the British during the Great War and offered to facilitate American entry into the conflict in exchange for the *Balfour Declaration* was considered a betrayal in Germany. Anti-Jewish sentiments increased in the period of the Weimar Republic, a time when the influence of Jews, although they constituted only 1% of Germany's population, was consolidated in all areas: in addition to being the apostles of communism, they controlled the economy, culture and were widely predominant in the legal and judicial professions, health care, show business.... All this led the Nazis, rightly or wrongly, to regard them as a perverse element in the community, because they considered their values decadent and saw them as a factor in the degeneration of German cultural life. Convinced of their harmful influence, they tried to promote their complete emigration from Germany. As we have seen, a large majority of German Jews had already emigrated with much of their property by 1939. In its publication *Unity in Dispersion*, the World Jewish Congress states that 'the majority of German Jews managed to leave Germany before the outbreak of hostilities' and acknowledges that around 400,000 Jews left the country before September 1939. The Prague Jewish Emigration Institute also stated that 260,000 Jews had left the former Czechoslovakia. To these must be added 220,000 of the 280,000 Austrian Jews, who also emigrated before the outbreak of the war. On the basis of these figures, it is estimated that only 360,000 Jews remained in the three countries.

As a preamble and starting point, it is worth recalling some facts already outlined in previous chapters in order to situate the issue of the persecution of the Jews, desired by international Zionism in order to encourage the influx of people to Palestine. As we know, while the economic boycott and the declaration of "holy war" against Germany had the effect of exacerbating anti-Jewish sentiments among German citizens, the ZVFD, "Zionistische Vereinigung für Deutschland" (Zionist Union of Germany) took advantage of the circumstance and hastened to seek agreement with Hitler that German Jews would be sent to Palestine under the best possible conditions. The Nazis naively played along and began to collaborate with Zionism. Jewish authors such as Lenni Brenner, Klaus Polkhen, Ralph Schönman and others have shown that there is no doubt about this fact, which was denounced by the CV "Centralverein deutscher Staatsbürger Jüdische Glaubens" (Central Union of German Citizens of Jewish Faith). This organisation, which was in favour of the assimilation and integration of Jews into the society in which they lived, declared that the actions of the ZVFD, whose aims were exactly the opposite, had been "a stab in the back" for them. Thus, while the Zionists acted freely and published the newspaper *Jüdische Rundschau* without hindrance, Hitler began to take action against non-Zionist Jewish organisations. Let us also remember that the B'nai B'rith lodge was only banned when the war began in 1939.

We refer the reader to chapter eight, where the secret pact between the Third Reich and Jewish Palestine has been explained in detail. At the 18th Zionist Congress in Prague in August 1933, an anti-Hitler resolution was overwhelmingly defeated, while a resolution banning all forms of anti-Nazi protest was passed. We know that the Haavara Agreement, the cornerstone of the understanding between Nazis and Zionists, was signed by the ZVFD, the German Ministry of Economic Affairs and the Anglo-Palestinian Bank, which was an instrument of the Jewish Agency. In 1937 the collaboration was intense and the Zionists, whose priority objective was to outnumber the Arabs in population, asked the Nazis to maintain their anti-Semitic pressure and intensify the emigration of Jews to Palestine. Recall that in 1938 a thousand Jews were trained in camps in Germany and Austria to prepare them for work in Palestine.

Fearing that Jews emigrating from Germany and Poland would be able to settle safely in America or other European nations, the World Zionist Organisation refused to participate in the Evian Conference held in France during the second week of July 1938. Nothing was more contrary to the interests of the Zionists than resettlement in host countries: their aim was to provoke the persecution that would enable them to direct the emigration of Europe's Jews to Palestine. Germany offered 3 billion marks to the International Red Cross or the League of Nations to manage the money and give it to countries willing to receive Jews the Nazis did not want on their territory; but the unwillingness of most countries to accept the emigrants served the purposes of international Zionism. The Evian Conference was a disgrace in every respect and made it clear to the world that the Zionists were concerned only with getting millions of Jews into the Holy Land as soon as possible in order to proclaim the State of Israel in Palestine.

From emigration to deportation

Needing to preserve its position vis-à-vis the Arab countries of the Middle East, Britain began to toughen its stance with on Jewish immigration to the Holy Land. In May 1939 London published the White Paper and the entry of Zionists into Palestine was reduced to a trickle. Germany, however, continued its policy of encouraging emigration and evacuation in order to get rid of them for good, and it was only in 1941 that plans for deportation to Eastern Europe began to be outlined. Volume 13 of the Nuremberg Military Trials (NMT) contains a report submitted by the US prosecution. It is file NG-2586, a multi-part document summarising Germany's policy on the deportation of Jews. Arthur Robert Butz reproduces the text in full in *The Hoax of the Twentieth Century*, a work published in 1976 that remains essential to understanding much of what happened during the war. The author of the memorandum, dated 21 August 1942, was Martin Luther, a senior Foreign Office official. Similarly, in *Les Mythes fondateurs de la politique israélienne* (1996), Roger Garaudy cites several texts that coincide with the extensive document presented by Arthur R. Butz.

According to the documents uncovered by these and other authors, the Nazis decided to promote by all means Jewish emigration from their territory. Marshal Göring, plenipotentiary for the implementation of the Four Year Plan, established in 1939 the Reich Central Department for Jewish Emigration and handed over its direction to SS Lieutenant General Reinhard Heydrich, head of the Security Police. The Foreign Office became a member of the committee of the Reich Central Department in February 1939. It is of interest to recall, as almost no one does, that Chaim Weizmann, President of the World Zionist Organisation and the Jewish Agency, declared war on Germany on behalf of Jews everywhere on 5 September 1939, only days after the invasion of Poland. On 8 September the *Jewish Chronicle* reproduced Weizmann's words: "The Jews make common cause with Britain and will fight in the camp of the democracies.... The Jewish Agency is prepared to take immediate steps to utilise the manpower, technical competence and resources of the Jews."

In the file NG-2586 submitted by the Americans in Nuremberg, it is stated: "The present war offers Germany the opportunity and also the obligation to solve the Jewish problem in Europe". This document states that after the overwhelming victory over France, it was proposed in July 1940 "the expulsion of all Jews from Europe and the request to France for the island of Madagascar as a reception territory for Jews". The philosopher Roger Garaudy, Communist deputy and member of the Central Committee, vice-president of the National Assembly between 1956-1958, clarifies that it was on 24 June 1940, after the French defeat, that Heydrich sent a letter to Ribbentrop proposing "eine territoriale Endlösung" (a territorial final solution), which consisted of the deportation to Madagascar. In this letter Heydrich informed Minister Ribbentrop that "the problem of the approximately 3,250,000 Jews in the areas under German control could no longer be solved by emigration, so a territorial final solution would be necessary".

The head of the Jewish Department of the Foreign Ministry, Franz Räder, warned in July 1940 that it would take four years to move all the Jews to the French island and that the operation would require "considerable means". In other words, in the midst of the euphoria of the fantastic success of the blitzkrieg against France, the Nazis went from seeking the emigration of Jews from Germany to expulsion from the conquered countries. To this end, the Reich Foreign Office agreed to undertake the groundwork for this operation. The Reich Security Main Office (RSHA, "Reichssicherheitshauptamt") accepted the task of implementing the evacuation and supervising the Madagascar plan, a large-scale deportation that could only be undertaken by this state body. The detailed plan for the evacuation and settlement of the Jews in Madagascar drawn up by the RSHA was approved by the Foreign Ministry in August 1940. The project, which involved several phases, was to be financed by an inter-European bank. Dr. Paul Schmidt, Hitler's interpreter, in his book *Hitler's Interpreter. The Secret History of German Diplomacy 1935-1945* recalls that Hitler told Mussolini that "a State of Israel could be founded in Madagascar".

In France, Holland and Belgium, the German administrative authorities received orders regarding the actions to be taken in these countries. With the approval of the German Embassy in Paris, the military command in France was the first to issue a decree on the treatment of Jews in occupied France on 27 September 1940, followed by similar texts in the Netherlands and Belgium. As in the German laws, these decrees did not consider the citizenship of Jews, and criticism from abroad immediately followed. The US embassy lodged a note of protest. NMT document NG-2586 contains the following comment on the matter: "The Reich Foreign Minister has decided in the case of the American protests that he does not consider it wise to have military regulations issued to make an exception for American Jews. It would be a mistake to reject the objections of friendly countries (Spain and Hungary) and on the other hand to show weakness towards the Americans".

In addition to being an extremely costly and complicated logistical operation, the transfer of European Jews to Madagascar required the use of trains, ships and other means of transport that were a priority for the continuation of the war effort. With the invasion of Russia in June 1941, things took a definite turn: the Madagascar plan was recognised as unworkable, and the idea began to take hold that it was easier to move the Jews to eastern Europe, where opened up new areas for resettlement. On 31 July 1941, Göring, again under the influence of the intoxication of victory produced by the rapid advance into the USSR, sent the famous letter to Heydrich often quoted by Jewish historians such as Raoul Hilberg, Gerald Reitlinger and Leon Poliakov to support his exterminationist theses. The following is an excerpt from the letter reproduced by Arthur R. Butz in *The Hoax of the Twentieth Century*, taken from vol. 13 of the NMT (Nuremberg Military Trials):

> "As a supplement to the task entrusted to you in the decree of 24 January 1939, namely to solve the Jewish question through emigration and evacuation, which is the most favourable way according to the conditions prevailing at present, I now charge you to carry out all preparations relating to the organisational, factual and financial questions for a

complete solution of the Jewish question in those territories of Europe under German influence.

If the competence of other central organisations is affected in relation to this issue, these organisations should be involved.

I also ask you to send me as soon as possible a draft outlining the organisational, operational and financial measures already taken for the implementation of the planned final solution of the Jewish question".

Those who claim that this text is proof that the "Final Solution" amounted to the mass murder of European Jews usually suppress the reference to "emigration and evacuation". Jewish historians and gentile supporters claim that it was at the Wannsee Conference, near Potsdam, that the extermination of European Jewry was decided. The Wannsee Conference was held on 20 January 1942. Heydrich, following the instructions he had received, called together all the departments concerned with the task of evacuating the Jews to the East. Martin Luther, the author of memorandum NG-2856 submitted by the US prosecution at NMT, writes the following in that document:

"... SS Lieutenant General Heydrich organised on 20 January 1942 a conference of all the organisations involved, which was attended by State Secretaries from other Ministries and myself as a member of the Foreign Ministry. At the conference General Heydrich explained that Reich Marshal Göring had appointed him on the instructions of the Führer and that the Führer had now authorised the evacuation of the Jews to the East instead of emigration....

At the conference of 20 January 1942, I demanded that all questions relating to countries outside Germany should first have the consent of the Foreign Office , a demand with which Lieutenant General Heydrich agreed and which was faithfully complied with, as indeed did the Reich Security Main Office (RSHA) handling Jewish affairs, which from the beginning took all measures in frictionless co-operation with the Foreign Office. The RSHA proceeded in this matter in an almost exaggeratedly cautious manner".

Many German Jews had already emigrated, some to Palestine, taking advantage of the Haavara Agreement, others to the United States or other European countries. After the Wannsee Conference, those who had not done so began to be evacuated. Likewise, the governments of Slovakia, Croatia and Romania agreed to the evacuation policy and did not demand the repatriation of Jews from their countries who were on German territory, but accepted their deportation to Eastern Europe. Thanks to the report of Martin Luther, Under-Secretary of State in the Foreign Ministry who was present in Wannsee, it became known in the NMT that since the manpower did not cover the required needs, the Slovaks were asked to organise the deportation of 20,000 young Jews, to which the Slovak government agreed. The Slovaks informed the Reich Foreign Office that they were prepared to contribute 500 Marks for each Jew evacuated. This decision prompted the Slovak Episcopate to raise its objections to the deportations with the Slovak government. There is a very significant paragraph in Luther's memorandum about the effect of the Slovak Church's protest:

> "... In the meantime 52,000 Jews had been taken out of Slovakia. Due to the influence of the Church and the corruption of some officials, 35,000 Jews had obtained special legitimisation. However, Minister-President Tuka wanted the evacuation of the Jews to continue and therefore requested help through the diplomatic influence of the Reich . The ambassador was authorised to lobby the head of state, Dr. Tiso, who was informed that the exclusion of 35,000 Jews came as a surprise in Germany, especially since Slovakia's cooperation on the Jewish problem had hitherto been highly appreciated. These instructions had been passed on by the Under-Secretary of State in the Political Division and by the Secretary of State."

There is another source of Jewish origin that complements Martin Luther's memorandum, namely the *Report of the Budapest Jewish Rescue Committee*, a 188-page handwritten document by Dr. Rudolf Israel Kastner (Rezsö Kasztner), published in part by fellow Jew Lenni Brenner in his *51 Documents. Zionist Collaboration with the Nazis* (2002). According to Kastner's writing, in March 1942 waves of Slovak Jews entered Hungary as refugees. In the same month of March, the leaders of the Bratislava Jewish Rescue Committee, Erwin Steiner, Gisi Fleischman and Rav Weissmandel, contacted the Nazis to stop the deportations of Slovak Jews for ransom. Kastner's text continues as follows:

> "The German in charge, Captain Wisliczeny, declared that after the deportation of 55,000 Jews, he was prepared to give up the deportation of the remaining 25,000 Jews for $50,000, two dollars for each life. The money was supposed to come from abroad, but it did not arrive or arrived very slowly. Wislizceny waited many weeks for the agreed sum, then sent his own request for payment by transferring three thousand Jews to Poland. After this, the money arrived and the deportations ceased".

In 1948 the International Committee of the Red Cross (ICRC) published in Geneva a report in three volumes, the *Report of the International Committee of the Red Cross on its Activities during the Second World War*, to which we will refer from now on, since Arthur R. Butz reproduces pages 641 to 657 of the first volume, which belong to chapter VI ("Special Categories of Civilians") and refer specifically to the situation of Jews in various European countries. It confirms that thousands of Jews were forced to leave Slovakia; but it adds: "a large part of the Jewish minority was allowed to remain in the country and at certain periods Slovakia was even regarded as a safe haven for Jews, especially those coming from Poland. Those who remained in Slovakia seem to have enjoyed safety until the end of August 1944, when there was an uprising against the German forces." As for the Slovak Jews interned in camps, the report says: "While it is true that the law of 15 May 1942 had resulted in the internment of several thousand Jews, they were taken to camps where the conditions of food and lodging were tolerable and the inmates were allowed to perform paid work on terms similar to those of the free labour market. By 1944 the Jewish community had achieved almost a complete cessation of forced immigration into German-controlled territories."

On the other hand, the Croatians also saw fit to deport Jews from Croatia, although the evacuation of some 4-5,000 Jews from the Italian-occupied areas of Dubrovnik and Mostar did not meet with Rome's approval. From May 1943 to the end of 1945, the ICRC report states that the Red Cross delegation "assisted the Jewish community of Zagreb, which was paid an average of 20,000 Swiss Francs per month by the American Joint Distribution Committee in New York". The report adds that in October 1944, "the German authorities, in accordance with measures taken in neighbouring countries, arrested the Jews of Zagreb and confiscated their food stocks." The Red Cross delegation, however, succeeded in getting the Croatian government to return these stocks.

The deportation of foreign Jews on French territory also posed a problem. Otto Abetz, the German ambassador in occupied France, regarded them as elements who could not be given privileged treatment under any circumstances, since many of them had been shown to be responsible for acts of terror and sabotage. Again, the Italian Jews in France constituted an additional setback. Italy's economic interests played a decisive role, and the Germans felt that if they could not be evacuated, they should at least be repatriated by Mussolini. Members of the International Committee of the Red Cross visited the camps in southern France, where in the Gurs camp there were six thousand Jews from the Bavarian Palatinate, who were assisted with "appropriate measures". In addition, the ICRC report provides information on Jews from Poland in France who had obtained permission to enter the United States. Thus, according to the Red Cross, "they were taken for American citizens by the German occupiers, who agreed to recognise the validity of about three thousand passports issued to the Jews by South American consulates". The report reveals that "they were accommodated in camps exclusively for Americans in Vittel."

As for the Bulgarian and Romanian Jews, the negotiations with these countries confirm once again that the so-called "Final Solution" was territorial and aimed at the expulsion of the Jews from Germany's sphere of influence in Europe. In Romania, in particular, the worst time for Jews came when the "Iron Guard", with the support of the Gestapo and the SS, took power in September 1940. Jews were then subjected to persecution and deportation, but in September 1941 Marshal Antonescu seized power and collaboration began. The Red Cross delegate in Bucharest received a letter from Antonescu in which he said: "The Romanian government repudiates any practical solution contrary to civilised customs and to the detriment of the Christian spirit which dominates the conscience of the Romanian people. The ICRC worked closely with the Romanian Red Cross. The document we have been using states that from 1943 "the Committee's task in Romania was made easier because the delegate was able to inspire confidence in the Romanian Government." In December 1943, as certified in the ICRC report, "Mr. Mihan Antonescu met with this delegate which greatly facilitated the Committee's activities on behalf of the Jews." Let us look at the full excerpt:

> "These talks focused on the case of Jews deported across the Dniester to Ukraine, who were natives of Bessarabia and Bukovina. These provinces were returned to Romania after World War I, but under the German-Soviet treaty fell back under Soviet rule at the beginning of World War II. After the 1941 changes, Romania, which had become Germany's ally against the USSR, reoccupied these two provinces. The Jews, whom the Romanians considered guilty of having welcomed the return to the bosom of Russia too well, were deported. The Romanian government's plan, prepared in agreement with Germany, seemed to be to settle these Jews in territories in the Sea of Azov region. However, this could not be done unless the USSR was defeated. In view of the Russian victories, the Romanian government decided at the end of 1943 to repatriate the survivors of this deplorable deportation, the number of whom fell from 200,000 to 78,000. Mr Mihan Antonescu supported the delegate's efforts in Bucharest to be entrusted with the task of providing the means for this repatriation and authorised him to travel throughout Transnistria distributing clothes and aid to these unfortunate people. In addition, the delegate succeeded in getting the Jews of Czernowitz, the only ones who were still obliged to wear the yellow star, to stop wearing it, since this mark exposed them to the brutality of the German troops with whom they came across".

The fact that 122,000 deportees did not return does not imply that they were exterminated, nor does it imply that all of them necessarily lost their lives. It is possible that many chose to remain in the Soviet Union. In a December 1944 report, the Bucharest branch of the Red Cross states: "Thanks to the dispatches of the New York Joint Committee and the collections made on the spot, it was possible to come to the aid of 183,000 repatriated Jews". In short, the surviving German documents show that Germany's plans had nothing to do with the mass extermination of European Jewry. All the Red Cross reports also show that the Germans did what the documents said, and this has been confirmed by neutral authorities and sometimes even by hostile sources.

Arthur R. Butz provides in *The Hoax of the Twentieth Century* texts from the proceedings of the Wannsee Conference, contained in document NG-2586-G presented at Nuremberg (NMT) by the Americans. "The emigration programme," it reads unambiguously, "has been replaced by the evacuation of the Jews to the east as a more complete possibility, in accordance with the prior authorisation of the Führer." While these references to evacuation to the east are repeated again and again, not a single text has been found that proves that there was a programme of extermination. This is acknowledged by Jewish professor Aryeh Leon Kubov of the Israel Center for Jewish Documentation in Tel Aviv, who states bluntly: "There is no document signed by Hitler, Himmler or Heydrich that speaks of extermination of the Jews... and the word 'extermination' does not appear in Göring's letter to Heydrich in connection with the final solution of the Jewish question". The Allied press also reported repeatedly during the war on the resettlement programme. Here are some significant paragraphs from NG-2586-G, which, astonishingly, are wielded by Holocaust propagandists to try to prove that the "final solution" was an extermination programme:

> "Appropriately enough, the Jews will now, in the area of the final solution, be brought to the East in a suitable way to be used as labour. In large work groups, with separation of the sexes, the Jews capable of work will go to these areas and will be employed in road construction, in the task of which a good part will undoubtedly fall by natural selection. The remainder who are finally able to survive - undoubtedly those who are more resilient - must be treated appropriately, for these people, representing natural selection, will be regarded as the germ of a new Jewish evolution if they are granted freedom. (See the experience of history).
>
> In the programme for the implementation of the final solution, Europe is to be combed from west to east. The Reich area , including the protectorate of Bohemia-Moravia, will have to be taken care of in advance, solely for reasons of accommodation and other social-political needs. The evacuated Jews will first be moved group by group to so-called transit ghettos, so that they can later be transported from there to the east.
>
> An important provision for the complete execution of the evacuation, as SS General Heydrich explained, is the exact determination of the categories of persons to be included. It is not planned to evacuate Jews over sixty-five years of age, but to take them to an old people's ghetto - Theresienstadt is being built. Alongside these groups of elderly people - of the perhaps 280,000 Jews who on 31/10/1941 were in the old Reich and in Austria, perhaps 30% are over sixty-five - Jews with serious war

wounds and war decorations (Iron Cross, First Class) will also have to be included in the ghettos for the elderly....
In connection with the problem of the effect of the evacuation of the Jews on economic life, Secretary of State Neumann reported that the Jews employed in important war industries could not be evacuated for the time being, since no suitable substitutes would be available. General Heydrich pointed out that these Jews, in accordance with the directive approved by him for the execution of the present evacuation, would not be evacuated."

In order to completely uproot the Jews who were evacuated, they were stripped of their property: money, furniture, jewellery, businesses, etc. so that they would have nothing to push them to return one day. This was precisely what the Zionists needed: people with nothing to lose who would be offered protection and a new life in the future state of Israel. It is therefore undeniable that hundreds of thousands of Jews were deported and their property confiscated. Their situation and that of other prisoners, as will be seen below, became progressively worse as conditions in the camps deteriorated as a result of Germany's inevitable defeat. Establishing figures for the number of deportees is not easy, as many European Jews emigrated to the United States, Palestine or ended up in Soviet territory, as was the case with Polish Jews in the territories occupied by the USSR. In addition, some 300,000 left Poland after the German invasion and moved to the communist zone as well.

On the other hand, the fact that Jews migrating from Europe to the United States did so on German, Austrian, Dutch, Polish, etc. passports makes it impossible to have reliable figures. It is known, however, that after the end of the war Jewish immigration to the United States was very significant, even though the Zionists operated freely in the displaced persons camps and worked to send as many as possible to Palestine. These camps were controlled by UNRRA, a UN agency that was headed first by Herbert Lehman and then by Fiorello La Guardia. These two Zionists allowed British and American officers out of uniform to give military training to thousands of Jews, preparing them for the invasion of Palestine. By 1944 nearly half a million Zionists were already in the Holy Land. Five years later, in 1949, the Israeli government reported that there were 925,000 Jews in Palestine. By 1957 almost a million Arabs were refugees in neighbouring countries, while the Jewish population had doubled to 1,868,000.

Reitlinger and Hilberg, based on German documents and Dutch Red Cross reports for Dutch Jews (about 100,000), give very similar figures for the total number of deportees from a dozen Western European countries: Germany, Austria, Czechoslovakia, Denmark, France, Belgium, Luxembourg, Norway, the Netherlands, Italy, Yugoslavia and Greece. According to Reitlinger there were 816,000, while Hilberg puts the number at 870,000. Since both are exterminationists or exterminationists, they assume that all were killed.

By contrast, revisionists insist that Jews and Gentiles were used as labour and argue that it made no sense to set up a resettlement programme in the east and organise a complicated and costly logistical operation in the middle of the war just to liquidate the Jews . The questions they ask are: What was the point of wasting money, thousands of tons of fuel, personnel and countless trains needed to transport troops and ammunition if the purpose was to kill Jews thousands of miles from their places of origin? Why was the construction of the camps undertaken if they were only to serve as places of extermination? Would it not have been easier to execute the Jews after their arrest if that was indeed what was intended?

It is especially difficult to know more or less exactly what happened in Poland. One Jewish source, the *American Jewish Year Book 1948-1949*, puts the number of Jews living in Poland at 390,000 at the end of 1945. On the other hand, a Canadian Jewish journalist, Raymond Arthur Davies, a staunch Communist who lived in the USSR during the war, published *Odyssey through Hell* in New York in 1946. In it he reveals that Schachmo Epstein, the leader of the Jewish Anti-Fascist Committee, confessed to him that through evacuation and other measures the Soviet Union had saved at least 3,500,000 European Jews. According to Davies, 250,000 Polish Jews living in German-occupied Poland fled to the Soviet Union in 1939. He details the prominent role of Jews in the USSR, where thousands of factories and war plants were run by Jews. A very large number of them, Davies notes, reached leading positions in the army and the administration. This is confirmed by another Jewish author, Ralph Nunberg, in *The Fighting Jew* (1945), also published in New York, in which Nunberg proudly acknowledges that no fewer than 313 Soviet generals were Jewish. R. A. Davies, for his part, recounts his contacts with Jewish officers in the Red Army, who boasted to him that they had eliminated German soldiers in mass executions. This Canadian journalist reveals that he had credible information that no fewer than 35,000 European Jews were fighting alongside Tito's partisans.

Arthur R. Butz refers to a twenty-page study written by Meir Korzen and published by the Government of Israel (*Yad Vashem Studies*, vol. 3). According to Korzen, hundreds of thousands of Polish Jews were dispersed within the USSR under an evacuation programme that began in June 1940. From September 1941 onwards, many of these refugees were granted Soviet citizenship, but were prevented from leaving the USSR. At the end of the war, as we have seen, Beria chose the new leaders of the Polish communist regime from among these Jews. Korzen writes that "they changed their names to Polish-sounding ones in order to keep their Jewish origin secret." The Joint Distribution Committee in New York maintained contact with Jewish refugees in the Soviet Union during the war and assisted them in their post-war displacements. In his work on Polish Jews deported and dispersed within the Soviet Union, Korzen, although he was assisted by the Zionist government in his research, acknowledges that his report contains huge gaps in the figures. As for the Jews already living in the USSR, a census of early 1939 states that there were more than three million. Of these, according to the first post-war census, some two and a half million remained in the country despite the wave of migration to Palestine and the United States and the casualties they must inevitably have suffered during the war.

Of these casualties, it should be noted that there is a legend that the "Einsatzgruppen" (operations groups) exterminated Russian Jews by means of mobile gas chambers and mass executions. At the Nuremberg trials, the Soviet representative of the Public Prosecutor's Office, Roman Rudenko, accused the Einsatzgruppen of murdering no less than one million Jews. In *The Destruction of the European Jews* Raul Hilberg puts the figure at 900,000. The fact is that these operations groups, four special units composed of elements of the Gestapo (Secret State Police) and the SD (SS Security Service), totalling some three thousand men, ruthlessly eliminated Jews and non-Jews who were part of the partisans who continually harassed the Germans on Russian territory. Their activity constituted a major threat to the army, so Hitler gave Himmler carte blanche to act as he saw fit on his own responsibility. Thus, in retaliation for the attacks on German troops, partisans, commissars and communist functionaries were hanged or shot immediately after their capture. It should be noted that the partisans were not sparing when it came to liquidating soldiers who fell into their hands.

SS Reichsfuhrer Heinrich Himmler visited Mussolini in Rome on 11 October 1942 and complained to the Duce that thousands of Jews in the occupied territories were partisans engaged in sabotage and espionage. Himmler acknowledged that women and children were collaborating with the partisans in the USSR and admitted that many captured Jews had been summarily executed by German units. Mussolini apparently used the interview to remind Himmler that the Catholic Church was opposed to extreme measures against the Jews and warned him that a policy of excess could change the attitude of Pius XII, who advocated an Axis victory over the Soviet Union.

There is no doubt, therefore, that the number of Jews who swelled the ranks of these partisan groups operating in the rear was considerable, so that indeed tens of thousands of them, perhaps around 80,000, including women and children, were executed. In wartime, such crimes are common practice in armies. Recall that the Americans in Vietnam, for example, had no qualms about napalming civilian populations in villages that supposedly offered cover or shelter to "Viet Cong" guerrillas. It should be noted, on the other hand, that many murders attributed to the Einsatzgruppen were committed by Ukrainian nationalists who had deeply hated Jews since the time of the civil war following the 1917 Revolution. Moreover, between 22 June and 2 July 1941, the communists mass-murdered many Ukrainians before retreating. In the eyes of the civilian population, Soviet Jews were held responsible for the killings, as they were considered accomplices of the communist criminals.

For security reasons, Polish Jews were grouped together during the war in ghettos located in the largest cities. Various Jewish authors refer to the large ghettos in Lodz, Warsaw, Bialystok, Lwow and Grodno. In Lithuania and Latvia, there were ghettos in Vilna, Kovno and Riga. As always throughout history, in these ghettos the Jews themselves governed themselves through the "Judenrat", a Jewish Council with its own police. The Jewish Council inevitably cooperated with the German authorities, who often asked it for manpower that was recruited by the Jewish authorities themselves. As a result, there were organisations opposed to the "Judenrat", whose members were considered puppets in the service of the Germans. However, thanks to this collaboration, the Germans lifted the initial ban on Jewish schools, and Jewish children were educated in schools operating under the authority of the Ghetto Council or privately. Books were produced in the ghetto's cultural life, as well as theatrical and musical performances. In addition, a Jewish social welfare agency, the "Jüdische Unterstützungsstelle" (JUS), supplied the ghettos with food, medicine and clothing, which it obtained from the German civil administration. The JUS also maintained contacts with the German Red Cross and foreign organisations that provided money and other goods. Until December 1941, most of this foreign aid came from the Joint Distribution Committee, but the entry of the US into the war made these activities illegal.

Eugene M. Kulisher, a recognised authority in the field of demography and migratory movements, studies the problem of the expulsion and evacuation of the Jews in an extensive section of *The Displacement of Population in Europe* (1943), a text accessible online on the Internet. This book, which is considered absolutely reliable because the author uses up to two dozen European institutions as sources, reveals what Germany's enemies certainly knew about National Socialist policy towards the Jews, regardless of the misleading propaganda campaign. Regarding the ghettos, Kulisher reports that the first ones were established in Lodz in the winter of 1939-1940. The Warsaw ghetto was established in the autumn of 1940. All Jews living outside it were ordered to enter its confines and Poles living inside it were ordered to leave. On 18 October 1941 *The New York Times* reported that the German authorities had had to send numerous ambulances to Warsaw for the disinfection of the ghetto, where some 400,000 people lived on an area of 6.4 km2 surrounding the former medieval ghetto. Epidemics in the ghettos were known to be frequent and were attributed by the Germans to the "lack of discipline" of the inhabitants. Many Jews from abroad were transported to the Warsaw ghetto, and by the spring of 1942 about half a million people lived there.

According to Polish circles in London, some 1,300,000 Jews had been grouped into eleven ghettos scattered in different parts of the country. In early summer 1942 the Institute of Jewish Affairs put the figure at 1.5 million. On 28 October and 10 November 1942, the Secretary of State for Security in the Polish General Government issued regulations on Jewish ghettos in five districts of the General Government: Warsaw, Lublin, Kraków, Radom and Galicia. According to Kulisher, in November 1942 all Jews in the General Government were confined in two types of areas: ghettos inside the large cities and purely Jewish-inhabited towns from which the non-Jewish population had been evacuated. In total there were thirteen ghettos and forty-two Jewish towns throughout the Polish General Government.

After the invasion of the USSR, ghettos were established in western Ukraine, western Belarus, the Baltic States and also in occupied Russia. Had the invasion of the USSR ended in a Soviet defeat, the policy of resettlement of Jews to Eastern Europe would surely have continued as planned, and the masses gathered in the Polish General Government would have ended up in these ghettos in countries further east. Hundreds of thousands of Jews passed through the transit camps, considered extermination camps by official historiography, on their journey further east. When a new resettlement was announced, it was up to the ghetto's Jewish Council to submit lists of those to be displaced to the German authorities.

The uprising of the large Warsaw ghetto on 19 April 1943 led to an accelerated transport of Jews to the east. After fierce resistance and a battle that enjoyed worldwide coverage and publicity, the uprising was put down on 16 May and the ghetto was finally liquidated. There were an estimated 12,000 casualties and about 60,000 of its inhabitants were moved further east. Treblinka became the transit camp for this new resettlement. Three months later the Bialystock ghetto was also evicted. There were clashes for a few days, but resistance was weak. According to the *Holocaust Encyclopaedia*, on 18 August deportations began to Treblinka, where exterminationists insist that deportees were gassed, Majdanek, Poniatowa or Auschwitz. A train with 1,200 children, initially planned to be sent to Palestine, passed through Treblinka at and was finally directed to Theresienstadt, the so-called "model camp", where numerous cultural and artistic activities, especially in the field of music, were taking place.

Deportation of the Hungarian Jews

Thanks to the *Report of the Budapest Jewish Rescue Committee* (*The Report of the Budapest Jewish Rescue Committee*) we have very interesting information about the activities of the Zionists in Budapest during the war. Rudolf Israel Kastner, also known as Reszö Kasztner, chairman of the Committee and author of the handwritten report, submitted the document in 1946 to the WZO (World Zionist Organization). Since Kastner was liquidated on 15 March 1957 in Tel Aviv by Zeev Eckstein, a former Israeli secret service agent, it is useful to look briefly at this assassination before addressing the controversy over what happened to the Hungarian Jews.

The assassination of Dr. Kastner in March 1957 was the first political crime in Israel's history. Someone decided that Rudolf Kastner had better disappear, apparently because he knew too much about Zionist collaboration with the Nazis and about his responsibility for certain events. The criminal, Zeev Eckstein, although repentant, never gave up the people who had ordered him to eliminate Kastner. It all began in 1952, when a Jerusalem hotelier named Malquiel Grünwald accused members of the Labour government of collaboration with the Nazis. Kastner, who in 1952 was spokesman for Dov Yosef, the Minister of Industry and Trade in Ben Gurion's government, was particularly targeted. In 1953, the Labour government, urged by Kastner, sued Grünwald for libel. During the trial, Grünwald's lawyer, Shmuel Tamir, accused Kastner of having testified on behalf of SS Colonel Kurt Becher at Nuremberg, and produced a letter from Kastner to Eleazer Kaplan, an official of the Jewish Agency over which David Ben Gurion and Moshe Sharett presided, in which he wrote: 'Kurt Becher was a colonel in the SS and served as liaison between Himmler and myself for our rescue work. He was released from prison in Nuremberg by the Allied occupation forces thanks to my personal intervention". Judge Halevi wanted to know who had given Kastner permission to advocate for Becher on behalf of the Jewish Agency and the World Jewish Congress. Kastner then spat out a list of leading Jewish Agency figures in Israel.

Things became so complicated that on 29 June 1955 *The New York Times* reported that the Israeli government, which was on trial along with Kastner, was being asked to resign. The trial lasted three years. Joel Brand, a close associate of Kastner's whom many would have liked to see dead, testified in court and it was established that David Ben Gurion, Moshe Sharett and Chaim Weizmann himself were also implicated in the alleged extermination of the Hungarian Jews: a non-existent extermination that propaganda had certified and could no longer be denied. Ultimately, Judge Hálevi, considering all the evidence, ruled in favour of Malquiel Grünwald, and the Government of Israel appealed to the Supreme Court. Kastner's murder took place before the decision of the Supreme Court, which finally ruled in 1958 that he was not guilty of collaboration, because, as one of the judges wrote, "There is no law which can impose obligations on a leader in an emergency situation with regard to those who depend on his leadership and follow his instructions". However, the Supreme Court found that he had committed perjury on behalf of a Nazi.

Having explained this, we can now look at the report submitted by Kastner to the WZO in 1946, bearing in mind that his editor, Lenni Brenner, publishes only excerpts selected by himself in *51 Documents. Zionist Collaboration with the Nazis*. Kastner, one of the leaders, if not the chairman, of the "Vaadat Ezra Vö-Hazalah" (Jewish Relief and Rescue Committee) in

Budapest, confirms that, in addition to a horde of Jews from Slovakia, waves of Polish Jews entered Hungary as refugees in March 1942. Many of them were provided by the Committee with financial aid, accommodation and forged legal documents. To help the great multitude of Slovak and Polish refugees it would have been necessary to draw on the funds of "Keren KaYemeth" (Jewish National Fund) and "Karen HeYesod" (Foundation Fund), but the Zionist leaders who controlled them refused to provide them on the grounds that they had already been collected for Palestine. However, in the autumn of 1942 the aid organisations of the Jewish Agency in Istanbul, headed by Chaim Barlas, sent the Budapest Committee a "modest sum" to be used for the relief of Polish Jews. Along with the money they sent a message from Palestine Jewry: 'Help the refugees! Help the Polish Jews!' According to Kastner, the organisation for the rescue of Polish Jews was codenamed 'Tikhul' and headed by Joel Brand, whose testimony at Kastner's trial in Tel Aviv raised eyebrows.

All went relatively smoothly until March 1944, when the Germans occupied Hungary, fearing that the Hungarians would break their alliance with them. The first to learn that the occupation was imminent were the leaders of the Jewish Rescue Committee, who on 14 March received confidential information from Joseph Winniger, one of their collaborators in the Military Intelligence Service, which put them on alert. A conference was immediately convened, attended by Otto Komoly, Joseph Fischer, Ernest Marton, Hillel Danzig, Moshe Schweiger, Joel Brand and Rudolf Kastner. The Budapest Jewish Rescue Committee decided to immediately alert Istanbul. In addition, contacted the Bratislava Committee, which had good connections with SS officials, in order to find out what the Germans' intentions were towards Hungarian Jewry. On the other hand, the Haganah, the instrument of Jewish protection, was to be immediately activated. The Haganah refused to make its presence felt during the first three or four months after the occupation, not least because Moshe Schweiger, its leader in Hungary, was arrested by the SS.

During the first days of the occupation, which began on 19 March, members of the 'Vaadah' (the Jewish Rescue Committee) and Zionist leaders held several meetings to plan the work to be done. Otto Kolmony was charged with contacting Hungarian politicians and the Christian churches, whom he asked for assistance. Moshe Krause was instructed to place himself under the protection of the Swiss Embassy and to ask for the intervention of neutral diplomats. Dr. Kastner and Joel Brand were put in charge of establishing relations with the Germans. Dieter Wisliczeny, Adolf Eichmann's assistant and head of the "Judenkommandos" in Budapest, was the contact who enabled them to enter into negotiations with the SS.

On 5 April 1944 Kastner and Brand were received by Wisliczeny, to whom they presented their aspirations, which, according to Kastner's report to the WZO, were as follows: to safeguard the lives of Hungarian Jews; that they should not be ghettoised; to prevent deportations; and that Hungarian Jews with visas should be allowed to emigrate and enter other countries. Here is what Kastner wrote about the response: "...Naturally," said Wisliczeny, "we insist that the influence of the Jews in all spheres must be radically reduced. But we do not insist on placing them in ghettos or in deportations. This possibility could only occur if we received orders from our superiors directly from Berlin." Let us look at the fragment of Wisliczeny's reply which refers to immigration to other countries: "As far as Immigration is concerned, I must ask my superiors for instructions. Personally, I do not believe that our high command would be interested in immigration in limited numbers. But if you were willing to devise a plan for the immigration of at least a hundred thousand Jews, we would try to influence Berlin to make it possible."

Kastner's report adds that Wisliczeny asked for two million dollars and demanded, as a sign of 'goodwill' and that the Jews had the capacity to raise the money, that ten percent be paid in advance, i.e. two hundred thousand dollars to be paid in pengös, the then current Hungarian currency. The conversion amounted to six and a half million pengös and was to be made on the black market. The Jews decided to pay this amount in order to keep the connection open and buy time. It should be noted that Budapest had for years been a city that had sheltered refugees from Central and Eastern Europe and had thus become an epicentre of the "Alijah" (Jewish immigration to Palestine). As for Captain Dieter Wisliczeny, he was later head of the Gestapo in Slovakia and ended up in the hands of the Czech communists, who tortured him into a wimp in Bratislava prison in November 1946 before executing him. Poliakov and other exterminationists use his statements to support the extermination of six million Jews.

Adolf Eichmann[1], the director of Jewish policy at the Reich Security Main Office (RSHA) of the SS and a specialist in all matters Jewish, had remained in the background, but came into the picture as soon as negotiations began to take shape. Joel Brand was received by Eichmann on 25 April 1944. The meeting took place at the Majestic Hotel in Budapest. Kastner reproduces verbatim in his report the words with which the interview began:

---

[1] The case of Adolf Eichmann became a world event when on 2 May 1960 he was captured in Argentina by Mossad agents, who transferred him to Israel to stage a show trial. Media from all over the world lent their support to the Jerusalem travesty. On 28 November and 5 December 1960, *Life* magazine published Eichmann's alleged memoirs in order to prepare international public opinion. Although he had never been accused of participating in executions of Jews, after appropriate torture and brainwashing, he testified at the trial that he had been responsible for the extermination of more than six million Jews. Furthermore, even though he knew he was going to be executed, he was forced to write "authentic confessions" in which he ratified and increased the number of Jews he had eliminated. Readers interested in learning more about the affair can read Paul Rassinier's *The Truth About the Eichmann Trial*, published in 1962.

"I have made enquiries and found that the 'Joint' is able to make the payments (after the experience in Austria and Czechoslovakia, anything to do with Jews and money was synonymous with 'Joint'). Naturally, I know about the conferences between Krumey and you, but that is just a trifle. Now I offer you the great opportunity to save a million Hungarian Jews. I have heard that Roosevelt in a radio speech expressed his fears for the lives of the Hungarian Jews. Now I will give you the opportunity to do something for them. I don't need money. I don't know what to do with it. I need war materials, especially trucks. Therefore, I have decided to allow you to travel to Istanbul so that you can pass on this generous German offer to your friends there. I will transfer all Hungarian Jews to Germany, they will be picked up at a certain place. I will wait two weeks for a reply from Istanbul. You will return immediately from Istanbul to bring me the answer from your friends. If the answer is positive, you may take all the Jews as far as I am concerned, but if the answer is negative, you will have to abide by the consequences."

It should be noted that the parenthesis in the fragment is verbatim, and is therefore a statement by Kastner, who admits that the Germans were well aware of the power of the Joint Distribution Committee in New York, whose agents in the USSR, as we have seen, were fiercely opposed by Stalin. As for Hermann Krumey, the name given in the text, he is a collaborator of Eichmann. Kastner notes in his report that Eichmann's sentences were brief and biting, and that Brand tried to convince him that it would be easier to reach an agreement if the Germans gave up their deportation plans. Joel Brand asked Adolf Eichmann to put these plans on hold because "it would be easier to conclude this matter". It seems logical that if the final solution had been a plan to exterminate the European Jews, Eichmann's offer would not have been possible. Had there been a superior order and a plan to exterminate them, Eichmann's proposal to exchange them for trucks would not have been feasible.

Joel Brand flew to Istanbul on a German courier plane. Before the trip, between 8 and 17 May, he was negotiating with Eichmann in Budapest. Eichmann, convinced of the powerful influence the Jews exerted over the Allies, especially the Americans, was confident that the offer of ten thousand trucks for one million Jews, i.e. one truck for the lives of one hundred people, would be accepted. "You can assure your friends," he guaranteed, "that we will not use the trucks at the front, but in the interior. At most, in case of emergency, they could be employed abroad on the Russian front." As soon as Joel Brand left for Turkey, contacts with Eichmann were taken over by Kastner and Hansi Brand (Joel's wife). By May, the deportations had already begun. On what Eichmann told them about them, Kastner wrote in his report: "There was absolutely no chance that he would suspend or stop the deportations. We were not to think that he was so stupid, because if he stopped the deportations no one abroad would negotiate with him. We would have to make an effort to be more effective in Istanbul. He would not allow himself to be taken for a fool and his patience had limits." After the interview, they hurried to send a telegram to Istanbul to announce that the deportations would not stop, so they had to act quickly because time was against them.

Kastner reports of a further meeting on 22 May, during which Eichmann confirmed his authorisation for six hundred selected Jews to emigrate; however, because of Hitler's obligations to the Grand Mufti of Jerusalem, he did not allow them to travel to Palestine via Istanbul, but they were to go to Germany, then on to France and Spain, from where they could go on to Africa. During the following days telegrams were received from Istanbul in which Brand said that he was holding hopeful discussions and that several British and American delegates of the Jewish Agency were backing him; however, it all ended in a big fiasco and Brand never returned to Budapest. In our opinion, if the delivery of ten thousand trucks was supposed to save the lives of hundreds of thousands of Jews, it is incomprehensible that the operation was not authorised. If the extermination of Hungarian Jewry had indeed taken place, the Zionist leaders who thwarted it would be guilty before history and before their people.

The following is a very brief summary of Joel Brand's vicissitudes. In the fourth volume of *The Collapse of the West: The Next Holocaust and Its Aftermath*, Francisco Gil-White devotes Chapter XXI, entitled "The 'Kastner Case'", to a detailed account of what happened. Gil-White claims to be indebted to Ben Hecht, who attended the trial as a journalist and in 1961 published a documented account of the trial in *Perfidy*, which is Gil-White's primary source. The information on the Tel Aviv trial against Kastner is of great interest, but we are now interested in Brand's handling of the case since he arrived in Istanbul with Bandi Grosz. According to this American author, no one waited for them at the airport and they found accommodation in a hotel, where they were visited by a representative of the Jewish Agency who took them to the Istanbul Relief and Rescue Committee.

Brand explained that he was to return to Budapest in two weeks to liberate the first 100,000 Jews. It was decided, however, that the presence of a senior official from the Jewish Agency Executive was required, so Venia Pomeranietz was appointed to bring Moshe Sharett to Istanbul. In view of the British refusal to allow Sharett to enter Turkey, Chaim Barlas, head of the Jewish Agency in Istanbul, suggested to Brand that he travel to British Syria to meet him, but Brand feared arrest by the British and, since Eichmann had told him that his return and his word would suffice, he asked to be allowed to return to Budapest with a letter from the Relief and Rescue Committee saying that the deal was approved. After an acrimonious discussion, Barlas forced Brand to travel to Syria in the company of Ehud Avriel of the Halutzin (Pioneers) movement.

When the train stopped in Ankara, Brand told Judge Halevi, Avriel got off the train for a few minutes and then two agents, one from Vladimir's Revisionist Party Jabotinsky and one from Agudat Israel, a religious Zionist party, got on to warn him not to continue his journey, as the British were waiting for him in Aleppo to arrest him. In his statement Brand claimed that Avriel reassured him and encouraged him to continue the journey. As soon as they arrived in Aleppo, Ehud Avriel got out of the carriage on the pretext of making arrangements, at which point British agents proceeded to arrest Brand. They took him to their headquarters, where, in their presence, he was finally interviewed by Moshe Sharett, the leader of the Jewish Agency's Political Department who would later become Israel's foreign minister and prime minister. Sharett, who maintained excellent relations with the government in London, told him that he could no longer return to Istanbul or Budapest. "I was surprised and bitterly objected," Brand told Judge Hálevi, "but he told me there was no alternative."

Ultimately, Joel Brand was taken to Cairo via Palestine. There he was interrogated again and again by the British and began a 17-day hunger strike in protest. Four months later he was released, but forced to enter Palestine. Brand naively wrote to Chaim Weizmann, president of the World Zionist Organisation (WZO), telling him what had happened, asking him to accept Eichmann's offer and explaining that the Jews were being betrayed by their leaders in Palestine. Weizmann's reply, dated 29 December 1944 in Rehovot, was submitted to the Tel Aviv court as evidence by Shmuel Tamir, the lawyer of the whistleblower Grünwald. Here is the text:

"Dear Mr. Brand,
Please forgive me for taking so long to reply to your letter. As I am sure you saw in the press I have been travelling a great deal and generally have not had a spare moment since I arrived here. I have read your letter and the enclosed memorandum and will be happy to meet with you one day next week - say about the 10th of January.
Miss Itin - my secretary - will contact you to arrange the interview.
I send you my warmest regards.
Sincerely, Chaim Weizmann".

Interestingly, after writing to Brand offering him an interview, Weizmann reneged on his promise and the meeting never took place. Joel Brand concluded his testimony before Judge Halevi thus: "Whether I was wrong or wrong, whether for good or for evil, I have cursed the official leaders of the Jews ever since. All these things will plague me until the day of my death. It is much more than a man can bear."

The deportation of Hungarian Jews in the spring of 1944 has been the subject of constant discussion among revisionist researchers, who have debated back and forth among themselves in order to find out as accurately as possible what actually happened. The official version offered by the exterminationists accepts the estimates of the World Jewish Congress in 1945 and 1946, according to which some 600,000 Jews died. As late as 2000, Arthur R. Butz debated Jürgen Graf in an extensive article entitled "On the 1944 Deportations of Hungarian Jews", published in *The Journal of Historical Review*. Graf, a well-known Swiss-born writer and activist who in 1992 published the book *Der Holocaust auf dem Prüfstand*, published in Argentina for the first time in Spanish under the title *El Holocausto bajo la lupa* (1997), accepts that 438,000 Jews were deported to Auschwitz between May and July 1944, but denies that they were gassed.

In 2001, Samuel Crowell, another revisionist author, joined the debate with a new article, "New Light on the Fate of Hungarian Jews", also published in *The Journal of Historical Review*. This American researcher recalls that Jean-Claude Pressac, the author who maintains the thesis that between 600,000 and 700,000 people died in Auschwitz, considerably reduces the number of Hungarian Jews deported to Auschwitz to between 160,000 and 240,000. Samuel Crowell disputes the mass deportation to Auschwitz and argues that many Hungarian Jews were transferred to various camps, including Dora, Buchenwald, Bergen-Belsen, Gross Rosen, Mauthausen, Szeged, Strasshof..., and provides evidence that in June 1944, 20,000 Jews were sent to Strasshof.

One of Crowell's sources is the Hungarian historian Szabolcs Szita[2], who lists almost 400 camps and their satellites where Hungarian Jews arrived. In addition, Szita adds the names of more than five hundred localities, many of which were not associated with concentration camps, that received Jews deported from Hungary. Among these, he cites Unterlüss, near Hannover, or Moerfelde-Walldorf. There is evidence that a large number of Hungarian women worked in Unterlüss. It is also known that about 1,700 Hungarian women, after being transferred in May from Auschwitz, worked in Moerfelde-Walldorf on an airstrip for the firm Züblin, a construction company. Szabolcs Szita also mentions Hungarians working in different concentration camps near the Baltic countries, such as Kovno, Klooga, Riga-Kaiserwald, Stuthoff and others. In the Dundaga sub-camp, between 2,000 and 5,000 Hungarian women, who arrived from Auschwitz from May onwards, worked. In other words, Szita and other historians confirm that instead of the intended extermination, there was a wide distribution of Jews from Auschwitz to various German-occupied areas, where they were forced to work.

---

[2] Szabolcs Szita was appointed by Viktor Orbán's government as director of the Holocaust Memorial Center in Budapest. Szita's book *Coexistence-Persecution-Holocaust*, published in 2001 and awarded by the Ministry of Education of the first Orbán government, provides important information on the history of Hungarian Jews. Since the contents of Szita's work did not please Jewish leaders, a campaign of criticism of his views began.

The 1948 ICRC report confirms that, as in Slovakia, Hungarian Jews enjoyed a certain freedom of action. There were anti-Jewish laws, but there was no danger. Until March 1944, those who obtained visas for Palestine were free to leave the country. Then, to prevent Hungary from abandoning its alliance with Germany in the face of Hitler's expected defeat, German troops occupied the country. On 18 March, the Führer summoned the regent, Admiral Horthy, to his headquarters. According to the ICRC report, he "expressed his indignation that nearly one million Jews in Hungary enjoyed unrestricted freedom". After the occupation, a new government under German authority suspended Jewish emigration and persecutions began. It was between May and July that the largest deportations took place in order to employ Jews as labourers.

Arthur R. Butz not only denies that Hungarian Jews were gassed at Auschwitz, but also considers it impracticable to transfer 438,000 of them to the notorious camp at a critical time in the war when the means of transport were required for the needs of the war. This author cites a text dated 19 April 1944 in which the German authorities allude to the "greater difficulties" in finding available trains for the transfer of the 10,000 Jews they needed as manpower. On 27 April, a new report confirms that it was finally possible to transport 4,000, who arrived at Auschwitz around 1 May. There is documentary evidence of a second transport of 4,000 Jews to the labour camp, 2,000 of whom were registered on 22 May and another 2,000 on 24 May. However, the shortage of trains prevented the deportation of the fifty thousand needed. It should also be noted that on 6 June 1944, D-Day, the Normandy landings began and the Germans faced a desperate situation on both fronts. The railways were vital for the transport of troops and materials to avoid collapse. It is impossible to understand how huge numbers of trains could have been allocated for mass deportation to the detriment of the army's priorities and operational capacity. In defence of his thesis, Arthur R. Butz argues that the figure of 438,000 Jews, allegedly deported in two months, is equivalent to two-thirds of the deportations from Germany, Austria and Western Europe in three years (1941-1944). Another incomprehensible fact that the exterminationists fail to explain is why the Germans wasted time and resources deporting hundreds of thousands of people to Auschwitz in order to kill them, when they could have done so, if that was indeed the aim, by shooting them in Hungary or in the Slovakian mountains through which the trains passed.

Before proceeding further, it is pertinent to clarify that at the beginning of 1944 the Hungarian Jews numbered about 750,000, according to figures provided by the Germans themselves. It is not clear whether this figure includes Polish and Slovak refugees who crossed the border en masse because Hungary was considered a safe haven. Since the Zionists used Hungary as a springboard for channelling immigration to Palestine, it must be assumed that there was also an additional influx of Eastern European Jews entering the country for this purpose. 300,000 of them were living in Budapest in the spring of 1944. If the number of deportees in the months of May and June were the figure given by the exterminationists, it would be tantamount to accepting the disappearance of all Hungarian Jews living in the provinces, since the Jews in the capital had not been evacuated. Furthermore, it should be noted that in November 1944, 100,000 Jews arrived in Budapest from different parts of the country, which means that the number of deportees was lower than the number of Jews deported in November 1944.

The fact that in March 1944 the Germans publicised their intention to deport the Hungarian Jews was immediately seized upon by Jewish propagandists to launch a campaign on the history of the extermination of the Hungarian Jews, which included all sorts of atrocities. Arthur R. Butz quotes in *The Hoax of the Twentieth Century* some twenty reports published between February and August 1944 in *The New York Times*, the flagship of the Jewish print media in the United States. Let us look at just a few of them. On 10 May there was a report by Joseph M. Levy stating that Hungary was preparing "the annihilation of the Hungarian Jews by the most diabolical means". Gratuitously, without the slightest proof, it was stated that the Sztójay government was "about to begin the extermination of nearly a million human beings." With utter impudence, Joseph M. Levy wrote: "The Hungarian Government has decreed the establishment in various parts of Hungary of 'special baths' for Jews. These baths are nothing but huge gas chambers ready for mass murder, just like those opened in Poland in 1941". A week later, on May 18, the same article claimed that eight hundred thousand Jews from the Carpathian provinces had been "sent to the murder camps in Poland."

Citing Hungarian sources reporting from Turkey, *The New York Times* on 2 July inserted on page 12 a story stating that "350,000 Jews were ready to be deported to death camps in Poland". The same report stated that 400,000 had already been sent on 17 June and added: "it is believed that the remaining 350,000 will be executed by 24 July". On 6 July it said on page 6: "The World Jewish Congress was informed more than a fortnight ago that one hundred thousand Jews recently deported from Hungary to Poland have been gassed in the major German concentration camp of Oswiecim" (Polish toponym for Auschwitz). On 4 August, a Polish resistance courier was credited as a source, announcing "that Hungarian Jews were being sent to Oswiecim at the rate of twelve trainloads every twenty-four hours". To further shock American public opinion, it added that "in their haste the Germans began to kill small children with truncheons". Also during the First World War, propagandists, as we know, launched a campaign against Germany. Their soldiers were accused of eating Belgian children and throwing them into the air to skewer them with their bayonets. The difference is that the British then retracted and their foreign secretary apologised to

Germany in the House of Commons, where he acknowledged that it was war propaganda; but today, in the 21st century, the propaganda about Nazi atrocities against the Jews is growing and growing.

Professor Butz reproduces in his work up to fifty documents presented at the Nuremberg trials, which are used by the exterminationists to prove that more than 400,000 Jews were deported between 15 May and early July 1944. An example of the unreliability of some of them is NG-2233, which absurdly states that the extermination programme enjoyed priority over military production in terms of railways. There is reasonable doubt to suspect that many of these texts are forgeries, with the post-war collaboration of Nazis who were granted immunity and escaped prosecution. Most are mimeographed copies of telegrams sent to the Foreign Ministry by Edmund Veesenmayer, the Ministry's plenipotentiary in Hungary. Veesenmayer was a defendant in the Wilhelmstrasse trial, the 11th NMT case, one of twelve trials organised by the Americans between 1946 and 1949. The Jewish prosecutor Robert Kempner, who took over the 'political ministries section', used the dirtiest strategies to get the statements he wanted. According to the *Encyclopedia Judaica*, Kempner was "chief prosecutor"[3]. Veesenmayer testified that he could receive up to twenty orders a day and that some of them contradicted each other. He stated that his reports were drawn up by assistants and that he signed them after reviewing them at a glance. He was eventually sentenced to twenty years in prison, but by the beginning of 1952 he was free.

In our opinion, some documents demonstrate the inconsistencies and uncertainties of the Germans, especially while Eichmann was negotiating with the Jewish Rescue Committee in Budapest and was awaiting Joel Brand's demarche in Istanbul, where the Zionists were expected to secure ten thousand trucks to save all the Jews of Hungary from deportation. Three documents dated between 28 and 30 April 1944, NG-5595, NG-5596 and NG-5597, confirm the arrest of 194,000 Jews as a result of "special

---

[3] We have already written about this Robert Kempner in chapter eleven, more specifically in the section on the Nuremberg assembly. We will now add that this German-born Jew had emigrated to the United States in 1939 and that during the war he was one of the many Jews who worked within the OSS (the Intelligence Service), including, as a curious example, Herbert Marcuse, the famous Frankfurt School philosopher and author of *One-Dimensional Man*. As has been explained, coercion was a regular tool of Kempner's in his Nuremberg interrogations, where he stole numerous original documents. Kempner concealed the Schlegelberger document, which showed that Hitler ordered in March 1942 that the solution of the Jewish question be postponed until the end of the war. David Irving published it in 1977 in *Hitler's War*. In 1951 Kempner was Israel's representative in Bonn and played a leading role in the negotiations on compensation from Germany to the Zionist state and to those affected by Nazi persecution. In 1952 he appeared again in the United States in connection with the House of Representatives investigation of the Katyn Forest massacre, about which Kempner had testified in favour of the Soviets in the IMT despite knowing that there was evidence of USSR guilt, thus exposing his dishonesty.

operations". In document NG-2059, dated 8 May 1944, Veesenmayer states: "A certain number of Jews who were to be deported have been put to work on military projects in Hungary". Particularly revealing is a typed report contained in document NG-2980, which admits that the special counsellor for Jewish affairs at the German Embassy in Budapest, von Adamovic, "has no idea for what purpose or in what way to implement the anti-Jewish measures." The report also refers to Adamovic's visit to Eichmann's office, where he learned that 116,000 Jews had been deported to the Reich and that the deportation of another 200,000 was imminent. In this connection, it is specified that the concentration of 250,000 Jews from the provinces north and northwest of Budapest was to begin on 7 June.

Thanks to Kastner's report, we know that on 9 June 1944 Eichmann was still waiting for Joel Brand's efforts in Istanbul to bear fruit, so that the members of the "Vaadah" (the Jewish Rescue Committee) enjoyed the protection of the Germans and Hungarians, which enabled them to continue helping the Polish and Slovak refugees. Kastner acknowledges that Zionist youth leaders visited them daily and that Ambassador Wesenmayer interceded on their behalf with the Hungarian government, all of which gave them hope. If the hopes related to Istanbul did not make possible the salvation of all Hungarian Jewry," wrote Kastner verbatim, "we should at least protect some of them from the gas chambers". Since the report was submitted to the WZO in 1946, it is logical that Kastner mentioned the gas chambers, since the official version and propaganda had already established that millions of Jews had been gassed.

Lenni Brener, the editor of *The Report of the Budapest Jewish Rescue Committee*, selects an excerpt from the report that records Kastner's negotiation with Eichmann during June for the transport of 1,300 Jews to Palestine. The day on which our 'Aliyah' was to begin," writes Kastner, "was approaching. The group had not been fully assembled..... In the meantime, we haggled with Eichmann over the number of participants. Under the heading of 'inclusion of the Klansenburger group' an increase of a thousand was achieved. In consideration of the large number of important people from the provinces, he gave permission to increase the number of places by two hundred. On the day of the departure the number of participants with official authorisation amounted to thirteen hundred". Reading these words there can be no doubt that in the month of June 1944 Eichmann was collaborating with the Zionists to save the lives of "Prominents". This is the English word in the text. Naturally, the lives of those who were not prominent were of less value. For its interest, we translate from English the excerpt "A Noah's Ark: The composition of the transport for abroad".

> "The group's departure was set for 30 June. Once again we had to compile a 'first' list. The 1,300 places were distributed among the following categories, in accordance with the Vaadah.

> 1. Orthodox (refugees from Budapest. Compiled by Philip Freudiger)
> 2. Polish, Slovakian and Yugoslavian refugees (according to their own lists).
> 3. Leading neurologists (Samuel's list Stern).
> 4. Zionists, holders of certificates (on the recommendation of the Presidium of the Department of Palestine)
> 5. Halutz, Hungarian and refugee youth: Dror Habonin, Makkabi, Hazan, Hashomer, Hazair, Noar Hazioni, Mizrachi Akiba (according to their own list).
> 6. Revisionists (on the recommendation of the revisionist leader Gottesman).
> 7. Paying persons, whose contributions helped to defray the cost of all transport.
> 8. Those rescued from the provinces.
> 9. Prominent Jewish personalities from the religious, scientific and cultural spheres.
> 10. Orphans. A group of Budapest orphans, plus 17 orphans from Poland. Their case was in the hands of Dr. Georg Polgar, a prominent leader of the Jewish Health Bureau, who was also on the transport."

Once again, it becomes clear that most of the Nazi victims were the poorest Jews, those who could not avoid persecution and deportation because they had neither the means to flee nor sufficient influence to be considered by the organisations negotiating with the German authorities in the various occupied countries. The text stresses that the spiritual elite of Hungarian Jewry was invited to leave the country, as well as personalities from all walks of life. The report cites as examples the names of an architect, an oculist, a psychologist, an X-ray specialist, an internist, a pianist, and even an opera singer. Kastner insists in another paragraph on mentioning prominent people that he and his team have managed to rescue:

> "Also, many personalities from public life in Siebenbürgen brought from Klausenberg could have been saved in this action. Some of them should be named here. Doctors Theodor and Joseph Fisher, Joel Titelbaum, the world famous Hasidist rabbi who was a convinced opponent of the Zionist movement . With the exception of Otto Kolmony and Dr. Rezsö Kasztner (himself), who remained in Budapest to continue the work, the following personalities left the country in the transport: The leadership of the Hungarian Zionist Organisation, the collaborators of the National Fund, also some collaborators and members of the Vaadah: Ernst Szilagy, Moshe Rosenberg, Joseph Weinberger, Ede Morton, Dr. Sarah Friedlander, Dr. Elisabeth Kurz. Other prominent orthodox personalities and rabbis complete the picture."

Other projects of collaboration with the Nazis appear in Kastner's report, where he notes as a success of the Budapest Jewish Committee the rescue of 17,000 Jews from the provinces who were taken to Austria. He also mentions that at 15:30 on 19 August 1944 they travelled to Switzerland with a list of 318 Jews, whom they intended to liberate from the Bergen-Belsen camp, a goal they achieved once again: on 21 August the group was taken to Basel from a small German border post. Lenni Brenner also reproduces in his *51 Documents* a letter from the Swiss representative of the War Refugee Board, Roswell D. McClelland, which Kastner enclosed with his report to the WZO. It has become known that between the autumn of 1944 and the spring of 1945, negotiations between the German leadership and Saly Mayer, the Swiss representative of the Joint Distribution Committee, continued under the mediation of Rudolf Kastner. As a result of these meetings, two groups of Hungarian Jews who had been deported from Budapest in June 1944, a total of 1,673 persons, were released from the Bergen-Belsen concentration camp and arrived in Switzerland in December 1944. As far as can be ascertained, the alleged exterminators repeatedly consented to facilitate the rescue of groups of Jews and, as they had done from the beginning of the Nazi rise to power, continued to negotiate and collaborate with Zionist organisations.

The report of the International Committee of the Red Cross also confirms that the Hungarian government was prepared to support the increase in Jewish emigration, and so in August the ICRC contacted the British and American governments and obtained a joint statement from them expressing their readiness to support Jewish emigration from Hungary in every way possible. The ICRC transmitted the following message from the American government to Budapest:

> "The United States Government has been informed by the ICRC that the Hungarian Government is prepared to allow certain classes of refugees to emigrate from Hungary.... in view of the humanitarian considerations concerning Hungarian Jews, the United States Government again expresses its belief that it will thereby be negotiated for the good of all Jews who are permitted to leave Hungary and reach Allied or other neutral territory and that temporary safe havens will be found for them where they can live in safety. The governments of the neutral countries have been advised of such intentions and have been asked to allow Hungarian Jews who reach their borders to enter their territories."

By the end of August, the course of the war clearly indicated that the Germans would not be able to hold their ground in Hungary for long, since the setbacks they were suffering were already continuing and they were in retreat on both the eastern and western fronts. The Vaadah, which had been negotiating with Eichmann until the end, began to cooperate with the Jewish groups operating in the resistance, to whom it provided money, arms and ammunition. "The 'Haluzim' groups still remained in Budapest," Kastner's report says, "prepared for the possibility of an armed confrontation with the

Germans on the streets of Budapest." On 8 October 1944, the Hungarian authorities announced the suspension of deportations and announced that they had dismantled the Kistarcea camp, where Jewish intellectuals, doctors and engineers were concentrated and liberated. Once again, therefore, we see the special treatment of an elite group of Jews. On 15 October, Admiral Miklós Horthy, who had been Regent of Hungary since 1 March 1920, requested an armistice from the Allied powers, which put the Jews, who had been waiting for the moment, on alert. The ICRC report notes that German troops were fired on from houses by members of these resistance groups, but Horthy's plan failed and the regent was arrested. On 16 October, Ferenc Szálasi's Arrow Cross Party seized power and a state of siege was declared in Budapest. From this point on, policy towards Jews was tightened and repression began to intensify.

The Jews were immediately expelled from Budapest and their property was confiscated. It should be noted that half of the city's real estate was in the hands of Jewish owners. In the interwar period, the power of this ethnic minority, which accounted for six percent of the population, had only grown throughout the country, despite the fact that many Hungarians hated them as a result of the crimes of the communist dictatorship imposed by Bela Kun and other Jewish communists in 1919-1920. No doubt this hatred in some Hungarians led to theft and other excesses for a few days, prompting the immediate complaint of the Red Cross delegate to the Ministry of the Interior, which on 20 October issued a decree banning looting. The delegation was immediately offered as a refuge to members of the Jewish Council or Jewish Senate, and the delegate got the Hungarian government to announce over the radio that ICRC buildings would enjoy the same immunity as embassies.

Szálasi's pro-German government sent 6,000 able-bodied Jews from Budapest to Germany in groups of 1,000. The march, which was to pass through Vienna, was conducted on foot, causing the commandant of Auschwitz, the "great exterminator" Rudolf Höss, and Colonel General Jüttner, who had arrived in Budapest at the invitation of Kurt Becher, to take pity on the Jews and order the march to be halted. "The commandant of Auschwitz, against the march on foot". With this sentence Kastner begins Chapter VI of his report, entitled "The seizure of power by the Arrow Cross". His own words follow:

> "At Becher's invitation, important German visitors arrived in Budapest on 16 November, the head of the Waffen SS, Colonel General Jüttner, and the commandant of Auschwitz, Lieutenant Colonel Höss. On the road between Vienna and Budapest they witnessed the horrific march on foot. Bodies piled up along the road, exhausted people, made a painful impression on the German horsemen.... Jüttner ordered the Budapest Judenkommando to suspend the march immediately."

Logically, such incoherence is beyond comprehension, and we do not see how it is possible that Höss, the monster who supposedly gassed thousands of Jews every day without the slightest scruple, could experience humanitarian feelings and order a halt to the march. In any case, the interruption was short-lived; on 21 November Eichmann returned to the Hungarian capital after a temporary absence and five days later ordered the march to resume. Both the ICRC and the Jewish Rescue Committee reports give full details of the means they mobilised to assist the marchers with supplies, medicines and other resources. The Swedish Red Cross, Division A of the International Red Cross, the Swiss Embassy are some of the organisations mentioned by Kastner. The ICRC report also acknowledges the generous help of the bishop of Gyor, a town west of Budapest, halfway between the Hungarian capital and Vienna. The bishop placed at the disposal of the Red Cross delegate the abbey of Panonalma, a Benedictine monastery which took in 1,000 orphans "without distinction of race or religion". As for the convoys of Jews who walked 25-30 kilometres a day on their way to the labour camps in Germany, the report states that the bishop worked closely with the delegate:

> "He organised an 'en route' relief centre which he himself financed and which was run by representatives of the Committee. It sheltered thousands of Jews from bad weather, at least for a few hours, during their terrible exodus. The delegation's 'transport groups' sent them food as they went along, paid peasants to carry the weakest, 15 or 20 at a time, in their wagons, provided medical care and dispensed supplies of medicine."

The new Hungarian government forced men between the ages of sixteen and sixty and women under forty to work in the fortification of Budapest. The rest of the Jewish population was confined to four ghettos near the capital. Nevertheless, Jews who had passports or visas for Palestine, Switzerland, Sweden, Spain or Portugal managed to escape evacuation. In November, those remaining in Budapest were herded into a ghetto along with 100,000 Jews who came to the capital from the provinces. Despite the constant bombardment of the city and the general shortage of supplies, the Red Cross managed to send relief and supplies to the ghetto. As soon as Budapest was liberated," the ICRC report states, "the delegate and local Jewish organizations set up, with funds from the Joint Committee in New York, stores of food and much-needed medicines. The Russian authorities had ordered all foreigners to leave Budapest...".

It is cruel sarcasm to call the communists' entry into the city a liberation, especially when one considers what happened. The order for foreigners to leave Budapest was probably intended to suppress witnesses to the crimes that followed the "liberation". As later in Germany, hundreds of thousands of Hungarian women, perhaps close to a million, were raped by Soviet soldiers thanks to the permissiveness of their officers, many of whom, as far as we know, were Jews. In addition to 600,000 prisoners of war, 230,000 civilians were dragged into the Soviet Gulag, the real death camps that nobody wants to remember. According to the most conservative estimates, half a million Hungarians lost their lives in the internment camps, shot in the streets or murdered in No. 60 Andrássy-út, in whose cells Jewish henchmen usually operated.

After forty years of communist dictatorship, in 2002 the building on Budapest's Andrássy Avenue was converted into a museum known as the "Terror Háza Múzeum" (House of Terror). Hungarian nationalist writer Louis Marschalko, author of the book *The World Conquerors*, denounces that the middle classes, intellectuals and national leaders were murdered and that those who presided over the so-called "revolutionary tribunals" were Jewish judges. Marschalho denounces that in Western Europe, an American-born Hungarian Jew, Colonel Martin Himmler, led the campaign of revenge against 300,000 Hungarians who had escaped from the communists. In Zionist publications, Martin Himmler is considered to have "avenged the shedding of innocent Jewish blood".

Since, as we have seen with the example of the Bishop of Gyor, the Hungarian Church took a stand against the persecution of Hungarian Jews and helped them, we will end by mentioning the case of the Catholic Cardinal Jozsef Mindszenty, who protected Jews during the war and after the war tried to do the same for Christians persecuted by the communists. As Bishop of Veszprem in 1944, Mindszenty rescued Jews the Germans wanted to deport by giving them papal safe-conducts. After the Szálasi government came to power, he was arrested, as he was considered an enemy of the Germans and a protector of the Jews. After the war, as he had done with the Jews persecuted by the Nazis, the Cardinal considered it his duty to defend persecuted Christians and to denounce the campaign of revenge unleashed by Jewish communists. Because of this attitude, he was considered an anti-Semite.

In 1948 he was arrested and tried in 1949. Louis Marschalko denounces the two main Jewish communists who went against Mindszenty: Mátyás Rákosi-Roth (Mátyás Rosenfeld), secretary general of the Workers' Party who in 1952 became president of the Council of Ministers, and Jozsef Revai (Moses Kahana), the minister of education who orchestrated the campaign against the Catholic cardinal. Among the priests who betrayed him, he cites Istvan Balogh (alias Izrael Bloch). Other Jews who testified against him were: Ivan Boldizsar, (Bettelheim), head of propaganda for the Communist government; Yuli Reismann, head of the Publicity department; Gera-Grünzweig, also a government propagandist; Hanna F. Sulner, a handwriting expert who forged the Cardinal's manuscripts presented at the trial, and her husband Laszlo Sulner.

The Sulners escaped to Austria on 6 February 1949, where they denounced the trial against Cardinal Mindszenty as a sham and exhibited the microfilm of the false documents they had been working on. Laszlo died at the age of thirty in Paris, and Hanna, convinced that her husband had been poisoned by communist agents, emigrated to the United States in 1950, where she became one of the country's foremost authorities on manuscript identification.

Part 2
About the camps in Germany

There are now numerous works that prove beyond doubt that the extermination camps did not exist as such. Those who insist on deceiving students of history the world over by taking this propaganda-fabricated thesis for granted are either ignorant or dishonest teachers. In the following parts of the chapter we will try to present all the evidence that revisionist researchers have uncovered so that the reader can judge whether or not it deserves any consideration. If the function of the camps was the mass extermination of the inmates, how can it be understood that on 28 December 1942 Heinrich Himmler, the Reichsführer of the SS, issued an order with this text: "The death rate in the concentration camps must be lowered at all costs". On 20 January 1943 SS General Richard Glücks, who was in charge of the Inspectorate of Concentration Camps, sent a circular to all camp commandants in which he ordered: "All means must be used to lower the death rate". Are these orders compatible with the goal of extermination?

The measures taken to combat the typhus epidemic which spread throughout the camp in the summer of 1942 will be discussed in detail in the section on Auschwitz that follows. We shall then have occasion to place these orders in the context in which they were issued. According to data presented to Himmler by SS General Oswald Pohl, head of the WVHA ("Wirtschafts-Verwaltungshauptamt"), there were 115,000 prisoners in the concentration camps in August 1942, of whom 12,217 died in that same month, or 12.21%. As a result of hygienic, nutritional and other procedural measures, the death rate had fallen to 2.80% by May 1943. Of the 203,000 inmates in the camps on this date, 5,700 died. This was presented as a success of the measures taken in carrying out the orders of the SS Reichsführer. It should be noted that these total numbers of prisoners in the camps, as reported by the German authorities, coincide with those of the Red Cross, which in its 1948 report put the number of detainees in August 1943 at 224,000. In the same report the Red Cross states that only one year later, i.e., in August 1944, there were 524,000 prisoners in the entire German concentration camp system.

In the pages that follow, it will be seen that the camps collapsed completely as a consequence of the defeat of Germany, whose civilian population was deprived of the most basic necessities during the final years of the war and was being massacred en masse by the saturation bombing of the major cities. Before this collapse of the concentration camp system, the German camps were well designed to do their job and were by far the best equipped. Recall that Eisenhower's death camps had no shelter for prisoners and that camp conditions in the Soviet Gulag were utterly depressing.

A German woman of Jewish origin, Margarete Buber, after spending several years in a concentration camp in the USSR, returned to Germany in August 1940 with a contingent of deportees. Unfortunately, she was not liberated, but interned in the Ravensbrück camp. In 1950 she published *Under Two Dictators* in London, in which she recounts her experience. She found the German camp immaculately clean, with spacious lawns and flowers. Baths were regular, sheets were changed weekly, which she found an unimaginable luxury after her previous experience. Meals were served with white bread, sausage, margarine and sweet porridge with nuts. Margarette Buber ate for the first time in Ravensbrück on 3 August 1940 and asked her neighbour if it was a special meal or a party. The man was expressionless, and she insisted on asking whether they always ate like this. After answering in the affirmative, the inmate expressed surprise that anyone could be so pleased about it. Frau Buber considered the barracks in Ravensbrück to be a palace compared to the overcrowded mud of the Soviet camp. On the first Sunday she ate beef stew, red cabbage and potatoes, a real feast according to her. In 1943, however, prisoners from other camps began to arrive and crowd the facility, and everything changed. By early 1945, inmates from Auschwitz and other camps in the east were arriving exhausted and hungry, but not only them, but also the tens of thousands of German refugees fleeing the Soviets.

Initially, between 1933 and 1939, the Nazis used the camps to imprison elements who had been arrested for their anti-regime activities: liberals, social democrats and above all communists. The Jewish historian Gerald Reitlinger admits that before the war the population of the camps was around 20,000, including fewer than three thousand Jews detained not because they were Jews, but because of their anti-Nazi activities. Compared to the millions of Soviet prisoners who were treated as slaves in the camps of the USSR, this figure is derisory. In 1939 there were six main camps in Germany: Dachau, opened in 1933; Sachsenhausen, in the town of Oranienburg, operated from 1936 and from 1940 onwards had the satellite camp Gross-Rosen; Buchenwald, near Weimar, established in the summer of 1937; Flossenbürg (1938); Mauthausen, near Linz (1938); and Ravensbrück, a women's camp published in Mecklenburg (1939).

The Jewish author Lion Feuchtwanger puts the number of Jews imprisoned in Dachau in 1936 at one hundred, sixty of whom had been there since 1933. Hans Beimler, another German Jewish communist who was murdered in Spain in 1936, spent a month in Dachau in 1933. In the same year his book *Four Weeks in the Hands of Hitler's Hell-Hounds. The Nazi Murder Camp of Dachau* (*Four Weeks in the Hands of Hitler's Hell-Hounds. The Nazi Murder Camp of Dachau.*) In this sensationalist, pamphlet-like work, he was already trying to spread the idea that Dachau was an extermination camp.[4]

Buchenwald: the testimonies of Paul Rassinier and Eugen Kogon

If we disregard Beimler's pamphlet, the first works of interest about the concentration camps were written by two Buchenwald prisoners. The first, *Der SS-Staat. Das System der deutschen Konzentrationslager (The SS State. The German concentration camp system)*, appeared in 1946. It was published in Spain in 1965 under the title *Sociología de los campos de concentración (Sociology of the Concentration Camps)*. Its author, Eugen Kogon, a German Jew who spent six years in Buchenwald, never doubted the existence of the gas chambers, although he only knew about them through propaganda and accounts of alleged witnesses. The second work, *Le Mensonge d'Ulysse (The Lie of Ulysses)*, first published in English in 1961, is by Paul Rassinier, considered the first revisionist historian. The fact that Rassinier comes from the radical left makes his work even more valuable, since few left-wing militants are honest enough to face up to the historical truth. Ideologically, intellectually, emotionally, no one could have been less inclined than he to defend Hitler and National Socialism. At the age of 16, Rassinier joined the French Communist Party in 1922, but was excluded because of his extreme left-wing positions in 1932. With the Jew Boris Souvarin, he participated in an independent communist organisation until 1934, when he joined the French section of the Workers' International. Arrested on 30 October 1943 for his activities in the French Resistance, Rassinier was deported to Buchenwald and from there to Dora-Mittelbau. Released in 1945, he returned to France as an invalid. His political views soon earned him many enemies, to the point of physical attacks, trials and social ostracism. Some had the gall to call him a "neo-Nazi". When he wrote

---

[4] Hans Beimler took part in the Spanish Civil War. He was a member of the Thälmann Battalion, of which he was a political commissar. Officially he died at the end of November 1936 defending Madrid. His funeral was exploited by political propaganda. A funeral procession of six or seven cars was organised from Madrid to Albacete. Even the radio announced the arrival of the international hero, who was accompanied by Santiago Carrillo, Fernando Claudín and other communist leaders. His corpse was exposed and the workers of Albacete paraded before the comrade's coffin. What is certain, however, is that Beimler was shot in the back by the NKVD, which suggests that he was a Trotskyite. His friend Antonia Stern accused Richard Steimer, General Hoffman, of being the perpetrator of the murder. It is now known that after the funeral ceremony, the forensic and Civil Government doctor, José Carrilero, examined the body when Carrillo and company had already left Albacete. He took photographs of the head and it was found that there was a bullet entry wound behind the middle part of the right ear and exit through the opposite cranial vault. Doctor Carrilero also ruled that the bullets were from a revolver or pistol and not a rifle.

The Lie of Ulysses, Rassinier did not yet dare, despite his doubts, to deny the existence of the cameras; but as he continued his research he became convinced that they did not exist.[5]

The combined contents of the two books give a full and complete picture of how Buchenwald functioned, which was initially a prison camp ("Straflager"), then became a labour camp ("Arbeitslager") and finally ended up as a concentration camp ("Konzentrationslager" or KZ). The two authors explain in detail what categories of prisoners there were and how they related to each other, who actually exercised control, and what the camp facilities were. The fact that Rassinier's work was four years later allowed him to comment on Kogon's book in *Ulysses' Lie* and to criticise at times its lack of objectivity and its tendentiousness in many instances. The two authors agree, for example, that the concentration camps were initially designed to imprison enemies of the National Socialist regime. They also agree that the camp management, the "Haftlingsführung", was in the hands of the detainees themselves. The SS, which according to Rassinier numbered about fifty men in charge of running the camp in Buchenwald, was soon overwhelmed and had to organise the prisoners and appoint among them the first "Lagerältester", a prisoner-in-chief in charge of maintaining discipline, who reported to an SS officer called the "Lagerführer". Reporting to the Lagerführer was the "Lagerschreiber", a prisoner with administrative duties. Normally, at the suggestion of the Lagerältester, the Lagerführer appointed prisoner-block leaders, the "Blockaltesten".

---

[5] Paul Rassinier, who taught history at the Lycée de Belfort until 1943, is certainly worthy of more attention, but the length of our work does not allow us to devote to him the space that the importance of his figure deserves. With this note, we intend to introduce him briefly to readers who did not know him and to pay a modest tribute to the courage and honesty of this great intellectual, to whom revisionism owes so much. After the hardships suffered in Buchenwald and Dora, the most logical thing would have been resentment and the search for a little peace of mind; nevertheless, despite his precarious health, Rassinier devoted the God-given years of his life to the search for historical truth and justice for Germany. After his communist comrades had succeeded in November 1946 in depriving him of his deputy's seat in the Constituent Assembly, he began his research into what happened, which resulted in eleven books. We have already used his last work, *Les Responsables de la Seconde Guerre Mondiale* (1967), as a source. Of particular importance are *L'opération Vicaire* (1965) and *Le véritable procès Eichmann ou les vainqueurs incorrigibles* (1962). In the Eichmann trial, several witnesses committed the crime of giving false testimony and testified that they had seen prisoners leaving for the gas chambers. Paul Rassinier rejected the lie of the intrinsic evil of the Germans and considered the claim that they gassed European Jews en masse to be an imposture. After reading the works of various propagandist fakers, Rassinier denounced as shameless the book *Doctor at Auschwitz* by Miklos Nyizli, a cynical liar who claims that 25,000 people were gassed daily at Auschwitz for four and a half years, for a total of more than forty million. Trying to find an eyewitness to the exterminations in the gas chambers, Paul Rassinier travelled all over Europe, but found not one.

In this way, the SS secured only the outer guard of the camp, so that they were usually hardly seen inside the camp. When they did appear, they were accompanied, Rassinier writes, "by a veritable company of marvellously trained dogs, always ready to bite and capable of searching a few dozen kilometres for a prisoner who might have escaped". Also the commandos who left the camp every morning to work outside and went five or six kilometres on foot were, of course, guarded by two or four members of the SS, depending on the size of the group, who wielded a weapon and carried a muzzled dog. This guard rarely intervened, for it was the prisoners who served as the camp's labour police, the famous kapos (Konzentrationslager Arbeitspolizei), who made sure that everyone worked. Thousands of Jews played the role of kapos and "oberkapo" (head of the kapos). The latter wore an armband with a blue Star of David on which was written the inscription OBERKAPO, usually in capital letters.

When it came to appointing the Lagerältester, it seems that, given the choice between a criminal, identified by a green triangle, or a political prisoner, who wore a red triangle, the SS initially chose the criminals, who in turn appointed the Kapos and block leaders (Blockaltesten) from their own world. Thus it was the criminals who were charged with helping to maintain discipline and control. Rassinier writes the following in this regard:

> "Only when the camps took on a certain development, when they became real ethnographic and industrial centres, was it really necessary for men of a certain moral and intellectual standing to give the SS-Führung effective help. The SS-Führung realised that the criminals were the dregs of the population, in the countryside as elsewhere, and that they were far below the effort required of them. So the SS turned to the politicians. One day a green Lagerältester had to be replaced by a red Lagerältester, who immediately began to liquidate the green Lagerältester from all posts to the advantage of the red Lagerältester. Thus was born the struggle between the Greens and the Reds, which quickly became permanent . This also explains why the old camps, Buchenwald and Dachau, were in the hands of the politicians when we knew them, while the young camps, still in the Straflager (prison) or Arbeitslager (labour) period, remained, except by the most extraordinary chance, in the hands of the Greens".

As for the colour coding of the triangles worn by the inmates, we would like to explain this in passing. As has been noted, green was the colour of criminals. If the criminal was also Jewish, the green triangle was superimposed on a yellow triangle to form the Star of David . A red triangle was also superimposed on the yellow triangle in the case of politicians of Jewish origin in protective custody. In addition, the red triangles specified the origin of the prisoner with a letter inside: an "F" indicated French nationality; an "S", Spanish nationality; the red triangle without a letter was for German political prisoners. The black triangle was reserved for asocial prisoners. Again, black on yellow indicated that the prisoner was a Jewish asocial. The brown triangle was for gypsies and the pink for homosexuals. There were a few other variations, but it is pointless to dwell on these details.

As for the Buchenwald facilities, both Kogon and Rassinier provide ample information peppered with varied anecdotes. Eugen Kogon spent a year in command of the wardrobe store ("Effektkammer") before becoming secretary to the camp's chief physician, Dr Ding-Schuller. Both positions show that his position was one of privilege. In the infirmary he had access to documents of great interest, some of which he reproduces in his book. For example, the above-mentioned order of SS Reichsführer Heinrich Himmler on the urgent need to reduce mortality in the camps, which in Buchenwald was recorded in the secret correspondence book under the number 66/42. It bore the signature of General Kludre. It stated:

> "The camp doctors must monitor the prisoners' food more closely than they have done up to the present and, in agreement with the administrations, must submit their proposals for improvement to the camp commandant. However, these should not remain a dead letter, but should be regularly checked by the camp doctors..... The mortality rate in each camp must be reduced considerably, for the number of prisoners must be brought up to the level required by the SS Reichsführer. The chief camp doctors must work to achieve this with all their means..... The best doctor in a concentration camp is not the one who thinks he has to call attention to himself with unwelcome harshness, but the one who keeps the work capacity as high as possible by vigilance and by moving from one work station to another".

Kogon's account provides detailed details of the research carried out in the "section for the study of typhus and viruses", the primary purpose of which was to evaluate possible vaccines against typhoid fever. The head of the section was the head physician at Buchenwald, the aforementioned Ding-Schuller. Located in Blocks 46 and 50, this research section was, according to Kogon, "a model of apparent cleanliness and was well installed". There, Kogon continues, "all typhists who were naturally contaminated in the field or who were already contaminated when they were handed over to him were isolated. They were cured there to the extent that they resisted this terrible disease". The reader may think that the existence of infirmaries in Buchenwald was something exceptional; but this is not so: there were infirmaries in all camps, including the so-called extermination camps. Hundreds of Jewish children were born in Auschwitz, which is a "contradictio in terminis" according to the principles of logic. "The Dachau concentration camp," writes Kogon, "had a dental service very early on. In Buchenwald one was established in June 1939 with a very modern facility, but without staff trained in the speciality." Undoubtedly, having access to a dental service is a luxury that many people in Europe today cannot afford; yet Kogon seeks in his account to detract from this. Here is an excerpt:

> "... Gradually, prisoner dentists were admitted to the dental service; in the course of time, a situation developed in which the prisoners were not treated as SS henchmen, but, on the contrary, the SS men were treated as prisoners. Since 1938, there had been two dental services for the SS in Buchenwald, one for the command and the skull battalion, the other for the troops and their families. Both were modernly equipped. There was a big difference between the treatment given to the commanders and that given to the soldiers. While the latter had all diseased teeth extracted, every effort was made to save those of the SS commanders. All dental prostheses for the SS commanders were made with gold from the mouths of dead or murdered prisoners. In the production of dental prostheses, a strict distinction was also made between soldiers and commanders. Bridges were only made for SS commanders.
> The staff made up of prisoners sought from the beginning to help the comrades as much as possible. In all services, work was carried out illegally and at great risk, in a way that is hard to imagine. Dentures, prostheses and bridges were made for prisoners whose teeth had been broken by the SS or for those who had lost them due to the general situation in the camp....".

Illegal work is not really understood. As for the SS being the ones who knocked out prisoners' teeth, apart from the absurdity of knocking someone's teeth out and then repairing them, it must be remembered that the ill-treatment was usually inflicted by kapos and other henchmen chosen from among the prisoners to maintain order and discipline. Kogon himself contradicts himself when he writes: "Some prisoners who mistreated their comrades or even beat them to death were evidently never punished by the SS and had to be killed by prisoner justice." Paul Rassinier certifies that it is true that the SS camp headquarters did not usually intervene in arguments between prisoners, so justice could not be expected. According to Kogon, the SS "were really unaware of what was going on behind the barbed wire." As an example, Kogon himself relates that one morning he found a prisoner hanging on a block. He had died "after being horribly beaten and kicked." The block leader or "Blockältester", a Green named Osterloh, had hanged him to simulate suicide and thus protect the perpetrator of the crime. It should not be understood that the SS did not practise violence on the prisoners, but that usually the kapos and block leaders spared them the trouble. Occasionally," writes Rassinier, "one of the SS distinguishes himself from the rest by his brutality, but this happens rarely and, in any case, he never shows himself to be more inhuman than those mentioned above".

Paul Rassinier devotes chapter V of his work, some forty pages, to commenting on Kogon's book. After reading it," he writes, "I closed the book again. Then I opened it again. And under the title of the flyleaf I wrote as a subtitle: "o plegaria pro domo" (prayer in favour of his interests). Rassinier considers that Kogon gave assurances to the preponderant communist nucleus in the camp in order to get the post in the infirmary. Kogon himself admits that, as the doctor's secretary, he suggested and drafted petitions which he submitted for signature. "I had Dr. Ding-Schuller in my hands", he openly admits. Here is a significant paragraph:

> "During the last two years that I spent as the doctor's secretary, I wrote, with the help of specialists from Block 50, at least half a dozen medical reports on exanthematous typhus signed by Dr. Ding-Schuller.... I will only mention in passing the fact that I was also in charge of some of his private correspondence, including letters of love and condolences. Often he would not even read the replies, he would throw the letters at me after he had opened them and say: 'Send this Kogon. You already know what to reply. It's some widow looking for comfort...".

Particularly criticised by Rassinier is Eugen Kogon's statement in which he acknowledges his subservience to the "clandestine camp leadership", referring to the Häftlingsführung, in whose actions there was, by the way, no clandestinity. Kogon implies that feared that his book might compromise certain communist or socialist politicians who controlled Buchenwald. The text deserves to be quoted in full:

> "In order to allay certain fears and to show that this account was in no danger of becoming an indictment of certain prisoners who had occupied a dominant position in the camp, I read it, at the beginning of 1945, when it was almost finished and only the last two chapters of a total of twelve were missing, to a group of fifteen persons who had belonged to the underground camp leadership, or who represented certain political groups of prisoners. These people approved of its accuracy and objectivity. They attended the reading:
> 1. Walter Bartel, Communist from Berlin, Chairman of the International Camp Committee.
> 2. Heinz Baumeister, a Social Democrat from Dortmund, who for years had been a member of the Buchenwald secretariat; deputy secretary of Block 50.
> 3. Ernst Busse, communist from Solingen, Kapo of the prisoner infirmary.
> 4. Boris Banilenko, head of the Communist Youth in Ukraine, member of the Russian committee.
> 5. Heins Eiden, Communist from Tèves, first Lägeraltester.
> 6. Baptist Feilen, Communist from Aachen, Kapo of the laundry.
> 7. Franz Hackel, left-wing independent, from Prague. One of our friends without a role in the camp.

8. Stephan Heymann, communist from Mannerheim, from the camp information office.
9. Werner Hilpert, Zentrum Leipzig, member of the international field committee.
10. Otto Horn, Vienna Communist, member of the Austrian committee.
11. A. Kaltschin, Russian prisoner of war, member of the Russian committee.
12. Otto Kipp, Communist from Dresden, additional Kapo in the prisoner infirmary.
13. Ferdinand Römhild, Communist from Frankfurt am Main, secretary of the prisoners' infirmary.
14. Ernst Thappe, Social Democrat, head of the German committee.
15. Walter Wolf, communist, head of the camp information office".

That is to say, the objectivity and accuracy of what Kogon says is attested to by his communist cronies, a cadre of the top people in the leadership of Buchenwald, which, as is clearly demonstrated, was in the hands of the Reds. In 1945 there was not a single camp leader who was not a communist or socialist. Rassinier considers it clear that Eugen Kogon avoided any comments that might serve as an indictment of the Häftlingsführung and directed most of his grievances at members of the SS: "No historian," Rassinier candidly writes in 1950, "will ever accept this. On the contrary, one can fundamentally believe that in so doing he has paid a debt of gratitude to those in the camp who gave him a quiet job and with whom he has common interests to defend in the public eye." Kogon himself admits in *Der SS-Staat. Das System der deutschen Konzentrationlager* (*Sociology of the Concentration Camps*) that the prisoners who served as kapos, who also had foremen, were the most violent towards their fellow inmates, as most of them were depraved people. In some commandos, especially in the construction, ditch and canalisation commandos, as well as in the mines," writes Kogon, "there was for the ordinary prisoner no other means of preserving his life than bribery, which reached unimaginable limits and took unimaginable forms.

Since Buchenwald was an experimental camp for SS doctors and Kogon was in the right place to know what was being done, there is ample information in his book about the operations and experiments that were carried out. Kogon takes the opportunity, however, to discredit and accuse SS personnel of the worst practices. According to him, "the conscious murder of patients in the infirmary was more commonplace for the SS than experimentation". In his eagerness to defame the SS, he adds: "There were concentration camps, such as Auschwitz, where it was carried out systematically. When the number of sick people exceeded a certain number, they were 'sprayed'. This was done by holding the prisoner by two people and injecting 10 cc. of phenol directly into his heart". Logically, in 1944, the year in which the book was already finished, Eugen Kogon could not have been aware of these criminal practices in the Auschwitz infirmary. The only thing he achieves with these assertions is to embarrass himself and discredit his book, in which, on the other hand, there are interesting facts about the sanitary services, such as the information that in the hospital there was outpatient treatment, stable treatment, dental service and convalescence.

As for the other facilities that made the harshness of life in Buchenwald more bearable, they were those that were generally available in most camps, including Auwschitz, the theoretical death camp, which had a concert hall, dance halls, swimming pool, bookshop, a non-denominational church where weddings were held, post office, football fields, cinema and theatre hall, brothel for workers, art centres, crèches for mothers and babies, and a state-of-the-art kitchen. In Auschwitz, as in Dachau, Westerbrook, Ravensbruck, Buchenwald and other camps, coins or money for internal use served to stimulate prisoners' work. Let us see what Kogon and Rassinier have to say about the functioning of these services and facilities in Buchenwald.

Regarding the postal service in Buchenwald, Kogon explains that correspondence between the prisoner and his next of kin was always permitted: one could write twice a month. The sending of parcels containing food, clothing, tobacco, etc. was also generally permitted from 1941 onwards. The receipt of money, which was used to buy food in the canteen, was limited to 30 Marks per month per prisoner. Kogon notes that "one third of the concentration camp occupants were in a position to receive money from their relatives". We give him the floor:

> "The prisoner had only two possibilities to use the money: buying in the canteen and bribery. Some kapos had not hundreds, but thousands of marks. They led a life that was in keeping with the money they had. In this respect there were irritating differences. The canteens in the concentration camps were centrally supplied, until 1943, by the Dachau concentration camp administration. In the pre-war period, it was possible to buy a lot of things there, including cakes and fine preserves. I remember a kapo who, when the canteen could still offer it, used to eat the following for breakfast: half a litre of milk with biscuits and cakes, sardines and tinned meat with bread rolls and strawberry jam and cream".

Rassinier refers to the "Bank" as the issuing institute for the special paper money which was only valid inside the concentration camp. This money, which was distributed in the form of performance bonuses, was introduced into Buchenwald in the autumn of 1943, says Kogon, who adds that from 1942 onwards Red Cross parcels began to arrive in the camp "for those foreigners whose names and prisoner numbers were known to the Red Cross in their homeland or to the Red Cross in Geneva". According to figures provided by the International Red Cross itself, from the autumn of 1943 to

May 1945 about 1,112,000 parcels with a total weight of four and a half thousand tons were sent to the concentration camps.

Regarding the sports that were played in Buchenwald, Kogon recounts that the younger prisoners got permission from the SS to play football. It seems," he adds, "that the SS regarded it as a kind of propaganda for the prisoners' good health and good humour". Be that as it may, several teams were formed, up to twelve, which were able to train and organise tournaments. The prisoners took to the field "in impeccable sporting attire", which our source attributes to the "secrets of corruption in the camp". In addition to football, handball, pelota and baseball were also played. The prisoners also managed to introduce boxing. It is absurd," opines Kogon, "but true: the concentration camp had athletes who even gave performances of their unwavering strength and skill."

From 1938 there was a rudimentary brass band in Buchenwald, which was improved and refined over the years. In 1940 the camp commandant, Hermann Florstedt, ordered the formation of a regular band with wind instruments. From then on, the prisoners in the band were exempted from hard physical labour and were given free time to rehearse. In 1941, the musicians were given the uniforms of the Yugoslav Royal Guard. "From then on, the band members, with their costumes and all the other apparatus, looked like circus conductors," says Kogon, who also reports that string quartets gave "some estimable recitals". On public holidays, the band played for the comrades in the blocks, and concerts were also given at the place de revue. On Sunday afternoons, the camp radio played the philharmonic concerts of the German stations. Today, remembering these concerts," Kogon comments freely, "I don't want to think of the tens of thousands of victims who, at the same time, were martyred to death or taken to the gas chambers in so many camps".

Shortly before the outbreak of the war, there was a library in Buchenwald with about 14,000 volumes and some 2,000 unbound works. After the outbreak of war, according to Kogon, who admits that the libraries "had very valuable books", the lending of books written in the languages of countries at war with Germany was forbidden, although they continued to be available for consultation in the library. From 1941 onwards, there were film screenings in Buchenwald, where cultural or entertainment films were regularly shown. Paul Rassinier notes that every time there was a film session, all seats were reserved for the kapos and other prisoners who were part of the camp leadership, the "Häftlingsführung".

In the summer of 1943, a decree signed by Himmler provided for brothels in the concentration camps. There were brothels in Dachau, Mauthausen, Sachsenhausen and others. Buchenwald seems to have had the first one. Kogon explains that in each brothel there were between eighteen and s girls from the Ravensbrück women's camp, who "had voluntarily presented themselves on the promise that they would be released in six months". On the purpose and use of the brothel, known by the euphemism "Sonderbau" (special house), Kogon states that its main function was "to corrupt politicians". In this connection, he writes that the Häftlingsführung, which he absurdly insists on calling the "illegal camp management", asked politicians not to frequent it. The politicians," Kogon assures us, "followed the instructions, so that the SS's aim was frustrated.

Rassinier disagrees with Kogon's comments and interpretations and considers his interpretation as a demonstration of puritanical and hypocritical prudery and clarifies that the brothel, like the cinema, "was only accessible to people of the Häftlingsführung". To expose the inconsistency, Rassinier reproduces in *The Lie of Ulysses* these words of Kogon: "Some prisoners without morals, and among them a large number of politicians, have had horrible relationships, first through homosexuality, then with pederasty after the arrival of young people". Rassinier argues that praising politicians because they did not allow themselves to be corrupted by the brothel makes no sense if one then admits that many did corrupt the young and ends by saying, "I would add still further that it was precisely to remove all excuse and justification for this corruption of minors that the SS had planned the brothel in all camps."

Eugen Kogon's book was published in France in 1947 under the title *L'Enfer organisé. Le système des camps de concentration.* In his eagerness to present the SS as the main organisers of the "organised hell", this author, who testified as a witness on 16 April 1947 at the Buchenwald trials, has no qualms about attributing to the SS crimes that he could never have known about in 1945. We should remember that he read his book before his political colleagues as early as that year. Thus, for example, he writes: "When the pregnancy of a woman was noticed in an outside women's command, she was sent, if she was Jewish, to Auschwitz to be gassed, and if she was not Jewish, to Ravensbrück to be gassed and aborted". Later he insists: "When the gassings at Auschwitz were stopped because evacuation was already being considered, the pregnant Jewish women, and then all the others, were transferred to the Bergen-Belsen 'residence camp' to be starved to death." By ironically quoting the phrase "residential camp", all that Kogon achieves, in our opinion, is to display a disgraceful cynicism and shamelessness. With these shameless statements, he shamelessly lends himself as a propaganda mouthpiece without any proof. If the intention was to starve the pregnant women to death, what need was there to transfer them to Bergen-Belsen to do so: they could have been executed directly at Auschwitz or simply left to the Soviets. What is certain is that many Jewish women gave birth in Auschwitz and that by the end of the war famine was raging not only in the camps, including the Bergen-Belsen "residence" camp, but throughout Germany.

To conclude the comparison between the works of Paul Rassinier and Eugen Kogon, which is tantamount to comparing an honest intellectual who emerged from Buchenwald physically ruined with an unconscionable Holocaust propagandist, we shall see what they both have to say about the punishments meted out to the prisoners. Once again it is worth remembering that it was the block leaders and kapos, who had their foremen, who reported inappropriate behaviour to the SS when they did not themselves punish it with slaps, kicks, insults and other humiliations. In fact, when it was the camp management who, because of the seriousness of the offence, intended to impose corporal punishment, they had to request and receive confirmation from Berlin. Rassinier states that traces or evidence of mistreatment were concealed not only from foreign visitors, "but even from the highest personalities of the SS and the Third Reich ". Here is his reasoning:

> "I imagine that if these personalities had been present at Dachau and Birkenau they would have been given as relevant explanations about the gas chambers as about the 'rack' at Buchenwald. And I ask the question: How can it be claimed after this that all the horrors of which the camps have been theatres were part of a concerted plan at the highest levels? As soon as Berlin, despite all that was hidden from it, discovered something unusual in the administration of the camps, calls to order were sent to the SS leadership".

Rassinier then reproduces the text of an order dated 4 April 1942, also quoted by Kogon, which stipulated the following:

> "The Reichsfuehrer SS and Chief of the German Police has ordered that when in his decrees on corporal punishment (both for male prisoners in protective and remand prisons and for female prisoners) the word 'aggravated' is added, the execution of the punishment is to be carried out on the naked buttocks. In all other cases, the method hitherto used in accordance with the previous instructions of the SS Reichsführer will be followed."

Eugen Kogon confirms that the camp management was supposed to certify by the camp doctor that the prisoner was healthy; but he hastens to add that "the practice was quite different", thus confirming Rassinier's assessment that the excesses were carried out in violation of the orders. Kogon, who praises and extols the moral superiority of the Reds, the communist prisoners, always above the other prisoners, certifies: "The doctor attended the procedure. Very few cases are known in which the camp doctors put an end to the administration of the blows for the benefit of the prisoners." And then he adds:

> "Sometimes prisoners were forced to inflict corporal punishment on their comrades themselves. Some did not have the courage to bring the consequences of refusing to do so upon themselves; occasionally there

was someone who was willing to do so. Political prisoners refused outright or beat in a way that was not to the liking of the SS. Then they were sentenced to the same punishment or 'softened up' in another way."

The proof that Rassinier is right that mistreatment by SS officers constituted violations of the regulations are the executions of two camp commandants: Karl Otto Koch and Hermann Florstedt. The former was commandant of Buchenwald when he was arrested in 1943 and replaced by Hermann Pister. His arrest came in the context of the investigation into a network of corruption in the camps that included the murder of some prisoners who knew too much. Koch was executed by the SS in 1945. As for Florstedt, a notorious commandant at Majdanek, after being tried and convicted by a court, he was also hanged in 1945 in the presence of the detainees. Both cases were investigated by SS Judge Dr. Konrad Morgen, who investigated up to 800 cases of cruelty and corruption in the concentration camps. As a result of his investigations, two hundred SS men responsible for the concentration camps were convicted.

On 13 March 1944, Paul Rassinier was sent to Dora-Mittelbau near Nordhausen, the labour camp where the famous V1 and V2 and also aircraft engines were being built in an underground factory, actually a tunnel. Civilians were also employed in the various factories in the tunnel. There, with twelve-hour working days, the conditions were extremely harsh, unbearable for the weakest. Add to these conditions typhus and other diseases, and it is understandable that the mortality rate was very high. The reader can get a good idea of the situation from this text by Rassinier:

"31 March 1944. For eight days the Kapos, the Lagerschutz and the block leaders (all prisoners) have been particularly irritated. Several prisoners have died under the blows: lice have been found not only in the tunnel but also in the commandos outside. The SS-Führung (SS Management) has held the Häftlingsführung (Prisoner Management) responsible for this state of affairs. In addition, the weather was appalling all day: the cold was harsher than usual and a freezing rain interspersed with showers fell uninterruptedly. In the evening, we arrived at the square freezing, soaked and hungry beyond description - let's hope that the training doesn't last too long! Bad luck: at ten o'clock at night we are still standing in the downpours, waiting for the "break ranks" that will free us. At last it arrives, it's over, we're going to be able to drink our hot soup in a hurry and drop onto the straw. We arrive at the block: shoes are cleaned, then, keeping us outside with a sign, the block leader, standing at the edge of the door, gives us a speech. He announces that, as lice have been found, the whole camp will be disinfected.... It will start tonight: five blocks, including the 35th, have been designated for disinfection. Consequently, we will not eat the soup until after the operation...".

As the war drew to a close, services and facilities progressively deteriorated in all the camps. At night, Rassinier explains, two ambulances arrived in the blocks: one ("Aussere Ambulance") provided immediate care for the sick with accidents who did not qualify for hospitalisation; the other ("Innere Ambulance") hospitalised those who required it after an examination. In the summer of 1944 "the whole camp was festering", says Rassinier, who describes the constant deterioration of the inmates' health: furunculosis, oedema, nephritis, wounds on hands and feet, cut fingers, broken arms and legs were the subject of ambulance care. By December 1944, Dora had become a large camp and no longer depended on Buchenwald. By January 1945, its facilities, designed for 15,000 people, housed some 50,000. Bread and flour were no longer available. The prisoners had to make do with two or three small potatoes, and the ration of margarine, soup and sausage was halved.

The progressive collapse in Dora had an impact on Paul Rassinier, whose endurance was stretched to the limit. On 8 April 1944, after crawling feverishly through the camp with a swollen body, Rassinier managed to enter the infirmary for the first time, from which he emerged on 27 April. On 5 May he had to return and remained in convalescence for four months, until 30 August. Six times he was in and out of the infirmary. On 10 March 1945 he was admitted for the last time. "I was ill, that goes without saying, even seriously ill, because I am still ill, but...". Thus, with these suspensory points, Paul Rassinier ends the only complaint about his ill health.

On the other hand, acts of sabotage in the Dora tunnel were continuing. The SS finally discovered that Russian prisoners were disabling a large number of V1 and V2 by urinating on the radio equipment. The Russians," explains Rassinier, "masters of looting, are also masters of sabotage and stubborn: nothing stops them. They also supply the largest contingent of hanged people. They supply it for an additional reason: they believe they have succeeded in developing a technique of evasion!" Rassinier comments that from March 1944 to April 1945 there was not a week without three or four hanged for sabotage. After that," he adds, "they were hung in groups of ten or twenty, in full view of each other. The operation was carried out in the square, in the presence of everyone". Thus, between continuous incidents, bombings, sabotage, hangings and starvation, Paul Rassinier, the father of revisionism, spent his last days in the camp. On 7 April 1945 he was included in an evacuation transport, a convoy of old wagons, and his liberation came.

What remains to be said about Buchenwald is the fame it achieved after the war for the alleged activities of Karl Koch, the commandant arrested in 1943 and shot in 1945, and his wife Ilse Koch. In large part, this fame was due to the book by Christopher Burney, a former prisoner who in 1945 published *Solitary Confinement: The Dungeon Democracy* in London, a pamphlet for which some booksellers dare to ask 135 euros for the first edition, perhaps thinking that it is a work of personal experience that has testimonial value. Nothing could be further from the truth, for when Burney arrived at Buchenwald in early 1944, Koch had already been arrested and Hermann Pister, the concentration camp commandant, was one of the gentlest on record. In describing Karl Koch, this opportunistic author paints him as the cruelest being he has ever known, who spent his time plotting cruel ways to kill prisoners. Burney adds that Ilse Koch made out with prisoners because her husband was homosexual and then sent them to the crematorium. Those with artistically tattooed skins were skinned beforehand to make artistic lampshades out of their skins.

Eugen Kogon refers to two orders of SS Reichsführer Himmler, one dated 23 September 1940 and one dated 23 December 1942, according to which dentists were to remove gold teeth from dead prisoners and gold from living prisoners "which was not suitable for repair". Significantly, however, a small amount of money was paid into their account. The gold from the teeth of the dead," continues Kogon, "with precise proof of origin, the name and number of the deceased, as well as proof of the weight, was sent to the Berlin headquarters, where it was processed into new gold for dentures. According to the monthly reports, between 182 and 504 grams of gold were collected in this way each month. Kogon explains that Major Koch had a gold pendant made for his watch chain, on which he engraved the birth dates of his children. As with the gold teeth, anything of value was taken from the bodies of the deceased. Christopher Burney himself explains that when an inmate died, the camp doctors would examine the corpse and salvage anything of interest. Arthur R. Butz recalls that medical experiments were carried out in Buchenwald and, without giving the slightest credence to Burney's story about Ilse Koch, believes that this is where the tattooed skins must have come from.

As for Ilse Koch, after she had been convicted before an American military tribunal, General Lucius Clay, the US military governor, reviewed the case and determined that, despite the testimony presented at her trial, Mrs. Koch could not be linked to the tattooed screens and other objects found in the Buchenwald commandant's residence in 1945 for one simple reason: she had not lived there since 1943, since she had been arrested with her husband. As soon as her sentence was commuted, Rabbi Stephen Samuel Wise and other influential people protested vehemently, but General Clay did not change his position and stood firm. When in October 1949 Ilse Koch was released from the detention centre where she had been held, the Americans pressured the German authorities to proceed against Mrs. Koch, "the bitch of Buchenwald", who was re-arrested and prosecuted for the tattooed skins affair and her treatment of prisoners. Although the defence proved that the statements given in the two trials were contradictory, Ilse Koch was found guilty and sentenced to life imprisonment. In 1967, she committed suicide by hanging herself in her cell.

Following the capture of Buchenwald by US troops, German citizens from Weimar, some six kilometres away, were forced to visit the camp in May 1945 and paraded en masse in front of tables lined up outside. The idea was to show them Nazi atrocities through a display of objects, including pieces of tattooed skin, a lamp shade made of human skin, and two heads reduced to the size of a fist. It was an operation conceived by the Psychological Warfare Division, on which the renowned Jewish Hollywood director Billy Wilder, who was in Buchenwald making propaganda films, was working at the time. Eugen Kogon also collaborated with the Department of Psychological Warfare ("Sykewar"), which was responsible for producing many of the false documents about Buchenwald.

The macabre idea of exhibiting the shrunken heads, obtained from some museum or anthropologist's collection, came from another Jew, Albert G. Rosenberg, who like Wilder was part of the Psychological Warfare Division. The heads almost certainly came from South America. Some Amazonian tribes, such as the Jíbaros, reduced the heads of their enemies in a ritual intended to trap their spirit in the head in order to prevent it from escaping through the mouth or eyes and harming them in the future. On 13 December 1945, documentary evidence USA-254, consisting of a shrunken head of a supposed Jew, which had been embalmed and preserved, was exhibited at one of the Nuremberg trials.

To conclude these pages on Buchenwald, it only remains to add that the propaganda film that was made was widely distributed. Alongside the Weimar citizens forced to visit the camp, a number of extras were brought in to simulate the necessary reactions: weeping, horror, shame, indignation. The aim was to instil feelings of guilt and remorse in the Germans and then show them to the world. The aim was to begin to prepare for the denazification of German society. The use of doctored photos and films was one of the repeated instruments of propaganda. The English revisionist Richard Harwood (pseudonym of Richard Verrall), author of the book *Did Six Million Really Die?*, describes in this work a revealing case of these forgeries reported in the British magazine *Catholic Herald* on 29 October 1948. In Kassel, all Germans were forced to watch a film about the "atrocities" at Buchenwald. A doctor from Göttingen who attended recognised himself on the screen, although he had never been there. He immediately realised that the images were of the victims of the Dresden genocide, whom he had assisted after the criminal Allied bombing. As will be recalled, the bodies of the dead were burned for several weeks in piles of between four and five hundred corpses.

Dachau

Before we begin to study in detail the camps in Poland where exterminationists claim that six million Jews were killed, it is necessary to say something about two concentration camps much quoted by Holocaust spokesmen: Dachau and Bergen-Belsen. As early as 14 July 1959, the Catholic weekly *Our Sunday Visitor*, a Huntington (Indiana) publication with a circulation of about one million copies at the time, published a letter by attorney Stephen S. Pinter, who had been in Dachau for about a year and a half, in which he flatly ruled out the existence of gas chambers in the camp.

"I was in Dachau for seventeen months after the war as a prosecutor for the US War Department and I can testify that there was no gas chamber in Dachau. What visitors and onlookers were shown and mistakenly told was a gas chamber was in fact a crematorium. There was no gas chamber there or in any of the other concentration camps in Germany. We were told that there was one at Auschwitz; but since it was in a Russian occupation zone, we were not allowed to investigate, as the Russians would not allow it...".

Eleven years earlier, in 1948, an American Association for the Advancement of Science (AAAS) publication had already presented a report that nobody paid much attention to. It explained the causes of death of the corpses found when US troops captured the camp. As the US Army moved deeper into Germany, the report said, its medical services anticipated what they might find:

"In the months of April and May Germany looked astonishing, a mixture of humanity travelling in every way, homeless, hungry and carrying typhus with them.... The more territory was discovered, the more cases appeared, for in West Germany, along the line of the American advance, typhus was spreading uniformly.... An estimated 35,000 to 40,000 prisoners were found in Dachau living in appalling conditions.... Extreme filth, lice infestations and overcrowding reigned in every building of the camp. Several wagons full of corpses were found in hangars in the railway station adjacent to the camp: they were remnants of the shipment of prisoners from camps further north who had been moved to Dachau in the last days of the war to escape the advancing American troops. The number of patients with typhoid fever when the camp was taken over will never be known.... Several hundred were found in the prison hospital, but they were few compared to those still living in the barracks with their comrades, bedridden, neglected, lying on four-tier bunks with two and sometimes three men per narrow, shelf-like floor; the sick and the healthy, crowded together, reeking of filth and neglect. And everywhere the smell of death."

In 1947, a year before this AAAS report appeared, the International Red Cross had submitted another report estimating that in the first months of 1945 some 15,000 Dachau prisoners died of typhus, most of them in the final two months of the war. Paul Berben, author of *Dachau 1933-1945. The Official History* (1975), confirms that more prisoners died in the last four months of the camp's existence than in all the preceding years. Even after the arrival of the Americans, some 2,000 prisoners died of starvation. For many years, a plaque commemorating the 238,000 who died there could be seen in Dachau, and during the 1950s anyone in Germany who denied the existence of a gas chamber in Dachau risked imprisonment. Today the death toll in this camp has been established at 32,000 and it is an accepted fact that no prisoners were gassed.

Today, even Jewish historians admit that there were no extermination camps on German territory. On 19 April 1960 Martin Broszat, director of the Institute of Contemporary History in Munich, declared that there were no gassings on Reich territory and that there were only a few camps in Poland. In April 1975, the well-known Nazi hunter Simon Wiesenthal published a letter in the British newspaper *Books and Bookmen* in which he acknowledged that "no one was gassed in any camp on German soil". On 24 January 1993 he confirmed this in the newspaper *The Stars and Stripes*, where he said: "It is true that there were no extermination camps on German soil and no mass gassings such as occurred at Auschwitz, Treblinka and other camps. A gas chamber was in the process of construction at Dachau, but was never completed." Even an American Jewish Committee publication, *The changing shape of Holocaust Memory*, admitted in 1995 that "there were no extermination centres 'per se' in Germany and although Dachau's conditions were horrific, its gas chamber was never used." As Wiesenthal accepts, it is not that it was not used, but that it did not exist.

Despite all this, people who waste their time visiting the Dachau museum near Munich continue to be misled and manipulated with false information. These naïve tourists are shown small rooms and told that they were used as gas chambers. What they see in reality are facilities used for disinfection or crematoria for dead prisoners. One of the rooms was a fumigation chamber used for delousing clothing. Also shown are photos taken in 1945 showing the famous door with a skull and crossbones above it with the warning: "Vorsicht! Gas! Lebensgefahr! Nicht öffnen!" ("Caution! Gas! Danger to life! Do not open!").

It has already been mentioned that Dachau began operating in 1933 and was therefore the oldest camp. Austrian political prisoners, common criminals and prisoners of all kinds, including Catholic priests, were interned there. More than 2,000 Catholic priests from various countries were imprisoned in the German camps, most of them in Dachau. The detainees usually worked in factories outside the camp. At the end of the war, the myth began to be fabricated that Dachau had been an extermination camp. As in the case of Buchenwald, it was American propaganda driven by Eisenhower, the man responsible for the death camps where almost a million Germans died, that was responsible for distorting the facts as soon as American troops took control of the concentration camp.

There are several versions of the Americans' arrival at Dachau, which we will summarise without going into too much detail. The Red Cross, thanks to international conventions, had access to prisoners of war, the POWs (Prisoners of War), who thus enjoyed international protection, but concentration camp prisoners were not included. In the early months of 1945, conditions in all the camps were already so catastrophic that on 29 March the German government, through SS General Ernst Kaltenbrunner, decided to allow a delegate of the International Committee of the Red Cross to be stationed in each camp in order to distribute relief supplies. It was made a condition that the delegates should remain in the camps until the end of the war. It was thanks to this agreement that the ICRC organised the transport of aid by road, since the use of the railways, which were completely collapsed, was reserved for the needs of the military. At this point in the war, the chaos was immense, so Kaltenbrunner's order did not reach some camp commanders. Some initially refused to allow the Red Cross to enter.

The Red Cross issued a document with a watered-down version of how Dachau was surrendered. Victor Maurer was the delegate authorised to move into the camp, where he arrived on 27 April with five truckloads of food for the prisoners. The camp was cut off due to Allied bombing. On 28 April a number of officers and guards began to escape. SS Lieutenant Heinrich Wicker, who also intended to flee at the head of the remaining guards, became the highest authority in Dachau. Maurer convinced him to surrender the camp to the Americans. With a white towel attached to a broomstick and accompanied by Lieutenant Wicker, the Red Cross representative left the camp. A motorised unit spotted them and they soon found themselves in the presence of a general, whose name is not specified, although other sources state that it was Brigadier General Henning Linden, for it was he who on 2 May submitted his report to General Headquarters confirming that on the night of 28 April, Victor Maurer, the representative of the Swiss Red Cross, arrived flying a white flag accompanied by SS Lieutenant Wicker and his assistant.

General Linden admits that he was told that there were some 42,000 "half-crazed" prisoners, many of whom were infected with typhus. He had reports that a trainload of corpses had arrived in Dachau from the north, of which Victor Maurer was unaware. General Linden asked the Red Cross delegate and the German officer to accompany him to the camp. His intention was to take pictures of the wagons full of corpses for the newspapers. According to the Red Cross report, when General Linden arrived at the camp at around 3 p.m. on 29 April, other American soldiers were already there, having been informed by civilians and journalists on their way to Munich about the existence of the concentration camp.

Apart from the Red Cross account, other accounts of the capture of Dachau state that it was these troops who, on approaching the camp, discovered the train with the bodies of some five hundred depressing-looking dead. This train, which had arrived on 26 or 27 April, was carrying starving prisoners evacuated on the 7th from Buchenwald and had been delayed because Allied planes had bombed the tracks and strafed the convoy, killing the prisoners in open wagons. Despite the efforts of the delegate Victor Maurer to get the Germans to hand over the camp in an orderly manner, as agreed with General Linden, the disorder was complete and a massacre took place: the Americans shot and killed almost all the guards and did not prevent some armed prisoners from also liquidating numerous German soldiers. Other prisoners tore down the wire fences and escaped without the Americans doing anything but firing into the air.

On these events, Lieutenant Colonel Walter J. Fellenz, an officer of the 222nd Regiment, reports how his men killed the SS guards who were still in the guard turrets: "The SS tried to point their guns at us, but we killed them quickly before they could shoot at us. We killed at least seventeen SS. Then in a fit of rage our men threw the bodies off the turrets and emptied their rifles into the chests of the dead SS." None of this appears in the Red Cross report. Nor does it say that Lieutenant Wicker, with whom Victor Maurer had engaged to safeguard the lives of the soldiers, was killed after the surrender of the camp.[6]

Two inmates wrote about Dachau. One was Father Johann Maria Lenz, who was commissioned by the Vatican to write a book about Dachau, *Christ in Dachau* (1960); the other was Nerin Emrullah Gun, a journalist of Turkish origin who in 1944 had worked in the press department of the Turkish Embassy in Budapest and was imprisoned by the Germans in April 1945, probably because of the anti-German content of his reports. In 1966 Nerin E. Gun published a book entitled *Dachau*. The work was translated into several languages, including Spanish. In Spain it appeared under the title *Dachau. Testimony of a Survivor* (1969). According to Gun, when the Americans arrived, they were not satisfied with just killing the SS guards, but even liquidated the dogs in their kennels. Father Lenz, for his part, in

---

[6] Lieutenant Heinrich Wicker was a very tall man, so that his corpse lying on the ground with his head smashed in is easy to recognise in several photos. This SS lieutenant had supervised between 28 March and 2 April 1945 the evacuation of prisoners from Neckarelz, a sub-camp of Natzweiler, to the main camp at Dachau. He also supervised between 5 and 15 April the evacuation of about 1,700 prisoners from Hessental, another sub-camp of Narzweiler, to München-Allach. His mother and sister had arrived in Dachau on 12 April to visit him. His fiancée and their two-year-old son were also in Dachau. These relatives never saw him again and subsequently reported his loss to the International Red Cross tracing service.

addition to declaring that he had never felt so close to God as in Dachau, says that the American general ordered a two-hour bombardment of the defenceless town of Dachau to take revenge for the dead found in the camp; but he later clarifies that he was finally dissuaded and gave the counter-order. There is no record of these events in the ICRC document.

It was not until forty years later that the full extent and details of the American war crime at Dachau became known. In 1986, medical colonel Howard Buechner published in the United States the book *Dachau. The Hour of the Avenger,* in which, in addition to his personal experience, he gives various eyewitness accounts, some of whom claim to be ashamed of what happened. Although in his communiqué on the liberation of Dachau General Eisenhower merely stated that 32,000 prisoners had been liberated and "300 SS soldiers were neutralised", Colonel Buechner claims in his book that the actual number of German soldiers executed was 520, of whom 346 were machine-gunned en masse on the orders of Lieutenant Jack Bushyhead. About half a hundred were killed by the inmates themselves, who according to several witnesses beat them to death with shovels and other tools. Some kapos were also torn to pieces by the prisoners. In another book about the liberation of Dachau, *Inside the Vicious Heart* (1985) by Robert H. Abzug, an eyewitness reveals that some American soldiers handed the inmates over to the Germans to be killed. Although the killing did not stop completely until 2 May, some order was established on 30 April and food was distributed. On 1 May, members of an ICRC delegation entered the camp, reporting that they witnessed piles of corpses and "also the execution chamber, the gas chamber, the crematorium ovens, etc.".

Since there is now a general consensus among researchers of both persuasions that there were no gas chambers at Dachau, these statements in the 1947 Red Cross report must be interpreted as reflecting American propaganda, which regarded as gas chambers showers of which the propaganda circulated a photo showing several US congressmen examining the holes in the artichokes. During the 1980s, these same showers were shown to tourists at the Dachau Museum and it was insisted that they were intended as gas chambers, although they were never used. A sign reads in German and English: 'Gas chamber. Camouflaged as a bath room - never used as a gas chamber." Revisionists warned that it had been proven that this facility was not a gas chamber, and the Museum authorities replaced the sign with one that reads: "Gas chamber. Here was the centre of potential mass murder". It was added that "up to 150 men could be gassed at a time". That is to say, absurdly, it was intended to silence the revisionists with the terms "potential" and "could". The propaganda also claimed that the disinfection or fumigation chamber, whose inscription on the door has been quoted above, was also a gas chamber for the extermination of prisoners. Under the photo distributed by the US Army showing a soldier is the following text: "Gas chambers conveniently located next to the crematorium are examined by a soldier of the U.S. Seventh Army. These chambers were used by Nazi guards to kill prisoners at the infamous Dachau concentration camp". Note that the plural is used, thus implying that there were several.

Since it is now time to write about the disastrous Bergen-Belsen camp, it must be emphasised once again that Germany was a maelstrom of death and misery in early 1945 and was to remain so for a long time to come, as has been explained in Chapter 11, where the plight of millions of refugees fleeing the Soviets in deplorable conditions has been recounted. In January 1945, for example, 800 German refugees were found frozen to death inside a train arriving in Berlin. The railway network was in a chaotic state, as evidenced by the fact that the train from Dachau in which the five hundred corpses were found had taken twenty days to arrive from Buchenwald. In the last note, it was noted that Lieutenant Heinrich Wicker had supervised the transfer of prisoners from one camp to another. It is not clear who gave these orders, nor what the purpose of transferring thousands of dying prisoners from one camp to another was. Perhaps the explanation is that the commandants intended to minimise the number of casualties in their camps and to shift the responsibility to others.

Bergen-Belsen

Bergen-Belsen is the paradigmatic camp of the tragedy experienced by concentration camp prisoners in the last months. So much so that it became the masterpiece of Holocaust propaganda. The images of unburied skeletal bodies of prisoners who had died of typhus, starvation and other diseases went around the world. This time it was not necessary to resort to forgeries, as the images were real. Footage of the burial of mountains of corpses at Belsen is regularly shown on television to prove the existence of camps where Jews were exterminated. However, it has been shown above that between August and December 1944, before the supply lines were cut off by bombing and the concentration camp system collapsed, some two thousand Jews were liberated from Bergen-Belsen through the joint efforts of the Jewish Rescue Committee in Budapest and the Joint Distribution Committee in New York.

We believe that at this point in our account it has been sufficiently proven that there was no deliberate policy of killing prisoners, whether Jews or gentiles, and that the hecatombs in the camps were the result of an absolute loss of control. Time and again different sources attribute the main cause of the death toll to typhus epidemics, which became a constant threat in all the camps. As is well known, exanthematous typhus is transmitted by lice. Consequently, the Germans tried to combat this disease as effectively as possible as long as possible, hence numerous hygienic measures were taken and these undesirable parasites were combated by disinfecting rooms, clothes and people. The fact that one of these insects, the human pediculus, lives on the scalp, where each louse can deposit up to ten nits per day, was the reason why prisoners were shaved as soon as they entered the camps. Since a slightly larger subspecies, pediculus humanus corporis, lives in the seams and folds of clothing, disinfection chambers were created, where hydrogen cyanide, also known as hydrocyanic acid and prussic acid, was used. The trademark used in the camps was "Zyklon B", which was manufactured by I G Farben. In all camps the ritual was the same: as soon as a batch of inmates arrived, they were stripped naked, their hair shaved, then showered and given new clothes, if not the old ones already disinfected.

Bergen-Belsen had originally been a Wehrmacht camp for prisoners of war and wounded, but in mid-1943 the SS took it over and turned it into an exchange camp, i.e. a transit camp where Jewish prisoners were exchanged for German prisoners. It seems that the first Jews to arrive came from Salonika and some had Spanish passports, so it was hoped that they would be sent to Spain. The largest group of Jews were those of Dutch origin, of whom there were about 5,000. Many of them were experts in diamond cutting who came from Amsterdam. The Jews were housed in lodgings specifically for them and formed what was called the "star camp", which was completely separated from the rest of the camps and was therefore not greatly affected by the typhus epidemic of the last few months.

It was the British and Canadians who on the afternoon of 15 April 1945 entered Bergen-Belsen, some fifty kilometres north of Hannover, the surrender of which had been agreed beforehand. The existence of the typhus epidemic was well known. There were even signs in the vicinity of the camp warning: "Danger. Typhus". There was therefore a danger that the epidemic could spread and affect troops on both sides. Many of the camp guards fled before the British arrived, but Josef Kramer, the camp commandant, remained in the camp with eighty of his men who voluntarily stayed behind. Kramer and his assistant Irma Grese met the British officer Derrick Sington at the gate, to whom they expressed their willingness to cooperate in dealing with the situation. On the same day Kramer was arrested and five months later appeared before a British military court as a war criminal.

In 1957 Derrick Sington published the book *The Offenders* in London, in which he gives the testimony of a political prisoner who explains how the typhus epidemic broke out. According to this prisoner, at the end of October 1944, a transport was admitted for the first time without being disinfected. The people who arrived in the camp brought lice with them, and they began to spread gradually. In January 1945 the disease began to appear, and by the end of February typhus was already a serious threat to the entire camp. In the last months Belsen was considered a "Krankenlager", a camp for the sick. Many of the people working in the camp were also sick. The British were unable to control the situation immediately, and a quarter of those affected by the epidemic died within the first four weeks.

Faced with the Dantesque spectacle of thousands of unburied corpses scattered across the countryside, the British began digging large rectangular pits in which to bury the dead. Two days after the entry of the troops, the first medical units arrived and set up a hospital. On the same day, all SS personnel, fifty men and thirty women, who had helped the British to cope with the catastrophe, were arrested. On the same day, 17 April, the Jews rushed to organise a Jewish Committee in the camp, which was led by Josef Rosensaft. On the 18th the burial of the corpses began. Most of the emaciated bodies of the dead were already piled up in the common graves. Bulldozers had been loading them onto trucks or pushing them directly into the graves. The British liberators forced the German women to work unprotected and without gloves, exposing them to typhus and other diseases. In some pictures, these women are seen dragging and carrying the limp dead in vehicles before dumping them in the graves. These images are shown in the famous film footage that has shocked generations of viewers. When six Red Cross detachments arrived to help on 23 April, the epidemic was still raging out of control and hundreds were still dying daily. Despite the treatment provided by the Red Cross and British Army medical units, 9,000 people died in the first two weeks after the camp was liberated, and another 4,000 died during the month of May.

As for the trial of SS Captain Josef Kramer, nicknamed in propaganda 'The Beast of Belsen', it was held in August 1945. It was the so-called 'Belsen trial', conducted by a British military tribunal outside the IMT (International Military Tribunal at Nuremberg). Because he had previously served at Auschwitz-Birkenau, Kramer was linked to the extermination of Jews through gas chambers. He made two statements before the tribunal, which are reproduced in full by Arthur R. Butz in an appendix to *The Hoax of the Twentieth Century*. In the first statement, which is seventeen pages long, Kramer recounted his experience in the various fields in which he had worked. Because of their interest, several excerpts are quoted below, some of which confirm facts already reported.

Kramer was in Auschwitz-Birkenau from mid-May 1944 until 29 November 1944. He was commandant of Birkenau, where prisoners whose ability to work, either because of illness or age, was no longer adequate, were sent. According to his statement, between 350 and 500 people died of natural causes each week. He justifies this high mortality rate by the fact that many of the inmates entering Birkenau from Auschwitz were sick: "The mortality rate," he argues, "was slightly above normal due to the fact that I had a camp with sick people coming from other parts of the camp". Kramer confirms that all prisoners who died were cremated and that they were not normally ill-treated:

> "No prisoners were flogged; there were no executions, shootings or hangings. I made frequent inspections in my camp. It was the sole

responsibility of the doctor to certify the cause of death when a prisoner died. The doctors changed all the time. One of these doctors was Hauptsturmführer (Captain) Mengele.... During my inspections I never saw prisoners who had died of physical violence. When a prisoner died, a doctor had to certify the time of death, the cause and details of the death. A doctor signed a certificate and sent it to the Camp Central Office".

On the work of the doctors, Kramer reiterated that "these doctors did everything in their power to keep the prisoners alive". According to his statement, they worked twelve-hour days and worked daily from eight o'clock in the morning until eight or nine o'clock at night. In relation to the accusations of having participated in mass murder, he said:

"I have heard allegations from former Auschwitz prisoners about a gas chamber there, about mass executions and floggings, about the cruelty of the guards and that all this happened in my presence or with my consent. All I can say is that it is false from beginning to end".

Josef Kramer was stationed in Belsen from 1 December 1944 until 15 April 1945. In his testimony, he relates that on 29 November he went to Berlin to report to "Gruppenführer" Glücks, who was in charge of the organisation of all concentration camps in the Reich under the orders of "Obergruppenführer" Oswald Pohl. Kramer quoted in his statement the words spoken by Glücks during his interview, some of which coincide with Rudolf Kastner's report and confirm that many Jews came to Belsen from other camps because they were exchanged or liberated from there. Here is an excerpt:

"'Kramer, you are going to Belsen as commandant. In Belsen there are at present many Jewish prisoners who will eventually be exchanged'. It was only later, when I was in Belsen, that I learned that these Jewish prisoners were being exchanged for German citizens from all over. The first exchange took place between 5 and 15 December 1944, and was personally supervised by an officer who came from Berlin on purpose. I cannot remember his name. His rank was 'Regierungsrat' (government adviser). The first transport contained between 1,300 and 1,400 prisoners. Glücks told me in the Berlin interview: 'It is planned to convert Belsen into a camp for sick prisoners. This camp will take in all sick prisoners and inmates from all concentration camps in northern and north-eastern Germany and also all sick people among the prisoners working in enterprises or industries...'."

Once again it can be seen that the Jews were not only not systematically exterminated, as propaganda continues to preach after more than seventy years, but that they received special attention, for bodies such as the Joint, the World Jewish Congress, the Red Cross and the Jewish Committees operating in many countries and other organisations were in contact with the German authorities and held frequent negotiations. Concerning the development of the number of prisoners and deaths in Belsen, Kramer said the following:

> "When I took office on 1 December there were approximately 15,000 people in the camp; about two hundred died in December. On 1 January there were approximately 17,000 people in the camp; six hundred died in January; on 1 February there were 22,000 prisoners in the camp. From the 15th of February onwards I couldn't say how many prisoners I had, because no more records were kept in the books, because it was totally impossible because of the flood of transports coming in from the Silesian camps, which were being evacuated, and, as I said, the records I had kept were destroyed in March.
> I do not know the number of deaths during this period, but conditions in Belsen worsened from mid-February to mid-April 1945, when the Allies arrived. I inspected the camp daily during this period and was well aware of the conditions and the large number of people dying. Mortality during the months of February, March and April increased steadily until it reached 400 to 500 a day....".

Many aspects of Kramer's statement are worthy of note. For example, the impossibility of continuing to cremate the corpses because the coal to feed the crematorium had run out, or the measures he took when he detected a case of cannibalism. With regard to the famine, the 1948 ICRC report notes that supplies to the camps were disrupted by air raids on all lines of communication. On 2 October 1944 the ICRC had warned the Foreign Office of the imminent collapse of the transport system and predicted that it would lead to starvation for all those in Germany. On the food shortages, Kramer points to the shortage of bread:

> "It was absolutely impossible for me to get enough bread to feed all the prisoners I had. At first the bread was supplied to us by the bakeries in Belsen. Then there were so many prisoners in the camp that the local bakeries could no longer supply the required quantities, and I sent trucks to Hanover and elsewhere to fetch bread, but even then I was unable to get half the bread needed to feed the prisoners on normal rations. Apart from the bread, the rations were never cut."

As for the epidemic of "rash fever" that spread through the camp in February 1945, Kramer explained that it was certified by the Bacteriological Institute in Hanover, so he closed the camp and sent a report to Berlin: "The answer I received from Berlin was that I should keep the camp open to receive convoys from the east, fever or no fever." In early March Kramer sent a full report to his superiors on the conditions in the camp. On 20 March Oswald Pohl personally went to Belsen to monitor the situation and agreed with the camp commandant that something had to be done. Before the court Kramer explained this:

> "The first measure he suggested was to close the camp and not to bring in any more people. I proposed two measures to Pohl to deal with the situation: (a) to stop the arrival of more transports and (b) to carry out immediately the exchange of the Jews in the camp. The result of this was that from my office he sent a letter to Berlin stating that the exchange of Jewish prisoners had to take place at once. This exchange finally took place during the last days of March. I don't know where the exchange was to take place, but they left Belsen for Theresienstadt. Between 6,000 and 7,000 people were sent out to be exchanged (three trainloads). These 6,000 to 7,000 constituted the total number of prisoners to be exchanged. They were transported in three convoys, each of which had 45 to 50 wagons. I received orders to dispatch three consignments on three different days. Each time I assigned a few guards - I cannot remember how many - and there was an N.C.O. (colloquially a non-commissioned officer) in charge of each train, probably a Scharführer (first sergeant), but I cannot remember. I don't know to whom these N.C.O.s had to report on the other side. All I knew was that he had to dispatch three trains. I never saw again these N.C.O.'s that I sent."

This information is of significant importance, as it would prove that among the thousands of corpses found in Bergen-Belsen there were few Jews, since most had been evacuated in three long trains at the end of March 1945. Kramer ended his lengthy testimony before the British court by stating that when Belsen was finally taken by the Allies he was quite satisfied that he had "done everything possible in the circumstances to remedy the conditions in the camp."

In a second statement, Kramer abandoned the firmness with which he had defended his actions and recanted, evidently in an attempt to save his life and on the advice of his lawyer. The logic of the defence was to offer a version that would offload onto Kramer's superiors all responsibility for the alleged mass murders in Birkenau, since the claim that Auschwitz-Birkenau was not an extermination camp had no chance of being accepted by the court. The second statement, also reproduced in full in *The Hoax of the Twentieth Century*, was much shorter and consisted of eight points that fit on two pages. In it Kramer testified that there was a gas chamber at Auschwitz, that he was not responsible for it, and that the exterminations were the responsibility of the central camp administration in Auschwitz 1. He mainly claimed that he had given Oswald Pohl his word of honour that he would keep silent. In any case, it was of no use for him to accuse Rudolf Höss, the camp commandant, and the RSHA of the crimes of which he was accused by the court, Josef Kramer and his assistant Irma Grese were hanged on 13 December 1945.

We do not want to end these pages on Bergen-Belsen without recalling the most famous of the camp's victims, the famous Anne Frank, the Jewish girl who supposedly died there and was turned into a myth by propaganda. Although we could write at length about the well-known *diary of Anne Frank* and the cult it enjoys around the world, we will only record that the diary has been proven to be a forgery - not just another forgery, but the most fruitful in every way: on the one hand, thanks to this adulterated account, hundreds of millions of children all over the world have been and continue to be deceived and manipulated, for through their identification with the feelings of the protagonist they have incubated the virus of antipathy towards the Germans as a whole; on the other hand, the fraud gave rise to a fabulous business for those who fabricated the fabrication. In 1947 the first edition appeared in the Netherlands, and in 1952 the book was published in Paris. Since then it has been published continuously throughout the world and in almost every language. In Germany it was imposed as compulsory reading in schools and teachers who doubted its authenticity were threatened with the withdrawal of their permission to teach, "venia docendi". In Spain, hundreds, if not thousands, of teachers of Spanish and Catalan continue today to propose *The Diary of Anne Frank* as compulsory reading in secondary schools. Of course, Hollywood produced a worldwide successful film, and theatre adaptations have also been made in several countries. In short, a multimillion-dollar business that has been going strong for seventy years.

Since it is necessary to argue how it was proven to be a forgery, we will now outline what happened. First of all, must be said that Anne Frank died at the age of fourteen and would therefore have been about twelve when she hypothetically wrote the diary, which is said to have been written secretly in school notebooks. In other words, a few pages in notebooks turned into a book of between 250 and 300 pages, depending on the edition. The whole thing became quite clear when Otto Frank, Anne's father, claimed sole ownership of the profits from the "business". Between 1956 and 1958, a trial was held at the County Court House in New York to settle the lawsuit between the Jewish writer Meyer Levin and Otto Frank. Levin, the plaintiff, had sued Mr. Frank for having sold the "Diary" and the "stage dramatisation" of it in ignorance of his copyright. Judge Samuel L. Coleman, who was also Jewish, ruled in favour of Meyer Levin, forcing Otto Frank to pay him $50,000 at the time for "fraud, breach of contract and unlawful use of ideas". In the verdict, Judge Coleman stated that Mr. Frank should pay Mr. Levin "for his work on Anne Frank's diary". The copious private correspondence between Another Frank and Meyer Levin, which was adduced at the trial as evidence by the parties, clearly shows that Meyer Levin was the author of the "Diary". In defence of his copyright, the writer, who had been a correspondent in Spain during the Civil War, also sued the film producer Kermit Bloombarden.

There is further evidence that Anne Frank was not the author of the diary. The British historian David Irving discovered that the original manuscript in Otto Frank's possession was written in biros, a device invented in 1949 and marketed from 1951 onwards. On the other hand, a Jewish handwriting expert, Minna Becker, ruled out that the manuscript could have been written by little Anne after comparing it with authentic texts by the child. Readers interested in more information are advised to read the work of the Spanish revisionist Pedro Varela, entitled *The Case of Anne Frank*.

Part 3
Belzec, Treblinka and Sobibor, three "extermination camps"

On 7 June 1979, John Paul II visited Auschwitz, "the place of the terrible devastation," he said, "which meant death for four million men from various nations". Thus the Pope, who announced to the world that he had gone as a pilgrim, ratified in his words the death toll on the plaque at the time, which read: "Four million people suffered and died here at the hands of Nazi criminals between 1940 and 1945". Twenty-seven years later, on 28 May 2006, another Pope, Benedict XVI, again made a pilgrimage to the camp and referred to it as "a place of horror, of an accumulation of crimes against God and against man that has no parallel in history." However, something had changed: in 1990 the old plaque had been replaced by a new one on which two and a half million dead had disappeared in one fell swoop. The new legend read: "Let this place forever be a cry of helplessness, a warning to mankind. Here the Nazis murdered around one and a half million men, women and children, mostly Jews from different countries of Europe. This official rectification of the Auschwitz death toll did nothing to alter the propaganda figures - acknowledged as false by the new plaque - whose cabalistic number of six million remains unchanged.

In official historiography, there were three other main extermination camps in occupied Poland besides Auschwitz: Belzec, Treblinka and Sobibor, all captured by the communists, who spared no millions in calculating the number of victims. In August 1944 a Soviet commission of enquiry issued a report that three million people died in Treblinka alone. In view of the fact that seven million people had already died in two camps alone, and that it was claimed that Jews had been exterminated in all of them, the number of deaths in Treblinka had to be lowered to 870,000, which was officially established as 870,000. Something similar happened with the figures for Belzec and Sobibor. The exterminationists certified that 1,720,000 people were killed in these three camps. However, Raul Hilberg, the most prestigious of Jewish Holocaust scholars, in a display of accounting rigour reduced the victims in the three camps to 1,500,000 in *The Destruction of the European Jews*, a three-volume work considered the "Bible of the Holocaust". Since the fourth part of this chapter will deal entirely with Auschwitz, we will now consider what is considered a third part of the Holocaust.

The Committee for Open Debate on the Holocaust (CODOH) has produced an admirable work entitled *One Third of the Holocaust*, in which 27 videos highlight the impossibility of accepting the canonical version of dogma about what happened in these three camps. On the other hand, the revisionist historians Carlo Mattogno and Jürgen Graf published *Treblinka: Extermination Camp or Transit Camp?* in 2002, an essential work on the camp. In 2004, Italian revisionist Carlo Mattogno continued his research with a new book, *Belzec in Propaganda, Testimonies, Archeological Research, and History*. These and other works, which we will discuss as we proceed, will allow us to contrast and refute the theses and data of exterminationists such as Raul Hilberg, and Yitzhak Arad, among others.

Belzec

Occupied Poland was reorganised by the Nazis, who established the General Government of Poland. Once it had been proven and accepted that there were no extermination camps on German territory, it was in the General Government, which after the war remained in the hands of the Red Army, that the Holocaust apostles placed all the extermination camps: Auschwitz, Belzec, Treblinka, Sobibor, Majdanek, Chelmno... Already during the last years of the war, propagandists launched quite a number of books on the mass extermination of Jews in Belzec, the camp closest to the border with the USSR, which were in fact pamphlets written without the slightest scruple. There are also numerous booklets about Treblinka, as we shall see later.

Before it began operating as a labour camp, Belzec, located between the Lublin and Galicia districts, had housed Roma detainees in April 1940. From the summer of 1940 onwards, it became part of the so-called "Otto-Programm", a strategically important road construction project to improve the transport infrastructure in the General Government. In September 1940, 6,000 Jews from Warsaw were transported to Hrubieszów, a town near the Burg River, the natural border between Poland and the USSR, to work on a road. These detainees were housed in a camp where a hospital was set up and where a Jewish doctor named Abraham Silberschein worked. In 1943 he left Poland and in 1944 he was a member of the Polish Parliament and a delegate to the World Jewish Congress. Even then he published in Geneva *Die Hölle von Belzec (The Hell of Belzec)* and several horrifying propaganda pamphlets in which he claimed that Jews were being exterminated in Poland. Silberschein claims that in August 1940, Jews from the city and district of Lublin were arrested and sent to work in Belzec. According to this Jewish doctor, "most of them died of wounds from the blows they received while working, others from typhus and other diseases, while others were simply shot". Nevertheless, he reports that their main job was to dig anti-tank ditches about ten kilometres from the Soviet border. Initially, then, Belzec was the centre of about ten forced labour camps employing some 15,000 Jews, of whom 2,500 were housed in Belzec.

In September 1940, a medical inspection took place in the Belzec group camps. The subsequent report was extremely negative, complaining that the conditions of the detainees in the network of camps were very harsh, especially in the northernmost camps. Carlo Mattogno reproduces part of the text:

> "The rooms are absolutely inadequate to accommodate so many people. They are dark and dirty. The lice infestation is out of control. About 30% of workers have no shoes or trousers. They all sleep on the floor, without any straw. The ceilings are damaged everywhere, there is no glass in the windows.... There is a shortage of soap and it is even very difficult to get water. The sick are with the healthy and sleep next to them.... All natural needs must be met locally. It is not surprising that in these conditions there are multiple cases of sickness. It is extremely difficult to be excused from work even for a day. Therefore, even the sick must go to work".

Clearly, these facilities were far from resembling those in Germany described above. Such a tragic situation was in theory unacceptable, and it seems that the dissolution of the group of camps in Belzec was considered. At least this is what emerges from the memorandum of an official of the Department of Population, Internal Affairs and Social Welfare of the General Government Administration, which is written in response to "your telephone enquiry regarding the dissolution of the Belzec camp and its current deficiencies". This report acknowledges that due to the lack of cooperation on the part of SS Brigadeführer (Major General) Globocnik it was not clear whether the Jewish camp in Belzec ("das Judenlager in Belzec") had already been closed. The memorandum, the text of which is also reproduced by Carlo Mattogno, reads:

> "The Jews from the Belzec camp are to be disbanded and put to work in the Otto-Programm. Those from Radom and Warsaw are to return to their homes. The Jewish Councils are even prepared to go in search of their racial comrades. In connection with the execution of this task, there is a disconcerting lack of clarity, and the proper cooperation of the SS organs and of the Polizeiführer (SS and Police Chief) cannot always be achieved in practice...."

From a new report it is known that during the month of October 1940 the demand for Jews for forced labour continued, so that they were required in other districts of the General Government. "From the Jewish camp in Belzec," it is specified, "4,331 released Jews were assigned to the construction of roads and buildings for the Otto-Programm. Their condition was such that they could not be regarded as entirely suitable for work".

We can add little more about Belzec up to 1942, since we have no other texts that might be useful. The next text quoted by Carlo Mattogno in his study on Belzec is dated 2 February 1942 and is a directive from the commander of the order police in the district of Galicia on the labour service of Jews ("Arbeitseinsatz von Juden"). It should be remembered that Germany is already at war with the USSR, which helps to understand the severe tone of the text:

> "With reference to a number of notes which I have received from German authorities and agencies, I must strongly emphasise the following: Recently we have seen more and more cases in which Jewish workers assigned to urgent work for war aims are being rounded up by various official agencies and are thus being withdrawn from the necessary work for which they have been designated. Jews who have been recruited for important Wehrmacht war projects as well as for projects of the Four Year Plan possess a corresponding identity card bearing the stamp of the agencies or authorities to which they have been assigned.
> I request once again that all units under my command, and in particular the Ukrainian auxiliary police, be informed so that those Jews who have been ordered to perform a work service are forbidden to be grouped together. If this order is violated, I shall punish the guilty."

Once again, it is clear from the text that there were first-, second- and even third-class Jews. For one reason or another, many of the Jews who were available for work in connection with the war effort were being protected through the efforts or pressure of various agencies. Indignation led the commandant to threaten sanctions against those who unjustifiably allowed Jews to be removed from their assigned workplaces.

Extermination by electrocution in Belzec

According to official historiography, from the end of 1941 Belzec became an extermination camp, implying that the Jews deported to the camp were murdered as soon as they arrived. Exterminationists have established that the mass killings began on 17 March 1942 and ended in December of the same year. As for the methods of extermination, there is something for everyone. Sometimes, in order to paint a picture of the extreme degeneracy of the Germans, the crimes were spiced up with sadistic stories, for example, that the soldiers, after forcing the Jews to dig a ditch, threw them into it and ordered their comrades to defecate on them until they were covered with faeces. On 10 July 1942, the Polish government-in-exile in London received the first report of extermination by electric shock. Since this method was progressively perfected in the imagination of extermination propagandists, it is worth devoting some space to it, as Carlo Mattogno provides explicit texts on this sophisticated technique of mass murder.

This report of 10 July stated that the trains were unloaded as soon as they arrived. The men went to a hut on the right and the women to another hut on the left. There they undressed, presumably to take a shower. They were then all taken together into a third shed with an electrified metal plate or sheet, where they were executed. According to this report, the bodies of the victims were taken by wagons to a pit some thirty metres deep dug outside the perimeter of the camp by Jews who had all been murdered. On 15 November 1942, Dr. Ignacy Schwarzbart, a prominent Zionist who was one of the Jewish representatives in the Polish National Council, confirmed the facts: "The victims are ordered to undress apparently to take a bath and then they are taken to barracks with a metal plate as a floor. The door is then closed, electric current is passed through the bodies of the victims and their death is instantaneous. The corpses are loaded into wagons and taken to a mass grave some distance from the camp." A fortnight later, on 1 December, the report of 10 July was published in a Polish magazine written in English. The headline was as follows: "Extraordinary Report on the Jewish Extermination Camp in Belzec". The newsletter of the "Jewish Telegraphic Agency" immediately echoed Dr. Schwarzbart's statement and published an article entitled: "250,000 Warsaw Jews led to mass execution: Electrocution introduced as new method of mass murder of Jews". The propaganda campaign was already well underway and Schwarzbart held a press conference in London at which he claimed that one million Jews had already been murdered. On 20 December 1942 it was the turn of *The New York Times*, the all-powerful Jewish media. The article published by the paper stated among other things: "No up-to-date data are available concerning the fate of the deportees, but there is news - irrefutable news - that execution sites have been set up at Chelmno and Belzec, where those who survive the shootings are killed en masse by means of electrocution and lethal gas".

As time went on, new variants circulated that "embellished" the sophisticated story of the killings by means of electric currents. On 12 February 1944, *The New York Times* published a report entitled: "Fugitive Tells of Mass Executions in Electrified Vats". The story, dated 11 February in Stockholm and distributed by the Associated Press, quoted as its source a young Polish Jew who had managed to escape. According to his account, "the Jews were forced to stand naked on a metal platform operated by a hydraulic lift that lowered them into a huge tank, which was filled with water up to the victims' necks. They were electrocuted by shocks of current through the water. The elevator would then lift the bodies up to a crematorium above."

As for the pamphlets on the extermination of the Jews in Poland circulated by Abraham Silberschein, we cannot resist the temptation to reproduce significant excerpts from *The Hell of Belzec*, published in Geneva in 1944, as mentioned above. Silberschein was a member of the Zionist Action Committee and directed clandestine activities in Poland from Switzerland. The following quotations come from *Belzec in Propaganda, Testimonies, Archeological Research, and History*, the work by Carlo Mattogno that we have been consulting as an indispensable source, although

Jurgen Graff in *Der Holocaust auf dem Prüfstand* (1992), published in Spain under the title *El Holocausto bajo la lupa*, also cites some of these writings:

> "The Jews deported to Belzec were ordered to undress, as if they were going to the toilet. They were, in effect, taken to a room capable of holding several hundred people. However, they were executed en masse by means of an electric current. A boy who managed to escape," Silberschein said, "told me what happened after the electrocution. The fat was extracted from the bodies in order to make soap out of it. The remains of the bodies were thrown into anti-tank ditches dug along the Russian border by the super-sergeant Major Dollf. The burial of the sacrificed had to be carried out by the strongest Jews, selected from among the condemned. It often happened that they had to bury their own relatives.... The Jews buried in Belzec came mainly from Lublin, Lemberg (Lvov) and other towns in eastern Galicia. About 300,000 Jews were buried there.
> Having dumped so many bodies in the mass graves, it was impossible to cover them with a sufficiently thick layer of earth. This caused the stench of rotting flesh to spread throughout the area. This stench is still perceptible (i.e. in April, at the time of the writing of this report by the witness). Travellers on the Zawada-Rawa Ruska line close their windows, as the dreadful stench penetrates into the compartments and makes them vomit. I myself had to travel on this line on several occasions and was able to convince myself of this. On 10 April 1943, I passed through there for the last time. The Christian population of Belzec has left the place because of this stench".

In *Belzec Execution and Extermination Camp* (*Hinrichtungs und Vernichtungslager Belzec*), another of Silberschein's libels, he introduced the variant of extermination through the heat of an electric furnace. In his delusions, Silberschein went on to invent other means of extermination in Belzec, which, in his words, "had become a fortress of the Inquisition such as had never before been seen in the history of mankind". The idea that the suffering the Jews endured was unparalleled in all of history is one of the fundamental elements of Holocaust propaganda. The more atrocities they were able to conceive of, the better this thesis could be substantiated. As if electrocution and the heat of the electric furnace were not enough, Silberschein wrote:

> "Special buildings for gas experiments were built there. Special factories for the production of soap and bitumen made from Jewish fat. Hospitals were built for the purpose of first carrying out transfusions of blood taken from Jewish children. Special types of hanging equipment were devised. Even the Wehrmacht soldiers could not believe it, but even so, those installations were seen by reliable witnesses."

As if the writings of Zionist leader Abraham Silberschein were not enough, the propaganda ideologues used a new town crier to deceive and manipulate public opinion, Stefan Szende, another unscrupulous fake, a Jewish journalist of Hungarian origin who wrote in German and Swedish. Szende published *The Last Jew of Poland* in Stockholm in 1944, which was translated into English and German the following year. In 1945 the book was also published in the United States, where it appeared under the title *The Promise Hitler Kept*. Thanks to the Jewish Virtual Library, we discovered that Willy Brandt, Chancellor of West Germany from 1969 to 1974, was Szende's "lifelong comrade-in-arms" and wrote the foreword to his memoirs, published in 1975. Stefan Szende's boldness and unscrupulousness in the aforementioned work break all records. After locating Belzec near the border with the USSR and confirming the large-scale fortification work undertaken in the area by the Germans, he writes: "It was in these unfinished fortifications that the Nazis set up their slaughterhouse in which millions of Jews were exterminated. For the first time, then, it goes from hundreds of thousands to millions. The text is not to be missed and deserves an extensive quotation and further commentary:

> "Exterminating five million people is an enormous task, and even in our age of technical perfection it requires much preparation and organisation, and there are many problems to be solved for those who planned to carry it out. Tens of thousands, even hundreds of thousands of Jews had been taken to Pjaski. Tens of thousands, even hundreds of thousands had died as a result of mistreatment, starvation and disease. But there were still millions left, and they were all to be exterminated in accordance with the Fuehrer's orders.
> Even the effective removal of headbands and lice on a large scale requires a certain technique. However, no one can doubt that the Germans are a very talented people in technical matters. Among them were highly skilled death engineers. These men had received instructions from the Gestapo and set to work to solve the technical problems that might arise in the mass extermination of millions of defenceless men, women and children. They solved them brilliantly. Their Führer, Adolf Hitler, and Himmler, the head of the Gestapo, can be well satisfied with them and their work.
> Months of planning and construction operations were necessary, but the Germans are a patient people and the goal was worth the time taken to achieve it. The extermination of millions of Jews with the latest means of modern technology - what a tempting goal! Hundreds of thousands of man-hours were required. Tens of thousands of tons of valuable materials were employed in the process. But at last, in the spring of 1942, the scientific slaughterhouse at Belzec was ready.
> The mass extermination facility at Belzec occupied a plot of land almost five miles wide. This area was surrounded by barbed wire and all sorts of modern devices to keep the prisoners in and the others out. No one was

allowed near the place except authorised persons or those who could never leave it alive. But despite all these precautions there were one or two people who saw inside Belzec and still managed to escape. Desperation sometimes brings ingenuity.

Selected SS men guarded the Belzec extermination camp. Men without nerves. There is a lot to do in a slaughterhouse, and the commanding of the victims gives great pleasure to the sadists. For example, the clothes and belongings of millions of victims had to be collected and sorted. For this purpose the SS picked out a few Jews from each arriving convoy. Of course, these Jews were not spared. Their execution was simply postponed. Two of these Jews did indeed manage to escape. They escaped to the ghetto that still existed at that time in Rawa-Ruska. In Rawa-Ruska they reported the details of the technically perfect massacre that was taking place in Belzec.

As far as I know, no Jew ever managed to escape from Belzec and reach neutral or Allied territory. The two Jews who managed to escape from Belzec to Rawa-Ruska in the summer of 1942 were probably killed later when the ghetto was liquidated, but a group of people who heard the testimonies of these two Belzec escapees fled. The following description of the Belzec slaughterhouse comes from them.

Trains entering Belzec loaded with Jews were taken to a tunnel in the underground facilities of the execution building. There the Jews were unloaded and ordered to divest themselves of all their belongings. In 1942 the Jews who went to Belzec did so dressed and carrying with them all kinds of belongings. Fully loaded trains arrived in Belzec from Germany, Austria, Czechoslovakia, Belgium, Holland, France and the Balkan states, and all were treated in the same way. These Jews were told to take all their belongings with them, as they were to be resettled in the East. In this way tens of thousands of Jews showed up with all kinds of belongings, typewriters, sewing machines, crockery, silverware, etc.

Everything was taken from them. The seized goods were carefully sorted, numbered, labelled and subsequently used by the master race. The Belzec staff had to be spared this tremendous task, which, of course, hindered their real work, so the Jews were subsequently sent to Belzec naked.

When the trainloads of naked Jews arrived, they were herded like a flock into a large hall capable of holding several thousand people. This room had no windows and a metal floor. Once the Jews were all inside, the floor of this room was lowered like a lift to a large water cistern below until the Jews were waist-deep in water. Then a powerful electric current was sent through the metal floor and within seconds all the Jews, thousands at a time, were dead.

Then the metal floor rose again and the water emptied. The bodies of the slaughtered Jews were now piled up on the floor. Then it switched to a different stream and the metal floor turned incandescent red so that the bodies were incinerated as in a crematorium and only ashes remained. The floor was then turned over and the ashes slid into prepared receptacles. The smoke from the process was evacuated through large factory chimneys.

This was the whole procedure. As soon as he had finished, he could start all over again. New consignments of Jews were constantly pouring into the tunnels. Each of the trains brought between three thousand and five thousand Jews at a time, and there were days when the Belzec line received the arrival of between twenty and thirty of these trains.

Modern industry and technical engineering in the hands of the Nazis overcame all difficulties. The problem of how to exterminate millions of people quickly and effectively was solved.

From the underground slaughterhouse a terrible stench emanated throughout the neighbourhood, and sometimes whole districts were covered with the foul-smelling smoke of burnt human bodies."

These agents of propaganda, who had no financial problems getting their works translated and published in different countries, nourished each other and each took advantage of some of the other's witticisms and reiterated them. The theme of the stench or stench of bodies spreading around, for example, had already been narrated by Abraham Silberschein. What is truly outrageous about the barbarities of Willy Brandt's colleague Stefan Szende is that he does not even bother to make the lies plausible. He is so brazen that he assumes the stupidity of the readers and understands that they will not even bother to try to rationalise his nonsensical stories. If we analyse the text paragraph by paragraph, it is easy to see that Szende is lying through his teeth.

He begins by saying that "exterminating five million people is a huge task". Besides being enormous, it is impossible when you consider the demographics. To put five million Jews in Belzec is an unbelievable barbarity. We know that in Hungary, where there was no persecution until the spring of 1944, there were more than half a million Jews, and there were also waves of refugees pouring in from Poland and Slovakia. Belzec, according to the exterminationists, ceased to function at the end of 1942. It has also been said that even before the war the emigration of European Jews to the United States and Palestine was massive. On the other hand, it is an accepted fact that the Soviets evacuated more than a million Jews from Red Army-occupied Poland to the interior of the USSR. Another 300,000 Jews from other parts of Europe, according to Jewish historian Gerald Reitlinger, entered the Soviet Union between 1939 and 1941. Based on these and other available data related to emigration statistics, there could not have been more than three million Jews in German-occupied Europe. Far more surprising are the figures from *The World Almanac and book of facts*, the prestigious annual international reference publication, according to which there were 15.3 million Jews worldwide in 1940. Surprisingly, by 1947 their number had risen to 15.6; in other words, the Jewish population had not only not decreased by six million, but had actually increased.

Szende, whose ability to lie must be pathological, claims that it took "hundreds of thousands of hours of work" and "tens of thousands of tons of valuable materials" to build the technologically advanced complex. We know that in September 1940 medical inspectors visited Belzec and reported that it was an infamous camp lacking the most basic facilities: no water, damaged roofs, broken windows, no latrines. Yet Szende claims that a little more than a year later, thanks to hundreds of thousands of hours of work, had been converted into a sophisticated centre some five miles wide, more than eight kilometres long, with trains running in underground tunnels. Yitzhak Arad, author of *Belzec, Sobibor, Treblinka* and director of the Holocaust Museum in Israel, encloses plans of the three camps in his book, but they are not to scale. The problem is solved if we look at the letters on display in the Museum, which make it clear that each side of the camp was about 270 metres long. Szende is lying here too. Furthermore, Luftwaffe aerial photographs show that Belzec was shaped like an irregular rectangle of about 250 x 300 metres.

As usual, the sources of information are people who say what others told them they had seen. In this case, Szende alludes to two Jews who escaped and turned up in 1942 in the Rawa-Ruska ghetto, whose existence in the midst of so much merciless extermination is nothing short of astonishing. He soon makes it clear that both must be dead, and that his account of the "technically perfect massacre" was told by people who heard what the deceased witnesses had said.

Above the immense windowless room with a metal floor capable of holding several thousand people, which functions as a huge lift that descends to a pool or tank where the victims receive a shock that electrocutes them all witheringly, there would be no need for commentary were it not for the fact that Szende continues his hallucinations and adds that the fantastic contraption went up again, drained and turned into a gigantic incineration chamber capable of turning the piled-up bodies of thousands of Jews into relics. The fantastic mechanisms of the marvellous metal plate also allowed it to rotate one hundred and eighty degrees and to discharge the ashes into large containers installed "ad hoc". And so on and so forth, because immediately more trains came and the whole operation was repeated. Since Szende states that on some days between twenty and thirty convoys arrived loaded with three or five thousand Jews, a further multiplication makes it possible to calculate that more than one hundred thousand Jews were exterminated daily. In other words, in one week a population equivalent to that of the entire island of Majorca could be wiped out cleanly and without any problems - an enormous task!

And yet, from Szende's ideas, new variants emerged. In a text dated 7 October 1944, a Soviet commission of enquiry presented an extract from a statement made by a woman named Rozalja Schelevna Schier, who claimed that her husband worked in Belzec and told her that two trains of fifty or sixty wagons loaded with Jews arrived daily and were directed to baths powered by gas and a high-voltage electric current. Within five minutes," she said, "all the people in the baths were dead. Inside the hangar, the floor automatically folded up and the bodies fell into a pre-dug trench where the victims were doused with a flammable liquid and burned."

Other means of extermination in Belzec

Another famous agent of extermination propaganda in Belzec was Jan Karski (Jan Kozielevski), who passed for a Christian Jew and a practising Catholic. Today he is considered a hero in Israel, in the United States and in Poland. Bronze statues of him have been erected in several American and Polish cities. In Tel Aviv, too, there is a statue of Karski, who in 1982 was designated "Righteous Among the Nations" by Yad Vashem. In the same year, a tree bearing his name was planted in Jerualen on the Avenue of the Righteous Among the Nations. In 1994 he was made an honorary citizen of Israel. According to his personal mythology, Karski, who adopted as many as half a dozen noms de guerre, operated underground in Warsaw during the years 1940-41 and became a courier for the Polish government in exile in London. This propagandist claims that, after bribing an Estonian soldier, he was smuggled into Belzec in October 1942 disguised as a guard. This is unlikely, or at least does not seem credible, since when he described the camp in 1944, he made gross errors: he placed it "on a large flat plain", when in fact it was on the side of a hill. Moreover, there were never any Estonian guards at Belzec. Karski did not even bother to locate Belzec correctly. He placed it 160 kilometres from Warsaw, when in fact Belzec is 300 kilometres southeast of the capital.

In November 1942 he began to fabricate part of his story, according to which "death trains" transported Jews from the Warsaw ghetto to Belzec, Treblinka and Sobibor in order to kill them. Since the invention of the electrified metal plate had already appeared in the report to the Polish government of 10 July 1942, which was subsequently subscribed to by I. Schwarzbart, one of the many Zionists who swarmed around the exile government, Karski also took up the idea and adopted it for his reports. On 25 November 1942 he arrived in London and delivered a new document to the Polish Government, which was transcribed under the title "The Polish Government in London receives news about the liquidation of the Jewish ghetto in Warsaw". In his report, Karski claimed that the German occupation of Poland had hardened since March 1942, "when Himmler ordered," it read, "that the extermination of 50% of the Polish population in the General Government should be completed by the end of 1942." How Karski could have known of the existence of an order from Himmler to eliminate only half of the Jews is not explained. However, the text immediately adds that, although the "German murderers" had begun their work "with extraordinary gusto," Himmler was not satisfied, so during his visit to the General Government in July 1942 he personally decreed "the total destruction of Polish Jewry." Karski detailed in his report savage Gestapo and SS scenes, similar to those depicted in Hollywood movies: "The chase in Warsaw," he recounts, " began on 21 July, when German police cars suddenly appeared in the ghettos. The soldiers rushed into the houses, shooting the inhabitants on sight, without explanation. The first victims were mainly from the educated classes".

Carlo Mattogno reproduces the report in its entirety. We shall quote only a few excerpts. Karski relates that the SS were characterised as "utterly ruthless, cruel and inhuman". In one passage, it is related that the Jews were led to a square, where the old and the crippled were separated, taken to the cemetery and shot. The rest were loaded into wagons with a capacity of forty people, in which he crammed one hundred and fifty. The text continues as follows:

> "The wagon floor is covered with a thick layer of lime and chlorine sprayed with water. The doors of the wagons are closed. Sometimes the trains leave as soon as they have been loaded, sometimes they remain on the siding for a day or two or even longer. The people are so crowded that those who suffocate to death are squeezed side by side between those who are still alive and those who are slowly dying from the lime and chlorine fumes, from the lack of air, water and food. Wherever the trains arrive, half the people are dead. The survivors are sent to special camps in Treblinka, Belzec and Sobibor. Once there, they are exterminated en masse.
> Only young and strong people are left alive because they are valuable slave labour for the Germans. However, their percentage is very small, for out of a total of 250,000 'relocated' only 4,000 have been sent to auxiliary work on the battlefronts.... Thus, under the guise of relocation to the east, the slaughter of the Jewish population is being carried out. It began on 22 June 1942 and has continued ever since. By the end of September 1942, 250,000 Jews had been eliminated. The extent of this operation is reflected in a few figures: In the Warsaw ghetto, according to official German statistics, about 433,000 people lived in March 1942. Despite the high mortality caused by hygienic conditions, epidemics, starvation, executions, etc., the number of Jews in the ghetto remained more or less stable, because to replace the dead, Jews from other parts of Europe, Germany, Austria, Holland, were sent to Warsaw. According to leaked information from the Department of Labour, only 40,000 people are to remain in the ghetto, to be employed in the German war industry.... Simultaneously with the extermination of the Jews in the Warsaw ghetto, ghettos in the provinces, in Falenica, Rembertow, Nowy Dwor, Kaluszyn and Minsk Mazowiecki are being liquidated. In the Wilno district there is only one Jewish community left, in the same town, consisting of only 12,000 people. According to news reaching London recently, the

Germans have murdered 60,000 Jews in Wilno, 14,000 in Kowno and 50% of the Jewish population of Lvov; similar news reaches us from cities in eastern Poland, such as Stanislavo, Tarnopol, Stryj, .
The methods applied in this mass extermination are, apart from firing squads, electrocutions and gas chambers".

The account of the arrival of the trains and the immediate electrocutions follows, with only a few variations, which is why we are sparing you the account of the train arrivals and the immediate electrocutions. What is new, apart from the trains with lime and chlorine to suffocate the deportees, is that the use of gas chambers as a means of mass extermination is already announced, although no details are given as yet.

By the end of November 1942, therefore, Ignacy Schwarzbart and Jan Karski were very active in England, and they had allies. Richard Law, the British Under-Secretary of State for Foreign Affairs, announced on 26 November that he had received a request for an audience with Mr Silverman and Mr Easterman, two English Jews. Samuel Sidney Silverman, president of the British section of the World Jewish Congress, and Alexander L. Easterman, political secretary, wanted to talk "about the extermination of the Jews in Europe". Easterman, in particular, gave the Under-Secretary of State the documents, i.e. the pamphlets placed in his hands by a member of the Polish National Council. On this subject, David Irving provided very interesting information in a lecture given in Madrid in 1989. The British historian said that as early as August 1942 the Political Warfare Executive and the Foreign Office knew that the Jews were launching a propaganda campaign based on falsehoods. Irving claimed to have documents from the British archives and read a text from August 1943 sent to Churchill by the head of propaganda, in which he said: "I don't know how much longer we can maintain that the Germans are killing Jews in gas chambers. It is a grotesque lie, like the lie that the Germans in World War I were making butter from the corpses of their enemies, and it made our propaganda lose credibility.

In December 1942 Karski was back in Poland. He is credited with a visit to a regrouping camp fifty kilometres from Belzec, which he is said to have entered disguised as a Polish policeman. In March 1943 the newspaper *Voice of the Unconquered* published Karski's alleged report, entitled "Recent eyewitness report of a secret courier from Poland", which again painted a Dantesque spectacle: "When I was there," he says, "some 5,000 men and women were in the camp. Yet every few hours new transports of Jews, men and women, young and old, would arrive on the last journey to death." There is nothing missing in the story: living skeletons, a dying child staring at the ceiling, the guards shooting into the crowd indiscriminately, bodies strewn everywhere, dehumanised, expressionless, cold guards, picking up corpses and piling them by the fence, etc., etc., etc.. The story ends with a train loaded with thousands of men, women and children parked on a siding for days on end:

> "The doors never open. Those inside suffer inhuman agony. They have to perform their natural needs on each other's heads. Many wagons are painted with lime, which begins to burn with the dampness of urine and increases the torture of the barefoot and naked. Since there are not enough wagons to kill the Jews in this relatively cheap way, many are taken to nearby Belzec, where they are killed with poisonous gases and the application of electric currents. The bodies are burned near Belzec. Thus, over an area of fifty kilometres huge pyres burn the bodies of Jews day and night."

In 1944 Karski finally published a memoir entitled *Story of a Secret State*. In it he reveals that in October 1942 he entered the Warsaw ghetto, where he made contact with the Jewish socialists of the "Bund", whose leader revealed to him the deportation of some 300,000 Jews to extermination camps and told him that he obtained information about Belzec because many of the Estonian, Latvian and Ukrainian auxiliaries who worked in the camp for the Gestapo were in the service of Jewish organisations for money. Karski explains that it was thanks to this Bund leader that he obtained the uniform and papers of one of the Estonians and got into Belzec. In the book, he narrates the adventure of entering the camp, followed by the episodes invented by this fake. In the American edition of the book, it is added that disguised as an Estonian guard he visited other death camps besides Belzec. Today, it seems, Karski's stories have fallen into disrepute even among official historians. Nevertheless, he enjoyed international recognition until his death in July 2000 and even post mortem: in 2012 the Polish Senate posthumously honoured him as a hero for his revelations about the Nazi genocide in Poland; in the United States, President Obama posthumously awarded him the Presidential Medal of Freedom, the nation's highest civilian honour.

Before the end of the Second World War, the story of the soap factory made from the fat of the Jews of Belzec, a story that had previously been launched by A. Silberschein, was also explored. By the post-war period, the idea had caught on and was recreated in several propagandistic works. One of these is the famous *Black Book*, whose main authors were Vasily Grossman and Ilya Ehrenburg, both pro-Red Army progandists. *The Black Book* was arguably the brainchild of the famous Jewish Anti-Fascist Committee, later purged by Stalin, although the American Jewish Community collaborated closely with their Soviet colleagues. Elsewhere, also in Belzec," write Ehrenburg and Grossman, "there was a soap factory. The Germans selected the fattest and killed them to make soap. Arthur Israelevitch Rosenstrauch, a bank clerk from Lvov to whom we owe the information, got his hands on a bar of 'Jewish soap'. The Gestapo bandits did not deny the existence of the factory. When they wanted to frighten a Jew, they would say: 'We will make soap from you.'

In 1946 Simon Wiesenthal published an article entitled 'RIF' in *Der Neue Weg*, a Jewish magazine published in Vienna. In it he wrote that in Folticeni, a small Romanian town, at the end of March 1946, twenty soap boxes had been solemnly buried in the town's Jewish cemetery. It was stated in the article that the boxes "had recently been found in a German army depot". On the boxes was the acronym RIF, which according to Wiesenthal stood for "pure Jewish fat" ("Rein jüdisches Fett"). The boxes were for the Waffen-SS and "on the wrappings," wrote the notorious Nazi hunter, "it was said with cynical and total objectivity that the soap was made from Jewish bodies. The real meaning of the acronym was "Reichsstelle für industrielle Fettversorgung" ("Reichsstelle für industrielle Fettversorgung"), . On 9 January 1991, the Jewish historian Yehuda Bauer finally acknowledged in a letter that the acronym RIF had nothing to do with Jewish grease. In 1946, however, Wiesenthal recreated the fable in these terms:

> "At the end of 1942 the terrible expression 'transport for soap' was heard for the first time. It was in the General Governorate, and the factory was located in Galicia, in Belzec. In this plant, from April 1942 until May 1943, 900,000 Jews were used as raw material.... Some solid parts of the bodies were separated and sent to northern Germany, where a special oil for submarine engines was produced. The human bones went to a bone mill in Lemberg, where they were turned into fertiliser.... What was left over, the residual fat, was required for the production of soap.... To the civilised world it is perhaps incomprehensible how the Nazis and their wives looked upon this soap in the Generalgouvernement. In every bar of soap they saw a Jew, whom they would have bewitched and thus prevented a second Freud or Einstein from growing up. The burial of the soap in a small Romanian town will seem supernatural. The bewitched pain, enclosed in this small everyday object, tears at the already insensitive human heart of this century. In this atomic age, the return to the darkest sorceries of the Middle Ages seems like a phantom! And yet, it is true!"

From high voltage currents to tailpipes

Incredible as it may seem, after having been spread throughout the war that Jews were exterminated en masse by modern electrocution techniques, another version began to be constructed in the post-war period . Before the beginning of the Nuremberg trial, the Polish and Soviet authorities had officially adopted the story of electric currents. In a report on the German extermination camps in Poland prepared in 1945 for the Nuremberg trials, Dr Jerzy Litawski, the official in charge of the Polish War Crimes Office, insisted that from the spring of 1942 'special electrical installations were used in the camp for a rapid mass extermination of Jews. Under the pretext of bathing, completely naked Jews were led into a special building called 'baths' whose floor consisted of plates through which high-voltage electric current flowed." The Soviet Communists, without whose collaboration the fabrication of the myth of the six million would not have been possible, drew up Document USSR-93 for the Nuremberg trial, which was taken over and presented by the Polish government. In it, the version of the electric currents through the ground was once again accepted. Still during the session of 19 February 1946, Document USSR-93 was quoted by the Soviet prosecutor, Colonel L. N. Smirnov, who recalled that, although the camp was founded in 1940, it was not until 1942 that "special electrical apparatus for mass extermination" was installed.

Contradictions arose in early 1946 as a result of investigations by a Lublin court judge, Czeslaw Godzieszewksi, and the Zamosc prosecutor, Jan Grzybowsky, who, after questioning dozens of indirect witnesses, created confusion as to what the method of extermination had been. Some said that people spoke of gas; others that electric currents were used; some maintained that they were killed in a room from which air was extracted and asphyxiation was provoked. Still in March 1946 a Polish witness insisted that Ukrainian guards serving in the camp had told him that several hundred Jews had been stuffed into a room and killed by means of an electric current. On 11 April 1946, Prosecutor Grzybowsky issued a tortuous report in which he acknowledged the existence of gas chambers, but admitted that "it had been impossible to determine how people were killed in them". This statement included the name of Rudolf Reder, who on 29 December 1945 had testified as a witness before Judge Jan Sehn, a member of the Commission for the Investigation of Nazi War Crimes.

Rudolf Reder was to go down in history as one of the two Jews considered to be the sole survivors of Belzec. The other, Chaim Hirzsman, collaborated with Beria and his henchmen in the repression of resistance to communism in Poland. Hirzsman was involved in the torture, summary executions and deportation to Siberia of 50,000 political "undesirables", for which he was killed in March 1946 in the course of an anti-communist uprising against the reign of terror in the country. For a change, many historians described the insurgents as anti-Semites. Thus Reder, who, according to him, was already 61 years old when was arrested in Lvov on 16 August 1942, became until his death in 1968 a museum piece, a kind of rara avis who had survived the Belzec extermination. Thanks to his statements, the thesis began to take shape that there was a rectangular building in Belzec with six gas chambers, three on each side of a central corridor that ran lengthwise through the plant. These chambers were equipped with lift doors that opened and allowed the corpses to be evacuated on ramps located on the outside, on the sides of the building. In *Belzec, Sobibor, Treblinka: The Operation Reinhardt Death Camps* (1987), Yitzhak Arad notes that this facility measured 24 x 10 metres. According to Reder's testimony, as soon as his train arrived in Belzec five thousand people were taken to this building and exterminated in these gas chambers. In his description of the process, he claimed that from a shed attached to the alleged gas chambers a tube 2.4 cm in diameter was introduced, but he could not detail the chemical process that caused death.

In 1946, Reder finally published *Belzec*, a booklet of some seventy pages, published in Kraków and written in Polish. In the opinion of some exterminationists, this booklet is the best and most important account of what happened in Belzec. In 2000, Polish historian M. M. Rubel published its English translation in volume 13 of the journal *Polin: Studies in Polish Jewry*. This translation, which happens to be one of the most reliable and accessible, is commented on by Thomas Kues, a revisionist scholar of Belzec, Treblinka and Sobibor, the camps of the so-called Aktion Reinhardt, in an extensive article published on 26 April 2008 on the website of CODOH (Committee for Open Debate on the Holocaust). Kues points out that Rubel reveals in his introduction that before testifying before Judge Jan Sehn on 29 December 1945, Rudolf Reder had already testified twice before the Jewish Historical Commission. Kues also stresses that Reder did not write the book alone, but in collaboration with a woman named Nella Rost, who wrote the foreword. Professor Rubel believes that Rost not only wrote the foreword to *Belzec*, but was the actual author of the pamphlet. Her full name was Nella Rost Hollander and she was the daughter of a Zionist rabbi named Abraham Ozjasz Thon, one of the forerunners of Jewish nationalism[7]. Nella Rost was linked to the World Jewish Congress in Uruguay. So much so that in 1963 the Stephen Wise Institute and the World Jewish Congress published her work *Belzec. Gas Chamber. Tomb of 600,000 Jewish martyrs*. All this invites

---

[7] Abraham Ozjasz (Osias) Thon, a first-generation Zionist, collaborated with Theodor Herzl in the preparations for the First Zionist Congress in Basel in 1897, the year in which he became the rabbinate of Kraków, a position he held until his death in 1936. At the Versailles Peace Conference he represented the Jewish National Council of Galicia. In *Diaspora Nationalism and Jewish Identity in Habsburg Galicia*, Joshua Shanes places Thon alongside two other Jewish nationalist leaders, Mordechai Ehrenpreis, who between 1900 and 1914 was Chief Rabbi of Bulgaria in Sofia and later also an organiser of the Basel Congress, and Markus Braude, who married Natalia Buber, sister of the famous philosopher, and was also a delegate to the First Zionist Congress. In his book, Shanes quotes Nella Rost Hollander's words about her father, who studied in Berlin with Ehrenpreis and Braude: "In Berlin the fate of the three friends was the same. All three pursued the same goal, which they expressed in the same way: 'The three of us will be the first to create a new type of rabbi and we will be the princes of a spiritual aristocracy'.... My father believed that first of all it was necessary to obtain a general science and Jewish knowledge as first-class weapons against all attacks and all arguments about national ideas." Nella Rost confirms that her father, in addition to a spiritual leader, aspired to be a political leader who from the pulpit would preach "the revolution of the contemporary generation."

the suspicion that Rudolf Reder was chosen in Poland by the Jewish Historical Commission for its propaganda purposes.

Since the official version that finally prevailed was that in Belzec, Treblinka and Sobibor the Jews were exterminated by means of carbon monoxide emanating from the exhaust pipes of diesel engines, it is worth knowing what Reder says about it in *Belzec*. Taking Professor Rubel's translation in the journal *Polin*, Reder describes the deadly agent as follows:

> "The machine was big, about a metre by a metre and a half. It consisted of an engine and wheels. The motor whirred at intervals and worked so fast that you couldn't see the spokes of the wheels turning. It would run for twenty minutes. Then it was switched off. The doors from the chambers leading to a ramp would open. The bodies were thrown out onto the ground in a huge pile several metres high. Those who opened the doors took no precautions. We didn't smell any special stench; I didn't see any balloons filled with gas or any powder being thrown out. What I saw were petrol cans.... But once, when the engine failed, I was called to fix it. In the camp they called me 'Ofenkünstler' (artist or oven maker?). That's why I was selected. I looked around and saw glass tubes connected to metal pipes, which led to the gas chambers. We thought that the engine was working well, producing high pressure or sucking in air, or that the petrol was producing exhaust fumes that were suffocating people. The cries for help, screams and the terrible groans of the locked-up people who were slowly suffocating lasted between ten and fifteen minutes."

Certainly, it is hard to believe that if the Nazis really wanted to eliminate hundreds of thousands of people, they would decide to use such rudimentary and shoddy mechanisms. Nor is it understandable that after having credited the Germans with the invention of sophisticated means of mass electrocution, after having acknowledged that they had mastered high technology, the exterminationists decided to adopt as the official version a rudimentary technique, an impossible piece of junk. Perhaps our English translation was unfortunate, so it may be pertinent to refer to the version offered by Yitzhak Arad in his 1987 book, which states that these were diesel engines with 200 horsepower and eight cylinders, which came from tanks captured from the Soviets. According to Arad, these diesel engines released a mixture of carbon monoxide and carbon dioxide, which were introduced into the gas chambers through pipes installed in adjoining rooms. However, it should be noted that a diesel engine does not emit carbon monoxide, but black soot containing oxygen. In 1984, the American engineer Fritz Berg published a technical study entitled *Diesel Gas Chambers: Myth within a Myth*. In it he claimed that the amounts of carbon monoxide produced by a diesel engine were insufficient to kill under the intended conditions. Berg's work shook the foundations of the official version and a translation appeared in Germany in 1994 under the title *Diesel Gas Chambers: Ideal for Torture, Absurd for Killing*.

The "Gerstein Report" on Belzec

Nella Rost Hollander argues in *Belzec. Gas Chamber. Grave of 600,000 Jewish Martyrs* that Rudolf Reder's report is consistent with that of Kurt Gerstein, the other key witness who testified that Jews were exterminated en masse in Belzec. Nella Rost considers that the fact that the two statements are identical confirms their veracity. The "Gerstein Report" is, together with Rudolf Höss's statement on Auschwitz, one of the main documents used by exterminationist historians to prove the existence of the Holocaust. It is therefore pertinent to dwell on it and the circumstances in which it was obtained. Since there are handwritten parts, the first thing that revisionist historians admit is that the writing is indeed by Gerstein's hand. What they question, therefore, is the credibility of what he says and its veracity.

Kurt Gerstein, considered the SS with a heart, was apparently the historical model on which Rolf Hochhuth was based to conceive the character of *The Vicar* (1963), the famed play in which Pope Pius XII is unjustly accused of having done nothing to prevent the Holocaust, which is a slanderous and blatant falsehood. This famous play, translated into more than twenty languages and adapted several times for the cinema, was instrumental in attacking the Catholic Church, and Hochhuth has been accused of being a nattering nincompoop at best. There are critics who argue that Hochhuth was not a fool, but worked in the service of obscure interests. But this cannot now be the subject of our attention, for we are concerned here with the statement of Gerstein, an SS officer who was head of the technical disinfection services of the sanitary corps and as such supervised the delivery of disinfection materials to the camps. In order to supply Zyklon B to some of the camps of the Polish Government General, Gerstein was reportedly in August 1942 in Belzec, where, it is alleged, he watched in horror the extermination of Jews in the gas chambers.

There are as many as six statements, mostly typed, although there are some partially handwritten ones, attributed to Kurt Gerstein. The main version, considered the 'Gerstein Report', was submitted to the IMT in Nuremberg on 30 January 1946 under the number PS-1553 and is typed mostly in French. What happened to Gerstein at the end of the war is unclear. According to one version, he initially fell into the hands of American interrogators in Rottweil, near the Black Forest, to whom he allegedly handed over a seven-page typed document. Gerstein allegedly told them that he had held a responsible position in the NSDAP, although in reality he had acted as an agent of the Reverend Martin Niemöller, an anti-Nazi Lutheran pastor. He confessed that he had been operating in gas chambers and was willing to testify as a witness in court. Another version places Kurt Gerstein three months later in the Cherche Midi military prison in Paris, where he hand-wrote in French a document enclosing invoices for Zyklon. According to the official story, Gerstein was found hanged in his cell on 25 July 1945, but in fact it can be said that he mysteriously disappeared after leaving his reports, as his body was never found.

In his report, Gerstein begins by recounting biographical aspects that trace the facts back to his Christian upbringing. After having been a member of the Nazi party for three years, he was expelled in 1936 because of criticism of his religious beliefs. In 1938 he was arrested by the Gestapo and spent six weeks in the Welzheim concentration camp. Gerstein then tried to regain membership in the NSDAP in order to infiltrate it, but was refused. On 10 March 1941 he applied for admission to the Waffen SS and, despite his record, was surprisingly admitted on 15 March. By January 1942 he had already become head of the technical disinfection services. Kurt Gerstein's hagiographers have taken advantage of his autobiographical account to elevate this Holocaust religious saint to the altars. The whole story smells rotten; but the part about his experience in Belzec is absolutely unbelievable. The fact that historians like Raul Hilberg and Gerald Reitlinger accept it as a reliable source only discredits them.

In the revised edition of *The Hoax of the Twentieth Century* (2003) Arthur R. Butz reproduces in full in an appendix the basic text of Gerstein's statement, as well as additional reports. He extracts them from the book *The Confessions of Kurt Gerstein*, by Henri Roques, published by the IHR. Roques, also known under the pseudonyms of Henri Jalin and André Chelain, became world famous because of his doctoral thesis, read on 15 June 1985 at the University of Nantes under the title *The Confessions of Kurt Gerstein. A comparative study of the different versions*. The thesis was a devastating refutation of the so-called "Gerstein Report" and was awarded a "very good" mention by a committee of university experts. In the course of a fulsome dissertation, Roques convincingly concluded that the accusations of mass gassings made by Gerstein were baseless and that the alleged cover-up of the massacre by the Catholic Church was false. The French Jewish lobby, supported by left-wing organisations, began a campaign of harassment and demolition and demanded a retraction from the university authorities. In 1986, for the first time in eight centuries of university history in France, the University revoked Roques' legally obtained doctoral degree. It did so pursuant to an order from the French government, whose intervention in the affair provoked a scandal.

Carlo Mattogno clarifies how Kurt Gerstein's statement became the official version. On 30 January 1946, Charles Dubost, deputy attorney general of France, submitted to the Nuremberg tribunal a set of documents classified as PS-1553, which included a report in French dated 26 April 1945 and signed by Kurt Gerstein. In this document, Gerstein recounted one of his alleged visits to the Belzec camp. Mattogno points out that half a year before the presentation of PS-1553 in Nuremberg, on 4 July 1945, *France Soir* had published the article 'A Nazi camp executioner confesses: 'I exterminated 11 000 people a day'', whose author, Geo Gelber, publicised the story of the engine-operated gas chambers. On 16 January 1947 a German translation of document PS-1553 was presented as documentary evidence before the IMT in the "doctors' trial". Thus, although Reder and Gerstein did not agree exactly: Gerstein spoke of a diesel engine and Reder of a petrol engine, the method of extermination reported by Kurt Gerstein was officially established by Western jurisprudence. The "Gerstein report" monopolised the attention of historians as soon as it was published and would become the cornerstone of the evidence that the extermination at Belzec was a historical fact. In 1948, the Polish government, which years earlier had certified that electrocution was the method of extermination at Belzec, endorsed the thesis of asphyxiation by carbon monoxide emanating from an engine exhaust pipe:

> "With the victims in the gas chambers, the final phase of the liquidation process began. The doors were closed behind the victims who crowded the chambers. The engine was started and carbon monoxide was pumped into the chambers through special exhaust pipes. Within minutes the screams of the suffocating people would subside and after 10-15 minutes a special team of Jews would open the outer doors of the chambers."

Since Gerstein's texts are available, it is best to refer to them in order to evaluate them. We shall begin with the report dated 26 April 1945 in Rottweil, in the central, most detailed part of which he describes his visit to Belzec. Before going to the camp, the memorandum states that he travelled to Lublin in the company of Wilhelm Pfannenstiel, where on 17 August 1942 they were met by SS Gruppenführer Globocnik, who told them that they were about to learn the greatest of secrets, that anyone who revealed them would be shot immediately, and that the day before he had already executed "two chatterboxes". Here is a quote from this conversation:

> "... Your other duties will be to change the method of our gas chambers (which now run on the exhaust gases of an old diesel engine) by employing more poisonous material which produces a more rapid effect, prussic acid. But the Führer and Himmler, who were here on 15 August - the day before yesterday - ordered that I should personally accompany all those who had to see the installations. Professor Pfannenstiel then asked: 'What did the Führer say? Globocnik, now Chief of Police and SS for the Adriatic Riviera and Trieste, replied: 'Faster, faster, carry out the whole programme!' he said. And then Dr. Herbert Lindner, head of the Ministry of the Interior said: 'But wouldn't it be better to burn the bodies instead of burying them? A future generation might think differently about these matters!' And then Globocnik replied: 'But, gentlemen, if ever such a

rotten and cowardly generation should arise after us who did not understand the goodness and necessity of our work, then, gentlemen, all National Socialism would have been for nothing. On the contrary, bronze plates should be buried with the inscription that it was we who had the courage to carry out this gigantic task'. And Hitler said: 'Yes, my good Globocnik, exactly, this is also my opinion'".

Apart from the fact that Hitler never travelled to Lublin and therefore the words attributed to him by Globocnik's mouth are pure invention, it is portentous that there are historians who can grant credibility to this puerile propaganda pamphlet for the gullible. Globocnik's bluster, whose claim to claim for posterity responsibility for the extermination of the Jews is approved by Hitler with the words "yes my good Globocneck", is perhaps intended to exemplify the absolute evil that nested in Germany's Führer. The report continues with the journey from Lublin to Belzec, which took place the following day. Once in the camp, the report recounts the arrival of the first train shortly before 7 a.m. on 19 August 1942: a convoy of forty-five wagons carrying 6,700 people, of whom 1,450 arrived dead. After ordering the Jews to undress and to deposit valuables and money in a place set aside for this purpose, women and girls were directed to the hairdresser to have their hair cut with one or two snips, which was then put into sacks to make mattresses, etc. Then the march to the gas chambers begins:

> "I am with Wirth, the police captain, just to the right of the gas chambers. Completely naked men, women, children, babies, even one-legged people are approaching. In one corner a sturdy SS soldier tells the poor devils in a loud, deep voice: 'Nothing will happen to you. All you have to do is to breathe deeply, it strengthens the lungs; this inhalation is a necessary measure against contagious diseases, it is a good disinfectant!'... Mothers, ayas, with babies at their breasts, naked, many children of all ages, naked too; they hesitate, but enter the gas chambers, most of them without saying a word, pushed by those who follow behind, pressed by the whips of the SS men. A Jewish woman in her forties, with eyes like torches, throws the blood of her children in the face of her murderers. Five lashes to the face, delivered by Captain Wirth himself, drive her into the chamber.... Captain Wirth orders: 'Fill her up well'. Naked, the men stand on each other's feet. 700-800 crammed together in 25 square metres, in 45 cubic metres! The doors close. Meanwhile, the rest of the transported, stark naked, are waiting..."

Anyone who stops to think for a few seconds can understand that it is absolutely impossible to cram seven or eight hundred people into a room of 25 square metres and two metres high, because there would be about thirty bodies in each square metre. Only with the use of a scrap metal press could so many people be squeezed into such a small space, in which case the use of gas would be superfluous, as the people would have been crushed to death first. The story continues with more scenic effects in order to highlight for the umpteenth time the Nazis' boundless cruelty. When the chamber is emptied and reloaded, for example, the Gerstein Report reads: "The bodies are thrown out, blue, wet with sweat and urine, their legs covered with excrement and menstrual blood. Everywhere, among the others, the bodies of children and infants...". As for Captain Christian Wirth, after the five lashes to a woman's face and the order to fill the gas chamber to the brim, another scene worthy of the best Hollywood pamphlets takes the opportunity to portray him as an unscrupulous beast greedy for riches, which, of course, symbolises the German nation as a whole. This is the familiar rhetorical device of putting the part (Wirth) for the whole (the Germans):

"... Two dozen workers are busy inspecting the mouths, opening them by means of iron hooks: 'Gold on the left, without gold on the right!'. Others inspect the anuses and sexual organs for money, diamonds, gold, etc. Dentists with pliers pull out gold teeth, bridges or caps. At the centre of it all is Captain Wirth. He moves here like a fish in water. He hands me a big jar full of teeth and says: 'Calculate for yourself the weight of the gold. This is only from yesterday and the day before yesterday! You wouldn't believe what we find every day! Dollars, diamonds, gold! But see for yourself!' Then he takes me to a jeweller who deals with all these values...".

Then follows the story of the burial of the bodies in large ditches, which according to Gerstein measured 100 x 20 x 12 metres and were located near the gas chambers. Gerstein explains that after a few days the bodies swell up, so that the contents of the trenches are pushed upwards by two to three metres. However:

"After a few more days the swelling will stop and the bodies can crumble. The next day, the trenches were filled again and covered with ten centimetres of sand. I heard that a little later they built grills out of railway rails and burnt the bodies on them with diesel oil and petrol to make them disappear. In Belzec and Treblinka no one bothered to record the approximate number of people killed. The figures announced by the BBC are inaccurate. In reality about 25,000,000,000 million people were killed; not only Jews, but especially Poles and Czechoslovaks, who, in the opinion of the Nazis, were of bad stock".

Obviously, the figure of 25,000,000 was untenable, since, as has been said, there were only about three million Jews in German-occupied Europe. Even including Czechoslovaks and Poles in this figure could not be credible, especially considering, as will be seen, that no trace was left of the alleged victims. Aware that the death toll was unacceptable nonsense, the comment about the BBC and the 25,000,000 victims in the gas chambers was deleted from the text printed in the NMT (Nuremberg Military Tribunals) volumes. Gerstein's interrogators allegedly induced him to write a second report in Rottweil, which is dated 4 May 1945. It is more likely that it was written a year after his death. His wife helped to clarify the matter by stating that she had discovered the document in 1946 among her husband's belongings at the Hotel Mohren in Rottweil. According to Mrs. Gerstein, her late husband had deposited it there without her having known about it until then. It can be assumed that this report is the German translation of document PS-1553, submitted to the ITM on 16 January 1947, typed and unsigned. Arthur R. Butz wryly notes that "the discovery of such a document in the dark days of 1946 naturally underpinned her status as the wife of St. Gerstein rather than the wife of an ordinary SS officer." The death toll alleged in this second memo would already be in line with the official figure of six million.

Wilhelm Pfannenstiel, witness in Belzec

Carlo Mattogno devotes ten pages in *Belzec in Propaganda, Testimonies, Archeological Research and History* to studying the statements and attitude of Wilhelm Pfannenstiel, a medical doctor and SS officer, whose name appears in the different versions of Kurt Gerstein's statement. As will be recalled, Gerstein claims that he travelled with him to Lublin and there they both met SS Gruppenführer Odilo Globocnik, whom Pfannenstiel asked about Hitler's opinion. The following is therefore a review of the information provided by Mattogno, whose authority on the subject is undisputed.

Arrested by the Allies after the war, Pfannenstiel was interrogated as one of the defendants in the IG Farben trial, held between August 1947 and June 1948. He was then questioned about his relations with Gerstein. In order to save his own skin, he tried to find a loophole and confirmed that he had witnessed gassings through the exhaust pipe of a diesel engine. Although he denied that he had been in Belzec or Treblinka, he admitted that he had heard that gassings took place in Belzec. Although he replied to Prosecutor von Halle that he had not been to Belzec, he did not hesitate to state the following:

> "Answer: There were - I think - six chambers in a slightly elevated building.
> Question: Were the people inside naked and cramped together?
> Answer: Yes, the chambers were filled piece by piece.
> Question: Were there children?
> Answer: Yes.
> Question: How was the diesel exhaust pipe introduced?
> Answer: From a 1,100 horsepower engine. The exhaust pipes were inserted into the chambers".

Mattogno considers it obvious that prosecutor von Halle knew about the Gerstein Report, which was known to Pfannenstiel. Moreover, he assumes that the prosecutor knew that Pfannenstiel was aware of it when he questioned him, which is why the interrogation was full of conditions. It was in this way that from 1950 onwards Pfannenstiel became the guarantor of the veracity of the Gerstein Report, a fact that was exploited by Holocaust historiography. As a result of his collaboration, Dr. Wilhelm Pfannenstiel was eventually acquitted for lack of evidence in the three trials in which he was involved. All passages on in which Pfannenstiel was implicated were excised from the first official publication in Germany of the Gerstein Report of 4 May 1945, prepared by the historian Hans Rothfels in 1953. Richard Harwood reports that this version was published in Bonn in 1955 by the Federal German government for distribution in German schools under the title *Dokumentation zur Massenvergasung* (*Documentation on Mass Gassings*).

Having thus assumed the role of endorser of the Gerstein Report. In all his court appearances, Dr. Pfannenstiel continued to confirm the official lies and historiographical dogma, although his statements became progressively more moderate, and he toned down Gerstein's uncontrolled excesses. On 9 November 1959, for example, he showed that he was aware of all the works published by exterminationist historians and even cited Gerald Reitlinger's *Die Endlösung (The Final Solution)*. Although eleven years earlier he had denied having been in Belzec, in this 1959 interrogation he stated that he had travelled with Gerstein from Lublin to Belzec, where he witnessed the arrival of a transport with some five hundred Jews, some of whom had died on the way because of overcrowding in the wagons. Four years later, on 8 November 1963, at the so-called Belzec trial, he maintained at another hearing that he had witnessed the arrival of a twelve-car train carrying between three and five hundred people, from which "occasionally" women and children got off. If that number of people were travelling in twelve carriages, it can be estimated that there were between 25 and 42 detainees in each carriage. Gerstein had referred to convoys of 6,700 deportees, of whom 1,450 had arrived dead. What Pfannenstiel did recover with precision, however, was his memory of dates. On 30 October 1947 he gave none; in his statement of 6 June 1950 he spoke of the "summer of 1942"; but on 9 November 1959 he confirmed that he had gone with Gerstein to Lublin on 17 August 1942 and that they had gone to Belzec on the 18th or 19th. Finally, on 25 April 1960, he gave the exact date of the alleged gassing: "If you ask me about executions of Jews," he said, "I must confirm that I witnessed the execution of Jews on 19 August 1942 in the Belzec extermination camp".

Finally, Professor Pfannenstiel was one of the fourteen witnesses who in January 1965 testified at the Belzec trial of Josef Oberhauser in Munich[8]. According to Yitzhak Arad, Oberhauser was in charge of building the camp and in the second half of December 1941 became an assistant to Captain (SS Hauptsturmführer) Christian Wirth, who was appointed commandant of Belzec. In his work, Arad tries to make him the scapegoat for the alleged gassing of 80,000 Jews. Josef Oberhauser denied any responsibility and claimed that he had always acted on superior orders. To save himself, he confessed to lies at the trial and admitted that Jews had been gassed in Belzec. The criminal section of the Munich court sentenced him to four years and six months of hard labour for complicity in 300,000 cases of first-degree murder. In the end, he served only half of the sentence.

Archaeological investigations in Belzec

From the ultramodern technology of electrocution and mass incineration, in one go, they switched to the crude system of exhaust pipes. Since then, it has been maintained that hundreds of thousands, if not millions, of Jews were exterminated in Belzec by this rudimentary method. On 22 September 1944 Rudolf Reder testified before the Lvov prosecutor that three million people had been eliminated in Belzec. On 11 April 1946, T. Chrosciewicz, the Polish prosecutor in Zamosc, summarised the results of his investigation in a report and lowered the number of victims to 1,800,000. Finally, in 1947, the Central Commission for the Investigation of German Crimes in Poland set the death toll at the Belzec camp at 600,000, a figure accepted by official historiography and questioned only by revisionist researchers.

Thus, it is claimed that between March and December 1942, 600,000 people were murdered in Belzec by means of an absurd, almost home-made system. In Chapter 16 of *Belzec, Sobibor, Treblinka*, entitled "Improving extermination facilities and techniques", Yitzhak Arad writes: "The new gas chambers that had been built in Belzec in June/July 1942 served as a model in the other two camps". Arad insists that the same extermination technique was used in Belzec, Treblinka and Sobibor. According to this Jewish historian, with the construction of new gas chambers, the capacity for execution was expanded and improved; but the system of diesel engine exhaust pipes as an extermination technique not only remained unchanged, but served as a model for the other camps. Yitzhak Arad himself writes the

---

[8] Josef Oberhauser had been captured, tried and sentenced by the Soviets, who released him in 1956. When the Belzec trial began in 1963, he was one of eight accused of crimes in the camp. On 30 January 1964 the trial collapsed and all were acquitted. Shortly afterwards, however, they were re-arrested. Oberhauser appealed and in 1965 he was the only defendant in the trial which took place from 18 to 21 January.

following about the burials and incineration of the alleged 600,000 victims at Belzec:

> "In Belzec, the 600,000 victims had already been buried when the cremation began. Over a period of four or five months they had to be dug up and burned. This was the only reason why the camp continued to exist with full staff until the spring of 1943, even though the transports with Jews had arrived and were liquidated in November 1942. The fact that during the cremation operation no more convoys arrived made it easier for the authorities to carry out their task."

That is, at Belzec, the extermination operations ended in November/December 1942; but, although no more trains arrived, the camp was not closed because the entire staff spent three or four months digging up the dead for cremation, supposedly to erase the traces of genocide. It seems that the Nazis, previously described as masters of technical engineering and exemplary in the use of revolutionary technologies, suddenly became models of improvisation and disorganisation, unimpressive bunglers incapable of planning elementary tasks. It has already been said that the Belzec area was about 250 metres wide and 300 metres long. It is hard to understand how in such a small space, minus the space occupied by the various camp facilities, 600,000 bodies could have been buried, dug up, burned and reburied in just a few months - as many as the entire population of Malaga, Spain's sixth largest city in terms of population.

Carlo Mattogno devotes Chapter IV of his work on Belzec, entitled 'Belzec in Polish Archaeological Research', to commenting on the work of a group of archaeologists who between 1997 and 1999 worked in the area of the former Belzec camp under the orders of Professor Andrzej Kola. The excavations were jointly decided by the "Rada Ochrony Pamieci Walk i Meczenstwa" (Council for the Safeguarding of the Memory of the Struggle and Martyrdom) and the "Holocaust Memorial Museum" in Washington. During separate excavation periods lasting two years, 33 graves were found in two separate areas of the camp, occupying a total area of 5,919 square metres and a volume of 21,310 cubic metres. The smaller one measured 5 x 5 metres, i.e. 25 square metres, and had a depth of 1.70 metres. The largest had a volume of 2,100 cubic metres, measuring 24 x 18 and a depth of between 4.25 and 5.20 metres.

The two main witnesses to the alleged extermination, Kurt Gerstein and Rudolf Reder, gave detailed descriptions of the mass graves. In 1945, in a statement to the Jewish Historical Commission, Reder reported: 'One pit was 100 metres long and 25 metres wide. A single pit contained 100,000 people. In November 1942 there were thirty graves, that is, three million bodies". In another statement made before Judge Jan Sehn on 29 December 1945, the witness Reder further specified the dimensions of the enormous graves: "the graves were all of the same dimensions and measured 100 metres long, 25 metres wide and 15 metres deep". Thirty graves of these dimensions would be equivalent to a large grave measuring three kilometres long by 750 metres wide, i.e. 225 hectares. However, after having declared that all thirty pits were the same, Reder declared that the area he had seen covered about 7.5 hectares. Kurt Gerstein, for his part, in the famous report of 26 April 1945 stated the following: "The naked bodies were then thrown into large ditches of about 100 x 20 x 12 metres located near the death chambers. In his report of 6 May 1945 he stated: "The naked bodies were loaded onto wooden carts and then thrown into pits situated a short distance away measuring 100 x 20 x 12 metres". To top it all off, in his report of 11 April 1946, the Zamosc prosecutor wrote:

> "All the mass graves had the same dimensions: 100 metres long, 25 metres wide and 15 metres deep. The bodies thrown into the graves were covered with lime. The detainees then covered the piles of bodies with sand. There may well have been thirty or forty or even more such pits in the camp."

Although according to Arad the bodies had been dug up and burned, in two of the larger graves archaeologists found bodies that had neither been exhumed nor cremated. Robin O'Neil, a British Holocaust researcher, claims in *Belzec: The 'Forgotten' Death Camp*, published in the quarterly *East European Jewish Affairs*, that there were "many thousands", but does not specify how many. For his part, Michael Tregenza, a singular exterminationist who declares that the testimonies of Reder and Gerstein are unreliable because they are full of embarrassing lies and absurdities, dares to estimate the number of bodies found in these graves at 15,000. The curious thing about Tregenza is that, despite his contempt for the statements of Reder and Gerstein, he gives credibility to other witnesses and in the article "Belzec Das vergessene Lager des Holocaust" (Belzec the forgotten camp of the Holocaust, 1999) he writes that, although the Belzec facility only operated for 133 days, "several hundred thousand Jews were exterminated in Belzec. Today there is official talk of at least 600,000 people murdered. However," he adds, "in the light of new research and excavations, a considerably higher number of victims, possibly close to a million, must be assumed".

Tregenza, although the bodies found in the two large graves were not dug up, puts the number of bodies found there at 15,000. It is hard to understand why the Polish authorities did not do as the Germans did when they discovered the bodies of Polish officers murdered by Beria's NKVD in the Katyn graves. Then, in the middle of the war, the graves were opened, the bodies were exhumed, autopsies were performed and attempts were made to identify the victims. "Why," asks Carlo Matogno, "were the bodies not exhumed from the mass graves in Belzec?" The answer is that of the first 236 samples taken initially Professor Andrzej Kola only published the result of 137, obviously the ones he considered most significant. Even so, only two of them bore the explicit designation of "human bodies". In the analyses published by Kola there are human remains in three of the seven samples taken from grave number 10, the largest one, and in two more samples out of the ten taken from two other graves, number 3 and number 20. This leads to the conclusion that in the above-mentioned graves there were rarely any scattered bodies.

Of course, the presence of bodies in other layers of the graves cannot be excluded. It is very likely that in the same grave number 10 there were more human bodies, since the examination of the samples indicates the presence of bodies in a state of saponification. During the two years of work, samples continued to be taken from the 33 graves, and new human remains were found. As early as 1998, a year before the archaeological investigation was completed, Robin O'Neil was quick to announce that the remains of the bodies found belonged to victims of the gas chambers who had not been exhumed and burned. Since the official interpreters have taken the presence of bodies as proof that mass extermination took place in Belzec, Carlo Matogno writes these words of response in emphatic terms:

> "The claim of these commentators - that the number of bodies found at Belzec disproves the revisionist thesis - is not only false, but grotesque. Of course, no revisionist historian would allow himself to declare that there were never any deaths at Belzec. As will be seen in the next chapter, there were deaths among the detainees because of epidemics, hard labour and misery..... If anyone really wants to refute these theses, he should prove that there are burial places in the camp containing hundreds of thousands of victims."

Carlo Mattogno concludes that the results of the excavations are incompatible with the exterminationists' thesis and that the most likely interpretation that can be drawn from Professor Kola's archaeological research "is that the pits contained at most several hundred bodies". Kola published the results of his excavations in a book containing 37 colour photographs. They show all sorts of insignificant objects: horseshoes, keys, padlocks, the remains of pots and pans, rusty scissors, pieces of glass and porcelain, combs, bottles, coins, etc.; but not a single photo shows a body or part of a body. In any case, thousands of people, probably tens of thousands, died in Belzec. Many probably died in 1940, when the conditions in the camp were, as has been said, extremely inhumane.

It may be argued that few bodies were found because they were burned. Yitzhak Arad claims that in the spring of 1942 Himmler paid a visit to Treblinka in which he decided that all the bodies should be burned; but there is no record of such a visit and there is every indication that it never took place. In any case, Arad himself states in his book on the Operation Reinhardt camps that at Belzec the exhumation and cremation work began in December 1942. The truth is that almost nothing is known about this gigantic operation. In his aforementioned report of 11 April 1946 the Zamosc prosecutor wrote this:

> "In December 1942 the transports of Jews to Belzec stopped. The Germans then began to systematically erase the traces of their crimes. The bodies were dug up with special excavators and burned on piles of wood soaked with flammable material. Later the cremation process was improved by using railway rails to build scaffolding, on which layers of bodies were placed alternating with layers of wood soaked, as before, with an easily flammable liquid. To separate any valuables that might be contained in the bodies, the ashes of the cremated bodies were filtered through a grain separator and then buried again. The cremation of bodies ended in March 1943. Then all camp buildings, fences and watchtowers were dismantled, the area was cleared, levelled and replanted with young pine trees."

We can see that the idea of depicting the Nazis as insatiable thieves is being put forward again and again: after having insisted that before burying the victims their mouths and even their anuses and genitals were inspected, it is now said that time was again wasted looking for something of value in the ashes, as if it were not difficult enough to burn 600,000 putrefying corpses in three months. A witness named Kozak testified to the Zamosc prosecutor: "Two or three pyres were burning at the same time. Meanwhile, a terrible stench of rotting bodies and burnt bones and corpses hung over Belzec. This stench could be smelled for fifteen kilometres around. The cremation went on without interruption for three months."

As for the weather conditions under which the cremation allegedly took place, it should be noted that during the winter the average temperatures in the Belzec area are on average 3 to 4 degrees below zero and hardly ever rise above zero. Every month of the year has an average of at least 12 days of rain, which suggests that rain, snow and wind must have been a constant during the three winter months.

In his reference work, Carlo Mattogno presents an approximate calculation of the amount of wood needed to carry out the gigantic task of burning 600,000 bodies to ashes for three months without interruption. According to his estimates, 96,000 tonnes of wood would have been needed, which would be equivalent to the deforestation of 192 hectares of fifty-year-old spruce forests. Aerial photographs of the forests near Belzec show that they looked the same in 1944 as they did in 1940. "Where did this immense quantity of wood come from," Mattogno asks. To transport it to the camp would have required ninety-five trains of forty wagons each. However, none of the inhabitants of the area could testify to having seen the arrival of trains or trucks loaded with firewood. The cremation of 600,000 bodies in three months would correspond to a rate of 6,650 per day, which would require 1,042 tons of logs per day.

As for cremation itself, just consider the amount of ash that eight or nine medium-sized logs leave daily in a kitchen chimney. Carlo Mattogno again makes a careful calculation of the amount of ash that the bodies would produce and the wood needed to incinerate them. The results are as follows: the 600,000 bodies would leave 1,350 tonnes of ash with a volume of 2,700 cubic metres; the wood would produce 7,680 tonnes of ash, corresponding to 22,600 cubic metres. In total, therefore, 9,030 tonnes or 25,300 cubic metres. As mentioned above, the 33 pits excavated by Professor Kola between 1997 and 1999 had a total volume of 21,310 cubic metres. Furthermore, it should be noted that the analyses presented by Kola show that the ashes were mixed with layers of sand and that among the human remains there were also animal residues.

Officially, the cremation operations ended in March 1943, but a small garrison of SS men remained at the camp until September. It is therefore unclear why a number of corpses were not burned. According to O'Neil, the bodies were not dug up and burned because, perhaps, "panic set in because of insufficient time to destroy all the evidence". This thesis is implausible considering that there were soldiers in the camp for half a year longer. Moreover, graves containing saponified bodies were scattered all over the camp, which invites the suspicion, argues Carlo Mattogno, "that these graves belonged to the previous camp administration and therefore dated from 1940, when Belzec was used as a camp for gypsies until it was later integrated into the 'Otto Programme'. In both periods many victims were buried in the camp. At that time the structure of the camp was very different from what it was later and there was more space. This would explain the position of these mass graves." There is evidence that in the spring of 1940 thousands of detainees died due to epidemics, including typhus , and also because of the extremely harsh working and living conditions in the camp.

But thousands also died in Belzec in 1942. On 28 April 1943 the deputy for the resettlement of Jews in the Lublin area, SS Major Höfle (Sturmbannführer), sent a report to Lieutenant Colonel Heim (Obersturmbannführer) giving the figure of 434,508 persons transferred to Belzec up to 31 December 1942. This document, deciphered by the British Secret Services, has only recently become known. In some trains the conditions of the deportees were deplorable. There is another report dated 14 September 1942 entitled "Resettlement from Kolomea to Belzec". Its author, Josef Jäcklein, a railway guard of the protection police, recounts the calamitous transport from Kolomea to Belzec, which left at 8:50 p.m. on 10 September with 8,205 Jews on board. Kolomea, a district of the Ukraine, had been occupied by the Germans in their advance into the USSR. Jäcklein explains that the Jews carried hammers and tongs. They later testified that they were told that these tools would be useful to them in their new destination. Evidently, the first thing the detainees did was to use these tools to open holes in the roofs of the wagons in order to escape. The train had to stop at every station to repair the damage. Jäcklein confirms that the train escort ran out of ammunition and went so far as to use bayonets and stones to prevent repeated escape attempts. When the train arrived in Belzec at 18:45 the next day, two thousand dead were inside. Mattogno also reports a second report on this transport from Kolomea, also dated 14 September 1942. It bears the signature of a lieutenant named Wassermann, also of the protection police. It states that 180 to 200 people were travelling in each wagon. In the first part of this report, Wassermann refers to actions carried out on 7, 8, 9 and 10 September 1942 in the Kolomea area and confirms the execution on the 7th of September 1942 of 300 Jews. The reasons given to justify the murder were that they were "old, infected, weak or untransportable". Basically, these shootings prove that Jews were not sent to Belzec to be gassed. It cannot, however, be denied that thousands, if not tens of thousands, of Jews died in Belzec.

But the purpose of the Polish investigators' excavations was not only to find human remains, but also to identify the buildings detailed by witnesses. One of the priorities was, of course, to locate the famous building so often described, where the six gas chambers were located. Yitzhak Arad and Raul Hilberg, the most prestigious of Jewish historians, recount the expansion of the three camps and the construction of these gas chambers. In fact, both of them take at face value Rudolf Reder's description of the new Belzec chambers, theoretically built in June/July 1942. In *The Destruction of the European Jews* Hilberg writes: "Solid structures, of stone in Belzec and of brick in Treblinka, containing at least six gas chambers, replaced the old facilities. In the new buildings, the chambers were lined up on both sides of the corridor, and in Treblinka the engine room was situated at the end". Accordingly, a stone building was sought which, according to Arad, was 24 metres long and 10 metres wide.

It was hoped that the excavations would uncover the original structures of the facility. While Kola and his team avoided digging up and thoroughly examining the human remains in the mass graves, they did proceed to unearth and carefully examine any structures that might lead to the discovery of the gas chambers built in the second phase of the camp. After describing six irrelevant finds, Andrzej Kola focused on "Building G", a wooden construction partially buried in the ground, whose rectangular base at a depth of 80 centimetres measured approximately 3.5 x 15 metres. Its description goes like this:

> "The wooden building probably served as a gas chamber in the second stage of the camp's operation, in the autumn-winter of 1942. Such an interpretation could be confirmed by its location on the camp plan. Exploratory drilling of the northeastern and eastern parts of the building

excavated only mass grave pits. The location of the gas chamber near the burial places in the second phase of the camp's existence was confirmed by some of the witness reports."

Carlo Mattogno, from whose book the quotation again comes, is indignant at the frivolity of Professor Kola's argumentation, since, based solely on the location of the building, he claims without providing any archaeological evidence that the building in question must have housed the alleged homicidal gas chambers. As for his claim that a wooden structure housed the gas chambers, the Polish archaeologist refers to Rudolf Reder in his report and says: 'According to him (Reder), however, the chamber was made of concrete. Excavations carried out in the area do not prove any existence of bricks or concrete in the buildings, which makes this report unreliable". Mattogno, without coming out of his astonishment, lets slip between the lines that Andrzej Kola does not even stop to consider that the wooden structure could have belonged to the initial phase of the camp. The problem is that if Rudolf Reder's statement is considered untrustworthy, so are the others, for they all agree that the gas chambers of the second phase of the camp were built in a brick structure. The judgement of January 1965 in the Belzec trial in Munich mentions this explicitly: "a solid stone building with a total of six chambers measuring 4 x 5 metres". Also in the *Encyclopedia of the Holocaust* one reads under the entry "Belzec" that the existing gas chambers in the first phase were demolished "and in their place was erected a new building made of concrete and brick containing six chambers measuring 4 x 5 metres". It seems incredible that Professor Kola would allow himself to discredit the witnesses with such poor expertise. Moreover, the dimensions of his wooden structure, 3.5 x 15 metres, also do not match the officially accepted 24 x 10 metres. If it was already impossible to fit hundreds of people in chambers measuring 4 x 5 metres, 20 square metres, what about the hypothetical chambers in the construction imagined by Kola?

Belzec, transit camp

We believe that the arguments of the revisionists are powerful enough to discredit the thesis that Belzec was an extermination camp: propaganda professionals like Jan Karski have been exposed; the witnesses are lying and some of their accounts are the stuff of science fiction; the method of extermination claimed by the official historiography is not credible; the material possibilities for cremation are impossible; archaeological research has disproved the theories of the exterminationists. In short, the hypothesis that 600,000 were massacred in Belzec in gas chambers is unacceptable if it is considered with the slightest rigour. Revisionists therefore maintain that

Belzec, like Treblinka and Sobibor, was a transit camp for the transfer of Jews to the East.

Letters and postcards from deportees to Treblinka in 1942 from the Warsaw ghetto arrived from the occupied Soviet territories to the Polish capital, indicating that they had been resettled there after transit through Treblinka. Some of these messages came from camps in Belarus and Ukraine. Mark Weber and Andrew Allen report on these texts in a paper published in the summer of 1992 in *The Journal of Historical Review*. According to these authors, some of these letters and postcards arrived by post, others clandestinely. The senders wrote that they were working hard, but confirmed that they, and in some cases their children, were being fed.

Several documents confirm that Belzec was not an extermination camp, but a transit camp. One of them, dated 17 March 1942, comes from the Department of Population and Social Assistance of the Governor General's Office for the Lublin District. It is a text by Fritz Reuter, a civil servant in this Department, in which he records an interview held the previous day with SS Major Hermann Höfle, the delegate for the resettlement of Jews in the Lublin area. The text is taken from Mattogno's work:

> "... In the course of the discussion Hauptsturmführer Höfle explained the following:
> It would be desirable to divide the transports arriving in the Lublin district into fit and unfit Jews at the station of origin. If it is not possible to make this separation at the station of origin, then this division will have to be made in Lublin. All Jews unfit for work have to go to Belzec, the station closest to the border in the Zamosz district.
> Hstuf. Höfle is thinking of building a large camp in which Jews fit for work can be registered in a file according to their occupations in order to be required from there.
> Piaski is becoming free of Jews and will be the collection point for Jews leaving the Reich .
> Trawniki is not currently occupied by Jews.
> H. asked where on the Deblin-Trawniki route 60,000 Jews could be unloaded. Informed of the transports of Jews currently departing from here, H. explained that of the 500 Jews arriving in Susiec, those deemed unfit for work could be sorted and sent to Belzec....
> In conclusion, he reported that he could accept daily 4-5 transports of 1,000 Jews to the Belzec terminus. These Jews would cross the border and never return to the General Government".

We agree with Mattogno on the importance of this document. In his paraphrase of the text, this revisionist researcher explains that Hermann Höfle was the chief of staff of Odilo Globocnik, the SS commander who acted as the first police authority in the Lublin district. The official historiography acknowledges that H. Höfle coordinated "the construction of the Belzec extermination camp and the deportations there from the Lublin District". Moreover, the official version assumes that on 17 March 1942, i.e. the date given in Reuter's report, the murderous activities had already begun. Once again, however, the text reflects the need to use the employable Jews as labour. The idea of organising "an archive according to their occupations" is further proof that there were no plans for extermination. It would have been absurd to waste time on these formalities if the intention was to wipe out all the Jews as soon as they arrived at the camp, as the propagandists of the Holocaust myth claim. Finally, it is clear from the text that Belzec was to serve as a base for the transfer across the border of Jews who would no longer return to the General Government, implying that they would have to be resettled in the Ukraine, the Soviet Union or elsewhere in the East. The idea of Belzec as a transit camp is thus reaffirmed in this document.

A second text dated 7 April 1942, also quoted by Mattogno, confirms the above. Its author is Richard Türk, director of the Population and Social Welfare Department of the Lublin District Governor's Office . The report, which refers to the month of March, contains a paragraph entitled "Jewish Resettlement Operation of the Chief of Police and SS". In it Türks reports on meetings with Höfle:

> "Accommodation possibilities, limited to sites along the Deblin-Rejowiec-Belzec railway line, were and are being discussed with the representative of the Chief of Police and the SS. Alternative possibilities were studied.
> From my proposal, there is a fundamental agreement that, since Jews coming from the West are being settled here, local Jews, if possible, should be evacuated in similar numbers. The present situation of the settlement process is that approximately 6,000 Jews from the Reich were settled here, approximately 7,500 have been evacuated from the district and 18,000 from the city of Lublin."

The report continues with a chronology of dates in March, listing the movements carried out, the cities of evacuation, the number of deportees and the places of settlement in different districts. These and other directives on the resettlement of Jews in the Lublin district run counter to the thesis that Belzec, Treblinka and Sobibor were camps where Jews were exterminated as soon as they arrived. As for the evacuation of Jews from Western Europe, documents show that between 5 May and 28 November 1942, some 35,000 people were deported directly to Eastern European territories without passing through transit camps, including Minsk, Maly Trostinec, southeast of the Belarusian capital, Riga, and Raasiki, an Estonian city east of Tallinn.

Regarding the closure of Belzec as a transit camp, Carlo Mattogno has brought to light a document, 'Police Regulation regarding the formation of quarters for Jews in the Warsaw and Lublin districts', dated 28 October 1942. Its author was SS General (Obergruppenführer) Friedrich Wilhelm Krüger,

SS High Commander, Chief of Police in the General Government and State Secretary for Security Services. This regulation established twelve residential areas for Jews. On 10 November 1942, Küger established four more areas in the Radom district, five in the Kraków district, thirty-two in the Galicia district and two more in the municipality of Rawa Ruska. Shortly thereafter, trains stopped arriving in Belzec, which according to Holocaust historiography had been built specifically as an extermination camp.

Treblinka

Before turning to what happened at Treblinka, it is worthwhile to think again. In the first part of Chapter XII, which deals with the persecution and deportation of the Jews, we have seen that the Nazis were initially determined to promote by all means the emigration of Jews out of Germany: the Haavara Agreement, the fruit of collaboration with Zionism, and the Evian Conference are good examples of this. The policy of encouraging emigration was replaced by evacuation and expulsion plans, the most famous of which, the Madagascar Plan, had to be abandoned and replaced by deportation to the East. After the invasion of the USSR in June 1941, half a year before the Wannsee Conference, the Nazi hierarchs, convinced that the blitzkrieg would bring them a quick victory as had happened in France, began to think of deporting Jews to the conquered territories in the Soviet Union.

Martin Broszat, in *Hitler und die Genesis der "Endlösung". Aus Anlaß der Thesen von David Irving* (*Hitler and the Genesis of the "Final Solution". On the occasion of David Irving's theses*), he quotes an entry from Goebels' diary dated 25 September 1941, in which a conversation with Heydrich is noted. It says: "in the end, they are all supposed to be transported to camps built by the Bolsheviks". Carlo Mattogno and Jürgen Graf in *Treblinka: Extermination Camp or Transit Camp* refer to another text of 7 October 1941 in which the same idea is repeated. Its author, Werner Koeppen, one of Rosenberg's liaison men, notes Hitler's own words: "All Jews must be evacuated from the Protectorate (Bohemia and Moravia) and indeed not only to the General Government, but further to the east". Six days later, on 13 October 1941, Alfred Rosenberg and Hans Frank, Governor General of the occupied Polish territories, took up the subject of the deportation of Jews from the Government General. The following quotation is also taken from the work of Mattogno and Graf:

> "The Governor General then spoke of the possibilities of deportation of the Jewish population of the General Government to the occupied territories in the East. Reichminister Rosenberg noted that similar requests were already reaching him from the Military Administration in Paris. For the time being, however, he saw no possibility yet of

implementing resettlements of this kind. But he announced that he himself was prepared in the future to promote the evacuation of Jews to the east...".

In other words, the deportation eastwards of the Jews of the Protectorate and also of those living in the territories of the General Government was already being contemplated in October 1941. As we know, it was at the Wannsee Conference on 20 January 1942 that the "territorial final solution" was officially announced, i.e., the determined will to expel the Jews from all areas of life of the German people and their territories, for which purpose their deportation to Eastern Europe was imposed. Considering that on 5 September 1939 Chaim Wezmann, the top leader of international Zionism, had declared war on Germany in the name of all Jewry and announced that they would fight in the camp of the democracies, the Wannsee Conference definitively banned Jewish emigration, as it was considered a danger in wartime. The policy of emigration or expulsion thus gave way to deportation, and the Madagascar Plan was officially abandoned on 10 February 1942. The evacuation of Jews to the eastern territories accelerated. The concentration of Jews deported from various parts of Europe in the General Government of Poland, where they were joined by Jews native to the region, was intended as a temporary measure, the ultimate goal being to transport them all, as soon as technically feasible, to territories further east. The impossibility of winning the war quickly ruined all plans.

Consequently, no one denies that Jews were deprived of freedom of movement and were concentrated in cities and ghettos. Those able to work were conscripted for forced labour according to the needs of the time. Such labour could be carried out outside the ghetto and sometimes inside the ghetto. The fact that the Nazis considered Jews to be the architects of communism prompted some generals to recommend an iron fist. The fight against Bolshevism," said Field Marshal Wilhelm Keitel in a directive, "calls for toughness and energetic measures, especially against the Jews, the main promoters of Bolshevism. The policy of deportations of Jews to the East was decided by Hitler in September 1941 and began in October of the same year. This is recorded in a letter from Himmler to Arthur Greiser, former chairman of the Danzig Senate and head of the district (Gauleiter) of Posen. In this epistle dated 18 September 1941, filed in the "Bundesarchiv" in Koblenz and quoted by Mattogno and Graf, Himmler wrote:

"The Führer wishes Germany (Altreich) and the Protectorate to be cleared of Jews as soon as possible, from the West to the East. It is therefore my intention, if possible this year, to transport the Jews from the Altreich and the Protectorate initially to the eastern territories incorporated into the Reich two years ago, as a first stage, in order to deport them still further east next spring."

This is yet another document, one more, that shows what the Nazis' real intentions were. The deportation order was issued on 24 October 1941, and the final destination of the deportees was to be the eastern territories. At the time, these territories were the "Reichskommissariat Ostland", divided into the four general districts of Estonia, Latvia, Lithuania and White Russia (Belarus), whose civil administrator was Heinrich Lohse; and the "Reichskommissariat Ukraine", administered by Erich Koch. Both were subject to the authority of Alfred Rosenberg, Reich Minister for the occupied territories in the east. However, these territories, unlike those of the General Government Poland, occupied since 1939, had just suffered the disastrous consequences of the war and were not yet ready to receive hundreds of thousands of Jews. This is borne out by various messages and telegrams from German officials on the ground. Heinrich Lohse, "Reichkommissar" in Ostland, informed of the deportation to Minsk and Riga of 50,000 Jews from the Protectorate and Germany, asked Rosenberg on 9 November to move the deportees further east.

In January 1942, it was the city commissioner of Minsk, Wilhelm Janetzke, who, without consulting Lohse, who chastised him for it, and bypassing the proper channels, went directly to Rosenberg to oppose the deportations and to let him know that it would be a catastrophe. Some 100,000 people lived in the city, which had been left in ruins. In these conditions, with the bitter cold and the ground frozen, Janetzke said, "there was no possibility of feeding either the population or the Jews", so it was not possible to accommodate the deportees there. This is the context in which the official historiography imposes its thesis that Treblinka, Belzec and Sobibor were camps designed solely and exclusively to exterminate European Jews.

Second only to Auschwitz, Treblinka is considered the second largest extermination centre. Unlike Auschwitz and Majdanek, which according to official historians became killing centres after having functioned as concentration camps, Treblinka, like Belzec Sobibor and Chelmno (Kulmhof), was theoretically operated for the sole purpose of eliminating Jews. As will become clear, the major evidence provided by Holocaust hawkers to justify such a claim is based exclusively on witness statements; in other words, the story of Belzec is being repeated.

Treblinka consisted of two camps: Treblinka I and Treblinka II. The first, whose construction order was published on 16 December 1941 in the *Official Gazette of the General Government for the Warsaw District*, was located two kilometres from the second and served as a labour camp: its prisoners produced gravel in a nearby stone quarry. Construction of Treblinka II reportedly began in March 1942. Located four kilometres from a small village of the same name and less than two kilometres from the Burg, it was intended to be the centre of mass annihilation. In fact, at the entrance to the camp, a stone inscription today proclaims in several languages that 'more than 800,000 Jews' were murdered there between July 1942 and August 1943.

The revisionists' thesis about Treblinka is the same as the one they defend for Belzec. They point out that Treblinka was primarily a transit camp set up to receive the population of the Warsaw district. According to figures of the Warsaw Jewish Council, from 22 July to 9 December 1942, 263,243 Jews were evacuated from the Warsaw ghetto, of whom 251,545 were supposedly deported to Treblinka and murdered there. A further 11,315 supposedly fit for work are said to have gone to the Treblinka I ghetto. Eugen Kulisher, an expert on demography and migration, confirms that on 22 July 1942 the Jewish Council in Warsaw was ordered to prepare six thousand people daily for evacuation. Interestingly, the Jewish Council itself acknowledges that it was their own hand-picked doctors who decided whether those admitted to Jewish hospitals on the day of evacuation could be discharged. That Treblinka was a transit camp is indicated by the fact that all Jews evacuated from the Warsaw ghetto in 1942 received three kilos of bread and one of jam. Quite a waste in times of war and scarcity if the real intention was to exterminate them on arrival at the camp.

In the following months, paradoxically, letters and postcards arrived in the Warsaw ghetto from deportees writing to their relatives. Some came from Belarusian towns such as Minsk, Brest Litovsk, Pinsk, Brzezc or Babruisk; others came from Polish towns further east, such as Bialystock, some sixty kilometres from the Belarusian border. Since the authors of the letters were supposedly being exterminated in Treblinka, resistance organisations in the ghetto, already peddling the gas chamber stories, spread the rumour that they were fabricated by the Germans to deceive Jews. The resistance labelled those who reported receiving letters as Gestapo agents. Official historiography later chose to support the thesis that the postcards and letters were written in Treblinka under duress.

Confusion over method of extermination at Treblinka

Propaganda about Treblinka as an extermination camp began to be fabricated in August 1942. At first it was not specified how the gas chambers functioned, and there was talk of toxic fluids mixed with gases emanating from exhaust pipes. The first reports of mass murder at Treblinka reached London and were taken up by the Polish government in exile. It has already been mentioned that British Jewish agents soon put pressure on the Foreign Office, which had information from the Political Warfare Executive as early as August and knew it was all false. One of the documents most often cited by Jewish historians proclaiming the Holocaust was produced on 15 November 1942 by the underground resistance movement in the Warsaw ghetto. The article in question, entitled 'Liquidation of the Warsaw Jews', originally written in Polish, runs to six pages in *Treblinka: Extermination*

Camp or Transit Camp, where it is reproduced in full. The report was received by the Polish government in London on 6 January 1943 and after being translated into English it was widely distributed. Although it is a reference document, it suffers from a fundamental flaw: it states that Jews were killed in steam chambers. Yitzhak Arad, considered an expert on Treblinka, uses and modifies it as he sees fit in his book on the Operation Reinhardt camps and has no problem transforming the steam chambers into gas chambers. Below we will comment on the text and quote some excerpts.

The report begins with a description of the site. The two camps are designated Treblinka A and Treblinka B. The former is erroneously said to have begun operating in 1940. According to this document, Treblinka B is said to have been built between March and April 1942 by Polish prisoners from Treblinka A and Jews taken from neighbouring villages. Another major error concerns the size of Treblinka B: it is stated that it was 5,000 hectares in size, when in fact it was only a little over 13 hectares. A branch line connected the camp to the main railway line. The Treblinka guards, "Lagerschutz", were mostly Ukrainians armed with machine guns. The drafters of the report note that supervisors or execution staff were few in number and that the "Slaughterhouse" was commanded by an SS major named Sauer, who is once again painted as a monster whom even his own men feared. In all," he is quoted as saying, "there are ten Germans and thirty Ukrainians". As for the workings of the "slaughterhouse", it is best to keep to the quotation:

> "... A large building of unusual shape: it is an unfinished single-storey brick construction, over 40 metres long and 15 metres wide (when we received the report on Treblinka B in the first half of September, this building was nearing completion). The Germans began the construction of the building after the action began, probably in mid-August, with the help of Jewish craftsmen collected from among the Jews taken to Treblinka to be murdered.... According to an eyewitness report, the interior of the building is as follows: a corridor three metres wide runs down the centre. There are five chambers on each side, the height of each chamber is about two metres and its area is 35 square metres. The execution chambers have no windows, but have doors that open onto the corridor and a kind of lift doors on the outer walls.... Pipes were installed in the walls from which water vapour is supposed to be poured into the chambers".

A second building of smaller blocks than the previous one is described below, with three chambers into which steam was fed through pipes from a steam chamber with a large tank to produce it. The floor of the chambers had a terracotta layer which made it very slippery when water was poured over it. It should be noted that the only well in the camp was located outside, next to the steam chamber. The work of emptying the chambers and burying the corpses was carried out by Jewish auxiliaries who obeyed the prisoners who served as kapos. As for the cruelty of SS chief Sauer, it is said that he personally eliminated the weak who were not fit for work:

> "The executions took place in a special place. The victim stood over a pit and the chief shot him in the back of the head. The next victim had to stand nearby and throw the body of the dead man into the ditch, and a little later he shared the fate of his predecessor. These young Jews are so overwhelmed that their will to resist has disappeared; and on the other hand the terror of the Germans is so atrocious that they even wish to die so that they would no longer have to suffer the inhuman tortures. On one of the first days of September, the head of Treblinka murdered 500 young Jews in this way by shooting one after another with his pistol; the amazing thing is that not one of this group of hundreds of men tried to resist death. The execution lasted from 7:30 in the morning until 15:00 in the afternoon."

As for the scenes of the introduction of the victims into the chambers and the execution process, they are very similar to those of Belzec: whippings, blows and punches abound, which crescendo until the figure of the inhuman monster who commanded the camp appears once again:

> "The sobbing and wailing of the women together with the shouts and insults of the Germans disturb the silence of the forest. At the entrance to Slaughterhouse No. 1 stands the chief himself with a whip in his hand, beating them in cold blood. He leads the women into the chambers. The floors are slippery. The victims slip and fall, they cannot get up because new victims are brought in and fall on top of them. The chief throws small children into the chambers over the women's heads. When the execution chambers are full, the doors close tightly and the slow suffocation of the people begins, carried out by the steam emanating from the numerous ducts in the pipes. At first, stifled screams are heard from outside, gradually they cease to be heard, and fifteen minutes later the execution is complete".

The spectacle described in connection with the evacuation of the chambers and the burial operations also differs little from that of Belzec. Here it is said that the bodies have become a homogeneous mass due to the victims' perspiration: "In their death throes, arms, legs and trunks are intertwined in a gigantic, macabre tangle". To separate such a jumble of corpses in order to be able to bury them, cold water must be poured over the jumble of human bodies.

Finally, the report asserted that the new slaughterhouse made it possible to liquidate between 8,000 and 10,000 people a day: "Two million Jews, or the greater part of Polish Jewry, already buried in the Treblinka area, have been murdered". Thus it was claimed that in less than half a year ten Germans and thirty Ukrainians, aided by Jews who worked piece-work before also being murdered, had exterminated two million people. The same figure was announced on 8 August 1943 by *The New York Times, which,* citing as its source an article in a London newspaper, reported the news with this headline: "2,000,000 Murders Attributed to Nazis. Polish newspaper in London says Jews are exterminated in Treblinka slaughterhouse". The subhead responded to the how: "According to the report, steam is used to kill men, women and children at a place in the woods." The Polish newspaper in London was the *Polish Labor Fights,* which on 7 August 1943 had published the report of 15 November 1942 that we have discussed.

This report was the mother of all reports, as the vast majority of those that followed drew on it. With the entry of the Soviets into Treblinka in August 1944, a forensic-type military investigation was carried out on the camp ground, and witnesses and survivors began to come forward. A Polish-Soviet commission of enquiry was soon formed, which as early as 15 September 1944 issued a report on the results of its findings, which we will spare you the commentary so as not to waste any more time. We will mention only a few witnesses, since two of them, Jankiel Wiernik and Samuel Rajzman, became essential sources for Raul Hilberg and Yitzhak Arad, the two established historians of the Holocaust.

At the end of 1945, Judge Zdzislaw Lukaszkiewicz was leading the interrogations of the Commission of Inquiry into German Crimes in Poland. At that time, the confusion was still going on: steam, air suction, chemicals, exhaust pipes... In 1946, Lukaszkiewicz wrote a long article in Polish entitled *The Treblinka Extermination Camp,* in which he based all the evidence on the statements of thirteen Jews. Among them were the names of Samuel Rajzman and the ineffable Jankiel Wiernik, author of the famous *One Year in Treblinka.* Wiernik is also cited as Jakob Wernik in Nuremberg.

In January 1946, Rachel Auerbach, a member of the Jewish Historical Commission who had not been to Treblinka, published a book in Yiddish based on prisoner accounts, in which it was not clear what the method of extermination was. In 1979 Alexander Donat, another Jewish concentration camp survivor and founder of Holocaust Library Publications in New York, published Auerbach's work in English as *In the Fields of Treblinka*. In her book, Rachel Auerbach criticised Vassili Grossman, who in 1945 had published *The Hell of Treblinka,* an example of propagandistic rubbish, , in which the number of dead in the camp was put at 3,000,000. According to Auerbah, there was no need to exaggerate, since the number of victims was only 1,047,000.

Samuel Rajzman was still unable in 1946 to specify how the alleged gas chambers functioned. On 27 February 1946 he appeared as a witness in Nuremberg and referred to the gas chambers, but could not detail their structure or the type of gas that caused death. In the same year Rajzman wrote an eight-page report in Polish, "My stay in Treblinka", in which he stated, without explaining the method, that 25,000 people were killed daily in Treblinka. The victims, according to Rajzman, were painted like a flock of sheep running over each other to enter the slaughterhouse: "As they walked naked to the gas chambers, the Germans beat them very hard; many died from the blows alone. Everyone was pushing to get into the gas chamber quickly because the Ukrainians and the Germans were hitting extremely hard. Everybody was stampeding forward. The place was completely covered with blood.

Carbon monoxide is also a must for Treblinka

As at Belzec, where the hallucinatory story of electric currents was initially spread, but the carbon monoxide thesis was eventually adopted, so at Treblinka, too, this version prevailed. Some historians admit that the method of diesel engine exhausts as a means of exterminating more than 1.5 million Jews is hardly credible, but they refuse to agree with the revisionists and scorn the accounts of dubious witnesses in the service of propaganda.

The idea of the exhaust pipes introduced into the chambers without the specification of the type of engine that produced the gas was picked up by Jankiel Wiernik, who stated that he had been in Treblinka from 23 August 1942 until 2 August 1943, the day of the prisoners' revolt. In May 1944, based on the parent text of November 1942, he published a report in Polish about Treblinka, which was sent to London, where it was translated into English before it travelled on to the United States, where it was published the same year. In December 1944 it was also printed in Palestine. After confirming that ten chambers were added to the initial three, Wiernik proceeds to give some details about the new facilities. From *Treblinka: Extermination Camp or Transit Camp,* a significant excerpt follows:

> "The new construction work between Camp No. 1 and Camp No. 2 that I was working on was finished in a very short time. It turned out that we were building ten additional chambers more spacious than the old ones, 7 by 7 metres or about 50 square metres. Between 1,000 and 1,200 people could be crammed into one gas chamber. The building was designed according to the corridor system, with five chambers on each side. Each chamber had two doors, one leading to the corridor and through which the victims entered; the other leading to the outside and used for evacuating the bodies.... There was a Star of David facing the countryside on the frontispiece of the façade, so that the building looked like an old synagogue...
> The engine that generated the gas in the chambers was defective, so helpless victims had to suffer for hours before they died.... When the chambers were opened, many victims were only half dead and had to be finished off with rifle butts, bullets or kicks.

The most significant difference from the report of 15 November 1942 is that Wiernik replaced steam chambers with gas chambers. The fact that Wiernik's text was included in the official report on German crimes sent by the Polish Government to the Nuremberg Tribunal, the USSR-93 document submitted by the Soviets, caused the Soviet prosecutor, Colonel L. N. Smirnov, to cite it on 25 February 1946. However, the Polish Government's report did not state that the method of extermination was the fumes emanating from an engine exhaust pipe, as Wiernik had suggested. In fact, at the session of 19 February 1946 Smirnov read out the passage from the Polish Government text which still stated that electrocution was the method of extermination in Belzec: "Under the pretext of taking people to the bath, the condemned were undressed and taken to a building where the floor was electrified in a special way; there they were killed.

Judge Lukaszkiewicz, who conducted the interrogations, was among the first to realise that the method of mass murder by the introduction of steam into the chambers was quite unbelievable. Already in his report of 29 December 1945 he discarded the most ridiculous methods reported by witnesses and retained only the one he considered most feasible, i.e. the gases produced by an engine. With the appearance of the Gerstein Report, which spoke of a diesel engine, historians clung to this method of extermination, which eventually prevailed at Treblinka as well. Gerald Reitlinger, author of *Die Endlösung (The Final Solution)* in 1956, admitted that "it was difficult to understand how people could be exterminated by steam". As discussed in the sections on Belzec, the Gerstein Report overturned the Polish government report, which spoke of electric currents for Belzec and steam chambers for Treblinka, and became the definitive proof for the official historiography, which adopted the version of diesel engine fumes as the method of extermination for all three camps.

It was on 24 December 1947 that Eliyahu Rosenberg, relying in part on Gerstein's statements, wrote "Tatsachenbericht. Das Todeslager Treblinka" (Report of the facts. The Treblinka death camp), in which the version of diesel exhaust fumes as a method of extermination was given. Carlo Mattogno points out that this Rosenberg text, however, remained in the archives until it was used in the Demjanjuk trial in 1987. Mattogno adds that in 1951, Leon Poliakov drew on the Gerstein Report to write in *Harvest of Hate*: "There is little to add to this description, which applies to Treblinka and Sobibor as well as Belzec. The facilities were built in much the same way and used carbon monoxide fumes from diesel engines as an agent of death. A few years later, Reitlinger also pointed to this method of extermination for all three camps. Thus, the carbon monoxide version had already acquired the status of certain historical fact by the time Raul Hilberg and Yitzhak Arad subsequently wrote their works.

We must dedicate a few lines to Friedrich Paul Berg's *The Diesel Gas Chambers: Ideal for Torture - Absurd for Murder*, an excellent thirty-five page study that occupies a chapter in *Dissecting the Holocaust*, Germar Rudolf's compendium of the best revisionist research[9]. Fritz Berg, an automotive engineer, exposes in his work the irrational and incoherent nonsense of the choice of carbon monoxide as a method of mass execution. Since the Nazis were not stupid, and their detractors are the first to admit that they were not, they would never have chosen such a crazy way to liquidate their enemies. If it were true, as the official historiography claims, that the extermination of the Jews was one of the fundamental objectives of the Third Reich, a state policy, it is logical to think that it would have been thoroughly planned and a safe and effective way would have been found. Fritz Berg's study shows that the chosen method is as absurd as trying to catch flies with slingshots.

Berg argues that if the Germans had really wanted to use exhaust pipes from an engine for mass gassing, they would certainly have turned to a petrol engine, since it produces more carbon monoxide and much less oxygen. This engineer focused his work on the two types of diesel engines that existed at the time and naturally chose the one whose gases contained the highest percentage of carbon monoxide (CO). At idle speed, this engine produced about 0.03% CO, while at high revs it increased the emission to 0.4%. According to the laws of toxicology, it would take a person exposed to this concentration of carbon monoxide, , almost sixty minutes to die, provided the diesel engine could be kept at full throttle for one hour. On the other hand, a diesel engine generates a large surplus of air, namely 18% oxygen at idle speed (the air we breathe contains 21% oxygen and 78% nitrogen). By contrast, the gases emanating from a petrol engine contain 7% carbon monoxide and 1% oxygen. Fritz Berg points out that with an appropriate modification of the carburettor, a petrol engine could increase its CO content by up to 12%.

In his paraphrase of Fritz Berg's study, Carlo Mattogno points out that during the war the shortage of petrol was one of the Germans' main problems. To alleviate this, all diesel vehicles were required by law to be equipped with generators that produced gas from coal or wood. This generated gas contained up to 35% CO. Berg points out that hundreds of thousands of these truly poisonous generators operated in Germany and the occupied territories and that this technology, which would have been more efficient, was then well known to German politicians. "How absurd to believe," Berg writes, "that anyone with a modicum of technical knowledge

---

[9] Readers interested in reading the full article can access it through the *Journal of Historical Review*, which has it published in PDF. In *Treblinka: Extermination Camp or Transit Camp*, Jürgen Graf and Carlo Mattogno also devote a few pages to commenting on Fritz Berg's impeccable work.

would try to use the fumes from a diesel engine to kill when the gas generator itself was a thousand times more lethal!"

Treblinka, a fabled camp where anything is possible

When the Soviets arrived at Treblinka, they carried out forensic investigations and examinations at Treblinka I and Treblinka II between 15 and 23 August 1944. After exhuming several hundred corpses, a report was issued concluding that three million human beings had been exterminated in the camp. Samuel Rajzman, whose testimony on 27 February 1946 before the Nuremberg Tribunal would be worth reproducing if we had the space, was able to detail to the commission of enquiry as early as September 1944 the exact number and nationality of the victims. According to this witness, as brazen as Jankiel Wiernik, there were clandestine groups who carried out a thorough search of the contingents of Jews arriving at the camp from different countries of Europe. These are Rajzman's milkmaid's accounts: 120,000 Jews came from Germany, of whom 40,000 were Austrians; from Poland, 1,500,000; from Czechoslovakia, 100,000; from Russia, 1,000,000; from Bulgaria and Greece, 15,000.... We will not, therefore, dwell on commenting on or refuting these impossible figures.

However, it is worth reflecting on the fact that the Germans, in addition to choosing the most inappropriate and ineffective method to carry out this gigantic slaughter, had not even thought of building crematoria to dispose of hundreds of thousands or millions of corpses. Can anyone believe that the Germans would build an extermination camp without realising this peremptory necessity? How is it possible that there were crematoria in concentration camps such as Mauthausen, Dachau, Buchenwald, Sachsenhausen, Rabensbrück and so many others, but not in Treblinka, which is claimed to be a "pure extermination camp"? According to Arad, only the astute Himmler realised the planning error in 1943:

> "During his visit to the camp in late February or early March 1943, Himmler was surprised to discover that in Treblinka the bodies of some 700,000 murdered Jews had not yet been burned. The fact that cremation began immediately after this visit suggests that it was Himmler, who was very touchy about the disposal of the crimes committed by Nazi Germany, who personally ordered the cremation of the bodies there. A place for this purpose was erected in the extermination area of the camp.

Yitzhak Arad himself recounts how the bodies were placed once they had been dumped in the ditches:

> "The bodies were placed in rows for burial. To save space, they were placed with their feet on their heads. Each head was between the feet of

two other bodies and each pair of feet between two heads. Sand or bleach was spread between the layers of bodies. Approximately half of the burial team worked inside the pits placing the bodies and at the same time the other half was covering the layers of bodies with sand. When the trench was full, it was covered with earth and another pit was opened.

Although Hilberg puts the number of victims at 750,000 and other exterminationists put it at 800,000, the *Encyclopaedia of the Holocaust* and much of the official historiography insist that between 860,000 and 870,000 bodies were buried at Treblinka before being incinerated. Therefore, if this is true, in four or five months, between March and July 1943, these fabulous numbers of rotting, decomposing corpses were dug up, roasted on large grills, the bones crushed, and the ashes reburied. About the titanic task of pulverising tens of millions of bones, Raul Hilberg writes barely a paragraph in *The Destruction of the European Jews*, his monumental work of 1,300 pages in three volumes. Yitzhak Arad, on the other hand, goes a little further in describing the operations. Let us read his version:

> "The burning of bodies was done day and night. The bodies were carried and laid out on the large grills during the day and when night came they were set on fire and burned all night. When the fire was extinguished there were only skeletons or bones scattered on the grills and piles of ash underneath. Another special team of prisoners known as the "ash column" (Aschkolonne) had the job of collecting the ash and removing the remains of charred bones from the grills and placing them on aluminium sheets. Round wooden sticks were used to break the bones into small fragments. These were then filtered through a wire grate. Bone fragments that did not pass through were separated for re-crushing. The insufficiently burnt bones that did not fragment were returned to the fire and re-burned along with new piles of bodies."

In the twenty-seven *One Third of the Holocaust* videos produced by CODOH (Committee for Open Debate on the Holocaust), two of them, No. 23, about six minutes long, and No. 24, more than seven minutes long, are devoted to examining the real possibilities of cremation of the bodies and crushing of the skeletons. In doing so, the indications of the witnesses as recorded by the official historiography are followed to the letter. Arad describes that the railway rails stood on concrete bases 70 centimetres high. CODOH investigators therefore place a large leg of lamb on a grill elevated to that height above the ground, fill the space with logs to the height of the grill, about twenty-one kilos of firewood, sprinkle gasoline on the meat and logs, and set it on fire. After thirty minutes, the pile of wood has dwindled and a space has been created between the grill and the fire, which no longer fully reaches the meat, which is scorched only at the bottom. After an hour of burning, the wood has almost been consumed and only the embers burn half a metre from the meat. The lower part of the leg of lamb is blackened, but cutting the upper part with a knife shows it to be raw. Since the conditions were not optimal: the day was windy and the flames did not have a good effect on the grill, it was decided to wait until it was whitewashed, which happened at night. The operation was then continued without wind and with forty-two kilos of wood, twice as much, placed not only under the grill, but also on the sides. In addition, the fire continues to be fed with an additional twenty kilos of logs so that the fire permanently envelops the leg. One hundred and twenty minutes later, so three hours in total, the meat is finally charred. In India, where cremation of corpses is common, the bodies are placed directly on the wood, so they are lowered as the wood is consumed and are always in contact with the fire and the burning embers.

The following video is filmed the next day. The cold, charred leg is placed on a metal sheet and crushed with wooden mallets similar to those described by Arad. The bones break easily until the innermost part of the leg shows a good chunk of flesh that cannot be turned into ash and flattens out as it receives the impacts of the mallet. The authors of the video then invite us to reflect on the conditions in which the cremations were supposedly carried out in Treblinka, where the flames could not pass through the bodies piled in huge heaps of more than three thousand corpses due to lack of air.

On the other hand, how long would it take to manually pulverise 860,000 skeletons? In the fabulous Treblinka camp, thirty Ukrainians and ten Germans were able to direct and control the Jewish prisoners, who, in little more than four months and before being murdered, not only crushed the bones of the victims, but had enough time to carry out all the colossal operations described above with great competence. Between October 1964 and September 1965, the Treblinka trial was held in Düsseldorf. There it must have been realised that the version of the thirty Ukrainians and ten Germans was not credible, and so it was established in the verdict that the Germans numbered forty and the Ukrainians one hundred and twenty.

Most of the implausibilities considered in the Belzec case arise again in Treblinka. The questions are the same: How many pits were required to bury so many bodies and how big they had to be; where they were located in the camp; how many grills there were; how many corpses were burned in them and how they were placed; where the wood came from, how it reached the camp and how much was needed; how much ash the burning would have produced, etc.... All these questions are dealt with by Jürgen Graf and Carlo Mattogno and also by Arnulf Neumaier, to whom these two authors dedicate their indispensable book on Treblinka. Neumaier's *The Treblinka Holocaust* is considered a milestone in scientific research on the notorious "extermination camp", which is why Germar Rudolf is publishing it in its entirety in *Dissecting the Holocaust*. Readers interested in finding out more will find these monographs on Treblinka at their disposal. We will only offer a brief outline of these questions, since the aim of our work is more general and we cannot afford to do otherwise.

In 1965, the Court of Assizes (Court of Cassation) in Düsseldorf had to admit in its verdict that the number and size of the graves could not be established because the versions differed from one another. However, it concluded that it could be accepted that there were around 80,000 bodies in each grave. In any case, Eliyahu Rosenberg gave precise details, stating that the graves were 120 metres long by 15 metres wide and 6 metres deep. According to the researchers' calculations, each of these gigantic graves would hold 79,200 corpses before they were cremated, which would require eleven mass graves of this size, occupying an area of 19,200 square metres. The total area of Treblinka II was 14,000 square metres. Since in the above-mentioned work the researchers have left no aspect of unstudied, we will note in passing that the excavation of eleven graves of this size would have produced 118,800 cubic metres of earth, enough to cover the entire area of the camp with a layer one metre high.

Much has been written about the enormously complex problems of the cremation of 860,000 bodies on grills, but we cannot help but comment on some of the nonsense. Konnilyn G. Feig, an American-born Jewish historian, claims that the organisers of the massacre decided to bring an "expert" named Herbert Floss to the camp, who had the ingenious idea of erecting four concrete pillars 76 centimetres high to form "a rectangle 19 metres long by 1 metre wide", which was called a "rotisserie" by the prisoners, according to Feig, who adds that a witness testified that the primitive grills could hold 2,600 bodies. Feig states that Floss discovered that "old bodies burned better than new ones, fat ones better than thin ones, women better than men, and children not as well as women, but better than men". Therefore, on the basis of this anthological discovery, Floss ordered that the bodies of fat women be lined up at the base of the grate and the corpses continued to be placed according to these criteria. Considering that the corpses had previously been dug up and the stench of decomposition must have been unbearable, it is hard to understand how time could be wasted on such nonsense. Carlo Mattogno comments: "The idea that Himmler, who had at his disposal the best engineers and technicians in the field of cremation - such as those of the firms J. A. Topf & Söhme (Erfurt) Hans Bori (Berlin) and Didier Werke (Berlin), who had supplied crematoria to all the German concentration camps, would send a nobody called Herbert Floss to Treblinka, is unintelligible".

According to Jankiel Wiernik, whose testimony was extensively considered by the Düsseldorf court, there were two grids on whose concrete pillars five or six rails 25 to 30 metres long were laid. The official version that has prevailed specifies that the two grids were 30 metres long by 3 metres wide. The cremation is supposed to have taken place from the beginning of April to the end of July 1943, so that in 122 days, theoretically

860,000 bodies were cremated, which is equivalent to burning 7,000 bodies daily between the two grids. In *One Year in Treblinka*, Wiernik conveniently seasons the spectacle with gimmicky ideas about the intrinsic evil of the executioners, whom he paints as an army of drunks: "The Germans," he writes, "stood around with satanic smiles on their faces, brimming with satisfaction at their mad deeds, toasting with choice liquors, eating and enjoying themselves around the heat of the fire.

On 27 November 1986, an article by Arnulf Neumaier was published in *The Schenectady Gazette* of New York, according to which 6,433 tons of wood were required daily in India for the cremation of 21,000 corpses, which is equivalent to 306 kilos per body. It should be noted that in Indian funeral ceremonies, the bodies lie individually on the wood, as mentioned above, so that the ventilation and other conditions for cremation are adequate. In *Treblinka: Extermination Camp or Transit Camp*, Carlo Mattogno presents the result of his calculations. He decides to make the estimate on the basis of a body weighing 45 kilos, which would require approximately 160 kilos of wood. Consequently, to incinerate 3,500 bodies, half of the 7,000 that were hypothetically burned every day, 560,000 kilos of wood would be needed. However, based on the spatial dimensions underneath the barbecue, only 30,780 kilograms of wood could fit there, which would be equivalent to 8.8 kilograms per body. That is to say, instead of eating, drinking and enjoying the warmth of the fire, there would have to be constant activity to feed the fire, which would require getting close to a gigantic bonfire: according to witnesses, the pile of bodies lined up in layers on the grills reached a height of more than eight metres, although one of them, Szyja Warszawski, specifies that it reached a height of sixteen metres. He does not explain, of course, how they managed to place the corpses on top of the heap. In short, it would take 139,200,000 kilos of wood to incinerate 860,000 bodies weighing 45 kilos. The accumulated ashes would amount to 13,000 tonnes, which would occupy a volume of 36,500 cubic metres.

As in the case of Belzec, aerial photographs taken between May and November 1944 in the Treblinka area show that there was no deforestation: a thick forest of 100 hectares appeared to the north and east, of which one hectare was within the camp itself. Today, the surroundings of Treblinka are surrounded by spruce trees. The same question arises that we asked about Belzec: How did the camp administration obtain the 139,200 tons of wood needed to incinerate the corpses? Witnesses claim that there was a "Holzfällerkommando" which felled the forests to supply the wood needed for the cremations, but in order to get the required tons, 278 hectares of forest would have had to be felled. According to official historiography, it was not until Himmler's alleged visit to Treblinka in March 1943 that it was decided that the bodies were to be dug up and burned. Therefore, it must be considered that it was only thereafter that the supply of wood became a necessity. Richard Glazar states in *Trap with a Green Fence* (1995) that the

"Holzfällerkommando" consisted of twenty-five men. If this were true, two dozen men would have felled and transported more than a thousand tons of timber a day to the field. We see, then, that one impossibility is followed by another impossibility.

Unfortunately, despite all the technical and scientific evidence, the courts of justice have been behaving like the official historiography, as all their judgements have been based on the testimonies of survivors. In the numerous trials of "Nazi criminals" in Germany, despite the lack of documents and material evidence, it was assumed that millions of people had been gassed because witnesses and defendants testified so. Of the testimonies of those who pleaded guilty, we have already commented on that of the famous Kurt Gerstein, and later we will have occasion to refer to Rudolf Höss. Before the Düsseldorf tribunal on Treblinka, as in the Nuremberg trials, the dynamic of the lawyers was to advise their defendants to acknowledge the facts narrated by the witnesses and to plead obedience to the orders of their superiors, to whom all responsibility had to be delegated. In the section on Belzec we saw the case of Josef Oberhauser, who, despite being found guilty of assisting in the mass murder of 300,000 people, was only sentenced to four and a half years in prison because of his cooperative attitude. In the camp trials, the defendants generally followed the instructions of the lawyers and admitted without exception to their participation in the murder of Jewish men, women and children on an industrial scale. They knew that if they did not do so, if they persisted in stubbornly denying what they were asked to ratify, they could only expect harsher sentences, including the death penalty.

John Demjanjuk's trial in Jerusalem

An example of the unreliability of witnesses is the trial in Jerusalem between 1987 and 1988 of John Demjanjuk, whom several survivors identified as "Ivan the Terrible". The Zionist state had succeeded in February 1986 in getting the United States to strip him of his American citizenship and extradite him to Israel. During the fourteen months of the trial, Treblinka became the centre of world attention. Accepting witness testimony as evidence, the Israeli trial court, composed of Judges Dov Levin, Zvi A. Tal and Dalia Dorner, found that Demjanjuk operated the gas chambers that killed more than 850,000 Jews between July 1942 and August 1943 and sentenced him to death in April 1988.

Thanks to the contribution of Dr. Miroslav Dragan, Jürgen Graf and Carlo Mattogno had access to the verdict document of "Criminal Case 373/86, State of Israel v. Ivan (John) Demjanjuk". Witnesses portrayed him as a brutal being who enjoyed torturing victims. One of them, Pinchas Epstein, recognised him as the man who ran the engine. According to

Epstein, when the gas chambers were emptied, Demjanjuk would appear and act like this:

> "Sometimes he would show up with a dagger, sometimes with a bayonet and crack skulls, cut off ears, brutalise prisoners, it's absolutely unbelievable, unbelievable. He stood next to the bodies and looked at them. I mean, honourable court, it was horrible to look at the bodies when they were taken out of the chambers. People with smashed faces, people with knife wounds, pregnant women with wounds in their bellies, women with their foetuses hanging, young girls with stab wounds in their breasts, with their eyes gouged out.... He was standing there contemplating the results of what he had done.... He was standing there enjoying the scene.... He was always close to me, a few metres away... He was always close to me, just a few metres away... He was baiting the prisoners, he was cutting off a nose, he was wounding someone in the head... Almost a million human beings, souls, were massacred, children, old people, babies... Because they were Jews. This Ivan was a monster from another planet."

Eliyahu Rosenberg also identified Demjanjuk as the Satan of Treblinka. His statement is also included in the Jerusalem court verdict. Rosenberg said that he saw him every day when he worked on the ramp and new consignments of Jews arrived for extermination. Like Pinchas Epstein, this witness also attributed bestial acts to Demjanjuk; but added that he also committed them when the prisoners entered the chambers: "...I also saw that he had a knife, I saw him with these destructive instruments and how he beat, punished, cut the victims at the entrance to the gas chambers". In his eagerness to denigrate the alleged Ivan the Terrible as much as possible, Rosenberg related the following to the court:

> "I was on the ramp, we had taken the bodies out of the gas chambers. Ivan came out of his cabin. He saw that I was there, the place was full of bodies, he told me.... pull down your trousers... lie down with them... I understood immediately... Lefler (one of the SS men) was standing there. He was standing and watching. I ran to him and said in German: 'Ivan wants me to have sex with a dead woman'. Then he turned to him and reprimanded him. Ivan just said to me (in Russian): 'I will give her back to you.' He gave her back to me and found the opportunity."

Carlo Mattogno and Jürgen Graf still reproduce the testimony of a third witness, Yehiel Reichmann, who, according to the verdict, gave the following statement to the court in Jerusalem:

> "I want to tell what happened with my friend Finkelstein near the well. While I was still brushing my teeth with him, with Finkelstein, this Ashmadai (devil) Ivan came with a drilling machine to dig holes. He spun

the drill on Finkelstein's buttocks and said to him: 'If you scream I will kill you'.... He wounded Finkelstein, he was bleeding and in great pain, intense pain, but he was not allowed to scream, for Ivan had given him an order: 'if you scream, I will kill you'.... Ivan was a devil, the super-annihilator of Treblinka."

Forty-five years after the events on trial, the Zionist authorities intended to make the Demjanjuk trial a Hollywood-style re-enactment in order to impress the world in general and the population of Israel in particular. It was initially planned to hold the trial in a football stadium. When it was realised that the show-trial aspect would have been too obvious, a theatre was chosen as the venue. It all ended, however, in a monumental fiasco, a complete failure for the Zionist state of Israel.

After the death sentence had been passed, the family of John Demjanjuk, a Ukrainian by birth who had acquired US citizenship, was able to uncover evidence suppressed by the Soviets. Thanks to the new evidence, it became clear that the alleged "Ivan the Terrible" was in fact another Ukrainian named Ivan Marchenko (or Marczenko). Thus, the testimony of the five survivors who had identified Demjanjuk without a shadow of a doubt as the sadistic mass criminal of Treblinka was discredited. Yoram Sheftel, one of the lawyers, appealed and the court had no choice but to admit that John Demjanjuk was not the monster the perjurers had described. In late 1988 Sheftel was assaulted by a criminal who threw acid in his face with a spray bottle. A few days after this attack, another Demjanjuk lawyer, Dov Eitan, was killed when he fell from a skyscraper. Nevertheless, in September 1993 Demjanjuk finally managed to return to the United States. He never received a single dollar in compensation for the unspeakable injustice he had suffered. By contrast, in 2002, the 82-year-old Demjanjuk faced further persecution for his service in Sobibor, Majdanek and Flossenbürg. Perhaps there will be an opportunity to write a few lines about this later.

Treblinka investigation with GPR (Ground Penetrating Radar)

In October 1999, an Australian team led by electronics engineer Richard Krege carried out six days of research on the Treblinka site. The researchers worked under the auspices of the Adelaide Institute, a revisionist think tank chaired by Dr Frederick Töben, who in 1999 was imprisoned for seven months in Germany for questioning the Holocaust. The researchers used an $80,000 ground-penetrating radar (GPR), which sends visible signals to a computer monitor. The device, used by geologists, archaeologists and police around the world, detects any large-scale disturbances in the earth's structure at a depth of four to five metres and can sometimes reach up to ten metres. Krege's team also drilled holes with an auger to take soil samples.

Treblinka II was examined: the places where the exterminationists placed the mass graves and also the surroundings of the area. No significant disturbances were found to indicate that hundreds of thousands of bodies were buried there or signs that the earth had been disturbed. Furthermore, Krege's team found no evidence of bone remains, human ashes or wood. With these scans," Krege said, "we were able to identify clearly undisturbed horizontal stratigraphic layers, better known as horizons, in the soil beneath the field." Krege pointed out that in previous scans in pits and at other sites where there had been ground disturbances, such as quarries or excavations, it was perfectly possible to identify whether natural soil layers were missing or had been massively disturbed. Geological processes normally occur very slowly and disturbances in soil structure would have been detected even after sixty years. The Australian team's work therefore suggests that there were never any large mass graves at Treblinka. Personally," Krege commented, "I don't believe there was an extermination camp here at all.

In January 2000, Krege gave a lecture in Melbourne and presented the results of his research. The engineer requested that a UN-sponsored commission travel to Treblinka with a GPR and initiate a scientific investigation in order to detect possible omissions in his findings, but there was no response. Richard Krege, however, acknowledged to Jürgen Graf that the data was incomplete and suggested that further research should be undertaken. It was in this way that Graf, a polyglot able to speak fifteen languages who had been sentenced to 15 months in prison in 1998 by a court in his native Switzerland, proposed to Krege that they work together.

Since the expensive GPR had only been rented for a fortnight, Graf was able to raise the necessary money from friends and sponsors to maintain the aircraft. On 21 August 2000, Graf, Mattogno and Krege met in Kraków. The latter had to return to Italy for family reasons, so only Krege and Graf travelled to the alleged extermination camps. Jürgen Graf himself gives an account of the trip in an article published in 2004. Krege wanted to compare his research on Treblinka with the study of a place where mass graves had been dug, so he and Graf travelled to Auschwitz-Birkenau, where in the summer of 1942 nearly 20,000 people had died of a terrible typhus epidemic. This huge death toll forced the camp to close and led to the construction of more crematoria at Auschwitz. Since the existing ones were totally inadequate, most of the corpses were buried in mass graves, which were clearly visible on aerial photographs taken by the Allies. The two researchers had no trouble locating one of the graves with the GPR, and Krege and his team worked for two days. The second site was Belzec, where Krege was able to work in ideal conditions for days without being disturbed, as there is no museum there and few people visit the site. The next station was Sobibor, where there is a museum at the entrance to the camp. There the employees demanded a permit, which they had to obtain in Warsaw, so they gave up and continued their journey to Treblinka. They stayed in a cottage near the small town of Ostrow, close to Treblinka. For several days Krege worked tirelessly checking every square metre of the area of the alleged mass graves. Since buses with (often Israeli) Holocaust tourists were constantly arriving," says Graf, "I was on edge all the time. Fortunately, my companion's industrious activity did not arouse suspicion among the Holocaust pilgrims and we left Treblinka without incident".

With the objectives accomplished, Krege returned home via Germany and Graf went to Lviv in Ukraine, where he worked for several days in the city's archive and then travelled on to Moscow, where he now lives in exile. Richard Krege presented the initial results of his research, displayed on slides, at two conferences: the first in June 2001 in Washington and the second in January 2002 in Moscow. While scans of Auschwitz-Birkenau reflected evidence of massive earthworks showing that there had once been a mass grave there, no trace of significant disturbance was found at either Belzec or Treblinka. As usual, not a single major media outlet provided the slightest information about the contributions of the revisionist researchers.

Sobibór

Jürgen Graf, Thomas Kues and Carlo Mattogno published *Sobibór: Holocaust Propaganda and Reality* in 2010, a definitive work of over 400 pages on this third camp of the so-called "Einsatz Reinhard" (Operation or Reinhard Action). English-language readers interested in learning more can turn to this work, available online in PDF format, as it is the main source for the pages that follow, which, again, will have to be scarce. Much of what we have written about Belzec and Treblinka also applies to this camp, yet another example of the falsification of reality that has been maintained against all odds.

The *Holocaust Encyclopaedia* states that the extermination camp was located near the railway station in the village of Sobibór, in the eastern part of the Lublin district. Built in March 1942, it was in the form of a rectangle measuring 400 x 600 metres and was controlled, as usual, by about 20 German SS personnel and about 100 Ukrainians. According to this source, the camp consisted of three zones: administration (Camp I), reception (Camp II) and extermination (Camp III). In this third part were located the gas chambers, mass graves and barracks for the Jewish prisoners working there. These chambers, built inside a brick building, were square and measured 4 x 4, i.e. 16 square metres, into which between 160 and 180 people were placed. The carbon monoxide was produced by a 200-horsepower engine in a nearby shed, from which the exhaust pipe was fed into the gas chambers.

The *Holocaust Encyclopaedia* reports that the victims were deceived: they were told that they had arrived at a transit camp from which they would go on to labour camps after disinfection of their bodies and clothes. Men were separated from women and children. After being ordered to undress and hand over their belongings, they were directed to the gas chambers, which appeared to be showers. According to this source, about 500 people entered the chambers and, as usual, they were beaten, threatened, shouted at.... In thirty minutes they were all dead. Then it was the same as in the other two camps: the chambers were emptied, the gold teeth were removed, etc., and the bodies were buried. All this took place in two or three hours, during which time the trains of twenty wagons, after being cleaned, had left in search of more Jews and were already entering the camp again with a new consignment of victims for extermination.

Holocaust preachers establish two phases of extermination in Sobibór. During the first, from the beginning of May to the end of July 1942, about 100,000 Jews were allegedly murdered. There was a lull in the killings, and in August and September the gas chambers were enlarged in order to be able to kill more and better. The second phase lasted from October 1942 to June 1943, and another 150,000 Jews were gassed. Here, too, the corpses from the first phase were dug up and cremation began at the end of September 1942. On 14 October 1943, an uprising took place, allowing some 400 prisoners to escape. At the end of 1943, the camp was raised and the area was ploughed and cultivated. In 1987, Hollywood produced a propaganda film, *Scape from Sobibor*, directed by Jack Gold. The hero, Alexander Aronovitch Pechersky, "Sasha", was played by Golden Globe winner Rutger Hauer.

This is the brief summary of the official version, formulated on the basis of witnesses and court verdicts which have accepted the testimonies as irrefutable evidence. There is, however, an official document, a secret directive of Reichsführer-SS Heinrich Himmler issued on 5 July 1943, which reads as follows: "The Sobibór transit camp in the Lublin district will be converted into a labour camp. A unit for the dismantling of armaments captured from the enemy will be installed in the concentration camp." Mattogno, Kues and Graf, from whose work the quotation comes, warn that Holocaust literature regularly distorts the content of this directive and give as an example the *Encyclopaedia of the Holocaust*, which reads: "On 5 July 1943 Himmler ordered the closure of Sobibór as an extermination camp and its transformation into a concentration camp". It is clear, therefore, that official Holocaust historians have had knowledge of Himmler's document and have deliberately manipulated it in order to distort reality. It is an undeniable fact that in the secret instruction Himmler uses the noun phrase "Durchgangslager" (transit camp). What need did he have for it if he was addressing exclusively his subordinates whom he could not and did not intend to deceive? Himmler's full text, sent to the SS-WVHA, SS-Wirtschafts-Verwaltungshauptamt (Main Economic and Administrative Department), and to seven sections of the SS, can be read in the work of the revisionist authors:

"The Sobibór transit camp in the Lublin district will be converted into a labour camp. A unit for the dismantling of armaments captured from the enemy will be installed in the camp.
2. All senior police and SS commanders must hand over the enemy's ammunition there, insofar as it is not needed for the artillery captured from the enemy.
3. All metals, but especially blasting powder, must be recycled in a prudent manner.
4. Simultaneously, a production site will be built for our multiple launchers and/or for other munitions."

In the end, the conversion into a concentration camp did not take place. On 15 July 1943, Oswald Pohl, head of the SS Department of Economic Administration, advised Himmler to abandon the idea of converting the Sobibór transit camp into a concentration camp, since the dismantling of weapons captured from the enemy could be carried out without the need for such a measure. Therefore, Pohl also referred to Sobibór as a transit camp:

"Reichsführer!
According to his earlier directives, the Sobibór transit camp in the Lublin district is to be converted into a concentration camp.
I have discussed this with SS-Gruppenführer Globocnik. We both propose that this conversion be abandoned, since the intended purpose, namely to set up in Sobibór a facility for the deactivation of enemy munitions, can be achieved without this conversion...".

There is documentation that Himmler visited Sobibór twice, on 19 July 1942 and in March 1943. A letter from Odilo Globocnick, SS and Police Chief in the Lublin District, to SS-Gruppenführer Maximilian von Herff records the March visit, in which Himmler inspected Sobibór and approved the promotion of some officers. Orthodox historians claim, as always on the basis of witness testimony, that during this second visit Himmler personally attended the gassing of between 300 and 500 Jewish girls, who were brought from Lublin for the occasion and murdered in his honour.

The first information about Sobibór as an extermination camp began to be fabricated in July 1942. On 23 December of the same year there was an official report from the Polish Government in exile that alluded to the extermination of Jews by gassing, although without specifying the method. During the first months of 1943 the Polish underground press continued to publish news about Sobibór. On 1 April 1943, for example, the daily *Informacja Biezaca* referred to Sobibór as a "death camp" to which transports of Jews arrived from France and Holland, who, it was said, "were convinced that they were going to work in war industry factories. On 14 March," the informants add, "Dutch Jews were received in Sobibór by an orchestra; the next day, not one of them was still alive". The claim that the Germans had the luxury of welcoming the deportees with an orchestra before liquidating them is, of course, a ridiculous device. It is curious, however, to note how the propagandists liked to introduce absurd details of this kind into their stories.

Since the lies and inconsistencies narrated in the sections on Belzec and Treblinka are repeated with few variations, there is no point in repeating them again. Basically, the witnesses said that the disinfection facilities were the gas chambers. Pechersky, the hero of *Scape from Sobibor*, stated that the chambers appeared to be baths: "At first glance, everything looked as a bath should look, taps for hot and cold water, showers for washing". Mikhail A. Razgonayev testified in 1948 that "everyone was given a bar of soap." According to another witness named Feldhendler, "the bath was arranged as if it was really a place to wash (taps in the showers, a pleasant atmosphere)." In other words, when in 1943 the population of Germany was suffering all kinds of deprivation, lacking essential consumer goods and desperately struggling for survival, the Nazis were wasting time and resources - soldiers, trains, fuel, etc. - to send Jews to the East in order to kill them thousands of kilometres away. There, in the Polish General Government, the Germans staged a grotesque performance: they had the luxury of welcoming them with an orchestra, handing them bars of soap and putting them in nice showers with hot water taps, which turned out to be gas chambers. All this in order to finally exterminate them with the most inefficient and unsafe method of all they had at their disposal.

Despite our initial intention not to dwell too long on Sobibór, we cannot resist the temptation to quote an excerpt from Jules Shelvis' book, which reproduces the harangue that the deportees heard when they arrived at Sobibór, for all indications are that, although he refuses to admit it, it was exactly what was to happen. The first edition of Shelvis' book was published in 1993 in Dutch under the title *Vernietiginskamp Sobibór* (*Sobibór Extermination Camp*). It was translated into German in 1998 and an English edition appeared in 2007. As one of a group of 3,006 Dutch Jews, Shelvis, his wife Rachel and other relatives were deported to the camp on 1 June 1943. The merit of his book is that it is well documented, citing official sources and abundant bibliography. In all editions, Jules Shelvis had accepted the official figure of 250,000 Jews gassed; however, in 2008 a new Dutch edition appeared in which he acknowledges that only 170,000 Jews were deported to Sobibór, thus reducing the number of alleged victims by 80,000. While authors such as the Zionist Miriam Novitch recount the usual lies of the type: the Germans urinated in the mouths of the prisoners, hacked the bodies of babies to pieces and other such barbarities, Shelvis merely records the SS beatings of the Jews when they did not work well. In the chapter entitled "Arrival and Selection", reproduced by Mattogno, Kues and Graf, from whose work we have taken it, Shelvis writes the following text:

> "The process following the arrival of the transports at the camp soon became routine. [...] After leaving the sorting barracks, the men were separated from the women and directed to the undressing area in Lager (camp) 2; the women to another part of the camp. Unless it had already been done on the platform, this was the time when an SS man made a short speech. Usually - until his transfer to Treblinka - it was made by Oberscharführer Hermann Michel. Nicknamed 'the doctor' by the Arbeitshäftlinge (labouring prisoners) because of his habit of wearing a white coat, he delivered his speech in rapid German [...] Michel's words followed this pattern: 'In wartime we all have to work. You will be taken to a place where you can prosper. Children and old people will not have to work, but they will still be well fed. You must keep yourselves clean. Because of the conditions in which you have travelled, with so many of you in each carriage, it is appropriate that we take precautionary hygienic measures. That is why you will soon have to undress and shower. Your clothes and luggage will be put away. You must put your clothes in a neat pile, and your shoes, matched and tied together. You must place them in front of you. Valuables such as gold, money and watches should be handed over there at the counter. You should carefully remember the number given to you by the man behind the counter, so that you will be able to retrieve your property more easily afterwards. If valuables are found on you after your shower, you will be punished. There is no need to bring a towel and soap; everything will be given to you. There will be one towel for every two persons.' [...]
> Michel was so convinced while delivering his speech, even though he was deceiving the victims, that the Arbeitshäflinge also nicknamed him 'the preacher'. Sometimes he made them believe that the camp was a transit camp, that the journey to the Ukraine was only a matter of time, and that the Jews would even be granted autonomy there. At other times he would tell them that they would all go to Riga."

According to Shelvis, people would soon afterwards march credulously to the gas chambers. In other words, this spiel would prove once again that the Germans were masters of the art of representation, and that they took care of their staging down to the smallest detail in order to conceal from their victims that they intended to exterminate them: welcome orchestras, pep talks, soaps, towels, hot showers and, finally, carbon monoxide. In Sobibór, too, however, the Gerstein Report's version had to be relied on in the last resort, since the witnesses, as usual, disagreed in their accounts of the method of extermination by gassing. The report on Treblinka of 15 November 1942, received by the Polish Government in London in January 1943, referred to three steam chambers. According to this document, 'steam was generated by a large vat. The hot steam was fed into the chambers through pipes installed there, each of which had a neat number of ducts". This description clearly fits a steam disinfection plant. Even a Holocaust defender like Jean-Claude Pressac admits that at Belzec as well as at Treblinka and Sobibór there were delousing facilities for the purpose of preventive hygiene and the fight against typhus. It is apparently these facilities that propagandists described as gas chambers, but since it was implausible that steam from a kind of sauna could exterminate hundreds of thousands of Jews, the version of Gerstein and the diesel engines prevailed.

Graf, Kues and Mattogno devote a significant part of their work on Sobibór, some seventy pages, to analysing the forensic investigations carried out in the field. A team led by Andrzej Kola, the same Polish professor who had previously carried out the excavations in Belzec, undertook archaeological research in 2000, the aim of which was to locate mass graves in Camp III and to produce a proper report in memory of the victims. It was also intended to locate artefacts for later display in the museum established in Sobibór. Of course, the location of the much-talked-about gas chambers was also one of the objectives. The excavations continued throughout 2001.

According to the *Encyclopaedia of the Holocaust*, the 100,000 Jews eliminated in the first phase of the extermination were exhumed, and at the end of September 1942, work began on cremating their corpses. However, in the seven mass graves discovered and described by Kola in his reports, in addition to the remains of cremated bodies, saponified bodies were found that had not been burned. Kola also noted that the camp was in a marshy area. On the western edge, he discovered an old sewage ditch near which a bog emerged. In their examination of Camp III, the archaeologists discovered a well not far from the pits that had been filled with sand. When excavating, they found groundwater at a depth of 3.60 metres, and when they reached a depth of five metres they had to stop because of the constant inflow of water. A map of Sobibór shows that the camp was in a place where, in addition to several marshy areas, there were half a dozen lakes within a radius of less than three kilometres. Lake Spilno, located one kilometre to the west, had an elevation of 164 metres. The Bug River, on the other hand, was 2.5 kilometres to the east. The Sobibór railway line itself was at an elevation of 167 metres and the tracks ran through a marshy area. The court in Hagen, where the Sobibór trial was held between 1965 and 1966, established in its verdict that in the summer of 1942,

> "... As a result of the heat, there was a pushing up of the bodies in the graves that were already full, and the liquids from the corpses attracted maggots, which caused the camp area to produce a dreadful smell. In addition, the camp commander feared that the drinking water, which came from the camp's wells, would be contaminated."

The danger of groundwater contamination due to the decomposition of the bodies was precisely the reason why the camp authorities decided to exhume the corpses and cremate them. Since the Germans visited the Sobibór area several times before starting the construction of the camp, there is no doubt that they were familiar with the geological characteristics of the area. It is logical to argue, therefore, that if they had intended it as an extermination camp, they would not have built it without crematoria, knowing that the terrain did not permit mass burials. If they did not contemplate cremation of the dead, it must have been because they did not foresee that higher than usual mortality rates would occur there.

Kues, Graf and Mattogno proceed to examine the findings of the Kola excavations, which cannot confirm the claims of the official historians, by means of rigorous calculations, exhausting for the reader, taking into account all possible parameters. The three revisionists absolutely reject the possibility of drawing from Professor Kola's work the conclusion that Sobibór was an extermination camp. However, since a new team of archaeologists led by Isaac Gilead and Yoram Haimi of Ben Gurion University, and by Wojciech Mazurek of the Polish company Underground Archaeological Surveys, began new research in October 2007, the three revisionists also comment on these latest archaeological studies in *Sobibor Holocaust Propaganda and Reality*.

In 2009, the American contemporary history journal *Present Pasts* published a thirty-page article by Gilead and Mazurek, less than twelve pages of which are devoted to Sobibór. The article acknowledges that they too failed to find the alleged gas chamber that Kola's team had been unable to locate. In their paper, instead of providing scientific evidence, Gilead and Mazurek quote Hilberg and Arad and shamefully write the following: "In addition to these sources, the evidence also consists of oral accounts of the survivors and SS criminals who worked in the killing centres and committed the murders.... Thus, the extermination of the Jews in general, and the extermination of Jews in Sobibór and other centres, is an established historical truth which does not need to be proved by archaeological excavations". It seems to us that comments are superfluous, since such an argumentation completely discredits these "scientists".

How many people died and were buried at Sobibór? This is the question posed by Mattogno, Kues and Graf. The difficulty in quantifying the forensic evidence and the lack of documentation on the number of deportees prevent an exact answer. In 2000-2001 and in 2007-2008, archaeologists neither excavated the graves in depth nor provided an estimate of the number of human remains, which is significant. Nevertheless, after reviewing Professor Kola's findings from the Sobibór graves, the revisionists establish three categories of the dead in their quest for an answer. In the first they place those who died of various diseases or epidemics such as typhus and prisoners executed for escape attempts and other violations of camp rules. These would include the nearly 400 who were shot after being recaptured following the mass escape in October 1943. In total, about 1,000 people. In the second category are the deportees who died en route, as the conditions under which the Jews from France and the Netherlands, some 38,000, travelled were very poor, if not inhumane. Of the total number of 170,000 deportees, it can be estimated that about 3% must have died on the trains from disease, dehydration and other causes. The calculation therefore gives a further 5,000 victims. In addition, Mattogno, Kues and Graf acknowledge that about 3,500 people were euthanised in Sobibor: the dying, the mentally ill, seriously ill prisoners and others suffering from contagious diseases. To these, accepting the figure calculated by Polish historians, they add another 1,000 non-Jewish patients from the Lublin mental hospitals, who were also allegedly euthanised. The total number of dead in the three categories would amount to some 10,500 people.

Since *Outlawed History* is a handbook covering some two hundred and fifty years of contemporary history, it is obligatory to finish these pages devoted to the camps of the so-called Reinhard Action, named after Reinhard Heydrich, who was assassinated on 4 June 1942. Heydrich, as is well known, chaired the Wannsee Conference in January 1942 and had been head of the Gestapo and the Reich Security Main Office . Official historiography has ruled that "Einsatz Reinhard" was a code name intended to camouflage the mass murder of Jews in the three camps we have been studying. Nevertheless, all Holocaust historians insist that the star extermination camp was Auschwitz.

Part 4
Auschwitz

Auschwitz in Upper Silesia, near Kraków, had a population of about 13,000,000 in 1939. In May 1940, the concentration camp that was to go down in history as Nazi Germany's largest killing centre was founded there. Auschwitz was ideally situated because it had good transport facilities and three rivers, the Vistula, Premsza and Sola, ran nearby. It was also located south of the Silesian coal fields in the Katowice mining region. The notorious Rudolf Höss was appointed commandant. Höss, who had been imprisoned between 1923 and 1928 for his part in the murder of a communist, had experienced the harshness of prison life and was therefore sensitive to the accommodation and food needs of the prisoners.

On 20 May 1940, the camp was opened on the basis of brick barracks of the Polish army. Its first prisoners were some 700 Polish criminals from Tarnów. For the first two years, Auschwitz was used primarily to intern Poles, although it also held prisoners from Germany. In 1941, construction began on Birkenau (Auschwitz II), located to the west of the city, about three kilometres from the main camp. In the autumn of 1941, looking deplorable due to the long marches, Soviet prisoners of war began to arrive and were used in the construction of Birkenau, which was to be completed in April 1942. On 16 November 1941, it was decided to build Monowitz (Auschwitz III), just under five kilometres east of the city. Soviet prisoners were also employed to build this third enclave, which began operations in May 1942 and became a huge industrial complex that was the largest of all the labour camps. From then on Auschwitz I became the administrative centre of a complex whose main camps were Birkenau and Monowitz, although there were also a large number of smaller camps within a radius of forty kilometres, also administered from Auschwitz I. Auschwitz thus became the largest set of camps in the German concentration camp system. It was in mid-1942 that the Jews, who were being deported eastwards, became the main element of these camps.

When honest witnesses established that there had been no gas chambers in Dachau and Bergen-Belsen, public attention began to shift to the camps in the east: Belzec, Treblinka, Sobibór and, particularly, Auschwitz. Since these camps remained in communist Europe, there was no way to confront the veracity of the claims of those spreading the news about the gas chambers. It took a decade before the Soviets finally allowed visits to the alleged Auschwitz extermination camp. During these ten years there was enough time to modify its appearance in order to make credible the claim that four million people had been exterminated there. This was the sensational figure announced by the Soviets after controlling the camp. At the time, in the midst of the Nuremberg trials, they were trying to pin the Katyn massacre on the Germans.

As seen in the previous section, testimonies about the extermination camps in Poland were collected after the war by official Polish commissions of enquiry and by the Central Jewish Historical Commission of Poland. The alleged mass murder of millions of Jews took place in Auschwitz-Birkenau between May 1942 and October 1944. If we take into account the figure of 4,000,000 on the memorial plaque when John Paul II visited the site in June 1979, the Germans must have eliminated more than 130,000 people every month, which is equivalent to about 4,400 a day. If the figure of 1,500,000, which Benedict XVI encountered in May 2006, were to be taken as a good one, 50,000 detainees would have had to be liquidated each month. Moreover, Gerald Reitlinger himself acknowledges in *The SS: Alibi of a Nation* that between May 1940 and February 1945 there were only 363,000 registered detainees in Auschwitz. Despite this finding, however, Reitlinger claims that the camp was equipped to exterminate 6,000 people daily. There were even more grotesque and blatant exaggerations, such as those of the Hungarian Jew Olga Lengyel, who in her book *Five Chimneys* (1959) claims that she was detained in Auschwitz and that no less than 729 corpses per hour were incinerated. She adds that 8,000 people were burned every day in the 'death pits'.

Considering that Auschwitz was the site of an extremely important industrial complex producing all kinds of materials for the war industry, it is incomprehensible that the prisoners who were the essential labour force for maintaining the necessary production activity were exterminated on a monthly basis. In Auschwitz, there were synthetic rubber and coal-derivative factories located in the camp by I.G. Farben. Krupp also had an arms factory there. In addition, there was an agricultural research station with laboratories, nurseries and livestock breeding. Numerous firms had branches in the camp, and the SS itself had its own factories there. In March 1941 Himmler visited Auschwitz accompanied by the directors of I.G. Farben in order to check the industrial capacity of the camp. It was then that he ordered that the facilities be enlarged in order to accommodate 100,000 new prisoners who were to work as labourers for I.G. Farben. This is, of course, incompatible with the claim that a systematic extermination policy was pursued at Auschwitz. It is also worth considering that there were free workers living in the area, . The number of prisoners working for I.G. Farben was less than thirty percent. About fifty percent of the workforce were foreigners who had signed up voluntarily. Ordinarily employed German workers made up twenty percent of the total workforce.

All SS administrative functions in Auszchwitz were centralised in the main camp (Auschwitz I). These competencies included guarding, feeding, clothing, housing, prisoner discipline, medical services, and recreational activities: concerts, cabaret artists, films, sports competitions, brothel.... For the maintenance of such extensive services, the companies that used the prisoners' labour rented them out to the SS. As in all other German concentration camps, the working day in Auschwitz was eleven hours six days a week, although in an emergency it was possible to work on Sunday morning.

I. G. Farben

Antony C. Sutton notes in *Wall Street and the Rise of Hitler* that on the eve of World War II, the German chemical complex I. G. Farben was the largest chemical manufacturing company in the world. With substantial financial assistance from Wall Street, six major German chemical companies - Badische Anilin, Bayer, Agfa, Hoechst, Weiler-Ter-Meer and Griesheim-Elektron - merged in 1925. Thus was born the cartel "Internationale Gesellschaft Farbenindustrie Aktiengesellschaft", better known as I. G. Farben. The organisational genius was Hermann Schmitz, who twenty years later was tried in Nuremberg and sentenced to four years in prison. By contrast, the members of the North American subsidiaries were not disturbed at all.

It has already been remarked in the account of Hitler's rise to power that it was Jewish Wall Street capitalists who financed Nazism. In chapter 8 we have devoted some fifteen pages to uncovering the contacts of Germany's future Führer with James Paul Warburg (Sidney Warburg), the son of Paul Warburg, the grey eminence who in 1913 planned and organised the banking cartel that made up the Federal Reserve System. The criminal oppression imposed on the German people with the financial burden of debt was used by Wall Street bankers, who took advantage of the situation to make profitable loans to German big business. In 1924, these international financiers came up with the Dawes Plan, devised by J. P. Morgan, which was approved and sponsored by the US government. It was thanks to these loans that I. G. Farben and Vereinigung Vereinigung were created and consolidated. G. Farben and Vereinigte Stahlwerke, a second conglomerate of iron, steel and coal companies.

In 1928 the Dawes Plan was replaced by the Young Plan, a perfect ploy of the international bankers for the invasion of Germany through financial capital from the United States. It should be noted that German companies with American subsidiaries evaded the conditions of the Young Plan through the manoeuvre of provisional foreign ownership. Thus, for example, A. E. G. (Allgemeine Elektricitäts Gesellschaft), affiliated with General Electric in the United States, was sold to a Franco-Belgian company and evaded the conditions of the Young Plan. It is worth noting, by the way, that Owen Young was Franklin D. Roosevelt's biggest financial backer. After the implementation of the Young Plan, the German bankers on Farben's supervisory board included Max Warburg, the Jewish banker from

Hamburg who was the brother of Paul Warburg, who in turn, not coincidentally, was also on the board of I. G. Farben in the United States, Farben's American subsidiary owned by American capitalists. Between 1928 and the outbreak of World War II, I. G. Farben doubled in size, an expansion made possible in large part by American technical assistance and bond issues from banks such as the National City Bank.

Carrol Quigley explains in *Tragedy and Hope* that all these operations were part of an ambitious plan of international cooperation and alliances for global domination. According to Quigley, the aim was to "create a worldwide system of financial control, in private hands, capable of dominating the political system of each country and the economy of the world as a whole". According to Quigley, the "apex of the system" was the "Bank for International Settlements", based in Basel. This Bank for International Settlements, Sutton writes, "was during World War II the means by which bankers - who were apparently not at war with each other - continued to benefit from each other's exchange of ideas, information and plans for the post-war world."

The importance of I. G. Farben during the war was related to the production of synthetic fuel and synthetic rubber from coal, which had already been experienced by the Germans during World War I. The Germans had already experienced during World War II. At that time, the shortage of rubber and other resources caused by the British blockade was a determining factor in Germany's capitulation. In Europe, only Romania had significant oil resources, but there was no natural rubber anywhere on the Old Continent. By contrast, coal was plentiful in Germany and other European countries. In an effort to prevent Germany's extreme vulnerability to raw material shortages, the Nazis subsidised scientific and technological research in this field, and Germany led all countries in these areas of knowledge. By means of a coal treatment technique known as hydrogenation, they succeeded in obtaining oil, from which a wide range of chemicals such as explosives, dyes, medicines, etc. could be manufactured. Another state or process of hydrogenation produced gasoline. More problematic was the production of synthetic rubber, needed for tyres for all types of vehicles; however, before the outbreak of war, they managed to resolve the technical difficulties. The product obtained, particularly suitable for tyre manufacture, was called "Buna-S" rubber.

With the annexation of a large part of Poland in 1939 following the partition of the country with the USSR, Germany was able to rely on the coal mines in Upper Silesia. Naturally, it was decided to exploit them immediately, and so the idea of setting up a hydrogenation and buna production plant in Auschwitz was born. The rivers flowing into the area ensured an abundance of water, and the mining camps were close by. In 1941, I. G. Farben built a Buna production plant in the Auschwitz industrial complex, where 3,000 tons of Buna were produced each month. I. G. Farben had three other Buna-S production plants in Germany: the first, with a capacity of 6,000 tons per month, was erected in Schkopau; the second was in Hüls and produced 4,000 tons; a third produced 2,500 tons per month and was located in Ludwigshafen, where the research centre and headquarters were located. However, it was at the Auschwitz plant that the most modern and advanced techniques for the production of synthetic rubber were developed.

When the United States entered the war in December 1941, Japan came to control natural rubber from the East Indies and the Malaya region, from which the Americans had been almost 100 per cent supplied. Thanks to a series of technical cooperation agreements with I.G. Farben maintained until the outbreak of the war with the consent of the German government, John D. Rockefeller's Standard Oil, the parent company of the American oil companies, had basic knowledge of the Buna rubber manufacturing process. The American side was the great beneficiary of these concessions, as the profit to the Germans was irrelevant. The sudden inaccessibility of the rubber sources caused a political crisis in the United States in 1942. The government took immediate notice of the emergency, for three days after the attack on Pearl Harbour, it banned the sale of new tyres for civilian purposes and decreed rubber rationing. From this point on, there was an urgent need to achieve the industrial capacity to produce synthetic rubber. On 6 August 1942, President Roosevelt appointed a committee to study the problem and make recommendations. An old acquaintance, the ubiquitous Bernard Baruch, who had controlled the War Industries Board during World War I, chaired the committee, hence it became known as the Baruch Committee. After meeting with representatives of Standard Oil, the Baruch Committee issued its final report on 10 September, urging the acceleration of the synthetic rubber production programme and recommending learning from the experience of others. At the time, , the most technically advanced site for Buna developments was Auschwitz.

All this is explained in detail by Arthur R. Butz in *The Hoax of the Twentieth Century* and is relevant because Auschwitz, the alleged centre for the systematic extermination of Jews, was at all times under the magnifying glass of US Intelligence, which necessarily knew what was going on in the industrial complex in 1942. Moreover, Allied military intelligence knew throughout the war much of what was going on in Germany, since Wilhelm Canaris himself, head of the Abwehr, the Military Intelligence Service, was a traitor, a spy who always passed information to the British Secret Service. If a major criminal programme had been launched in 1942 in the largest German camp, there is no doubt that it would have been detected, for the Americans attached strategic importance to the synthetic rubber operations of I.G. Farben in the Auschwitz industrial complex. US intelligence had taken numerous aerial photographs of the camp and the manufacturing facilities, had established the basis of the German chemical company's operations, and was following with the greatest interest the hydrogenation and other chemical processes involved in the production of gasoline and rubber.

When in August 1942 the Baruch Committee was gathering information, photographs of Auschwitz and the I. G. Farben factories surely came into the hands of the commissioners. Since the Buna plant was closed on 1 August, the lack of activity and the ghostly appearance of the facilities must have come as a surprise in the United States. It is likely that they soon learned that the closure was motivated by a terrible typhus epidemic. Over two months, thousands of people died, some sources say perhaps as many as 20,000, and production activities could only resume at the end of September. It was in this context that the German authorities realised that the crematoria in the camp were insufficient to incinerate the corpses quickly and prevent contagion. As a result, many of the victims were immediately burned in the open air, although many probably had to be buried temporarily. Fifteen new crematoriums were ordered to be built at Auschwitz-Birkenau, but they were not operational until March 1943.

The Birkenau ovens were located in buildings containing cellars, rooms and other spaces that the exterminationists took to be gas chambers. The first allegations about the extermination of Jews at Auschwitz originated not from Allied intelligence information, but from propagandistic misrepresentations by Rabbi Stephen S. Wise, president of the World Jewish Congress and the American Jewish Congress, supported by Secretary of the Treasury Henry Morgenthau. The State Department, on the other hand, was reluctant to accept the fable without proper cross-checking . It has been seen in chapter 10, specifically in looking at the Morgenthau Plan for Germany, that divergences and disagreements between the Treasury and State Departments grew in the final years of the war.

Propaganda by Jewish organisations in the USA

In the pages on the transit camps transformed into extermination camps by propaganda, it has been seen that the Zionist Action Committee, the World Jewish Congress and other Jewish organisations were well established in Switzerland, where works and pamphlets were published. From there, much of the propaganda campaign directed at Europe and the United States was organised. The first allegation that Jews were being exterminated, however, came in London, where the World Jewish Congress (WJC) branch claimed in June 1942 that one million Jews had been murdered in "a great slaughterhouse for Jews" somewhere unidentified and unlocated in Eastern Europe. The only evidence was information received by the Polish government in exile in the English capital. Nevertheless, *The New York Times* picked up the information and published it in the United States. It has been noted above that in August 1942 both the Foreign Office and the

Department of Psychological Warfare knew that the whole thing was a propaganda hoax and let Prime Minister Churchill know so.

On 8 August 1942, Gerhart Moritz Riegner and Paul Guggenheim, two representatives of the WJC, used the American ambassador in Bern, Leland Harrison, and the consul in Geneva, Paul C. Squire, to send reports to the United States about alleged killings of Jews in Eastern Europe. Auschwitz, for the time being, was not linked to the death camps. Riegner, who would later become secretary general of the WJC between 1965 and 1983, sent Rabbi Stephen Wise through diplomatic channels the so-called "Riegner telegram", considered the first official information on the alleged planning of the Holocaust. The State Department, which received the text through the embassy in Bern, did not initially agree to allow publication of the message, and Under Secretary of State Summer Welles told Rabbi Wise, who intended to release it immediately. Welles argued that other ambassadors and consuls in Europe needed to verify the facts. In reality, the State Department, like the Foreign Office, gave no credence to the allegations.

Wise had to agree, as publication of the telegram without State Department authorisation would have been counterproductive to WJC interests. Stephen Wise would later explain that as chairman of the WJC in the United States he was able to maintain contact with all its European agencies through the State Department's communication network. Zohar Zegev writes in *The World Jewish Congress during the Holocaust* that "the unauthorised publication of the Riegner telegram, sent through the Embassy in Bern, would have meant that it would have been the last telegram sent in this way and would have effectively ended the WJC's operations in Europe". This statement is clearly exaggerated, given the enormous power of the Zionists in the Roosevelt Administration, but it gives an idea of what Rabbi Wise's considerations were. In any case, two days later, on 10 August 1942, the Foreign Office received from Berne the same information from S. S. Silverman, chairman of the British section of the WJC, and from Gerhart Riegner, secretary of the WJC in Geneva. The text of the Riegner telegram, which is in the UK National Archives, reads as follows:

> "Received alarming report that, at the Fuehrer's headquarters, a plan has been discussed and is being considered, according to which all the Jews in the German occupied and controlled countries, between 3.5 and 4 million, are, after deportation and concentration in the East, to be exterminated at once, in order to solve the Jewish question in Europe once and for all. The action is reportedly planned for the autumn. The methods of execution are still under discussion, including the use of prussic acid. We pass on this information with the necessary reserve, as we cannot confirm the accuracy. Our source has close connections to the highest German authorities and their reports are generally reliable. Please inform and consult with New York."

Gerhart Riegner later alluded to the fact that his telegram was not given credibility and stated: "I have never felt so deeply the sense of abandonment, helplessness and loneliness as when I sent messages of disaster and horror to the free world and nobody believed me. After this first official document, the campaign that has been explained in the pages on the camps of the so-called "Einsatz Reinhard" was unleashed, which included such nonsense as: corpses used for fertiliser, soap made of pure Jewish fat, glue and lubricants from Jewish bodies, etc.

In the United States, J. Breckinridge Long, the Deputy Assistant Secretary of State who was to go down in history as one of the villains who did not believe the propaganda hoaxes, headed the State Department group that resisted the pressures of Rabbi Wise, Morgenthau, Dexter White and their Treasury minions. During the autumn of 1942, Stephen Wise launched a campaign to demand that the Allies take a public stand and condemn the alleged extermination of Jews in Europe. On 10 October 1942, however, the Vatican informed US representatives that it had been unable to confirm the alleged massacres. Finally, Wise led a delegation to the White House on 8 December 1942 to deliver to President Roosevelt a twenty-page document entitled *Blueprint for Extermination*. The pressure paid off, and on 17 December the Allies, led by Washington, issued a statement condemning the massacres. Two days later a second, related statement from Washington pointed to Belzec and Chelmno; but Auschwitz remained unmentioned. Despite these public statements Breckinridge Long not only refused to accept the propaganda claims, but tried to resist. On 21 January 1943 he got Summer Welles, the Under-Secretary of State, to sign instructions to the Ambassador in Bern, Leland Harrison, which had been drafted by himself or one of his staff:

> "In the future, reports given to you for transmission to private persons in the United States will not be accepted unless extraordinary circumstances make it advisable. We believe that by sending these private messages which circumvent the censorship of neutral countries we risk that these neutral countries may find it necessary to take action to restrict or abolish our secret means of official communication."

Morgenthau's Treasury Department, true to its habit of meddling in areas of State Department policy that did not fall within its competence, was quick to protest the forwarding of these orders to the ambassador to Switzerland. The following month, February 1943, the dispute between the two Departments escalated when the State Department learned that the Zionists had persuaded the Romanian Government to transfer 70,000 Jews to Palestine on Romanian ships carrying Vatican banners. Considering that this massive illegal migration could provoke an Arab uprising, which would have had catastrophic consequences at the height of the war, the British

Foreign Office warned the United States that if so many Jews were to be taken out of Europe, camps would have to be set up in North Africa to accommodate them. This provoked a new disagreement between Morgenthau's men, staunch Zionists, and the State Department.

In addition, the Romanian Government had been bribed with a promise to pay him $170,000. At the end of July 1943, both the Treasury Department and the WJC proposed that this sum be taken over by Romanian businessmen of Jewish origin. Brekinridge Long and his colleagues in the State Department chose to oppose the operation and became even more convinced that the extermination allegations were war propaganda, as they kept hearing of proposals to remove from Europe people who had supposedly been exterminated: in late summer it became known that six thousand Jewish children could be evacuated from France.

Brekinnridge Long began to be beaten up from all sides and was openly accused of contributing to the murder of the Jews. As a result, he began to be questioned within the government. At the moment," he declared bitterly, "I am in the centre of the bull's eye". One of Morgenthau's deputies, Josiah DuBois, drafted the famous "Report to the Secretary on the acquiescence of this Government in the murder of the Jews", which was used to convince Roosevelt of the need to establish the War Refugee Board (WRB). Finally, at the end of 1943, Wise and Morgenthau's campaign produced results and they got their way. In December, arrangements were finalised with the Romanian government for the evacuation of Romanian Jews. The money was deposited in an account in Switzerland controlled by Riegner and Morgenthau himself. In addition, in December 1943, Romania also tested the ground for peace, which was offered on condition that the Jews were treated well. In 1940 the Romanian Jews had been deported to the Sea of Azov region, and the Romanian government decided in December 1943 to repatriate them in cooperation with the International Red Cross, as explained above.

The War Refugee Board (WRB), at the origin of the Auschwitz fable

The victory of the Treasury Department over the State Department led President Roosevelt in January 1944 to authorise his close friend Henry Morgenthau, the Jewish potentate installed in the Treasury since 1934, to create the War Refugee Board (WRB), which, in addition to Secretary Morgenthau, included the Secretary of State, Cordell Hull, and the Secretary of War, Henry L. Stimson. The WRB's executive director was John W. Pehle and its general counsel, the aforementioned Josiah DuBois, two of

Morgenthau's boys at the Treasury[10]. In reality, the WRB was Morgenthau's Board, whose main concern was the evacuation of Jews from Europe, so it became an instrument of WJC and other Zionist organisations. Since Harry Dexter White was responsible for foreign relations in the Treasury Department, the WRB's operations were soon dominated and controlled by this Lithuanian-born Jew, the amazing communist spy who was Morgenthau's right-hand man, in reality an internationalist/globalist in the service of the international bankers. Since we have already written at length about both of them in chapter ten, namely in part five, which focuses on the Morgenthau Plan for Germany, no further comment is necessary.

Rabbi Wise, Zionists and other propaganda agents used the WRB to intensify their campaign in the United States. In November 1944 the War Refugee Board finally issued a report, a booklet entitled *German Extermination Camps: Auschwitz and Birkenau*, which can be considered the WRB's greatest success in propagating the Auschwitz lie. This booklet is the document which formally originated the official thesis of extermination in Auschwitz by means of gas chambers. It already contains the essential components of the fable, so much so that the accusations at Nuremberg were based on this WRB text. Breckinridge Long and other members of the State Department suspected that the report had been transmitted to Washington from Berne. In any case, it was no longer of any use for them to go on thinking and commenting privately that it was all a campaign by Morgenthau and his Jewish helpers. Of course, the German newspapers also denounced to no avail that an abominable propaganda campaign ("Greuelpropaganda") was being fabricated on the basis of lies.

On 26 November 1944 the WRB pamphlet, received in Switzerland on 6 August 1944, was published on the front page of *The New York Times*, which gave several summaries. It consisted of two reports, the first written by two Slovak Jews who escaped on 7 April, the second by a Polish officer. All claimed to have been in Auschwitz from the spring of 1942 to the spring of 1944. The report also had a brief supplement attributed to two other Jews who escaped on 27 May. The anonymity of all of them was preserved in the interests of security: "Their names will not be disclosed for the time being, it is argued, in the interests of their own safety. Everything invites the suspicion that the text, in addition to the fabricated part, contains information obtained

---

[10] Josiah DuBois acted at the Nuremberg Military Trials as chief prosecutor in the I.G. Farben trial. In 1952 he published the book *The Devil's Chemists*, in which he gives his version of the trial of what he calls the "24 conspirators of the Farben International cartel". In it, he notes that as early as November 1942, he received information from an Auschwitz prisoner working at the Buna plant that the shooting of prisoners was a constant occurrence. DuBois writes that in two messages received from Switzerland, sent by Riegner in January and April 1943, colleagues in the State Department were warned that 6,000 Jews were being murdered daily in Auschwitz. He thus denounces once again the alleged obstructionism put in place by the State Department to prevent the mass issuance of visas to European Jews seeking to enter the United States.

through intelligence services, since official data are given, such as, for example: numbers of detainees in April 1942, description of the prisoner registration system, causes of internment, nationalities, a detailed map of the area, dimensions of Auschwitz I, death certificates due to natural causes, a detailed breakdown of the numbers and classifications of prisoners in Birkenau in April 1944, a new registration system put into operation in May 1944...

In the account attributed to the Polish soldier, it is said that in the summer of 1942 the Jews were gassed in special enclosed buildings that appeared to be showers, which were located in a birch forest very close to Birkenau. Since the construction of the crematoria had not been completed, the bodies were buried in mass graves and putrefied. When the ovens at Birkenau were ready in the autumn of 1942, many corpses were exhumed and burned. Concerning the ovens at Birkenau, the report states that in the spring of 1944 four buildings housed crematoria I, II, III and IV. Each building consisted of a room for the furnace boilers, a large hall or foyer and a gas chamber. The first two buildings each contained 36 ovens (mouths or doors are understood) and the other two 18. According to the report, each oven could hold only three bodies at a time and their cremation lasted one and a half hours, which meant that 6,000 bodies could be burnt per day. Finally, the famous Zyklon B appeared, the packaging of which bore the inscription: "for use against pests", as the specific product used for mass murder in the gas chambers. It is added in this section of the pamphlet that prominent people in Berlin attended the opening of the first crematorium in March 1943. The "programme" consisted of the gassing and cremation of 8,000 Jews from Kraków. The names of those invited to the spectacle are not revealed, but it is noted that they were extremely pleased with the results.

The report includes a table that meticulously records by nationality the number of Jews gassed at Birkenau between April 1942 and April 1944. It is contained in document 022-L in the public record of the IMT trials, the heading of which reads: 'Summary of a Report of the War Refugee Board, Washington, D. C., November 1944, on the German extermination camps - Auschwitz and Birkenau - giving an estimate of the number of Jews gassed at Birkenau between April 1942 and April 1944'. Arthur R. Butz appends it in the appendix of illustrations to his reference work. Thanks to this, we can comment on some figures. It specifies that 900,000 Polish Jews, 600,000 of whom arrived by train and 300,000 by truck, were gassed during these two years in Birkenau. The French Jews exterminated numbered 145,000; the Dutch, 100,000; the Germans, 60,000, etc., to reach the figure of 1,765,000 Jews murdered. As for the Hungarian Jews, about whom we have written above, they do not appear in document 022-L, since as we know they began to be deported in May 1944. The WRB pamphlet states, however, that some 15,000 began arriving daily at Birkenau from 15 May, ninety percent of whom were eliminated immediately. It is stated that the capacity of the crematoria was overwhelmed by the arrival of so many Hungarian Jews, which is why they were burned in ditches.

Concerning the operation of the Auschwitz I Hospital, it is recorded that in the autumn of 1942 the death rate was so high that Berlin demanded explanations. We know that the typhus epidemic forced the closure of the Buna plant of I. G. Farben during the months of August and September. However, the report states that the camp doctor was found to have administered lethal injections to the weak and sick, to certain prisoners on death row and to some teenagers considered to be orphans.

It took sixteen years for the names of the alleged authors of the WRB report to be revealed. In the first edition of *The Final Solution,* Gerald Reitliger continued to refer to the anonymity of the writers, which was clearly not conducive to the credibility of the document and must have been understood as such, since it was Reitlinger himself who in 1960 was responsible for locating a certain Rudolf Vrba, whom in the revised edition of his work, published in 1968, he considers to be the author of the most important part of the account. Thus, at Eichmann's trial in Jerusalem in 1961, the names of the two Slovak Jews, Rudolf Vrba and Alfred Wetzler, finally came to light. The prosecutor then submitted an affidavit from Vrba, which the court rejected on the grounds that there was no excuse for the prosecution not to bring him before the court to testify. In 1963 Rudolf Vrba published the book *I Cannot Forgive,* in which he does not explain why it took him sixteen years to show signs of life. In 1964 he and Wetzler finally appeared in Frankfurt to testify as witnesses at the Auschwitz trial. Naturally, the WRB pamphlet is spurious and the appearance of these two characters does nothing to prove its purported authenticity.

Rudolf Höss' confession, second pillar of the Auschwitz fable

Holocaust historiography has in Rudolf Höss its brightest star in the universe of witnesses and defendants on which the Auschwitz fable has been built. If the WRB report was the first pillar on which the myth of Auschwitz as an extermination camp began to be built, Höss's confession, obtained under severe torture, constitutes the second pillar and fundamental framework of the story. Höss was presented as a witness before the International Military Tribunal (IMT) on 15 April 1946. His testimony was an unexpected bombshell that stunned all the defendants and the international journalists attending the IMT sessions. He stated unequivocally that Himmler had ordered him to exterminate the Jews and claimed that some 3,000,000 people had been murdered at Auschwitz, 2,500,000 in gas chambers. Since Höss ceased to be camp commandant on 1 December 1943, it is assumed that these figures refer only to that date. In the winter of 1986-87 *The Journal of Historical Review* (Vol. 7, No. 4) published an article by Professor Faurisson entitled "How the British Obtained the Confessions of

Rudolf Höss". We turn to it for an account of how the signed statement of Höss was obtained.

At the end of the war, Rudolf Höss was captured by the British. His captors were unaware of the importance of the prey in their hands, and since he was an expert agronomist, a labour office found him a job on a farm in Flensburg, near the Danish border, and he was released. He was wanted by the military police, and his family, whom he managed to contact, was closely guarded. Nevertheless, Höss remained in hiding on the farm for about eight months, until 11 p.m. on the night of 11 March 1945, when he was arrested again. Confirmation that Höss was tortured, a fact that revisionists regarded as a certainty, came in 1983, when the anti-Nazi Rupert Butler's book *Legions of Death* appeared. Butler boasts of his research in various UK institutions and expresses his gratitude to Bernard Clarke, a British Jew who was a sergeant in the 92nd Brigade of the Field Security Section, who he says "captured Auschwitz commandant Rudolf Höss". Butler quotes excerpts from the written or recorded reports of Clarke, who, instead of showing remorse, is proud to have tortured a Nazi. In fact, Rupert Butler himself considers that there is nothing to criticise and explains that it took three days of torture to produce "a coherent report".

According to Butler's account, on 11 March 1946, a captain named Cross, Sergeant Bernard Clarke and four other intelligence specialists wearing British uniforms entered the home of Mrs. Höss, Hannah Höss, who lived with her children in a flat block in the Schleswig-Holstein town of Heide, in a threatening attitude. The six men, Butler stresses, "were experts in sophisticated techniques of prolonged and ruthless investigation." Clarke shouted at the woman, "If you don't tell us where your husband is, we will hand you over to the Russians and put you in front of a firing squad. Your children will go to Siberia." Clarke explains that suitable threats to the son and daughter had the desired effect: Mrs. Höss burst into tears, revealed the location of the farm where her husband was hiding, and also revealed the false name he had adopted: Franz Lang. Captain Cross, the Jewish sergeant and the other "third degree interrogation" specialists[11] went looking for Höss at midnight and found him in a room in the farm's cattle slaughterhouse. "What is your name?" shouted Clarke. Each time he answered "Franz Lang" he was punched in the face. After the fourth punch, Höss admitted his true identity. In the book Butler relates that the parents of the Jewish sergeants who were part of the arrest party had died in Auschwitz on an order signed by Höss. As a result, he was stripped naked and placed on a plank in the slaughterhouse, where he was bludgeoned to within an inch of his life. The medical officer urged the captain: "Tell them to stop, unless they want to take a corpse. They then placed a blanket over Höss's swollen body and bundled

---

[11] "Third Degree Interrogation" is a euphemism to avoid using the word torture. In these interrogations, physical and/or mental pain is inflicted on the person being interrogated in order to obtain a confession or a report.

him into Clarke's car, where after making him drink a good swig of whisky, Clarke poked his eyelids with his service stick and ordered him in German: "Keep your pig's eyes open, you swine!" The group reached Heide at about three in the morning. The wind was whirling snow and Höss was forced to walk naked across the prison yard to his cell.

A private named Ken Jones, stationed at Heide with the 5th detachment of the Royal Horse Artillery, confirmed in an article published in the *Wrexham Leader* on 17 October 1986 that it took three days to get a coherent report out of Hoss. Jones recalls that he and two other soldiers were preparing him for the interrogation: "We sat with him in his cell," Jones writes, "day and night, armed with sticks. Our job was to prod him every time he fell asleep to help break his resistance." Jones explains that when Höss was taken out into the cold outside for exercise, he wore only a thin cotton T-shirt. After three days and three nights without sleep came the confession. According to Clarke, who personally censored the letters Rudolf Höss sent to his wife and children, once the prisoner began to talk it was impossible to stop him.

Rudolf Höss was extradited to Poland on 25 May 1946. There he faced a new trial for war crimes. The trial was held in Kraków on 2 April 1947, where Höss lowered the figure of 3,000,000 he had given in Nuremberg to 1,135,000. Two weeks later, on the 16th, he was hanged at Auschwitz. Paradoxically, though for various reasons which we will spare you, the communists allowed him to tell his story in a memoir which he wrote in pencil in Krakow prison. Martin Broszat, a member of the Institute of Contemporary History in Munich, who on 10 August 1960 admitted in *Die Zeit* that no one had been gassed in Dachau, Bergen-Belsen or Buchenwald, published them after retouching them in 1958 under the title *Commandant in Auschwitz*. In them, Höss confirms that at his first interrogation he was beaten to get his statement: "I don't know what is in the document, although I signed it. The alcohol and the whip were too much for me. The whip was mine, which they happened to have got from my wife's suitcases. I had hardly touched my horse, let alone the prisoners. However, one of my interrogators was convinced that I had used it permanently to whip the prisoners." In this memoir Höss denounces that it was only after three weeks that the British removed his handcuffs, which he had worn from the time of arrest, cut his hair, allowed him to wash and shaved him. In *Commandant in Auschwitz* we read the following:

> "I was in Nuremberg because Kaltennbrunner's lawyer had asked me to testify as a witness for his defence. I have never been able to understand, and it is still not clear to me, how, of all the people there, I could have helped to acquit Kaltennbruner. Although the conditions in the prison were in all respects good - there was a well-stocked library and I read whenever I had time - the interrogations were extremely unpleasant, not so much physically, but much more because of their strong psychological

effect. I can't really blame the interrogators - they were all Jews. Psychologically I was devastated. They wanted to know everything about everything, and that was also done by Jews. They left me in no doubt about the fate they had in store for me".

Höss's statements are the cornerstone of historians' claims that the extermination of millions of Jews in the gas chambers of Auschwitz is a historical reality. Robert Faurisson explains in the article published in *The Journal of Historical Review* that Höss actually made four statements, which is why we can strictly speaking speak of the confessions of Rudolf Höss. The first is a typewritten text of eight pages, document NO-1210. There is no indication of location, it is dated 14 March 1946 and was signed at 2:30 a.m., possibly already on the 15th. After examining it, Professor Faurisson, a specialist in text analysis and document criticism, comments that under normal circumstances no court in a democracy would have taken it into consideration.

The second affidavit, document PS-3868, was signed 22 days later, on 5 April 1946. It is a twenty-page text in English. On the last page is this text: "I understand the English text. The above statements are true: I have made this declaration voluntarily and without coercion; after reading the declaration, I have signed and formalised it in Nuremberg, Germany, on the fifth day of April 1946". Faurisson, whose formal criticism of the document is devastating, finds the text unpresentable and less acceptable than the first: there are lines added in capital letters, lines crossed out in pen, and no annotations in the margin to justify or explain the corrections. In order to justify that Höss had signed an affidavit in a language that was not his own and to make the erasures and additions disappear, the text was restructured in Nuremberg and presented as a translation from German into English.

The third confession is the spectacular oral statement before the IMT on 15 April 1946, ten days after the signing of document PS-3868. Absurdly, Höss's appearance in court was at the request of Kurt Kauffmann, Kaltenbrunner's lawyer, whom he sought to defend by attributing all responsibility to Himmler. Finally, the fourth confession is the texts in the book *Commandant in Auschwitz*, written under the watchful eye of his communist jailers while awaiting trial. It is clear that this last version of Höss must be approached with all sorts of reservations, since it could not alter what he had declared before the IMT and is again riddled with lies in the aspects relating to the alleged extermination and the means used.

Before going on to comment on the impossibilities of Höss's statement, it must be remembered that only some 400,000 individuals of all nationalities were registered at Auschwitz. Moreover, when in April 1945 the Red Army seized the records of Oranienburg, a town 35 kilometres north of Berlin, they discovered that the total number of dead in all labour camps over ten years was 403,713. The Soviets kept these documents secret for forty-five years. On the other hand, there existed at Auschwitz a register of the dead recorded in forty-six volumes. The problem is that the total number of deaths recorded cannot be determined exactly because the books for 1940, 1941, most of 1944 and January 1945 are missing. In other words, only the deaths for 1942, 1943 and incompletely for 1944 are recorded in the forty-six books. Nevertheless, several revisionist authors have attempted to calculate the numbers of deaths in the camp on the basis of the known data and the total number of prisoners registered in Auschwitz.

Arthur R. Butz extrapolates and gives a figure of 125,000 dead, many, if not most, of whom were Catholic Christians. In 1992 the Jewish revisionist researcher David Cole, about whom we will report later, filmed a famous documentary on Auschwitz, in which he interviewed Dr. Franciszek Piper, director and curator of the archives of the Auschwitz State Museum. Dr. Piper acknowledged on camera that 197,820 inmates had survived. Franciszek Piper, on the other hand, wrote that "when Soviet soldiers liberated the camp in January 1945, they found documents confirming only 100,000 dead." In 1999 Vivian Bird published *Auschwitz: The Final Count*. This English author insists that the statistics in the books are complete and authentic, but also acknowledges the drawback of not having the full record. Bird concludes that 73,137 inmates succumbed to the harsh working conditions in Auschwitz, of whom only 38,031 were Jews.

Given these figures, it is clear that we cannot give any credibility to the "affidavits" of Rudolf Höss, obtained after his capture at through third-degree interrogation. In fact, even the exterminist author Gerald Reitlinger does not believe them and calls Höss's testimony in Nuremberg "irretrievably recusable". Reitlinger admits that Höss's testimony was an enumeration of insane exaggerations, such as the claim that 16,000 people were killed every day. Unfortunately, he and other Holocaust historians, instead of admitting the true nature of Auschwitz and the great importance of its industrial activities to the Germans, argue that Höss's delusional statements were motivated by a kind of "professional pride".

Only one reference to the industrial nature of Auschwitz has survived in the transcripts of all the witnesses who testified before the IMT. This is the testimony of a political prisoner named Marie Claude Vaillant-Couturier, who refers in passing to a munitions factory, the Krupp plant, and to a large factory in Buna, about which she cannot say anything because she did not work there. Other allusions, if any, were deleted. The fact that the camp commandant hardly mentions in his testimony the first-rate interest of the factories in the camp is very significant. By contrast, the barbarities invented in Höss's confession are so absurd that they would hardly merit refutation. Let us see:

> "I was commandant of Auschwitz until December 1943 and I estimate that at least 2,500,000 victims were executed and exterminated there,

gassed and burned, and that at least another half a million succumbed to starvation and disease, making a total of about 3,000,000. This figure represents 70 to 80 per cent of the total number of people sent to Auschwitz as prisoners. The remaining percent were selected for use as slave labour in the concentration camp industries. Among those executed and burned were approximately 20,000 Russian prisoners of war (previously screened by the Gestapo from prisoner-of-war cells), who were delivered to Auschwitz in Wehrmacht transports operated by regular Wehrmacht soldiers and officers. The total number of victims included some 100,000 German Jews, and large numbers of citizens, mostly Jews from Holland, France, Belgium, Poland, Hungary, Czechoslovakia, Greece and other countries. We executed about 400,000 Hungarian Jews in the summer of 1944 alone."

Of particular note is this mention of the 400,000 Hungarian Jews, about whom there seems to have been a special interest in adding to the cabalistic figure of 6,000,000. Since we have already devoted space to what actually happened to the Hungarian Jews, we will not add to it, although it should be noted that Rudolf Höss was no longer in Auschwitz in the summer of 1944. However, since in December 1943 he was promoted to the Inspectorate of the Concentration Camps at Oranienburg, it is credible that he could have known that the alleged executions were continuing. That said, it seems clear that the inclusion of the Hungarian Jews was a further imposition by the drafters of the declaration submitted to him for signature. The total number of victims thus stood at 3,400,000, very close to the figure of 4,000,000 given by the Soviets, which appeared on the first plaque installed at the camp for tourists. On the other hand, if the figure of 3,000,000 was only seventy or eighty percent of the total number of people sent to Auschwitz, it must be deduced that there were about 4,000,000 camp prisoners, which is ten times the number recorded.

Another paragraph of the statement records that, although his command in Auschwitz ended on 1 December 1943, his position in the Camp Inspectorate enabled him to be aware of what was happening in the concentration camps:

"Gas executions began during the summer of 1941 and continued until the autumn of 1944. I personally supervised the executions in Auschwitz until December 1943 and I know from my continuing duties in the WVHA Concentration Camp Inspectorate that the mass executions continued as stated above. All executions by gassings took place under direct order, supervision and responsibility of RSHA. I received all orders to carry out the mass executions directly from the RSHA."

We know that the Reich Security Main Office (Reichssicherheitshauptamt), abbreviated RSHA, was established by

Heinrich Himmler on 27 September 1939, so Höss thus implies that he received the extermination order from Himmler himself. In *The Hoax of the Twentieth Century*, Arthur R. Butz comments that in his testimony, which appears in volume 11 of the ITM, Höss said that in the summer of 1941 he had been summoned to report directly to the Reichsführer SS and that during his interview with him, Himmler gave him the order to exterminate the Jews, but told him that he was to maintain "the strictest secrecy", not allowing his immediate superior Glücks to know what he was doing. Richard Glücks was at that time the inspector of the concentration camps and was subordinate to Reichsführer Himmler. It goes without saying that it is absolutely absurd to claim that Himmler, without informing Oswald Pohl, head of the SS Economic and Administrative Department (SS-WVHA), ordered Major Höss to secretly exterminate millions of Jews and to conceal the killing from Glücks, his superior, who was at the same time under Himmler's orders. Can greater nonsense be conceived? Let us see more:

> "The 'final solution' of the Jewish question meant the complete extermination of all the Jews of Europe. I received the order to set up extermination facilities at Auschwitz in June 1941. At that time there were already three other extermination camps in the General Government, Belzec, Treblinka and Wolzek. These camps were under the Einsatzkommando of the Security Police and SD. I visited Treblinka to find out how they carried out their killings. The camp commandant at Treblinka told me that he had liquidated 80,000 in half a year. He was mainly interested in the liquidation of the Jews in the Warsaw ghetto. He used gaseous monoxide and I didn't think his methods were very effective. So when I built the extermination building in Auschwitz, I used Zyklon B, which was crystallised prussic acid, acid that we dropped into the gas chamber through a small opening. It took between three and fifteen minutes to kill people inside the chamber, depending on the weather conditions. We knew when they were dead because their screams stopped. We usually waited half an hour before opening the doors and removing the bodies. After they were removed, our special commandos would take off their rings and extract the gold from their teeth."

Another improvement we made over Treblinka was that we built our gas chambers to hold 2,000 people at a time, whereas the ten gas chambers in Treblinka held only 200 people each. The way we selected our victims was as follows: we had two SS doctors in Auschwitz to examine the prisoners who arrived in the transports. Those who were fit for work were sent to the camp. Others were sent immediately to the extermination plants. Children of a few years of age were invariably exterminated because of their condition they were not useful for work. Another improvement we made over Treblinka was that in Treblinka the victims almost always knew that they were going to be exterminated and in Auschwitz we tried hard to make them believe that they were going to go through a delousing process. Of course they often realised our true intentions and sometimes there were disturbances and difficulties because of this. Often the women would hide their children under their clothes, but naturally when we discovered them we sent the children to extermination. We were asked to carry out these exterminations in secret, but of course the foul smell given off by the continual cremations of corpses permeated the area completely and all the people living in the surrounding villages knew that exterminations were being carried out in Auschwitz."

As we can see, the declaration insists that the extermination order took place in the summer of 1941, thus half a year before the Wannsee Conference took place. It seems clear that historical rigour did not adorn the intellect of those who presented Höss with the confession for his signature. In contrast, Gerald Reitlinger soon realised that inconsistencies of this kind detracted from the credibility of the confession and hastened to rectify the date. According to Reitlinger, Höss meant the summer of 1942, not 1941. Moreover, Reitlinger himself places the first major transport of two thousand Jews to Birkenau in March 1942. "At that time," reads the statement, "there were already three other extermination camps in the Central Government, Belzec, Treblinka and Wolzec." This is another major blunder, for even in 1941 there was still no Treblinka II, the construction of which began in March 1942. It has been reported that an inscription on a stone now indicates that the extermination of 800,000 Jews took place there between July 1942 and August 1943. And on and on it goes, for the contradictions and inconsistencies are the logical consequence of the outright lies that make up the "affidavit". Robert Faurisson comments that in NO-1210, the text of the first affidavit, the British made Höss sign that the Wolzec extermination camp was "near Lublin". In reality, Wolzec does not and did not exist. It seems unlikely that they meant Belzec, since it is not near Lublin, but more than one hundred and thirty kilometres away, and it is mentioned together with Wolzek, a mysterious place name which is not to be found on any map of Poland.

Arthur R. Butz comments extensively on the references to Zyklon B in Höss' confession. He confirms that there was indeed no deadlier gas and that it was a well-known and widely used insecticide, which had been marketed worldwide before the war. The "Deutsche Gesellschaft für Schädlingsbekämpfung" (DEGESCH), a pesticide company, supplied it during the war to the German Armed Forces and the entire camp system. As mentioned above, during the months of August and September 1942, work at Auschwitz had to be stopped because of a terrible typhus epidemic. We know that the cessation of disinfection measures in the Bergen-Belsen camp at the end of the war had devastating effects. The death toll there provided the shocking images that constitute the reference footage for Holocaust propagandists. Zyklon B, which was packaged in green cylindrical cans, was therefore essential in the camps as a disinfectant to preserve the lives of the prisoners, but not to kill them. Rooms and barracks were sealed before the gas, which killed lice and other insect pests, was emptied. Afterwards it was properly ventilated. Clothes were also deloused in the "killing chambers". The US Army also used a powerful insecticide in its concentration camps, DDT, which was more versatile and advanced than Zyklon and therefore less lethal to humans. Precisely because Zyklon was so poisonous, it is quite impossible, as Höss's statement says, that only half an hour after the gas was released they entered the chambers to remove the bodies in order to strip them.

It is incredible nonsense, moreover, to claim that the Nazi hierarchs delegated to a camp commandant the choice of material and method of execution for the systematic extermination of millions of Jews. According to Höss's delusional statement, it was he who, after visiting Treblinka and seeing that his commandant was using a shoddy extermination procedure, decided to look for a more effective way to put an end to the Jewish problem. Reitlinger, overwhelmed by such an unacceptable confession, ends up saying gratuitously that "without a doubt" it was Hitler who finally made the decision. Such seriousness and historical rigour are impressive. We will not comment now on the assertion that two thousand people were put into a gas chamber at a time, as there will be time to discuss this when we present the *Leuchter Report*. As for women hiding their children under their clothes and children being systematically exterminated because they were useless for work, there is no point in saying anything, for it has been said in the pages on Belzec, Treblinka and Sobibor that painting the Germans as ruthless beasts was a propaganda ploy. Let us remember that already in the First World War it only remained to say that they ate children with french fries after they had skewered them with their bayonets.

In the final lines of the quotation it is stated that the area was impregnated by the pestilence produced by the "continuous cremations of corpses". According to Höss and other exterminationists, before the construction of modern ovens, cremations were carried out in ditches or on pyres. It has already been seen that this issue of the stench of burning bodies was a recurring theme of the propagandists in the camps of the so-called Operation Reinhard. In the case of Auschwitz, however, the stench is confirmed, and there is an explanation that should not be ignored: there were numerous industries in the camp working with highly polluting materials. Hydrogenation and other chemical processes that took place in the factories were characterised by the stench they generated. The coal used by the Germans was a dirtier source than crude oil. It is therefore reasonable to conclude that the stench in the area must have come from the I.G. Farben Buna plant and the various industrial activities of the other factory complexes.

On the crematorium ovens at Auschwitz-Birkenau

Since Arthur R. Butz provides considerable information on the construction of the four buildings containing the crematoria, we will once again turn to this reliable and rigorous source in order to discredit the famous report of the War Refugee Board, which states that in the spring of 1944 there were four crematoria (I, II, II and IV) in Birkenau. In reality the four buildings in Birkenau which contained the crematoria were II, III, IV and V. Building I was in Auschwitz I and would have been an inactive crematorium that had four openings. Butz reveals that the plans for the construction of the four structures with the crematoria were dated 28 January 1942 on . On 27 February of that year, an SS engineer colonel, Hans Kammler, head of the Construction Department of the WVHA, visited Auschwitz and held a meeting during which it was agreed to install five crematoria instead of the two originally planned. It was therefore decided to build five ovens with fifteen crematoria in each of the four crematoria, which would make a total of sixty crematoria in the four crematoria. However, while there are documents that show that the works were completed in buildings II and III, there is no documentary evidence to confirm this in crematoria IV and V, although there is evidence that there were operating ovens in them. The work was commissioned on 3 August 1942 from the company Topf und Söhne of Erfurt. Each furnace, like all normal crematoria, was designed to cremate one body, and there is no evidence that unconventional furnaces designed to hold more than one body at a time were installed.

The WRB report states that in two crematoria there were 36 ovens in each and in the other two buildings, 18 ovens in each. If we accept the information in the previous paragraph as valid, we must assume that it refers to 36 openings or doors, so if we consider that each oven had three openings, in two buildings there would be 12 ovens with three openings each and in the other two buildings, 6 ovens with three openings each. This would give a total figure of 108 mouths, which in reality was the number of mouths necessary to burn 6,000 bodies per day by introducing three bodies into each furnace, provided that, as the report assures us, the three bodies were incinerated in only half an hour and the furnaces were working non-stop twenty-four hours a day, which is technically impossible. Generously, it can be accepted that with the technology of 1943 each furnace could reduce a body to ashes in one hour. If, as claimed in the WRB Report, three bodies were introduced at a time, the incineration time would necessarily be longer. On the other hand, downtime was unavoidable, as various maintenance and cleaning operations were required.

Before calculating the maximum number of corpses that could have been cremated in the crematoria at Auschwitz-Birkenau, it is of interest to examine further the information and documents provided by Arthur R. Butz in his masterly work. The plans of the four buildings containing the crematoria show that in each there was a large room or hall, the "Leichenkeller" (mortuary cellar or corpse cellar), which in the case of Crematoria II and III were below ground level and in Crematoria IV and V at ground level. The first five ovens, each with three openings, were installed in building II. Construction continued until January 1943. Butz reproduces the text of document NO-4473 from Volume 5 of the Nuremberg Military Tribunals (NMT), which confirms the completion of the construction work:

"29 January 1943
To the Commander of Amtsgruppe C, SS Brigadefuhrer and Brigadier General of the Waffen SS, Dr. Ing.
Subject. Crematorium II, building conditions.
Crematorium II has been completed - with the exception of a few minor works - using all available forces, despite tremendous difficulties and intense cold, in 24-hour shifts. The furnace fires were lit in the presence of the chief engineer Prüfer, representative of the contractors of the firm Topf und Söhne, Erfurt, and are working to full satisfaction. The planks of the concrete ceiling in the cellar used as a mortuary (Leichenkeller) have not yet been removed because of the ice. However, this is of no further importance, as the gas chamber can be used for this purpose.
Topf und Söhne was unable to deliver the ventilation and ventilation systems requested by the Central Building Department in time due to restrictions on the use of railways. As soon as they arrive, work will begin to install them, so it is to be hoped that everything will be ready for use by 20 February 1943. Attached is a report from the test engineer of the firm Topf und Söhne, Erfurt.
Head of the General Directorate of Construction, Waffen SS and Auschwitz Police, SS Hauptsturmführer.
Ditsributed to: 1 -SS Ustuf. Janisch u. Kirschnek; 1 Office archive (crematorium archive), Certificate of authenticity of copy (signature illegible) SS Ustuf. (F)".

It is therefore certain that all 15 of the five ovens in the crematoria in Building II could have been used by the end of January 1943. However, it took several months for the other crematoria to become operational. On 12 February 1943 Topf und Söhne wrote to Auschwitz acknowledging receipt of the order for the construction of five units of three-shaft furnaces for the crematoria in Building III, which, if there were no obstacles, were to be completed by 10 April. Arthur R. Butz points out that he has not, however, been able to find any reliable documents proving that the construction of the ovens in Crematoria IV and V was completed, although he mentions a letter dated 21 August 1942 from an SS lieutenant in Auschwitz, in which he notes a proposal by Topf a Söhne to install two units of three-hole ovens each. In any case, there is evidence that ovens were eventually built in crematoria IV and V as well, and that these would have been in operation throughout 1944.

Butz himself admits that there is at least one record of a working "Kommando" which on 11 May 1944 was assigned to the crematoria in buildings IV and V. In the *Leuchter Report*, which we will discuss below, it is definitively established that in Crematoria IV and V there were two furnaces with four bays each ("retorts" is the technical term used by Leuchter). Reitlinger assumes that between the four buildings there were twenty furnaces with a total of sixty openings; but in reality there were only fourteen furnaces with 46 openings.

These findings make it possible to establish that from the end of January until April 1943 there were only five ovens with three burners each in Auschwitz-Birkenau. If the ovens in Crematoria III could indeed be put into operation on 10 April 1943, there were ten ovens with thirty bays during eight months of 1943. Since the alleged exterminations were completed in the autumn of 1944, only ten or eleven months would have seen the operation of all twenty ovens with their sixty bays, provided that the ten ovens of crematoria IV and V had been in operation since January 1944, as Reitlinger assumes. Arthur R. Butz offers an estimate on the basis that there could have been as many as 46 burners operating at full capacity daily in 1944, stopping for only one hour, and calculates that about 1,000 corpses per day could have been cremated in this way, which would amount to 360,000 corpses in a year. When we study the *Leuchter Report*, we will see that Professor Butz's figures are far removed from reality.

As for the operation of crematoria ovens, a gas furnace was used which produced a mixture of air and gasified fuel that was introduced into the furnace to start, control and stop the ignition. These crematoria are known as gas-fired ovens because they use gas as a fuel, which is injected under pressure. The German word used for the concept in question is 'Gaskammer', but in document NO-4473 the word 'Vergasungskellker' appeared, which Reitlinger erroneously translated into English as 'gassing cellar'. Arthur R. Butz explains that the word "Vergasung" has in a technical context the meaning of gasification, carburation or vaporisation, i.e., he points out, "to turn something into a gas and not to expose something to a gas". A "Vergasser" is a carburettor. The ovens at Birkenau," Butz adds, "seem to have been coke or coal-fired.

There are two processes for producing gaseous fuel from coke or coal: the first is passing air through a layer of burning coke to produce 'coke oven gas'; the second is passing steam through the coke to produce 'water gas'. The German term used to generate these processes is "Vergasung". In any case, writes Butz, "it is obvious that the crematoria at Auschwitz required 'Vergasung' equipment to introduce the air-gas mixture into the ovens and that the translation in NO-4473 should possibly be replaced by 'gas production cellar'. I have confirmed this interpretation of 'Vergasunskeller' with technically reliable sources in Germany."

In short, Arthur R. Butz claims that, if properly interpreted, document NO-4473, like so many others, tends to contradict the claims of the prosecution. Butz insists that Crematorium II had at least two cellars: a "Leichenkeller" (corpse cellar) and a "Vergasungskeller" (gas production cellar), neither of which was a "gas chamber". NO-4473, included in the NMT volumes in a selection of accusatory evidence from the Concentration Camp Administration trial (Case 4) is, Professor Butz laments, the most documentary evidence the exterminationists have been able to produce to prove that gas chambers existed in the Birkenau crematoria. As for Raul Hilberg's interpretation, he writes: "Inexplicably, he skips over NO-4473 without addressing the problem it raises. He quotes the document, but not the sentence containing the word 'Vergasungskeller'. He simply says that the 'Leichenkeller' in Crematoria II and III and the 'Badenanstalten' (baths) in Crematoria IV and V were in fact gas chambers. He presents absolutely no evidence for this. The documents cited by Hilberg on this subject do not speak of gas chambers". Consequently, Butz concludes, "there is no reason to accept, and plenty of reason to reject, the allegations that these installations are gas chambers."

The high mortality rate in Birkenau

The fact that there were no mass executions or gas chambers does not, however, exonerate Birkenau from being the camp with the highest death rate in the entire German concentration camp system. During the period 1942-44, death had one of its favourite domains there, so that in this sense it can be called a "death camp". But if we consider that in Dresden more civilians died in a few hours than in Birkenau in two years, and that in Hiroshima and Nagasaki it took only a few seconds to massacre more than 150,000 innocents, Birkenau was only one of many favourite fiefdoms of death, the implacable enemy of the human race, which during World War II struck the planet with an unprecedented slaughter that involved the sacrifice of more than sixty million lives.

We know that Birkenau (Auschwitz II) and Monowitz (Auschwitz III) were built as dependencies of Auschwitz I, where the administrative centre of the entire camp system in the area was located. Commenting on the testimony before the IMT of Josef Kramer, commandant of Birkenau from May to November 1944, it has been said that Kramer admitted in his statement that between 350 and 500 people died weekly in Birkenau. "I had a camp with sick people," he said, "who came from other parts of the camp." In his first statement, Kramer insisted that doctors, who worked twelve hours a day, were required to certify the causes of death of prisoners, who were not normally mistreated and were cremated when they died. By claiming that people from the other camps who were no longer able to work, "sick people", went to Birkenau, Kramer sought to justify the high death rate. In other words, Birkenau would have been designed to house sick prisoners, old people, children, the dying and those who could no longer work. All sick prisoners from Monowitz who were unfit to work were sent to Birkenau. Prisoners in transit were also accommodated in Birkenau. In fact, there was an area of the camp exclusively for Gypsies and another area where the families of Jews coming from Theresienstadt were accommodated. Birkenau, which, like Auschwitz I, was initially intended to provide labour for the Krupp plant, the Siemens electrical factory or I.G. Farben and its subcontractors, became a larger camp than Auschwitz I, used by the SS for a variety of needs.

According to Reitlinger, between the summer of 1942 and the summer of 1944 only a fraction of the Birkenau population worked. In April 1944, as the war entered its most critical period for Germany, of the 36,000 inmates in Birkenau almost half were considered unfit for employment as labourers; by contrast, in Auschwitz I, of 31,000 prisoners, only ten percent were considered unfit for work. As we have seen, it was at Birkenau that the largest facilities were built for the disposal of corpses by incineration in crematoria. NMT documents show that in May 1944 there were 18,000 male prisoners in Birkenau, two thirds of whom were classified as 'paralysed', 'unusable' and 'unassigned', and were therefore quarantined in sick blocks, showing that being sick did not mean immediate execution. Some exterminationists seem to have regarded the fact that the clothes of the prisoners transferred to Birkenau were returned to Monowitz as proof of their elimination. Professor Butz rejects this claim, arguing that the return was due to the fact that they were being transferred from the I.G. Farben budget to that of the SS. As 1944 drew to a close, Germany's defeat became irreversible and the situation at Birkenau became increasingly disastrous, as the camp received inmates being evacuated from other camps and the population swelled to 100,000. Then, as Josef Kramer hinted, up to 2,000 people could die in a month.

It is not an easy task to determine the number of deaths at Auschwitz-Birkenau. There are estimates by the Dutch Red Cross of the death rate during the typhus epidemic that forced the closure of the I.G. Farben Buna plant in August and September 1942. According to this source, between 16 July and 19 August the average death rate in Birkenau was 186 per day among men alone. The Dutch Red Cross specifies the number of deaths between 28 September and 2 October 1942. In these six days alone, 1,500 people died. The same report gives data for two other periods: between 30 October 1942 and 25 February 1943 the average death rate was 360 people per week, while from 26 February to 1 July 1943 the figure of 185 deaths per week is given. Under these circumstances, it is understandable that the immediate construction of crematoria was chosen in order to dispose of the bodies cleanly and prevent the spread of epidemics.

In the second part of the chapter, which deals with the camps in Germany, it has already been reported that the high death rate set off all the alarm bells. Himmler's order of 28 December 1942, in which he demanded that deaths in the camps be reduced "at all costs", was discussed. It has also been seen that on 20 January 1943 Richard Glücks, the SS General in charge of the Camp Inspectorate, ordered in a circular "to use all means to reduce the death rate". Oswald Pohl presented Himmler with official data from the Main Department of the Economic Administration, according to which in August 1942 alone 12,217 prisoners died out of a total of 115,000 concentration camp detainees. Since manpower was essential to sustain the war effort at its height, these figures were intolerable. It is ridiculous to pretend that these blunt orders about the need to keep prisoners alive were strategies to conceal planned mass extermination.

On 15 March 1943 Pohl went so far as to complain to Himmler that the prisoners sent by the Ministry of Justice from the prisons were suffering from "physical weakness" and many of them were "sick with tuberculosis". On 10 April 1943 Oswald Pohl asked Himmler to approve a draft letter to the Reich Minister of Justice in which he lamented that of 12,658 prisoners delivered to concentration camps, 5,935 had died by 1 April. Arthur R. Butz reproduces an excerpt from the letter, in which Pohl complained in these terms: "The surprisingly high number of deaths is due to the fact that the prisons transfer inmates who are in the worst possible physical condition". Professor Butz is of the opinion that there was a rivalry or conflict of interest between Departments. According to him, "the prisons in Germany undoubtedly had their own economic-productive interests and were not only reluctant to give up their healthiest prisoners, but were even eager to give up the weakest or sickliest."

Arthur R. Butz, in summary, admits that half of all deaths in German concentration camps between 1942 and 1944 occurred in Auschwitz-Birkenau, a fact which was used by Jewish propagandists to launch the claim that it was an extermination camp. This was done by using the lie of turning the gas used as a means of disinfection into the agent used to massacre millions of Jews. In reality, Jewish families with children lived for months in Birkenau in barracks that had previously been disinfected with Zyklon-B.

The *Leuchter Report* on Auschwitz-Birkenau and Majdanek

In 1985, the first of the trials against Ernst Zündel, a celebrated German revisionist fighter, took place in Toronto, about whom it will necessarily be necessary to write more later, when we devote to the persecution of revisionists the space it deserves. Denounced by a Jewish organisation called the "Holocaust Remembrance Association", he was brought to trial on the charge of "publishing false news". They relied on an English law of 1275, rarely enforced, which forbade the vulgar to mock knights in satirical verse. Zündel had published Richard Harwood's book *Did Six Million Really Die?* through "Samisdat Publishers", a small publishing house he had founded in 1978, which eventually became a producer of videos, radio interviews, television programmes and other historical documents of great value to the revisionist movement.

The trial lasted seven weeks, during which Raul Hilberg and Rudolf Vrba testified at the request of the Canadian Jewish lobby. Lawyer Douglas Christie, almost as legendary as Zündel himself, cornered Hilberg, who was unable to produce a single document proving the existence of the extermination plan. Nor could he produce any technical expert report on the gas chambers or an autopsy report proving the death of any inmate by Zyklon gas. The prosecution's expectations then fell on the witnesses Arnold Friedman and Rudolf Vrba. The former, at the mercy of lawyer Christie's skilful cross-examination, eventually lost his nerve and had to admit that he had seen nothing and that what he knew "he had heard from credible people". Vrba, the theoretical source of the WRB report, made numerous contradictions, errors and inaccuracies that exposed him. To remedy this, he argued that in his book *I Cannot Forgive* he had resorted to poetic licence, which irritated even prosecutor Griffiths. Nevertheless, Zündel was sentenced to 15 months in prison. The West German government confiscated his passport and demanded his extradition. In January 1987, however, the Ontario Court of Appeal quashed the trial, finding that the judge, Hugh Locke, gave instructions to the jury and withheld evidence from the defence. A retrial was ordered, which began on 18 January 1988.

This second trial, which lasted four months, was to mark a turning point: the publication during the trial of a technical-scientific expert opinion, the *Leuchter Report*, definitively challenged the claims of the exterminationists about Auschwitz-Birkenau and Majdanek. After the second trial against Ernst Zündel, revisionism gained momentum and began to grow internationally. Today it is a dangerous and exciting intellectual enterprise of the first order, as historians and researchers who demand historical truth are persecuted as criminals and convicted of thought crimes, yet insist on their theses. It was Professor Robert Faurisson who, at the beginning of the trial, had the brilliant idea of turning to Alfred Leuchter, then considered an undisputed expert in executions, as he designed and manufactured various equipment for US penitentiaries: gas chambers, electric chair and lethal injection. Hence his nickname "Mr. Death".

Alfred Leuchter himself explains how it all began: "In February 1988 Dr. Robert Faurisson contacted me through the process of Mr. Ernst Zündel and asked me to consider a commission to investigate the alleged execution gas chambers operated by the Nazis in Poland, and at the same time to provide an engineering opinion as to their operability and efficiency. Moreover, I was asked to carry out a forensic evaluation of existing crematoria." Leuchter met with Zündel, lawyer Christie and other members of the team, who explained that they intended to use his opinion in the case "The Queen v. Zündel", which was being heard in the Toronto District Court.

Once Fred Leuchter had accepted the assignment, it was decided that the investigation would include all crematoria and alleged execution gas chambers at Auschwitz, Birkenau and Majdanek (Lublin).

On 25 February 1988, Leuchter began his historic trip to Poland with his wife Carolyn, a technical draftsman named Howard Miller, cameraman Jürgen Neumann and interpreter Theodor Rudolf. On site, all the necessary facilities were inspected, measurements were taken, forensic samples were taken, manuals on the design and operation of the DEGESCH disinfection chambers, on Zyklon-B gas, as well as materials on the execution processes were reviewed. After the work was completed, Leuchter and his team returned on 3 March 1988. On 20 and 21 April, Fred Leuchter participated as a witness in the trial against Zündel.

Before going on to discuss the *Leuchter Report*, it may be of interest to readers to know that there is a wonderful film entitled *Mr. Death: The Rise and Fall of Fred A. Leuchter, Jr.* Its author, Errol M. Morris, a New York filmmaker of Jewish origin, is renowned for the quality of his documentaries. Morris, after hearing in the press that Fred Leuchter was being publicly shredded because of his report on the gas chambers, decided to make a documentary that took him six years to produce. In it, exterminationists like Shelly Shapiro, who warns viewers not to be fooled by the "racist" and "anti-Semitic" Leuchter, or chemist James Roth, who testified during the trial that he found no trace of Zyklon-B in the samples tested and in the film shamefully says: "If I had known that the samples came from those places, my test results would have been different". Alongside Leuchter, English historian David Irving and Ernst Zündel appear in the documentary. Zündel, who in 2005 was eventually extradited to Germany, where he was formally charged with "inciting hatred" and sentenced to five years in prison, took some time to decide to participate in the film, as he doubted Errol Morris' objectivity. It was Morris himself who personally convinced him that he was not part of the Zionist financial and journalistic lobby and that he intended to act honestly and objectively. Zündel then agreed to help the Jewish documentary filmmaker and offered him materials of all kinds. Morris did not lie and was able to complete an impeccable film, which was screened at the Toronto International Film Festival in September 1999. The film ends up showing a Fred Leuchter destroyed by the Holocaust lobby, without a job and without a family, who disappears walking along a motorway. Despite all this, he gives the image of a man of integrity, who holds fast to the truth, and who maintains the validity of his work.

Short review of the *Leuchter Report*

The main purpose of the investigation was to verify whether the gas chambers and crematoria had functioned as the exterminationists claimed. To this end, the facilities were physically inspected, their design was studied, and a description of the procedure was made in order to determine the amount of gas used, the necessary execution and ventilation times, the space and capacity of the chambers, and the time for handling and burning the corpses. The aim was to determine the veracity and credibility of the accounts that make up the official story. In the words of Fred Leuchter, the aim was to "provide scientific evidence and information from the actual sites and to state an opinion based on the scientific, quantitative and engineering data available".

Methodologically, we proceeded with absolute rigour. The first thing that was carried out was a general study of the background of the materials. Hydrogen cyanide gas or hydrocyanic acid, used as a fumigant since before World War I, had also been used with air vapour and hot air. The Allies used it with DDT during World War II. The gas, Leuchter points out, "is obtained by a reaction of sodium cyanide with dilute sulphuric acid. The product of the chemical reaction, HCN, used for pest and insect control in ships, buildings, chambers or other structures designed for that purpose, is projected into the air with a remnant of prussic acid (hydrocyanic acid)". In his review of the background to this dangerous chemical fumigant. Leuchter recalls the context and places around the world where HCN was used for disease control.

After explaining in detail the packaging conditions of the product, marketed as Zyklon-B in tablet and pellet form, how it should be spread, the required air temperature (25.7°C), the minimum time to complete the fumigation (24 to 48 hours) and other technical specifications such as vapour density, melting point, vapour pressure, appearance, colour and odour, Leuchter writes the following in his report:

> "After fumigation, ventilation of the area requires a minimum of ten hours, which depends on the premises (and volume) and longer if the building has no windows or skylights. The fumigated area must then be chemically tested for the presence of gas before entry. Gas masks are sometimes used, but they are not safe and should not be worn for more than ten minutes. A full chemical suit should be worn to prevent skin poisoning. The warmer the temperature and the drier the environment, the safer and faster the handling will be.

After learning about all these precautions that must be taken to preserve the safety of those who interact with hydrocyanic acid, it becomes clear that things could not possibly have happened as Holocaust mythologists relate. According to them, shortly after the poisonous gas was introduced through fake showers or special ducts in the roof of the chambers, the bodies of the dead Jews were immediately removed and piled up outside. In order to maximise the output of the "extermination facilities", the chambers were soon filled with new batches of victims awaiting their turn for mass murder. The unfortunate Rudolf Höss, who became the star of Nuremberg, related in his confession that German soldiers smoked cigarettes (hydrocyanic acid is highly flammable and explosive) and ate while removing the bodies from the chambers only minutes after they had been gassed. Since HCN is a fast-acting poison that can be fatal if inhaled or absorbed through the skin, it would have been extremely dangerous to remove the corpses from the chambers without protective suits and gas masks.

No one knew the details of the gassing process and the problems with leaks better than Alfred Leuchter, who had designed the gas chamber for the Missouri State Penitentiary in Jefferson City. His 192-page report, including appendices, explains in detail how a fumigation facility, and in particular a gas chamber for executions, should be designed, which should have a welded pressure-proof shell. Among other features, he describes the sealing, how it should be heated, the importance of circulation and exhaust capacity for the air, alludes to the need for a chimney at least twelve metres high or an incinerator for the exhaust, and insists that it should have means for even distribution of the gas. All in all, Fred Leuchter's explanations make us realise that a gas chamber is a very complex installation that must meet exhaustive requirements. Let us look at an excerpt as an example:

> "Gas detectors are used for safety. First, in the chamber, where an electronic locking system prevents the door from opening before the chamber is secure. Second, outside the chamber, in the witness and personnel areas, which triggers an audible alarm, and in the air intake and exhaust system to protect the witnesses, as well as to stop the execution and evacuate the chamber. The security system also contains alarm bells, horns and light signals. In addition there are emergency breathing apparatus (air tanks) at the chamber site, HCN first aid kits, emergency medical equipment for HCN and a resuscitation apparatus at the adjacent site for medical personnel. The design of a gas chamber involves consideration of many complicated problems. A mistake somewhere could, and probably will, cause death or injury to bystanders and technicians".

After referring to the first gas chambers in the United States and describing their characteristics and operation, Fred Leuchter gives a brief history of the alleged German gas chambers, including Rudolf Höss's confession that "executions by gas began during the summer of 1941". Leuchter refers to official texts obtained from the state museums in Auschwitz and Majdanek, where the first gassing is said to have taken place in two peasant houses that were later modified. Since his assignment did not include the alleged carbon monoxide gassings in Belzec, Treblinka and Sobibor, he did not visit these places. However, he notes, like all experts, the unsuitability of CO as a gas for executions. As for the sites that were the focus of his work, in 1988 he found the alleged execution facilities at Auschwitz I (Crematorium I) and Majdanek in their original form. At

Birkenau, by contrast, crematoria II, III, IV and V were collapsed and razed to the ground. At Majdanek, the first crematorium with the fuel burner had been destroyed and the crematorium with the alleged gas chamber reconstructed, with only its original ovens remaining. After recalling that, according to information in the Auschwitz Museum, crematorium I in Auschwitz, crematoria II, III, IV and V in Birkenau and the existing crematorium in Majdanek were combined crematoria and gas chambers, Leuchter writes: "The first crematorium in Auschwitz, crematoria II, III, IV and V in Birkenau and the existing crematorium in Majdanek were combined crematoria and gas chambers. Leuchter writes as follows:

> "On-site inspection of these structures proved an extremely poor and dangerous design for facilities that were to serve as gas chambers for executions. There are no provisions for gaskets on doors, windows and vents; the structure is not covered with tar or other sealant to prevent gas seepage or absorption. Adjacent crematoria constitute a potential explosion hazard. Exposed, porous bricks and plaster would accumulate HCN and make these facilities hazardous to humans for several years. Crematorium I is located next to the SS Hospital in Auschwitz and has floor drains connected to the main sewer, which would allow gas to enter all buildings in the complex. There were no extraction systems to vent the gas after use and there were no heaters or mechanisms for dispersing the Zyklon-B gas or for its introduction or evaporation. The Zyklon-B was allegedly dumped through roof vents and windows, which does not allow for the distribution of the gas or pellets. The facilities are always damp and unheated. As noted above, humidity and Zyklon-B are incompatible. The chambers are too narrow to physically fit the intended occupants; and all doors open inwards, which would prevent removal of the bodies. With the chambers filled to capacity with occupants, there would be no circulation of HCN within the room. Furthermore, if the gas had actually filled the chamber for an extended period of time, the people who poured the Zyklon-B through the ceiling vents and verified the death of the occupants would have died themselves, as they were exposed to HCN. None of the alleged gas chambers were built according to the design for disinfection chambers, which apparently functioned safely for years. None of these chambers were built according to the known and approved designs of operational facilities of the time in the United States. It does not seem logical that the purported designers of these so-called gas chambers ever consulted or considered the technology of the United States, which at the time was the only country that executed prisoners with gas."

This is, as can be seen, an impossibility on top of another impossibility. The disinfection chambers, however, did meet the required safety requirements perfectly; therefore, says Leuchter, "they functioned safely for years". It will be seen later that the samples obtained in them contain the unmistakable evidence of Zyklon. The walls of these disinfection facilities show the typical bluish colour of prussic acid that the walls of the alleged gas chambers would have had if it had been used inside them. Even half a century later, the blue colour of HCN is clearly visible on the outside walls of the disinfection chambers. Germar Rudolf, the graduate chemist and author of the *Rudolf Report*, which will be discussed below, photographed himself inside and outside a disinfection chamber in order to show the unmistakable signs of the prussic blue colour.

Leuchter's meticulous description of the facilities in Majdanek confirms that they were incapable of fulfilling the purposes attributed to them, but we will not repeat the same incompatibilities, because we must now talk about the crematoria. At a historical overview, Leuchter notes that cremation of corpses has been practised for centuries by many cultures. He also recalls that orthodox Judaism prohibited it and that it was frowned upon by the Catholic Church until it softened its position at the end of the 18th century. After explaining that the first crematoria in Europe consisted of ovens heated with coal or coke, he goes on to describe their description and operation. The furnace used to burn corpses is called a 'retort'. It is of interest, since the exterminationists claim that 1,800,000 bodies were burned in the open air in Belzec, Treblinka and Sobibor, to quote from Leuchter's text, who clarifies that "the old retorts were merely ovens which extracted from the corpse all the liquid by boiling and reduced it to ashes. Bones," he adds, "cannot be burned and to this day must be reduced to powder. Nowadays the old mortars have been replaced by grinding machines". Reading these lines, it is impossible to avoid bringing to mind the fabulous images of Jewish prisoners crushing with sledgehammers and hammers the bones of burnt bodies on great pyres in the freezing nights of the harsh Polish winter. Here is an excerpt from the *Leuchter Report* on the retorts:

> "The old retorts were simple brick ovens for drying or cooking, and only dried human remains. Modern steel retorts, lined with refractory, now throw fire through pipes, directly at the bodies, igniting them, which causes their rapid combustion and burning. Modern retorts also have a second burner or afterburner to re-burn all the contaminating particles of the gaseous material burnt... These modern retorts, or crematoria, burn at a temperature of over 2,000° F (about 1,100° Celsius). With the second burner the temperature is 1,600° F. This high temperature causes the body itself to burn and waste away, which allows the burner to close... At 2,000° F, or higher, modern retorts burn a body in 1:25 hour. Theoretically this gives 19.2 bodies in a 24 hour period. Factory recommendations for normal operation and continued use allow for three or fewer cremations per day.
> The crematoria used in the German installations were of the old type. They were constructed of bricks and cement mortar, lined with refractory bricks. All the ovens had multiple retorts (as we have called them above),

some with air insufflators (although none had direct combustion), none had afterburners, and all were coke ovens, except for one installation which no longer exists, at Majdanek. None of the retorts inspected in all the locations visited were designed for multiple incineration of corpses. It should be noted that unless specifically designed for a higher rate of heat, which reduces the remains to bone, retorts do not consume the materials placed inside them."

One of the eight tables in the *Leuchter Report* contains a study of the theoretical and actual output of seven crematoria: the four at Birkenau, the two at Majdanek and the one at Auschwitz I, totalling 73 retorts. According to Leuchter's calculations, the theoretical output of these crematoria would be 469.2 bodies burned in 24 hours, while the actual output would be 207 bodies. In other words, if these ovens had operated for a thousand consecutive days, a total of 207,000 corpses would have been burned. Let us recall that, in a display of voluntarism, Professor Butz had estimated that the 46 retorts of the four Birkenau crematoria, stopping for only one hour, would have been able to cremate a thousand corpses a day.

Cyanide, if it does not come into contact with other chemicals which produce a reaction, remains for long periods of time in cement mortar, bricks and concrete. Fred Leuchter selectively took thirty-one samples from the alleged gas chambers in crematoria I, II, III, IV and V of Auschwitz-Birkenau. A control sample was taken from the delousing chamber where the gas was known to have been used. Cyanide combines with iron in bricks and cement mortar and is transformed into ferrocyanide, a very stable complex of iron and cyanide also called Prussian blue pigment. Chemical examinations of this sample from the disinfection chamber, number 32, indeed showed a very high concentration of cyanide. In contrast, almost all samples from the alleged gas chambers of the crematoria showed negative results. Only a few of them showed very low, barely significant levels. According to Leuchter, "the small amounts detected would indicate that at some point in time those facilities were disinfected with Zyklon-B, as were all buildings and constructions in those facilities". The Report therefore concludes that these sites were not gas execution chambers.

The detailed study of Crematorium I at Auschwitz I shows that the alleged gas chamber was in fact a morgue and later an air-raid shelter. Leuchter was able to obtain the plans from the museum officials and made a detailed analysis of them. He decided to append to his report a scale drawing made by himself on 23 March 1988, which is included in Appendix V together with those of the other crematoria and the disinfection chambers at Majdanek, also made by Leuchter himself. The locations where the samples were taken are indicated on these drawings. Crematorium I is officially said to have been reconstructed for the period from 25 September 1941 to 21 September 1944, and the official Auschwitz museum guide states that the building is physically in the same condition as it was found on 27 January

1945. Leuchter describes this crematorium precisely: the dimensions of its rooms, the openings in the ceiling, the cooker chimney in the morgue area, its doors, gates and even the frames that had no door, the lighting system, which was not explosion-proof, etc. As for the claim that the morgue was used as a gas chamber, he wrote the following:

> "The alleged gas chamber is not, as stated above, designed to be used in this way. There is no indication or evidence of the presence of an exhaust system or ventilator of any kind in this building. The ventilation system for the alleged gas chambers consisted simply of four square openings in the roof, which evacuated the gases to within two feet of the roof. By venting the HCN gas in this way, it would inevitably reach the vicinity of the SS hospital, a short distance away on the other side of the road, killing patients and medical staff. Due to the fact that the building has not been sealed to prevent leakage, as no doors have seals to prevent gas from reaching the crematorium, and that there are drains which allow gas to reach all the buildings in the camp, and that there is no heating system and no circulation system, no ventilation system or chimneys and no gas distribution system, plus constant humidity, and no circulation due to the number of people in the gas chambers, and no way to introduce the Zyklon-B material, it would be suicide to attempt to use this morgue as a gassing chamber. The results would be an explosion or a gas leak that would affect the entire camp."

As for the four buildings at Birkenau. II and III were identical facilities with three morgues in the basement and a crematorium with five ovens and fifteen retorts, which was located on the first floor. The transport of the bodies from the morgues to the crematoria was done by lifts: the three morgues, which had no doors, led to a room where the freight elevator went up to the vicinity of the ovens. We investigated the areas where the official historiography places the supposed gas chambers, which in the sketches drawn by Leuchter and based on the original plans correspond to morgue no. 1. Everything mentioned in the previous quotation is repeated: no ventilation, no heating or circulation system, no evidence of doors or frames? Since parts of the building of crematorium III have disappeared, Leuchter acknowledges that he could not determine the same. He points out, however, that both buildings have reinforced concrete ceilings, without any perceptible openings. As for the claim that the columns were hollow in order to conduct gases, according to some reports, this possibility is completely ruled out. Leuchter states that they are all solid, reinforced concrete, exactly as the plans captured from the Germans indicate. The report concludes once again: "Such installations would be extremely dangerous if used as gas chambers and such use would probably result in the death of the person using them and an explosion when the gas reached the crematoria.

Table V of the *Report* gives an estimate of hypothetical executions and proportion of use of crematoria II and III. Morgue No. 1, the alleged gas chamber in Crematoria II and III, had an area of 232.25 square metres. By rigorous calculation, Leuchter concludes that it could hold up to 278 persons. To fill this room of 566.40 cubic metres (height 2.5 metres) with HCN gas, 2.26 kilos of Zyklon-B would be needed. The ventilation time after such an execution would be at least seven days, if one is very optimistic. According to these estimates, 556 people could have been gassed in one week between the two crematoria, which is equivalent to 2,224 per month and 26,688 per year. On the basis of this expertise, one easily realises that it takes a great deal of candour to give any credibility to the statement of Rudolf Höss, who said: "Another improvement we made over Treblinka was that we built our gas chambers for 2,000 people at a time. On the use of the crematoria, Leuchter estimates for each of them a hypothetical ratio of 714 persons per week and 315 in real time.

As for crematoria IV and V, they were identical. Each of them had two ovens with four retorts, although this could not be verified on site. Leuchter does not dare to state their exact physical appearance, as the buildings were razed to the ground. Apparently, the building was made of red brick and plaster with a concrete floor and no basement. In any case, if the plans of the buildings are correct, the report states, there were no gas chambers in these facilities for the same reasons as those given for the earlier crematoria.

As for the Majdanek facility, we shall avoid any further discussion so as not to repeat the same or similar considerations unnecessarily. Leuchter attaches Table VII ("Hypothetical proportions of executions at Majdanek"), where he fixes the number of persons who could have been executed per week in Chambers No. 1 and No. 2 at 54 and 24 respectively. He concludes: "My engineering opinion is that Chambers No. 1 and No. 2 were never, and could never have been, used as gas chambers for executions. Neither of the Majdanek facilities is suitable and they were not used for execution purposes." The *Leuchter Report,* ends with a paragraph where in a few lines the following general conclusions are drawn:

> "Having reviewed all the material and inspected all the sites at Auschwitz, Birkenau and Majdanek, the author finds the evidence overwhelming. There were no gas chambers for executions at any of these sites. It is the opinion of this author that the alleged gas chambers at the sites surveyed could not have been used then or now. Nor should opinions that they functioned as gas chambers for executions be taken seriously.
> Done on 5 April 1988 in Malden, Massachusetts
> Fred Leuchter Associates.
> Signed
>
> Fred A. Leuchter, Jr.
Chief Engineer".

In short, the alleged gas chambers were not such: they would have been constantly leaking because they were not sealed, they had no gas distributors or heating mechanisms, and the ventilation was inadequate. Moreover, the Germans would never have been stupid enough to build them next to the crematoria, as the official historiography claims, because it would have been suicidal. The Zyklon-B would have remained in the chambers for at least a week, and only with special suits and masks would it have been possible to operate in them for a short time. In reality, they were mortuaries. As for the crematoria, their cremation capacity could only have eliminated a small fraction of the alleged millions touted by Holocaust propagandists. Samples taken from the "gas chambers" and the disinfection chambers show that in the former the traces of cyanide were very small, while the latter contained very high doses. As mentioned above, the cyanide analysis was not carried out by Leuchter himself, but by an American chemist named James Roth, who did not know where the samples came from.

Of course, no media paid the slightest attention to the *Leuchter Report*. There were, however, two attempts at refutation: in 1989 the Frenchman Jean-Claude Pressac published *Auschwitz: Technique and Operation of the Gas Chambers* in New York, which despite its title does not report on the operation of the gas chambers; and in 1990 the German Werner Wegner in *Die Schatten der Vergangenheit (The Shadows of the Past)* also tried to refute Fred Leuchter's technical expertise. Both objections were broken down point by point by Udo Walendy in issue 50 of *Historische Tatsachen* (*Historical Facts*). Alfred Leuchter himself published a report in 1991 (discussed below) to reject and discredit Pressac's reasoning in no uncertain terms. Professor Faurisson also demonstrated in issue 3 of the *Revue d'Histoire Révisionniste* that Pressac was unwittingly reinforcing revisionist views: in his book, Jean-Claude Pressac goes so far as to admit that 95% of the Zyklon-B was used by the Germans in the disinfection chambers and only 5% for homicidal purposes.

On 12 March 1992, Walter Lüftl, President of the Austrian Federal Chamber of Engineers and sworn court expert, was forced to resign as President of the Austrian Federal Chamber of Engineers. Lüftl had dared to say in the so-called "Lüftl Report" that the alleged mass gassings at Auschwitz were technically impossible [12]. Finally, the German chemist Germar Rudolf published the *Rudolf Report* in 1993, in which he reached the same conclusions as Leuchter, whom he criticises in some minor respects. In

---

[12] What happened to Walter Lüftl was a disgraceful scandal. The Austrian Masonic institutions were particularly belligerent in demanding the resignation of Walter Lüftl as president of the Chamber of Engineers. Under the pseudonym Werner Rademacher, Lüftl himself explained at length what had happened in *Der Fall Lüftl* (*The Lüftl Case*), a pamphlet published in Tübingen in 1944, included by Germar Rudolf in *Dissecting The Holocaust*.

his excellent work, praised by experts from all over the world, Rudolf relies on incontrovertible documents to refute Pressac's book in a resounding manner. We will devote time and space to Germar Rudolf in a moment.

This section on the *Leuchter Report* cannot be closed without referring very briefly to the other three Leuchter reports on the gas chambers. In May 1988, Ernst Zündel was nevertheless sentenced to nine months in prison. The sentence was appealed and on 27 August 1992 it was overturned, as the Court declared the "publication of false news" law to be archaic and unconstitutional because it violated fundamental rights. In the meantime, instead of cowering, Zündel, encouraged by the findings of the Auschwitz-Birkenau and Majdanek expertise, contacted Fred Leuchter again in March 1989 and asked him to investigate three other alleged execution sites with gas chambers: Dachau in Germany, and Mauthausen and Hartheim Castle in Austria. The task was to produce an engineering report and a forensic study of these facilities. The result of the work was the second Leuchter Report.

On 9 April 1989 a team led by Fred Leuchter, including Dr Faurisson, Mark Weber and five other members, inspected Dachau. The next day they travelled to Austria and worked in the other two camps near Linz. It has already been said in recounting the events at Dachau that even Holocaust propagandists acknowledge that there were no extermination camps in Germany and that no one was gassed at Dachau. This was confirmed by the second Leuchter Report, dated 15 June 1989 in Massachusetts. For the two Austrian camps it was also established that there were no gassing chambers at either of these sites. The conclusions end with this blunt statement: "It is the full conviction of this investigator as an engineer that the alleged gas chambers at the sites inspected could not then, nor could they now, have been used or seriously considered to be suitable for use as gas execution chambers".

The third Leuchter Report originated from another request by Ernst Zündel, who in October 1989 commissioned the engineer to inspect a gas chamber in operation in the United States. The task was to produce a document with accompanying photos and a video. The facility surveyed was the Mississippi State Penitentiary gas chamber, which used hydrogen cyanide gas (Zyklon-B) for execution. The purpose was to demonstrate the design and fabrication requirements of an execution gas chamber, the operating protocol and safety conditions for personnel using hydrogen cyanide. This was intended to support and corroborate the criteria set out in the original *Leuchter Report* of 5 April 1988. The document was submitted on 6 December 1989. We cannot, for obvious reasons, go into the technical details at the heart of the text, which served, as intended, to show that the Germans had taken into account the guidelines described in the design and construction of the Zyklon-B delousing chambers and had ignored them in the chambers where mass gassing was supposed to take place. The larger the chamber," Leuchter concluded, "and the greater the number of persons executed, the more imperative it is to apply the basic principles in its design."

On 17 October 1991 Alfred Leuchter submitted a fourth and final report: *A Technical Evaluation of Jean-Claude Pressac's Book*, which constitutes a forceful refutation of the book *Auschwitz: Technique and Operation of the Gas Chambers*, which Leuchter considered "a blatant attempt to promote exterminationist propaganda". Once again it was Ernst Zündel who asked Leuchter for a scientific and technical evaluation of Pressac's text. In Leuchter's opinion, Pressac's inability to prove the existence of executions by gas chambers with his technical documentation was obvious. After commenting on and refuting the twenty-two chapters into which Pressac divides the five parts of his work, Leuchter regrets that "an author who presumably passes for a man of science tries to make reality coincide with his preconceived theses".

David Cole, a Jewish revisionist, exposes Auschwitz fable

In September 1992, David Cole, a 23-year-old American Jew, travelled from the United States to Europe with the idea of personally investigating several concentration camps. After the publication of the *Leuchter Report*, revisionism was experiencing an international boom and Cole, who frequented revisionist circles in the United States, decided to do his bit. With the idea of filming a documentary, he visited Auschwitz wearing his kipa (Jewish cap) on his head and accompanied by a cameraman. His filming made him famous and, although he was later forced to retract it, the value of the documentary and his contribution to the revisionist movement have remained. The following is a summary of this document, although the interested reader can watch it in its entirety on You Tube and in English.

David Cole does not initially appear in the video: he is the narrator, and his distinctive voice is heard as he points to the plan of the camp, with the barracks inside a quadrangular area once surrounded by barbed wire. Outside, on the right-hand side, he shows the SS buildings and the hospital, next to which is the crematorium and the "gas chamber". Then there are images of the camp. Cole explains that the guided tour takes visitors to the former prison, which is described as a "death block". The young revisionist recounts that tourists are also presented with a "wall of death" and a series of displays arranged to endorse atrocity legends and present Auschwitz "as a death machine, the place where detention meant extermination." What is not shown on the sightseeing tour is a building outside the area surrounded by barbed wire, which in Cole's words "might well be called the life block, a mass disinfection complex where Zyklon-B gas was used to combat lice and the diseases they carry." The theatre building, where Carmelite nuns who prayed there for all those who died in Auschwitz were installed, is also not shown. In April 1993 John Paul II invited them to move to another location after a Jewish group entered the convent in 1989 and demanded their evacuation. The tour climaxes with the gas chamber. David Cole then quotes: "At this point the group is emotionally conditioned to believe anything. The gas chamber is like the bottom course after a two-hour upward preheating. Literally, the gas chamber is the objective proof that everything they heard during the tour is true, the proof of the Holocaust. But is it?"

In this moment, the young Cole is seen for the first time, dressed in his kippah and holding a microphone with a personal guide named Alicia, for whom he has paid a premium in order to have her exclusively at his disposal. Cole explains that he has donned the kipa so that he will not be taken for what he is, a revisionist, but as "a virtuous Jew who seeks to know the truth and to counter those who say the Holocaust never happened." She merely tells him what she tells other believers who make the annual pilgrimage to the Auschwitz I shrine, monopolised exclusively by Holocaust dogma propaganda. Alicia shows him evidence that proves nothing, which is presented to all tourists as material evidence of the extermination. She starts with the piles of hair. "But what do they prove?" asks Cole, and adds:

> "It has been acknowledged that every inmate was shaved because of lice, that is not denied, so why shouldn't there be piles of human hair? That is not denied, so why shouldn't there be piles of human hair? And what about the piles of shoes and clothes? Do they constitute evidence? It is a fact that prisoners were given a uniform on arrival that included shoes. So why shouldn't there be piles of shoes and clothes from the inmates? That does not prove that anyone was killed. And that gives Poles and Soviets the benefit of the doubt that such clothes and hair genuinely came from the camp. And what about the gas canisters? No one denies that Zyklon-B was used to disinfect clothes and buildings? And what other evidence is offered? Well, there are the traditional photos of sick inmates which prove the shattering thesis that people got sick in the camp. No one denies the typhus epidemic which caused many deaths...".

Finally, Cole appears in front of the building that passes for the gas chamber. He explains that the exterminationists claim that what was the morgue was used as a gas chamber, although they admit that it was later an air raid shelter. Followed by the cameraman, Cole enters the large room without the guide and points out holes in the floor that show that there was a toilet there. He also shows the evidence of old walls that compartmentalised the space of the great hall and ends by stating that at one time there were five rooms and a bathroom. He adds that there are no blue Zyklon-B stains on the walls as in the disinfection rooms. He then gives a close-up of the rudimentary wooden door with a glass top. Four square openings in the ceiling are shown below. These are the famous holes through which the gas was supposedly thrown when the chamber was full of people. David Cole clarifies: "Revisionists argue that the holes were added after the liberation of the camp and that it was then that the walls were demolished and the toilet removed to make the room look like a large gas chamber".

Back outside, he asks the guide if there has been any reconstruction. Alicia replies that everything is in its original state. He goes back into the room with her, asks her about the four holes and points out the obvious evidence that walls had been knocked down. The guide insists that the holes are original, that Zyklon-B was dropped through them and that no walls were knocked down. Sensing that her explanations do not convince the young Jew, Alice suggests that he speak to the guide supervisor at the Auschwitz State Museum, who eventually suggests that he ask for an interview with Dr. Piper, chief archivist and senior commissioner of Auschwitz. Before saying goodbye, however, Cole coaxes a confession out of the supervisor that the holes in the ceiling are not original and were reconstructed after the war.

Franciszek Piper, author of the book *Auschwitz. How many perished*, in which he accepts that the Soviet figure of 4,000,000 is wrong and puts the number of victims at 1,100,000, appears on camera in his office in the Auschwitz Museum. He is suspicious and suggests that the interview should not be filmed, but finally agrees to appear in the documentary. Cole's first question is about the changes made to the theoretical gas chamber. Piper replies that the room was a gas chamber that was later converted into an air-raid shelter in which interior dividing walls were erected, the holes in the ceiling were covered up and a door was opened on one side. He notes that after the liberation of the camp, the walls were torn down and the holes reopened, but the door remained. Cole asks why tourists are not told the truth. The filming of the interview is interrupted. Cole points out that the holes in the ceiling are not visible in any of the aerial photographs he has studied. He then offers the two versions written in black background. Official version: "The Soviets and the Poles created the gas chamber in an air raid shelter that had previously been a gas chamber". Revisionist version: "The Soviets and Poles created a gas chamber in a bomb shelter that had previously been a bomb shelter."

The interview resumes. Second question: "Why are there so few traces of Zyklon-B in the homicidal gas chambers compared to the large quantities of residues present in the disinfection chambers?" The answer is surprising: "Zyklon-B was used for a very short time, about twenty or thirty minutes in twenty-four hours, whereas in the disinfection chambers it was used day and night." That is to say, contrary to what witnesses and exterminist historians say, according to whom it was gassed continuously, Piper assures us that there was only one gassing a day. Cole then takes the opportunity to ask him if he knows how many groups were gassed in crematoria II and III at Birkenau. Piper painfully contradicts what he said earlier: "It is difficult to say because there were periods when the gas chambers were used day after day for hours at a time. Such actions were repetitive: gas, cremate, gas, cremate, cremate". To an interpellation about the four million figure, Piper says: "It was estimated by the Soviet commission investigating Nazi crimes at Auschwitz, since the Nazis destroyed the camp documentation." This is another lie, as it was not destroyed. The interview is interrupted and this text appears on a black background, read aloud by the narrator: "In reality, the records of those who died in the camp were captured by the Soviets, who did not make them public until 1989". The documentary ends by recalling the Katyn massacre and other Soviet lies assumed by the Allies at Nuremberg.

As a result of his contribution to revisionism, David Cole was considered a traitor and began to be harassed by the JDL (Jewish Defence League), which published his details on the internet. He and his family received anonymous death threats and he was kept in hiding for three years. The JDL published a text entitled "David Cole, monstrous traitor", which ended with the words: "JDL would like to know the location of Holocaust denier David Cole. Anyone who provides us with his correct address will receive a financial reward." Frightened, he contacted and begged to have his details removed from the internet because his family was under constant threat of death. JDL President Irv Rubin[13] received a notarised letter from the young revisionist in January 1998 retracting his statement. The text was published on 8 February 1998. In it Cole stated: "The Nazis tried to kill all the Jews of Europe, and the sum total of this attempted genocide is six million".

After a prolonged silence of eighteen years, David Cole, who had adopted a new identity under the name of David Stein, reappeared publicly on 22 February 2014 at a meeting held by the IHR (Institute for Historica Review) in California. Mark Weber, director of the Institute, introduced him to an audience that subjected him to numerous questions. After recalling that JDL thugs had physically assaulted him at an event at the University of California at Los Angeles and that he had been forced to recant. Cole stated that he stood by what he had said in the 1990s about Auschwitz and the Holocaust.

The *Rudolf Report* and the forensic investigation at Auschwitz

Germar Rudolf, a brilliant graduate in chemistry from the University of Bonn, received a government scholarship that enabled him to do doctoral research at the prestigious Max Planck Institute in Stuttgart. He was working on his doctoral thesis when in 1991 he agreed to prepare a forensic study for the defence of Otto Ernst Remer, accused in a trial for "Holocaust denial". He was asked to study various documents, take samples, analyse them and

---

[13] Irv Rubin, president of the JDL from 1985 to 2002, was eventually charged by the FBI with murder and terrorism. He committed suicide in his jail cell while awaiting trial. His family decided to take legal action against the government.

issue a report. Germar Rudolf tested some of the Auschwitz buildings for residues of hydrocyanic acid, i.e. chemical traces of the notorious Zyklon-B. The result of his investigations was recorded in the report. The result of his investigations was recorded in an expert report entitled *Technical Report on the Formation and Detectability of Cyanide Compounds in the "Gas Chamber" of Auschwitz* (*Gutachten über die Bildung und Nachweisbarkeit von Cyanidverbindungen in den "Gaskammern von Auschwitz*), which was used as evidence by Remer's defence. Years later, Rudolf wrote in *Resistance is Obligatory* that the purpose of the expert opinion was to correct the omissions and deficiencies of the *Leuchter Report*. Between 1992 and 1994 this report was introduced as evidence in seven or eight criminal trials in Germany. In all cases it was disallowed because according to German jurisprudence , the facts that took place in the Auschwitz camp during the Third Reich are considered obvious and therefore do not require proof or demonstration. Since 1996 it has been a criminal offence to try to argue otherwise. Thus, as unheard of as it may seem, the technical analyses were roundly rejected.

Otto Ernst Remer, one of the defendants for whose benefit the report had been prepared, published the results of Germar Rudolf's research in July 1993. The pamphlet of some 120 pages became known as the *Rudolf Report*, a chemical study on the formation and detection of hydrogen cyanide in the alleged Auschwitz gas chambers, an ideal complement to the *Leuchter Report*, since both documents agreed that hydrocyanic acid murders never took place in the camps of the Auschwitz complex. This led to the indictment of Germar Rudolf. The German press, which consistently supported the decisions of the courts of law, reacted angrily and associated the young chemist with the accused Remer.

The outcome of the whole affair was catastrophic for Germar Rudolf, who was refused by the Max Planckt Institute in 1993 to submit his thesis for the final doctoral examination. In 1995, he was sentenced to fourteen months in prison and was also charged with new offences for continuing his forensic research activities. The copies of *Grundlagen zur Zeitgeschichte* (*Foundations of Contemporary History*), in which Rudolf had published under the pseudonym Ernst Gauss an up-to-date collection of research papers on the problem of the Holocaust, were seized and destroyed by court order. Germar Rudolf managed to flee to England in 1996, where he spent a few years in hiding before seeking political asylum in the United States. Years later, in the March/April 2001 issue of *The Journal of Historical Review*, Rudolf himself published an extensive article in which he brilliantly reviewed all the forensic examinations carried out at Auschwitz and, at the same time, criticised the unacceptable attitude of those who not only reject the results of scientific research, but also criminalise the technicians and experts.

The first reproach went to the Max Planckt Institute, which in late spring 1993 made public the memorandum informing about the expulsion of Germar Rudolf for the research carried out at Auschwitz. The Institute, disdaining that forensic examination is a moral obligation in any criminal investigation, argued that it was repugnant to discuss the specific way in which the Nazis had murdered Jews. In defence of his research, Rudolf wrote in his article a definition of forensic examinations: "Forensic science is generally seen as a supporting science to criminology. Its aim is to collect and identify physical evidence of the crime, and from this to draw conclusions about the victims, the criminals, the weapons, the time and location of the crime, as well as the manner in which it was perpetrated, if at all. This science is relatively new, entering the courts of law only in 1902, when for the first time an English court accepted fingerprints as evidence". The revisionists' demand for material evidence, therefore, "is absolutely consistent," Germar Rudolf insisted, "with customary practice and modern application of the law. As is generally admitted, forensic evidence is more decisive than witness statements or documentary evidence." With these principles established, Rudolf reviewed in his extensive article the forensic investigations carried out at Auschwitz.

In 1945 the Forensic Research Institute in Kraków produced a forensic report on Auschwitz which was presented as evidence in 1946 at the Auschwitz trial in Kraków. Considering that the Polish communist regime readily accepted the Soviet hoax about the Katyn graves, one must at the very least doubt the rigour of the Polish judicial proceedings. Polish forensic experts conducted qualitative, not quantitative, analyses and took hair, theoretically from the inmates, and hair accessories found by the Soviets in suitcases. In both cases cyanide residues were found. A chrome-plated lid with zinc was also examined and tested positive. The Krakow Institute claimed that this metal lid covered the exhaust duct of an alleged gas chamber at Birkenau. These analyses do not prove whether hydrocyanic acid gassings took place in Auschwitz, among other things because there is no way to check where the hair, hairpins and other head ornaments came from. In addition, it is known that hair was cut for hygienic reasons and that longer hair had to be deloused before being recycled. As for the origin or provenance of the metal cap, this does not seem to be sufficient evidence to prove anything.

Another Auschwitz trial was held in Frankfurt between 1964 and 1966, but no forensic analysis was presented there. Among the most publicised reports was that presented by the Institute for Contemporary History in Munich. Although it was a mammoth trial, neither the court nor the prosecution nor the defence suggested the need for material evidence of the alleged crimes. Moreover, the lack of documentary evidence was considered irrelevant. As usual, almost everything was proved by witness statements and statements of persons attributed responsibility for the crimes perpetrated. These testimonies were considered sufficient to establish beyond doubt the existence of a programme to exterminate the Jews in Auschwitz. Also in 1966 the Auschwitz State Museum commissioned the Polish company Hydrokop to carry out an excavation at Auschwitz-Birkenau to analyse soil samples. Rudolf points to the possibility that the research was carried out in the context of the Frankfurt process. Since the findings were not made public and faded away in the museum archives, it is reasonable to assume that they did not yield any significant results.

The first sensible report on Auschwitz came during the trial held in Vienna between 18 January and 10 March 1972. The defendants at the time were Walter Dejaco and Fritz Ertl, two architects responsible for the design and construction of the crematoria at Auschwitz-Birkenau. The court was presented with the report of an expert who interpreted the plans for the alleged gas chambers at Auschwitz and Birkenau. This technical study concluded that the rooms in question could not have been gas chambers, nor could they have been converted into gas chambers. Thanks to this methodologically sound report, Dejaco and Ertl were acquitted.

It took a decade from the time Robert Faurisson began to doubt the existence of the gas chambers to the *Leuchter Report*. In 1978, after a critical study of witness statements and an intensive examination of documents, Professor Faurisson formulated the thesis that "there was not a single gas chamber under Hitler's regime". At the end of 1978, *Le Monde* allowed Faurrisson to present his considerations in an article. Ten years later, as mentioned above, the trial of Ernst Zündel in 1988 was a milestone in the history of the revisionist movement. Fred Leuchter's pioneering work gave rise to a series of publications whose scope of research gradually expanded to include interdisciplinary studies of the material and documentary evidence. The most important work was that of Germar Rudolf, who fully corroborated Fred Leuchter.

Germar Rudolf began his research at the beginning of 1991 in order to verify the assertions made in the *Leuchter Report*. He was particularly interested in verifying that cyanide residues remained stable for a long time and could therefore be found in the murder gas chambers if Zyklon-B had been used in them. Initially," Rudolf writes, "I was only interested in finding out whether the resulting mixture, ferrocyanide or Prussian blue, is stable enough to survive forty-five years in harsh environmental conditions. Having confirmed it, I sent the results to about twenty people who might have an interest in them". Among them were engineers and lawyers. The former could help him in his forensic investigation; the latter needed the evidence to defend Otto Ernst Remer. Germar Rudolf travelled twice to Auschwitz, and for eighteen months he worked with the intention of putting the results of his investigation into a report that ran to seventy-two pages and was ready in January 1992. The so-called *Rudolf Report*, which was distributed to opinion leaders in Germany, corroborated Fred Leuchter's assertion that for various technical and chemical reasons the mass gassings attested by witnesses could not have occurred. Improved and updated, the *Rudolf Report* was finally published in July 1993. Dutch and French versions appeared in 1995 and 1996, but the English version had to wait until 2003.

In his eagerness to confront his research work, Germar Rudolf contacted the Institute of Forensic Medicine in Kraków, which in 1990, at the request of the Auschwitz State Museum, had conducted its own forensic tests in order to refute Fred Leuchter's research. The forensic institute team, headed by Jan Markiewicz, Wojciech Gubala and Jerzy Labedz, extracted samples from the 'gas chambers', but the Polish chemists who analysed them found even smaller traces of cyanide than those found by Dr Roth. They then decided to take samples from the disinfection chambers and, although the walls had been bleached, there were much higher traces of cyanide in them, but they were unwilling or unable to recognise it. Markiewicz and company claimed that they did not understand how the walls of the disinfection chambers exposed to hydrocyanic acid could have become impregnated with the Prussian blue colour and went so far as to suggest that it came from another source "It is difficult to imagine," they said, "the chemical reactions and physico-chemical processes that could have led to the formation of Prussian blue at that site. They even expressed the nonsense that the walls of the disinfection chambers had been painted Prussian blue.

In 1994 the Polish researchers presented a paper on their findings. Rudolf, after reading it carefully, came to the conclusion that they had not actually done anything to find out whether prussic colour can form on walls that have been exposed to hydrogen cyanide gas. He contacted them to ask for a scientific explanation of their methods of analysis and gave them irrefutable proof that prussic blue does form on walls exposed to hydrogen cyanide gas. Finally, Rudolf received a letter from the Kraków researchers in which they clearly admitted that their purpose was not to establish the scientific truth, but to reject the "Holocaust deniers" and to avoid the laundering of Hitler and National Socialism. Let us learn how Germar Rudolf explains the process scientifically:

> "... When hydrogen cyanide and certain iron compounds mix, they form Prussian blue. That is exactly the phenomenon one can observe when entering the Zyklon-B delousing facilities that operated in Europe during the Third Reich . A few of them, for example in the concentration camps of Auschwitz, Birkenau, Majdanek and Stuthoff, are still intact today. All these facilities have one thing in common: their walls are impregnated with Prussian blue. Not only the inner surfaces, but also the mortar between the brick blocks and even the outer walls of these delousing chambers are filled with ferrocyanide and show an irregular blue colouring. Nothing similar can be observed in the alleged gas chambers of Auschwitz and Birkenau. The iron compounds necessary to form Prussian blue are an integral part of all building materials: bricks,

sandstone and cement always contain an amount of oxide (iron oxide, usually between 1 and 4 percent). That is what gives bricks and most sands their red or ochre colour".

In other words, Markiewicz and his colleagues decided for political reasons to reject what they did not want. As scientists, they should have proved that the prussic blue colour could not form on walls exposed to hydrocyanic acid. To do this, they had to prove whether or not it was true that the iron compounds contained in bricks and cement formed the ferrocyanide in contact with the gas. Instead of accepting this, they preferred to defend the thesis that disinfection chambers and homicidal "gas chambers" had similar levels of cyanide residues.

Germar Rudolf always claims that the scientific method is the best way to reach irrefutable conclusions. He believes that forensic science has always been used to decipher historical crimes, such as Katyn. Rudolf bitterly regrets that no influential group dares to demand a forensic investigation at Auschwitz-Birkenau and that those in power show no interest in establishing the truth about Auschwitz and the Holocaust. Instead, he writes:

> "Authorities around the world are pursuing and prosecuting those who propose or attempt such research. This may slow us down, but it will not stop us. When revisionist researchers achieve a sudden breakthrough through forensic research, they are countered not only with defamation and persecution, but also with academic forgery and professorial deception, a glaring example of which is the Krakow forensic report. How desperate must the keepers of the flame of the Holocaust legend be to resort to such methods? By protecting the alleged graves and the ruins of the Auschwitz 'gas chamber' from scientific enquiry they risk the burial of their own reputation and the ruin of the Auschwitz myth."

PART 5
THE PERSECUTION OF REVISIONISTS FOR THOUGHT CRIMES

As a tribute to the many honest people who have risked their careers and their lives to defend freedom of expression and research in the search for historical truth, we will end Chapter XII of this *History Outlawed* with a broad overview of the essential work of these unsung heroes of revisionism, unknown to the general public. Many of them have already been mentioned in the course of our work, but we will now present them in greater detail and thus outline the value and scope of their contributions. The persecution of revisionists for thought crimes is one of the most shameful things that can happen in self-proclaimed free and democratic societies. It is outrageous, intolerable, indecent that intellectuals from all fields of knowledge are imprisoned for exercising their right to study and research historical facts. This unjustifiable fact should be enough to make us realise that reality and history have been falsified and that the lie is being maintained at all costs.

The victims of the thought police are numerous in Europe, especially in Germany, where since the end of World War II the German people have been subjected to all sorts of humiliations with the connivance of their leaders. In France and Austria, too, there are many cases of people being persecuted, prosecuted and imprisoned for exercising their right to freedom of expression. In order to facilitate the presentation and to bring together in these pages the main cases of which we are aware, we will proceed to present them by country and will also try to keep a chronological order, in order to follow the process from a historical perspective. We will begin in Germany, where the ideological control that has been exercised since 1945 is not perceived to its full extent by the majority of the population, whose brainwashing, begun in childhood, has reached unprecedented levels.

We will see below how far the deterioration of civil rights has gone in Germany, a country that has accepted the censorship of its national anthem, mutilated, with banned verses that no one dares to sing in public. The idea of political correctness is the tool used by those who want to paralyse German society at all costs. Anything that does not conform to the official version of events is considered politically unacceptable. This state of paralysis is maintained by the irreplaceable support of the so-called anti-fascist movement, which viciously attacks and disqualifies those who seek to revise history, especially that of the Third Reich . Unlike anti-capitalist or anti-communist movements, which are the expression of personal convictions, anti-fascism in Germany is institutionalised, rooted and structured at all levels of society, so that those who do not express anti-fascist sentiments are morally disqualified.

It should be remembered that it was only in 1955 that Germany was granted partial sovereignty. Until then, there was neither freedom of the press nor academic freedom. To ensure that political changes could not take place, the Department for the Protection of the Constitution was set up. In addition to combating communist political parties, this department did everything necessary to legally nullify national parties and media considered to be right-wing. As a result, there are neither universities nor political parties in Germany, nor any significant right-wing newspapers or media. However, in 1968, thousands of students, incited by the teachings of left-wing, socialist and even communist professors installed in the universities by the Allies during the occupation, took to the streets with pro-communist slogans. As a result of the student revolt of 1968, the progressive entry of these leftists into the country's institutions began.

At the end of the last century, this generation with ideas ranging from socialism to communism reached the height of its power and influence on German society. Its representatives were well placed at all levels and formed a powerful political elite. In this way they can maintain extensive influence and control over public opinion and immediately silence with accusations of "fascism" those who dare to be politically incorrect. Their methods are wide-ranging and include everything from press campaigns to intimidation if necessary. The main mechanism of these leftist circles in which German Jews abound is to keep up to date the feelings of collective guilt, collective shame or collective responsibility, which have kept the German people anaesthetised for more than seventy years.

Before I begin to present the victims of the thought police in Germany and other countries, it is interesting to know that every year the German government presents the figures of its persecution of peaceful dissidents, whom it groups together with violent criminals as "enemies of the Constitution" (Basic Law that came into force on 23 May 1949). In 2011, for example, the *Report on the Protection of the Constitution* (*Verfassungschutzbericht*) indicated that of the 13,865 criminal investigations, 11,401 cases were for "propaganda offences". Of these cases, 2,464 were individuals who had said or written something deemed capable of "disturbing the order of the people". Most of these transgressions are attributed to "right-wing extremists". Crimes committed by radical leftists or foreigners are not grouped in the category of "left-wing extremists". Thought crimes in Germany can only be attributed to nationalists or patriots who are considered "Nazis", "right-wingers", "fascists", labels that are synonymous with "evil".

1. MAIN VICTIMS OF PERSECUTION IN GERMANY:

Joseph Burg, a Jewish revisionist persecuted by Nazis and Zionists

It is only fair to begin these pages on the persecution of the Revisionists with an admirable character if ever there was one, Joseph Ginsburg, better known as Joseph Burg, a German Jew of integrity and honesty like few others, who ended up being persecuted and attacked several times by extremist thugs of the Jewish Defence League. The contempt and hatred of his co-religionists went so far as to deny him the right to be buried in the Jewish cemetery in Munich. Joseph Ginsburg was born in Germany in 1908 and was persecuted by the National Socialist regime during the 1930s. At the outbreak of war in September 1939, he was living in Lemberg, Poland, from where he fled with his family to Czernowitz in the Romanian province of Bukovina, which was occupied by the Red Army in June 1940. When Germany attacked the USSR a year later, Red soldiers fled the region and gangs of Ukrainians began pogroms against Jews. German and Romanian troops stopped these actions and prevented further violence. Ginsburg and his family were deported east to the Transnistria region, where at least they could live. The German-Romanian front collapsed in 1944, and Ginsburg and his family returned to Czernowitz, where the Red terror reigned and all was chaos and hunger.

After the war ended, in 1946 Ginsburg and his party went to Breslau and from there to an UNRRA displaced persons camp near Munich, which was run by an American Jew, whom he served as factotum. In *Schuld un Schiksal, Europas Jugend zwischen Henkern und Heuchlern* (*Guilt and Destiny, European Youth among Executioners and Hypocrites*), a book published in 1962, Joseph Burg recalls his experiences in the camp and tells how he organised the police, the prison, the newspaper and cultural activities. In 1949 he was living in Munich, but chose to emigrate to Israel. There he immediately rejected the sectarianism and racism of the Zionists, so in August 1950 he decided to return to Munich, where he worked as a bookbinder.

It was in Germany, therefore, that he began his struggle to establish the historical truth. His testimony in 1988 in the trial against Zündel is an invaluable source of information. Ernst Zündel, with whom Burg worked closely, has acknowledged that reading the book *Guilt and Destiny* was a determining factor in his life, for it prompted him to begin the struggle against the false accusations against the German people and made him a revisionist. Joseph Burg's courage and stature became evident when he dared to accuse the Mossad of being responsible for the burning of a Jewish old people's home in Munich on the night of 13 February 1970, a terrorist action that claimed the lives of seven people, five men and two women. Also in the 1970s, the so-called "Kreisky-Wiesenthal affair" broke out in Austria. Bruno Kreisky, a Jew persecuted by the Gestapo, was Chancellor of Austria from 1970 to 1983. Simon Wiesenthal accused him in 1975 of appointing five ministers with Nazi backgrounds. Kreisky reacted indignantly and accused Wiesenthal of being a 'racist' who had collaborated with the Gestapo and promoted anti-Semitism in Austria. Joseph Burg came to the Chancellor's support and corroborated the accusation against the notorious "Nazi hunter". Burg publicly declared that Wiesenthal had been an informer for the Gestapo.

In 1979 Joseph Burg published his second work, *Majdanek in alle Ewigkeit?* (*Majdanek in all Ewigkeit?*), in which he recounted his visits to the Majdanek camp in late 1944 and autumn 1945. On this second occasion he also went to Auschwitz. In it he boldly criticised the imposture of the Holocaust and denounced the swindle of the financial reparations paid by the Federal Republic of Germany. The book was immediately banned and all copies were destroyed by order of the German judiciary, which invoked Article 130 of the Criminal Code. The accusation against Joseph Burg was as follows: "Hateful statements against Zionism and attempts to rehabilitate the criminals of the extermination camps". Burg was accused of having mental problems and was forced to undergo psychiatric treatment. When he sought refuge at his wife's grave in the Jewish cemetery in Munich, he was physically assaulted by a Zionist commando because of his testimony.

The friendship between Ernst Zündel and Joseph Burg developed over the years. Burg continued to write books denouncing the situation in Germany. In 1980, for example, he published *Zionnazi Zensur in der BRD* (*Zionazi Censorship in the Federal Republic of Germany*). Zündel not only visited him, but also corresponded with him on an ongoing basis. In 1982, Zündel wrote to him twice for advice and help, as he was having problems with the Zionists in Toronto. Therefore, when the second trial against Ernst Zündel for "publishing false news" began, Burg travelled to Canada to testify as a witness for the defence. His testimony took place on Tuesday 29 March and Wednesday 30 March 1988.

Among other things, Burg stated that he had spoken to hundreds of people who worked in the crematoria, but that he could never find anyone who had worked in the gas chambers. About the crematoria in Auschwitz and Majdanek, he explained that they were operated in three shifts a day by prisoners who did the work voluntarily. The request for volunteers was made by the Jewish council or the Jewish police, who collaborated with the German SS. On the emigration of Jews from Nazi Germany, he charged that the Zionists made it difficult for Jews who did not go to Palestine to emigrate to other countries, since their only interest was to populate Palestine at any cost. Burg claimed to have discovered that it was German Zionist leaders who as early as 1933 asked the Nazis to force Jews to wear the yellow star.

The Zionists did not see this as an insult, but as a heroic gesture, just as the SS saw it as a heroic gesture to display the swastika. In 1938, Burg said, the Zionist leaders of the Third Reich caused Jews to wear the yellow star against the wishes of Göring and Göbbels. In his statement, Burg was particularly critical of the State of Israel and the Zionist leaders, whom he accused of inventing the Holocaust in order to fleece Germany of exorbitant compensation, which was accepted by Dr. Adenauer.

A prolific writer and practising Jew, Joseph Burg was the author of more than a dozen works, today very difficult to find because more than half of them were confiscated by court orders. In *Sündenböcke, Grossangriffe des Zionismus auf Papst Pius XII un die deutschen Regierungen* (*Scapegoats, Zionism's General Offensive against Pope Pius XII and the German Governments*), he denounced Zionism's slander against Pius XII and attacks on Germany. In 1990, two years after testifying at the Toronto trial, Burg died in Munich. Considered a traitor, he was denied burial in the Jewish cemetery as he would have wished. Otto Ernst Remer and Ernst Zündel came to the Bavarian city to pay tribute and bid farewell to the remains of this self-sacrificing revisionist to whom history will never do justice.

Thies Christophersen convicted of "bringing the state into disrepute".

Few Germans dared to speak out during the harsh years of National Socialist purge and repression. One of those who rebelled against the imposed silence was Thies Christophersen, a farmer who was in Auschwitz from January to December 1944. Wounded at the beginning of the war, he was disabled for combat. On behalf of the Kaiser Wilhelm Institute, he arrived in Auschwitz as a Wehrmacht high commander with the task of cultivating vegetable rubber. As the labour force in the camp was too large, the plant cultivation institute was moved from Berlin-Müncheberg to Auschwitz. There, research was carried out in the laboratories at the Bunawerk plant. Christophersen was housed in the Raisko camp, and two hundred female prisoners held in the camp worked with him on his experimental farm. In addition, 100 men arrived daily from Birkenau, although civilians, mainly Russians, were also employed. Among other things, the prisoners analysed the percentage of rubber in the plants in the laboratory in order to select the plants that contained the most rubber for breeding. According to Christophersen, the prisoners worked there eight hours a day, with an hour's rest at noon.

After the war, Christophersen resumed his farming activities. In his efforts to defend the interests of German farmers, he edited and published a quarterly magazine, *Die Bauernschaft* (*The Farmers*). In 1973 Thies Christophersen dared to publish in German the book *Die Auschwitzlüge (The Auschwitz Lie)*, a booklet of which 100,000 copies were printed, in which he denies that Germany exterminated six million Jews during World War II. At the end, he concludes with these words: "I have written my memoirs as I have experienced them and as I remember them. I have told the truth, so help me God. If I could contribute to giving our youth a little more respect for their fathers again, who as soldiers fought for Germany and who were not criminals, then I would be very happy". The book caused a sensation and was soon banned for "stirring up the people". Christophersen, who in addition to the book had published other writings that insisted on denouncing the lies against Germany, was eventually charged and sentenced to a year and a half in prison for "discrediting the state" and for "offending the memory of the dead".

He was politically persecuted and received numerous letters containing insults and threats, forcing him into exile. After passing through Belgium, he settled in Denmark, where legislation protected him, but this did not prevent him from falling victim to "anti-fascist" thugs: hundreds of them attacked his modest house in the small town of Kollund, located just across the border in Germany. The criminals stoned the house, daubed it with insulting graffiti, set fire to the storeroom where he kept his books and, using corrosive acid, smashed his car and photocopying equipment. The German authorities asked the Copenhagen government to take action against him and went so far as to suggest that the Danes review their laws on racism in order to be able to take action against Thies Christophersen. Fortunately, speech and thought crimes were not prosecuted in Denmark and a Danish court rejected an extradition request from the Federal Republic. Finally, as the Danish police failed to prevent the constant harassment and abuse to which he was subjected, he was forced to leave Denmark in 1995. Seriously ill with cancer, he sought treatment in Switzerland, but in December 1995 he was also forced to leave the country. Finally, he found a temporary refuge in Spain. Meanwhile, the printer of the *Bauernschaft* magazine in Germany was fined DM 50,000.

Despite all the tribulations, Christophersen managed to travel to Canada in 1988 to testify as a witness in Toronto in the Zündel trial. His appearance in court preceded that of Joseph Burg. The cross-examination of Doug Christie, Zündel's lawyer, took place on 8 March 1988. Months later, Thies Christophersen himself reproduced it in full, word for word, in the June issue of his magazine *Die Bauernschaft*. Lawyer Christie asked numerous questions about the prisoners, who, like the soldiers, were housed in barracks. Christophersen explained that there were bunk beds, cupboards and bathrooms with hot and cold water. Sheets, towels and clothes were changed regularly. The interrogation went on like this:

-Did prisoners receive correspondence?

- Mail was regularly delivered and parcels were opened if the contents were not very clear in the presence of the prisoners. Some things were not delivered.
- What things were not delivered?
- Money, drugs, chemicals, propaganda material...
- Were prisoners mistreated?
- No ill-treatment was allowed, and if it did occur, the perpetrators were severely punished.
- Did prisoners have the opportunity to complain?
- Yes, at all times. Even the camp commandant, Nöss, and his successor, Captain Lieberhenschel, had authorised the prisoners to speak to them whenever they wanted.
- Did you hear the complaints and grievances of the inmates?
- To tell the truth, these were not complaints, but rather requests. The greatest joy I was able to give the prisoners was when I allowed them to pick mushrooms and blackberries or to bathe in the Sula. Sometimes I would also sequester a prisoner's private letters if the contents were not very clear."

Christophersen admitted during interrogation that he did not know the capacity of the crematoria at Birkenau and that he did not see them in operation, although he had often been in the camp, where he brought material from the aircraft scrapyard and selected labour for the rubber plantations. Concerning the cremation of corpses, he claimed that medical aid was given to sick prisoners and attempts were made to save their lives, as there were ambulances and sick wards in the military hospital. As usual, Christophersen alluded to the many deaths from typhoid fever and noted that the wife of his superior, Dr. Cäsar, herself died of typhoid. As for questions about the gas chambers, he repeatedly claimed that he only heard about them after the war and that he never saw any or met anyone who had seen them.

During the last months of his life, Thies Christophersen was willing to return home to stand trial if he was allowed to present experts and witnesses of his own choosing, but the German courts treated him as an enemy of the state and refused him. His bank account was blocked. In early 1996 he applied to return to Germany to attend the funeral of one of his sons, who died in a car accident, but a court rejected the request. Despite the fact that Christophersen was suffering from cancer, the German authorities cancelled his insurance cover and stopped paying his modest retirement pension, which had been paid to him for 45 years, and his army service pension. Seriously and terminally ill, he risked returning to spend the last days of his life with his family, but was arrested for the last time. A German judge found that he was too ill to go to prison, so he was allowed to remain under the guardianship of a son. On 13 February 1997, he died in the northern German district of Molfsee, where he was denied the right to a funeral.

Wilhem Stäglich, the judge who demanded justice for Germany

During the months of July to September 1944, Wilhelm Stäglich was assigned to a detachment near Auschwitz as an air defence officer. Based in the town of Osiek, some nine kilometres south of the camp, he maintained contact with SS commanders and had access to the main camp facilities. After the war, he received a doctorate in law from the University of Göttingen in 1951. For years he worked as a financial judge in Hamburg, where he wrote numerous articles on legal and historical topics. After years of silence, outraged and emotionally disturbed by the stories about Auschwitz imposed on the public, which clashed head-on with his own experience, the German judge and historian decided to undertake an investigation. When he began to express publicly what he understood about Auschwitz, he faced several legal proceedings against him as a result of his articles. Finally, in 1974, a disciplinary hearing was held against Judge Stäglich and in 1975 he was forced to retire from the judiciary. The forced retirement was accompanied by a reduction of his pension for a period of five years. There followed a series of inquiries and raids on his home in an attempt to find out his background.

Instead of shrinking back, Stäglich continued to work on the issue and in 1979 published a landmark book for German revisionism: *Der Auschwitz-Mythos: Legende oder Wirklichkeit* (*The Auschwitz Myth: Legend or Reality*), a thorough and detailed work in which he critically and systematically examined documents, testimonies, confessions and accounts describing Auschwitz as a killing centre. Stäglich denied the existence of the gas chambers and denounced the documents proclaiming the Holocaust as forgeries. In 1980 the book was banned and seized nationwide by order of a Stuttgart court. On 11 March 1982, order no. 3176 of the "Bundesprüfstelle für jugendgefährdende Schriften" (Federal Department for Dangerous Writings for Youth), listed it as harmful material which should not be distributed to young readers. In 1983 the German police confiscated all unsold copies by order of the Federal Court of Justice. On 24 March 1983, ironically invoking a 1939 law enacted in Hitler's time, the dean's council of the University of Göttingen, after a cumbersome process, withdrew Wilhelm Stäglich's doctoral degree, which it had awarded him in 1951. A judicial-administrative appeal was rejected, as were his written protests in court, which were dismissed by the Constitutional Jury of the Federal Republic of Germany.

On 23 November 1988, Judge Stäglich, with commendable fortitude and aplomb, addressed a reproachful letter to Richard von Weizsäcker, President of the Federal Republic of Germany from 1984 to 1994, enclosing the *Leuchter Report*, which for the revisionist movement was the incontrovertible ratification of its theses. We consider this document worth reproducing. *Die Bauernschaft*, Thies Christophersen's journal, initially published the text, which was also reproduced in the autumn of 1990 by *The Journal of Historical Review*, from which we have taken and translated it:

"23 November 1988
The President of the Federal Republic
Richard von Weizsäcker
5300 Bonn

Mr President:
You have repeatedly made public pronouncements on matters relating to Germany's history in this century (the first time was on the occasion of your speech of 8 May 1945 before the West German Parliament). The content and style of his statements show that they are based on what is at least a biased perspective, namely that of the victors in the two world wars. In his pamphlet *On Weizsäcker's Speech of 8 May 1945* (J. Reiss Verlag, 8934 Grossaitingen, 1985), of which you are no doubt aware, the publicist Emil Maier-Dorn convincingly demonstrated this, providing many examples of the tendentious bias. Evidently unimpressed, in subsequent years you continued, even more stridently if possible, to accuse the German people at every opportunity. Finally, you even felt it necessary to support historians by your attendance at the 37th Historians' Conference in Bamberg, whose guidelines, so to speak, included dealing with the Auschwitz problem, which had been the subject of academic discussion for at least the last decade. Is it possible that you are unaware of Article 5, paragraph 3 of the Basic Law, which guarantees academic freedom and freedom of research? The applause for your completely partisan and unreserved comments from our enemies in the world wars and from the West German media, who evidently still follow your orders, should have reminded you of a maxim of Bismarck, who once remarked that when his enemies praised him, he had undoubtedly been wrong.
Unfortunately, Maier-Dorn had to omit from his pamphlet any commentary on his statements on the issue of the extermination of the Jews, since the official version of this issue is, in his words, legally protected in West Germany. Although this is not entirely correct, Maier-Dorn's assessment hits the nail on the head insofar as a politically pressured and therefore not independent judicial system manipulates the facts and the law in order to prosecute and, if not, harass those who doubt or even refute the annihilation of Jews in the alleged 'gas chambers' in the so-called 'extermination' camps. This phenomenon is undoubtedly unique in the history of justice.
Now, however, an event that occurred about six months ago has forced a rethinking of the official story. The defence in the trial of Ernst Zündel, a German-Canadian, in Toronto presented the testimony of the American gas chamber expert Fred A. Leuchter (as is known, gas chamber executions are still carried out in certain states of the USA), according to

whom those places in Auschwitz, Birkenau and Majdanek which were identified by alleged witnesses as gas chambers could not have functioned as such. This technical expertise, which has meanwhile become world famous, cannot in future be ignored by any serious historian who claims objective scholarship. In addition to the technology of the gas chambers, the Leuchter Report deals with the composition and modus operandi of the pesticide Zyklon-B, allegedly used to kill the Jews, as well as the technology in the crematoria. As early as 1979, on page 336 of my work *Der Auschwitz Mythos*, which was significantly confiscated on the orders of a court following instructions from above, I pointed out the urgent need to clarify these questions about the approach to the problem of extermination. Neither judges nor historians have bothered about this state of affairs, not to mention politicians, including yourself.

Unfortunately, the Leuchter Report, like everything else that can historically exonerate our nation, is officially ignored with a deathly silence. That is why I take the liberty of forwarding this important document to you in its original English, Mr. President, so that you may gain a clear understanding of things. This text only differs from the original report in the omission of the chemical analyses carried out by the American chemist Professor Roth, whom Leuchter involved in the analysis of the samples he had collected during his personal enquiries at those places in Auschwitz and Birkenau officially designated as 'gas chambers', in addition to samples taken in the former disinfection chambers for the purpose of comparison. These analyses are included only in summary form (on page 16) in the text of the Leuchter Report intended for public distribution. Mr. President, you can now familiarise yourself with the most up-to-date and authoritative research on this subject of such importance to our nation.

I dare say that from now on, even if you do not correct your past accusations, you will at least refrain from unjustifiably imposing guilt on our nation. The high office you hold requires, in accordance with the promise you made when you assumed it, that you act as the protector of the German nation, instead of stripping it of the last shred of political self-confidence. In your speeches you have repeatedly called for 'courage to face the truth', even though the 'truth' you proclaimed was already dubious because it was so one-sided. Now is the time to show your own courage to face the whole truth, and nothing but the truth, Mr. President! Otherwise you must later justifiably face reproaches for your hypocrisy.

With greetings from a citizen,
Wilhelm Stäglich".

Wilhem Stäglich died in 2006 at the age of ninety. In February 2015, Germar Rudolf published a corrected and slightly revised edition of his book by Castle Hill Publishers, the publishing house he founded, under the title *Auschwitz: A Judge Looks at the Evidence*. This publication proves the continuing value of Stäglich's work. Robert Faurisson, who admired the magistrate's honesty, wrote these words of respect and tribute: "Dr Wilhelm Stäglich, German judge and historian, has saved the honour of German judges and historians. He has lost everything, but not his honour".

Ernst Zündel, "Revisionist Dynamo", model of resistance

The time has now come to pay our modest tribute to Ernst Zündel, the indispensable man, the revisionist of distinction, who has had the courage and fortitude to stand undaunted throughout his life against the mighty tyrants who impose the falsification of history on the world. Perhaps that is why one of the nicknames he has justifiably been given for his stellar role is "revisionist dynamo". A sketch on his life and the milestones of his unequal struggle to redeem Germany before the world will help uninitiated readers to understand and appreciate the stature of this irreplaceable figure in the history of historical revisionism.

Born in Germany in 1939, he came to Canada in 1958 and married a Canadian woman named Janick Larouche. In 1961 he left Toronto and settled with his family in Montreal, where he set up a successful graphic arts business. Zündel considered communism "a threat to our civilisation", and in Canadian politics he became involved in anti-communist activities and campaigns. One of the figures who most influenced him during these years was Adrien Arkand, a French Canadian nationalist who spoke eight languages and was imprisoned for six years during the war. It was Arkand who provided books, articles and other texts that helped the young Zündel to develop intellectually. As mentioned above, Joseph Ginsburg, who published under the pseudonym J.C. Burg, was another essential person who had a profound influence on him during the 1960s. Burg went to Canada to record with Zündel and spent a month as a guest in his home. Their love for truth and justice led to mutual admiration. Burg called Zündel "a fighter for truth for his people". But Burg was only one of the important Jewish intellectuals whom Zündel asked to collaborate with him. He also made contact with Benjamin Freedman, the Jewish billionaire convert to Catholicism[14], and Rabbi Elmer Berger, president of the American Council

---

[14] Chapter I has already introduced Benjamin H. Freedman and discussed his famous letter to David Goldstein, edited under the title *Facts are facts*, in which he revealed the Khazar origin of Ashkenazi Jews. Freedman had personal relationships with Bernard Baruch, Woodrow Wilson, Franklin D. Roosevelt, Samuel Untermayer and other Jewish Zionist leaders, so he knew very well who was behind what he called *The Hidden Tyranny* in a booklet so titled. In 1961 Benjamin Freedman delivered at the Willard Hotel in Washington the famous speech warning America, later known as "A Jewish Defector Warns America". In it, he insisted that the Zionists and their co-religionists ruled America as if they were the absolute masters of the country and warned America's patriots of the imperative need to react.

for Judaism. Zündel travelled to New York in 1967 to meet Berger, who provided him with new knowledge and information about Zionism. Later, in one of the trials, Zündel explained his relationship with Rabbi Berger in this way:

> "... I went to New York and interviewed Rabbi Berger, with whom I have been in contact ever since. He was the person who, for the first time, made it very clear to me what the differences were between Zionism and Judaism. His particular philosophy of life and of the people he represents is that they are first and foremost Americans and Jews by religion, whereas Zionists are Jews first, at least that's how I understand it, which leads them in practice to the exclusion of anything else. They reside in different countries, but their only allegiance is to the principles of Zionism, the aims of Zionism, the policies of Zionism. He felt it was a dangerous ideology because it called into question in the eyes of public opinion the loyalty of Jews living in America or Canada."

In 1968 Zündel was denied citizenship without explanation. On 27 August 1968 he received a letter from the Canadian authorities stating: "the information on the basis of which the decision has been taken is confidential and it would not be in the general interest to disclose it". In 1969 Zündel and his family returned to Toronto, where he re-established his graphic arts company, which went on to publish books with large print runs and circulation, earning him substantial profits. This facilitated the publication of texts and interviews he had conducted with revisionist writers and historians such as Robert Faurisson and the aforementioned rabbi. Berger and Burg were not the only Jews who collaborated with Zündel in his titanic struggle to expose the falsifiers of history. Roger-Guy Dommergue Polacco de Menasce, a French professor of Jewish origin, philosopher, essayist and doctor of psychology, was another honest intellectual who influenced Ernst Zündel, with whom he corresponded for years. Zündel, who received texts from Roger-Guy Dommergue in which he stated unequivocally that the Holocaust was a historical lie, would eventually travel to France to record a long interview in Professor Dommergue's house.

Ernst Zündel and his wife separated in 1975, as Zündel refused to give up his "political activities", as she herself declared, which caused the family to feel uneasy and fearful. Nevertheless, the friendship and contact between them and their children was not broken. In these years, in 1978 to be precise, Zündel founded a small publishing company called Samisdat Publishers Ltd., which produced a series of interesting films to help spread the ideas of revisionism through various testimonies. These and other resistance activities undertaken by Ernst Zündel provoked prominent columnists such as Mark Bonokoski of the *Toronto Sun* and other columnists in league with Jewish leaders such as Ben Kayfetz, president of the Canadian Jewish

Congress, to launch a smear campaign to portray Ernst Zündel as a "neo-Nazi fanatic".

From this moment on, the German government's attacks were joined by those of Jewish organisations that sought to silence Zündel through their harassment in Canada and Germany. Accusations of "incitement to hatred" and "spreading false news" became commonplace. Various Jewish lobby groups put pressure on governments and used the media to provoke public outrage. It was in this context that the JDL (Jewish Defence League), the infamous FBI terrorist organisation, and "Anti-Racist Action", groups stepped up their harassment of Zundel with demonstrations in front of his home. These terrorists came to besiege him by patrolling the surrounding area with dogs and, in addition, by banging on the walls of the house, shining spotlights on the windows at night and threatening him with incessant phone calls.

On 22 November 1979, the *Toronto Sun* reported that the Ontario Attorney General was going to file hate speech charges against Samisdat Publishing Ltd. In response to this threat, Zündel mailed thousands of copies of Richard Harwood's *Did Six Million Really Die?* to Canadian lawyers, politicians, journalists, professors and priests. He asked them to evaluate the information contained in the book. In the accompanying text, he insisted that he was driven only by the search for truth and that Zionists and their sympathisers were using words like "racism" and "hate" to try to suppress his freedom.

The next major setback to Ernst Zündel's rights came from Germany. In January 1981, the Federal German government seized his postal bank account in Stuttgart, through which Zündel received numerous donations and handled payments for books and tapes. On 23 and 24 March 1981, the German Ministry of the Interior ordered one of the largest raids in German history: some two hundred private homes were raided for the purpose of seizing books and recordings labelled as "Nazi literature". Some ten thousand police officers and three hundred judges and prosecutors were mobilised for the operation. About this Zündel testified: "the police obtained the addresses of people who had helped me monetarily by violating German banking laws, taking the addresses of the donation receipts and raiding the homes of these people". Zündel was then charged with "agitation of the people", a crime in Germany.

In Canada, raids ordered by the German Interior Ministry were reported in the press, and Ernst Zündel was publicly accused of spreading "Nazi propaganda" in West Germany from Canada. On 31 May 1981, a mass demonstration by Jewish groups took place near Zündel's home in Toronto. The demonstration had been announced in Jewish media with the following statement: "Neo-Nazism in Canada: Why is Canada the export centre for Nazi propaganda? Why do hate-mongers freely spread the lie that there was no Holocaust? Why do war criminals move unpunished? Demonstration to protest against racism and hate speech." The organisers were the B'nai Brith Lodge of Canada and the Jewish Congress of Canada. The Jewish Defence League was not among the promoters, but its extremists were in the majority and stirred up a crowd of fifteen hundred people, who with cries of "Burn him! Kill him!" they tried to attack Zündel's house. Of course, the organisers did not try to contain them. Only the action of about 50 police officers who barricaded the house prevented further incidents. Zündel, who received bomb and death threats before and after the demonstration, recorded everything that happened and produced a tape entitled *C-120 Zionist Uprising! in* which one can hear the shouts calling for the storming and burning of the house and the killing of Zündel and all the inhabitants.

Against all odds, in unequal combat, Zündel continued to withstand all kinds of attacks. The next outrage was the ban on receiving mail. In July 1981, two months after the mass demonstration outside his home, Sabina Citron, a Zionist activist with the Holocaust Remembrance Association, complained to the post office that Zündel was spreading anti-Semitic literature and requested that his postal privileges be revoked. On 17 August 1981, postal inspector Gordon Holmes visited Zündel. He showed him some leaflets he had sent and Zündel, for his part, presented him with photos, texts and recordings of the May demonstration outside his home and explained that he was engaged in a mail campaign to expose his views through the service. Holmes' report to his superiors confirmed that Zündel had been cooperative throughout and had provided him with books and writings. Finally, on 13 November 1981, an Interim Prohibition Order was issued against Samisdat Publishers. It was argued that Zündel's company used the postal service to incite hatred.

Zündel requested that the Interim Prohibition Order be investigated by an Evaluation Commission to see if it violated the Canada Post Corporation Act. During the hearing, held on 22, 23 and 24 February and 11 and 12 March 1982, Toronto lawyer Ian Scott, representing the Canadian Civil Liberties Association, intervened on Zündel's behalf and successfully argued that the freedom of expression recognised in the Charter of Human Rights was being violated. In his statement, Zündel showed a tape entitled *German-Jewish Dialogue,* which Benjamin Freedman had given him permission to sell. Zündel boasted of his friendship with the Jewish billionaire, whom he had known for fifteen years and with whom he had spoken on many occasions. Proving that he did not hate Jews, Zündel gave the names of Jewish intellectuals he had interviewed who had given him permission to sell the tapes. Among others, he cited Haviv Schieber, the former mayor of Beersheba in Israel; Roger-Guy Domergue Polacco de Menasce, the Jewish professor at the Sorbonne; Rabbi Elmer Berger and Professor Israel Shahak, chairman of a human rights commission in Israel.

While in Canada the final opinion of the Evaluation Commission was awaited, despite a hysterical campaign in Germany and Canada about the importance of the seized material from Samisdat Publishers, on 26 August 1982 Zündel was acquitted in Germany by a district court in Stuttgart, which found that the texts in question were not hate literature. In addition, the court ordered the Federal German government to pay the legal costs of the proceedings and to return to Zündel the money seized from the accounts together with interest. Of course, the Canadian press remained silent and continued to describe Zündel as a "neo-Nazi" who sent "Nazi propaganda" to Germany. The German government reacted to the Stuttgart court ruling by refusing to renew his passport. Sarcastically, a law enacted by Hitler against Jewish refugees who published anti-Nazi materials in exile was used for this purpose.

In Canada, finally, on 18 October 1982, the Evaluation Commission recommended in its report to the Canadian government the revocation of the order suspending Ernst Zündel's postal rights. In accordance with this well-argued recommendation, Government Minister André Ouellet signed the revocation of the order on 15 November 1982, and Zündel's rights were reinstated, with the result that the Canada Post Corporation had to return numerous mailbags to him. All the cheques had expired, so that Zündel's business incurred almost ruinous losses. The Canadian Jewish Congress announced through Ben Kayfetz that they were appalled by the decision. Nevertheless, Jewish organisations immediately resumed their harassment and in 1983 launched a campaign to prosecute Zündel. The Holocaust Remembrance Association and Sabina Citron wrote to Ontario Attorney General Roy McMurtry asking him to prosecute Zündel for incitement to hatred under the Criminal Code. On 13 October 1983, the *Toronto Star* reported that B'nai Brith was demanding that Zündel be prosecuted for racial hatred.

Zündel's lawyer in Germany had meanwhile appealed the authorities' decision not to renew his client's passport. During the appeal proceedings in 1985, the lawyer was allowed in the presence of a court policeman to study, but not copy, in the government archives various documents used in the proceedings against Zündel. It was in this way that they learned that the Ministry of the Interior, which had no competence in passport matters, had been incessantly lobbying the Ministry of Foreign Affairs since 1980 to have Ernst Zündel's passport withdrawn. The documents showed that senior officials of the German Federal Intelligence Service had travelled to Ottawa in order to get the Canadian government to ban Zündel from using the postal system. The German files also indicated that Ben Kayfetz of the Jewish Congress of Canada had written to the German Consul General in Toronto requesting copies of Zündel materials they wished to examine, but Consul Koch initially refused. The German authorities apparently conceived the idea that if they succeeded in depriving Zündel of a passport, the Canadians would deport him. In November 1982, Consul Koch was prepared to proceed with the renewal of the passport; but, as the files examined by Zündel's lawyer show, the Ministry of the Interior put pressure on the Ministry of Foreign Affairs to send a directive to the Consul in Toronto to do the opposite, which he did. Zündel appealed the consul's decision not to renew his passport. On 9 May 1984, the Cologne Administrative Court decided that the Federal Republic of Germany was not obliged to renew the passport. A further appeal was then lodged with the Higher Administrative Court of North Rhine-Westphalia. It was in the course of this appeal that Zündel's lawyer was granted access to the government archives, which made it possible to establish that since 1980, the German authorities had been trying viciously to have Zündel deported.

Let us now turn to the pressure from Jewish organisations on the Canadian authorities to bring a case against Ernst Zündel, as it would eventually lead to the 1985 trial. The hate speech charge did not seem likely to succeed, so on 18 November 1983 Sabina Citron of the Holocaust Remembrance Association pressed for charges of "spreading false news" in publications such as *Did Six Million Really Die?* and *The West, War and Islam*. Sabina Citron's charges were admitted by the Crown, which meant that the state bore all the costs of prosecution on behalf of the Zionists. Thus began Zündel's nine-year legal battle to defend his civil rights.

On 9 September 1984, a few months before the start of the trial, a bomb exploded at the back of Zündel's house, damaging the garage and two cars. Shrapnel flew out and pieces were embedded in the bedroom wall of two Jewish neighbours. On 10 September, the Toronto newspaper *The Globe & Mail* reported, "A man phoned *The Globe & Mail* last night on behalf of a group he called the Jewish Defence League (JDL) People's Liberation Movement to claim responsibility for the bombing." No arrests were made and Zündel issued a press release denouncing the escalation of violence by the JDL and related groups against him, supported by certain media outlets. He demanded a police reaction against the terrorism of this Zionist organisation, since, he argued, "the police, politicians and the media were well aware of the JDL's reputation for arson, bombings, shootings, attacks and assassinations".

Every appearance of Ernst Zündel in connection with court summons was used by members of the JDL, who were waiting for him at the courthouse gates, to threaten, insult and assault those who accompanied him. As a result, they appeared wearing construction helmets to protect themselves. Both Zündel and his lawyer Lauren Marshall received phone calls in which they received death threats. The *Toronto Sun* quoted Marshall as saying: "In a trembling voice, she said she and her client and their families were harassed daily and received death threats. She later told reporters that in one phone call her seven-year-old daughter was told: 'If your mommy goes to court, we'll kill her. Zündel addressed an open letter to members of Parliament and the media, warning that the administration of justice in Canada was in danger if it allowed intimidation and attacks by Jewish mobs.

The trial began in January 1985 and lasted thirty-nine days. The Crown sought to prove the Holocaust through the intervention of experts such as Raul Hilberg and former inmates who testified as witnesses. Since we have already reviewed Hilberg's testimony under cross-examination by lawyer Doug Christie in the space devoted to the *Leuchter Report*, we will now add that among those called by Zündel's defence, in addition to the already well-known Faurisson and Christophersen, were, among others, Dr. William Lindsey, a chemist who had been head of research at the American chemical company Dupont; Dr. Russell Barton, who as a young man was a former researcher for the American chemical company Dupont; and Dr. Russell Barton, who as a young man was a former researcher for the American chemical company Dupont, a former researcher for the American chemical company Dupont. Russell Barton, who as a young doctor had attended the liberation of Bergen-Belsen; Frank Walus, an American of Polish origin falsely accused of being a Nazi criminal; Pierre Zündel, son of Ernst Zündel; and a hitherto unmentioned Swedish-born Austrian researcher Ditlieb Felderer, well known in revisionist circles, whose activities are worthy of recognition and will therefore have their own section below.[15]

On 28 February 1985 Zündel was convicted by a jury and on 25 March received a fifteen-month prison sentence, but was released on bail under strict conditions prohibiting him from writing, publishing or speaking publicly. Between these two dates, B'nai Brith, the Jewish Congress of Canada, the Holocaust Remembrance Association and the JDL organised a public and private campaign for the Canadian government to deport Zündel to Germany. The most prominent event was a demonstration of thousands of people, culminating in a rally. On 11 March 1985, the *Toronto Star* reported on the massive demonstration against Zündel, which culminated at Toronto's O'Keefe Centre. There, all the speakers demanded deportation amidst shouts and incessant cheers from the crowd. But not all Canadians were indifferent

---

[15] Ditlieb Felderer testified in both trials against Zündel. In 1988 he was the first witness called to testify by the defence and his collaboration with Zündel's team was outstanding. Felderer was a conspicuous Jehovah's Witness until he was expelled when he discovered that the extermination of the sect's members was a falsehood. He did research at the Jehovah's Witnesses' headquarters in New York, as well as in the archives in Toronto, in Switzerland and in Scandinavia. He succeeded in getting it acknowledged that the figure of 60,000 Jehovah's Witnesses killed by the Nazis was false, since only 203 of them had died in concentration camps. Although the New York leadership forbade members of the organisation to speak to Felderer, a subsequent yearbook published by Jehovah's Witnesses themselves acknowledged that Felderer's figure was correct. Ditlieb Felderer was among the first to denounce Anne Frank's diary as a forgery. In his famous book *Anne Frank's Diary, a Hoax* (1979), he exposed the fraud, which was later confirmed by other researchers. Felderer, relentlessly pursued by the henchmen of the Jewish lobby, was imprisoned several times in Sweden. Recently, he has publicly accused Johan Hirschfeldt, a Jewish judge in Sweden, of being responsible for acts of terrorism against him and his Filipino wife.

to the spectacle. On 21 March, four days before the verdict was announced, the *Toronto Sun* published a letter to the editor in which J. Thomas criticised the excesses of the demonstrators, whose demonstration of hatred he considered evident: "The spectacle of 4.The spectacle of 4,000 Jews, very well organised," Thomas wrote, "marching from City Hall to the O'Keefe Centre and the loquacious statements of numerous interveners, all symbolically shouting 'Barabbas, Barabbas, give us Barabbas,' was a frightful exhibition of mob rule.... The strident and continued demand that Zündel be deported far exceeds the bounds of justice and reveals itself as hatred of anyone who dares to question the power of a small minority of Canadians."

The *Toronto Sun* itself reported on 27 March 1985 that, following a government meeting, Flora MacDonald, Minister of Immigration, had instructed officials in her Department to begin proceedings to deport Zündel as soon as they received a report on his sentence. On 29 April 1985, without considering his legal rights of appeal, Ernst Zündel was ordered deported. On 30 April the *Toronto Star* reported in its pages the jubilation of B'nai Brith: "We are very pleased to see that the government has acted swiftly. We think it is the right procedure and the right decision". However, Ernst Zündel, a seasoned fighter, immediately appealed and the expulsion process was halted as a matter of law.

In 1987, Zündel won two very important victories that reaffirmed his will to resist at all costs. On 23 January 1987, the Ontario Court of Appeal, which had allowed the appeal against his conviction, ordered a retrial on the grounds that Judge Hugh Locke had acted in a biased and improper manner. Among other excesses, he had rejected various evidence presented by the defence and had shown the jury films about Nazi concentration camps in order to influence their decision. Half a year later came Zündel's second triumph: on 7 July 1987, the deportation order was invalidated on the grounds that it had been issued contrary to Canadian law.

And there was yet a third victory for Zündel in 1987 against Sabina Citron and the usual Jewish organisations. On a CBC Radio programme, Zündel publicly told the Zionist leader that "the Germans were innocent of the charge of genocide against the Jews". Further, addressing the host, David Shatsky, he recalled that at the January trial Sabina Citron had been unable to show any document proving that there was an extermination order "because there wasn't one". Citron told the press that she was stunned by Zündel's appearance on the programme. Shortly thereafter, they sued CBC Radio for damages. On 25 August 1987, Citron sued Zündel again for spreading "false news" on the radio show. The complaint was dismissed by the Crown on 18 September 1987 on the grounds that "Zündel's statements during the broadcast constituted an opinion that did not fall within the scope of the 'false news' section of the Criminal Code".

The second trial against Zündel for "spreading false news" finally began on 18 January 1988. It lasted sixty-one days and has gone down in revisionist history for the transcendent importance of the revelation of the *Leuchter Report*. Raul Hilberg declined to return to Canada to testify, no doubt so as not to be subjected again to cross-examination by lawyer Christie, who had cornered him in the first trial. The Crown presented seven witnesses. The defence called 23 to prove that there was no "fake news" in the book *Did Six Million Realy Die?* but that its contents were true. The most striking of the statements made by the witnesses presented by Zündel was, of course, that of Fred Leuchter, who was recognised by the presiding judge as an expert on the workings of the gas chambers. Leuchter explained his inspection work at Auschwitz, Birkenau and Majdanek and asserted that the alleged gas chambers could never have fulfilled the murderous function attributed to them. The *Leuchter Report*, submitted to the court as an illustrated exposition, was subsequently translated into numerous languages and widely distributed throughout the world. Among the defence witnesses was David Irving, a British historian of Jewish origin, who was convinced that the implications of the Report would be devastating for Holocaust historiography. Significantly, media coverage of the trial was almost non-existent compared to that of the first trial.

Despite all the evidence presented, Zündel was again convicted at the end of the trial and received a nine-month prison sentence. Again, Jewish organisations were quick to call for his deportation to Germany. Zündel, who in 1988 again requested the reasons for the rejection of his citizenship application without receiving a reply, again appealed the verdict to the Ontario Court of Appeal. Before the outcome of his appeal was known, the Consul General of Federal Germany, Dr Henning von Hassell, addressed several letters to the Ontario Court in which he falsely accused Zündel of having distributed leaflets to the crew of a German ship in the port of Toronto. According to the consul, the text of the leaflets had as its main theme Holocaust denial, which was a violation of his bail conditions.

On 5 February 1990, the Court of Appeal dismissed the appeal, so Ernst Zündel had to apply for leave to appeal to a higher court, the Supreme Court of Canada, which he did on 15 November 1990. At this point in the persecution, the legal battle of a single man against colossal enemies already had epic connotations. It took almost two years to hear the Supreme Court's decision, but it stood firm in its application of the law and on 27 August 1992 acquitted Zündel. The Court found that the freedom of expression protected by the Canadian Charter of Rights and Freedoms had been violated. Despite the media campaign against Zündel over the years, some editorialists eventually recognised the relevance of the Supreme Court's decision, as the right to freedom of expression of all Canadians was threatened under the guise of the "fake news" law.

As usual, organised Jewry in Canada went ballistic and did not accept the Supreme Court's verdict on Zündel's right to peacefully express his views on the "unquestionable" Holocaust. With the usual brazenness, this minority group in Canadian society arrogated to itself the right to lecture and criticise judges and the judicial system. By mid-September 1992, Jewish organisations had formed a large coalition, which included some gentile groups, and began a new campaign, including posters and advertisements. The September issue of the *Covenant,* B'nai Brith's monthly publication, featured a full-page photograph of Zündel on its front page with the words: "Arrest this man, says B'nai Brith: Coalition campaigns to bring new charges against Zündel". The accompanying article said they were going to fill the streets with thousands of posters made by the Human Rights League in order to put pressure on Ontario Attorney General Howard Hampton. The Holocaust Remembrance Association took out advertisements reading: "Zündel must not escape justice! Urgent Demonstration". Evidently, the justice referred to was not the justice in Canada, but his own. The rally was held on 4 October 1992, at which Sabina Citron called for a "declaration of war" on the Canadian legal system. In its 15 October 1992 edition, the *Canadian Jewish News* reproduced Sabina Citron's words verbatim, in which she urged everyone to "continually harass the lives of politicians. Zündel must be charged and deported. We have had enough and we will not stand for any more".

In the midst of this frenzied maelstrom of anti-Zündel hysteria, a young Jewish acquaintance, David Cole, came to his aid. Cole, who had returned from Auschwitz with the film footage discussed above, published a letter to Attorney General Howard Hampton in the *Kanada Kurier,* a newspaper of the ethnic German group in Canada. For its interest, it is reproduced in full, excerpted from *The Zündelsite*:

"Dear Mr. Hampton,

I am writing to you regarding the case of Ernst Zündel and your forthcoming decision on whether to bring new charges against him. I am a Jew, and I am also a Holocaust revisionist. I am not a crackpot who comes out from under the rocks to spread hatred and anti-Semitism, quite the contrary. I have been rationally explaining to people for years that there are two sides to the Holocaust story, and that based on the available evidence, the revisionist side is simply more credible. Revisionism has nothing to do with hatred and malevolence, but with objectivity and the attempt to discern truth from falsehood. If I were trying to harm Jews, it would mean that I am trying to harm my whole family. This would be a serious accusation against me.

I have been featured on a network television programme in the United States (the prime-time news programme '48 Hours' hosted by Dan Rather) and I have also debated the issue with survivors and 'experts' on a national talk show (the Montel Williams show sold to local repeaters). I have never been accused of being a racist, a Nazi or a Jew-hater (I am none of those things).

The purpose of this letter is to ask you to stop the legal persecution of Mr. Zündel. I am aware that there are pressure groups trying to convince you to do otherwise, and I also realise that it must be difficult for these people to separate their emotions from what is best for intellectual freedom in Canada. It would therefore be your job, as a representative of the people and the law, to look at things objectively and do what is best for both the people and the greatness of the law. How has the continued persecution of Mr. Zündel benefited the people of Canada, except as an example of how to waste tax money, and how has the gross double standard regarding the rights of Germans compared to the rights of other ethnic groups benefited the integrity of the law?

Please remember that the subject of the Holocaust does not only concern the Jews; the Germans were there too and, as part of their history, they have as much right to study it as the Jews. In future years, perhaps many years, perhaps only a few, when sanity has prevailed and the Holocaust can be reviewed objectively, and we see that the world as we know it does not disappear as a result, the hypocritical and miserable persecution of Ernst Zündel will in retrospect seem quite pointless and history will not look favourably on those who were involved in it.

Yours sincerely
David Cole"

For months, the media were used to put pressure on the authorities and to tighten the noose around Zündel, who, unwavering in his will to resist, even sent letters to London newspapers, the effect of which was the opposite of the desired one, provoking angry and irrational reactions from the Jewish communities. However, on 5 March 1993, for the umpteenth time, the Jewish organisations failed in their attempt to break the stubborn resistance of the "revisionist dynamo". The police forces involved in the investigation did not understand that he could be charged. The Hate Literature Section of the Ontario Provincial Police reported that no charges could be laid under the hate propaganda law, as Zündel's comments did not constitute the crime of hate speech. Zündel issued a press release reiterating his position:

> "The facts are: my material, my ideas, my appearances on radio and television do not generate anti-Semitic incidents, because they are not anti-Semitic. My material is trying to counter anti-German hate speech in the media, in films and in textbooks. There is a simple solution to the problem: stop telling untruths, half-truths and outright lies about Germans and their role in history and I won't have to retort with uncomfortable and unpopular truths. Simple! Remember: a lie does not become the truth just because it has been repeated millions of times."

Ernst Zündel's legal successes and his persistent fighting spirit could only further inflame his enemies, who saw how a single individual stood up to them without them being able to finish him off as usual. Sabina Citron and her cronies stepped up their campaign with all kinds of pressure that reached the highest levels of political power. Citron threatened again: "He must be indicted; if not, we will lose our respect for the law in Canada". A signature campaign was launched among university students: all student federations were asked to take a stand against Zündel, including the African Students' Association. Jewish agitators arrived on university campuses, lecturing young people with fierce diatribes. In addition, the call was extended to the gay, lesbian and bisexual community, women's centres and other social organisations. Further demonstrations were called in various cities and in May 1993 the Jewish Student Network organised a sit-in outside the Ontario Attorney General's building.

B'nai Brith and the Canadian Jewish Congress extended their tentacles and decided to use leftist and anarchist groups. The aim was to mobilise all sectors of Canadian society to finally put an end to "the largest international purveyor of Holocaust-denying materials". In the summer of 1993, Zündel launched an international shortwave programme via radio and satellite television. His programmes, entitled "The Voice of Freedom", touched on revisionist issues and general historical interest. These programmes expanded and gained access to public television in the United States, where Zündel's supporters and sympathisers sponsored the programme in various American communities.

On 24 October 1993, Zündel opted to apply for Canadian citizenship for the second time. Of course, if he had been granted citizenship at the time when the campaign against him was at its height, it would have been a humiliating defeat for his persecutors. The Department of Citizenship and Immigration made him aware that his activities constituted a threat to Canada's security. The Canadian Jewish Congress (CJC) and B'nai Brith put pressure on the government. The Jewish Masonic Lodge issued a statement in the *Montreal Gazette* on 28 July 1994 calling for his extradition to Germany instead of citizenship: "This man does not deserve the privilege of Canadian citizenship. Not only would it be an affront to Canada's minorities, but it would be tantamount to a message to those who spread hatred around the world that Canada is a haven for racism:"

A detailed account of the attacks on Zündel would take up too much space. Since what has been written gives a full picture of his titanic struggle, we will only list the most brutal ones. On 24 November 1993, a group called ARA (Anti-Racist Action), after calling on its supporters with hundreds of posters, gathered in front of Zündel's house to throw eggs and paint it. Since Zündel's house had police protection, the same group had months earlier set fire to the unprotected house of a friend named Gary Schipper. On 7 May

1995, however, Zündel's house was also burned down. An arsonist threw flammable liquid on the porch: the fire destroyed the front of the building and completely consumed the third floor. A JDL henchman named Kahane Chai claimed responsibility. Two weeks later, Zündel received a package that he found suspicious. He took it to the police, who found it to be a bomb containing shrapnel and nails. Once exploded, the device left a crater half a metre deep. Police confirmed that it would have killed anyone who opened the package and could have injured, if not killed, anyone within ninety metres of the explosion.

More interesting is the appearance of *The Zündelsite* on the Internet, also in 1995. Interested readers can find further information on this website. This burst into cyberspace was made possible thanks to the collaboration of his friends at "American Free Speech". In September 1995 Jamie McCarthy, co-webmaster of *The Nizkor Project*, a project of websites promoting the Holocaust and debunking revisionist arguments, sent an email to Zündel inviting him to connect or link the two sites so that users could have a view to determine who was telling the truth. McCarthy wrote: "Since you maintain, time and again, that 'truth needs no coercion', I trust you will not insult the intelligence of your readers by withholding an alternative point of view." Surely contrary to expectations, Zündel gratefully received the offer: "Thank you wholeheartedly for your proposal to make the internet the open forum in which we can discuss, in a sensible and civilised manner, what is of such importance to all of us." After explaining that since the early 1980s he had already offered a public debate to Canada's Jewish community, he said he "would be delighted if the offer was genuine and shared by the people who supported *The Nizkor Project*, as it was precisely what I had long been hoping for". It did not take long for the two sites to become connected (linked).

On 5 January 1996, Zündel invited the Simon Wiesenthal Centre to link its website to *The Zündelsite*, but received no response. Two days later, on 7 January, Zündel announced a global electronic debate on the Holocaust on his site. In preparation, the webmaster of *The Zündelsite* started uploading all texts and documents, including the *Leuchter Report* and *Did Six Million Really Die?* to the File Transfer Protocol (FTP). Almost immediately the files, even the restricted ones, were downloaded by someone unknown, which led Zündel to believe that there had been continuous surveillance of his site and his activities. In an editorial on the website he later asked: "Who has the money, the ability, the equipment and the staff to do that? Two days later, the Simon Wiesenthal Center sent hundreds of pages to internet providers and university presidents asking them to refuse to transmit messages promoting "racism, anti-Semitism, chaos and violence". *The Zündelsite* began to be attacked, its mail stolen, tampered with or destroyed. E-mail "bombs" even came from Russia. Falsified messages from Zündel began to circulate on the net in order to damage his reputation. On 25 January

1996, the media reported that German prosecutors were preparing charges of hate speech against those Internet providers in Germany who helped distribute Ernst Zündel's site. Zündel made a desperate call for help: "If there are any patriotic Internet experts anywhere who can help us defend ourselves through technical or legal means, please call. Surely we can use your help!"

Patriots or not, advocates of freedom of thought, regardless of whether or not they believed in the Holocaust, reacted against any attempt to censor the internet. At universities in the United States, supporters of free speech, understanding that freedom was at stake for all, began to set up electronic clones (called "mirror pages") on their own initiative. These electronic safe havens were set up at the universities of Stanford, Pennsylvania, Massachusetts, among others. Dean McCullagh, a graduate student at Carnegie Mellon University (CMU) wrote: "If the German government forces Deutsche Telekom to block access to the web servers of CMU, MIT (Massachusetts Institute of Technology) and Standford University, it will be cutting off communications with three of the most respected universities in the United States". One of the mirror pages contained this statement by the webmaster: "This is a mirror file of most of Zündel's revisionist page. My reasons for this mirror are not my agreement with Zündel's political ideas. I do not agree..., but I think that the questioning of any creed deserves some space. Therefore, I think Zündel's project is good for our society". On the battle to maintain *The Zündelsite*, it remains to add that the webmaster of the site was Ingrid Rimland, whom he met in January 1995. Born in Ukraine and naturalised US citizen, Rimland, a woman of great intellectual stature, has been an irreplaceable support for Zündel ever since.

After more than four decades in Canada, where two applications for citizenship were rejected, Ernst Zündel decided to settle in the United States, where Ingrid Rimland managed his website. In January 2000, they married in Tennessee, making Ingrid, who had also been married before, Zündel's second wife. Being married to an American citizen, one might have thought that he would finally be able to live without being constantly harassed, and so he was initially. For two years he lived peacefully in a mountainous region of East Tennessee, but on 5 February 2003 he was arrested at his home in the presence of his wife. Three Immigration and Naturalisation Service agents and two local agents handcuffed him and took him away. Thus began an ordeal that was to end in Germany seven years later, on 1 March 2010 to be exact.

Ingrid asked for help from her husband's friends and supporters to publicly denounce his arrest, as he had committed only a minor violation of immigration laws: he had allegedly failed a procedural hearing and was therefore technically illegal in the US. On 10 February 2003, Ingrid explained on a radio programme all the efforts and unsuccessful efforts she had made to have her husband released and expressed her fear that if Ernst was deported to Germany he could be imprisoned for years because it was a crime there to hold anti-Holocaust views. Mark Weber, director of the Institute for Historical Review, also participated in the programme at Ingrid's request. Weber was honoured to be a friend of Zündel, whom he described as a civil rights activist who had fought costly and endless battles in Canada for basic freedoms. Days later, on 14 February, it was reported in the newspapers that the US authorities planned to deport Zündel in the coming weeks, but it was unclear whether he would be sent to Germany or Canada. Finally, after two weeks behind bars, Ernst Zündel was deported to Canada on 19 February 2003.

Zündel applied for refugee status, but on 24 February 2003 the Department of Citizenship and Immigration Canada notified the Refugee Protection Division to suspend consideration of the application, as it was considering whether Ernst Zündel constituted a threat to national security. Finally, on 1 May 2003, the Canadian authorities issued a certification stating that Zündel could not remain in Canada for national security reasons. On 6 May, Zündel's lawyer Barbara Kulaszka filed a constitutional challenge in the Federal Court of Canada and subsequently challenged his detention in the Ontario Superior Court of Justice. All to no avail: on 21 January 2004, a magistrate ordered Zündel's continued detention on the grounds that he posed a danger to national security. On 1 March 2005, Ernst Zündel was deported to Germany, where he was arrested for publicly denying the Holocaust. A lifetime of patriotic struggle to defend the honour of his country and demand justice for Germany ended in the most depressing way. The Simon Wiesenthal Centre, the Canadian Jewish Congress, the Holocaust Remembrance Association, the Human Rights League (equivalent to the JDL in Canada) had finally won: Ernst Zündel was at the mercy of the judicial terrorism of his native country.

Locked up in Mannheim prison, Zündel, who had already spent more than two years incarcerated in Canada, was to face the bitterest years of his heroic life. Due to the conditions of prolonged solitary confinement, without being able to speak to other prisoners, Zündel was already suffering from depression when he entered the German prison. As Barbara Kulaszka complained in a submission to the UN Human Rights Committee, the most basic human rights were violated during the Canadian period of detention: she was not allowed to have a chair in her cell, whose lights were on 24 hours a day and dimmed only slightly at night; she was not allowed to take her natural herbs for arthritis and high blood pressure; her request to be seen by a dentist was refused; she was not allowed to exercise physically; she was not allowed to have a chair in her cell, whose lights were on 24 hours a day and dimmed only slightly at night; she was not allowed to take her natural herbs for arthritis and high blood pressure; her request to be seen by a dentist was refused; he could not exercise physically or even walk; the cold in the cell in winter forced him to cover himself with blankets and sheets, which were only changed every three months; he had no pillow; he could not wear shoes; the food was always cold and of poor quality. Barbara Kulaszka reported that Zündel had a lump in his chest that could be cancerous, but she had no right to a diagnosis.

On 29 June 2005, the Mannheim public prosecutor formally charged him with "inciting hatred". According to the text submitted by the prosecutor's office, some of Zündel's writings "condoned, denied or minimised" genocidal actions by the German regime that "denigrate the memory of the dead Jews." Thought criminals in Germany cannot plead not guilty. If the defendant's lawyer proclaims his client's innocence, he is in danger of being arrested for "Holocaust denial" or "hate speech". In the height of the absurdity of German judicial terror for thought crimes, the judge can prohibit the presentation of evidence in favour of the accused. Sylvia Stolz, Zündel's lawyer in Mannheim, was herself sentenced to three and a half years in prison for Holocaust denial during her client's defence and five years of disbarment. Since Sylvia Stolz is a major victim of the thought police in Germany, we will comment on the details of the trial below, where she will have her own space, for she has suffered and continues to suffer a disgraceful persecution for the honest practice of her profession, degrading for any judicial system worthy of the name.

For his part, Zündel insisted before the "court of justice" that the alleged murder of millions of Jews was a falsification of history. In his final words before the court, he called for an independent international commission to investigate the Holocaust and promised that if it was proven that Jews had been gassed, he would "call a press conference to apologise to the Jews, to the Israelis and to the world". Finally, two years after he was imprisoned in Germany, the Mannheim court convicted him on 14 February 2007 of incitement to racial hatred and Shoah (Holocaust) denial and sentenced him to five years in prison. In Canada, Jewish organisations that had persecuted him welcomed the court's ruling. Bernie Farber of the Jewish Congress said the sentence sent a strong message to the world and would serve to "comfort" Holocaust survivors.

When he was released from prison on 1 March 2010, exactly five years after his deportation, Ernst Zündel was seventy years old. His face was a poem of infinite sadness and pain. A disturbed look, undoubtedly the result of prolonged suffering, was visible in his visionary blue eyes, which, wide open, gazed raptly, illuminated by a strange, unsettling light, bordering on madness. A group of twenty people were waiting for him on the other side of the iron prison gates and took his first photos of him at liberty. They greeted him with applause, bouquets of flowers and shouts of "bravo". His first words were: "I am free again after seven years, three weeks, three prisons and three countries".

Germar Rudolf: persecution and destruction of an eminent scientist

In connection with the persecution of Germar Rudolf and revisionists in general, it should be known that the West German government, following the example of the Israeli parliament (Knesset), passed a law in 1985 according to which "denying the systematic annihilation of the majority of European Jews perpetrated by Nazi Germany" constitutes a criminal offence. That said, it can be said that the persecution of Germar Rudolf, about which we now know when and why it began, is the story of an infamy, the story of a blatant insult to intelligence, cynically consummated by the authorities of the Federal Republic of Germany. There is no better source of information on the life, work and persecution of this intellectual than *Germar Rudolf's Site*. There, the interested reader will find everything he could wish for and more. For example, the site contains all the essential and complementary documents of his case: reports, verdicts, asylum requests, expert statements, affidavits, lawsuits, appeals and other texts of various kinds. Most of what follows is therefore taken from this source, but also from Germar Rudolf's books and IHR publications.

Before recounting the drama of his ordeal, Rudolf reflects on the semantic nuances of the terms "prosecution" and "persecution". Prosecution is legal if it takes place in accordance with internationally recognised civil rights and freedoms; but it becomes persecution if these are not respected, as in his case. During the trial of Ernst Zündel, a magistrate ordered that Sylvia Stolz be replaced by a public defender while she was acting as counsel for her client. Stolz was sentenced to three and a half years' imprisonment and five years' disbarment for questioning the Holocaust in court. Naturally, a judicial system that not only prevents lawyers from working freely but also prosecutes and persecutes them does not meet international models or benchmarks. Section 130 of the German Criminal Code allows for the removal of civil rights of disruptive citizens, who are usually those who question the Holocaust or oppose multiculturalism. These undesirables commit an offence that can lead to five years' imprisonment.

Since we know that Germar Rudolf decided to flee to England to avoid prison, we will resume the story of his persecution there. It should first be recalled that, in addition to the indictment that brought him before the Stuttgart District Court, which sentenced him to fourteen months, three other indictments were in progress on charges brought against him. One of them concerned an exchange of correspondence with the Kraków Institute for Forensic Research, which Rudolf had approached, as discussed in the fourth part of the chapter, in order to clarify technical questions related to the Polish institution's research at Auschwitz. As a result, Rudolf's house was searched three times, and on each occasion books, files, correspondence and computers were seized, ruining his work and his scientific research. When in

March 1996 the Federal German Supreme Court confirmed the sentence of fourteen months imprisonment, Rudolf decided to leave Germany with his family. Initially they settled in southern Spain, but their stay was short-lived, for in May 1996 Rudolf was informed that the Spanish government was also planning to enact an anti-revisionist law. After consulting with his wife, he decided to settle with his family in the South East of England, where he hoped that freedom of thought and speech would be more than just talk. His contact was David Irving, who in 2006, as will be seen below, would also end up imprisoned in Austria.

Once in the UK, problems began as early as 1997: the *Telegraph* reported that German embassy officials in London were working on the extradition of Germar Rudolf, a fugitive from justice. In 1998 his wife began to feel uncomfortable with the new situation: life in exile was not fulfilling her expectations: she was homesick for her family and friends and could not find new friends. In addition to homesickness, the constant fear of extradition hung over her head like a sword of Damocles. She decided to leave her husband and return with her two children to Germany, where she began divorce proceedings against Germar, who was left alone in exile.

In June 1999 Rudolf, after a few moments of uncertainty at Heathrow airport, was able to travel to the United States to give a series of lectures there. It must have been on this occasion that he gauged the possibility of emigrating there. At the end of September he made his second trip to the United States and received an offer from a small publishing house called "Theses & Dissertation Press". In the autumn of 1999, a campaign against the "neo-Nazi fugitive" began in the British media, which led to a halt in his family's visits. Since he was no longer tied to England and in order to avoid persecution in Europe, he finally decided to emigrate to the USA, even though he did not have a "green card" (work permit). One of the most important events of his English period was the founding of a modest publishing company called "Castle Hill Publishers", now famous in revisionist circles.

Once in the United States, his hopes of obtaining the longed-for work permit were dashed in July 2000. To avoid problems with the immigration authorities, he settled temporarily in Rosarito, Baja California (Mexico), where he rented a small house near the home of Bradley Smith, the head of CODOH (Committee for Open Debate on the Holocaust). During the ten-week stay in Rosarito, a close friendship between the two revisionists was born. In August Rudolf learned from his mother that his parents had decided to disinherit him in favour of their children. Previously, his father had asked him to be sterilised so that he would no longer be able to procreate. On 29 August 2000, increasingly depressed, Germar Rudolf sent out a distress call to several friends. He finally decided to fly to New York via Iceland and in October 2000 he applied for political asylum in the United States. At the end of the month, he received a notice from the Immigration Service announcing that his application had been formally accepted and that he would have to attend an interview with Department officials at the end of November 2000. The interview took place on the 29th.

On 4 April 2001, a date of 24 September 2001 was set for an immigration court to hear the case. Rudolf therefore had almost half a year to prepare documents on the deterioration of civil rights in Germany and get them into the hands of a specialised lawyer. Days before the big day, the attacks of 11 September had occurred and the immigration judge, after a brief discussion, decided to postpone the hearing until 18 March 2002. The asylum application process thus dragged on and on for years. In the meantime, Rudolf married a US citizen named Jennifer in 2004 and applied to have his immigration status upgraded or changed to permanent resident status. At the end of 2004, the US Immigration Service informed him that his application had been rejected and shortly thereafter he was informed that he was not eligible to file a petition for permanent residence because of his marriage. Consequently, Germar Rudolf filed an appeal with the Federal Court in Atlanta. In early 2005, he became the father of a baby girl.

Despite the fact that the Immigration Service had said that he was not eligible for permanent residence because he was married to a US citizen, almost a year later, on 19 October 2005, the couple was summoned by the Immigration and Naturalisation Service for an interview. It was supposedly intended to verify that the marriage was "bona fide" (genuine, in good faith). The couple confidently went to the appointment with their baby in the pram. Within seconds of returning the certificate of recognition, Rudolf was told by two officials that he was under arrest. The reason for this arbitrary decision was his failure to keep an appointment that was supposed to have taken place five months earlier. Rudolf's lawyer tried to convince the officers that the arrest was unjustified and the police officer seemed willing to accept the arguments, but claimed he needed to consult with someone in Washington. After an hour of phone calls back and forth, the order was given from Washington for the arrest to be finalised and for deportation to Germany to begin without further ado. With shackles on his hands and feet, Rudolf was added to a chain of criminals being taken to the Kenosha County Jail. There he awaited deportation. According to the identification bracelet he was given at the jail, he was the only inmate in the entire facility who was not a criminal, a fact that surprised guards and prisoners alike.

Neither his marriage nor the clear evidence that he was politically persecuted by legal publications in the United States were sufficient considerations for the Federal Court in Atlanta to prevent his deportation. It should be noted that Rudolf had filed an appeal with the Atlanta Federal Court against the decision to deny him the right to asylum and that the decision had not yet been rendered and was therefore still pending. Although the Fifth Amendment to the Constitution guarantees due process for all persons - not just US citizens - present on US soil, the Federal Court rejected the request to postpone deportation until a final decision on the asylum claim had been made. The Supreme Court did not even bother to consider an emergency claim, which was dismissed without explanation. The question Germar Rudolf asks himself is: "What is the point of an application for political asylum, if the government deports the applicant before the court examining the case has decided whether there are grounds for granting it?"

On 14 November 2005 Germar Rudolf was deported to Germany. He was immediately arrested to serve his outstanding sentence of fourteen months and transferred to Stuttgart prison, where he was informed that new proceedings had been initiated against him for his publications in England and the United States. It is incomprehensible how the German Criminal Code can be applied to activities carried out in other countries where they are perfectly legal. Thus, the new trial against Rudolf began in Mannheim on 15 November 2006. Accused of "inciting the masses", which theoretically would have been done through the publication of the results of his historical research, summarised in the book *Lectures on the Holocaust* (2005), Rudolf was sentenced in February 2007 to 30 months in prison. According to the prosecution, the aforementioned book was the main reason for the new conviction, since all reprehensible opinions were set out in it in an exemplary manner.

Germar Rudolf published in 2012, now legally residing in the United States, the book *Resistance is Obligatory*, which contains the presentation he made in his defence before the Mannheim District Court. All motions submitted by the defence team of lawyers to prove that their defendant's writings were of a scientific nature and therefore protected by the German constitution were rejected by the court, which also prohibited academics willing to testify on the scholarly nature of Rudolf's texts from testifying. During the trial, Rudolf's defence lawyers were prohibited from making submissions in support of their client's views under threat of prosecution.

Faced with this Kafkaesque situation, Germar Rudolf gave a speech to the court that lasted for seven full sessions. For days on end, Rudolf brilliantly presented in a perfectly structured text a dissertation on what science is and how its manifestations can be recognised. Furthermore, although jurisprudence was not one of his specific fields of expertise, he demonstrated that German laws designed to repress peaceful dissidents are unconstitutional and violate human rights. It explained in detail why it is everyone's obligation to nonviolently resist a state that throws peaceful dissenters into dungeons. The Mannheim court did not bat an eyelid and, in addition to sentencing him to thirty months in prison, ordered all copies of *Lectures on the Holocaust* to be confiscated and burned under police supervision.

We will now look at some faint glimpses of this defence speech by Germar Rudolf, the text of which forms the core content of the book *Resistance is Obligatory*. Rudolf tried to publish his dissertation in court while serving his sentence, which prompted a new criminal investigation by the prosecutor's office. On 10 August 2007, already months after the end of the trial, the Mannheim court issued a warrant to search Rudolf's cell for documents showing that he was in the process of publishing his defence speech. On 25 September 2007, he was visited by several Mannheim police officers who confiscated all the documents he had used during the trial. The reasons given to him were that his plans to publish the speech were once again evidence of his intention to disseminate the contents of *Lectures on the Holocaust*, for which he was serving a sentence. He was made aware that he could incite the masses with the use of adjectives such as "alleged", "pretended", "supposed" or "claimed".

Faced with the evidence that few lawyers were willing to take on his defence for fear of being charged, and convinced that those who would take the risk would try to convince him during the trial to recant, which was tantamount to hiring them to waste time and money, Germar Rudolf decided to approach the trial as an opportunity to expose the Kafkaesque legal conditions prevailing in the Federal Republic of Germany. His intention was to write a book after the trial was over. For seven sessions, Rudolf delivered a lengthy speech that was exhausting for the judges, for the audience and for himself. Aware of this, Rudolf writes: "I prepared these lectures not primarily for the listeners, but rather for posterity and for the whole world, for you, dear reader, who are now holding the book in your hands". For this to be possible, Rudolf acknowledges that it depended on the judges, despite their constraints, being rational enough to authorise such a defence, which they were. The presentation to the court began with a principled clarification of his position throughout the trial, headed "General remarks on my defence", which, because of its relevance, is reproduced in full:

> "1. Statements on historical matters shall be made only for the purpose of
> a. Explain and illustrate my personal development;
> b. Illustrate by examples the criteria of a scientific nature;
> c. Put the prosecutor's charges about my exposures in a broader context.
> 2. These statements are not made to back up my historical views with facts.
> 3. I will not formulate proposals asking the court to consider my historical theses for the following reasons:
> a. Policy: German courts are prohibited by superior orders from accepting such requests to present evidence. As stated in Article 97 of the German Basic Law. Judges are independent and subject only to the law'. Please excuse my sarcasm.
> b. Timeliness: Point a) above does not prohibit me from submitting proposals for evidence. However, since they would all be rejected, it would be a wasted effort. We will all be spared the waste of time and energy.

c. Of reciprocity: Since current law denies me the right to defend myself historically and on the basis of the facts, I deny my accusers the right to accuse me historically and on the basis of the facts, in accordance with the maxim of equality and reciprocity. Thus, I consider the historical allegations of the accusation to be non-existent.

d. Legal: In 1543, Nicolaus Copernicus wrote:

'If perchance there should be stupid speakers, who, together with those who are ignorant of everything about mathematics, should dare to make decisions in relation to such things, and by some page of the Law twisted in bad faith for their purposes, should dare to attack my work, they do not deserve the least importance, so much so that I despise their judgment as foolhardiness.'

No court in the world has the right or the competence to rule authoritatively on scientific questions. No Parliament in the world has the power to use criminal law to dogmatically prescribe answers to scientific questions. It would therefore be absurd for me as a publisher of science books to ask a court of to determine the validity of my published works. Only the scientific community is competent and authorised to do this".

Germar Rudolf, Stuttgart, 4 November 2006".

On the basis of this statement before the court that was to try him, Rudolf put together a coherent discourse arranged around four axes: scientific considerations, legal considerations, specific considerations, resistance to the state. On the first of these axes, he reviewed his academic training. The demonstration of scientific and technical knowledge was considerable: biochemistry, chemistry in electronics, nuclear chemistry, theoretical chemistry, quantum mechanics, organic and inorganic chemistry, physical chemistry, mathematics, were some of the optional subjects that he did not want to give up, until, overloaded with work, he ended up studying nuclear chemistry and electrochemistry in depth. Rudolf tried to make the court understand the importance of curiosity for any self-respecting scientist. When a state tries with all the means at its disposal to suppress certain research and declare its results illegal, "automatically," he told the judges, "it exposes itself to the suspicion that it is trying to conceal something extraordinarily interesting and important. Then no sincerely passionate scientist can resist any longer". Rudolf said he was convinced that the need to know the truth was part of human dignity.

As a contrast to the lack of scientific rigour and the desire to conceal the truth and impose lies, Rudolf brought up before the Mannheim court the study on the Auschwitz crematoria by the French pharmacist Jean-Claude Pressac, which appeared in 1993 and was constantly used by the media and official historians as a refutation of the revisionist theses. He denounced that at no time had Pressac had the capacity to confront, let alone refute, a single one of the revisionist arguments. Rudolf reminded the court that he and other researchers had analysed and criticised Pressac's work in a book published in 1996 (*Auschwitz: Nackte Fackten*). For the specific reason that our book, in contrast to Pressac's book," Rudolf reminded the judges, "complied with scientific procedure, the German government ordered it to be seized and destroyed and initiated a new criminal case against me. In his eagerness to contrast the attitude of the two, exterminationists and revisionists, Rudolf insisted that the attitude of any scientist worthy of the name is to examine any attempt at refutation and to discuss it rationally, as the revisionists do. He regretted that the official historiography and the German and international courts support their theses almost exclusively on witness statements instead of presenting documents and conclusive evidence, and deplored the attacks on researchers who ask for something more.

The judicial considerations in Rudolf's exposition take up half a hundred pages. Without being a lawyer, he demonstrated his ability to study and analyse the German judicial system, which he compared with the Soviet judicial system, using quotations from Alexander Solzhenitsyn's *Gulag Archipelago* to show that in both, political prisoners are treated as criminals. He acknowledged, however, that at least in Germany detainees are not tortured, for which he was grateful. The definition of a political prisoner and the progressive deterioration of civil rights in German law were addressed by criticising the heavy-handed application of certain articles of the Basic Law of the Federal Republic of Germany. "The present trial," he said, "is taking place only because the prosecutor alleges that a conflict has arisen between my scientific freedom and freedom of expression on the one hand and the human dignity of a particular group of the population on the other." Germar Rudolf insisted in court that the law recognises that there can be no conflict between the publication of the results of scientific research and human dignity, however much one might want to put the human dignity of a certain group above that of the rest of the citizenry. Of course, he did not accept the charge that he had violated the Youth Protection Act, through which freedom of expression in Germany is limited.

Of particular interest in the judicial remarks was the consideration of the arbitrary interpretation of certain terms systematically made by judges and prosecutors in Germany, "an illegitimate tactic," he said, "of immunisation against criticism. The expressions, taken from his own indictment, used to charge researchers, writers or publicists were: "incitement to hatred", "in a manner capable of disturbing public order". In relation to the writings, they are interpreted as "insulting", "maliciously disseminated to belittle", "denigrate" and/or "despise", and, among other things, "deny" historical facts or present them "knowingly untruthfully". On the latter assertion, Rudolf told the judges verbatim that the claim of consciously going against the truth "was the most absurd expression of German jurisprudence, which seriously thinks that it can determine historical truth and knowledge through verdicts. History - he added - cannot be treated in this way in courts of law". Rudolf insisted once again that it cannot be established that a piece of writing is "insulting", "contemptuous", "repudiatory", "defamatory", "denigrating" or "toxic to the mind" just because a reader subjectively interprets it in this way. His presentation on the dangerous arbitrariness of the terms used against dissidents in courts of law concluded with quotes from jurists such as Dr. Thomas Wandres and Dr. Florian Körber, who in different dissertations had expressed the opinion that Germar Rudolf's books should enjoy the protection of Germany's Basic Law, which protects freedom of speech and scientific research.

Dr. Körber had published in 2003 *Rechtsradikale Propaganda im Internet -Der Fall Töben* (*Radical right-wing propaganda on the Internet - the Töben case*), a monograph on an Australian revisionist, Dr. Töben, whom the German authorities would like to prosecute (his prosecution will be dealt with later). Rudolf quoted verbatim before the court several theses from Körber's work:

> "The protection of historical truth through the criminal code harbours the danger of removing or withdrawing parts of history from an essential social discussion.
> Despite its neutral wording, Section 130 III of the German Criminal Code grants problematic special protection to the Jewish part of the German population by means of a 'privileium odiosum'. There is a danger that, in the eyes of the people, one group appears to be more protected than the majority, which strengthens the perception of antipathy towards the protected group...".

After citing these and other theses, Rudolf endorsed before the court the views of Dr. Körber, who was in favour of the complete repeal of Section 130 of the Criminal Code, and supported the idea that "special protection" for Jews could end up being "counterproductive for them", which should be avoided. Rudolf ended this part of the speech on judicial considerations with these words:

> "What is certain is the fact that my writings and those I have published do not, if objectively considered, contain content that 'incites hatred', 'disparages or insults', etc., nor can they be considered to 'disturb the peace'. That the accusation uses such terms - for lack of any other explanation - only shows what it really intends: to shock, to create taboos and to ostracise me by making false assertions."

"Specific considerations" is the heading of the third major block of content in the defence speech before the court. In it, Rudolf referred to specific issues contained in the indictment, among which he alluded to his theoretical sympathies with National Socialism and, above all, to his famous book *Lectures on the Holocaust,* considered by all, including himself, to be his main work, in which, over five hundred pages, he offers readers a comprehensive overview of revisionist research and its results in relation to the Holocaust. After recalling that the indictment called for the seizure and destruction of the book, and after comparing this attitude to that of the Nazis themselves, he asked that, before handing the book over to the flames, the members of the court should at least be aware of its contents. To this end, he submitted a request that the book be read during the court proceedings. The court decided that the magistrates should read it in private, so the trial was interrupted for three weeks to allow the judges to read the book.

We will devote a few more lines to the fourth block of the speech, entitled "Resistance", which begins with quotes from various authors, including our own Ortega y Gasset and his work *La rebelión de las masas (The Rebellion of the Masses)*. Ortega warns that when one renounces a shared life based on culture, one returns to the everyday life of barbarism. In accordance with this idea, Rudolf said: "That you do not try to persuade me to change my mind with arguments, but on the contrary reject any discussion and try to send me to prison, is exactly this return to barbarism". He then singled out the German state as the main target of non-violent resistance, advocated among others by Gandhi, because it restricts the freedom of peaceful citizens from whom it claims to protect itself. Rudolf, drawing on texts by authoritative intellectuals, recalled the Cuban missile crisis, the Vietnam War, the attempt by NATO to deploy nuclear missiles on German soil and the social rejection of nuclear energy as examples of resistance and/or civil disobedience in the Federal Republic. "In the case of revisionism or in my case," he said, "disobedience or resistance is directed against an unconstitutional law and consists only in deliberately ignoring and violating this, and exclusively this, law." Rudolf turned to a quotation from the Basic Law, specifically Article 20 paragraph 4, to legitimise his right to resistance: "All Germans have the right to resist against anyone who tries to eliminate this order, if there is no other remedy." Hence, the accused eventually declared in court that he was in fact fulfilling his constitutional duty by resisting and fighting to reverse a situation in which the state is acting in an unjust and totalitarian manner.

Germar Rudolf ended this fourth part of his defence speech by completely rejecting any kind of violent resistance, because violence begets violence. He did, however, appeal to collectives and institutions capable of remedying the situation. In particular, he appealed to parliamentary and legal initiatives, social organisations, intellectuals, the media and the German people as a whole to demonstrate in defence of freedom of expression. With regard to the latter means of protesting against injustice, he noted that, unfortunately, the remedy through public protests was proving impossible, since in April 2006, while awaiting the start of his trial, a demonstration in Mannheim had been banned on the grounds that prohibited opinions could be expressed during the course of the demonstration. "Well, you know,"

Rudolf commented, "if it wasn't so deeply sad, one should really write a satire about it."

After seven days of gruelling sessions, it was time for Rudolf to formulate his own "Conclusion" before the judges. He began by recalling the principles he had upheld as a publisher and insisted that none of the books he had published denied human rights to others, proposed or justified it, which did not rule out that he had edited texts with which he disagreed. He claimed to have acted along the lines of an idea attributed to Voltaire, who would have written: "I detest what you say, but I will defend to the death your right to say it". It appears that the attribution of the quote to Voltaire is erroneous, as acknowledged in a footnote in *Resistance is Obligatory*. We will, however, take the opportunity to quote another thought also attributed to Voltaire, which Rudolf himself could perhaps have used: "To find out who dominates you, simply find out who you cannot criticise". On his vital need to express himself in freedom, we highlight this fragment of the Conclusion:

> "Professor Faurisson once said that he is like a bird whose nature is to sing. Even if he were locked up in a cage, he would still sing. And this is also my way of being. It is part of my character, my personality, yes, it is even in my genes that I cannot keep my mouth shut, that I have to express my opinion, in particular if I think I discover an injustice. In this case nothing will shut me up. Just as a black man can't help being black, I can't help speaking my mind. Punishing this is as unjust as punishing a black man for the fact that he is black".

Addressing the presiding judge, Matthias Schwab, he reminded him that a retired colleague of his, Günther Bertram, former president of the District Court, had expressed in an article in a legal weekly, *Neuen Juristischen Wochenschrift*, all the problems related to paragraph 130 of the Criminal Code. Rudolf read the text in full before the court, since, he said, it was an article written by an expert who "clearly emphasised the unconstitutional nature of the law under which he was being prosecuted." He expressed, however, his disagreement with Bertram's opinion on the Shoah, which according to the jurist justified the German taboo on Auschwitz, and also disagreed with the Federal Minister of the Interior, Wolfgang Schäuble, who had not only justified the taboo, but, unlike Bertram, had supported its judicial implementation. Schäuble, who was twice Minister of the Interior from April 1989 to October 1991 and from November 2005 to October 2009, was appointed Finance Minister of the Federal Republic of Germany by Angela Merkel on 28 October 2009, a position he still holds at the time of writing. Since he is a key figure in the economic policy of the European Union, it is of interest to know the text that Rudolf Schäuble quoted before the judges who were trying him, published in the *Frankfurter Allgemeine Zeitung* on 24 April 1996 in the context of an exchange with Ignatz Bubis, then president of the Central Council of Jews in Germany:

"With regard to whether lying about Auschwitz is a criminal act and with regard to the banning of National Socialist symbols, I will only say this: in an abstract place we could have wonderful discussions about whether it is nonsense or not, from a legal point of view, to repress the expression of opinions. Nevertheless, this is what must be done, because we are simply not acting in an abstract place, but we have had concrete historical experiences. I do not believe that these legal provisions will remain in force for all eternity; but here and now it is right to say, through laws that could be considered problematic from purely legal considerations: there are limits and barriers in this regard and this is where the joke ends."

Rudolf obviously found the text unacceptable and called it "absurd mental censorship". In order to highlight the pseudological nature of the reasoning, he used a text from his book *Kardinalfragen*, published in 1996, which he also read out to the judges:

"Now everyone knows: the persecution of revisionist historians does not take place for legal reasons, since laws created for the punishment of those who hold fastidious opinions can be qualified as problematic nonsense. On the contrary, some alleged 'historical experiences' must serve as an excuse so that an open debate on precisely those historical experiences can be outlawed. Or to put it another way:
Art. 1: The party is always right.
Art. 2: If ever the party is not right, Article 1 shall automatically apply".

After the appointment, Rudolf indignantly addressed the court to declare that "the imprisonment of dissident historians was not a problematic nonsense but an outright crime" and asked the judges to review the passages of the Criminal Code where the persecution of innocent people and unlawful imprisonment were mentioned. He then recalled that on 3 May 1993, after the publication of the *Rudolf Report*, the director of the Max Planck Institute, Dr. Arndt Simon, informed him of the following in a personal conversation:

"Every era has its taboos. Even we researchers have to respect the taboos of our time. We Germans must not touch this issue (the extermination of the Jews), others have to do this. We have to accept that we, Germans, have less rights than others".

Drawing parallels between his situation and that of Galileo Galilei occupied the final part of his speech. One was born in 1564, the other four hundred years later, in 1964. Neither was able to take his final university exam. Both had had two daughters and a son. Both were scientists and authors. In both cases the main work was a 500-page volume that had been banned, confiscated and burned for the same reason: to reject a dogma of their time that subverted the claim of infallibility of powerful groups. Both had been tried and convicted for denying the dogma and both had lost their freedom. Germar Rudolf's lengthy speech ended with the following words:

> "In my opinion this trial is not really about me and my books. This trial is a turning point. It will be decided here whether it will be possible in the future to maintain or regain a leading position in Germany on the intellectual, cultural and scientific level, or whether Germany will remain on a second- or third-rate level. It is up to you to decide. Therefore, all I can do at the end of my statement is to call upon you:
> Gentlemen, grant us freedom of thought!' (from Schiller in *Don Carlos*)
> And following Martin Luther, I must conclude:
> I say all this; I can't do anything else, so help me God!'
> Thank you for your attention.

After forty-four months in prison, Germar Rudolf was released on 5 July 2009. When, in 2011, he was finally granted a "green card", the unrestricted permission to join his family in the United States, Rudolf was able to publish *Resistance is Obligatory* there.

Horst Mahler, from radical leftist to Holocaust denier

The case of lawyer Horst Mahler is, like those of Zündel and Rudolf, extraordinary in itself. Mahler began to be persecuted in 2003 for denouncing the hidden lie behind the attacks of 11 September 2001. Years later, in 2006, the first sentences for denying the systematic extermination of the Jews began. Now seventy-three years old, he was sentenced in 2009 to six years in prison, a sentence that was later extended to eleven years. While in prison, probably in 2010, Mahler married the much younger lawyer and close friend Sylvia Stolz, who was serving time for questioning the Holocaust while defending Ernst Zündel. Sick with diabetes, Horst Mahler's condition progressively worsened in prison due to lack of movement, poor nutrition and inadequate medical treatment, a fact denounced by his son in an open letter. On 29 June 2015, close to his eightieth birthday, he was hospitalised in critical condition with septicaemia, a severe infection that can spread throughout the body. To avoid the worst, his foot had to be amputated.

The son of a dentist, Horst Mahler was born in 1936 in Haynau/Schlesien. His father, a convinced National Socialist, committed suicide years after the Americans released him from captivity. With the head of the family gone, in 1949 his family settled in Berlin, where Mahler studied law at the Free University of Berlin. When he managed to set up on his own, he began defending defendants from the left-wing student movement and the extra-parliamentary opposition, APO (Außerparlamentarischen Opposition). In 1969 he defended Andreas Baader and Gudrun Ensslin, accused of setting fire to a department store. In the early 1970s, Horst Mahler was to become the father of the RAF (Red Army Faction), as it was apparently he who persuaded Baader and Ensslin to form a "guerrilla". In March 1970, the West Berlin District Court sentenced him to ten months in prison for his connection with riots outside the Axel Springer building in Berlin. He was granted parole, but in June he was ordered to pay a fine of 75,800 marks for damages to the Axel Springer publishing house. He then decided to flee to Jordan with Ulrike Meinhof, Gudrun Ensslin, Andreas Baader, who had escaped from prison with violence, and other sympathisers of the "Rote Armee Fraktion" (RAF), to join the Palestinian guerrillas. There they intended to train for the armed struggle. On 8 October 1970 Mahler was caught in a trap and arrested in Berlin's Charlottenburg district. He was accused of having planned and participated in the violent escape of Andreas Baader from prison.

It is clear that at this point in his life Horst Mahler had not discovered the true nature of communism and was at the antipodes of understanding the falsification of history and reality. In May 1972, the court trying him could not prove his involvement in Andreas Baader's escape from prison and acquitted him, but he remained imprisoned for other crimes. In October of the same year came the trial in which he was charged with organising and participating in a criminal organisation. On 26 February 1973, he was convicted of founding the RAF, also known as the Baader-Meinhof gang, and for his involvement in some of its violent actions. The sentence of twelve years' imprisonment was much discussed and considered inconsistent in legal circles. In July 1974, Mahler's licence to practise law was withdrawn.

It was in these stormy years that the scandal of the alleged suicide in their cells of the RAF leaders occurred. Andreas Baader, Gudrun Ensslin, Jan-Carl Raspe and Ulrike Meinhof had been arrested in 1972. Meinhof, who had testified at Horst Mahler's trial, faced very harsh conditions of imprisonment: after her arrest she spent 236 days in total isolation. After two years of preliminary hearings, she was sentenced to eight years in prison on 29 November 1974. On 19 August 1975 Meinhof, Baader, Ensslin and Raspe were jointly charged with four counts of murder, fifty-four counts of attempted murder and forming a criminal organisation. Before the trial was over, on 9 May 1976, U. Meinhof was found dead in her cell in Stammheim prison: she had allegedly hanged herself. At the request of her lawyer, an international enquiry in 1978 tried to get access to the first autopsy report, but the authorities refused. The international commission issued a report stating that "the initial claim that Meinhof had committed suicide had no basis in fact". On 18 October 1977, Andreas Baader and Jan-Carl Raspe had also been found dead in their cells from gunshot wounds, while Gudrun Ensslin had hanged herself by a rope made of speaker wire.

With this overview of Horst Mahler's circle of friends, we can now turn to the transformation that was to turn him into a stubborn Holocaust denier. In July 1979 Mahler was granted an open regime for the remainder of his sentence, and finally in August 1980, after ten years in prison, he was released on parole after condemning terrorism and publicly declaring that he repudiated the methods of the RAF. Interestingly, his lawyer was Gerhard Schröder, who later became Chancellor of Germany. In 1987, his application to be allowed to practise his profession again was rejected; however, again thanks to Schröder's good work, the matter was reconsidered in 1988 and his rights as a lawyer were reinstated.

Over the next ten years, Horst Mahler's thinking underwent profound transformations. Already in 1997 his political ideology had changed. One of the people who most influenced his evolution was Günter Rohrmoser. On 1 December 1997, at Rohrmoser's seventieth birthday celebration, Mahler gave a speech in which he denounced that Germany was an occupied country and that it had to free itself from debt slavery in order to re-establish its national identity. A year later he published an article in the weekly *Junge Freiheit* entitled "Zweite Steinzeit" (Second Stone Age), in which he explained his conversion to the "Völkisch" ideology (anti-materialistic romantic idealism based on the concepts of people, fatherland, blood and tradition). In 2000 he joined the National Democratic Party of Germany, NPD, of which he became an advocate.

By March 2001, he was already well identified with revisionist ideas. Proof of this is that he was among the participants in a conference entitled "Revisionism and Zionism", held in Beirut from 31 March to 3 April 2001. Horst Mahler's name appeared among speakers such as Robert Faurisson; Frederick Töben, PhD, director of the Adelaide Institute in Australia; Max Weber, director of the IHR; Henri Roques, author of the doctoral thesis on Gerstein's "confessions"; Oleg Platonov, Russian historian; and Roger Garaudy, the French philosopher who like Mahler came from the Marxist camp and who in 1998 had been sentenced by a Paris court to pay a fine of 45.45,000 for the publication of *The Founding Myths of the State of Israel*. Three of the most powerful Jewish organisations - the World Jewish Congress, the Andifamation League (ADL) and the Simon Wiesenthal Center - with the support of the US government and some members of Congress, lobbied the Lebanese government to ban the meeting. Predictably, the "friends" of freedom of speech and thought were successful and the Lebanese authorities announced nine days before the conference was due to start that the conference was cancelled.

As mentioned above, Mahler's persecution in Germany began because of his denunciation of the attacks of 11 September 2001. In 2003 he was charged with "disturbing the public order" and "inciting the people". Mahler testified in court that it was not true that Al-Qaeda had anything to do with the attacks. In 2004 he was charged with disseminating videos and other documents denying the Holocaust. In 2006 the German authorities withdrew his passport to prevent him from attending the "International

Conference for the Global Review of the Holocaust" in Tehran, which will be discussed further when we look at the persecution of Professor Faurisson. In 2007, new charges were brought against him as a result of a lengthy interview for *Vanity Fair* magazine on 4 October at the Kempinski Hotel at Munich airport. It was published on 1 November 2007 and the author of the interview, Michel Friedman, former vice-president of the Central Council of Jews in Germany, denounced Mahler on the grounds that he had greeted him with his arm raised in the Hitlerian manner and had shouted "Heil Hitler, Herr Friedman! Friedman portrayed the interviewee as a demented Nazi who inspired the German far right with his anti-Semitic theories and who had prevented the banning of the NPD when he was its lawyer. During the interview, Mahler told the Jewish journalist that the alleged extermination of the Jews in Auschwitz was a lie. As a result of Friedman's complaint, Mahler was sentenced to six months in prison without bail on 23 November 2007.

In February 2009, the international news agency Associated Press reported that Horst Mahler, a seventy-three-year-old neo-Nazi who in 1970 was the founder of the Red Army Faction, an extreme left-wing terrorist group, had been sentenced to six years in prison. He had been charged with publishing Holocaust denial videos on the internet and distributing CDs inciting anti-Jewish hatred and violence. Mahler, whose experience as a lawyer meant that he knew he could expect nothing from the court, wasted no time during the trial in trying to excuse himself or seek mitigation, but began his intervention by filing a lawsuit against himself. Upon hearing him, Judge Martin Rieder, who presided over the court in Munich, called his words "nationalistic squawking". According to the Associated Press, Judge Rieder accused him of "using the court to spread his message of hate." In his hour-long address, Mahler reaffirmed that "the Holocaust was the biggest lie in history" and had words of admiration for English Catholic Bishop Richard Williamson, who in a recent interview on Swedish television had denied the extermination of the Jews.

Rieder's indignation at Mahler's arrogance and defiance caused him to increase the sentence by one year over the statutory maximum of five years in his sentence of 21 February 2009. To justify himself, the judge explained that the defendant was "stubborn and impossible to re-educate". Of the verdict, the Simon Wiesenthal Center in Jerusalem said, "It reinforces the message that there is no tolerance for Holocaust denial and seriously reminds the courts that they must not allow themselves to be used by deniers to propagate their lies." Three weeks later, on 11 March 2009, the sentence was extended by four years and nine months by a court in Potsdam, which, considering Mahler's advanced age, amounted to a life sentence. Once again Mahler had denied the Holocaust and questioned many of the war crimes attributed to Germany.

Horst Mahler had chosen to bring charges against himself before the Munich court in order to set an example to the civil disobedience movement that was forming in Germany. Many of his supporters, however, understood that he would be more useful out of prison. "Why are you doing this?" they had asked him, unable to understand what they disapproved of. To answer them, Mahler managed to write a text for public opinion before his imprisonment. In it, which is considered a kind of political testament, he tried to make it clear that it was not only the right to express an opinion that was at stake, but also the right to survival:

> "If one realises, as I do, that the religion of the Holocaust is the main weapon for the moral and cultural destruction of the German nation, then it becomes clear that what is at stake here is nothing more and nothing less than the collective right to self-defence, i.e. Germany's right to survive. Survival affects everyone!
> Does the world really believe that we Germans will submissively allow ourselves to be destroyed as a People, that we will passively allow our national spirit to be extinguished without a fight? What jurists can argue that self-defence is a criminal act? As a People and as a collective entity we have a national and spiritual nature. The surest way to end Germany as a spiritual entity is to destroy our national soul and our identity, so that we will never know who or what we are. Destroying our national spirit is precisely the purpose of our enemy in demanding that we unquestioningly accept his Holocaust dogma and give up emphasising that his fantastic Holocaust never happened. There is no evidence of it! Once we grasp the fact that we face the threat of annihilation, we will have no doubt who our enemy is: it is the old nation-killer. If we understand this, we will no longer passively accept his lies and misrepresentations."

As can be seen, Mahler resolutely called for resistance as an existential necessity for Germany. Part of the text was devoted to explaining the years of armed struggle of the Rote Armee Fraktion (RAF). Mahler explained that he and his comrades intended then to fight against "the System" and that they believed what "the System" had taught them in schools about the Holocaust. He admits that they even "bought" the anti-German propaganda spread by the Americans. His realisation, it transpires from this writing, came in 2001 when he had to defend as a lawyer Frank Rennicke, a patriotic singer-songwriter who had been charged and convicted of Holocaust denial. As a result of taking on Rennicke's defence, he began an investigation that set him on the path to a new understanding of the historical facts. Let us look at another excerpt from Mahler's political testament:

> "It is clear that the victors or the victor of World War II (the only real victor was international Jewry) went to great lengths to ensure that the basis of Jewish domination, primarily the religious cult of the Holocaust, would be legally irrefutable. This was their goal when they created the Federal Republic, and it is clear that the Supreme Court long ago adopted

a judiciary designed to perpetuate the Holocaust. The mission to protect the Holocaust underlies both the Basic Law and the Federal Republic. This is the basis of Germany's domination by its enemies. German Foreign Minister Joschka Fischer explained this very clearly when he referred to the Holocaust and the support of Israel as the raison d'être of the Federal Republic."

In his writing, Mahler appealed to his compatriots to resist and to regain a sense of pride in being German. He reaffirmed his conviction that what he had done was the best he could do, and acknowledged that fighting alone and depending on himself, he could do nothing but "repeat the truth over and over again", since he had left a promise on the internet that he would "never cease to repeat this truth". As for the eleven years of imprisonment he was about to face, , he admitted that with his seventy-three years behind him anything could happen, a fact he assumed with a phrase from the Gospel of St. Matthew: "Whoever is not willing to take up his cross is not worthy of me." Mahler finally showed his hope in the power and strength of the Church. Despite lamenting that its leadership had been corrupted and undermined by the Jews, he was confident that "it could be the rock on which the ship of the Great Lie could crash and disappear." The text ended with the conviction that only truth would bring freedom:

> "I wanted to give an example. I have often said that ours is the easiest revolution that could ever be made. We need only a few thousand people to stand up and speak the truth clearly as Bishop Williamson has done and as I have tried to do, along with others who have suffered prosecution for speaking the truth and distributing Germar Rudolf's *Lectures on the Holocaust*. The final victory of the truth is inevitable, as is the defeat of the global Zionist empire."

Having examined the absolute control of nations and peoples through the economy, the media and co-opted politicians, and having seen what is happening in the courts of justice in Germany and other European countries, the idea of a revolution, the "easiest ever", of thousands of people shouting the truth does not seem right. It must be admitted that only by means of absolute power can the courts of a country be forced to proceed as they do in the Federal Republic of Germany. Whichever way you look at it, it is aberrant for a defendant to say in court that he is not lying, that he has proof that he is telling the truth, that he wants to show it, and for the judges to reply that they do not want to see this proof, because he has denied the Holocaust. The perversion reaches delirious heights when you consider that when the defence lawyer tries to prove that his client is telling the truth, he is warned that his actions are illegal, that he will be incapacitated and that he will go to jail. Specifically, the judge who removed Sylvia Stolz from Ernst Zündel's defence told her that he could understand a defendant behaving as Zündel did, but that it was then the lawyer's duty to tell his client that what he was doing was illegal. This is the monstrous formula for Holocaust justice.

Two years after Horst Mahler's imprisonment, Kevin Käther, a young German revisionist who wanted to follow his example, and his lawyer Wolfram Nahrath organised a demonstration outside the Brandenburg prison, some eighty kilometres from Berlin, where Mahler was incarcerated. The aim was to demand his release, that of Sylvia Stolz and the repeal of Article 130 of the Criminal Code. Käther, too, had pleaded guilty in court and, despite a 20-month sentence in 2010, had surprisingly been granted parole, . On 26 March 2011, around 300 people gathered in the prison car park, including revisionists who had travelled from France, Belgium, Great Britain, Austria, Switzerland, Japan and elsewhere in Germany.

Lawyer Nahrath addressed the demonstrators to let them know that the event was authorised from 12 noon until 4 p.m. He then read out a moving text in which he described Mahler as an idealist, a freedom fighter. He then read a moving text in which he described Mahler as an idealist, a freedom fighter. Wolfram Nahrath denounced the hypocrisy of so-called democracies, which condemn the repression of human rights in China while at the same time imprisoning their own dissidents for thought crimes. As an example of double standards, he recalled that while Horst Mahler was serving an inhuman sentence for a man of his age, the Nobel Peace Prize had been awarded to the Chinese dissident Liu Xiaobo. Dr Rigolf Hennig and Ursula Haverbeck, both of "Europäische Aktion", also spoke. Haverbeck, recently sentenced to ten months in prison despite being almost 90 years old, said with extraordinary lucidity that Germany "had been deeply wounded" and that the BRD (Bundesrepublik Deutschland) "was not the state of the German people". British politician Richard Edmonds spoke on behalf of a group of British revisionists and described what was happening not only in Germany but in the European Union as "scandalous" and "cynical". Lady Michèle Renouf, a well-known English revisionist model who runs the website *Jailing Opinions,* was the last to speak.

In January 2013 Horst Mahler had finished writing in prison a book that will never be published, but which can be read in German in PDF format, *Das Ende der Wanderschaft. Gedanken über Gilad Atzmon un die Judenheit (The End of the Walk. Reflections on Gilad Atzmon and Jewry).* The work had been born after reading a book sent to the prison by a friend, *The Wandering Who?,* a work published in 2011 by Gilad Atzmon, an anti-Zionist Jewish dissident exiled in London[16] . The book by Mahler consisted

---

[16] We could write a long article about Gilad Atzmon, for he deserves to be known and recognised. Born in Tel Aviv in 1963, after living through the war in Lebanon in 1982 as a Tsahal soldier, Atzmon became a friend of the Palestinian people and an activist for their cause. In 1994 he emigrated to the UK and became a British citizen in 2002. After studying philosophy at the University of Essex, he became known for his activities as a jazz saxophonist. Because of his criticism of Zionism and his revisionist views on the

of a series of historical considerations on the contents of Atzmon's book, to whom in the foreword dated 3 January 2013 he expressed his heartfelt thanks for his honesty and courage: "May God grant him long life, health and creative strength. The world needs Gilad Atzmon - and know: not only one Gilad Atzmon, but many Gilad Atzmons are needed. Two years later, on 11 June 2015, the Federal Department for Materials Harmful to Young People in Germany included Horst Mahler's book on the list of harmful books. Among the people who at 11.30 a.m. on 11 June appeared before the Department's board to argue that Mahler's work should not be banned were the parish priest Friedrich Bode and Gerard Menuhin, son of the famous Jewish-born violinist Yehudi Menuhin and author of *Tell the Truth and Shame the Devil*, in which he considers the Holocaust to be a huge historical lie.

At the end of June 2015, only a few days after the book was banned, Horst's son Axel Mahler wrote a letter to the parson Friedrich Bode to inform him that his father was in a critical condition in the ICU. Four years had passed since the demonstration in Brandenburg in favour of Horst Mahler, and the "revolution of thousands of people shouting out the truth" had still not taken place. Evidently, a few hundred meant nothing to the German authorities, who were also oblivious to the desperate prison situation of the revisionist dissident. Axel Mahler explained to Bode in his letter that his father's diabetes had not been properly treated and that he was suffering from a severe infection that made him fear for his life. Therefore, he said, they were considering "taking legal action against the judicial authorities for keeping him imprisoned".

On 4 July 2015, Ursula Haverbeck wrote to Prof. Dr. Andreas Voßkuhle of the German Supreme Court, demanding in a very stern and critical tone that he consider the suffering of the lawyer and philosopher Horst Mahler and that the German judiciary no longer submit to the dictates of Israel, represented by the "Zentralrates der Juden in Deutschland" (Central Council of Jews in Germany). With great courage and risk-taking, she referred to the Holocaust as "the biggest and most persistent lie in history" and wrote: "Eine Untat ohne Tatort ist keine Tatsache" (A crime without a crime scene is not a reality). Ursula Haverbeck concluded by pleading for swift action before it was too late. On 14 July 2015, the press reported that

---

Holocaust, he is considered an anti-Semite and many of his Zionist enemies accuse him of being "a Jew who hates himself for being Jewish". His discography now consists of more than a dozen titles, including the CD *Exile*, released in 2004 and considered album of the year by the BBC. It is a moving work in which almost all the tracks, including *Jenin*, *Al Quds* and *Land of Canaan*, refer to the suffering of the Palestinian people. Two Palestinians, musician Dhafer Youssef and singer Reem Kelani, collaborated with Gilad Atzmon on this album. Before publishing *The Wandering Who*, Atzmon had already written two other books. The present work is an investigation of contemporary Jewish identity politics and ideology. Among the many topics critically examined are the hatred of Jewish racists towards gentiles and the role played by the religion of the Holocaust.

Horst Mahler's left foot had been amputated and that he was in a stable condition after the operation. After the operation, Mahler remained incarcerated. Increasingly distressed, in October 2015 he finally decided to ask for help in a desperate note:

> "Dear friends, for a long time I have doubted whether I should ask for help. But now my life is in danger. My left leg has been amputated and the doctors are trying to prevent further amputations. Finally, a lawyer has agreed to defend me in court. However, since I am financially ruined, I cannot afford it. Moreover, the implementation of my parole has to be financed. If I were to get out of prison, some renovations to my house would be necessary to allow for the life of an invalid.
> Please help! Thank you in advance!
> Horst Mahler."

A few days after the publication of this petition, on 6 October 2015 some media outlets published the news that Horst Mahler, who was about to turn eighty, had been released from Brandenburg prison, where he had spent almost seven years incarcerated for a thought crime.

Sylvia Stolz, the uncompromising lawyer

What happened to the lawyer Sylvia Stolz has become clearer as we have narrated the vicissitudes of Zündel and Mahler. In any case, what happened to this brave woman is worthy of a proper place in our *Outlaw History*. We shall begin her unhappy "adventure" in December 2005, when she was a defence lawyer in the trial of Dr. Rigolf Hennig, a medical colonel in the reserves accused of having disparaged the "Bundesrepublik" in the newspaper *Reichsboten*, which he himself published. Hennig was accused of denying the legitimacy of the Federal Republic. On Monday, 12 December, prosecutor Vogel arrogantly threatened a defence lawyer, Sylvia Stolz. Vogel warned her that if she continued with her line of defence, she would also be charged with incitement and contempt for the "Bundesrepublik" and that he would not hesitate to prosecute her. Instead of being intimidated, the lawyer expressed gratitude to Vogel because, she told him, "by his attitude he was reinforcing his thesis that the trial was a show trial". Stolz expressed her opinion that it was not German law that was being applied, but the will of a foreign ruling power.

In the course of the trial, which lasted until almost the end of December 2005, Sylvia Stolz demonstrated commendable competence, citing texts by Jewish intellectuals such as Harold Pinter, who had just been awarded the Nobel Prize for literature, and Gilad Atzmon, whom we introduced earlier. Atzmon had just given a lecture in Bochum on 2 December 2005, , in which he had publicly stated that the history of the

Second World War and the Holocaust was "an absolute falsification initiated by the Americans and the Zionists". Stolz also quoted texts from Germar Rudolf's *Lectures on the Holocaust* and predicted that this work would "nip the Holocaust religion in the bud". In the end, Dr. Hennig was sentenced to six months in prison for denigrating the Federal Republic.

Almost simultaneously with the trial of medical colonel Rigolf Hennig, the Mannheim court that was to try Ernst Zündel had already begun preparatory preliminary hearings. Sylvia Stolz, whose experience and expertise in matters of nationalism and the persecution of revisionists were well known, was part of the team of lawyers chosen to defend Zündel, which also included Jürgen Rieger and the Austrian Herbert Schaller. Sylvia Stolz was assisted by the lawyer Horst Mahler. The first hearing took place on Tuesday, 8 November 2005. More than thirty journalists and about eighty Zündel supporters, some from Canada, France, the UK and Switzerland, gathered at the Mannheim courthouse, famous for its anti-revisionist fervour.

As soon as he had pronounced the name, date of birth, profession and address of the accused, the presiding judge, Ulrich Meinerzhagen, proceeded to attack the defence team. He read out the decision of a local Berlin court prohibiting Horst Mahler from practising his profession. Meinerzhagen quoted at length from Mahler's revisionist statements and comments relating to the Jewish question and the Reich. He then demanded that he be replaced as assistant to lawyer Stolz, who immediately pointed out that there was no reason. The judge insisted that he understood Mahler's influence on the defence to be considerable, to which Stolz replied that it was up to him to determine which writings he would use in his defence and that this was all his responsibility. The judge threatened to forcibly remove Mahler and detain him for a day. Lawyer Rieger then intervened to tell the judge that such attacks on the defence did not occur even in the Gulag. Sylvia Stolz insisted that she would not give up the assistance of lawyer Mahler; but without further words the judge ordered the policemen to take him away. Seeing that she could do no more, Stolz opted to take the decision to remove her assistant herself, which made it possible for her to sit in the audience, which was clearly shocked. Meinerzhagen then threatened to clear the room.

Further intimidating warnings for the team of lawyers followed: the presiding judge made it clear that any "incitement to hatred" would be vigorously dealt with and directly threatened the lawyers with the application of paragraph 130 of the Criminal Code. He then pointed out that he would not listen to "pseudo-scientific views, since the Holocaust was a historically verified fact". This statement provoked uproar and laughter among the audience. It did not end there, as Judge Meinerzhagen was just getting warmed up. He immediately went back on the attack and said that he was not sure that Sylvia Stolz was suitable for Zündel's defence, as she would probably end up being guilty of the violation of paragraph 130. Zündel made it clear that he wished to be represented by Ms. Stolz. The court then decided to adjourn to deliberate on the matter.

After deliberation, the court annulled the appointment of Stolz as Zündel's first lawyer. Dr. Meinerzhagen then added that Jürgen Rieger was not a suitable lawyer for the defendant either, since his revisionist views were well known and it was to be feared that he might proceed inappropriately in this matter. In order to give the entire defence team its share, the judge then turned to Dr. Schaller, whom he also considered unsuitable because of his age, which did not guarantee his suitability for the job. It became clear to everyone that the presiding judge intended to eliminate Ernst Zündel's brilliant team of lawyers in order to appoint others of his own choice. Naturally, the lawyers tried not to be intimidated. After Sylvia Stolz had been reproved as Zündel's lead counsel, Judge Meinerzhagen asked how the defendant was going to settle the case. Zündel declared that he would dispense with his third lawyer of choice (Ludwig Bock, who was not attending the hearing) and Sylvia Stolz would take his place[17]. On this occasion, the lunch break served as a pretext for interrupting the session.

In the afternoon, lawyer Rieger read a text in which he asked the court to abandon the discriminatory attitude. This was followed by Sylvia Stolz, who stated that the defence was being publicly threatened not to say anything forbidden by the court and that this was an outrage that could only be the result of a sick mind. Stolz then requested that the public be excluded from future sessions, arguing that the court was threatening to prosecute the defence for violation of paragraph 130 of the Criminal Code (this paragraph is only applicable when the "crime" is committed in public. By excluding the public, the defence intended to be able to express "forbidden thoughts" before the court without running the risk of prosecution). Counsel added that if the court wanted the trial to be public, the defence team would be in grave danger of prosecution. The court's response was to adjourn the proceedings until Tuesday 15 November 2005.

For the objective press and the public there was no doubt that presiding judge Meinerzhagen had tried to destroy Ernst Zündel's defence. Moreover, by threatening the lawyers before they had even begun their defence, the judge had violated basic rules of judicial procedure. Sylvia Stolz had developed a brilliant strategy, maintaining a calm attitude and a perfectly proper demeanour throughout. If the court decided that the trial should not be public, the judges would be confronted with the evidence contained in Germar Rudolf's *Lectures on the Holocaust* and Horst Mahler's request to "hear evidence on the Jewish question", which could be burdensome for the

---

[17] Since we are not lawyers, we are not competent to explain the functioning of German courts. It appears, in any case, that in regional courts German law requires the defendant to have a lawyer with specific powers authorised by the court and may have three more lawyers of his choice. In the case of the trial against Ernst Zündel, it was Sylvia Stolz who had these specific legal powers, which were overruled by the presiding judge.

court, which would have to explain why a secret trial was being held. In the event of an open trial, the defenders had been threatened with prosecution, thus embarrassing the Mannheim court in the eyes of public opinion and jurists around the world.

At 10.00 a.m. on 15 November 2005, a hundred or so supporters of Ernst Zündel had gathered outside the building. However, there were fewer journalists and only two cameras. At 10.40 a.m., access to the hall was granted and it was packed. Zündel's entrance was greeted with a round of applause. As soon as the judge appeared, he said he would tolerate neither applause nor rumours and warned that he had ordered the police to remove those who broke his rules and take their names. He then considered the claim that the court had adopted a discriminatory attitude to be unfounded and stated that there was no reason for the accused to have any doubts about the judges. Secondly, he corroborated his disapproval of Sylvia Stolz and repeated the reasons given in the previous session. Meinerzhagen insisted that Ms. Stolz was not suitable because she could not guarantee an orderly procedure, which would lead to conflicts between the defendant and the defence. The presiding judge rejected Ms. Stolz's request to exclude the public from the hearings. He stated that the public could only be excluded if it posed a threat, which was not the case. On the contrary, he claimed that it was the defence that posed a threat to the trial because of its intention to incite the public. Meinerzhagen added that it was to be expected that, if the public were absent, the defence would make inciting applications and submissions. Without giving any choice, the magistrate's next move was to announce that he was suspending the trial, as the court had to replace Ms. Stolz and the new lawyer would need time to familiarise himself with the materials. In the meantime, the defendant should remain in prison, which he considered fair, given the magnitude of his crime. To top it all off, Dr. Meinerzhagen claimed that the trial had been adjourned because of the defence.

At this point Jürgen Rieger expressed his disagreement and stated that the judge had not informed the defence of his intention to suspend the court proceedings, which he was obliged to do. Rieger claimed that the defence had not had the opportunity to prepare a statement on this decision. The judge replied that the defence had indeed been informed, which was a blatant lie. After a procedural battle over what decisions to make, Sylvia Stolz found the time to ask the court to allow her to make a statement about her substitution; but Meinerzhagen replied that this was not appropriate. Stolz retorted by telling the judge that his attitude was improper and out of place. "The trial is adjourned," the judge insisted. "I haven't had a chance to make my statement," the lawyer complained. "I don't care! The trial is adjourned!"

In little more than an hour the presiding judge had settled the matter. Naturally, the public reacted with indignation and shouts of protest and disapproval were uttered, such as "this is a carnival", "scandal", and the like.

Outside the courtroom, Zündel's lawyers and close friends met to assess what had happened and came to the conclusion that the trial would resume in February or March 2006 and that the judge would pursue the defence as soon as he began his proceedings. These events coincided with Germar Rudolf's arrival at Frankfurt airport, where he was arrested and immediately taken to Stuttgart prison.

As the lawyers had predicted, the trial resumed in February 2006. On Thursday, the 15th, Ulrich Meinerzhagen rejected three defence motions to exclude himself on the grounds of biased or tendentious views. As for Sylvia Stolz, he threatened to charge her if she questioned the Holocaust. The session on the 16th saw a serious confrontation between Stolz and Meinerzhagen. The lawyer interrupted on several occasions and raised a battery of objections and new requests. He denied that she had insulted the court and tried to sabotage the trial, accusations made by the judge. Specifically, Meinerzhagen said she suspected that Stolz "intended to make the judicial process impossible by causing the trial to collapse". He further announced that he would file a complaint with the relevant bar association requesting that action be taken against her. Instead of submitting, Stolz replied that she was "not prepared to bend to his will" and, turning to the room full of Zündel supporters, accused Meinerzhagen of wanting to "gag" her. The situation became extremely tense when the lawyer ignored the judge's demand for an apology. Meinerzhagen fined three Zündel supporters for singing banned verses of Germany's national anthem and sent another to jail for four days for insulting him. Lawyer Ludwig Bock then intervened, telling the court that he needed to study the authorship of dozens of statements and texts, mostly from *The Zündelsite*, submitted by the prosecutors. The presiding judge adjourned the trial again for three weeks so that the lawyers could analyse the publications in *The Zündelsite*.

On 9 March 2006, the sessions began again and the confrontation that was to be the ruination of Sylvia Stolz and the end of her career as a lawyer finally took place. At the height of her outrage, Stolz declared the court "an instrument of foreign domination" and described Jews as "enemies of the people". The judge requested the withdrawal of Silvya Stolz from the trial and adjourned the hearing again. On 31 March, a higher court in Karlsruhe removed Sylvia Stolz from the case for her illegal obstruction of the proceedings "with the sole aim of sabotaging the trial and making it a farce". Despite this verdict, on 5 April, Stolz disregarded the Karlsruhe ruling, which she considered to be without legal force, and appeared at the Mannheim court of justice. Judge Meinerzhagen ordered her to leave the courtroom, but she refused to obey. Two female police officers had to force her out, at which point the lawyer shouted: "Resistance! The German people are revolting!" Some of Zündel's supporters also left the courtroom. For the umpteenth time, the presiding judge suspended the trial, which was not to resume until June 2006.

The sentence of three and a half years' imprisonment and five years' disqualification from practising her profession came in January 2008. Sylvia Stolz was convicted by a Mannheim court, which found that she had incited racial hatred during the defence of Ernst Zündel. The verdict stated that the defendant had denied the Holocaust and declared that the extermination of European Jews during World War II was "the biggest lie in history". Sylvia Stolz served her imprisonment in three different facilities. When three hundred people gathered on 26 March 2011 in front of the Brandenburg prison where Horst Mahler was serving his sentence, most of the banners showed the same solidarity for Sylvia Stolz, whose imminent release was eagerly awaited at the time.

When she left Aichach prison in Bavaria at 9.00 a.m. on Wednesday 13 April 2011, a large group of international freedom of expression lawyers and supporters from France, Italy and Great Britain were waiting for her at the main gate to celebrate her release with flowers and gifts. Among them was Michèle Renouf, who had once again travelled from England to show solidarity with the revisionist lawyer. Sylvia Stolz emerged to applause, laden with a large number of written documents, carefully accumulated and organised during her years of captivity. After loading the material into a van, they all went together to a nearby tavern, where Günter Deckert had reserved the main room for the celebration.

On 24 November 2012, twenty months after her release, Sylvia Stolz gave a lecture in Chur, capital of the Swiss canton of Graubünden, entitled in German: *Sprechverbot-Beweisverbot-Verteidigunsverbot. Die Wirklichkeit der Meinungsfreiheit* (*Prohibition of expression-prohibition of evidence-prohibition of legal defence. The reality of freedom of thought*). This was the 8th Conference of the "Anti-Zensur-Koalition" (AZK). The conference organiser, Ivo Sasek, introduced Sylvia Stolz as a person uniquely qualified to speak on the subject and referred to her experience of the trial of Ernst Zündel, his arrest in the court of justice and his conviction. The presentation ended with these words: "Welcome Sylvia Stolz. If you were not allowed to speak there, we will let you speak here. We trust that you know your limitations. I am sure you do.

After thanking Ivo Sasek and the audience of more than two thousand people for their warm welcome, Stolz delivered a well-structured, calm speech without reading at any point, appropriately seasoned with eloquent silences. His voice, extremely warm and as soft as a child's, maintained a calm and serene tone throughout his speech, which was rigorous in its legal terminology, extremely sensible and entirely convincing. The lecture, delivered in German, can be viewed on You Tube with English subtitles. Of course, for reasons of space we cannot reproduce it in its entirety, but we will give a few outlines. In her presentation, Sylvia Stolz gave the audience a very beautiful thought by Johann Gottfried von Herder, which in her opinion embodied the essence of all human beings: "To believe in truth, to feel beauty and to love what is good".

The principles that should govern the functioning of any court of law worthy of the name occupied the first part of the lecture: the rights of the accused and the obligations of the court to prevent his or her defencelessness and to establish the truth through evidence. In relation to the need to present evidence, he drew a comparison with the evidence that courts usually require in murder cases, i.e. where it took place, when it was committed, what weapons the criminal used, possible fingerprints, where the victim's body was found, forensic analysis to determine the cause of death, and so on. However, Stolz insisted, in none of the "Holocaust denial" cases has any of this specific evidence ever been proven or presented:

> "There are no details regarding the crime scene, the method of murder, the number of victims, the time period of the crimes, the perpetrators, the bodies. We have no physical traces of the murder. The testimonies do not specify, there are no documents or similar evidence. The intention to exterminate all or part of Jewry during the National Socialist regime has not been proven anywhere. There are no documents proving prior decisions, plans or orders. When there are trials of Holocaust deniers, we do not find these things specified. Nor do we find references to other verdicts in which these things are specified. This is the problem. As long as the court does not record the crime sites where the alleged mass killings are supposed to have taken place; as long as the court does not claim at least one specific piece of evidence; as long as this is the case, these mass murders simply cannot be proven."

At another point, Sylvia Stolz read out to the audience an embarrassing excerpt from the verdict of the Auschwitz trials that took place in Frankfurt. In it, the lawyer said ironically, one might expect some specification of details of the Holocaust. These are the words of the court:

> "The court lacks almost all the means of evidence of a normal murder trial, necessary to get a true picture of the facts at the time of the crime. There were no bodies of the victims, no autopsy reports, no expert reports on the causes and time of death, no evidence on the killers, on the murder weapons, etc. Verification of witness testimonies was only possible on rare occasions..... Therefore, in order to clarify the crimes of the defendants, the court relied almost exclusively on the testimony of witnesses...".

Drawing on her own experience, Stolz complained that, by contrast, when evidence was presented on behalf of a Holocaust denier and the court was asked to establish that such and such was true because it had been corroborated by expert reports, then the court would not admit the evidence and the lawyers were accused of Holocaust denial. Sylvia Stolz regretted that the European public knew nothing about the treatment of defendants, about the threats and punishments that lawyers suffered just for doing their job, and about the way in which the administration of justice in German courts was aborted. He gave as an example his own case, when a Bavarian court decided to withdraw his licence:

> "I presented evidence in relation to the alleged 'obviousness' of the Holocaust. Again the evidence was not admitted and the reason given was that the court, in the light of available books and photos, had no doubt about the 'obviousness' of the Holocaust. Both I and my lawyer asked the court to point out which books and which photos gave them such certainty as to the 'obviousness' of the Holocaust. These requests were rejected because: 'the Holocaust and the violent crimes of the National Socialists against the Jews were obvious'. Therefore, we were given no answer as to what materials formed the basis of the court's finding. All we got were general references to 'newspapers, radio and television, encyclopaedias, dictionaries and history books'."

After recalling the most disappointing moments of her experience with Judge Meinerzhagen during the trial against Ernst Zündel, Sylvia Stolz ended the lecture by returning to Herder's phrase with which she had begun her speech. These were her final words:

> "I will return now to the phrase with which I began this lecture. Believing in truth, feeling beauty and wanting what is good' implies the ability to identify and label lies, the ability to identify the inhuman, the ability to identify and qualify injustice. It also involves character traits, which is of particular importance at our age. The knowledge of our immortality, of our constancy and incorruptibility. With this character we should be able to shape a world for the many children who were here earlier today. A world in which we are allowed to tell the truth without punishment."

In January 2013, a Jewish lawyer from Bern, Daniel Kettiger, filed a criminal complaint against Sylvia Stolz with the public prosecutor's office in Graubünden. Kettiger accused Stolz of having violated Article 261 of the Swiss Criminal Code, which relates to a Swiss racial law. Ivo Sasek, the organiser of the AZK event, was also denounced by this lawyer, an uncompromising guardian of censorship. The fact that during the conference Stolz had said that the Holocaust had never been proven in a court of law because the evidence had never been presented was sufficient grounds for criminal charges to be brought against her. On 25 February 2015, a Munich court rejected the arguments of Sylvia Stolz and her lawyer Wolfram Nahrath on the right to exercise freedom of speech in Switzerland and sentenced the lawyer to twenty months in prison for the lecture given in Chur in November

2012. At the time of writing, she is still in prison. We hope, of course, that this admirable woman will regain the freedom so unjustly taken away from her for a second time.

Günter Deckert, a persistent symbol of freedom of expression

Günter Deckert, leader of the NPD (National Democratic Party of Germany), lost his job as a high school teacher in 1988 because of his political activism. In November 1990 he took part in an event to present Fred Leuchter, at which he declared that the Holocaust was a myth perpetrated by an exploitative group that was using a historical lie to muzzle Germany. In 1991, he also shared a table with historian David Irving at a lecture in Weinheim, Germany. These events led to a criminal complaint and in 1992 he was sentenced to one year in prison. Deckert appealed against the verdict and in March 1994 the Mannheim District Court, which at that time was not yet the court we have seen in the persecution of Ernst Zündel and Sylvia Stolz, ordered a retrial on the grounds that the lower court had failed to prove all the necessary facts.

In the summer of 1994, the trial began again, in which two of the three judges on the court, Wolfgang Müller and Rainer Orlet, had words of sympathy for Deckert. Müller described him as "an intelligent man of character", who acted out of deep convictions. For his part, Judge Rainer Orlet declared that Deckert had "expressed legitimate interests" in questioning the Jews' endless political and economic claims on Germany fifty years after the end of World War II. In a sixty-six-page report, Orlet recalled that while people in Germany were being persecuted for expressing opinions, "mass criminals of other nations remained unpunished." The judge added that Deckert was "not an anti-Semite" and that he had made a good impression on the court as a "responsible person of good character." Nevertheless, the court found Deckert guilty and upheld his one-year prison sentence, but he did not have to go to prison because he was given the opportunity to remain on probation as long as he did not reoffend.

As usual, the howls of protest from Jewish lobby groups were automatic. At the centre of the target was Judge Rainer Orlet, whose views were deemed to be Holocaust denialist. Justice Minister Thomas Schäuble was quick to acknowledge that the judge's statement was "a slap in the face of the victims of the Holocaust." On the other hand, the Association of German Judges considered it "a blunder". A parallel trial then began which was to lead to Judge Orlet's voluntary retirement, a decision he took to avoid forced removal from office. On 23 January 1995, Ulrich Maurer, the Baden-Württemberg parliamentary leader of the SPD (Social Democratic Party of Germany), called for Judge Orlet's dismissal for having written a scandalous verdict on Günter Deckert in June 1994. This disciplinary measure was the only way to remove Orlet from the 6th Grand Criminal Division of the

Mannheim District Court. Minister Schaüble had to listen to accusations from the CDU (Christian Democratic Union) of double standards and double standards.

On 9 March 1995, the *Berliner Zeitung* published a report that Judge Rainer Olmert himself could end up in the dock. The newspaper commented that the dismissal of Rainer Orlet before the German Constitutional Court would be the first case of the dismissal of a judge in the history of the Federal Republic of Germany. In addition to the voluntary retirement of the judge, the campaign led to the retrial of Günter Deckert in April. In December 1995, Deckert was sent to the Bruchsal Detention Centre in Baden-Wurttenberg with an effective two-year prison sentence for "dangerous political arson".

While serving this two-year sentence, Günter Deckert was again brought to trial because of a letter he wrote from prison to Michel Friedman, vice-president of the Central Council of Jews in Germany. He allegedly asked him to leave Germany. This letter led to a new charge of incitement to racial hatred. A new trial was held in Mannheim and on 12 April 1997 Deckert was sentenced to an additional two years and three months in prison. His lawyer, Ludwig Boch, was fined 9,000 marks for basing his defence on the idea that the Holocaust was a "legend" invented by Jews. David Irving was quick to write a protest text to *The Daily Telegraph*, declaring himself a friend of Deckert's and denouncing the ongoing assault on freedom of expression in Germany.

After spending two years behind bars, instead of being released, Deckert began serving his new sentence on 31 October 1997. The international outcry was barely visible to the public, although letters were received by German embassies in several countries calling for the release of political prisoner Günter Deckert. On 10 December 1998, for example, Rainer Dobbelstein, a senior German official in London, justified in a letter of reply to an outraged Londoner, Milton Ellis, that the tapping of Günter Deckert's correspondence was justified by law because of his extremist views.

In October 2000, the "dangerous neo-Nazi" was released from Bruchsal prison, where he had spent almost five years. Just when it seemed that the revisionist fighter was past the worst, in 2012, at the age of seventy-two, he was once again sentenced to prison. What was Günter Deckert's crime this time? In 2007 he had translated *Auschwitz* into German. *The First Gassings, Rumours and Reality*, a book by Carlo Mattogno published in 1992 in Italian and in 2002 in English. In 2008, on the orders of Mannheim prosecutor Grossmann, the thought police raided his house. It was the twelfth "special visit", as she told a friend in a letter of March 2012. They took her computer and two copies of Mattogno's book. In the summer of 2009, a court in Weinheim, the town where Deckert lived, accepted the indictment. The charges were "promotion and incitement of the public by means of Holocaust denial and defamation of the memory of the dead." On 28 July 2010 Deckert went to trial without a lawyer. A single judge sentenced him to four months, but granted him probation, to be put on probation for a period of three years, and a fine of 600 euros. In addition, he had to pay costs. Both public prosecutor Grossmann, who had asked for six months, and Deckert himself appealed the verdict. Once again, the case came before the famous Mannheim district court. The retrial began on 14 November 2011 and ended on 2 February 2012 with a verdict sentencing Deckert to six months in prison. In the aforementioned letter, Deckert explains the following to her friend:

> "The trial lasted so long because I changed my tactics to make the court understand why I was in favour of revisionism. I offered all the arguments and evidence that could be presented in court without being charged again. At first it seemed that Judge Roos was hesitant about the problem of convicting a person for publicising and disseminating a book. But in the end he seized on the suggestion of prosecutor Grossmann, who said that the possibility of accessing the book via the internet fulfilled the requirements of paragraph 130."

On 2 February 2012, the verdict was delivered and on 6 February the six-month prison sentence was announced. Upon receiving it, Deckert courageously declared: "A prison sentence will not force me to believe." He announced that he would appeal to the court in Karslruhe; but the appeal was dismissed. Finally, on 23 November 2012, the Mannheim public prosecutor's office informed him that at 3 p.m. on 17 December he was to enter prison. Deckert protested vehemently, as he wanted to spend Christmas with his family. For once, there was understanding, and his admission was postponed until 2 January 2013. This confirmed a shameful fact: with hardly anyone protesting and without the media denouncing it, an honest and decent person in Germany could be sentenced for translating a history book. Here are the words of Günter Deckert:

> "Friends, comrades and fighters for the truth about the history of World War II, the time has come! Although my constitutional appeal has not yet been decided, I must soon enter prison to serve my five-month sentence. I have to report to prison on 2 January 2013. My release will take place on 2 June.... 'What doesn't kill me makes me stronger!' With this thought in mind, my best regards and comradely loyalty to our families and our people. I wish everyone a very good 2013 full of success and the best possible health."

When Sylvia Stolz was released from Aichach prison on 13 April 2011, Günter Deckert had organised a celebratory meal for her in a Bavarian tavern. In February 2013, Stolz, who must surely have known that a Jewish lawyer had denounced her for her lecture in Switzerland, wanted to show solidarity with her friend and published a long article, the English translation of which could be *El terror de opinar (The terror of giving an opinion)*. In it, he broke down the text of the sentence and technically demonstrated all the inconsistencies of the legal process that had been followed against Deckert, whose defencelessness was exposed by the procedural abuses that are common in all Holocaust denial trials.

Udo Walendy, imprisoned for publishing revisionist texts

Born in Berlin in 1927, Udo Walendy, who is approaching his 90th birthday, had time to serve in his country's army before the end of the war. After the war, he studied journalism and political science in Berlin, where he became involved in the publication of revisionist books. In 1956 he graduated in political science and for a time worked as a lecturer at the German Red Cross. As early as 1964 he published his own book *Wahrheit für Deutschland - Die Schuldfrage des Zweitens Weltkriegs* (*The Truth for Germany - The Question of Guilt for the Second World War*). In 1965 he established his own publishing house, "Verlag für Volkstum und Zeitgeschichsforshung" (Publishing House for Contemporary History and Folklore Research). In 1974, ten years after the publication of *Wahrheit für Deutschland*, Udo Walendy founded the journal *Historische Tatsachen* (*Historical Facts*), a serious journal focusing on the rigorous investigation of facts about National Socialism and the Third Reich which official historiography prefers to ignore. In issue 31 of the magazine, for example, he investigated the first Soviet reports on Auschwitz printed on 1 and 2 February in *Pravda*, in which there is no mention of burning pits, gas chambers, piles of shoes and spectacles, dentures or piles of hair.

The legal problems for Udo Walendy began in 1979, when the government blacklisted his book as dangerous or harmful material for young people. Walendy engaged in a lengthy legal battle that was to last fifteen years. Finally, in 1994, the Federal Constitutional Court ruled that the author's rights were being violated, since the book was defensible from an academic point of view. Proof of the value of this work is that *The Barnes Review* republished it in 2013 and a year later, on 1 September 2014, Castle Hill Publishers, Germar Rudolf's publisher in the UK, published an updated and corrected reprint of the book, again translated from the German. Also in 1979 Walendy delivered the first lecture of the Institute for Historical Review (IHR), which had been founded in 1978. From 1980 he was a member of the Editorial Advisory Board of the *Journal of Historical Review*, the Institute's prestigious publication. In the United States, he became personally acquainted with Arthur R. Butz, whose landmark work he translated into German and then edited. The book was soon banned by the German authorities. In 1988, Udo Walendy testified in Toronto at the second trial of Ernst Zündel. His revisionist activities also include his close association with the Belgian online magazine *VHO* (*Vrij Historisch Onderzoek*), where many of the books he has published in German can be found.

The persecution of this veteran publicist and revisionist historian took a qualitative leap forward when on 7 February 1996 a squad of twenty policemen raided his residence and his company. Without respecting the "data protection law", they seized documents, disks and downloaded copies of computer files and took Udo Walendy away for fingerprinting. Shortly afterwards, two German courts found that articles in *Historische Tatsachen*, the magazine he edited and published, incited hatred. On 17 May 1996, the Bielefeld District Court sentenced Walendy to fifteen months' effective imprisonment, despite the fact that he had no previous record. The court rejected any consideration of the academic value of the works in question. Half a year later, in November 1996, a Dortmund court fined him 20,000 marks for possessing twelve copies of *Mein Kampf*. Without any evidence, the court found that Walendy was preparing to distribute these copies of Hitler's book, which was banned in Germany: "The planned distribution of the books," the court declared, "manifests an extreme and therefore particularly dangerous mentality. The books are propaganda for the dismantling of the legal and constitutional system of the Federal Republic of Germany and the establishment of a National Socialist injustice system.... This must be judged with all severity."

A year later, in May 1997, another court in Herford finished the job off and sentenced Walendy to an additional fourteen months' imprisonment. Judge Helmut Knöner found that Walendy had not knowingly published lies, but had not offered alternative interpretations. The court quoted a passage from an issue of *Historische Tatsachen* in which Walendy reported approvingly on Fred Leuchter's research on the "gas chambers" at Auschwitz. The judgment said that the quotation from Leuchter's text "lacked critical sense and repeated the alleged findings of the 'expert'. The defendant endorsed them." The court also criticised Walendy for having reproduced in issue no. 66 of the magazine an article published on 13 June 1946 in the Swiss newspaper *Basler Nachrichten*, the title of which was "How high is the number of Jewish victims", discrediting the imposed figure of six million. The Herfod court did not want to take into account that this was not the editor's point of view, but that of the authors of the texts. As is well known, many newspapers warn in their opinion section that the editor is not responsible for the opinions expressed in the articles published. Walendy explained to the court that in order to ensure that the articles he published in *Historische Tatsachen* did not violate the law, he routinely submitted the texts to the supervision of four lawyers. The court rejected the opinions of the four lawyers as irrelevant.

In 1999, already in the midst of a campaign of legal harassment, the ownership of his publishing house was transferred to his wife. As if imprisonment were not enough, in 2001 there was a new attempt to censor *Wahrheit für Deutschland*, Walendy's book which had received a favourable ruling from the Federal Constitutional Court in 1994. With little chance of the Constitutional Court's ruling being overturned, the government authorities eventually abandoned the plan.

Ursula Haverbeck. The indecent condemnation of a venerable old woman

Ursula Haverbeck will be 88 years old in the year of writing. She was sentenced to ten months in prison in 2015 for denying the Holocaust. This aberrant and shameful sentence exposes the servitude and misery of the Federal Republic of Germany for all to see. Surely any honest person must condemn this abuse by a state that has long since lost its sense of decency. However, the media, instead of criticising the revolting condemnation, served up the news to their readers as if it were logical, since it was about "a Nazi grandmother". In reality, as the sentencing magistrate said from an obscene moral superiority, "there is no point in having a debate with someone who cannot accept the facts." However, even if the judge could not perceive it because of her limitations and short-sightedness, Ursula Haverbeck is a great lady and is recognised as such among revisionists. Despite her venerable old age, she expresses herself with astonishing intelligence and lucidity. There is not a single inconsistency to be found in her texts, speeches or interviews, which are perfectly cohesive.

Ursula Haverbeck was born in Berlin in 1928. When the World War ended in 1945, she was a seventeen-year-old teenager. As a result, she lived through the air terror, the barbaric rapes perpetrated by the communist armies, Eisenhower's death camps, the pogroms and ethnic cleansing of Germans throughout Europe, the famine brought about by the Morgenthau Plan... Her husband, Werner Georg Haverbeck, who died in 1999, was a professor, intellectual and historian who wrote numerous works of all kinds. He had been involved in the leadership of the NSDAP and fought as a soldier on the Eastern Front. Ursula Haverbeck was also a woman of great erudition who studied pedagogy, philosophy, history and linguistics, and thus holds several university degrees. In 1963, the two of them founded the "Collegium Humanum", which was a pioneer among the environmental movements. In the last decades of the 20th century they were very active in the defence of the German language and culture and in the struggle for the preservation of nature. Between 1983 and 1989, Ursula Haverbeck was president of the German section of the World Union for the Protection of Life.

In 2000, Ursula Haverbeck and other researchers, who had already focused on her revisionist activities, gained access to original National Socialist government documents on Auschwitz, which had been confiscated by the USSR at the end of the war. These are now in the hands of the Institute of Contemporary History and can be consulted by the general public for 124 euros. She and other historians have supplied some of these relevant documents to various German government ministries and the judiciary. Although they have asked for an official investigation, they have never received a response. It is clear from these papers that Auschwitz was not an extermination camp but a work camp for the defence industry and that there were orders to preserve the health of the prisoners as far as possible.

During these years she met Horst Mahler and on 9 November 2003 she took part in the founding of the Society for the Rehabilitation of Those Persecuted for the Refutation of the Holocaust ("Verein zur Rehabilitierung der wegen Bestreitens des Holocaust Verfolgten"), of which she was the director. Zündel, Faurisson, Rudolf, Töben, Stäglich, Honsik, Graf and other prominent revisionists joined this society, which was banned by the Ministry of the Interior in 2008. The first sanctions for its revisionist activities came as a result of articles published in *Stimme des Gewissens* (*The Voice of Conscience*), a publication of the Collegium Humanum: in 2004 it was fined 5,400 euros and in 2005 another 6,000 euros. On both occasions the publication was confiscated by the authorities.

In 2008 the Collegium Humanum was banned: Charlotte Knobloch, chairwoman of the Central Council of Jews in Germany, had publicly called for the banning of the Collegium Humanum and its publication *Stimme des Gewissens*. Haverbeck's response came in the form of an open letter, in which he indignantly asked Knobloch "not to interfere" in matters that did not fall within her competence. Alluding to the Ashkenazi Jews' Khazar origins, he invited Knobloch to return to Asia if he did not like life in Germany. These words and others like them led to the filing of a criminal complaint. In June 2009, the Bad Öynhausen District Court fined Haverbeck a further 2,700 euros for insulting Charlotte Knobloch.

Ursula Haverbeck took an initiative that may explain the harshness with which she was subsequently treated. On 20 November 2014 she filed a criminal complaint, an unprecedented event in post-war Germany, against the Central Council of Jews in Germany, which she accused of persecuting innocent people. The complaint was based on paragraph 344 of the Criminal Code and concerned prosecutions of innocent Germans for Holocaust revision. The crime of false prosecution is punishable by up to ten years in prison; however, as early as December 2014, the complaint was dismissed and the investigation dropped. In contrast, the public prosecutor's office examined the possibility of prosecuting Haverbeck for false accusations.

On 23 April 2015, the astonishing event occurred that led to Ursula Haverbeck being sentenced to ten months in prison. Incomprehensibly, ARD, the German public broadcaster founded in 1950, broadcast during its *Panorama* magazine slot a historical interview recorded in March with the grand dame of revisionism. The broadcast was one of the most disconcerting events in Germany since World War II. It should be noted that, after the

BBC, the ARD, a consortium of public broadcasters with 23,000 employees, is the second largest television station in the world. Millions of viewers were shocked at home by Ursula Haverbeck's unprecedented statements. Never before had a German public broadcaster allowed anyone to even hint at the truth about World War II. It is clear that the ARD ran the risk of a multimillion-dollar lawsuit for broadcasting a programme in which it committed the crime of denouncing the Holocaust as a lie sponsored by the Bonn regime in the hands of the criminal transnational Jewish financial occupation. We do not know what consequences the broadcast of the interview had for the *Panorama* journalists and the ARD management. In any case, this is of lesser concern to us, as it is the content of the statements that is of interest. Angela Merkel had declared in January 2013 that Germany "bears eternal responsibility for the crimes of National Socialism, for the victims of World War II and above all for the Holocaust." On the basis of these words, no moderately educated person can deny that the Germans have been subjected since the end of the war to the iron grip of Zionism. This is exactly what the great lady denounced.

The interview, an excerpt of which follows, is available on You Tube with English subtitles. It begins: "You have claimed that the Holocaust is the biggest and most persistent lie in history". After citing the works of Professor Faurisson, Haverbeck reaffirms himself and points out that it is a universal lie operating all over the world. He then mentions evidence of the non-existence of gas chambers, that Zyklon-B was a disinfectant and insists that the Holocaust is the biggest lie that has ever been imposed. The interviewer reminds him that this is a slap in the face, as everyone has learned that the Holocaust happened and resulted in the deaths of six million people. "Can you briefly explain once more why the Holocaust is for you the biggest lie in history?" Haverbeck reiterates that it is the most persistent and the one that has had and still has the greatest impact. He explains that instead of answers you get sentences and adds, "When you need a law that imposes the Holocaust and threatens with punishment if someone investigates freely there is a problem, isn't there? The truth doesn't need a law.

The interview goes on to consider the terrible suffering of the generation of Germans to which Ursula Haverbeck belongs. She recalls that fifteen million Germans, including herself, were driven from their homes. She denounces the murders, rapes and other criminal acts that no one in Europe remembers. In this thematic context, the great lady categorically denies the figure of 25,000 dead in Dresden offered by the authorities and gives a verified figure of 235,000 victims. She concludes with the statement that only the truth can reconcile everyone. Paragraph 130 of the Penal Code adopted in 1994, which is irreconcilable with Article 5 of the Constitution on freedom of expression and freedom of enquiry, is the next topic. Haverbeck reviews the known absurdities and mentions Germar Rudolf's chemical study, his conviction and Mahler's: "This must deeply outrage any decent person," she concludes in growing excitement.

Despite the octogenarian's obvious emotion, the interviewer insists: "So you maintain publicly that the Holocaust never existed?" "Yes, of course, that's right," replies Haverbeck, who immediately recalls that the orders in the concentration camps were strict, that the commandants could not overstep their bounds, and that two of them were even executed. "I understand, then," the journalist interrupts, "that concentration camps existed, but that there was no mass extermination programme as we understand it today." Haverbeck then explains the importance of industrial activity at Auschwitz and provides evidence, including the Leuchter and Rudolf Reports, which allow her to conclude that there were never any gas chambers because "Auschwitz was not an extermination camp, but a labour camp." The old woman wields texts and documents proving that she is not lying, which prompts another question: "If there are so many documents, why don't you talk about them?" Answer: "You could answer that yourself. Because it is not desirable. "For whom?" "For those who have set up the lie". There follows a conversation about the publication and concealment of banned or censored materials and texts, culminating in the lament that reversing the teaching received by Germans in schools for half a century is a serious problem. Haverbeck explains that there was no extermination of the Jews, but there was persecution, deportation and resettlement. The Zionists themselves wanted this," he adds, "and that's why they even collaborated. The Zionists wanted to have a state.... They had the same goal: they wanted their own state, and above all they wanted the German Jews because they were the smartest. The fraud of Anne Frank's diary, the falsehood that Germany was the cause of the two world wars, Eli Wiesel's hoaxes about the concentration camps, the realisation that the piles of bodies in Bergen-Belsen had died of typhus, starvation and disease, are other topics of the 49-minute conversation . At this point, Haverbeck recalls: "At the end of the war we were all starving. My mother weighed only 40 kilos. We were all skeletal..." The interviewer insists: "Do you think you could convince the majority of Germans that the Holocaust, as we know it, did not happen, that it never happened?" Haverbeck replies that someone must do so "because otherwise they will suffer uselessly for all eternity. And suffer they do. And they are told they have to. This guilt complex is deeply rooted. And then on top of it all there are the demands: give us more submarines, give us more of this, do that, and so on and so forth. It's all a function of our past..."

The interview takes place in Ursula Haverbeck's huge library. The subject of hatred comes up. Then the great lady mentions the *Talmud* as an example of the ultimate expression of Jewish hatred of gentiles: "All you have to do is read the *Talmud*. I have there," she says, turning her head, "all twelve volumes in the most recent and authoritative translation, a 2002 edition...". The dialogue ends with a warning, "The things you say that you believe, specifically, that the Holocaust did not take place, as you claim, could cost you prison." Response, "Well, then, if people think that's the best thing to do, that's just a risk I have to take.... It's the price to pay. I always think of Schiller, the Wallenstein Field: 'Rise, my comrades, to the horses, to the horses!.... And if you do not risk your lives, you will never receive life as a prize.'"

As a consequence of the expression of the ideas just summarised, in June 2015 the grand dame of revisionism was arrested. The public prosecutor's office ordered the Lower Saxony State Criminal Police to enter the home of Ursula Haverbeck and three other historian colleagues in search of evidence of her thought crimes. The operation took place at night. An armed group of political police kicked in the door and stormed in. It can be said that the house was razed to the ground, as most of the books and other objects ended up on the floor during the search for documents or other evidence that could be used to incriminate Ursula for incitement to hatred and Holocaust denial. The same scene also took place at the homes of the other three revisionists, whose books and documents were seized by the police. What is puzzling about the whole affair is that the ARD programme management allowed the interview to be broadcast, especially since the journalist warns the revisionist historian that she could end up in prison for what she has said. Ursula Haverbeck's arrest was foreseeable from the start.

On 11 November 2015, the Hamburg District Court sentenced her to ten months in prison for questioning whether Jews were gassed at Auschwitz. The defendant appeared at the trial without a lawyer and defended herself in good spirits. About fifty people who accompanied her tried to sit in the courtroom, but a group of "activists" had previously occupied the seats in order to keep out Ursula's friends, many of whom had to remain outside due to lack of space. She was accused of having given an interview to the television magazine *Panorama* in which she stated that Auschwitz had not been an extermination camp, but a labour camp, and that the mass murder of Jews had not taken place. Haverbeck's words to the judge were, "I stand by everything I said." Turning to the prosecutor, he asked: "How do you as a lawyer prove the accusation that Auschwitz was an extermination camp?" His request for a revisionist historian to testify and provide evidence that no one had been gassed in Auschwitz was rejected by Judge Jönsson, who said it was useless to argue with someone who does not accept the facts.

This magistrate, in the height of his arrogance, blithely disregarded the fact that the non-acceptance of the facts went the other way, given that it is the German courts that systematically refuse to examine them and reject proof and evidence of the crime on trial. Judge Jönsson equated the certainty of the Holocaust with the evidence that the earth is round: "I don't have to give evidence that the world is round either". Finally, after hypocritically expressing his sadness that the old woman used all her energies in "fomenting hatred", the judge ruled that "it was a lost cause." The state prosecution maintained that the defendant had not changed her "fanatical delusional thinking," so that, despite her advanced age, she should be sentenced to ten months' effective imprisonment. The judge agreed.

Reinhold Elstner, the revisionist who burned himself alive

In the Federal Republic of Germany about two thousand people are arrested annually for crimes of opinion and nobody cares about it because they are only "neo-Nazis". We could go on with other honest revisionists who, for no other crime than thinking freely, ended up behind bars, such as Dirk Zimmermann, who in 2007 sent copies of *Lectures on the Holocaust* to three local figures: the mayor of Heilbronn, a Lutheran clergyman and a Catholic clergyman. After sending the books, he filed a lawsuit against himself and in 2009 was sentenced to nine months in prison; or Gerhard Ittner, sentenced in 2015 by a Munich court to eighteen months in prison. To present more examples would unnecessarily take us too long. We will therefore end with an extreme, generally unknown case, that of Reinhold Elstner, to whom we have reserved the last place as the culmination of the persecution of revisionists in Germany. This 75-year-old retired chemist, engineer and veteran of the Wehrmacht went to the stairs of the "Feldhermhalle" (Hall of the Heroes) in Munich on 25 April 1995, doused himself with flammable liquid and set himself on fire. The people who saw him tried to rescue him in order to save his life, but twelve hours later Elstner was dead. The reasons for such an unfortunate action are explained in a text written before he committed suicide, in which he explains his sacrifice. We reproduce it in memoriam.

> "Germans in Germany, in Austria, in Switzerland and in the world, please wake up!
> Fifty years of endless defamation, of continuous hateful lies, of demonisation of an entire people are enough.
> Fifty years of unbelievable insults to German soldiers, of permanent blackmail costing billions, and of 'democratic' hatred are more than one can bear.
> 50 years of Zionist judicial vengeance is enough.
> Fifty years of trying to create a rift between generations of Germans by criminalising parents and grandparents is too long.
> It is unbelievable that in this anniversary year we are inundated with a flood of lies and slander. Since I am already 75 years old, I cannot do much more; but I can still take my own life by immolating myself, a last action that can serve as a signal to the Germans to come to their senses. If by my act a single German should wake up and find the way to the truth, then my sacrifice would not have been in vain.
> I felt I had no choice after realising that now, after 50 years, there is little hope that reason will prevail. As someone who was expelled from his

home after the war, I always had one hope, the same hope that was granted to the Israelis after 2000 years, namely that the expelled Germans would have the right to return home. What happened to the right of self-determination enacted in 1919, when millions of Germans were forced to live under foreign rule? To this day we have had to suffer for these mistakes, and I can say that the Germans cannot be held responsible for them.

I'm a German Swede, I have a Czech grandmother, and on the other hand Czech and Jewish relatives, some of whom were imprisoned in concentration camps such as Buchenwald, Dora and Theresienstadt. I never belonged either to the Nazi party or to any other group that was in the least connected with National Socialism. We always had the best relations with our non-German relatives and, when necessary, we helped each other. During the war, our grocery shop with bakery was responsible for the distribution of food to French prisoners of war and workers from the East who lived in the city. Everything was done correctly and this ensured that at the end of the war our business was not looted because the French POWs guarded it until their repatriation. Our relatives who had been detained in the concentration camps returned home as early as 10 May 1945 (two days after the end of hostilities) and offered their support. Particularly helpful was our Jewish uncle from Prague, who had seen the bloodbath of the remaining Germans in the Czech capital caused by the partisans. The horror of these cold-blooded murders could still be seen in the expression in his eyes. Obviously, a horror that he himself as a former prisoner of the Reich had not experienced during his imprisonment.

I was a soldier in the Wehrmacht of the great German Reich , fighting from day one on the eastern front. To this I must add a few years of slave labour in the USSR as a prisoner of war.

I remember well Kristallnacht (Night of Broken Glass) in 1938 because on that day I found a Jewish girl crying, a girl with whom I had studied. But I was much more shocked when I saw in Russia how all the churches had been desecrated, how they were used as stables and gun shops; I saw pigs grunting, sheep bleating and the clattering of guns in holy places. The worst for me was when I saw churches turned into museums of atheism. And all this happened with the active connivance of the Jews, that small minority of which so many members were Stalin's criminal thugs. The most prominent of these were of the Kaganovich clan, seven brothers and sisters, who were such mass criminals that the alleged SS murderers can be considered harmless by comparison.

After the return from the Russian prison camps to my "homeland" (what a mockery to speak of "homeland" to a prisoner who has been expelled from the land of his ancestors!) I heard for the first time about the brutalities of the concentration camps, but at first I heard nothing about gas chambers or the murder of human beings by the use of poison gas. On the contrary, I was told that in concentration camps like Theresienstadt and Buchenwald (Dora) there were even brothels for the inmates in the confines of the camp. Then, on the occasion of the 'Auschwitz trials', Mr Broszat of the Institute of Contemporary History stated that the famous figure of six million is only a symbolic number. Despite the fact that Mr. Broszat also declared that there were no gas chambers for the murder of human beings in the camps set up on German soil, for years the alleged chambers were shown to visitors in Buchenwald, Dachau, Mauthausen and others. Lies, only lies to this day. It all became very clear to me when I read dozens of books written by Jews and so-called anti-fascists. In addition, I could draw on my own experience in Russia. I lived for two years in the hospital city of Porchov, where already in the first winter the danger of a typhus epidemic arose and all hospitals and primary care centres were deloused with what we called then 'K.Z. Gas', specifically 'Zyklon-B'. There I learned how dangerous it was to handle this poisonous gas even though I was not part of the teams that fumigated the buildings. In any case, since then I have had no choice but to study all the works about the concentration camps that tell fabulous tales about the gas chambers. This must be the real reason why all the victims' reports about the concentration camps are regarded as the truth by the courts and do not need to be proven.

In 1988 German television broadcast a report on Babi Yar (a ravine near Kiev) where it was reported that the SS had stoned 36,000 Jews to death. Three years later a lady named Kayser wrote a report for the Munich newspaper *TZ* in which she said that these Jews had been shot and their bodies burned in deep ravines. Asked about this, Ms Kayser pointed to a bookshop in Konstanz that sells the book *The Shoah at Babi Yar*. The day the book arrived at my house, German television showed a report from Kiev on the findings of a Ukrainian commission: at Babi Yar were the bodies of 180,000 human beings, all murdered on Stalin's orders (before 1941). The Germans were not responsible at all. However, Babi Yar memorials blaming the Germans for the massacres can be found all over the world (Clinton visited Babi Yar on 10 May 1995 and in front of a Menorah alluded to the Germans as the slaughterers).

Because, as Mr Broszat said, we have been deceived about what happened in dozens of concentration camps. I am not prepared to believe the stories that are being told about what allegedly happened in the camps in Poland. Nor do I believe the post-war accusations that paint the Germans as particularly aggressive. After all, it was Germany that kept the peace from 1871 to 1914, while England and France, the leading democracies, conquered most of Africa and expanded their colonies in Asia. At the same time, the United States fought Spain in Mexico, and Russia waged war on Turkey and Japan. In these matters I consider the US Government to be particularly cynical, since it was the country that twice in this century crossed the ocean to attack Germany and bring us to 'democracy'. It must be considered that this was a government whose nation exterminated the original inhabitants, and which to this day treats its coloured population as second-class citizens.

During my years I found kind and helpful Jews not only among my relatives, but also among prisoners of war in Russia. In Gorky a Jewish teacher helped me back to health when I suffered from pleurisy and serious eye problems. But I also heard a lot of bad things about this small minority. Didn't Churchill write in the *London Sunday Herald* (8 February 1920) the following?

From the days of Spartakus Weishaupt to Marx, Trotsky, Bela Kun, Rosa Luxemburg and Emma Goldmann, there is a world conspiracy engaged in destroying our civilisation and changing our society by means events of appalling greed and with the implementation of the impossible dream of the equality of all. This conspiracy, with its relentless undermining of all existing institutions, was able to employ a band of unscrupulous people from the underworld of the great cities of Europe and America to seize power in Russia and make themselves masters of this vast empire. It is not necessary to overestimate the part which these atheistic Jews played in the establishment of Bolshevism.'

I believe I am entitled to quote the recipient of the prestigious Karls Prize. In the 18th century, Samuel Johnson wrote: 'I do not know which we should fear more, a street full of soldiers ready to plunder or a room full of writers accustomed to lie'.

Considering our experience after 1918 and after 1945, we Germans know who we have to fear the most!

Munich, 25 April 1995
Reinhold Elstner".

2. MAIN VICTIMS OF PERSECUTION IN FRANCE:

François Duprat, murdered by Jewish terrorists

The law that prohibits Holocaust revisionism in France is the Gayssot Law, also known as the Fabius-Gayssot Law, passed on 13 July 1990. Two Jews, the communist MP Jean Claude Gayssot and the wealthy socialist Laurent Fabius, were the fathers of the invention that since then has made it possible to prosecute those who question the existence of certain crimes against humanity, namely those defined in the London Charter, which was used as the basis for convicting Nazi leaders in the infamous Nuremberg trials. As usual, the Jewish lobby, using the supposed defence of human rights as a cover, succeeded in ensuring that in France, as in Germany, investigators are harassed for thought crimes and deprived of freedom of expression. Prior to the existence of this law, revisionists had already been subjected to coercive measures. It has been said that Paul Rassinier, one of the fathers of historical revisionism, had to endure from the publication of *The Lie of Ulysses* until his death in 1967 all kinds of slander and exclusion, as well as several legal proceedings.

Another precursor of historical revisionism in France was François Duprat, who in June 1967 published an article in *Défense de l'Occident* entitled "The Mystery of the Gas Chambers". Later, Duprat read *Did Six Million Really Die?*, the book by Richard Harwood whose publication was to cause Ernst Zündel so much trouble, and became involved in its publication and distribution in France. François Duprat, born in Ajaccio in 1941, is considered one of the ideologues of French nationalism and the creation of the National Front. One of his mentors was Maurice Bardèche, a propagator of Holocaust revisionism alongside Paul Rassinier. Influenced by Bardèche, Duprat suggested the dissolution of the Zionist state and supported the Popular Front for the Liberation of Palestine. Duprat promoted the translation and publication of key Holocaust revisionist texts. Thanks to him, Thies Christophersen's *Die Auschwitz Lüge* (*The Auschwitz Lie*) and Arthur Robert Butz's *The Hoax of the Twentieth Century* were circulated in France.

At 08:40 on 18 March 1978, a bomb killed François Duprat, who at the age of 37 became the first person to be murdered for his support of Holocaust revisionism. His wife Jeanine, who was with him, was seriously injured and, although she was able to save her life, she lost her legs and was paralysed. Duprat was driving his wife to school in Caudebe-en-Caux, where she was teaching. The car stopped at a petrol station to buy newspapers and the criminals took the opportunity to plant a bomb in the underbody of the vehicle. When they resumed driving, the car was blown up. The investigation showed that the device used was sophisticated and could only have been the work of skilled experts. Two groups claimed responsibility for the attack as a way of rejecting 'Shoah denialism': the self-styled Commando of Memory and the Jewish Revolutionary Group; however, Zionist organisations in France condemned the murder in the public eye and an intoxication campaign was spread to attribute the crime to ultra-left and/or rival nationalist groups. Duprat's funeral in the church of Saint-Nicolas-du Chardonnet in Paris was a massive event.

No one was arrested and the crime went unpunished. Today there is little doubt that Duprat's murder was the work of the Mossad. Thanks to the publication in 1990 of *By Way of Deception,* the book by former agent Victor Ostrovsky, international public opinion gained access to revealing details of how the Israeli Secret Service trains and arms so-called "Jewish defence groups" in different countries. Ostrovsky explains in his controversial book that young people from other countries are brought to Israel for various intelligence-related training. In Europe, the "Tagar", a branch of the Zionist Betar movement, is the most important terrorist group. Tagar/Betar, which is headquartered in Paris, has close ties to the Israeli government and is therefore used in Mossad covert operations. It is more than likely that this Tagar was linked to Duprat's assassination, as it has been credited with numerous criminal attacks against people considered 'enemies', including Holocaust revisionists.

Roger Garaudy, the philosopher pilloried for denouncing Israel

As we begin to write these lines on the philosopher Roger Garaudy, we are plagued by a few doubts. His life, a paradigmatic example of eclecticism, was so rich and varied that one is tempted to explain something of it to those who do not know this scholar, who wrote incessantly during his long life of almost a hundred years. Our limitations, of course, are imposed by the contents we have been dealing with. What basically interests us in his extensive oeuvre of more than fifty essays is what concerns historical revisionism. For this reason, we will focus mainly on the book that was to provoke the so-called "Affaire Garaudy", *Les Mythes fondateurs de la politique israélienne.* This essay, published in December 1995, probably came about as a moral necessity, as a compromise, since Garaudy was married to the Palestinian Salma Farouqui and had converted to Islam in 1982. Constrained by space constraints, we will nevertheless write a few paragraphs on his life trajectory. This will help us understand how Garaudy came to denounce the perversion of the Zionist state.

In the spring of 2013 we visited the Museum of the Three Cultures in the Calahorra Tower , a Muslim fortress whose use was ceded by the City Council to the Roger Garaudy Foundation in 1987. Ten years later, in September 1997, the Calahorra Tower, located opposite the mosque, on the other side of the Roman bridge over the Guadalquivir, was entered in the register of museums of the Autonomous Community. There we had the opportunity to acquire several of Garaudy's works translated into Spanish, including a memoir he began writing at the age of 75, *Mi vuelta al siglo en solitario*. We will therefore use his own voice to outline some moments in the intellectual, ethical and religious transformation of this synthetic and conciliatory thinker. His metamorphoses led him to move from militant communism to Islam, via Catholicism, and thus from supposed Marxist atheism to a profound faith in God.

Garaudy was born in Marseilles in 1913. His maternal grandmother was Spanish, a Menorcan exiled in Algiers in 1848. In the foreword to the memoirs he states: "The great quest of my life was precisely to find meaning in it. And also to history". In his twenties, he sought that meaning in Marxism and joined the French Communist Party in 1933. After having been a prisoner of Vichy France in Algeria, he lived through the liberation in Paris in 1945. He wrote some enlightening words on the situation in France: "In a country where the vast majority has accepted both the occupation and the Vichy regime, the illusion of a unanimous and heroic resistance is now being created. In 1945 in France there were more resistance fighters than inhabitants". Since the Communist Party had been predominant in the internal resistance, its prestige was transformed into power. Garaudy was elected in 1945 as a member of the first Constituent Assembly. He then began his career as a PCF deputy, followed by "fourteen lost years in Parliament", in his own words. At the end of October 1956, after the nationalisation of the Suez Canal by Nasser, Garaudy, as Vice-President of the Assembly, witnessed the pre-war atmosphere and the preparations for the Anglo-French intervention in Egypt.

It was during these years that his doubts began and he formulated the significant dichotomy between "responsible communists and responsible communists", which was to lead to his expulsion from the party in 1970. Increasingly in favour of establishing a dialogue between Christians and Marxists, he claimed the figure of Father Teilhard de Chardin, paleontologist and philosopher, as a meeting point. During the 1960s, his views against atheism and his constant meetings with Christian theologians and philosophers often provoked adverse reactions from many comrades. No creator," he wrote, "can deny God. He is aware of his presence. Even if he does not say so..." It can be said that Garaudy was the great animator in Europe and America of the Christian-Marxist dialogues. In 1969, in answer to the question "Who is Christ for you?", he wrote beautiful words about Jesus and about Christians:

> "... A bonfire has been lit: it is the proof of the spark or the first flame that gave it birth. This bonfire was above all an uprising of the destitute, without which, from Nero to Diocletian, the 'establishment' would not have persecuted them so harshly. For these men (the Christians), love

becomes something militant, subversive; if it were not for that, He (Christ), the first, would not have been crucified.
Up to this moment all wisdoms meditated on destiny and on foolishness confused with reason. He, the opposite of destiny, has pointed out its folly. He, freedom, creation, life. He is the one who has disfigured history".

A year before he wrote these words, what he considered "the turning point of dreams" had already taken place in his life: after the fiasco of May 1968, Warsaw Pact troops led by the USSR invaded Czechoslovakia on 20 August and aborted the so-called "Prague Spring". Garaudy condemned the intervention unreservedly, but the party denounced his "indiscipline". On 6 February 1970 he was expelled from the PCF.

Roger Garaudy's new phase was marked by his travels around the world. In his desire to delve deeper into the existence of God, he needed to see how God is conceived in the everyday life and artistic manifestations of other cultures and civilisations. To this end, he travelled to India, China and Japan. He came to the conclusion that "our western civilisation is at a standstill" and in 1979 he published *Appel aux vivants,* one of his best received books, translated from French into seven languages, including Arabic, Spanish and Catalan. The royalties brought him substantial profits and with them the opportunity to create the association "Appel aux vivants", which aimed to raise a movement of non-violent "resistance" against "the occupation of institutions and spirits by the ideology of growth and the anaesthesia of souls".

On 17 June 1982, a text by Garaudy appeared in *Le Monde* that was to mark a turning point in his life. As he denounces in *My Turn of the Century Alone,* the article was used "to throw me into the dungeons of oblivion". Jacques Fauvet, the editor of the newspaper with whom Garaudy had good relations, agreed to publish a paid page in which he and Father Michel Lelong and Pastor Mathiot harshly criticised Israel's massacres in Lebanon and explained their meaning: "We showed that this was not an oversight, but the internal logic of the political Zionism on which the State of Israel is founded". Garaudy explains in his memoirs the consequences of the text and denounces: "Through anonymous letters and by telephone I received up to nine death threats". LICRA (International League Against Racism and Anti-Semitism) filed a lawsuit in order to provoke a trial for "anti-Semitism and provocation to racial discrimination". Jacques Fauvet's lawyer insisted that the State of Israel could not be confused with the Jewish community; but the LICRA lawyer tried to prove that Garaudy was an anti-Semite.

Fortunately, it was all just a prologue to what years later would become the "Affaire Garaudy". On 24 March 1983, the Paris Court of Appeal ruled that it was a "lawful criticism of the policy of a state and the ideology that inspires it and not a racial provocation". Consequently, the lawsuit of the powerful Jewish lobby in France was rejected and LICRA had to pay the court costs. Instead of dropping the matter, they appealed; but again the judgment of the Upper Chamber of the Paris Court ruled in favour of Garaudy and the two clergymen who had co-signed the article. On 11 January 1984, a verdict was handed down confirming the previous court's judgement and once again ordering LICRA to pay the costs, which again appealed in cassation. It took almost four years. Finally, on 4 November 1987, the Zionists lost the legal battle. The Court rejected the cassation and ordered the plaintiffs to pay the costs. The defeat of the Jewish lobby was systematically ignored. Even *Le Monde*, whose former editor Fauvet was involved in the affair, confined itself to an insignificant review. Alongside the harassment in the courts, a much more pitiful one was launched for the philosopher:

> "But from that moment on, the media began to suffocate me: my access to television was blocked and all my articles were rejected. Up to that point, I had published forty books in all the major publishing houses, from Gallimard to Seuil, from Plon to Grasset and Laffont. They had been translated into twenty-seven languages. From that moment on, all doors were closed: one of my best publishers was told by the board of directors: 'If you publish a book by Garaudy, you will not have the right to translate any American work'. To accept me would have been to ruin the house. On the subject of another work, another 'big' (publisher) told his literary director, who, passionate about the book, had worked for three months to help me put the finishing touches to it: 'I don't want Garaudy in this house'. This is the story of the walling up of a man".

Garaudy refers to the period 1982-1988 as "my six years of wandering in the desert". The attempt to bury him literarily reflects perfectly the plans outlined earlier by Adam Weishaupt and also in the *Protocols of the Learned Elders Zion*. The former, already at the end of the 18th century, wrote that they had to ruin writers who were hostile to them: "When we shall gradually have the whole book trade in our hands, we shall make them (hostile writers) have neither publishers nor readers." In the Twelfth Protocol, which deals with the control of public opinion through news agencies, the press and publications in general, we read: "We shall surely defeat our adversaries because, in consequence of our measures, they will have no newspapers at their disposal in which they can give vent to their opinion."

In 1982 Roger Garaudy married the Palestinian Salma Farouqui and a fortnight after the publication in *Le Monde* of the paid page that sparked the storm, on 2 July, "fully conscious and fully responsible", he made his profession of the Muslim faith in Geneva before Imam Buzuzu: "God alone is God and Mohammed is his prophet". The news of his conversion was good news for the Muslim communities in the West, who sent him invitations one after the other. In a lecture in Belfort entitled "Jesus the Prophet of Islam", in which, as he admits in his memoirs, "the heart speaks more fervently of

Jesus than of Mohammed", he quotes the suras of the Koran which recognise Mary's virginity and Jesus as God's prophet: "The Messiah, Jesus, son of Mary, is God's apostle. He is His Word deposited by God in Mary. It is the spirit that emanates from Him". Garaudy notes that while God said to Mohammed: "Repent of your sins, past and present", the Koran considers Jesus and his mother the Virgin Mary to be the only human beings who have never committed sin.

Almost inevitably, he saw in Spain the historical example of the dialogue of civilisations that he preached and, consequently, he ended up in Cordoba, where the largest mosque in the world is located. A city, the philosopher points out, "which during the Muslim period of Spanish history, was the largest city in Europe, when Paris and London were but small towns. It was the centre of irradiation of the culture". In 1987, the city council of Cordoba granted him the Calahorra tower for a period of forty-nine years so that the evocation of Cordoba's heyday could be exhibited there: "That was the beginning for me," writes Garaudy, "of the marvellous adventure of realising a dream".

Unfortunately, dreams sometimes give rise to terrible nightmares, such as the one Garaudy experienced in 1996 following the publication in France of *Les mythes fondateurs de la politique israélienne* at the end of 1995. This work, which was published in Spain under the title *Los mitos fundacionales del Estado de Israel*, unleashed an unprecedented storm in France, since not even the books of revisionists such as Paul Rassinier, Arthur R. Butz or Robert Faurisson caused so much noise in the media and among the "intelligentsia". During the first half of 1996, the controversy did not cease and the affair was to go down in history as the "Affaire Garaudy". Previously, Garaudy had seen two of his books on the Palestinian question unofficially censored through the usual means used by Jewish pressure groups: intimidation and blackmail. Increasingly aware of the role of the Holocaust as an argument to silence criticism of Israel, Garaudy took up the offer of Pierre Guillaume, who in 1980 had relaunched the bookshop "La Vieille Taupe" as a publishing house specialising in revisionist books.

Robert Faurisson, who has been assaulted and threatened with death many times, and who knows first-hand the violence of these media storms, wrote a long article on 1 November 1996 entitled "Bilan de l'affaire Garaudy-abbé Pierre (janvier-octobre 1996)" (Balance of the Garaudy-Father Pierre affair (January-October 1996)). Professor Faurisson explains that Pierre Guillaume, in order to avoid "the rays of the Fabius-Gayssot law", sold Garaudy's book outside the trade as "a confidential bulletin reserved for friends of the Vieille Taupe". Faurisson claims that, religious and political considerations aside, the pages that unleashed the wrath of Jewish organisations in France and much of the Western world were the revisionist-inspired pages at the heart of the book. In them, for the taste of a meticulous and precise revisionist like Faurisson, Nuremberg, the Final Solution, the alleged gas chambers and, finally, the Holocaust were hastily reviewed. In an excerpt from the article Faurisson said:

> "But as it was, with all its inadequacies, Garaudy's book could only worry Jewish organisations, which already had an exaggerated tendency to see revisionists coming out of everywhere and which now discovered a man whose political views - he had been a Stalinist apparatchik of the most orthodox kind - could in no way be described as fascist. R. Garaudy had also been a Protestant, then a Catholic, before becoming a Muslim in the 1980s. In his various works, he had shown himself to be an opponent of all racism".

The first media to cry foul were *Le Canard enchaîné* and *Le Monde*. Then followed the anti-racist organisations, led by LICRA, which denounced it. On 11 March 1996, Pierre Guillaume tried to print a public edition as he had announced in the Vieille Taupe bulletin, but his usual printer refused, so Garaudy decided to clandestinely publish the remodelled work on his own. On 15 April, Henri Grouès, known as Father Pierre, wrote a long letter of support to his friend Garaudy. On 18 April Garaudy, accompanied by his lawyer Jacques Vergès, gave a press conference at which he mentioned the names of some of the personalities who had shown their solidarity with him, among them, in addition to Father Pierre, Father Michel Lelong and the Swiss essayist Jean Ziegler.

Faced with the virulence of the attacks, everyone, including Garaudy, soon tried to excuse themselves with arguments that sought to qualify their positions, a fact that Faurisson regrets: "It is regrettable that Roger Garaudy and Father Pierre did not show more courage. Since the media storm broke out in France, they have begun to beat a retreat". However, both Professor Faurisson and Henri Roques, accustomed to standing up, immediately publicly accepted a proposal from Chief Rabbi Joseph Sitruk, who on 27 April suggested a debate on the Shoah. The following day, the rabbi withdrew the proposal.

On 29 April, the newspaper *Liberation* headlined: "Father Pierre refuses to condemn Garaudy's denialist theses". It was the beginning of a general offensive: the Catholic hierarchy declared that it did not want to be dragged into the controversy. The Bishops' Conference deplored Father Pierre's attitude, reaffirmed that the extermination of the Jews was an indisputable fact and denounced the scandal of questioning the Shoah. The attacks grew louder and louder throughout the month of May. On 9 May, for example, Jean-Luc Allouche, one of *Liberation*'s star journalists, associated Garaudy and Father Pierre with Robert Faurisson, something both had tried to avoid, and accused the three of seeking only to delegitimise the State of Israel. In the United States, on the same day, 9 May, a certain J. Sobran accused Father Pierre of "having denied the divinity of Christ" in *The Wanderer,* a Catholic weekly in Ohio.

For his part, Roger Garaudy sought and found support. On 11 May *Tribune Juive* announced that Garaudy was planning to publish the book in the United States and that Rabbi Elmer Berger had written a text for him that he intended to use as a preface. On 23 May *Liberation* reported an editorial in *Al-Ahram*, a newspaper considered the unofficial voice of the Egyptian regime. The newspaper declared itself proud to have welcomed in its pages the author of a book persecuted in France and denounced the media campaign against him. The editorial reproached *Liberation* for being at the service of Zionist propaganda and reminded it that, on the other hand, it had defended Salman Rushdie's right to attack Islam. Finally, on 29 May, the press announced the withdrawal of Father Pierre, who had decided to go into seclusion in an Italian monastery, where he was visited by Garaudy. Father Pierre told the *Corriere della Sera* that the Church of France had intervened "to silence him under pressure from the press, inspired by an international Zionist lobby". These words provoked a worldwide scandal.

Back in June, Garaudy published a booklet entitled *Derecho de respuesta. Response to the media lynching of Father Pierre and Roger Garaudy*. In it he sought to clarify and qualify his views on revisionism. On the gas chambers, he insisted that no court had sought to examine the murder weapon and recalled the existence of the *Leuchter Report*. Acknowledging the persecution of the Jews, he denied Zionists the right to monopolise Hitler's crimes and recalled that sixteen million Slavs had died during the Second World War. Referring to the attacks in the press, he wrote: "Let the journalists know one thing: the great majority of those deported to the Nazi camps were not Jews, although all the media have credited the thesis that only Jews were deported and exterminated.

As for Father Pierre, in June he left Italy and settled in Switzerland, from where on 18 June he sent a twelve-page fax entitled "Long live the truth" to a journalist from *Le Monde*. Two days later, on 20 June, Monsignor Daniel Lustiger, the Jewish Cardinal Archbishop of Paris, declared in the weekly *Tribune Juive* that he had "experienced the controversy as an immense disaster". The archbishop issued a public reprimand to Father Peter and exonerated the Church of any responsibility. Months later, on 26 September, on the occasion of a debate at the Sorbonne on the Holocaust (the Shoah), the Archbishop declared that "denialism was the same kind of lie as that of the man who kills his brother to escape the truth". His friend Elie Wiesel echoed the statement and declared: "Denialists may have no soul".

Finally, the offensive continued throughout the summer of 1996. On 16 July, the modest "Librairie du Savoir" in the Latin Quarter, owned by Georges Piscoci-Danesco, a Romanian political refugee who sold revisionist works, including Garaudy's, was attacked. He was wounded by members of Betar and the bookshop was razed to the ground, some two thousand volumes were damaged. The damage amounted to 250,000 francs. As usual, the Betar terrorists went unpunished, since, enjoying the prurient protection of the

Ministry of the Interior, the police did not even bother to look for the criminals. In fact, more than fifty criminal acts perpetrated by Jewish organisations have gone unpunished in France, . Also in July, Father Pierre finally retracted his statement in a text published on 23 July in *La Croix*: "I have decided to withdraw my words, relying once again entirely on the opinions of the Church's experts, and I apologise to all those whom I may have hurt. I want to leave God as the sole judge of the integrity of each one's intentions".

The witch-hunt waged by the media in general generated multiple victims, especially people suspected of having committed the sacrilege of being revisionists or negationists. About the two main victims. Robert Faurisson wrote the following:

> "Two octogenarians, who thought they knew life and men, have suddenly and with childish surprise discovered that in reality their past existence had been, in short, easy. The two of them, in the space of a few days, have had to face an exceptional ordeal: that which Jewish organisations are in the habit of inflicting on individuals who have the misfortune to provoke their anger. There is no plot or conspiracy on the part of these organisations, but a kind of ancestral reaction. The media, who work for them with devotion, because to go against them could be very costly, know how to mobilise against 'anti-Semites', that is to say against people who, with a few exceptions, do not hate Jews, but are hated by Jews. Old Testament hatred is one of the most formidable in existence: nervous, feverish, frenzied, unlimited, it suffocates its victims through the suddenness and duration of its violence. It is an inextinguishable hatred because those who suffer from it cannot afford to reveal the true motive and thus mitigate, at least in part, their fury. For example, for months Faurisson has been picked at for his 'minimising' estimate of the number of Jews killed during the world war. But this was only artifice, the real motive lay elsewhere; it lay in the sacrilege of casting doubt on the existence of the gas chambers. However, revealing this doubt was tantamount to running the risk of creating or increasing doubt among the general public. Hence the need to talk about something else...".

Complaints filed by LICRA and MRAP (Mouvement contre le Racisme et l'Amitié entre les Peuples) prompted the French state to prosecute Roger Garaudy for violation of the Gayssot law. The trial began in January 1998. It was followed with expectation in the Arab and Muslim world, no doubt due to the fact that a Muslim intellectual was on trial. From the Persian Gulf to the Nile, hundreds, if not thousands, of writers, journalists, lawyers and politicians publicly expressed their solidarity and protests at the action of the French judiciary. Of course, Israeli Prime Minister Benjamin Netanyahu and the usual American Zionist groups were quick to point out that books like Garaudy's constituted "the main threat to

Israel". The Paris court that tried the case handed down the verdict on 27 February and found the philosopher guilty of "denial of a crime against humanity" and "racial defamation". The judges specified that the writer's "anti-Semitism" and not his "anti-Zionism" had been judged, arguing that "although he takes refuge in a political criticism of Israel, is in fact questioning the Jews as a whole". The court fined the defendant 240,000 francs and sentenced him to six months' imprisonment, which he did not serve. It should be noted that in 1998 Roger Garaudy was already 85 years old, so it would have been scandalous for a prestigious octogenarian intellectual to be sent to prison in France, as in Germany, for thought crimes. On 13 June 2012, Garaudy died at the age of 99 at his home on the outskirts of Paris.

Robert Faurisson, revisionism's essential alma mater

Robert Faurisson is one of the three main pillars of historical revisionism, the other two being Ernst Zündel and Germar Rudolf. The quantity and quality of Professor Faurisson's works place him at the head of revisionist writers. There is no subject on which he has not written, for he knows them all without exception. Moreover, his militant commitment to the intellectual and political challenge that revisionism demands has led him to intervene in one way or another in many legal proceedings in defence of other researchers harassed by "justice" in different countries: of particular relevance was his contribution to the two trials against Ernst Zündel in Canada. His complete work is compiled in four volumes totalling more than 2,200 pages entitled *Écrits révisionnistes*. In application of the Fabius-Gayssot law of 13 July 1990, this work cannot be disseminated and has been privately published outside the commercial circuits. Its content is therefore prohibited by law because the Holocaust (the Shoah) cannot be questioned in France. Interested readers who can read French can access it on the Internet. From the introduction to the first volume, we have translated Professor Faurisson's conception of historical revisionism:

> "Revisionism is a question of method and not an ideology.
> It advocates, for any research, a return to the starting point, examination followed by re-examination, re-reading and re-writing, evaluation followed by re-evaluation, re-orientation, revision, re-casting; it is in spirit, the opposite of ideology. It does not deny, but aims to affirm more accurately. Revisionists are not 'deniers' or 'negationists'; they strive to seek and find where, it seems, there was nothing to seek and find.
> Revisionism can be exercised in hundreds of activities of everyday life and in hundreds of fields of historical, scientific or literary research. It does not necessarily require the questioning of acquired ideas, but often leads to their nuance. It seeks to disentangle the true from the false.

History is essentially revisionist; ideology is its enemy. Since ideology is never so strong as in times of war or conflict, and since it then manufactures falsehoods in abundance for the needs of its propaganda, the historian will, in this circumstance, have to redouble his vigilance: by passing through the sieve of analysis the examination of what has been foisted on him as 'truths'. He will undoubtedly realise that, wherever war has claimed tens of millions of victims, the first of the victims will have been the verifiable truth: a truth that he will try to seek out and re-establish.
The official history of the Second World War contains a little truth combined with a lot of falsehoods".

Methodological rigour and intellectual honesty characterise all of Faurisson's revisionist writings, and this is a consequence of his academic training and extraordinary work capacity. Born on 25 January 1929 in Shepperton (England) to a Scottish mother and a French father, after spending a few years in Singapore and Japan, he completed his youthful education in France, where in 1972 he received a doctorate in letters and humanities from the Sorbonne, where he taught from 1969 to 1974. From 1974 to 1990, Faurisson was professor of French literature at the University of Lyon. The author of four books on literature, he is also a recognised specialist in the analysis of texts and documents, a skill that allows him to access historical writings with unquestionable professional competence.

Professor Faurisson was the first to publish important revisionist documents on Auschwitz. In the archives of the Auschwitz State Museum he discovered the technical and architectural drawings of the morgues, crematoria and other facilities. Aware of the value of his discovery, he decided to exhibit it. By 1978 Faurisson had already written several articles expressing his critical view of the history of the extermination of the Jews. On 16 November 1978, the newspaper *Le Matin de Paris* published an article about an unknown professor at the University of Lyon named Robert Faurisson and his views on Auschwitz and the Holocaust. The fact that the press picked up on his revisionist views brought him into the limelight and thus began the "Affaire Faurisson", which was to continue indefinitely. From the beginning, he wrote years later, "I never had any illusions: I would be dragged into court, I would be convicted, there would be physical attacks, press campaigns and turbulence in my personal, family and professional life".

Everything he had imagined was soon to come true, for on 20 November 1978, four days after making the headlines in *Le Matin de Paris*, Faurisson suffered the first attack, praised by Bernard Schalscha, a Jewish journalist from *Liberation* de Lyon who had reported on the day, place and time Faurisson was giving the courses. Members of the Union of Jewish Students who had travelled to Lyon by train from Paris attacked the professor at the University in the presence of Dr Marc Aron, a cardiologist who was president of the Liaison Committee of Jewish Institutions and Organisations in Lyon. Faurisson not only refused to be intimidated, but stepped forward: in December 1978 and January 1979 *Le Monde* published two articles by him in which he showed his scepticism about the gas chambers at Auschwitz. The response to such audacity was a new attack on the day he was trying to resume his courses. Marc Aron was again at the University that day.

In April 1979 he took part in an impressive debate on Swiss television, in the course of which he refuted the arguments of conspicuous advocates of exterminationist theories. The path had been mapped out and Robert Faurisson was determined to follow it without deviating from the marked route. It was also in these years that he had begun to contribute to *The Journal of Historical Review*, an organ of the Institute for Historical Review (IHR) in California, where in September 1983 he gave a lecture entitled "Revisionism on Trial: Events in France, 1979-1983", in which he explained the actions of Jewish organisations to silence revisionists through lawsuits and acts of intimidation.

Professor Faurisson faced a concerted campaign to silence him during those years and was forced to defend himself in French courts because of his statements and writings. His bank account was frozen and judicial officials repeatedly visited his home to threaten him and his wife with seizure of their assets to meet the financial burdens imposed by his comments. As a result of this campaign, his family life was disrupted and his health deteriorated. In December 1980, in an interview for the radio station "Europe 1", Robert Faurisson uttered the famous sentence summarising the result of his research in 60 words in French. The alleged Hitlerian gas chambers and the alleged genocide of the Jews form a single historical lie, which has allowed a gigantic political-financial swindle, whose main beneficiaries are the State of Israel and Zionism and whose main victims are the German people - but not their leaders - and the Palestinian people as a whole". Thirty-six years later, the professor considers that the phrase does not require the slightest change.

For these unbearable words, Faurisson was criminally prosecuted for racial defamation and incitement to hatred. Found guilty, , he received a three-month prison sentence in July 1981, but his sentence was suspended. In addition to a fine of thousands of francs, he was ordered to pay 3.6 million francs in costs for the publication of the verdict on television and in the written press. On appeal, a court in June 1982 dropped the charge of incitement to racial hatred and eliminated the 3.6 million francs. From this point on, Faurisson was tied to a chain of legal proceedings with ruinous effects, as he himself found it necessary to take legal action against outrageously false defamatory attacks. He soon realised that if he persisted in defending himself in this way, he would end up destitute, for if he won, he would receive one franc in damages, while if he lost, he would have to pay the other side considerable sums.

On 25 April 1983, after having been sued by Jewish organisations, which had hoped for an exemplary sentence, he heard a relatively favourable verdict, as the judges of the Paris Court of Appeal said: "Faurisson is a serious researcher; we see no frivolity, negligence, deliberate omissions or lies in his writings on the gas chambers, but he is perhaps malicious and he is certainly dangerous. We condemn him for this probable malice and the danger it entails, but we do not condemn him for his work on the gas chambers, which is serious. On the contrary, since this work is serious, we guarantee every Frenchman the right to say, if he thinks so, that the gas chambers did not exist." Verdicts like this explain why the Zionist Laurent Fabius and the Jewish communist Jean-Claude Gayssot sponsored the Fabius-Gayssot law in 1990. The verdict, handed down on 26 April 1983, can therefore be considered a political achievement, but one that was achieved at the expense of Professor Faurisson, who was ordered to pay the costs of publishing the full verdict, estimated by the judges at a minimum of 60,000 francs.

LICRA published the verdict in the journal *History*, but the text was so badly falsified that Faurisson sued the Jewish lobby. The result of the lawsuit was that the professor was awarded one franc in damages, but had to pay 20,000 francs, despite which LICRA never published the correct text of the verdict. Another lawsuit brought by Professor Faurisson was against Jean Pierre Bloch, president of LICRA and author of a book in which he portrayed him as a Nazi and a falsifier convicted in court. A third lawsuit was against the communist newspaper *L'Humanité*. He lost the lawsuits and also the appeals. The judges acknowledged that he had been defamed, but added that his adversaries had done so in "good faith". Consequently, the defendants were acquitted and he had to pay all legal costs. In February 1985, *Droit de Vivre*, an LICRA publication, gloated with the following headline on one of its pages: "Treating Faurisson as a forger is defaming him, but 'in good faith'". This was an invitation to consider him a forger, which was henceforth the case, always "in good faith".

Robert Faurisson's role in the 1985 and 1988 trials of Ernst Zündel in Toronto was of the highest order. Apart from his testimony as a defence witness, his work as a shadow expert alongside the legendary Doug Christie, Zündel's lead lawyer, was extremely important. This has already been discussed in the pages on the "revisionist dynamo", but now it is time to expand on his contribution in those historic days to the international revival of revisionism. In June 1984 Professor Faurisson travelled to Canada to help what was to become one of his great friends. In January 1985, he returned to Toronto to spend the seven weeks of the trial with Zündel's team, whom he has since considered "an exceptional person". In his *Revisionist Writings* Faurisson has left much of his experience of those trials for posterity.

The court was presided over by Judge Hugh Locke; the prosecutor was Peter Griffiths. Attorney Douglas Christie was assisted by Keltie Zubko, the mother of his two children[18]. The jury was made up of twelve people. The costs were borne by the state, i.e. the taxpayers, and not by Sabina Citron of the Holocaust Remembrance Association, who had brought the case. Faurisson spent hundreds of hours, sometimes late into the night, with Douglas Christie, whom he briefed and advised on all matters, as there was no greater expert in the field at the time. Together they prepared the devastating interrogations of Raul Hilberg and Rudolf Vrba, the two main witnesses for the prosecution. We now give the floor to Professor Faurisson:

> "In Douglas Christie, Zündel was able to find a lawyer who, in addition to being courageous, was heroic. It was for this reason that I agreed to support Doug Christie, day in and day out, as he prepared and developed his work. I might add that without the help of his friend Keltie Zubko we would not have been able to succeed in the 1985 trial, a gruelling ordeal that in retrospect seems like a nightmare. The atmosphere prevailing in court was unbearable, especially because of the attitude of the judge, Hugh Locke. I have attended many trials in my life, including those in France during the time of the purge, the post-war purge of 'collaborators'. I have never encountered a judge as biased, autocratic and violent as Judge Hugh Locke. Anglo-Saxon law offers many more safeguards than French law, but it only takes one man to pervert the best of systems: Judge Locke was that man. I remember Locke shouting in my direction, 'Shut up!' as, from a distance, without saying a word, he pushed a document in Doug Christie's direction."

It would be interesting to devote a few pages to the interrogations of Hilberg and Vrba, as they were absolutely exposed and their credibility was in tatters. Since this is not feasible, as we must prioritise the pursuit of Faurisson, we will offer just a few sample paragraphs. Raul Hilberg, haloed with prestige, arrived in Toronto with no books, no notes, no documents, apparently sure of himself and confident of his experience in other trials in which he had testified against alleged war criminals. "He testified," writes Faurisson, "for several days probably at a rate of $150 an hour." To questions

---

[18] Douglas H. Christie, nicknamed "The Battling Barrister" by his friends, died at the age of 66 in 2013. The mainstream press took advantage of his death to recall that he had defended a number of "scoundrels", "neo-Nazis", etc. etc. etc.; however, there was a pleasant surprise: at least one newspaper in Canada, the *Times Colonist* of Victoria , in British Columbia, where Douglas had lived, reminded its readers that Douglas Christie was an extraordinary lawyer who had always defended freedom of expression. Lucien Larre, the priest who officiated at the funeral mass, gave an emotional farewell address and referred to him as a free speech warrior who fought for the truth. "He did not care," Larre said, "about the threats to his life or the number of times the windows of his office were broken. He stood tall." His wife Keltie Zubko preferred to define him in the words of his daughter, "I think my daughter said it best, that everyone talks about his legacy as a lawyer, as a public speaker, as an inspirational speaker - a person who helped a lot of people who were homeless and couldn't pay - but she said his real legacy was as a father."

from the prosecutor, he answered the usual, viz: Hitler gave orders to exterminate the Jews, the Germans followed a plan, they used the gas chambers.... Hilberg defined himself in these terms: "I would describe myself as an empiricist who looks at materials".

Everything changed when the cross-examination began by Doug Christie, who, perfectly advised by Professor Faurisson, cornered the renowned Jewish historian, whose work is considered one of the bibles of the Holocaust. Faurisson himself tells the story:

> "For the first time in his life, he had to deal with a defendant who had decided to defend himself and was capable of doing so: Doug Christie, next to whom I was sitting, interrogated Hilberg harshly, mercilessly, for several days. His questions were incisive, precise, relentless. Until then I had had a certain respect for Hilberg because of the quantity, not the quality, of his work; in any case he stood head and shoulders above the Poliakovs, Wellers, Klarsfelds and the rest. As he testified, my regard was replaced by a feeling of irritation and pity: irritation because Hilberg was constantly engaged in evasive manoeuvres, and pity because Christie ended up scoring a goal almost every time. On every issue, if one had to conclude anything, it became clear that Hilberg was by no means 'an empiricist who looks at materials.' He was exactly the opposite; he was a man lost in the clouds of his ideas, a kind of theologian who had constructed for himself a mental universe in which the physical aspects of facts had no place."

Doug Christie announced to the "empiricist who looks at the materials" that he was going to read him a list of concentration camps. When he had finished, he asked him which ones he had examined and how often he had done so. Hilberg admitted that he had not examined any of them, either before publishing the first edition of *The Destruction of the European Jews* in 1961 or even for the publication of the definitive edition in 1985. In other words, the historian who had begun his research into the history of the Holocaust in 1948 and who was considered to be the leading authority on the subject had not examined a single camp and had only visited Auschwitz once and Treblinka once. When asked by lawyer Christie if he knew of any autopsy report of a prisoner's body which established that he had been killed by poison gas, Hilberg's reply was: "No". The transcript on pp. 828-858, Professor Faurisson explains, reflects Doug Christie's lengthy questioning of the two alleged orders that Hilberg claims Hitler issued for the extermination of the Jews. The Jewish historian was asked where they were, that is, where he had seen them. He had to admit that there was "no trace" of them. The lawyer then reminded him of a statement he had made in February 1983 at Avery Fisher Hall in New York, where Hilberg elaborated a thesis that had nothing to do with the existence of an extermination order. He said the following, verbatim:

"What began in 1941 was a process of destruction not planned in advance, not centrally organised by any agency. There was no blueprint or budget for destructive measures. They were taken bit by bit, step by step. Thus what was carried out was not so much the execution of a plan as an incredible mental agreement, a consensus - telepathy of a vast bureaucracy."

This mind-boggling explanation would have more to do with parapsychology, as it claims that there was no plan, no centralised orders, no blueprint and no budget for the extermination of six million Jews - a gigantic operation - but the mental consensus of a bureaucracy communicating telepathically.

Faurisson explains that he prepared with lawyer Christie the interrogation of Rudolf Vrba, author of *I Cannot Forgive* and theoretical germ of the War Refugee Board (WRB) report on Auschwitz. Arthur R. Butz's book was a fundamental source that provided them with very useful elements to unmask the impostor. The lies about the gas chambers and about Himmler's visit to Auschwitz in January 1943 to inaugurate a crematorium and to witness the gassing of 3,000 people were exposed. It was shown that Vrba was a fake who had never set foot in either the crematoria or the "gas chambers". Documents proved that Himmler had been in Auschwitz in July 1942 and not in January 1943. The impossibility of his opening any crematoria was also proven, as the first of the new crematoria was not opened in January, but much later. In *I Cannot Forgive*, Vrba describes Himmler's visit in detail and even reports on his reflections and conversations. Vrba, a bundle of nerves, was portrayed for what he was, a lying charlatan who even outraged prosecutor Griffiths with his inane verbiage.

After making an essential contribution to Zündel's defence during the first trial, Faurisson returned to France, where the witch-hunt against revisionists was continuing. In 1985, Claude Lanzmann's *Shoah* had been released. Faurisson devoted a review to it, denouncing the film's propagandistic function. Pierre Guillaume, the revisionist book publisher, had published the professor's text and had chosen a May '68 slogan as the title: "Open your eyes, break your television set! Lanzmann turned to France-Presse (AFP) and managed to get the French state agency to publish a long statement in which he gave vent to his indignation at the revisionist criticism of the film. Naturally, freedom of expression, which is constantly claimed when merciless attacks are launched against everything and everyone, could not be exercised in this case. Consequently, on 1 July 1987, France-Presse called on the judicial authorities to act to "put an immediate stop to the machinations of the revisionists", in the name of "respect for freedom of enquiry and human rights". The Federation of Journalists denounced the *Shoah* analysis as unspeakable. Among other examples of its particular respect for freedom of expression, it said: "The Federation believes that individuals like Robert Faurisson should not be able to write with impunity.... To tarnish a film like *Shoah*, which can only be viewed with appalling awe and infinite compassion, is an attack on the Rights of Man".

In the absence of the Fabius-Gayssot law, the insults and threats led to two new attacks. The first was carried out by a certain Nicolas Ullmann on 12 June 1987. This individual violently beat Faurisson at the Sporting-Club in Vichy. Two months later, exactly on 12 September, a group of Jewish militants attacked the professor at the Sorbonne. It was not only he who was attacked, but also the people accompanying him, including the publisher Pierre Guillaume. All were injured to varying degrees, but it was Professor Henry Chauveau who was the most seriously injured. On this occasion, Sorbonne guards managed to arrest one of the attackers, but a plainclothes policeman ordered his release and also expelled Professor Faurisson from the Sorbonne, where he had taught.

In January 1988 Faurisson was back in Toronto to assist his friend Ernst Zündel. As we know, it was his idea to hire Fred Leuchter to travel to Poland to conduct research at Auschwitz. It was indeed a momentous contribution, for Leuchter's technical expertise became the *Leuchter Report*, which was to be a landmark in the history of the revisionist movement. Faurisson reasoned that the United States was the ideal place to look for an expert on gas chambers, since it was there that gas executions regularly took place. Zündel's lawyers contacted William M. Armontrout, warden of the Missouri State Penitentiary, who in a letter recommended Fred A. Leuchter as the most qualified expert. I suggest," he said in the letter, "that you contact Mr. Fred A. Leuchter.... Mr. Leuchter is an engineer specialising in gas chambers and executions. He is well versed in all areas and is the only consultant in the United States that I know of." The reader interested in learning more about Robert Faurisson's contribution to the second Zündel trial should refer to Barbara Kulaszka's book *Did Six Million Really Die: Report of the Evidence in the Canadian "False News" Trial of Ernst Zündel* (Toronto,1992).

Between 20 November 1978 and 31 May 1993, Robert Faurisson was the victim of ten violent attacks. The most serious of these occurred on 16 September 1989, when he was already in his sixties. While he was walking his dog in a park near his home in Vichy, three men set him up. After spraying his face with a stinging gas that momentarily blinded him, the assailants threw him to the ground and began punching him in the face and kicking him in the chest. It seems clear that the criminals, three Jewish thugs who are members of the group "fils de la mémoire juive" (children of Jewish memory), intended to kill him. Fortunately, a person who saw the scene intervened and was able to rescue the teacher, who was seriously injured. He was taken to a hospital and underwent a long surgical operation in the emergency room, as his jaw and a rib were broken, as well as severe head injuries. The Jewish group that claimed responsibility for the attack said in a statement: "Professor Faurisson is the first, but he will not be the last. We leave those who deny the Shoah warned." Faurisson later stated that on the eve of the attack he had noticed in surprise the presence in the park of Nicolas Ullmann, who two years earlier had already beaten him in a sports club in Vichy. As usual, not a single arrest was made and the attackers went unpunished.

Robert Faurisson's merit is singular, since, as in the case of Ernst Zündel, we are looking at a man alone who does not shrink back, an intellectual of great stature, almost unrepeatable, who has been and remains capable of enduring anything rather than renounce his convictions. In April 1991, following an interview that appeared in September 1990 in *Le Choc du Mois*, the 17th chamber of the Paris Correctional Court, presided over by Claude Grellier, imposed a fine of 250,000 francs on Faurisson and another 180,000 on the editor of the publication. In the same year, the Jewish lobby succeeded in having him expelled from the university on the basis of the Fabius-Gayssot law. The professor appealed to the ICCPRHRC (International Covenant on Civil and Political Rights and Human Rights Committee) on the grounds that the Fabius-Gayssot Law violated international law; however the ICCPRHRC dismissed the appeal and said that the Fabius-Gayssot Law is necessary to counter "possible anti-Semitism". On 17 March 1992 Faurisson issued a challenge from Stockholm: he demanded a graphic display of the murder weapon and its operating technique. He demanded that someone show him or draw him a Nazi gas chamber. The response was a new aggression. A year later, on 22 May 1993, he was physically assaulted for the second time in Stockholm. On both occasions, the Swedish press reported the attacks on the French professor at some length.

Years later, when in April 1996 the 'Affaire Garaudy' was beginning to polarise attention in France, Robert Faurisson made a statement in which he expressed his solidarity with Roger Garaudy and confirmed 'the imposture of the gas chambers'. As a result of these words, Jewish organisations sued him for the umpteenth time on 25 September 1997. During the trial, Faurisson told the court: "We are only three years away from the year 2000 and millions of people are asked to believe in something they have never seen and do not even know how it worked". The prosecutor called for Faurisson to be jailed if he did not pay the appropriate fine, to which the professor replied, "I will neither buy nor pay for my freedom. No one has ever bought me and no one will ever buy me." Finally, on 23 October 1997, the court found him "guilty" and demanded that he pay 120,600 francs divided into three parts: 50,000 francs as a fine, 20,600 francs for the Jewish accuser, and another 50,000 francs to pay for the publication of the sentence in two newspapers.

Only three months later, in December 1997, the Jews sued again. Faurisson was subpoenaed by a Paris court because of an article published on a website on 16 January 1997: "Les visions cornues de l'"Holocauste", in which he began by stating that "the Holocaust of the Jews was a fiction". The professor responded to the summons with a letter announcing his refusal to continue to collaborate with the French justice system and police in their repression of revisionism. The harassment continued: three months later, on 16 March 1998, he had to appear before a Paris court to be tried for a definition of "revisionism", which appeared in a newspaper incorrectly.

And so it goes on and on. On 8 April 1998 it was the Dutch Jews who went against Faurisson. Seven years earlier, in 1991, in collaboration with the Belgian revisionist Siegfried Verbeke, he had published in Dutch *Het "Dagboek" van Anne Frank. Een Kritische benadering* (*The 'Diary' of Anne Frank. A critical evaluation*), a booklet which concluded that the 'diary' was a forgery, since the handwriting of the original manuscript could not have been that of a child. The book was banned in the Netherlands, but both the Anne Frank Museum in Amsterdam and the Anne Frank Fonds in Basel were not satisfied with the censorship of the book and took joint legal action. The Museum complained that Faurisson's work had forced them to provide "special instruction" to the guides and that the professor's criticism could reduce the number of visitors to the museum and, consequently, its profits.

The cancellation of the congress "Historical Revisionism and Zionism", which was to be held in Beirut from 31 March to 3 April 2001, was a major setback for revisionists from all over the world who had gathered in the Lebanese capital. The government of Lebanon, the victim of continuous Israeli attacks, yielded to pressure from the most important Zionist organisations, backed by the United States. Robert Faurisson then explained that Rafik Hariri, Lebanon's prime minister, was so trapped by his country's debt, which amounted to 24,000,000,000 dollars for four million inhabitants, that he had no alternative but to give in to blackmail and ban the congress. Since then, the holding of an international revisionist conference had been in doubt. When Mahmoud Ahmadinejad became president of the Islamic Republic of Iran in 2005, Tehran offered to host revisionists from all over the world. One hundred and thirty researchers from thirty countries converged on the Iranian capital, where the Tehran International Holocaust Review Conference finally took place on 11-12 December 2006, which was greeted in the West with all sorts of disqualifications and backlash.

On 11 December 2006, Professor Faurisson gave a speech based on a document entitled *The Victories of Revisionism*, which has since been translated into several languages, including Spanish, and published in many countries. In this text, dedicated to Professor Mahmoud Ahmadinejad and to Ernst Zündel, Germar Rudolf and Horst Mahler, whom Faurisson refers to as "our prisoners of conscience", up to twenty historical realities clarified by revisionist research are presented in detail, which have had to be explicitly or implicitly acknowledged by the exterminationists. 1. There were no gas chambers in the camps in Germany. 2. 2. There was no order from Hitler to exterminate the Jews. 3. At the Wannsee Conference, the extermination of the Jews was not decided upon, since the term "final solution" meant deportation to the East. 4. The formulation in which the German concentration camp system has been presented is doomed. 5. The Auschwitz gas chamber visited by millions of tourists is a fake. 6. No documents, traces or other material evidence of the existence of the gas chambers have been found. On 11 December 2006, Robert Faurisson gave a wide-ranging interview to Iranian television, during which he declared to millions of Iranian viewers that the Holocaust was a lie. This was bound to have consequences, as the usual people in France were waiting for him.

No sooner had the revisionist congress ended than the then President of the Republic Jacques Chirac condemned Faurisson's participation in the Tehran conference on 13 December 2006 and personally called for an investigation. Following the instructions of the highest authority of the state, the Minister of Justice instructed a Paris prosecutor to launch an investigation. On 16 April 2007, police lieutenant Séverine Besse and another colleague went to Vichy to question the professor. Obstinately, Faurisson refused to answer any of the questions and wrote the following in the official report: "I refuse to collaborate with the police and judicial system in the repression of historical revisionism".

Magistrate Marc Sommerer, assigned to the case, summoned Faurisson nine months later. At 9 a.m. on 24 January 2008, the professor presented himself at the local police station. As soon as he entered, three judicial police officers sent the day before from Paris, including Séverine Besse herself, notified him that he was in custody and that his home would be searched while he was being held. He, an old man who would have been 79 years old the following day, 25 January, had his body searched and his wallet, purse, pen, watch, belt, etc. were confiscated. Perhaps they were trying to intimidate the old professor, who said that his wife was ill at home, a fact known to the police, and that for serious medical reasons she needed his constant presence. Once again, Faurisson remained stubborn and did not answer any questions. He was then told that he was the subject of three criminal proceedings for which warrants had been issued by Judge Sommerer. The first two mentioned to him related to his participation in the Tehran Conference. In one, he was being prosecuted under the Fabius-Gayssot Law by the Public Prosecutor's Office and a host of "pious organisations" for "denying crimes against humanity". In another, the LICRA had sued him for "defamation". The third lawsuit had been brought by the daily *Libération* for tortuous reasons that we will spare you the explanation. Faurisson was then taken to his home, where the search continued for six hours. Finally, on 25 July 2012, a judge in Paris notified him of the trial of the three criminal complaints.

The persecution of Robert Faurisson for thought crimes has been ongoing for forty years. On the evening of 19 November 2014, two policemen from the neighbouring town of Clermond-Ferrand, one of whom was a major, turned up at his home at Vichy with a search warrant: they wanted to seize a computer and certain documents. They found neither. Once again, LICRA had asked the public prosecutor to take action against the appearance of an unofficial "Blog" by the professor. There is no doubt that Faurisson is endowed with an inner strength of a superior nature. Faced with the scale of the attacks and the sheer scale of the fight against such powerful enemies, any normal person would have given up, but Faurisson, who had a heart attack in 2014, has neither flinched nor broken down. He just turned 87 on 29 January 2016 and is still holding on with his 83-year-old wife, who has been able to stay with the professor despite the fact that she too has a heart condition. Faurisson has recently complained that he is constantly receiving threats, both by telephone and in writing, and has unsuccessfully asked the police to protect them, as his wife is being harassed more and more every day and is suffering more and more from her illness.

Vincent Reynouard, "Hearts go up!"

The case of the young revisionist Vincent Reynouard is another example of the will to resist: in the face of endless adversity, he has shown commendable courage and courage worthy of respect. Born in 1969, he married in 1991 and is now the father of eight children. A Catholic traditionalist, a convinced National Socialist and a revisionist, Reynouard has put everything at risk rather than give an inch in his denunciation of the falsity of official history. At the age of twenty-three, he had his first setback with the Fabius-Gayssot law. On 8 October 1992, a court in Caen sentenced him to a month's imprisonment, suspended, and a fine of 5,000 francs for having anonymously given twenty-four of his students texts questioning the gas chamber murders. Graduated as a chemical engineer with a diploma from ISMRA (Institute of Materials and Radiation), he worked as a high school teacher of mathematics and as a freelance historian specialising in the Second World War. In 1997, after revisionist texts were found on the hard drive of the computer he used at school, he was dismissed from the secondary school teaching profession by Education Minister François Bayrou. Since then, he has had to survive on his writings, his videos and his work as a researcher.

Author of a dozen essays and pamphlets on historical topics. Reynouard worked with Siegfried Verbeke on *Vrij Historisch Onderzook, VHO (Free Historical Research)*, a website that became the largest revisionist publishing site in Europe. He himself edited the publication *Sans Concession*. His most famous book was the result of an investigation into the Oradour-sur-Glane massacre. At 1400 hours on 10 June 1944, shortly after the Normandy landings, the Waffen SS entered this small, quiet village in the Limousin, where resistance fighters were sheltering. Six hours later, at 20:00, the Waffen SS left the village. Behind them lay a ruined place littered with corpses, five hundred of them charred women and children. Academic historiography attributed the massacre to the Germans. Officially, they retreated through the village and set fire to the church where women and children had taken refuge. This is exactly what Reynouard questioned in his 450-page book, published in Belgium in 1997. In France the book appeared in June 1997, after he had been expelled from teaching for his revisionist views. Three months later, in September, Interior Minister Jean-Pierre Chevènement ordered the book to be seized and banned its distribution and circulation throughout France.

Between 1998 and 1999, a team of Reynouard's collaborators produced a video cassette summarising the book and encouraging people to buy it. The film was released in 2000 and distribution began in January 2001. On 8 February 2001, the prefect of Haute-Vienne, a department in central France, issued a decree banning the cassette in the whole department. On 27 September 2001, four years after the banning of the book, the Ministry of the Interior banned the video throughout France. The proceedings against Vincent Reynouard led to a trial which took place in first instance on 18 November 2003. Reynouard was sentenced for "apology of a war crime" to one year in prison, a fine of 10,000 euros, and the confiscation of all his seized files. The appeal proceedings were held on 14 April 2004. Reynouard was sentenced to two years, of which six months was actual imprisonment and the rest was probation, but the fine of 10,000 euros was changed to 3,000 euros. In addition, he had to compensate the three civil parties that had appeared in the case, including the inescapable LICRA.

Nevertheless, Reynouard continued to pursue revisionist ideas and in 2005 wrote a sixteen-page pamphlet entitled *Holocaust? Here is what they hide from us*, in which he openly questioned the official history and presented a completely opposite view. The French judiciary was quick to pounce on him. The retrial took place on 8 November 2007 in Saverne, where a court sentenced him to one year in prison and a fine of 10,000 euros for "questioning crimes against humanity" through the aforementioned pamphlet. He was also ordered to pay 3,000 euros to LICRA. The judgment was appealed, but on 25 June 2008, the Colmar Court of Appeal upheld it and also imposed a new fine of 60,000 euros. Simultaneously, on 19 June 2008, six days earlier, the Brussels Court of Appeal had sentenced Reynouard and Siegfried Verbeke to one year's imprisonment and a fine of 25,000 euros for having written and published texts denying the Holocaust and questioning crimes against humanity.

Moreover, as Reynouard resided in Belgium, the French authorities issued a European arrest warrant in order for the Belgians to extradite him, since, in accordance with the ratification of the sentence by the court of appeal of Colmar, Reynouard was also to serve one year in prison in France. On 9 July 2010, he was incarcerated in Forest Prison (Brussels). On 23 July 2010, Judge Chambers in Brussels declared that the arrest warrant for

Reynouard issued by France was valid, so on 19 August 2010 he was extradited and imprisoned in Valenciennes prison. While awaiting extradition he declared: "When you have no other argument than prison to free yourself from a dialectical opponent, it is because you lack arguments".

Paul-Eric Blanrue, founding historian of the research group Cercle Zététique and author of the book *Sarkozy, Israël, et les juifs*, issued a press release denouncing the Gayssot law, calling for solidarity with Vincent Reynouard and launching a campaign to collect signatures in defence of freedom of expression and to demand Reynouard's release. Blanrue, in addition to denouncing the suspicious silence of the French and international media, noted the abnormality of the fact that not a single NGO had said a word in defence of Reynouard's freedom of expression and freedom of thought.

Early in the morning of Tuesday, 5 April 2011, the 42-year-old revisionist left Valenciennes prison. His wife Marina, his son Pierre and a group of friends, including Siegfried Verbeke, his wife Edna and a group of Belgian and German revisionists, were waiting for him outside the gate. Reynouard's seven other children were waiting in a café near the prison, making drawings to give to their father. After eating together in a joyful atmosphere, the Reynouard family had to separate again, as Marina and the children had to return to Brussels. Vincent could not go with them, as he was under judicial supervision and forbidden to leave France. In fact, the next day, 6 April, he was summoned by an examining magistrate in Amiens on another matter: he was suspected of having sent revisionist CDs to 120 high schools in France in 2009.

On the day of his release, Reynouard gave an interview to a journalist from *Rivarol* magazine. His first words were for his wife, whom he thanked for her attitude and congratulated for her heroism. Secondly, he thanked Paul-Eric Blanrue for his courage and all those who had assisted him financially and written to him. He expressed his intention to write a testimonial book and to resume the publication of the magazine *Sans Concessions*, which had been interrupted since his arrest, since all his collaborators had remained faithful to their posts. The last words of the interview were words of encouragement: "In spite of all the vicissitudes and all the pitfalls, the fight continues. Hearts go up!

In February 2015, a court of first instance in Coutances, Lower Normandy, again sentenced Vincent Reynouard to two years in prison for publishing a video in which he denounced the political manipulation and brainwashing inflicted on the youth of his country and refuted the theory of the systematic extermination of European Jews during the Second World War. He was also fined 35,000 euros. Faced with the severity of the sentence, as the Gayssot Law provides for a maximum of one year in prison for "Holocaust denial", the prosecutor himself appealed to the court of appeal in Caen, the regional capital. In a video posted on the internet, Reynouard had announced that he did not intend to pay a single cent. On 17 June 2015, in view of the evidence that the sentence imposed by the Coutances court was "illegal", the Caen court reduced it to one year and revoked the financial penalty. Reynouard did not appear before the Caen court, two months earlier, on 25 April 2015, he had announced in a video that he was going underground to flee the political persecution he was suffering in France: "So," he said in the video, "you can say that I am on the run. This time I have lost everything, or almost everything. Here I am without a home, with my rucksack. I have only been able to save a few fragments of files to try to make the promised videos". At the time of writing, we do not know what has become of Reynouard, as we have not been able to find out anything new about him.

3. MAIN VICTIMS OF PERSECUTION IN AUSTRIA:

Gerd Honsik, victim of PSOE's surrender to Zionism

Hans Strobl, president of the Burgenland Cultural Federation, wrote in 1988 in the epilogue of *A Solution for Hitler?* that the Austrian state police had threatened Gerd Honsik in 1978 with committal to a psychiatric clinic. He does not, however, explain why Honsik was so seriously intimidated, and instead of being sent to an insane asylum he ended up in prison. In prison he wrote two books of poems. The first, *Lüge, wo ist dein Sieg?* (*Lie, where is your Victoria ?*), was published in 1981; the second, *Fürchtet euch nicht! (Don't be afraid!)*, in 1983. Both manuscripts were smuggled out of prison with the help of prison guards sympathetic to the poet, who had been forbidden to write. The first book, composed in classical verse, was eventually confiscated and cost Honsik a fine of 41,000 shillings (then Austrian currency). The president of the Supreme Court, apparently an expert in literary criticism, ruled that it was "not art". As for the latter, an inquiry was also instituted to ban it.

In 1986, for political reasons, Honsik was dismissed from his job, where he had been employed for fifteen years. The persecution affected his school-age children, who were subjected to pressures to which even some teachers lent themselves. Between 1987 and 1988, Honsik had to go to court eighteen times: he had to spend 140,000 shillings in court fees and legal costs. The worst came in 1988 with the publication of *Freispruch für Hitler? (Solution for Hitler?)*, a book purporting to be a book of reconciliation. Gerd Honsik consulted a Catholic parish priest, Robert Viktor Knirsch, to find out whether the priest understood that there were any moral impediments. The parish priest wrote him a letter in which, as a Roman Catholic priest, he encouraged him to continue with the book:

> "...Truth is part of the retinue of good. Everyone who seeks the truth has the right to be able to doubt, to investigate and to weigh up. And where people are required to believe blindly, there is a haughtiness, with so much blasphemy, that it gives us pause for thought. While now those whose thesis you question have reason on their side, they will accept all questions calmly, they will give their answers with all patience. And they will no longer conceal their evidence and records. But if they lie, they will cry out to the judge. Thus they will be known. The truth is always calm; but a lie is always in a struggle for an earthly trial!
>
> With my compliments, I send you my best regards.
> Priest Robert Viktor Knirsh
> Kahlenbergerdorf, 2/6/1988".

After writing these words to Honsik, which the poet reproduced in his work, the parish priest was admitted to a psychiatric clinic, where he soon fell ill. He died on Monday 26 June 1989. Before his death, he expressed the wish that the German anthem should be played at his burial. At 9.30 a.m. on 30 June, a funeral mass was held in Kahlenbergerdorf, after which Knirsh's body was buried in the parish cemetery. About seven hundred people attended the funeral, among them Archbishop Krätztl and Provost Koberger, but also numerous secret agents and a police dog unit. When, at the end of the ceremony, Honsik asked for the priest's last wishes to be carried out, the police intervened and began asking the attendees to identify themselves. Gerd Honsik was momentarily detained and reproached for requesting the playing of the German anthem in circumstances where it was forbidden.

As for the consequences of the book's publication, the process dragged on for years and even led to the creation of an implementing law exclusively for the case. In January 1992, Honsik left the country after being publicly defamed on television, where Dr. Neugebauer, director of the Austrian Resistance Documentary Archives, accused him in the presence of the Minister of the Interior of planning a coup d'état. When it was proved to be slander and falsehoods, Honsik returned to Austria to attend the trial, which lasted several weeks. Gerd Honsik was sentenced on 5 May 1992 to eighteen months imprisonment for "revitalisation of National Socialist activities". The Austrian Supreme Court rejected the appeal. To avoid further imprisonment, he fled to Spain, where he had already lived for a year as an eight-year-old boy. In 1949 he crossed the Pyrenees in a special train with a thousand severely malnourished Austrian children fleeing the ethnic cleansing perpetrated in Europe against the German people between 1945 and 1948, the perfectly documented genocide that has been concealed.

In 1993, Honsik published another book for which he would also later be prosecuted, *Schelm und Scheusal* (*Rogue and Monster*), in which he denounced Simon Wiesenthal, who had expressed his satisfaction with the letter bomb sent from Austria to former SS Alois Brunner, who lost an eye and eight fingers. A close associate of Adolf Eichmann, Brunner lived in Damascus, where Zionist assassins had tried to kill him on several occasions. Wiesenthal was well aware of the details of the bombing and referred to the victim as his "most wanted murderer of Jews". However, in August 1988 Gerd Honsik had visited him in the Syrian capital and to the question "When did you learn about the gas chambers?", Brunner replied, "After the war, through the newspapers."

On 7 October 1993, the Spanish Prime Minister, Felipe González, travelled to Vienna. There, the Chancellor of the Republic of Austria, Franz Vranitzky, took advantage of the occasion to ask him to extradite Honsik. This clearly reveals the extent of the power of the Jewish lobbies, which are capable of getting a high-ranking European leader to ask another to hand over a political refugee because of the publication of a book. Gerd Honsik, aware of this, addressed an open letter to the Spanish Parliament in which he requested political refuge in Spain. In the text he recalled that Spain had taken him in as a child in the post-war period and that he had already learned Spanish. The letter ended with these words: "I am addressing the Spanish parliamentarians, both on the right and on the left, and the Spanish people, begging them to remain firm in the face of the international pressures that are calling for my extradition. In Spain then I found refuge from hunger. In Spain today I seek refuge from prison". The Austrian authorities requested the Spanish Government to extradite him, but on 7 November 1995 the Audiencia Nacional refused. The Public Prosecutor's Office objected and considered, as the defence pointed out, that it was "a political crime and therefore excluded from extradition". The reasoning of the Audiencia Nacional considered that "it was not feasible to frame such conduct as provocation to the crime of genocide, as this requires the purpose of destroying, totally or partially, a religious group", a purpose that could not be affirmed "from the facts (writing and publishing *A Solution for Hitler?*) for which the defendant has been convicted...". Both the judge and the Audiencia prosecutor agreed that Honsik's book did not violate Spanish law. Therefore, without any harassment by the Spanish authorities, Gerd Honsik lived in Malaga for nearly fifteen years.

Finally, a European arrest warrant issued by the Vienna court was served by the Spanish authorities: on 23 August 2007, police arrested Honsik in Malaga. In September 2007, the president of the Jewish Religious Community of Austria, tycoon Ariel Muzicant, a Haifa-born Israeli, told the newspaper *Die Gemeinde* (*The Community*) that the Jewish community was working for uniform European legislation against neo-Nazis and Holocaust revisionists. Commenting on Honsik's arrest in Spain, he said:

> "Gerd Honsik was arrested after spending fifteen years in Spain and will be extradited to Austria. Personally, I am delighted about this because it shows once again that my talks with the Spanish Prime Minister, the Foreign Minister and the Minister of Justice in January this year have helped to get the Spanish government to adopt a corresponding stance

Without a hint of dissimulation, on the contrary, Muzicant boasted shamelessly about his power and took credit for getting the Spanish socialist government to do the right thing, i.e. what Zionism wanted. In January 2007 there was a PSOE government in Spain headed by José Luis Rodríguez Zapatero. The foreign minister was the ineffable Miguel Ángel Moratinos and the justice minister was Juan Fernando López Aguilar. The judge who allowed the extradition was Baltasar Garzón, who four years later would be sentenced to eleven years of disqualification and expelled from the judiciary by a unanimous decision of the members of the Criminal Chamber of the Supreme Court. This unscrupulous judge, unfortunately defended by many sectarians of the Spanish left, put himself at the service of the Zionists without considering that Spain had twice refused extradition and that the Audiencia Nacional had ruled in a 1995 decision that Honsik's was "a political crime and therefore excluded from extradition". Gerd Honsik's surrender to Austria took place on 4 October 2007. The Austrian Minister of Justice, the Socialist Maria Berger, publicly expressed her special thanks to Judge Baltasar Garzón in a press release issued by the Ministry of Justice on 5 October.

Four years later, on 26 January 2012, Göran Holming, a retired Swedish army commander and member of European Action, movement for a free Europe, filed criminal charges against Baltasar Garzón and against Prime Minister Rodríguez Zapatero and the aforementioned ministers with the Audiencia Nacional. The letter denounced the meeting with Ariel Muzicant and the political agreements reached at the meeting in January 2007. It argued at length about the false pretexts invoked to grant the extradition and specifically accused Judge Garzón of prevarication and violation of the law and the Spanish Constitution, which prohibits extradition for political crimes unless there are "terrorist acts". Here is the text of the request:

> "I would like to ask the Public Prosecutor to verify whether the former Prime Minister José Luis Rodríguez Zapatero and his former Ministers of Justice and Foreign Affairs, in collaboration with Judge Baltasar Garzón, have to answer for the extradition of the Austrian poet and writer Gerd Honsik, promoted through a conspiracy with the foreigner Ariel Muzicant and Ms. Maria Berger and carried out with the purpose of carrying out an inhumane and unjust political persecution in Austria, and whether the aforementioned persons have cumulatively committed Maria Berger and carried out for the purpose of inhumane and unjust political persecution in Austria, and whether the aforementioned persons have cumulatively committed:
>
> I) A crime against humanity,
> II) the offence of abuse of power,
> III) for falsification of the EU Arrest Warrant,
> IV) of conspiracy in an agreement against the Spanish Constitution.
>
> I hereby request that the above-mentioned persons be brought to trial before the competent court for the above-mentioned offences.
>
> Sincerely
> Göran Holming, retired commander of the Swedish Army".

Let us now return to the case of G. Honsik. On 3 December 2007, the appeal hearing, which had been cancelled in 1992 due to "failure of the person concerned to appear", was held in Vienna. The appeal was dismissed and the sentence of eighteen months unconditional imprisonment was confirmed. In May 2008, the Vienna Public Prosecutor's Office brought new charges against Honsik for "revitalisation of National Socialist activities". On 20 April 2009, the trial before the Vienna Regional Court began and on 27 April Honsik was sentenced to five years imprisonment because of his views on the existence of the gas chambers in the National Socialist labour camps. The verdict was upheld by the Supreme Court; but on 1 March 2010 the sentence was reduced to four years by the Vienna Court of Appeal.

A new trial against Honsik for the publication of two books, one of which was *Schelm und Scheusal* and the other *Rassismus Legal?* took place on 20 July 2010. This was a "3g trial", which is under Section 3g of the Austrian Prohibition Act (Verbotgesetz) of 1947, which severely represses the "revival of National Socialist sentiments". Judge Andreas Böhm, who sentenced Honsik to five years in the April 2009 trial, had instructed prosecutor Stefan Apostol to exclude the incriminating books at the time, in order to subsequently open a new trial that would allow for an additional sentence. At the trial, the books were considered separately. Honsik, despite serving time in prison, or perhaps because of it, was not deterred and lashed out at Simon Wiesenthal. What information we have about the trial sessions comes from the Austrian press, servile as all of them are to the controlling Jewish lobbies, so we will spare you the quotes. In short, Honsik reiterated that it was an admitted fact that there was not a single gas chamber on German or Austrian soil and that the liar was not he, but Wiesenthal. The judge tried to get Honsik's lawyer, Dr. Herbert Schaller, to deny the existence of the gas chambers. He repeatedly asked him if he, too, claimed that there were no gas chambers; but the lawyer always avoided answering questions that in Germany were asked to incriminate the defendants' lawyers.

Theoretically, Honsik was not due to be released until 2013, but an appeal to the Vienna Court finally achieved the goal of a favourable sentence, which reduced the length of his sentence by eighteen months. His advanced age (70 years) and his "successful social integration" in Spain, where he returned after his release at the end of 2011 to settle again in Malaga, where he had been arrested in 2007, were reportedly taken into account. Throughout his life, Gerd Honsik has been imprisoned for nearly six years for expressing ideas considered thought crimes.

David Irving sentenced to three years in prison in Vienna

The second trial of Ernst Zündel in Toronto was a milestone in the evolution of the revisionist thinking of David Irving, who, together with Robert Faurisson, acted as counsel to lawyer Doug Christie and testified at the trial as a defence witness. It appears that it was Irving who contacted Bill Armontrout, and when he recommended Fred Leuchter, he flew to Boston in the company of Faurisson to meet with the gas chamber expert to convince him to provide the technical expertise. The *Leuchter Report* dispelled all of Irving's doubts about the alleged extermination of European Jewry, if he still had any. Upon his return to London after the trial, Irving published the American engineer's report in the UK under the title *Auschwitz the End of the Line: The Leuchter Report* and wrote the foreword. Neither pleased the political establishment, and so on 20 June 1989 Irving and Leuchter were convicted in a motion tabled in the House of Commons . It described David Irving as "a Nazi propagandist and apologist for Hitler". As for the text that was released, it was deemed a "fascist publication". Irving issued a scathing press release in response to the Commons motion. On 23 June 1989, Irving published a text in which he stated unequivocally that the Auschwitz gas chambers were a "fable".

On 6 November 1989, David Irving gave a lecture at the Park Hotel in Vienna that sixteen years later would cost him a three-year prison sentence. Jewish organisations and various communist and extreme left-wing groups brought five thousand demonstrators onto the streets in an attempt to prevent the event. About five hundred riot police had to form a protective cordon to prevent the most exalted from storming the building. As a result of the content of the two lectures given in Austria, the government issued an arrest warrant for Irving and banned him from entering the country.

In January 1990 David Irving gave a lecture in Moers, Germany, where he alluded to Allied air terror and claimed that as many people died in Auschwitz between 1940 and 1945 as died in any of the criminal bombing raids on German cities. On 21 April 1990 Irving repeated the same speech in Munich, prompting a court in the Bavarian capital to sentence him on 11 July 1991 to a fine of DM 7,000 for Holocaust denial. Irving appealed, and during the hearing on 5 May 1992, he on those present in the Munich courtroom to fight for the German people to "put an end to the bloody lie of the Holocaust that had been woven against the country for fifty years". Irving referred to Auschwitz as "a tourist attraction". In addition to a fine of 10,000 marks, he was henceforth banned from entering Germany.

Other countries followed suit and the veto against Irving began to become widespread. In Canada he was arrested in November 1992 and deported to the UK. He was also refused entry to Italy and Australia. On 27 April 1993 he was summoned before a French court on charges related to the Gayssot Law. As this law does not provide for extradition, the historian refused to travel to France and did not appear. In 1994, he was sentenced in the UK to three months in prison for contempt of court during a legal dispute over publishing rights. He was finally locked up for ten days in London's Pentonville Prison.

The legal confrontation between David Irving and the Jewish historian Deborah Lipstadt, well known in revisionist circles, was a turning point that marked the British historian. It was a long process in the United Kingdom, of which we will only note the essential facts, since Irving appears in these pages as a victim of persecution in Austria and we must not deviate from our objective. For readers who are not familiar with the issue, the controversy between Deborah Lipstadt, Professor of Modern Judaism and Holocaust Studies at Emory University (USA), and David Irving began in 1993, when Lipstadt disqualified Irving in *Denying the Holocaust: The Growing Assault on Truth and Memory*. In the book, Lipstadt referred to the British historian as "an anti-Semite who falsifies documents for ideological reasons" and concluded that he was "a dangerous Holocaust denialist spokesman". In 1996 Irving decided to sue Lipstadt and his British publisher Penguin Books Ltd. for libel, claiming that his reputation as a historian had been damaged. The trial began on 11 January 2000 and ended on 11 April with Judge Charles Gray ruling in favour of Lipstadt and Penguin Books. Gray found that Irving "for his own ideological reasons had persistently and deliberately misrepresented and manipulated the historical evidence". Despite the fact that, as Germar Rudolf revealed, David Irving has Jewish origins, Judge Gray argued in the verdict that Irving was an "active Holocaust denier"; that he was "anti-Semitic and racist"; and that he had "associated with far-right radicals to promote neo-Nazism". The trial and verdict went around the world.

On 11 November 2005 David Irving became the most notorious victim of the persecution of revisionists in Austria. He himself later recounted the whole story in an article published in the *American Free Press*. According to his account, he had travelled to the country to speak to a student association, the student fraternity "Olympia". The subject of the lecture, discussed earlier in this work, was Joel Brand's negotiation in Hungary with Adolf Eichmann to free Hungarian Jews in exchange for trucks. Irving planned to explain that the British secret services had cracked the communication codes and were aware of what was being discussed between the Zionists and the Nazis. Since there had been a warrant for his arrest issued by the Vienna Regional Court for Holocaust denial since November 1989, Irving did not want to risk entering Austria by direct flight and opted to travel by car from Zurich. After driving through the night, he arrived in Vienna at 8:00 a.m. after having driven 900 kilometres.

Once he had rested, he called from a train station to the student Christopher V. who had invited him: "Rendezvous A," Irving said without identifying himself, "in one hour. Security was necessary and everything had been arranged six months in advance. Christopher, a young man in his twenties, picked him up in the station foyer and drove him to where over two hundred students were supposedly waiting for him. The event was scheduled to start at 18:00. Once the car was parked, they approached the building on foot. Leaning against the wall, they saw "three burly bouncers". As soon as he realised that they were from the "Stapo" (State Police), the young man handed the car keys to Irving and they parted . As he walked back to the Ford

Focus, Irving recounts, "one of the bouncers was following me about eighty yards behind; the other two were chasing Christopher." Out of habit, he entered the car from the right, as if it were an English vehicle; but the steering wheel was on the other side. The man started to run. When he finally started, the policeman was only about ten yards away. In the rear-view mirror, he saw him writing down the car's details on a notepad. The plan was to try to get to Basel, where he was to catch a plane the next day. About 250 kilometres outside Vienna, two police cars forced him to stop: "Eight uniformed policemen suddenly jumped out and came running towards me, shouting hysterically". This is the tight summary of how Irving experienced his arrest.

A spokesman for the Austrian Interior Ministry, Rudolf Gollia, reported that the British historian had been arrested on 11 November by motorway police officers near the town of Johann in der Heide in Styria. The international press reported that he had been arrested for denying the Holocaust 16 years earlier in a lecture given in 1989. A spokesman for the public prosecutor's office was quoted in the media as saying that if he was tried and found guilty, he could be sentenced to between one and ten years in prison.

After three months in custody, he was sentenced to three years' imprisonment by the Vienna Regional Court on 20 February 2006. In the indictment, the prosecutor specified that in the two public speeches in 1989 Irving had said that "Hitler actually maintained his protective hand over the Jews" and had denied the existence of the gas chambers. According to the prosecutor, Irving had also maintained in 1989 that Kristallnacht was not perpetrated by the Nazis, but by individuals disguised as Nazis.

In all fairness, it must be said that Irving's concessions before the Viennese court deeply disappointed some revisionists, who would have wished for a more dignified, more stoic attitude. Irving declared that he had changed his mind about the Holocaust because on a trip to Argentina he had found new materials on Adolf Eichmann. He agreed to retract some of his claims and even admitted to the existence of gas chambers, thereby admitting his guilt of falsifying history. It seems that with this strategy he was hoping for an acquittal. So confident was he that he had even bought a plane ticket back to London in advance. However, the eight members of the jury were unanimous, and in the verdict the judge Peter Liebetreu said: "The previous confession did not seem to us to be an act of repentance and was therefore not taken into account in the weight of the sentence". The judge asked him if he had understood the sentence. "I am not sure about that," he replied dumbfounded. As he was led out of the courtroom he declared that he was shocked by the severity of the sentence.

The Court of Appeal, presided over by Judge Ernest Maurer, accepted an appeal. On 20 December 2006, Judge Maurer agreed to reduce the initial sentence to one year's imprisonment and two years' probation. Since Irving had already been in prison for thirteen months, he could be released. However, he was still banned from re-entering Austria. The verdict sparked the anger of Vienna's Jewish community and the Historical Documentation Centre of the Resistance. Brigitte Bailer, director of the centre, expressed her indignation. The verdict, she said, "is worrying because it is a sign that there are sectors in the Austrian justice system that minimise the crime of Holocaust denial." Bailer accused Judge Maurer of being a sympathiser of the far-right FPÖ party. As soon as he was in England, Irving reaffirmed his revisionist positions and stated that "there was no longer any need to show remorse".

Thus, David Irving resumed his activities and gave revisionist lectures in Europe and America. In December 2007, the Catalan government tried to ban one of the planned events in Spain. The Mossos d'Esquadra (Catalan regional police), in addition to searching and filming the attendees in order to intimidate them, proceeded to seize some books. The speaker was warned that he would be arrested if there was any indication of a crime of opinion. In view of the situation, it was decided to suspend the conference and David Irving held a press conference with his freedom of expression alibied.

We continue in Spain. On the occasion of the seventieth anniversary of the outbreak of World War II, the newspaper *El Mundo* prepared a special edition in 2009 with interviews with specialists of different tendencies, including Irving. Israel's ambassador to Spain, Raphael Schutz, sent a letter of protest to the newspaper demanding censorship of Irving's contributions. Schutz, with his usual victimhood, claimed that it was not enough to invoke the right to "freedom of expression". The newspaper called the ambassador "intransigent" and replied that the newspaper *El Mundo* did not deny the Holocaust, quite the contrary.

Let's finish with an anecdote. In March 2013, David Irving's ban on entering Germany, which was to last until 2022, was lifted. In July of the same year he tried to book a room in Berlin because a conference was scheduled to take place in the German capital on 10 September at which attendees had to pay 119 dollars to gain entry. Volker Beck of the Green Party contacted the German hoteliers' association to boycott Irving. In this way he managed to get Berlin's leading hotels to refuse to accommodate the British revisionist, who was supposed to have found other accommodation.

Wolfgang Fröhlich, the "canary" still singing in the cage

Wolfgang Fröhlich is on track to break all records, having already spent nine years of his life in prison and currently serving another five years, which amounts to fourteen years in prison for thought crimes. In an article published in *Smith's Report* in October 2015, Roberto Hernández equated Fröhlich with that canary to which Professor Faurisson alluded in his well-known phrase: "Putting a canary in a cage can't stop it from singing its songs." Wolfgang Fröhlich is an Austrian chemical engineer who is convinced that the thesis of the extermination of deportees in gas chambers is scientifically absurd. Fröhlich, our caged canary, is a specialist in disinfection processes and the construction of gas chambers for pest control and the elimination of microbes.

It has already been said that freedom of expression and freedom as a whole is prevented in Austria by a 1947 law, the "Verbotsgesetz" (Prohibition Law), which was originally intended to prevent the existence of anything that might be related to National Socialism. In 1992 this law was amended in order to punish Holocaust denial and any attempt to minimise Nazi atrocities. Despite the new implementation of the Prohibition Law, during the 1990s Fröhlich sent hundreds of texts to lawyers, judges, parliamentarians, journalists, etc., denouncing the alleged Nazi gas chambers as a lie. In 1998 he participated as an expert for the defence in the trial in Switzerland against Jürgen Graf and his publisher Gerhard Förster, to which we will return later. Now it must be said that the court was not at all pleased with his testimony on the technical impossibility of mass gassings, so that the prosecutor Dominik Aufdenblatten threatened to charge him. The passage from the interrogation is as follows:

> "Aufdenblatten: In your opinion, were mass gassings with Zyklon B technically possible?
> Fröhlich: No.
> Aufdenblatten: Why not?
> Fröhlich: The pesticide Zyklon B is hydrocyanic acid in granular form. It is released on contact with air. The boiling point of hydrocyanic acid is 25.7 degrees (Celsius). The higher the temperature, the faster the evaporation rate. The delousing chambers in which Zyklon B was used in the camps and elsewhere were heated to thirty degrees and even higher, so that the hydrocyanic acid was quickly released from its granules. However, in the semi-underground morgues of the crematoria at Auschwitz-Birkenau, where, according to witnesses, mass exterminations with Zyklon B were carried out, the temperatures were much lower. If one accepts that the rooms were heated by the bodies of the prisoners, the temperature would not have exceeded 15 degrees Celsius, even in summer. Consequently, it would have taken many hours for the hydrocyanic acid to evaporate. According to witness reports, the victims died quickly. Witnesses mention time periods from 'instantaneous' to '15 minutes'. In order to kill the prisoners in such a short time, the Germans would have had to use enormous quantities of Zyklon B - I estimate between 40 and 50 kilos in each gassing. This would have made any work in the gas chamber totally impossible. The special detachment (Sonderkomando), which according to witnesses emptied the chambers of bodies, would have collapsed immediately on entering, even

while wearing gas masks. Huge quantities of hydrocyanic acid would have flooded out and the whole camp would have been poisoned".

Fröhlich's statement was greeted with applause; but prosecutor Aufdenblatten reacted indignantly and said: "For this statement I ask the court to charge you with racial discrimination under Article 261, or else I will do it myself. Upon hearing these words, Förster's lawyer, Jürg Stehrenberger, stood up and informed the court that in view of the intolerable intimidation of the witness, he was withdrawing from the case. In the company of Graf's counsel, he left the courtroom for several minutes. When they returned, they both expressed their vehement objection to the prosecutor's behaviour, but announced that they would nevertheless continue with their duties as defence counsel.

In 2001 Wolfgang Fröhlich published *Die Gaskammer Lüge (The Lies of the Gas Chambers)*, a book of almost 400 pages, which earned him an arrest warrant and forced him to go into hiding somewhere in Austria to avoid capture. In hiding, he conceived the project of sending out CDs entitled *Gaskammerschwiendel (The Gas Chamber Fraud)*, in which he detailed his research findings and referred to the fraud as "psychological terrorism". On 30 May 2003, he wrote in a letter that he was well and that he was eager to continue his project of sending CDs to people across the entire spectrum of Austrian society. To date, he had sent out some 800 CDs in the hope that his action would hasten the end of the "Holocaust story that millions of Jews had been gassed". Fröhlich saw this as an unprecedented historical deception of an entire people ("Volksbetrug"). Finally, on Saturday, 21 June 2003, Fröhlich was arrested and imprisoned in Vienna. In early 2004 he was tried and sentenced to three years in prison for violating the Prohibition Act ("Verbotsgesetz"), of which he spent two years on probation. When he was released from prison on 9 June 2004, he found himself without a job and without resources.

While on parole, in June 2005, a new indictment was brought against him for issuing the 800 CDs proving the absolute impossibility of the gassings. He had to return to prison, where he awaited his retrial. On 29 August 2005, , Judge Claudia Bandion-Ortner sentenced him to two years imprisonment and annulled the suspension of the previous sentence, which meant that Frölich had been imprisoned for a total of four years. Fortunately, his appeal to the Supreme Court was successful, so that his sentence was reduced by 29 months and he was again granted provisional release. In December 2006, just out of prison, Wolfgang Fröhlich attended the International Holocaust Conference in Tehran, but did not speak, so that, despite allegations and pressure on the Austrian authorities, he was not charged for having travelled to Iran.

While on parole, the indefatigable Wolfgang Fröhlich asked a member of parliament and the provincial governors to abolish the prohibition law. For this reason he was re-arrested at the end of July/beginning of August 2007 and returned to prison, where he remained until a new trial was held. Judge Martina Spreitzer-Kropiunik of the Vienna Regional Court on 14 January 2008 returned a guilty verdict and sentenced him to four years' imprisonment, to be added to the 29 months that had been revoked by the Supreme Court. He was thus sentenced to a total of six years and four months imprisonment for simple offences of opinion.

Imprisoned as a political prisoner, Fröhlich, the "canary" who cannot stop singing, wrote to Barbara Prammer of the SPÖ (Austrian Social Democratic Party) National Council, Cardinal Chistoph Schönborn and others to explain his thesis that the extermination of millions of Jews in the gas chambers is technically impossible and that the death of six million Jews is "the most atrocious lie in the history of mankind". Wolfgang Fröhlich's irrepressible chant resulted in a new indictment against him: on 4 October 2010 he was sentenced to an additional two years in prison. And so it goes on and on. Half a year before he was due to be released, on 9 July 2015, the Krems District Court, presided over by Judge Dr. Gerhard Wittmann, sentenced him to a further three years' imprisonment. This time, prosecutor Elisabeth Sebek had brought charges against him for sending letters to Austrian Chancellor Werner Faymann, a Catholic Social Democrat, the news magazine *Profil* and other influential people. In these letters, he once again expressed his views on the Holocaust.

The latest we have heard from Wolfgang Fröhlich is that on 25 November 2015 he sent a letter of formal notice to the United Nations Human Rights Committee and the European Convention on Human Rights. Since both Robert Faurisson and Ernst Zündel unsuccessfully went to international bodies, the former to denounce the Gayssot Law and the latter to denounce the violation of his rights, it is unlikely that Fröhlich will obtain any protection. The hidden tyranny of global power does not allow the slightest concession when it comes to of revisionists who seek to unmask the imposture. In any case, the text will be recorded as a tribute to this honourable Austrian engineer who has tried everything and lost everything:

> "Ladies, gentlemen,
> I hereby formulate a
> REQUIREMENT
> in order that my human rights complaint no. 56264/09 against the Austrian Republic, which by criminalising my opinions is attacking my fundamental rights, in particular those relating to the freedom of scientific research, be re-examined and that justice be done!
> I had already turned to the ECHR as a complainant against several convictions handed down by the Vienna criminal court solely because I had used my freedom of expression. By letter of 15 May 2012 (GZ ECHR LGer11.2R), this complaint was rejected as inadmissible!

Through the press, I have recently learned that the ECHR had in the meantime modified its legal view concerning the human rights guarantees for freedom of expression. In October 2015, a Turkish politician who had been convicted in Switzerland for having expressed his opinion in public was ultimately cleared of all charges by the ECHR and Switzerland convicted of human rights violations. I refer to this matter in my letter of 13 July 2015 to the Council of Ministers of the Austrian Republic, which you will find in attachment no. 1.

To sum up my question: I have been imprisoned in Austria for one and the same 'crime' for more than ten years now! On 9 July 2015 I was sentenced by the Krems court to an additional three years in prison, because I persist in defending the fundamental right to express myself freely! I refer to this matter in a letter addressed on 13 July 2015 to the Austrian Minister of Justice, M. Wolfgang Brandstetter, which you will find in the attached document no. 2.

Since the Austrian Republic is bound by the same legal standards (UN CCPR and ECHR) as Switzerland with regard to human rights, I therefore request that my application no. 56264/09 be investigated.

With my warmest regards,

Wolfgang Fröhlich".

4. MAIN VICTIMS OF PERSECUTION IN SWITZERLAND:

Jürgen Graf and Gerhard Förster sentenced for writing and publishing books

Born in 1951, Jürgen Graf, who initially sympathised with the Palestinian cause and consequently rejected Zionism for its crimes, had no doubt until 1991 that the Nazis had exterminated the Jews by means of gas chambers. He then met Arthur Vogt (1917-2003), considered the first Swiss revisionist, who provided him with a series of books that opened his eyes and cleared his mind. From then on, "I decided to dedicate my life," Graf confesses, "to the fight against the most monstrous fraud ever devised by human minds. So profound was the impact of reading the revisionist texts that in March 1992 he visited Professor Robert Faurisson in Vichy, who corrected his book *Der Holocaust auf dem Prüfstand*, published in early 1993.

Jürgen Graf, who studied French, English and Scandinavian philology, speaks more than ten languages. As a result of his first revisionist publication, he was dismissed in March 1993 as a teacher of Latin and French, the languages he taught at a secondary school in Therwill, a town near Basel. A month later he met publisher Gerhard Förster, whose father, a native of Silesia, had died during the brutal ethnic cleansing of millions of East European Germans. Unable to stop himself, Graf visited Carlo Mattogno, living near Rome, in September 1993, who provided him with valuable materials written in Polish, which he had been studying and researching for a decade. From this first visit, the two began a close collaboration and a deep friendship, as Graf became the translator of many of the Italian revisionist's writings. Subsequently, they would make half a dozen research trips together (Poland, Russia, Lithuania, Belgium, Holland), which resulted in several books that they would end up co-signing. In September 1994, Graf flew to California to attend a revisionist conference organised by the Institute for Historical Review. There he met Mark Weber, director of the IHR, Ernst Zündel, Bradley Smith and other revisionists. In October 1994 he got a new job as a German teacher in Basel; but he was dismissed in 1998, after the trial in Baden, which, after this hasty introduction, will be dealt with in the following lines.

Since we have cited Jürgen Graf as a source throughout this work, his name should be familiar to us by now. The collaboration with the Italian revisionist Carlo Mattogno resulted, as has said, in important work on the transit camps in eastern Poland, which were turned into extermination camps by propaganda. *Treblinka: Extermination Camp or Transit Camp?* has been one of our main sources when studying the camps of the so-called "Aktion Reinhard". However, when Graf was convicted in 1998, it was for his early works, from which we have used *El Holocausto bajo la Lupa*, an English edition of *Der Holocaust auf dem Prüfstand*, one of the four books that led to his conviction. The five-member court was presided over by Judge Andrea Staubli, who, in justifying the verdict, rejected the defendants' arguments about the academic content of the books, which the court considered "cynical and inhuman".

In terms of the importance of his work and research and the number of books he has published, Jürgen Graf is the most important revisionist convicted in Switzerland. He and his publisher Gerhard Förster were sentenced on 21 July 1998 to fifteen and twelve months in prison respectively for writing one and publishing the other allegedly anti-Jewish books inciting "racial discrimination". The "Anti-Racism Law" which permitted the prosecution had been enacted on 1 January 1995 at the request of the Jewish community in Switzerland. It prohibited unspecified crimes such as "denial or trivialisation of genocide or other crimes against humanity". Gerhard Förster was found guilty of having published the writings of Graf and two other authors. Jürgen Graf was also convicted of sending "racist" CDs to Sweden for Ahmed Rami and to Canada for Ernst Zündel, who distributed them via the internet. In addition to imprisonment, the court in the northern Swiss town of Baden fined each of them CHF 8,000 and ordered them to return the CHF 55,000 they had earned from the sale of the books, of which CHF 45,000 went to Förster and CHF 10,000 to Graf.

The Journal of Hisorical Review published in its July/August 1998 issue an extensive summary of the trial, which began on 16 July. According to this source, all sixty seats in the courtroom were filled with Graf and Förster sympathisers. At the outset, the court refused to allow Robert Faurisson, whose erudition was already feared everywhere, to testify. Instead, it accepted the testimony of the lesser-known Wolfgang Fröhlich, an excerpt of which has been reproduced above. Jürgen Graf's testimony lasted about two hours and was characterised by a vigorous defence of the views and arguments of his books. It is of interest to quote some of the questions and answers from the cross-examination. In response to Judge Staubli's question as to whether or not there had been a Holocaust, Graf replied:

> "It is a question of definition. If by Holocaust is meant a brutal persecution of Jews, mass deportations to camps, and the death of many Jews from disease, exhaustion and malnutrition, then it is of course a historical fact. But the Greek term 'holocaust' means 'utterly burned' or 'sacrifice by fire', and is used by orthodox historians for the alleged mass gassing and incineration of Jews in 'extermination camps'. That is a myth."

The judge then tried to question Graf on the fact that he was not a qualified historian. She then reproached him for not caring about offending

Jews with his books. In his rejoinder, Graf cited examples of offences against the Swiss without anyone bothering about it. "Why is it that only the feelings of Jews are taken into account and never the feelings of non-Jews? The judge reminded him that the Anti-Racism Law was passed through a democratic referendum. "Shouldn't you respect that?". Response:

> "At the time, people were led to believe that the law served to protect foreigners against racist violence. In reality it serves exclusively to protect Jews against any criticism. This is irrefutably proven in the booklet 'Abschied von Rechtsstaat' (Farewell to the Rule of Law), to which I contributed two short essays. So far, not a single Swiss citizen has been charged for having criticised a black, an Arab or a Turk. Only people who have criticised Jews have been charged and convicted".

The public prosecution, represented by prosecutor Aufdenblatten, was very harsh in its conclusions and used expressions such as "pseudo-scientific", "anti-Semitic incitement" and "racist propaganda" to refer to the "criminal books". He concluded that Graf's writings fanned the flames of anti-Semitism, of hatred, and did not seek the truth, but distorted it. The prosecutor stressed that Graf showed no remorse, that he reaffirmed his revisionist views and was unlikely to amend them. He therefore asked the court not to consider a suspended sentence for either Graf or Förster, whom he said was as unreasonable as his colleague. As for the publicist's poor health, he said it was no excuse for leniency, as it was not for the court to consider whether he was too ill to go to prison, but for the doctors. Gerhard Förster died in September 1998, nine weeks after the trial.

After closing statements by Jürg Stehrenberger and Urs Oswald, the lawyers for Förster and Graf, Judge Staubli gave Graf ten minutes to make a final statement, provided that it was limited to relevant issues related to the trial. After thanking her for the gesture, Jürgen Graf insisted that the revisionists were seeking the truth: "We try to get as close as we can to the historical truth. To have our mistakes pointed out to us is what we want. There are indeed errors in my books, but do you know who has shown them to me? Other revisionists! On the other side, the only reaction has been insults, slander, threats, legal action and lawsuits." As for his possible conviction, he informed the court that since the beginning of the 19th century no one had been imprisoned in Switzerland for the non-violent expression of his opinion.

> Do you, ladies and gentlemen of the court," he appealed to the judges, "want to break this tradition on the threshold of the 21st century? And if you insist on imprisoning one of us, then please look to me and not to Mr. Förster, who is mortally ill! By putting me in prison, you will not humiliate me. If you do so, you will humiliate the whole country, Switzerland. A Switzerland in which freedom of speech has been

abolished. A Switzerland in which a minority of 0.6 percent of the population is allowed to decide what one can write, read, say or think is a dead Switzerland."

The fact that some of the books for which Graf and Förster were charged had been published before the enactment of the 1995 law was not considered relevant as a mitigating factor. The verdict, of course, was appealed by Dr. Urs Oswald, Graf's lawyer. On 23 June 1999, the court of the canton of Aargau upheld the verdict, whereupon an appeal was made to a higher instance, the Federal Court in Lausanne. The Swiss organisation "Verité et Justice", which is led by René-Louis Berclaz, Philippe Brennenstuhl and Graf himself and works for the restoration of intellectual freedom in Switzerland, published the documentation of the trial under the title *A Political Trial to Escaner. The Case of Jürgen Graf*, a report that was translated into several languages. In April 2000, Graf learned that his appeal had been rejected and that he was to be sent to prison on 2 October.

In those days he was already engaged to Olga Stepanova, a Belarusian historian from Minsk. The two decided that they did not want to be separated for so long, and Graf opted for exile. On 15 August 2000, his 49th birthday, he emigrated to Iran, where he lived until April 2001. For a polyglot like him, studying Farsi during the months he spent in Tehran was a diversion. From there he eventually moved to Russia, where he settled after marrying Olga. Since 2002 Graf and his wife have lived in Russia, where he earns his living by translating texts written in English, Russian and other European languages into German. In addition, of course, to his efforts to denounce the Holocaust religion, the lie that has been poisoning the world, he continues to publish books: *Sobibor. Holocaust Propaganda and Reality*, published by Castle Hill Publisher, Germar Rudolf's publishing house, is one of the latest.

Gaston-Armand Amaudruz, one year in prison for an octogenarian

Born in Lausanne, Gaston-Armand Amaudruz founded and published the *Courrier du Continent*, a newsletter written in French, in 1946. Amaudruz was only 28 years old when he challenged in his book *Ubu Justicier au Premier Procés de Nuremberg* (1949) the assertions about the murderous gas chambers. He can therefore be said to be one of the first revisionists. Amaudruz wrote that "the Nuremberg trial had made him realise that the victory of the Allies was the victory of decadence". Amaudruz, who in 1951 set up the "New European Order" in Switzerland, a nationalist, anticapitalist and anti-communist organisation, was sympathetic to such prominent Swiss as the Lausanne-born François Genoud, the Swiss financier who had been a convinced National Socialist all his life. A devoted advocate of the Palestinian cause and a great patron of the PLO, Genoud founded the

Arab Commercial Bank in Geneva in 1958. It was not for nothing that he was known as "Sheik François" among Arabs[19]. Genoud described Gaston-Armand Amaudruz as "a man of integrity, racist, disinterested, a man of the past".

It was precisely because of two articles published in 1995 in the *Courrier du Continent* that Gaston-Armand Amaudruz was denounced. In one of them he had written: "For my part, I maintain my position. I do not believe in gas chambers. Let the exterminationists present the proof and I will believe in them. But as I have been waiting for this proof for decades, I don't think I will see it any time soon." The trial against him followed that of Jürgen Graf, who had a personal friendship with Amaudruz and used the ten minutes given to him by Judge Staubli to vindicate at the end of his speech the figure of his friend before the court in Baden:

> "I would like to close my remarks by quoting a friend from Western Switzerland, Gaston-Armand Amaudruz, against whom a trial similar to the one here is being prepared in Lausanne against Förster and me. In issue 371 of his bulletin *Courrier du Continent,* Amaudruz writes: "As in the old historical times, trying to impose dogma by force is a sign of weakness. The exterminationists may win trials through laws that muzzle freedom of expression. But they will lose the final judgement in the court of future generations".

Shortly before the start of his trial, in April 2000, Amaudruz wrote an intentionally provocative article in issue 418 of his bulletin, entitled "Long Live Revisionism! In it, he again denounced the untouchable dogma of the Holocaust imposed on humanity, claimed that he was prepared to face impeachment and announced: "I prefer to obey my conscience rather than an immoral and criminal law. I stand by my convictions. Long live revisionism!" After the long investigation, the trial began on 8 April 2000, and the verdict was delivered on 10 April 2000. The court sentenced the defendant to one year in prison for "denying" the existence of homicidal gas chambers in German concentration camps during World War II. The 79-

---

[19] There are few people as extraordinary and as little recognised as François Genoud. The biographies that have been written about him fail to present him adequately because their authors show little courage and/or too much concern for political correctness. Genoud, besides being a banker and publicist, was an eminent international strategist who opposed the New World Order with all his might. After the war, he played an essential role in rescuing anti-communist and nationalist refugees fleeing the vengeance of the Judeo-communists who had taken over half of Europe. As early as 1936, François Genoud formed a lifelong friendship with the Grand Mufti of Jerusalem, the spiritual leader of the Muslims in Palestine. With the founding of the Arab Commercial Bank, he put himself at the financial service of Arab nationalist causes, which were trying to gain independence from the Rothschilds' financial empire. This exceptional man of privileged intelligence fought to the end against international Zionism and the global empire.

year-old retired publicist and professor was found guilty of violating the Anti-Racism Act, which makes it a crime to "deny, grossly minimise or attempt to justify genocide or other crimes against humanity." In addition to the year's imprisonment, the Lausanne court ordered Amaudruz to pay 1,000 Swiss francs to each of the parties to the case: the Swiss Federation of Jewish Communities; LICRA, which, despite being based in Paris, had appeared; the Association of Sons and Daughters of Jewish Deportees in France; and a Jewish concentration camp survivor. The costs of the trial and the publication of the verdict in three newspapers and an official gazette also had to be borne by the convicted defendant.

After the trial, Gaston-Armand Amaudruz narrated his judicial experience in a book including the inculpatory reports. In September 2000, "Verité et Justice" published the text in the third issue of its bulletin under the title *The Amaudruz Trial. A judicial farce.* In this way, the organisation helped to publicise the cruelties of the trial against a 79-year-old dissident. The authorities considered it a new violation of the Anti-Racism Law and sued Amaudruz and René-Louis Berclaz and Philippe Georges Brennenstuhl, co-founders with Jürgen Graf of "Verité et Justice". In March 2002, "Verité et Justice" was dissolved by court order. On 22 May 2002, the criminal court of Veveyse in the canton of Fribourg sentenced Amaudruz and Brennenstuhl to three months' imprisonment and Berclaz to eight months' imprisonment.

In the meantime, an appeal court had reduced to three months the April 2000 sentence against Gaston-Armand Amaudruz, who in January 2003, at 82 years of age and already in very poor health, entered the prison of Plaine de l'Orbe in Vaud, in the canton of Waadt, to serve the sentence imposed by the Swiss justice system.

5. MAIN VICTIMS OF PERSECUTION IN BELGIUM AND THE NETHERLANDS:

Siegfried Verbeke, stubborn fighter for freedom of expression

A Belgian of Flemish origin, Siegfried Verbeke is one of Europe's most prominent revisionists. He and his brother Herbert founded in 1983 the aforementioned *Vrij Historisch Onderzook* (*Free Historical Research*), known by the acronym *VHO*, which over the years became Europe's leading centre for the publication of texts critical of official historiography and Holocaust dogma. A whole range of books, pamphlets, leaflets and articles in English, Dutch, French and German have been published by *VHO*, which for a time also published a newsletter. Since 1991, when Verbeke and Faurisson published a 125-page booklet on the fraudulent diary of Anne Frank, a persecution has been unleashed that has increased over time. Government institutions, with the usual support of the usual Zionist organisations, have relentlessly harassed Verbecke, who has time and again been sentenced to prison and fined for his political dissent and his consistently peaceful views. The Belgian authorities have, moreover, for years confiscated tons of books and other texts produced by Verbeke, which have been systematically destroyed.

The first sentence imposed by a Belgian court on Siegfried Verbeke came in 1992: for distributing writings questioning the Holocaust, he was sentenced to one year in prison. Fortunately, his imprisonment was suspended, but he lost his civil rights and his right to vote for ten years. Nevertheless, Jewish lobbies continued the harassment and in 1992 the Masonic lodge B'nai B'rith, the Israel Information and Documentation Centre and the Anne Frank Foundation joined the National Department for Combating Racism and brought a civil suit against Verbeke for publishing materials including the *Leuchter Report*. At the end of the year a Dutch court ordered Verbeke to pay 10,000 guilders for each of the texts. In 1993, the Anne Frank Foundation in the Netherlands and the Anne Frank Fund in Switzerland sued Verbeke, Faurisson and a colleague of theirs at *VHO* for the publication of the booklet on Anne Frank's diary. In the indictment, it was pointed out that "Anne Frank had for years been a symbol of the Jewish victims of the Holocaust, and her name and diary had therefore acquired additional value".

While Switzerland passed the Anti-Racism Law in 1995, in Belgium the same year the parliament gave the green light to a new anti-revisionist law that made it a crime to question the official version of the Holocaust. According to the new law, denying, minimising or trying to justify the genocide of the National Socialist regime was punishable by up to one year's imprisonment and a fine. This was an anti-free speech legislation very similar to that which already existed in France and Austria. This showed that the offensive against revisionism was being pushed behind the scenes by the hidden forces that hold the puppet "democracies" born after the world war in their thrall. In fact, well before that, on 23 April 1982, the *Jewish Chronicle* (London) had already reported that the Institute of Jewish Affairs in London, a branch of the World Jewish Congress, was announcing a campaign to pressure and persuade governments to outlaw "Holocaust denial". The anti-revisionist thought crime laws introduced in several European countries reflect the success of this initiative.

In 1996, Siegfried Verbeke started co-operating with a German revisionist publicist to create a German-language division of *VHO* supervised by Germar Rudolf. In September 1997 Germar Rudolf launched the website vho.org on the internet, which became the largest revisionist website in the world. On 6 November 1997, in the course of a roundtable discussion in Antwerp (Belgium), Verbeke distributed hundreds of copies of a revisionist booklet written by himself, *Goldhagen and Spielberg Lies*, which was very well received, to the audience [20]. This activity, which followed the launch of *VHO* on the internet, was the straw that broke the camel's back. In a 2004 article, Germar Rudolf himself pointed to "the well-known Belgian witch hunter Johan Leman", who was allegedly in the audience in Antwerp, as the person who put pressure on the Belgian government to act against Verbeke. A series of raids on four of his premises took place on 21 and 29 November 1997 and 7 January 1998. Large quantities of books and documents were seized and the warehouses were sealed. On the basis of this experience, the German division of *VHO* became independent at the beginning of 1998. In order to escape prosecution, Castle Hill Publishers, Germar Rudolf's publishing house in England, took over the publication of the German texts. In 1998, the Frankfurt public prosecutor's office filed a criminal complaint against Siegfried Verbeke. The initiative had come from Ignatz Bubis, the head of the Central Council of Jews in Germany. The motive was the distribution of tens of thousands of copies of the German version of *Goldhagen and Spielberg's Lies* to German households. The booklet was confiscated and destroyed by order of a Munich court. The court proceedings lasted two years.

In the end, on 27 April 2000, a ruling by the Amsterdam Court of Appeal forbade *VHO* from continuing to publish and distribute the booklet by Verbeke and Faurisson, which questioned the authenticity of Anne Frank's alleged diary. In May 2001, the Belgian Ministry of Culture ordered all Belgian bookshops to remove Verbeke's works from their shelves.

---

[20] Daniel Goldhagen, whose father was one of the countless "Holocaust" survivors, had published *Hitler's Willing Executioners* in 1996, a work in which he criminalises all Germans who, according to this American Jew, not only knew about the extermination but supported it. About Steven Spielberg and his *Schindler's List*, we think that no comment is necessary.

Consequently, all revisionist texts were taken out of the shops and discreetly destroyed. With this unspeakable outrage against freedom of expression, the epic of this unspeakable publicist was reaching its climax.

During 2002, Verbeke's house was repeatedly raided by the Belgian police. On 12 February 2002, the Belgian authorities officially banned *Vrij Historisch Onderzook* and its post office box was temporarily confiscated. The publisher's premises were again searched and he was subjected to intense interrogation during the twenty-four hours he was under arrest. In the following months, the warehouses where Verbeke kept his materials were constantly visited by the police. As a result, Siegfried Verbeke decided to reorganise. After taking over new post office boxes, he renamed his foundation *Vogelvrij Historisch Onderzook* (*Proscribed Historical Research*). The French section or division became independent and became *Vision Historique Objective*. Months later, the confiscation of its former post office box was lifted and Siegfried Verbeke's organisation regained its original name and addresses.

On 9 September 2003, a court in Antwerp sentenced the two Verbeke brothers to one year's imprisonment and the payment of 2,500 euros. Both were released on probation and for the second time Siegfried Verbeke was deprived of his civil rights for a period of ten years. The reason for the conviction had been the distribution of materials that "minimised the Nazi genocide against the Jews". Only three weeks later, at the end of the same month of September, the Belgian police raided the premises of the publishing house for the umpteenth time, looking for evidence that revisionist materials bearing Verbeke's name and address were being distributed by him.

A year later, on 27 November 2004, following an arrest warrant issued by the German authorities, Verbeke was arrested at her residence in Kortrijk in Flanders. The European Arrest Warrant, allegedly introduced under the pretext of combating terrorism, is a legal decision issued by a Member State of the Union, which has been applied in most countries since 1 January 2004, . Such orders are usually executed discreetly and without any legal impediment. Germany immediately requested extradition to Belgium, but surprisingly a judge rejected the request on the grounds that Verbeke had already been convicted of the same crimes in Belgium in September 2003. Under Belgian law, a person cannot be charged or tried twice for the same acts .[21]

In any case, the harassment of Siegfried Verbeke did not stop. On 4 April 2005, a Belgian court again sentenced him to one year in prison and a

---

[21] Scandalously, in July 2005 the German Constitutional Court, in response to a Spanish request for the extradition of a German of Syrian origin suspected of involvement in the brutal 11 March 2004 Madrid bombing, ruled that the European Arrest Warrant was invalid in Germany. The German Constitutional Court argued that a German citizen is entitled to a verdict in German courts. Therefore, the German authorities released the alleged terrorist.

fine of 2,500 euros for denying the genocide of the Jews during World War II. Since he appealed the verdict, his imprisonment was once again postponed. Taking advantage of her freedom, Verbeke tried to travel with her Filipino girlfriend to Manila. When he was about to board the plane at Schiphol airport near Amsterdam on 4 August 2005, he was arrested by the Dutch police, as the European Arrest Warrant was still valid in the Netherlands. It is clear that, as his lawyer regretted, Verbeke made a serious mistake, since if he had wanted to travel from Brussels he would probably not have been arrested because the extradition request had been rejected by a Belgian magistrate.

After three months in detention in the Netherlands, he was finally extradited to Germany. The Dutch authorities ignored the fact that Verbeke had Belgian nationality and that a Belgian judge had given a perfectly good reason why he would not extradite him to Germany. Naturally, Verbeke was fighting against the impostors of history and was far more dangerous than any terrorist wanted by the Spanish police for alleged involvement in the murder of some 200 people. In Germany, where the German suspect of Syrian origin had just been refused extradition to Spain, Verbeke was held for half a year in solitary confinement in Heildelberg prison. Suddenly, we don't know why, he was allowed out on bail. In total, without having been convicted either in the Netherlands or in Germany, Siegfried Verbeke was imprisoned for nine months as a dangerous revisionist.

Back in Flanders, he was arrested again in November 2006 at his home in Kortrijk. The reason for the new arrest seems to have been the execution of a previous sentence of a Belgian court. This time he was imprisoned in Belgium. Verbeke told friends that he hoped to regain his freedom in July 2007. Verbeke's last conviction that is aware of was on 19 June 2008. We have already seen in the pages on Vincent Reynouard that the Brussels Court of Appeal sentenced them both to one year in prison and a fine of 25,000 euros for the publication of denialist texts questioning crimes against humanity. Since neither of them appeared, the Belgian authorities issued a national arrest warrant and prepared to prepare the European arrest warrant.

As we are about to conclude these pages on Siegfried Verbeke, we have learned that the Flemish-language *newspaper De Morgen* published an extensive three-page interview with the Belgian revisionist in its *Zeno* supplement on Saturday 9 January 2016. In it, unmoved, Verbeke insisted that the only gas chambers in Auschwitz were those used to disinfect the detainees' clothes. The Antwerp-based monthly *Joods Actueel* (*Jewish News*), which takes a belligerent stance against anything that moves against Israel, has taken *De Morgen* to task for welcoming a "stinker" like Verbeke into its pages. According to reports in the Belgian press, these Zionists are prepared to take the Flemish newspaper to court. Michael Freilich, editor and owner of the Jewish newspaper, told the *Jewish Telegraphic Agency* that he had filed a complaint against *De Morgen* and Verbeke with the ICKG (Interfederal Centre for Equal Opportunities and the Fight against Racism). Freilich stated that "*De Morgen* is to all intents and purposes an accomplice to this offence and should be held accountable for his actions". According to Freilich, officials from the state agency had assured him that they were considering legal action. The mayor of Antwerp, Bart de Wever, was quick to support the initiative.

6. Main Victims of Persecution in Spain

In Spain, the most blatant cases of political persecution of revisionists and submission to Zionism in the courts of justice are to be found in Catalonia. There, for example, Pilar Rahola, defined as "Zionist scum" by Antonio Baños, a member of the CUP in the Catalan Parliament after the 2015 autonomous elections, exhibits herself shamelessly, with absolute shamelessness, in the numerous media outlets that offer her day in and day out their sets and microphones. For years a leader of Equerra Republicana de Catalunya, a party with a deep Masonic tradition throughout its history, Rahola admitted in an interview to a pro-independence digital media her contacts with Israel. When the journalist asked her if she worked as a liaison between the president of the Generalitat, Artur Mas, and the Zionist government. His reply was: "The best answer I can give you is that I won't give it. Allow me to keep these things confidential. We will not show all the cards. When the journalist replied, "I understand that we do work", Rahola confirmed, "There is information that is too sensitive to give out.... We work a lot and talk little". It is therefore unquestionable that Zionism has in Catalonia a well-fertilised terrain in which it moves with arrogance thanks to the acquiescence and shameful servility of the media and the complicity of certain pro-independence politicians.

In Spain, the most blatant case, the most bleeding injustice, has been committed against a bookseller and publisher from Barcelona, Pedro Varela, whose dignified and honest struggle is known in all international revisionist circles. His case, however, is not the only one; other booksellers and publishers based in Catalonia have also been victims of harassment. Ramón Bau, Óscar Panadero, Carlos García and Juan Antonio Llopart are other names that should appear in this section, since they have been persecuted for publishing revisionist books or for expressing their opinions on political issues that have to do with revisionism. We shall therefore devote the first section on persecution in Spain to Pedro Varela and then present the second case.

Pedro Varela, an honest bookseller victim of hatred and sectarian intolerance

About Pedro Varela we will write adequately. Since our work was born in Spain, we know its hardships perfectly well, we have had access to sufficient information and we can explain the case as deserves. His name is associated with CEDADE (Círculo Español de Amigos de Europa), an organisation of National Socialist ideology created in Barcelona in 1966. The first congress of this group was held in 1969 and Jorge Mota was its first president and at the same time director of the magazine *CEDADE*. During these early years, militancy grew and the organisation spread to all regions of Spain, with fifty branches. The groups in Catalonia even displayed the Catalan "senyera" during the Franco years. Pedro Varela became president of CEDADE and editor of the publication in 1978.

Little by little, revisionist ideas became the fundamental basis of Varela's ideas and of the organisation he presided over. He contacted Robert Faurisson and brought about the publication of an extract from Arthur R. Butz's essential book. Likewise, other authors close to the Institute for Historical Review, as well as IHR publications and texts, were translated and introduced in Spain thanks to CEDADE. In 1989, for example, CEDADE published in Spain the explosive *Leuchter Report* with a foreword by David Irving. One of CEDADE's last events took place in Madrid in 1992, where a number of revisionist personalities gathered to demand the inalienable right to freedom of expression. The meeting was attended by Gerd Honsik, Thies Christophersen and others who were persecuted in their countries for speaking out freely. It should be noted that by this time the two trials against Ernst Zündel in Toronto had already taken place and that things were going from bad to worse in Germany. Finally, a new legal framework similar to the one being forged in Europe was also being created in Spain, so Pedro Varela announced his resignation as president of CEDADE and in October 1993 the organisation finally disappeared.

During the 1980s, Pedro Varela had become increasingly committed to historical revisionism, and in 1988 he travelled to Canada to attend the second Zündel trial in Toronto. There he met Faurisson, Irving, Zündel and other revisionists, and had the opportunity to meet Fred Leuchter in person. Around the same time, together with David Irving, he also staged a protest rally in Berlin in front of the German television headquarters. Holding placards reading "German historians, liars and cowards", Varela and Irving led a small group of demonstrators in calling for an end to the falsification of history. These were the years when revisionism had achieved the decisive success of engineer Leuchter's expertise at Auschwitz. At the same time, the enemies of the revisionists and of historical truth were becoming more radical: as we know, in 1989 Robert Faurisson was the victim of a cowardly attack by Jewish terrorists, who beat him to death.

In March 1991 Pedro Varela spoke in German at the "Leuchter Kongress", an open-air meeting in Munich which had been organised by Ernst Zündel. On 25 September 1992, thirty-five years old, with ideals, firm convictions and a lot of hope in his backpack, he was arrested in Austria, a country he was visiting as part of a tour of Europe. The reason for his arrest was that on a previous visit he had made a speech praising Hitler's policies. He was brought before the police and imprisoned in Steyr prison, a former Cistercian monastery, for the crime of propagating National Socialism. His correspondence was monitored. Before the letters were handed over to him, they were translated into German to be attached to the trial dossier in case they could be used as incriminating evidence. He spent three months behind bars before being arraigned on Wednesday, 16 December 1992 before a court of three judges and a jury of eight. In the end, he was surprisingly acquitted, as it was concluded that the defendant did not know Austrian law, which is why he could not have known that he was committing a crime when he expressed his opinion about a historical figure.

Compared to Austria or Germany, Spain remained an oasis of free speech in a Europe that was increasingly condescending to Jewish lobbies. In 1995, the year in which Switzerland and Belgium enacted anti-racist laws intended to combat 'hatred' and 'Holocaust denial', Spain finally embarked on the same path. On 11 May 1995, Parliament approved a revision of the Penal Code in order to bring Spanish legislation into line with that of certain European nations. In the preamble, the law justified itself as follows: "The proliferation in several European countries of incidents of racist and anti-Semitic violence, carried out under flags and symbols of Nazi ideology, obliges democratic states to take decisive action to combat...". We have already noted that the laws against "hatred" and "Holocaust denial" in Europe were not a consequence of spontaneous expression or justified indignation on the part of the people, but the result of a prefabricated and well-organised campaign in the service of Zionism. Three years later, in June 1998, the International Association of Jewish Lawyers and Jurists again called for new and tougher laws against Holocaust revisionism.

In 1991, four years before Spain submitted to outside pressure to modify its legislation, Pedro Varela had opened the doors of the Librería Europa at number 12, Calle Séneca. From there he tried to work honestly selling books; but the fanaticism and intolerance of the champions of "freedom of expression" were not going to allow it: insulting graffiti on the walls and windows of the shop have been a constant since then and the shop has been attacked on several occasions. It all started when in May 1995, the same month in which the Spanish Parliament approved the modification of the Penal Code, a self-styled "Civic Platform Anne Frank" tried to change the name of Seneca Street to the name of the unfortunate Jewish girl who died in Bergen - Belsen. Interestingly, the Bergen City Council had previously refused to name a school after Anne Frank and later also refused to name the street leading to the camp memorial after her.

Between 12 May 1995 and autumn 1996, this misnamed civic platform collected signatures and lobbied the two hundred and thirty families living in Seneca Street to support the renaming of the street. The promoters made no secret of the fact that the aim of the campaign was to "boycott the activities of the Europa bookshop". Quite an example of respect for freedom of expression (theirs, of course). The civic and, of course, democratic groups that were part of the platform were the usual left and extreme left. Seneca Street lost its tranquillity and the neighbourhood had to endure demonstrations of democratic violence and intolerance, i.e. insulting graffiti, stones, Molotov cocktails, etc. Pedro Varela, in order to offer the neighbours and public opinion in general information that could be contrasted with that provided by the promoters of the street name change, published in the form of a circular letter a text he had written while studying Contemporary History at the University. It was a text that offered a rigorously accurate overview or synthesis of the work of Faurisson, Verbeke, Felderer and Irving on the most fruitful and profitable literary forgery of the twentieth century. In this text, the only one written by Varela among all those presented against him by the Mossos d'Esquadra and the Public Prosecutor's Office, no evidence of hatred against anyone can be found.

On 12 December 1996, the Catalan police raided the Librería Europa. Pedro's sister Varela was working in the shop and his daughter was playing in the backyard. The Mossos seized some 20,000 books, as well as periodicals, magazines, posters, videos.... Varela was subsequently arrested at his family home. The operation, which, according to *El País*, had been three months in the making, was ordered at the behest of José María Mena, who in 1996 was appointed chief prosecutor of the Public Prosecutor's Office of the High Court of Justice of Catalonia. This "progressive" jurist, who had been a militant of the PSUC (Catalan communists) in the 1970s, was of the opinion that Varela "was pursuing hatred and not an ideology".

The information that appeared on 13 December 1996 in *El País*, a newspaper close to the Spanish socialists, was an example of a lack of objectivity: after praising the Mossos d'Esquadra for having had the honour of being "the first police force in Spain to arrest a person for genocide apologia", the newspaper said that the Librería Europa was a "centre for the sale and distribution of Nazi books published in South American countries". It went on to state that the residents of the Gracia neighbourhood welcomed the arrest and that the City Council was considering appearing in the case as a private prosecutor. He ended by confirming that the Plataforma Cívica Ana Frank, the Gay-Lesbian Coordinating Committee, the Asociación Amical Mauthausen and SOS Racismo were all very satisfied because they had dismantled "a neo-Nazi plot that used the bookshop as a cover".

The proceedings were delayed for almost two years because many of the books seized were in English, German and French, so the Prosecutor's Office insisted on translating them to find out what part of their contents violated the law. Finally, the head of Barcelona Criminal Court No. 3, Santiago Vidal, set Friday 16 October 1998 for the start of the first trial in Spain for advocacy of genocide and incitement to racial hatred. As soon as the date became known, the Anne Frank supporters, now a Civic Platform against the Spread of Hatred, called a rally against Pedro Varela in front of the court building. Supporting the demonstration were the B'nai B'rith lodge, the Comunidad Israelita de Barcelona, the Baruch Spinoza Foundation, the Anti-Defamation League, Maccabi Barcelona, Asociación Judía Atid de Cataluña, Asociación de Relaciones Culturales Cataluña-Israel, Amical

Mauthausen, Coordinadora Gai-Lesbiana, Sos Racismo and Unión Romaní. The participants carried cardboard coffins and candles in memory of the victims. Evidently, the purpose of staging a street spectacle was to exert social and political pressure.

The two trial sessions were held on 16 and 17 October. Shimon Samuel, president of the Wiesenthal Centre Europe, attended as an observer, escorted by police officers and accompanied by Israeli television cameras. "This trial," he said, "is a historic opportunity for Spain to join European jurisprudence and condemn the Spanish godfather of neo-Nazism." The prosecutor cited some thirty works sold in the Europa Bookshop that praised the Third Reich and its policies or presented revisionist arguments on the subject of the Holocaust. In the case against Varela, the Comunitat Jueva Atid (future) de Catalunya, SOS Racismo and the Israeli Community of Barcelona had filed a popular action. Varela's two lawyers made it clear from the outset that the law under which their client was being tried was unconstitutional, and therefore requested the suspension and annulment of the proceedings. The bookseller was questioned for more than four hours and rejected the charges: "I have never provoked racial hatred", he told the court, adding that as a historian he "had a moral obligation to tell the truth". As for revisionism, he said: "In my opinion, revision of history is necessary because it is an open subject and everything is subject to revision. Historians must be sceptical about everything and they must also revise what has been said so far". In relation to the books in his bookshop, he explained that he could not know the contents of the 232 titles he had in his shop and that he was not obliged to do so. He pointed out that in his shop he sold books of different ideologies and among the authors he mentioned the Basque nationalist Sabino Arana, Francisco de Quevedo and he also cited Marx's *Capital*. As for the text on Anne Frank, he acknowledged his authorship. In his final statement he said: "It has fallen to me to play the role of the bad guy in this film as the scapegoat for a deliberately created 'social alarm' (expression used by the prosecutor). I condemn, condemn and attack any form of genocide. I am not a genocidal person, nor have I murdered anyone. I have never desired the genocide of anyone or the murder of any ethnic or religious minority".

The public prosecution, which recalled that the facts of the case were a crime in the European Union, requested two years' imprisonment for advocacy of genocide and two years' imprisonment for incitement to racial hatred. This, despite the fact that the second paragraph of article 607 of the new Penal Code stipulated that the crimes contemplated in this article would be punishable "with a prison sentence of one or two years". For his part, Jordi Galdeano, the lawyer for SOS Racismo and the Comunitat Jueva Atid de Catalunya, called for an exemplary sentence of eight years in prison. "What is a crime and constitutes a risk to democracy," he said, "is the dissemination of an ideology that despises certain groups." On 16 November 1998, the court found Varela guilty of incitement to racial hatred and guilty also of having denied or justified genocide. Consequently, Judge Santiago Vidal[22], who in his sentence referred to Varela as "a university graduate with a brilliant academic record, expert in matters of historical revisionism", sentenced him to five years' imprisonment and a fine of 720,000 pesetas. It also ordered Varela to surrender his passport and to appear in court every month. As for the 20,000 books, they were ordered to be burned, despite the fact that only thirty of the nearly two hundred works seized were in violation of the law. The very severe sentence exceeded the provisions of article 607.2 of the Penal Code, which led Galdeano to express his "intimate satisfaction". Pedro Varela, for his part, declared that it was "a political sentence and a tremendous injustice" and recalled that for two years, from the police search of his bookshop to the trial, terrible pressure had been created. On 10 December 1998, Pedro Varela's lawyers appealed the verdict and sentence, and he was able to avoid imprisonment pending the decision of the court of appeal.

---

[22] Judge Santiago Vidal, who belonged to the "progressive" association Judges for Democracy, is now a famous figure in Spain. His relations with SOS Racismo were revealed when in September 2013 the General Council of the Judiciary banned him from collaborating with this NGO, as it was incompatible with his duties as a judge. In April 2014, it emerged that Vidal, who is deeply committed to Catalan separatist nationalism, was drafting a Constitution for Catalonia, in violation of the Spanish Constitution, as Catalonia is a community with a Statute of Autonomy. Once again, the General Council of the Judiciary summoned him to remind him of the limitations of his jurisdictional work. Vidal issued a statement in which he assured that his work was "on his own altruistic initiative, without any official commission from any public or private institution". He denied "political intentionality" and proclaimed his independence and impartiality. In October 2014, the judiciary opened a disciplinary case against him and pointed to a precautionary suspension, "given the extreme relevance of the facts and the evident public and social projection". In January 2015, after having said that he acted with independence, impartiality and without "political intentionality", this delusional judge presented the draft of the Catalan Constitution and declared verbatim: "I have a dream: to see the birth of the Catalan republic as a judge". In February 2015, the General Council of the Judiciary suspended him for three years, a sanction that entailed the loss of his seat in the Barcelona Court. Having become a martyr for the secessionists, in March 2015 the news came out that President Artur Mas had incorporated him into the Government of the Generalitat to "plan" and "design" the state structures linked to the judicial sphere. Vidal, without any political intentions, of course, then set about recruiting the 250 judges who would begin to practice in an independent Catalonia, which led the High Court of Justice of Catalonia to demand that the Generalitat take action against Vidal, as it understood that it was "undermining collective confidence in the judiciary". It then emerged that the Generalitat's Justice Department had signed a three-year contract with Vidal as temporary staff. Eventually, Vidal resigned from the contract to run for the Senate as head of the Esquerra Republicana de Catalunya list. As a senator, in January 2017 he revealed that the Generalitat had illegally obtained the tax data of Catalans, that the separatist authorities already had a selection of sympathetic judges in order to purge opponents, and that a non-European country (Israel) was training a unit of the Mossos in counter-espionage tactics. ERC forced him to resign.

As if the bookshop and its commercial activity had not been damaged enough for two years, a demonstration was called for Saturday, 16 January 1999 under the slogans: "Let's close the bookshop Europe, young people and workers in the struggle against fascism". "Against fascism: Let's close the Nazi bookshop." Two days earlier, on Thursday 14 January, Maite Varela, Pedro's sister who worked in the establishment, warned the National Police about what was being prepared and about the risk of an attack. On the same day, around 13:15 hours, a call was made to the regional police and the situation was explained to the Complaints Department. At 20:00 on Saturday 16, friends or acquaintances of the Librería Europa reported to 091 that the demonstration was heading towards Séneca Street. At 20:30 the bookshop was attacked. In order to enter and smash the shop, it was necessary to break through the shutters at the entrance. Some of the demonstrators hooded themselves, entered the shop and began the destruction: windows, showcases, displays, doors, shelves, photocopiers, telephone, fire extinguisher, stairs, even some tiles. Everything was razed to the ground. Once the furniture was overturned, they piled the books on the floor with the intention of burning them inside. In the end, they chose to throw some 300 volumes into the street and set fire to them on the asphalt. Naturally, some neighbours, who were frightened by the scenes of violence, made further calls for help, but no police force turned up. As for the Guardia Urbana escorting the demonstrators, they withdrew when the assault on the bookshop began.

El País, which from the outset supported the public lynching of a man who defended himself alone against almost everyone, reported the news with this headline: "Demonstration by 1,600 young people to demand the closure of the Europa bookshop". In the body of the news item it said: "The protest was peaceful, but on arriving at the bookshop a group of demonstrators burnt some books they had taken out of the shop, which was slightly damaged". Naturally, the news item was not illustrated with photographs, as only one would have sufficed to see how the bookshop was left after suffering "minor damage". In a well-known expression, Lenin described as "useful fools" those who are used as instruments for a certain cause or policy. It seems clear that the individuals who hooded themselves and razed the bookshop to the ground were political terrorists, probably paid, who were among the "useful fools" disguised as "peaceful demonstrators" in the service of the real power.

To complete the disgraceful action of the forces of law and order, the court dismissed the complaint on the grounds that the culprits were not known. However, television cameras filmed the aggressors and the City Council had the names of the two dozen groups that participated in the demonstration: Assemblea d'Okupes de Terrassa, Assemblea Llibertària del Vallés Oriental, Associació d'Estudiants Progressistes, Departament de Joves de CC.OO., Esquerra Unida i Alternativa, Federació d'Associacions d'Associacions de Veïns de Barcelona, Joves Comunistes, Joves Socialistes de Catalunya, Maulets, Partido Obrero Revolucionario, Partits dels Comunistes de Catalunya, PSUC viu, Amical de Mauthausen... As many as 23 associations were listed in the complaint filed by Pedro Varela in an ordinary court on 10 February 1999. The complaint included a list of the damages assessed and their estimated value, which amounted to 2,815,682 pesetas in "small damages".

Finally, on 30 April 1999, Pedro Varela received wonderful news: by unanimous decision, the three judges of the Third Section of the Barcelona Provincial Court, presided over by Judge Ana Ingelmo, upheld the appeal lodged by the lawyer José María Ruiz Puerta and questioned the sentence handed down by Judge Santiago Vidal. Considering that it violated the right to freedom of expression, they considered referring the case to the Constitutional Court in Madrid. The three judges considered that doubting the Holocaust could not be considered a crime under the Spanish Constitution. Instead of ruling on the conviction, they reflected in their ruling brief all doubts about the constitutionality of article 607.2 of the new Penal Code. The Provincial Court judges argued that the article for which Varela had been convicted conflicted with Article 20 of the Constitution, which upholds the right to freely express and disseminate thoughts, ideas and opinions by word, writing or any other means of reproduction. As was to be expected, the accusers reacted angrily. The intrepid Jordi Galdeano decided not to be outdone and ruled that the court's decision was "an attack on the democratic system". In other words, when instead of sympathetic judges and prosecutors they were faced with truly independent magistrates, they were accused of endangering freedoms. The lawyer for Amical Mauthausen, Mateu Seguí Parpal, described the court that doubted Pedro Varela's criminality as "unpresentable".

The Constitutional Court, however, before admitting the consideration of the constitutionality raised by the judges of the Third Section of the High Court, demanded as a formal prerequisite that the Barcelona High Court should first hear the appeal against the conviction, and so the Chamber of the Third Section then set the date of 9 March 2000 for the hearing of the appeal. A week earlier, the judge, Ana Ingelmo, had been challenged by SOS Racismo, which denounced her to the Public Prosecutor's Office for prevarication and requested that she abstain in the case. The Chamber upheld the challenge and agreed to a change of rapporteur, and therefore ordered the suspension of the oral hearing and processed the challenge in a separate piece. On 19 June 2000, an order of the Seventh Section of the Barcelona Provincial Court dismissed the challenge.

Finally, 13 July was set as the date for the oral hearing. Varela did not attend because he was in Austria. His lawyer described the five-year prison sentence as "scandalous". On the other hand, the prosecutor Ana Crespo and the private prosecutors asked the Audiencia to confirm the sentence imposed on the owner of Librería Europa. In the end, by Order of 14 September 2000, the Third Section of the Provincial Court again raised the question of unconstitutionality. Pedro Varela remained on probation and the case was pending the ruling of the Constitutional Court. Freedom of expression advocates and revisionists around the world considered that a victory had been achieved in Spain , at least temporarily, and awaited the decision of the high court, which was to take seven years to issue the long-awaited judgement.

During this temporary period, Pedro Varela continued his activities as a bookseller and publisher with the Asociación Cultural Editorial Ojeda, which he had founded at the beginning of 1998. The Librería Europa also began to organise conferences on its premises, often given by revisionist authors who came from abroad. Suddenly, on Monday 10 April 2006, the Catalan autonomous police unexpectedly burst into the premises of the Librería Europa. At 9:30 in the morning, about fifteen masked police officers began a search that lasted until five o'clock in the afternoon. Some six thousand books valued at more than 120,000 euros were seized. In addition, the officers of the Generalitat's political police removed from the premises eight large boxes full of documentation, hundreds of folders and thousands of photos and slides, catalogues ready to be sent out and thirteen thousand conference programmes. The six computers containing dozens of books corrected, typeset and ready for publication were confiscated. These computers also contained all the information about customers and friends of the publishing company and the bookshop. Hard disks, back-up copies, savings books, bank accounts, the bookshop's chequebooks, personal and business contracts were also confiscated. As if that were not enough, the "mossos" took away framed photographs that recalled events from the CEDADE era and even the flags of the autonomous communities that, together with the Catalan flag, adorned the conference room.

Pedro Varela was arrested. Once at the police station, he was forced to strip naked to pass the search and then locked in a cell. He then went on to "play the piano", which in prison jargon means inking his fingers to take fingerprints, and was photographed face and profile with the offender's number. He was told that on this occasion the reason for his arrest was that Editorial Ojeda was publishing books "contrary to the international community", books that were "against public freedoms and fundamental rights". In other words, in a "democracy" where freedom of expression, dissemination and communication are sacrosanct signs of identity, the publishing and sale of books became a criminal activity because the ideas contained in the texts were "contrary to the international community". If it were not so serious and pathetic, it would be laughable.

Two days after his arrest, Varela was released with charges. He was charged with crimes against an entelechy called the international community, against the exercise of fundamental rights and against public freedoms for the defence of genocide. Juan Carlos Molinero, deputy chief of the General

Criminal Investigation Office, explained to the media that the operation had not been directed against the bookshop, which had already been investigated in the 1990s, but against Editorial Ojeda, so neither the shop nor its website had been closed. In reality it was a "legal" ruse to be able to act again against Varela.

Given that we are historicising the events of Pedro Varela, victim of the greatest attack on freedom of expression and publication perpetrated in "democratic" Spain, it is pertinent to note that power in Catalonia in April 2006 was in the hands of a government known as the tripartite, which emerged after the signing of the so-called Pact of Tinell. Chaired by the Socialist Pasqual Maragall, the parties that formed part of it were the Partit dels Socialistes de Catalunya (PSC), Iniciativa per Catalunya Verds-Esquerra Unida i Alternativa (offshoots of the PSUC communists) and Esquerra Republicana de Catalunya (whose emblem, according to its leaders, is a Masonic triangle). This government was thus politically responsible for the persecution in Spain of a businessman for publishing books "contrary to the international community", the majority of which were published almost everywhere in Europe without any problem.

As is well known, when the aim is to criminalise a leader who somewhere in the world opposes the designs of the co-opted puppets at the head of the powerful countries that unleash wars, the latter claim to represent the "international community". The state or nation that does not submit is then accused of "defying the international community". In the unprecedented case we have just described, we understand that there would be an index of banned books whose contents threaten an inconceivable abstraction called the international community.

On 7 November 2007, the Constitutional Court finally issued STC 235/2007, the ruling on the question of unconstitutionality raised by the Third Section of the Provincial Court with respect to Article 607, second paragraph, of the Criminal Code. The rapporteur was Judge Eugeni Gay Montalvo. The ruling, after setting out the legal grounds at length, read as follows:

> "In view of the foregoing, the Constitutional Court, by the authority conferred on it by the Constitution of the Spanish nation, has decided to partially uphold the present question of unconstitutionality, and as a consequence:
> 1º Declare unconstitutional and null and void the inclusion of the expression 'deny or' in the first paragraph of Article 607.2 of the Criminal Code.
> 2. To declare that the first clause of Article 607.2 of the Criminal Code, which punishes the dissemination of ideas or doctrines tending to justify the crime of genocide, interpreted in the terms of legal ground 9 of this Judgment, is not unconstitutional.
> 3. Dismisses the remainder of the constitutional challenge.

This judgment shall be published in the Boletín Oficial del Estado.
Given in Madrid, this seventh day of November two thousand and seven.

In other words, since STC 235/2007, the dogma of faith of the Holocaust can be denied in Spain, just as, for example, the dogma of the Immaculate Conception, the existence of God or any other dogma of the Church can be denied. The Constitutional Court considered that such denial "remains at a stage prior to that which justifies the intervention of criminal law, insofar as it does not even constitute a potential danger to the legal interests protected by the rule in question, so that its inclusion in the precept entails the infringement of the right to freedom of expression". The judgement stated that "the mere denial of the offence is in principle inane". The Court, on the other hand, did consider the dissemination "by any means" of ideas justifying genocide to be a crime. But this is not the case of the revisionists who have been appearing in these pages: none of them justifies or has ever justified genocide. Pedro Varela assured again and again that he disapproved of it in his statement before the judge who sentenced him to five years.

Two months after the Constitutional Court's ruling, the Provincial Court, nine years after Pedro Varela was sentenced to five years, held the hearing of the appeal against the sentence on 10 January 2008. Pedro Varela's defence had requested more time to prepare, as the Constitutional Court's ruling was sufficiently important to study its legal implications thoroughly; but the Chamber rejected the request. Both the prosecution and the defence reiterated their demands. Finally, on 6 March, the judges of the Provincial Court issued the sentence partially upholding the appeal and reducing the sentence to seven months' imprisonment. It was considered that Varela had made an apology for genocide through his work of disseminating genocidal doctrines through the sale of books, but that he had not directly discriminated in a personal way, and was therefore acquitted of the crime of incitement to racial hatred. Pedro Varela did not have to enter prison and announced that he would consider filing an appeal for amparo.

In any case, the harassment of Varela was at its peak, since after his arrest in April 2006 he was still at liberty with charges and was awaiting a new trial. It was on 29 January 2010 when the hearing took place in the 11th Criminal Court of Barcelona. Faced with the obligation to comply with the doctrine of the Constitutional Court, according to which denying the Holocaust is not a crime, but justifying it is; the bookseller and publisher was accused of disseminating ideas that justified genocide and incited racial hatred, despite the fact that he had always said actively and passively that he condemned all forms of violence against any ethnic minority and, of course, all genocide. Prosecutor Miguel Angel Aguilar said that they were not judging ideas, "but the dissemination of the doctrine of hatred". From among the books selected, the prosecutor quoted fragments to support his ramshackle thesis. Pedro's lawyer Varela denounced that the paragraphs extracted by the prosecutor from more than a dozen books sold in the Europa bookshop were "taken out of context" and recalled that some of the books chosen, such as Hitler's *My Struggle*, could also be bought in department stores.

On 5 March 2010, Estela María Pérez Franco, an unopposed substitute judge, who was appointed on a discretionary basis to Criminal Court no. 11, handed down her sentence, which became known on 8 March. In the section on proven facts, this magistrate-judge dedicated fifteen pages to commenting on texts of the seventeen books that she ordered to be destroyed. Here are a few samples. From *Mi lucha* (36 copies seized), she insisted on quoting fragments that allude to race. It seems clear that this judge was unaware that the racial question has always been the raison d'être of the Jewish people. Suffice it to quote an embarrassing statement by Golda Meir, the revered Zionist leader and former prime minister of Israel, that "intermarriage is worse than the Holocaust". This racist, alluding to the Palestinians, said at her moment: "There is no such thing as the Palestinian people. They don't exist. Would the magistrate-judge consider that Golda Meir hated the Palestinians? From Joaquín Bochaca's *Los crímenes de los buenos* (2 copies tapped), the judge quoted as condemnable the sentence "It was not the Arabs, but the good guys, the Jews, who implanted terrorism in Palestine". If this assertion is considered false, one might wonder whether at the time of the sentencing of Pedro Varela the judge had the remotest idea of how the Zionist state came into being. The inclusion of *Yusuf's Green Rain* (222 copies seized), a work by the Jewish author Israel Adam Shamir, among the books to be destroyed is striking. In the sentence, the judge quotes, among others, the following statement by Shamir: "P. 35, lines 3-6, 'The world press, from New York to Moscow, via Paris and London, is perfectly controlled by the Jewish supremacists; not a gnashing of teeth can be heard without their prior authorisation'". Does Estela Maria Perez Franco believe that Shamir is a liar and an anti-Semite? Zionists could explain to her that they consider Jews who dare to criticise them to be "Jews who hate themselves because they are Jews" rather than anti-Semites. Israel Shamir, famous for his commitment to the Palestinian cause, is the author of a trilogy, which in addition to the above-mentioned work includes *The Spirit of James* and *Pardes. A Study of the Kabbalah*, both of which were sold in the Europa bookshop. Two months before the trial, at the invitation of Pedro Varela, Shamir had participated in a series of lectures given by Librería Europa: on Sunday 8 November 2009 in Madrid and on Monday 9 November 2009 in San Sebastián. The title of his lecture was *The Battle of Discourse: The Yoke of Zion*.

Analysing the selection of quotes from the sentence we could write at least fifteen pages, the same as those written by Estela María Pérez; but it is now time to look at the ruling, in which the judge sentenced Pedro Varela Geiss to one year and three months in prison "as criminally responsible as the perpetrator of a crime of spreading genocidal ideas", and to one year and six months in prison for "a crime committed in violation of the fundamental rights and public freedoms guaranteed by the Constitution". It is an unbearable sarcasm, a manifest injustice, that Varela was sentenced for a crime against fundamental rights and constitutional freedoms, when he was precisely the victim of the violation of these rights and freedoms in his person. It was also agreed "to confiscate all the books described in the proven facts... and to proceed to their destruction once the sentence is final".

The judgment did not become final until the end of October 2010. Previously, in May 2010, the Provincial Court heard the appeal. This court of the Audiencia at least kept the decorum it owed itself as a court of justice and acquitted Pedro Varela of the second offence, for which he had been sentenced to one year and six months' imprisonment; but upheld the first: "dissemination of genocidal ideas", for which had been sentenced to one year and three months. Finally, another judge in Barcelona, the head of Criminal Court no. 15, did not agree to grant Pedro Varela the suspended sentence he had requested. The judge stated in her ruling that in ordering the bookseller's imprisonment she had taken into account the fact that he had another seven-month prison sentence from 2008, a fact that from a criminal point of view showed "a criminal record that demonstrates his dangerousness".

Pedro Varela entered prison on Sunday 12 December 2010. It was a bright winter morning, clear of clouds, just as Pedro was clear of crime. He arrived in a small caravan of cars, accompanied by a large group of friends and supporters who surrounded him and cheered him on until the last moment. A large banner carried by several people read: "For the right to inform. No more editors in jail". Another companion carried an individual banner with the phrase "Books are banned and publishers are locked up". With admirable fortitude and dignity, aware of the need to set an example of fortitude, Varela urged his friends not to lose heart. He evoked Quevedo's imprisonment in the dungeons of San Marcos de León and assumed that the time had come to face imprisonment. He asked everyone to remind the world that books were being hunted down and publishers sent to prison. We can make sure," he told them, "that no one else is imprisoned for this reason". With hugs and kisses, he said goodbye after thanking them and crossed the gate. He walked away towards the access control offices to a backdrop of applause and excited shouts of "Come on Pedro!" "Bravo!" and "We won't forget you Pedro!". Fortunately, he was not forbidden to write, which allowed him to write a series of letters in cell 88 of the Can Brians 1 penitentiary centre, where he served his sentence. These texts were later published under the title *Cartas desde prisión. Thoughts and reflections of a dissident*.

On 8 March 2011, Isabel Gallardo Hernández, another substitute judge assigned to the 15th Criminal Court of Barcelona, issued an order in which she ordered the execution of the destruction of the books, as ordered in the sentence of 5 March 2010. We will quote a fragment of the operative part of the order so that there is a record of the index of banned books in Spain, a country where theoretically there is freedom of expression and, consequently, there are no banned books.

> "I DECIDE: to order the destruction of all copies of the books with the following titles:
> 1st My struggle. 2nd Self-portrait of Leon Degrelle, a Fascist. 3rd Hitler and his philosophers. 4th Hitler, speeches of the years 1933/1934/1935. Complete works (volume 1). 5th The crimes of the 'good guys'. 6th Foundations of biopolitics: forgetting and exaggerating the racial factor. 7. Race, intelligence and education. 8. Nobilitas. 9. The new man. 10th Revolutionary ethics. 11th Iron Guard. Romanian fascism. 12th The Protocols of the Elders of Zion. 13° Ecumenism on three sides: Jews, Christians and Muslims. 14° The green rain of Yusuf. 15° Wagnerian thought. 16° The history of the vanquished (the suicide of the West). Volume II. 17th The chief's handbook. Of the Iron Guard.
> The bust of Hitler, the iron swastika, military helmets, as well as the photographs and posters with National Socialist themes that have been removed should also be destroyed.
> Return the flags and stationery to the prisoner".

To note that everything is done in the name of democracy, freedom and fundamental rights is deplorable in the extreme. The question arises as to why busts of historical figures, swastikas, military helmets, photos or posters should be destroyed. If we are told that Hitler represents absolute evil, we have to argue that communism has produced the worst criminals in history. As far as we know, there are no rulings requiring the destruction of busts of Lenin, Trotsky, Kaganóvich, Beria or Stalin in private homes. It is a different matter that statues in public places have been removed in some countries, if not torn down by outraged populations after years of communist totalitarianism.

As for books, what can be said about the destruction of works that are read all over the world and can be freely consulted in Spanish libraries. How can one accept the banning of texts in Spain just because a court in Barcelona has considered it a proven fact that "the content of the occupied books reflects contempt for the Jewish people and other minorities". It is insulting sarcasm that works critical of Jews have to be destroyed, while in Israel racial hatred is at the basis of education. The Talmudists, who viscerally hate Christians, teach in "Abhodah Zarah" that "even the best of the goyim (gentiles or non-Jews) must be killed". Does this teaching not exude racial hatred and bigotry of the worst kind? Maurice Samuel (1895-1972), a Zionist intellectual, in Chapter XIV of his work *You Gentiles*, entitled "We, the Destroyers", writes these words to the gentiles: "We Jews are the destroyers and will remain so. Nothing you can do will meet our demands and needs.

We will destroy eternally because we want the world to be ours." Is this not criminal racism?

It is to be assumed that Judge Pérez Franco did not prevaricate and that if she had been sufficiently erudite on the subjects she was judging she would not have ordered the burning of, for example, *Wagnerian Thought* (12 copies of which were seized), a work by the British thinker Houston Stewart Chamberlain, because on page 83 the author dared to write that "the influence of Judaism accelerates and favours the progress of degeneration by pushing man into an unbridled whirlwind which leaves him no time either to recognise himself or to become aware of this lamentable decadence..."..." The quote comes from the "proven facts" section, in the distressing judgment of 5 March 2010.

"From the school of the war of life. - What doesn't kill me, makes me stronger". This phrase by Nietzsche in *Twilight of the Idols* is ideal to explain the state of mind in which Pedro Varela left Can Brians prison on 8 March 2012. "From now on, I will redouble my efforts", he declared after showing his determination to resume activities in his bookshop and to continue fighting against repression. A year later, on 5 March 2013, the European Court of Human Rights in Strasbourg ordered Spain to pay Varela 13,000 euros, as it found that the Barcelona Provincial Court should have allowed him to prepare and exercise his defence more effectively and with more time after the Constitutional Court's ruling in 2007. It was a moral victory , as the bookseller had requested 125,000 euros in compensation. The judges of the Strasbourg Court unanimously considered that "he was only belatedly allowed to learn of the change of qualification" of the offence for which he was sentenced to seven months' imprisonment.

The fact that Librería Europa and its owner had been able to continue with the lecture series and to reorganise its commercial and cultural activities again did not please its enemies. A dozen hooded henchmen were sent on 11 March 2014 to Seneca Street. These brave men showed up at the bookshop at around half past ten in the morning and in broad daylight, with the insolence of those who know they are unpunished, began the attack: from the street they smashed the windows of the shop windows with blunt objects and then threw paint cans at books and furniture. Fortunately, the staff of the bookshop were not attacked. According to eyewitnesses, the group consisted of about twenty people, but only the hooded men acted violently. Pedro Varela filed a complaint with the Mossos d'Esquadra, although with little hope, if any, of anyone being arrested, as there had never been any arrests before.

Germany, the state that persecutes its own shadow, could not remain on the sidelines without participating in the harassment of the Spanish bookseller and publisher. His appearance in the persecution took place in February 2009, when the German Consulate General in Barcelona filed a complaint against Pedro Varela for marketing *Mein Kampf* (*My Struggle*) without authorisation from the State of Bavaria. The publication of the work in Germany was an offence until 30 April 2015, when, seventy years after Hitler's death, the book fell into the public domain. Under this pretext, the indefatigable Miguel Ángel Aguilar, a "progressive" jurist from the ranks of Baltasar Garzón, Santiago Vidal, José María Mena and the like, known as the prosecutor of hate, since he heads the Service against Hate and Discrimination Crimes of the Barcelona Public Prosecutor's Office, charged Pedro Varela in September 2015 with a crime against intellectual property, a crime which, incidentally, has nothing to do with hate and discrimination. The hate prosecutor submissively asked for two years' imprisonment for Varela, his disqualification for three years as a publisher and trader, and a fine of 10,800 euros for publishing the book without authorisation or licence, despite knowing that the rights to the work belonged to the German state of Bavaria by virtue of a ruling by the Munich Chamber of Justice. In addition, he claimed a further fine of 216,000 euros and compensation of 67,637 euros from the State of Bavaria.

Regarding the rights to Hitler's work, we know that Paula Hitler, the "Führer's" sister, had entrusted François Genoud, "Sheik François" (see note 19), with the editorial management of numerous texts by her brother, including *Mein Kampf*. The Swiss banker was working on a global agreement with her to acquire the rights to all of Adolf Hitler's works, but Paula died in 1960. Even then, the Bavarian authorities, who had seized the contract between Hitler and the NSDAP publishing house (Franz Eher Verlag), anxiously claimed the rights for the State of Bavaria.

Be that as it may, the hatred of Pedro Varela should be among the proven facts, since *Mein Kampf* has been and is being sold all over the world. In India, for example, Hitler is a cult author. His famous work has become a classic and has long been a bestseller. It can be bought in street stalls and from time to time it makes the top ten bestseller list. Pedro Varela's lawyer, Fernando Oriente, rejected in his defence that the State of Bavaria and the Federal Republic of Germany had or had had the rights and argued that the German consul "lacked any legitimacy". The lawyer recalled that the first edition of the book in Spain dates back to 1935 and that the copyright of a person who died before 7 December 1987 is free, as established in a 1996 royal decree on the Law on Intellectual Property. Varela's lawyer regretted that Bavaria's intention was to "act as a censor of thought, preventing the free dissemination of ideas enshrined in the Constitution".

We were about to conclude, but we read in the 28 January 2016 edition of *El País* in Catalonia the following headline: "The prosecutor studies the act of a neo-Nazi in the Europa bookshop". The news reads: "the historic far-right leader Ernesto Milá will present there (in the Europa bookshop) his new book *El tiempo del despertar*, which extols the rise of Nazism". In other words, the prosecutor of hate understands that the presentation of a book can be a criminal act. After having buried more than a hundred million victims of communism all over the world, after the oppression of this totalitarian ideology in half of Europe for fifty years, a lecture on the communist champions is still "progressive"; but if the lecturer is "a neo-Nazi", we are faced with absolute evil, with the apology of national socialism, racial hatred, anti-Semitism.

Unfortunately, revanchism, resentment and hatred are the order of the day in Spain today, but they nestle in the chests of the ever so democratic "anti-fascists". Eighty years after the civil war, protected by a Law of Historical Memory that is used sectarianistically to remember only the crimes of one of the sides in the fratricidal conflict, the parties of the so-called "progressive left", which have gained power in the big town halls thanks to pacts of all against one, are dedicated to destroying monuments, removing plaques in memory of religious people who were shot, changing the names of streets... Armed with reason and moral superiority, as usual, they display an intolerance and fanaticism that threaten harmony and reconciliation among Spaniards, which seemed to be assured thanks to the 1978 Constitution. For this reason, in view of the atmosphere that prevails, one can suspect that the persecution of Pedro Varela will not cease.

Post Scriptum

Unfortunately, months after having written the last sentence, our suspicion has come true: having already concluded this *outlawed History*, we have learned that on 7 July 2016 a new complaint filed by the Public Prosecutor's Office against the Asociación Cultural Editorial Ojeda as a legal entity and against its vice-president Pedro Varela entered the Juzgado de Guardia (Juzgado de Instrucción number 18 of Barcelona). The complaint was also directed against Carlos Sanagustín García, Antonio de Zuloaga Canet, Viorica Minzararu and Nicoleta Aurelia Damian, persons linked to the association and to Librería Europa. Judge Carmen García Martínez immediately ordered "urgent precautionary" measures, which included: the cessation of the activities of Editorial Ojeda, the closure of Librería Europa and the blocking of the bookshop's two websites. Absurdly, the Barcelona Hate Prosecutor's Office invoked article 510.1 a, of the Spanish Constitution, which refers to Fundamental Rights and Public Freedoms, to continue its ruthless harassment of Varela.

On Friday 8 July, the Mossos d'Esquadra arrested the two shop assistants of the Librería Europa, both of Romanian origin, and the two members of the Asociación Cultural Editorial Ojeda at their homes. Pedro Varela was not in town, as he had travelled with his youngest daughter and was camping in the mountains somewhere in Spain. During the search of the bookshop, fifteen thousand books and computer equipment were confiscated. The Europa bookshop was sealed. At 7:00 the same morning, the Catalan police also raided the home of Pedro Varela. In addition to the computers, the officers seized all the cash he kept in his house.

After learning that an arrest warrant had been issued, Pedro Varela issued a statement announcing that he would appear in court, which he did on 15 July. Accompanied by his lawyers, the bookseller and publisher arrived at the Juzgado de Instrucción number nine, which had issued the arrest warrant. He refused to testify. The prosecutor, Miguel Ángel Aguilar, asked for him to be remanded in prison on the grounds that he was a flight risk and that his crimes were repeated. The judge ordered him to be remanded in custody on bail of 30,000 euros, which Varela was unable to pay. Luis Gómez and Javier Berzosa, the lawyers, tried to get a reduction. They argued that their client was not a rich man and that he could not use the money seized by the Mossos d'Esquadra at his home to pay the bail. What he has," said Berzosa, "was taken in the search of his house. Varela was thus admitted to the Modelo prison in Barcelona. Fortunately, a friend paid the judicial deposit the same day and Pedro was able to regain his freedom in the evening.

As for the other persons, after 24 hours in detention, they were released with charges of promoting hatred and discrimination for participating in the "organisation of conferences in the bookshop where the Nazi genocide is glorified and justified and the Jewish Holocaust is denied". The prosecution intended to imprison the two men, the president and treasurer of the Asociación Cultural Editorial Ojeda, but the judge released them. A few days after the sealing of the Librería Europa, a splendid wreath appeared in front of the zippered door, laid on a wooden easel with the following inscription: "From culture and freedom to Librería Europa".

On 18 July, Esteban Ibarra, a supposed champion of tolerance who presides over the Movement Against Intolerance, an NGO that has received nearly seven million euros in public subsidies since 1995, filed a lawsuit against Pedro Varela and the other managers of the bookshop and the publishing house. Ibarra announced that he was going to bring a popular action and that he was counting on the participation of the Federation of Jewish Communities of Spain, the International League Against Racism (LICRA), the Jewish Community Bet Shalom of Barcelona, etc., etc... To finish off the public lynching of a single man, the Barcelona City Council announced through the mouth of the deputy mayor Jaume Asens, state responsible for human rights in Podemos, that the City Council would appear as a prosecutor in the case "for the offence to the whole city". Jaume Asens, an "anti-system" turned separatist, declared that "Librería Europa was a headquarters of the extreme right in the city".

During Franco's regime there was censorship, which served to protect booksellers, as they knew which works they could not sell. Now there is no censorship in Spain and in theory no bookseller should fear anything. However, a businessman, a man capable of "offending a whole city" by selling books, is being viciously persecuted. We fear that this time Pedro Varela's enemies are determined to lock him up forever in a prison of silence. After more than twenty years of persecution, Varela has become a legendary dissident in Spain and one of the most tenacious in Europe. His convictions and his dignity as a person are exemplified by his exemplary attitude of peaceful resistance. His struggle for freedom of expression and thought deserves the recognition not only of those of us who share his revisionist views, but of all those who truly believe in freedom.

Other booksellers and publishers persecuted in Catalonia

The following case confirms the injustice done to Pedro Varela. Known as the Librería Kalki case, it involved four booksellers and publishers who were acquitted by the Supreme Court while Varela, also a bookseller and publisher, was serving a prison sentence for identical acts. Many and varied conclusions could be drawn from this, which we will leave for the end. We will now limit ourselves to a succinct account of the facts after outlining the characters: Óscar Panadero, Ramón Bau, Juan Antonio Llopart and Carlos García, convicted by the Provincial Court of Barcelona for disseminating genocidal ideas in a judgement of 28 September 2009.

The first, Óscar Panadero, son of a leader of the PSUC, nephew of anarchists and grandson of Falangists, was educated as a child in the discussions of the three ideological creeds and ended up choosing National Socialism. Born in Barcelona in 1977, he dropped out of school with excellent marks and opted for a self-taught education. Neither the teachers nor his parents managed to convince the young teenager, who confirmed that he had no intention of giving in to a school that taught falsehoods. After going through associations such as Alternativa Europea and the Movimiento Social Republicano, he ended up in the Círculo de Estudios Indoeuropeos (CEI), whose president was Ramón Bau. In January 2003, after selling his estate and giving up a good job, he opened the Kalki Bookshop, which he owned and managed. Only half a year later, his political persecution began: on 8 July 2003 and 25 May 2004, the regional police raided the establishment and, as in the case of the Europa bookshop, seized thousands of books and magazines, as well as catalogues, pamphlets, etc.

The second, Ramón Bau, also from Barcelona, participated at the age of seventeen in the founding of the Círculo Español de Amigos de Europa and worked with Pedro Varela in its publishing activities. Bau worked closely with Varela and became secretary general of CEDADE. In 1984 he set up Ediciones Bau, Bausp y Wotton and published more than a hundred magazines. In June 1998 he founded the Círculo de Estudios Indoeuropeos. Bau, an intellectual with a wealth of knowledge, is a convinced National Socialist and a self-proclaimed Wagnerian.

Juan Antonio Llopart, the third of the persecuted Catalans, was born in Molins de Rei into a Falangist family. Founder of Ediciones Nueva República, he was also the driving force behind the magazine *Nihil Obstat*. Llopart, from Ediciones Nueva República, sponsored and organised a series of conferences, Disidencia, which for several years were attended by international personalities, fighters against the current in the field of culture. He is the author of several works and has collaborated in different publications.

The fourth, Carlos García, a member of the CEI and also of Falangist tradition, claims to be a student of National Socialism. Secretary to Óscar Panadero, he told a significant anecdote about his arrest: when ten policemen burst into his home at night in 2004, the one who was calling the shots was in civilian clothes and wore a red communist star on his lapel. García believes that this was a way of letting him know who was after him.

Well, after being arrested in a humiliating manner and being held for several days in the dungeons, proceedings were opened against them in the Juzgado de Instrucción n° 4 de Sant Feliu de Llobregat (Sant Feliu de Llobregat Magistrate's Court n° 4). Once the opening of oral proceedings had been decreed, the case was referred to the Provincial Court of Barcelona, which handed down its sentence on 28 September 2009. The four were sentenced to prison terms of up to three and a half years for crimes of dissemination of genocidal ideas, crimes against fundamental rights and freedoms, and unlawful association. Ramón Bau, president of CEI, and Óscar Panadero, owner of Librería Kalki, received three and a half years; Carlos García, three years; Juan Antonio Llopart, administrator of Ediciones Nueva República, was not convicted of illicit association, and was therefore sentenced to two and a half years in prison.

The lawyers lodged an appeal in cassation before the Supreme Court for infringement of the law and of constitutional precepts, as well as for breach of form. On 12 April 2011, the Supreme Court handed down Ruling 259/2011, whose rapporteur was Judge Miguel Colmenero Menéndez de Luarca. The ruling considered that the cassation appeals for infringement of the Law and Constitutional precept, as well as for breach of form, were admissible. As a result, the defendants were acquitted of the crimes for which they had been convicted and all the rulings of the High Court judgement were rendered null and void. The sentence consisted of 218 pages. In the section on "Fundamentos de Derecho" (legal grounds), the same arguments were given which, when put forward by the defence of Pedro Varela, had been rejected by the Catalan courts which had tried and convicted him. An excerpt is quoted below:

> "Therefore, in the case of publishers or booksellers, the possession of some copies of such works, in greater or lesser numbers, with the aim of selling or distributing them, as would be the case with many other

possible works with similar themes, or even contrary ones in their deepest but equally discriminatory and exclusionary sense, does not in itself constitute an act of dissemination of ideas beyond the mere fact of making their documentary supports available to potential users, and therefore, nothing different from what is to be expected from their professional dedication, even if they contain some form of justification of genocide, they do not constitute direct incitement to hatred, discrimination or violence against these groups, or indirect incitement to the commission of acts constituting genocide, and even if these works contain concepts, ideas or doctrines that are discriminatory or offensive to groups of people, it cannot be considered that these acts of dissemination alone create a climate of hostility that entails a certain danger of materialising in specific acts of violence against them.

There is no description in the proven facts, as would be necessary to apply the offence, of any act of promotion, publicity, public defence, recommendation, praise or incitement or similar acts attributed to the accused which referred to the goodness of the ideas or doctrines contained in the books which they edited, distributed or sold because of their philhonazi content, discriminatory or genocide-prone or genocide-justifying content, or the desirability of acquiring them for the knowledge and development of those ideas or doctrines, or in any way advocating their implementation, which could be considered as dissemination activities, which had a wider scope and were different from the fact of publishing certain works or making copies available to potential customers.

Nor can the acts alleged in the factual account be seen to glorify Nazi leaders on account of their discriminatory or genocidal activities, and therefore, without prejudice to the opinion that such persons may deserve, in relation to what has been said so far, it cannot be considered as an indirect incitement to genocide or as an activity aimed at creating a hostile climate from which specific acts against the offended persons or against the groups of which they form part could be inferred".

In plain English ("in which the people usually talk to their neighbours"), the fact that booksellers or publishers, in the exercise of their professional activity, sell or publish certain books does not imply that they justify genocide, hatred or violence against anyone. The Supreme Court, and this would be applicable to the case of Pedro Varela, did not consider that in the "proven facts" there was anything related to acts of promotion or justification of the practice of the ideas contained in the books published or distributed. Nor did he consider that any incitement to genocide could be attributed to the convicted persons on the basis of the acts alleged in the account of the facts. As for the claim that the defendants formed part of an unlawful association, the Supreme Court explained in the ruling that "it is not enough to prove the ideology of the group or its members" and considered that the available data did not show that the group was "a structured organisation with the means to transform ideological orientation into the promotion of discrimination".

STC 235 of 7 November 2007 and Ruling no. 259 of 12 April 2011 of the Criminal Division of the Supreme Court protect the rights to ideological freedom and freedom of expression, so that any idea can be defended and disseminated. However, instead of congratulating themselves on two rulings that protect the freedoms of all, some "progressive" media, always subservient to the voice of their masters, tore their garments and considered the rulings to be a step backwards. In other words, when judges and prosecutors act in accordance with certain interests, even if they restrict fundamental rights, they are exemplary rulings; but otherwise the magistrates are conservative and carcas. In their sectarianism, these media and the groups behind them ignore the fact that the Constitution does not prohibit ideologies, whether they are at one end of the political spectrum or the other. According to the Supreme Court judges, the Constitution "does not prohibit ideologies", so "ideas as such should not be criminally prosecuted". The Supreme Court insisted that tolerance of all kinds of ideas allows for the acceptance of even those that question the Constitution itself, "however reprehensible they may be considered". In short, the Supreme Court relied on the jurisprudence of the Constitutional Court, according to which "in the protection of freedom of opinion there is room for any opinion, however mistaken or dangerous it may seem to the reader, even those that attack the democratic system itself. The Constitution also protects those who deny it".

The Supreme Court's ruling was a setback, a setback, for the Barcelona High Court. At the time, Pedro Varela was still in Can Brians prison. In June 2011, half a year after being voluntarily admitted, the prison's treatment board denied him permission to see his wife and young daughter, whom he had not seen since. Since the powers of prison enforcement have been transferred to the Generalitat de Catalunya, it is clear that the prison officials were obeying political instructions from the Catalan government. Pedro Varela had applied for the third degree and had been denied. On 3 March 2011, he lodged an appeal against the refusal. If justice had been served, as soon as the Supreme Court judgement acquitting the four booksellers and publishers convicted of the same offences became known, the corresponding Prison Supervision Court should have resolved the appeal against the denial of the third degree and automatically ordered the conditional release of the prisoner. Despite the fact that the case law of the Supreme Court does not consider the facts for which he was in prison to be a crime, Varela served his sentence in full. Thus, it was demonstrated once again that his case was political and had nothing to do with fairness and justice.

7. MAIN VICTIMS OF PERSECUTION IN SWEDEN:

Ditlieb Felderer, the mocking Jew using corrosive satire

This revisionist, who has been accused, prosecuted, convicted and imprisoned in Sweden, currently maintains an irreverent website, *Ditliebradio*, where he has opted for sardonic humour to denounce impostures. In a sarcastic, macabre way, he uses all kinds of ironic photographs, including pornographic ones, to mock the lies about the Holocaust, the crimes of Zionism, the Catholic Church's adherence to dogma, Jehovah's Witnesses and all the rest. Sometimes he uses bold and ingenious photomontages to better illustrate his denunciations. For all this, Felderer is known as the eccentric revisionist. His bizarre sense of humour has been used by exterminationists and propagandists to discredit him. He seems to care little for it, believing that the "sensibilities" of history falsifiers and compulsive liars should not be respected at all.

According to Elliot Y. Neaman, Ph.D. in history from the University of California at Berkeley and professor at the University of San Francisco, Ditlieb Felderer is Jewish, as was his mother, who was descended from a family of Jehovah's Witnesses. Born in Innsbruck in 1942, he fled the Nazis with his family: they went to Italy and from there emigrated to Sweden, where he was educated. He therefore has Swedish nationality. In 1976, working for a Jehovah's Witness publication, he began to travel to the camps. Years later, between 1978 and 1980, he made a second round of visits to what were supposedly extermination camps. He was one of the first researchers to look for evidence at Auschwitz. On these trips, he took nearly 30,000 photographs, recording even the most trivial details of the facilities. Many of them are used in his photomontages. At Auschwitz, Felderer photographed the swimming pool, the modern hospital and its gynaecology section, the theatre, the library, the classrooms where sculpture classes were held, the kitchen, which was one of the largest facilities in the camp. He had access to archives that required special permission and discovered in them the musical score of a piece entitled "Auschwitz Waltz", which was supposedly performed by the camp orchestra.

Among his main contributions as a revisionist was the discovery of the role played in the camps by Jehovah's Witnesses, who cooperated with the SS administration. We have already mentioned above that, as a prominent Jehovah's Witness, he was expelled from the sect when he denounced that it was false that the Germans had exterminated 60,000 members, since according to his investigations he established that only 203 of them had died (see note 15). It was at the same time as this dispute with the sect's leadership that Richard Verrall's (Richard Harwood) book *Did Six Million Realy Die?* fell into his hands, of which he published a Swedish edition in 1977 and distributed some 10,000 copies. Since then his commitment to historical revisionism has been permanent. After founding the magazine *Bible Researcher* in 1978, in 1979, the year he met Ernst Zündel, he published the book *Auschwitz Exit* under the pseudonym Abraham Cohen. As a result of his research, in the same year his *Diary of Anne Frank - A Hoax?*

Felderer was already fond of certain eccentricities, some of which disturbed Zündel, as he considered them counterproductive. One of them ended up costing him imprisonment. Since the Auschwitz Museum exhibits hair from alleged victims murdered in the gas chambers, Felderer came up with the idea of making fun of it in a widely circulated pamphlet entitled: 'Please accept this hair from a gassed victim'. The leaflet was sent to the officials of the Auschwitz Museum. Interspersed in the text of the leaflet were drawings and jokes mocking the museum officials and the exterminationists. In the first drawing, a smiling woman held a wrapped gift with the inscription: 'Please send us all your junk. We need it for our authentic exhibits and documentation". The second joke was a clown saying: "I am an expert exterminationist. Generously send us your documents to all our addresses. You will be remembered for it. The third illustration was a man crying crocodile tears, the text below read: "I was gassed six times! No! Ten times, No! ... and there are 5,999,999 others like me in Neu Jork! The six million gassed Jews are a hoax!". During Zündel's first trial he was questioned and explained that in his opinion satire was necessary to denounce an imposture supported by powerful states and the power of money.

In 1980, the Swedish police arrested Ditlieb Felderer for publishing the pamphlet. On this first occasion he spent three weeks in prison. In 1982 he was arrested a second time because of the controversial pamphlet. This time he was charged with agitation against an ethnic group, and a Stockholm court sentenced him to six months in prison. Felderer stated that during this imprisonment he was treated inhumanely. Not knowing whether it was day or night, he said, he spent most of the time staring at the wall of a two-by-three metre concrete bunker, as he was hardly allowed to go outside to breathe fresh air. The cell had no toilet and he was escorted and locked in a washroom when he needed to relieve himself. In protest at his situation and because he was prevented from writing, he went on three hunger strikes, until he was finally allowed to do some exercise and was provided with paper and pencil. Felderer reported that he was beaten several times and had to endure insults.

In 1988, at Zündel's second trial, he showed 300 leaflets taken during his visits to the camps and demanded protection for revisionism and freedom of speech instead of persecution. The Crown presented him with several of his pamphlets. He asked her to read one entitled "Three Jewish Contributions to Western Civilisation". The contributions referred to the atomic bomb, developed by Robert Oppenheimer; the hydrogen bomb, whose father was

Edward Teller; and the neutron bomb, by Samuel Cohen. All three were Jewish. Felderer testified that his flyer spoke volumes about certain people who had created these terrible weapons of destruction. Another of the leaflets he was shown alluded to his admission to a psychiatric hospital when he was on trial: he complained that in Sweden, detractors were interned and compared this practice to that used in the Soviet Union. The Crown Prosecution replied to Felderer that it could not accept that the Swedish authorities thought he was ill and needed help; but he insisted that the tests he had undergone showed that he was perfectly healthy.

It seems that after his testimony at the Toronto trial, he thought he had done all he could and his research had stopped. Ernst Zündel always acknowledged Felderer's excellent work on the camps and on Anne Frank's diary, but considered that satire was not an effective genre for a historian because it can call into question the seriousness of other work. Zündel came to regret that Feldererer had gone too far in his mockery through pamphlets and drawings. Despite his disappearance from the scene, Feldererer has reported repeated harassment and insults. Not for nothing is he considered one of the pioneering researchers of revisionism.

As we noted in footnote 15, the latest news we have had from Ditlieb Felderer is that in November 2013 he blamed Jewish judge Johan Hirschfeldt for being behind "terrorist actions" against him and his Filipino wife. On his website *Ditliebradio*, Feldererer referred to secret documents from the Swedish Foreign Ministry to make very serious accusations against Hirschfeldt, whom he accused of having instigated attacks against them by thugs on behalf of the ADL (Anti-Defamation League). It seems that in one of these acts, which Feldererer describes as state terrorism, his wife almost lost her life. According to Felderer, Carl Bildt, then foreign minister, could be held responsible for his inaction. Felderer also accused Judge Hirschfeldt of harassing Ahmed Rami, a Moroccan revisionist who has been attacked several times and has run the website *Radio Islam* for many years, with false accusations.

Ahmed Rahmi, the architect of *Radio Islam* and leading Muslim revisionist

This Moroccan of Berber origin was an officer in the Royal Moroccan Army when, on 16 August 1972, he took part in a failed coup d'état against King Hassan II, whom he considered a puppet of Jewish power. After going underground, Ahmed Rami went to Paris and from there to Sweden, where he applied for and was granted political asylum in 1973. Since then he has lived in Stockholm, where he has published five books in Swedish. His appearance in these pages is due to the revisionist activities that ended up costing him imprisonment in the country that had taken him in.

In 1987 he founded and ran a radio station called *Radio Islam*, which enabled him to communicate with Swedes and the eighty thousand or so Muslims living in the country. His slogan was "Radio Islam - The Freedom Fighter - Join the fight against Jewish domination and racism! In its radio broadcasts it began to launch revisionist content, in particular the works of Robert Faurisson. In 1988, the station reported on the Ernst Zündel trial in Toronto. A staunch supporter of the Palestinian cause, Rami linked the Holocaust to the Zionist usurpation of Palestine from the outset, and consequently linked the liberation of the Palestinian people to the uncovering of the lies imposed by Zionism. This frankness led to the radio station being branded as anti-Semitic, and in 1989 the Minister of Justice, under pressure from the Jewish lobby, brought a charge of incitement to racial hatred.

A trial against Ahmed Rami began in September 1989 and lasted until November. The trial began at the Stockholm District Court on 15 September. From the outset, Rami's defence rejected the accusations of grievance and defamation against an ethnic group and put forward the argument that freedom of expression could not be restricted because someone feels insulted. In addition, lawyer Ingemar Folke, insisted that Rami had merely quoted passages from the Bible in which Jews were depicted as blackmailers, greedy, sadistic, exploitative and criminal. The fact that the texts came from the Pentateuch led the Swedish press to believe that the court should ultimately interpret whether they contained expressions of racism or contempt for other ethnic groups. Prosecutor Hakan Bondestam called Rabbi Morton Narrowe and former Stockholm Lutheran bishop Krister Stendahl, an honorary professor at Harvard University, who flew in from the United States to testify against the Moroccan revisionist. Stendahl declared that Luther's *The Jews and Their Lies* was not Christian and that Luther was an anti-Semite. For his part, Rami presented as witnesses Jan Hjärpe, a renowned professor of Islam at Lund University, and Jan Bergman, a professor of religion at Uppsala University. Both testified that in their opinion freedom of expression in Sweden was under attack when it was intended to silence criticism of Israel and silence the Palestinian issue. Lawyer Folke insisted that a distinction had to be made between anti-Semitism and anti-Zionism and stressed that his client was seeking to defend the rights of the Palestinian people and that criticism of a state's policies could not be considered racial hatred. The newspaper *Expressen*, in a display of insidious bad faith, considered in its 23 October 1989 edition that it was "practically impossible to separate anti-Semitism from anti-Zionism".

On the other issues, Rami was accused of Holocaust denial. He maintained impassively that the alleged genocide of six million Jews "was a huge propaganda hoax". Some newspapers indignantly picked up on Rami's quotes from *The Protocols of the Elders of Zion* and his claim that Jews had not been exterminated in the gas chambers. The main defender of Rami and Professors Hjärpe and Bergman in the Swedish press was Jan Myrdal, son of

Nobel laureate Gunner Myrdal. As the trial progressed, prosecutor Bondestam realised that prolonging it was counterproductive because Rami was using it to "continue his anti-Semitic propaganda while on trial". On 14 November, the verdict was pronounced and Ahmed Rami was found guilty. At sentencing, he was sentenced to six months' imprisonment for "incitement against an ethnic group", for which he was sentenced to prison in February 1990. His *Radio Islam* licence was cancelled for a year. Robert Faurisson subsequently reported on the activities of his revisionist colleague in prison. According to the professor, Rami successfully explained his views not only to the prisoners, but also to the guards, which is why the authorities transferred him to another, smaller facility, where the result was the same.

As for the cancellation of the radio permit, the Stockholm Community Radio Council allowed the station to continue broadcasting until 28 November 1990. When the station resumed its activities in 1991, it did so under the direction of David Janzon, a Swedish nationalist member of the "Sveriges Nationella Förbund" (Swedish National Alliance), who was subsequently convicted of the same offence in 1993. The radio station thus remained inactive between 1993 and 1995. Programming was re-established under the leadership of Ahmed Rami in 1996, when he also launched his famous website, which kept the same name of *Radio Islam*. Initially, this website was very active in its criticism of Jewish racism and Zionist world domination. In addition, very interesting revisionist texts appeared in up to 23 languages. Today, and for some years now, the site, maintained by a group of self-styled "freedom fighters" from different countries who support Ahmed Rami, is rarely renewed. We do not know what the reason for this lack of activity is, although it is likely to be due to the harassment of Rami.

In his *Écrits révisionnistes*, Robert Faurisson recounts that between 17 and 21 March 1992, he travelled to Stockholm at the invitation of his Moroccan friend. On the afternoon/evening of the same day of his arrival, Rami, two young Swedes and Professor Faurisson were attacked and nearly lynched by individuals armed with sticks, knives and tear gas bombs. The leaders of the group of attackers were the heads of a Jewish student club. Thanks to these threats, the Jewish community in Stockholm succeeded in cancelling all the lectures that Ahmed Rami had organised for Professor Faurisson to speak; but it was not possible to prevent him from expressing himself freely and extensively on *Radio Islam*. The professor's second stay in Stockholm took place between 3 and 6 December of the same year. At the airport, the "Nazi prophet", as some media described him, was met by Rami, some Arab friends and a Somali. Paradoxically, two Jewish demonstrators were holding a banner with the inscription "Down with racism! Faurisson stayed at his host's house and recounts in the *Écrits* that there were two night-time attacks on Rami's home.

In October 2000 Rami was again convicted of "incitement to racial hatred". The Swedish court that tried him in absentia fined him about

$25,000. In both France and Sweden he was investigated for "hate crimes" because of his role in maintaining *Radio Islam*. In Sweden, the investigation ended in 2004 and the prosecutor was unable to provide evidence that Ahmed Rami was responsible for the content displayed on the site. The *Radio Islam* affair reached the Swedish Parliament in November 2005. The debate took place due to the large number of lawsuits that Jewish organisations filed in court, demanding that Ahmed Rami be prosecuted in Sweden or brought before an international court. This idea had been proposed in Morocco by Robert Assaraf, the leader of the Moroccan Jewish community, who in March 2000, in a statement to the magazine *Jeune Afrique*, asked rhetorically: "Shouldn't Moroccan Jews, who are scattered all over the world, mobilise in order to bring Ahmed Rami to trial?"

The debate in the Swedish Parliament took place on 10 November 2005. Jewish members of the chamber criticised the government for having abdicated to Ahmed Rami and his anti-Jewish activities in Sweden. Minister of Justice and Home Affairs Thomas Bodström defended himself with these words: 'In a state under the rule of law, it is not for me or the members of Parliament to charge or judge Ahmed Rami. This is a matter for the Prosecutor's Office. But the prosecution has not been able to find any evidence to prove that Ahmed Rami has violated Swedish law". To the discomfort of some MPs, the minister reminded: "Swedish law does not prohibit questioning or denying the Holocaust". Minister Bodström recalled that it had been agreed in Sweden that citizens could not be forced to believe in the Holocaust and that it was not possible to prohibit questioning its historical veracity. However, he suggested "the possibility of exerting some influence in Parliament by proposing a law and, of course, contributing to the work done in the European Union".

The latest we know about Ahmed Rami and *Radio Islam* is that in December 2015 the Italian police opened an investigation. The reason was the publication in Italian on the website of a list of influential Jews operating in the country. The names of journalists, businessmen, actors, and various personalities were listed, who were described as "Judeo-Nazi mafia". Representatives of the Jewish community considered this an incitement to sectarian violence and used adjectives such as "unacceptable" or "despicable" to refer to the issue. The leader of Rome's Jewish community told *Corriere della Sera* that "it was an unbearable representation of anti-Semitic hatred". Some lawyers called for the website to be shut down immediately. Meanwhile, Giuseppe Giulietti and Raffaele Lorusso, president and secretary general of the Italian National Press Federation, called the publication of the list "a miserable, racist and intolerable act". In a press release they wrote: "It offends first of all Muslims who have chosen the path of dialogue and respect. This list evokes the dark times and the walls that we should all tear down together".

These two hypocrites were, of course, referring to all the walls except the eight-metre high wall erected by the Zionists in Palestine. As for "dialogue and respect", it does not include, of course, the Palestinian people, let alone the 1.5 million Gazans living in subhuman conditions in their open-air prison. As is well known, in July/August 2014 some two thousand people, a quarter of them children, were killed and nine thousand were badly wounded, if not severely maimed. Of course, this was not "a miserable, racist and intolerable act". Two years after the "tolerable" bombardment of Palestinian civilians, Gaza, thanks to "dialogue and respect", is still in ruins and its inhabitants remain destitute.

8. MAIN VICTIMS OF PERSECUTION IN AUSTRALIA:

Frederick Töben, imprisoned in Germany, England and Australia

Dr. Fredrick Töben is one of the most illustrious and courageous victims of the revisionist movement. This German-born Australian could have been listed among the victims in Germany, as the "Bundesrepublik" is the country that has been most vicious in its persecution. However, we have chosen to dedicate an exclusive space to him and place him in Australia because it is there that he founded the Adelaide Institute in 1994, a institution dedicated to historical research that would be the equivalent in Australia of the Institute for Historical Review in California.

The Jewish lobbies in Australia have been relentless in their efforts to shut down the Adelaide Institute's website. In 1996 the powerful Jewish lobby "Executive Council of Australian Jewry" (ECAJ) took the first legal action to shut down the Institute's website. Dr. Töben, author of numerous works on history, education and political issues, has researched most of the concentration camps in existence today: Buchenwald, Dachau, Oranienburg, Sachsenhausen, Auschwitz-Birkenau, among others. In the latter, he inspected the alleged gas chamber in April 1997 and shot a highly recommendable video which is part of the documentary *Judea Declares War on Germany*, released by the IHR in Los Angeles.

In 1999, he travelled to Europe to conduct research in several countries, including Poland, Ukraine, Hungary, the Czech Republic and Germany. While in the office of a German prosecutor famous for his work against deniers, Hans-Heiko Klein, with whom he was supposedly discussing German legislation prohibiting dissent from the official version of World War II, he was arrested on 9 April 1999 for having published or forwarded to Germany revisionist texts from the Adelaide Institute. The arrest warrant stated: "since April 1996 and most recently between January and April 1999, he has mailed from Adelaide (Australia) to recipients in the Federal Republic of Germany, inter alia, a monthly newsletter of the Adelaide Institute, for which he is the responsible editor". A criminal offence, no doubt, which justified, as the arrest warrant stated, his being remanded in custody pending trial.

This pre-trial detention was ignominiously prolonged for seven months. On 3 May, the prosecutor's office of the Mannheim district court confirmed it in a new arrest warrant. The charges, in addition to the sending of the newsletter, specified that she was "one of the leading revisionists" and specified some of the inadmissible contents of the newsletter, such as the statement that "the extermination was a legend invented by the Jews for the purpose of subjugating the German people". This second arrest warrant accused him of incitement to hatred, attacks on the dignity of others and denigrating the memory of dead Jews, all of which disturbed the public peace.

As soon as news broke in Australia of the Adelaide Institute director's arrest, civil rights groups mobilised to denounce Fredrick Töben's arrest in Germany under "draconian free speech laws". John Bennett, a well-known Australian revisionist and activist who chairs the Australian Civil Liberties Union, urged people to go to German embassies and other institutions to protest. Bennett organised a fund for to secure Töben's legal defence and release. Another group, Electronic Frontiers Australia (EFA), an independent group promoting online freedom of expression, also spoke out against the arrest and expressed anger that the German authorities treated the material posted on an Australian website as if it had been published in Germany. EFA president, lawyer Kimberley Heitman, accused the German government of trying to legislate in practice for the whole world. Mark Weber, director of the IHR, also protested indignantly at the arrest and remand of his Australian colleague, but nothing changed Töben's situation in Germany.

After seven months in prison without bail, he was brought before a Mannheim district court presided over by Judge Klaus Kern on 8 November 1999. On the first day of the trial, Töben announced that he would not defend himself against the charges against him because this would only serve to bring new charges against him for additional violations of German laws on 'Holocaust denial' and 'incitement to hatred'. He rejected the German authorities' claim that the revisionists were dangerous neo-Nazis or anti-Semites. His lawyer, Ludwig Bock, also announced that he would not defend Dr. Töben either, as he risked being indicted as well. He therefore confined himself to reading a statement to the court in which he compared the persecution of Töben and other "Holocaust deniers" to the witch trials of the Middle Ages. He claimed that German laws against revisionism seriously violated the principle of freedom of expression. He justified his and his client's decision to a journalist: "If I say anything, I myself will go to jail, and if he says anything, he exposes himself to another trial.

Prosecutor Klein later confirmed that these fears were fully justified: "If they had repeated illegal things in court, I would have brought new charges". As has already been explained, the legal system in Germany renders defendants and witnesses defenceless and prevents lawyers from freely exercising their profession. Indeed, in November 1999, Ludwig Bock was awaiting the outcome of his appeal, because while defending Günter Deckert he had been convicted and fined DM 9,000 for having complained that political leaders and judges in his country prohibited debate on the subject of the Holocaust.

The trial ended on 10 November 1999. The court found Töben guilty of incitement to racial hatred, insulting the memory of the dead and public denial of genocide because in his writings sent to people in Germany he had questioned the evidence of Holocaust extermination. Klaus Kern, the presiding judge, said that there was no doubt that Töben was guilty of "Holocaust denial" and that, as he showed no signs of rectifying his conduct, he should be sentenced to prison. He was therefore sentenced to ten months in prison. Fortunately, Judge Kern took into consideration that the defendant had already spent seven months in prison and agreed to pay a fine of 6,000 Marks in lieu of the remaining three months of his sentence. Frederick Töben's German friends immediately collected the money, and within 24 hours of the verdict he was released.

Particularly important in the ruling was the decision on the internet, as the consequences could be far-reaching. The Mannheim court declared that German law had no jurisdiction over Dr. Töben's writings and online publications, and therefore refused to enter into the evidence presented by the prosecution in relation to the Adelaide Institute's website. Judge Kern argued that the court could only consider material that Töben had emailed or physically distributed in Germany. As soon as he was released, Töben declared this a victory for freedom of expression: "We have saved the internet," he said, "as a place where we can tell the truth without being punished for it". For his part, public prosecutor Hans-Heiko Klein was also aware that the court's verdict could set a dangerous precedent and immediately filed an appeal. This is the first time," he said, "that a German court has decided that some things said on the internet in Germany cannot be subject to German law. This is a very bad thing. It will weaken our legislation which is very important to ensure that history does not repeat itself in Germany."

Back in Australia, the fight continued with a new battle. As we noted at the beginning, in 1996 the ECAJ (Executive Council of Australian Jewry), the most powerful of Australia's Jewish lobbies, had filed a complaint aimed at banning the Adelaide Institute's website from the Internet. One year after Töben had won a victory for Internet freedom in the German court case, on 10 October 2000, the Human Rights and Equal Opportunity Commission (HREOC), under pressure from Australian Jewry, issued an injunction against the Adelaide Institute. HREOC Commissioner Kathleen McEvoy alleged that the Institute had violated Section 18C of the Racial Discrimination Act 1975 by publishing materials whose primary purpose was to denigrate Jews. McEvoy declared that such materials, "none of which were of sufficient historical, intellectual or scientific standard", should be banned because they were "intimidating, insulting and offensive". ECAJ vice-president Jeremy Jones was quick to reiterate that "Töben's Holocaust denialism was offensive, insulting and, as confirmed by HREOC, illegal". Jones added that the commissioner "had demonstrated that she understood the need to enforce laws that include the internet and had endorsed the view of other jurisdictions that anti-Semitism masquerading as pseudo-history is as pernicious as the worst form of racial hatred." Peter Wertheim, ECAJ's counsel in the legal proceedings and a Jewish community leader, referred to the case as "a landmark" because it "dealt with internet hate for the first time in Australia and most likely in the world."

Dr Töben's response was defiant: he claimed that he had no intention of complying with the HREOC (Human Rights and Equal Opportunity Commission) order and said he had no intention of apologising for the publication of "objectively correct material". Töben accused HREOC of considering only the interests of Jews and called its actions immoral. He said he had "no intention of doing anything" because the truth could not be considered an offence to anyone. In early November 2000 the Australia/Israel & Jewish Affairs Council joined ECAJ in petitioning the country's Federal Court to enforce HREOC's censorship order against Töben and the Adelaide Institute.

The attempted censorship of the Adelaide Institute set a shameful precedent for a country with a long tradition of respect for civil liberties and free speech. Terry Lane, a veteran columnist and television commentator, asked Commissioner McEvoy if she was "going to order every sincere person who dislikes one group or another to cease and desist and apologise." This journalist went so far as to say that Töben's claims about the gas chambers "could be proved or disproved by the evidence", so there was no need to censor them beforehand. If Töben is telling the truth," Lane added, "nothing can stop him. If he is a malicious writer, he will be ignored. We should check his claims, not ban them." Another author, civil rights advocate Nigel Jackson, referred to HREOC as a "pseudo-judicial" body and called its order "a victory of interests over principles". On 17 September 2002, the Federal Court, in response to the Jewish lobbies' application, upheld the application of anti-racial hate laws against the Adelaide Institute's website. In 2003, in the case of Töben v. Jones, the Court issued Australia's first ruling in relation to racial hatred against religious groups. Töben failed to remove the materials in question and also refused to apologise.

In 2004, a Mannheim court issued a European Arrest Warrant (EAW) against Frederick Töben, who was accused of publishing anti-Semitic and/or revisionist material online in Australia, Germany and other countries. Despite the existence of the European Arrest Warrant, Dr. Töben travelled the world without any problems. In 2005 he gave an interview to Iranian public television in which he denounced the State of Israel, "founded on the lie of the Holocaust". In December 2006 he took part in the Tehran Conference together with his revisionist colleagues. However, problems continued to arise in his own country as a result of his refusal to remove the censored texts from the Institute's website and, consequently, his confrontation with the Federal Court.

Jeremy Jones of the Executive Council of Australian Jewry (ECAJ) meanwhile continued his relentless pursuit in the courts. At the end of

February 2008, Dr. Töben, summoned to the Federal Court in Sydney, made strong accusations against two Jewish judges of the High Court, Alan Goldberg and Stephen Rothman, whom he accused of "propagating the Jewish Holocaust" in order to "protect a historical lie". On 7 August 2008, the Australian newspaper *The Advertiser* reported that "Holocaust revisionist Frederick Töben could be jailed for criminal contempt of the Federal Court if he could not face a fine." He was accused of continuing to publish racist texts on the Adelaide Institute's website, despite a Federal Court order in September 2002 and a further injunction in 2007.

Two months later, on 1 October 2008, Töben was travelling from the United States to Dubai. When his plane landed at Heathrow airport for a technical stop. British police boarded the plane and, in application of the 2004 EAW, arrested the Australian revisionist on board. He was brought before a Westminster District Court on the 3rd and British magistrates decided to hold him in London's Wandsworth prison pending a decision on his extradition request. Töben stated that he was protected by the Schengen treaty and would not accept extradition, but the hearing was set for 17 October.

British revisionists mobilised against the outrage perpetrated against their Australian colleague. A group of supporters, including David Irving, demonstrated in front of the court. The press devoted considerable attention to the affair. *The Telegraph* reported the Töben case appropriately, calling the arrest "a blatant attack on free speech". In an editorial, it warned: "The arrest of Dr Frederick Töben should alarm us all". In Parliament, Liberal Democrat Party spokesman Chris Huhne reminded the House that "Holocaust denial" was not a crime in Britain, and called on the British courts to reject Töben's extradition. Simultaneously, Andreas Grossmann, the prosecutor of the Mannheim district court, welcomed the arrest and said that despite attempts to avoid extradition to Germany, he hoped to have Töben in court next year. Grossmann warned in statements to Australian media that the defendant's stubbornness and obstinacy could cost him five years in prison in Germany.

On 17 October 2008 there was anticipation. Journalists with cameras and microphones gathered in front of the City of Westminster Magistrates Court. Kevin Lowry-Mullins, Töben's lawyer, declared before entering that they would fight every issue. Also speaking to journalists was Lady Michèle Renouf, the Australian-born British revisionist model who runs the website *Jailing Opinions*, which has been assisting Töben since she learned of his arrest. A staunch supporter of freedom of research, expression and thought, Renouf stressed the importance of the court decision for freedoms in the UK. However, the hearing was postponed until 29 October. Lowry-Mullins explained on the way out the scope of the ruling, as it was a question of whether a state could request the extradition to the UK of any person, even if the crime charged was not a crime in the UK.

Finally on 29 October came the victory awaited by Töben, Lady Renouf and so many revisionists around the world. Daphne Wickham, the judge at Westminster Magistrates' Court, ruled before a packed courtroom of Töben supporters that the European arrest warrant was invalid because it did not sufficiently specify the offences: it did not mention the name of the website, where or when the materials had been published, but only said publications on the internet around the world. Melanie Cumberland, the lawyer representing the German authorities, argued that the requested information could be provided; but the district judge said: "The requirement, in my view, cannot be met with a drop-by-drop information as and when provided by the authority of the issuing country. I consider the details to be vague and imprecise. I consider that the order is invalid, and I therefore disqualify the defendant." In other words, without even going into whether the alleged crimes of opinion were extraditable offences, the judge dropped the charges against Dr Töben on the grounds of formal defects in the arrest warrant. Cumberland announced that he intended to appeal to the Supreme Court. Pending such an appeal, Judge Wickham, after prohibiting him from making statements to the press, granted Töben provisional release on bail of £100,000 on condition that he give an acknowledged address, which would be that of Lady Renouf.

Michèle Renouf stated on the way out that they were not afraid of ending up before the Supreme Court, as this would allow Dr. Töben's case to gain greater international impact. Finally, perhaps considering that the filing of the appeal could end up being detrimental to the interests of the Holocaust lobby, Töben's lawyers were informed on 18 November that the German authorities were waiving their appeal. On the evening of 19 November, while the British Parliament honoured Zionist Shimon Peres with the Order of St Michael and St George, Fredrick Töben celebrated freedom with his friends. On 21 November Kevin Lowry-Mullins reported that his passport had been returned to him and that he was preparing to leave Britain. The lawyer regretted that his client had not received any compensation for the almost two months he had been held against his will in London.

By 3 December 2008, Töben was back in Australia; but far from enjoying a respite, he had to face the continuation of the prosecution that the Executive Council of Australian Jewry had initiated in 1996. In April 2009, Töben was convicted for ignoring a Federal Court order to remove material from the Adelaide Institute's website. Sentenced to three months' imprisonment, he argued that he did not have the money to pay a fine to avoid imprisonment, let alone the legal costs of such a lengthy court case, as demanded by Jeremy Jones, who had brought the case on behalf of Jewish organisations. Töben appealed the verdict in June.

The appeal hearing was held on 13 August 2009. Lawyer David Perkins told the court that the texts published on the Adelaide Institute's website were only "a drop in the bucket" compared to the amount of revisionist material available online. The judges insisted that the case was not about the Holocaust, the gas chambers or the execution of Jews during World War II, but about disobedience of Federal Court orders. Evidently, this was a quibble, i.e. a false argument put forward with sufficient skill to make it appear true. The Federal Court would not have ordered the removal of the material in 2002 without pressure from Jewish lobbies seeking the banning of texts that questioned the official version of history. The three judges of the Federal Court of Australia therefore rejected the appeal and upheld the committal to prison. "You follow orders blindly, gentlemen," Töben said to the judges as he left the courtroom.

Frederick Töben thus became the first prisoner of conscience in Australia's legal history. He initially spent a week in a maximum security punishment block at Yatala Prison in the northern suburbs of Adelaide, a prison where the worst criminals are held. He was subsequently transferred to a much less rigorous detention centre in Cadell, about 200 kilometres north-east of Adelaide, where he was able to receive the support of his friends, who kept visiting him. The Adelaide Institute was taken over by Peter Hartung, a businessman and political adviser with a spirit of resilience worthy of his predecessor and friend.

As for the costs of the proceedings, Dr. Töben had to bear them. On 25 June 2010, Jeremy Jones, who behaved like a hound that does not let go of its prey, submitted a statement of costs and expenses amounting to 104,412 dollars. On 30 June, the Federal Court decided to request $56,435 as a provision and on 15 September 2010 issued a valuation certificate stating that the amount requested by the Court was correct. Thus began another complicated legal battle between Jeremy Jones and Fredrick Töben that lasted for more than two years, and the amount demanded kept increasing. On 27 February 2012, Jeremy Jones asked for a new costs assessment. On 10 April, Dr. Töben filed an application for an interlocutory injunction in which, inter alia, he requested the removal or exclusion of the assessment of court costs. On 3 May 2012, Judge Mansfield rejected Töben's claim, and Töben also had to pay the costs relating to the interlocutory application. On 18 May 2012, Fredrick Töben wrote to Jeremy Jones in these terms:

> "Your claim against me in the matter of costs in excess of $175,000 is unjust and inadmissible. I have sold my house in which I had lived for twenty-seven years, the only asset I had, to satisfy your previous requests. I have no other funds or securities and will not be able to pay a penny. If necessary, you may petition for my insolvency. I have at all times exercised my right to freedom of expression. In order to demonstrate the injustice you have done me, I maintain a cross-claim against you in the Federal Court, claiming damages for breaches of sections 18 (1) and 20 (1) of clause 2 of the Competition and Consumer Act (we will not venture to translate the title of that Act). I also intend to bring an action for defamation. The grounds for this action go back to your article of 31

August 2009 ('The last word: contempt for the truth'), which you published on the internet and which is still there. If the lawsuits I am proposing are heard by the Court, I expect to receive a substantial amount in damages, sufficient to meet your claims for costs. However, I am prepared to waive my legal rights to sue you for the above actions, provided that you stay your claim for costs.
I look forward to your advice".

These lines, taken from the documentary archives of the Adelaide Institute, which contain the texts of the court proceedings, reflect the unequal struggle of a humble man, lacking in resources, against the Australian Jewish lobbies, whose wealth is practically unlimited. After serving time in prisons in Germany, England and Australia, Fredrick Töben had lost all his material possessions and was ruined, but he possessed an exemplary conviction and greatness, which today makes him a paradigm for all those who strive in one way or another to ensure that future generations of young people study a true world history, in which the impostors are unmasked.

Without space for further details, we will add that after seventeen years of legal persecution by representatives of Australia's Jewish community, on 24 September 2012 Dr. Fredrick Töben was declared insolvent by the magistrates of the Federal Court of Sydney . After the legal deadline for appeal had expired, *The Australian jewishnews* broke the news at the end of October with the headline "Töben tied up". According to Australian law , the declaration of insolvency entailed the confiscation of his passport in order to facilitate the control of his estate and income. Thus, "tied up", he was condemned to live as a pauper for the rest of his life as punishment for his "crimes".

9. OTHER VICTIMS OF PERSECUTION FOR THOUGHT CRIMES:

All Against Catholic Bishop Richard Williamson

The case of the English Catholic bishop Richard Nelson Williamson is internationally known because of the repercussions of his statements on the Holocaust. Monsignor Williamson belonged to the Fraternity of St. Pius X and was excommunicated by John Paul II in 1988. In November 2008, Swedish television recorded an interview with him in Regensburg (Germany), which was broadcast on 21 January 2009, a few days before Pope Benedict XVI issued a decree lifting the excommunication of him and three other renegade bishops. The bishop's words produced a media scandal, unleashed by Zionist organisations, and came to jeopardise the Vatican's relations with Jewish religious leaders. The interview begins as follows:

> P. "Williamson, are these your words: 'Not a single Jew was killed in the gas chambers. These are nothing but lies, lies, lies'. Are these your words?
> R. - I think you quote me from Canada, yes, many years ago. I think the historical evidence is overwhelmingly against six million Jews having been murdered in gas chambers as a result of a deliberate policy of Adolf Hitler.
> P. - But you said that not a single Jew was killed.
> R. - In gas chambers.
> P. - So there were no gas chambers.
> R. - I think there were no gas chambers, yes".

The dogma of faith of the Holocaust had just been publicly denied by a Catholic bishop. Anathema! For the rest of the interview, Williamson turned to the revisionists and said that according to them between 200,000 and 300,000 Jews had died in concentration camps, but none of them in gas chambers. After asking the interviewer if he had heard of the *Leuchter Report*, Monsignor Williamson enlightened the journalist when he replied that he did not know it: the research at Auschwitz, the conditions in a gas chamber, the characteristics of Zyklon B were the subjects explained by the priest. The interviewer reacted with a question : "If this is not anti-Semitism, what is anti-Semitism?" The answer was that historical truth could not be anti-Semitism.

The criticism of such a heinous thought crime was fierce and the demands immediate. As early as January, Regensburg's public prosecutor, Günter Ruckdaeschel, announced that an investigation had been opened against Williamson. Criticism extended to Pope Benedict XVI for lifting his excommunication. A Vatican spokesman immediately pointed out that the bishop's views were unacceptable and violated church teaching. In a front-page article, the Vatican newspaper *L'Osservatore Romano* reaffirmed that the Pope deplored any form of anti-Semitism and that all Catholics should do the same. Rabbi David Rosen of the American Jewish Committee, Rabbi Marvin Hier of the Simon Wiesenthal Center and the Jewish Agency, effectively the mouthpiece of the Israeli government, denounced the Vatican for pardoning a Holocaust denier.

Bishop Williamson, now back at his headquarters in La Reja, Buenos Aires province, thanked the Pope for his decision, which he described as "a step forward for the Church". On 26 January 2009, Cardinal Angelo Bagnasco, president of the Italian Bishops' Conference, defended the Pope's decision to rehabilitate Williamson, but criticised his views as "unfounded and unjustified". The president of the Bishops' Conference in Germany, Heinrich Mussinghoff, was also quick to "strongly condemn the explicit denial of the Holocaust". Monsignor Williamson issued a statement apologising to the Pope for having caused him "distress and trouble" because of his views on the Holocaust, which he himself described as "imprudent".

The outcry and pressure from Jewish organisations multiplied and exposed the Vatican's inability to respond other than obedience and docility. Charlotte Knobloch, president of the Central Council of Jews in Germany, announced that in these circumstances she was suspending her dialogues with Catholic leaders. On 3 February 2009, the Chief Rabbinate of Israel officially broke off relations with the Vatican and cancelled a meeting scheduled for 2 and 4 March with the Holy See's Commission for relations with Jews. Oded Weiner, director general of the Rabbinate, addressed a letter to Cardinal Walter Casper, in which he said: "without a public apology and retraction, it will be difficult to continue the dialogue".

On the same day, 3 February, Angela Merkel, faithful to the voice of her masters, demanded that Pope Benedict XVI clarify the position of the Church: "The Pope and the Vatican," she said, "must make it unambiguously clear that there can be no denialism. In Germany the whole machinery for stoking the "scandal" fire was in full swing: The *Bild Zeitung* warned the Pope that "the extermination of six million Jews could not be denied" without a reaction. The *Süddeutsche Zeitung* applauded the Chancellor's warning and recalled that a German Pope could not "back a Holocaust denier" without offending the Jewish community. The *Berliner Zeitung* wrote that Williamson had not only mumbled in private, but had spoken publicly, calling on the Pope to excommunicate him again. In an attempt to contain the criticism, on 4 February Benedict XVI ordered Richard Williamson to recant "publicly and unequivocally."

The bishop had been living in Argentina for five years, but on 19 February he was declared "persona non grata". The Argentine Ministry of the Interior, through the National Directorate of Migration, urged the British bishop to leave the country within ten days. The note stated that it took into account 'the public notoriety following his anti-Semitic statements to a Swedish media, in which he doubted that the Jewish people were victims of the Holocaust'. The Argentine government added in the note that Williamson's statements "deeply offended the Jewish people and humanity".

Monsignor Williamson, who travelled to England, nevertheless resisted all pressures and in an interview with *Der Spiegel* said that he had always sought the truth and therefore converted to Catholicism. He declared that he was convinced of what he had said: "Today I say the same thing I said in the interview with Swedish television: historical evidence must prevail and not emotions. And if I find other evidence to the contrary, I will retract it, but that will take time." The bishop drafted a written apology, but Federico Lombardi, Vatican spokesman, said he "did not meet the conditions for him to be admitted back into the Church". Of course, the Jewish community also rejected it. Marvin Hier of the Simon Wiesenthal Centre demanded: "If he wants to apologise he has to affirm the Holocaust".

Brigitte Zypries, Germany's Minister of Justice, eventually dismissed the possibility of issuing an EAW for the British authorities to arrest the bishop and extradite him to Germany. Finally, in April 2010, a trial was held in Regensburg at which Williamson did not appear. Nor did the three Swedish journalists who had taken part in the interview come to testify. Lawyer Matthias Lossmann applied in vain for acquittal. Monsignor Williamson was sentenced to a fine of 10,000 euros for "incitement to racial hatred". Following an appeal, in July 2011, again in absentia, Williamson was sentenced in the second instance to pay 6,500 euros, but due to procedural flaws, a review of the proceedings was forced. On 24 February 2012, he was acquitted. The court found that the charges had been brought incorrectly because the prosecution did not adequately specify the nature of the offence. The sentence was therefore quashed due to procedural errors. Since the possibility of new charges remained open, he was convicted in absentia for the third time on 16 January 2013. This time the fine was reduced to 1,600 euros. Williamson refused to pay and appealed again.

As can be seen, what was important in the case was the monumental uproar, the unrelenting harassment, the disproportionate reactions against a Catholic priest just because he dared to speak his mind. In our opinion, what was really regrettable was not the usual condemnations and threats from international Jewish organisations or the demands made on the Pope by the German press and Chancellor Merkel, the daughter of a Polish Jew and remarried to a Jewish professor, but the Vatican's and the Church's capitulation. "I have come into the world to bear witness to the truth," Jesus replied to Pilate as he was about to be handed over. "You shall know the truth, and the truth shall set you free", he taught his disciples. Unfortunately, the Catholic hierarchy has long since given up speaking the truth as Jesus Christ taught. Both the Vatican and the Red Cross know very well what the truth is about the so-called extermination camps; but their present leaders have capitulated, preferring to lie and painfully abide by the dogma of faith of the Holocaust.

On 25 March 2016, Good Friday, the Holy Father Francis presided over the Stations of the Cross in the Colosseum in Rome. The event was broadcast by numerous television stations to hundreds of millions of people around the world. The Pope commissioned Cardinal Gualtiero Basseti to write the meditations. For the Third Station, Jesus falls for the first time, Basseti referred to the sufferings of today's world. In the first place of the meditation he wrote: "...There are sufferings that seem to deny the love of God. Where is God in the extermination camps? And a little later, before praying the Our Father: "...We pray to you, Lord, for the Jews who have died in the death camps...". It is obvious that there was no need to mention among today's tragedies and in pride of place a suffering of seventy years ago. Only servitude justifies this mention by Cardinal Basseti, who, of course, forgot to write a single word for the unfortunate Palestinian people. Yes, like Monsignor Williamson, the Church knows that the death camps did not exist. It knows the truth, but it affirms the lie out of cowardice, because it is subservient to deception and ignores the words of Christ: "You shall know the truth, and the truth shall set you free".

Haviv Schieber, the Jew who slashed his wrists to avoid deportation to Israel

In *On the Wrong Side of Just About Everything But Right About It All*, Dale Crowley Jr. recounts attending Haviv Schieber's funeral with his close friends in a blizzard of snow, a fitting backdrop to the tormented and courageous life of this revisionist Jew. Dale Crowley quotes this line from Schieber: "My Jewish brothers love to hate. They do not know how to forgive. They are sick and they need the doctor, Jesus, and the medicine, the Bible." Schieber, then, was a Christian, and in his articles, interviews and statements he always expressed his desire for truth and justice. "Nazism," he once said, "made me afraid because I was a Jew. Zionism makes me ashamed to be a Jew." When asked if the Protocols of the Elders of Zion were authentic, he invariably replied, "It doesn't matter. It's all come true."

Ernst Zündel learned a great deal from Haviv Schieber, with whom he maintained a good friendship. Zündel regarded him as an extremely intelligent person. From him he obtained first-hand information about Zionism, as Schieber explained to him the reality of the State of Israel. In 1932 Schieber was a passionate Zionist who emigrated from his native Poland to live in British Mandate Palestine. He had Palestinian friends and lived and did business with them until 1936 when, disillusioned by the reality, he chose to return to Poland. There he saw how, instead of helping the neediest Jews, the Zionist organisations selected only young socialists who could be useful in their plans for the future state. In 1939, when the Nazis invaded Poland, he returned to Palestine, where he married, raised a family and became the Jewish mayor of Beersheba. His final disenchantment with Zionism came when he discovered its true nature during the 1948-1949 war of conquest. Fed up with murder and injustice, he flew to the United States from Israel on 18 March 1959.

The Zionists then began their persecution and pressured the US authorities to deport him. The legal battle to obtain political asylum lasted more than fifteen years. He was initially allowed to stay until 1 February 1960. On 4 April 1961 a court order ordered his deportation, but his claims that he would be physically persecuted in Israel were heard and deferred. Finally, on 5 August 1964, he was invited to leave the country voluntarily as an alternative to deportation, but was warned that if he did not leave the United States he would be deported. The asylum process lasted until the early 1970s. As late as 23 June 1970, an appeals court denied him indefinite political refugee status. When Zionist pressures were about to bear fruit, Haviv Schieber slit his wrists at the Washington D.C. airport to prevent being put on a plane to Israel.

In the United States, Schieber became the admired Quixote of a group of Americans, Jews and Christians, who saw in him an indomitable idealist. Schieber became a whirlwind of activity in defence of the rights of the Palestinian people and in denouncing the imposture of Zionism. Haviv Schieber died in 1987. During the last years of his life, despite two serious operations in 1985, he continued his work at the head of his "Holy Land State Committee", set up to fight for a state in which Jews, Arabs and Christians could live in peace.

Hans Schmidt, the American imprisoned for four words

Emigrated to the United States in 1949, Hans Schmidt became a citizen in 1955. In addition to marrying and having two children, he became a businessman in the restaurant industry, but he had also founded and chaired the German-American National Political Action Committee (GANPAC), an organisation dedicated to protecting the rights and interests of the country's largest ethnic minority. In 1985, his offices in Santa Monica (California) were attacked and damaged to some extent. Schmidt, who was in contact with the IHR and had attended some IHR conferences, edited and published two hard-hitting newsletters, the English-language *GANPAC Brief* and the German-language *USA-Bericht*. A civil rights activist, he was outspoken in his revisionist views and opinions, including denouncing the falsification of history and the Holocaust campaign. He was also ruthless about the betrayal and capitulation of German political leaders.

On 9 August 1995 he was arrested at Frankfurt airport. He was 68 years old and retired. He had travelled to Germany to visit his elderly mother and was about to fly back to Florida. Schmidt was arrested on the basis of an arrest warrant issued on 28 March 1995 by a judge in Schwerin, which was replaced by a second arrest warrant dated 5 October. The 'crime' had been the sending of a copy of his newsletter *USA-Bericht* (*USA Report*) to the home of Rudi Geil, a member of the 'Bundesrat'. The newsletter contained an open letter he had written in response to an article published in *Die Zeit*. Offended by what he read, Geil filed the complaint that led to the arrest warrant. The offending paragraph that prompted the arrest alluded to "the left, the anarchists, the Jew and the Freemason infesting the political system, together with the controlled press." According to the arrest warrant the expressions "the Jew infested" and "the Freemason infested" were directed against these two population groups in Germany. The charges against him related to the famous paragraph 130 (I, 2) and were the usual ones.

For the first time an American citizen was arrested for something he had written in an e-mail sent from the United States, for expressing an opinion that was absolutely legal in his country. US political leaders, so quick to condemn violations of human rights and freedom of expression when it is in their interest, remained silent. When questioned, they dismissed the matter with the familiar "domestic issue". Protests came from American civil rights activists, who sent a flood of letters to German officials and journalists and took out newspaper advertisements denouncing Schmidt's treatment. On 22 August, for example, a group of citizens stood outside the German consulate at New York holding a large banner entitled 'Travelers Alert', warning Americans planning to travel to Germany that they risked imprisonment if they expressed 'incorrect political views'.

While in prison, Schmidt accused the US Embassy of providing false information to Germany to facilitate his prosecution. Due to his delicate health, his lawyers managed to get him released on bail in January 1996. Thus, after spending five months in prison, he managed to return to the United States and was able to avoid further prosecution. There he wrote a book about his experience, entitled *Jailed in "Democratic" Germany*, which was published in 1997. Until his death in 2010, he continued to fight against the power of the Jewish lobbies and their influence in the United States and around the world.

Arthur Topham, convicted in Canada for "hatred" of Jews

Arthur Topham is a long-time revisionist fighter who in November 2015 was convicted in Canada of the crime of "hate". Topham maintains the website *The Radical Press*. For eight years now he has been resisting harassment from the enemies of free speech, so his fight has been long and heroic. The site has been sabotaged on several occasions. The first attack on the materials posted on the website took place in 2007. Charges were laid against Topham under the Canadian Human Rights Act. His first arrest and imprisonment, on 16 May 2012, coincided with further sabotage of the site. He was charged with "willfully promoting hatred against people of the Jewish race or religion". The two individuals who sued him are known to have acted at the behest of the Jewish Masonic lodge B'nai B'rith of Canada.

Topham himself has revealed that the text that contributed most to the filing of the lawsuit was a satirical article entitled *Israel Must Perish*, written in May 2011, in which Arthur Topham parodied Theodore N. Kaufman's famous *Germany Must Perish*, published in 1941. What he had done was simply to substitute the names in the sentences that exuded the most hatred for Germany. That is, where Kaufmann's book said "Nazis", Topham had written "Jews"; instead of "Germany", he had written "Israel"; instead of "Hitler", he had written "Netanyahu". He intended to expose the hypocrisy of Jews, who accused others of hatred. On 15 April 2014, a provincial court judge surnamed Morgan, emulating the practices of the Inquisition, prohibited the publication of the names of the two individuals who had filed the criminal complaint against Arthur Topham, publisher of *The Radical Press*, for "hate crime".

The trial against Topham began on 26 October 2015 and concluded on 12 November with a guilty verdict for Topham. At the time of writing, the sentence, which could be two years minus one day, is not yet known. Readers interested in more details about the trial can go to *The Radical Press* website, which contains a full transcript of the archives of each session of the trial. The jazz musician and Jewish revisionist Gilad Atzmon intervened in the trial and also published an excerpt on 8 November 2015. It explains that the Crown presented among the experts on Judaism and anti-Semitism Len Rudner, a "Jewish professional" who for fifteen years had been working for the Jewish Congress of Canada and its successor organisation, the Center for Israel and Jewish Affairs (CIJA). Prior to the start of the trial, he had tried to force the internet service provider to shut down the site. Rudner himself has filed civil lawsuits against Topham. As in the cases of Pedro Varela and Librería Europa or Fredrick Töben and the Adelaide Institute website, most of the books and texts listed by Rudner can be obtained on the Internet or freely purchased on Amazon and in bookstores.

Gilad Atzmon (see note 16), who is not only a musician but also a philosopher and author of several books, was the expert on Jewish issues presented by Arthur Topham and his lawyer Barcley Johnson to counter Rudner's arguments. Atzmon's competence in "Jewish identity politics" was recognised by the court. The jury listened with fascination to the precise and complex explanations of this unique Jew, who asserted that many of the apparently anti-Semitic writings were produced by early Zionists. Atzmon, a former soldier, experienced first-hand the perverse ideology of Zionism and the tribal mechanisms that are fanatically applied in Israel.

The latest we have learned is that on Friday, November 20, 2015, having been found guilty in the previous trial, Arthur Topham appeared in

Supreme Court in Quesnel for a hearing related to the bail issue and also additional claims related to the publication in *The Radical Press* of a photo of the jury in front of the court building. Jennifer Johnson, the Crown prosecutor, requested a number of extremely harsh conditions. It appears that while Topham and Johnson appeared in person, Bruce Butler, the Supreme Court judge, and defence lawyer Barcley Johnson appeared via telephone from Vancouver and Victoria respectively. The judge ruled that the publication of the photo of the jurors, who were standing in the snow and photographed from a distance where their faces could not be clearly seen, could not be a danger to their safety. In any case, he demanded its withdrawal.

10. APPENDIX ON THE RUTHLESS PERSECUTION OF NONAGENARIANS

The persecuted people listed in this last section, which we write as an appendix, are no longer revisionists, nor have they committed thought crimes. They are people who would never normally enter history textbooks. They would perhaps form part of what Miguel de Unamuno considered intrahistory. Their names have been in the headlines for a day or two and then disappeared forever. Precisely for this reason, so that they do not end up in oblivion, we have chosen to include them in our work, albeit concisely. They are nonagenarian victims of unspeakable persecution for the simple fact of having served as soldiers in the army during the Second World War. Normally, these elderly men who served their country as teenagers should be honoured and recognised, yet they are treated as criminals.

The famous case of John Demjanjuk, extradited, accused, tried and sentenced to death, has already been mentioned. Another well-known case is that of Frank Walus, Zündel's witness in the 1985 trial. Falsely accused by the Nazi hunter Wiesenthal of being the "Butcher of Kielce", he suffered a vicious campaign in the US media, which led to his public beating. The German-born American mechanic was attacked seven times by Jewish henchmen, who almost killed him in an acid attack. In order to finance his defence, he sold his house and was ruined. He also lost his US citizenship. After a long and costly appeals process, he won, but his health was already very poor and after suffering several heart attacks he died. There are more cases like these that could be recounted, but we prefer to give space now to the anonymous ex-soldiers, of whom we will present only a few examples.

In April 2013, it became known in Germany that prosecutors had decided to carry out a "final effort" to find Nazi criminals. To this end, a list had been compiled of the names of 50 living Auschwitz and other camp guards who were to be investigated in order to give satisfaction to Holocaust survivors. "We owe it to the victims," said Kurt Schrimm, head of the Central Office of the Judicial Authorities for the Investigation of National Socialist Crimes, who reported that the Auschwitz Museum had forwarded the list of names of former guards to them.

Efrain Zuroff, a furious Nazi-hunter, director of the Simon Wiesenthal Centre in Jerusalem and one of the masterminds of "Operation Last Chance", declared that the fact that most of the names on the list are octogenarians or nonagenarians is no reason why "justice" should not be done. Author of *Operation Last Chance: One Man's Quest to bring Nazi Criminals to Justice,* the vigilante avenger states in his book: "Don't look at these men and say they look weak and frail. Think of someone who at the height of his strength devoted his energies to murdering men, women and children. The passage of time in no way diminishes the guilt of murderers. Old age should not afford them protection". The famous Deborah Lipstadt, the Emory University professor, supported the idea that there is no age limit for prosecuting criminals.

Laszlo Csatary

It is the first name to appear on the list managed by German prosecutors and the SWC (Simon Wiesenthal Center). In July 2012, shortly after the arrival of Zionist Laurent Fabius at the Foreign Ministry, a meeting took place in France between Fabius, the Nazi hunters and Jewish community groups. As a result of the meeting, France asked Hungary to arrest Laszlo Csatary, who was living in Budapest under his own name. A spokesman for the Ministry declared that there could be "no immunity" for those who had carried out the Holocaust. On 18 July 2102 the SWC reported that Csatary had been arrested. His lawyer Gabor Horwath said that he was interrogated for three hours behind closed doors by a Budapest prosecutor, who accused him of anti-Semitism. No charges were brought against him, but he was placed under house arrest. According to his persecutors, he participated in the deportation of more than 15,000 Jews to Auschwitz in 1944. Csatary denied being an anti-Semite and cited examples of relations with Jews in his family and circle of friends. He also denied having been a commander of the Kosice ghetto in German-allied Hungary. Horwath said he "could easily have been mistaken for someone else". To apply pressure, vigilantes organised demonstrations outside the house with signs reading "Last chance for justice". A group from the European Union of Jewish Students, all wearing very indignant faces, formed a chain with their hands tied. Two "activists" climbed up to the floor and stuck crossed-out swastikas and a sign with the slogan "We never forget" on the door. In August 2013, Laszlo Csatary died at the age of 98 while awaiting trial. In reporting the death, the lawyer recalled that Csatary had only been an intermediary between Hungarian and German officials and had not been involved in any crime.

Samuel Kunz

On 21 December 2010, Christoph Göke, spokesman for the Dortmund prosecutors, reported that a 90-year-old man, Samuel Kunz, a former guard in Sobibor who had helped exterminate 430,000 Jews, had been charged. According to press reports, Kunz admitted that he had worked in 1942-43 in the Belzec "extermination camp". When his flat was raided by the police, the old man denied that he had been personally involved in any crime. The news reported that a "flurry of arrests" was taking place among people in their nineties and that Nazi hunters were pleased with the zeal of the police.

Alongside the bloodletting of people, the economic bloodletting continued: days before Kunz's arrest, on 9 December 2010, Ruediger Grube, chief executive of Deutsche Bahn, declared that the suffering of Nazi victims was not forgotten, and the state railway company was donating 6.6 million dollars to fund projects for survivors, given to EVZ (Foundation for Remembrance, Responsibility and the Future).

Johan Breyer

As a result of an arrest warrant issued by Germany, in July 2014 Johan Breyer, an 89-year-old man who had emigrated to the United States in 1952, was arrested at his home in Philadelphia, Pennsylvania, accused of having acted as an accomplice in the murder of hundreds of thousands of Jews. Breyer admitted that he had been a guard at Auschwitz, but said he had served overseas and had nothing to do with the murders. Although his lawyer, Dennis Boyle, warned that his client was in too frail health to be jailed while awaiting an extradition hearing, the judge said the detention centre was equipped to care for him and refused any bail. The Associated Press reported statements in Jerusalem by Nazi-hunter Efraim Zuroff, who reminded the American public that in 2013 the German authorities had displayed posters in some cities with the slogan "Late, but not too late" that the decrepit Breyer should be extradited. Zuroff added that Germany "deserved credit" for "making a last-ditch effort to maximise the prosecution of those responsible for the Holocaust."

Oskar Gröning

The shameful poster campaign deserves a comment, as Oskar Gröning was one of the thirty Auschwitz guards targeted in the context of the operation "Spät, aber nicht zu spät" (Late, but not too late). They depicted in black and white the main façade of Auschwitz in the background and the railway tracks on the snowy ground , which converged before the entrance to the camp. At the bottom, a red stripe with the above-mentioned inscription. The SWC offered rewards of 25,000 euros for those who denounced the grandparents. The Wiesenthal Centre reported that six cases were located in Baden-Würtenberg, seven in Bavaria, two in Saxony-Anhalt, four in North Westphalia, four in Lower Saxony, two in Hesse and one each in Rhineland-Palatinate, Hamburg, Schleswig-Holstein, Saxony and Mecklenburg-Western Pomerania. All of them were former guards.

One of the four prosecuted in Lower Saxony was Oskar Gröning, who was arrested in March 2014. When he was formally charged in September 2014, Gröning, known as the "Auschwitz accountant", was 93 years old and charged with complicity in the murder of at least 300,000 people. "Oskar

Gröning did not kill anyone with his hands, but he was part of the extermination machine," survivor Judy Lysy told retired judge Thomas Walter, who investigated Gröning in Toronto and Montreal. The trial began in April 2015, and Gröning's failing health forced the trial to be suspended for a few days. The verdict was made public on 15 July. Although the prosecutor had asked for three and a half years in prison, the Luneburg court, disregarding the fact that Gröning was already 94 years old and had not killed anyone, sentenced him to four years. Justice Minister Heiko Maas, a Social Democrat, said the trial had helped to alleviate the "great failure" of the German justice system, which had only managed to bring to justice about 50 of the 6,500 SS members at Auschwitz who survived the war.

Reinhold Hanning

In the summer of 2015, the court set to try Reinhold Hanning, a 93-year-old former Auschwitz guard accused of complicity in the murder of 170,000 people, was awaiting a medical report to determine whether the nonagenarian was mentally fit to stand trial. Anke Grudda, a spokeswoman for the court in Detmold, North Westphalia, told the Associated Press that the trial could not begin until the neurological report was completed. The British newspaper *Daily Mail* reported that there was insufficient evidence to show whether Hanning had made decisions himself or had merely assisted others in the work. The case was supplemented by statements from an alleged grandson of victims, Tommy Lamm, 69, who told the story from Jerusalem of his grandparents, who were shaved and gassed shortly after arriving at Auschwitz, and linked Hanning to their deaths. Lamm said he was willing to go to Germany to hang him with his own hands. Finally, in November 2015, neurologists concluded that Reinhold Hanning could withstand two-hour court sessions a day.

Siert Bruins

Accused of killing a member of the resistance during the World War, Siert Bruins, a 92-year-old Dutch-born former security guard, was brought to trial in Germany in September 2013. The public prosecution, despite the fact that he was a nonagenarian, asked for life imprisonment. The prosecutor argued that Bruins had killed Aldert Klaas Dijkema, who in September 1944 was working for the resistance against the German occupation of the Netherlands. Surprisingly, the judge found that there was insufficient evidence that the accused was the perpetrator of the alleged crime, which took place seventy years earlier. Detlef Hartmann, the lawyer for Aldert Klaas' sister, who was allegedly seeking revenge, said that his client was upset by the court's decision. For his part, Siert Bruins left the courtroom with a walker and was unable to express an opinion.

A 91-year-old woman

Many of the detainees were usually ill, as it is impossible to reach the age of ninety without serious physical and especially mental deterioration. In most cases, the full names of these elderly people were not even revealed to the press. So we end up with an anonymous victim, who will serve as a symbol of so many unknown people who have suffered and continue to suffer from the insatiable hatred which, eighty years later, is still displayed by the eternal "victims"; but also as a symbol of the moral and political misery of the Federal Republic of Germany, whose Chancellor Angela Merkel cynically declares that her country must pay "eternally" for the Holocaust. A state that persecutes old men who served their homeland and carried out the orders of their superiors has neither credibility nor dignity.

On 22 September 2015, *Fox News* carried this news item: "German woman, 91, charged in 260,000 Auschwitz deaths". The body of the story reported that an unidentified 91-year-old woman had been charged by German prosecutors with involvement in the deaths of 260,000 Jews at Auschwitz. *The Times of Israel,* one of *Fox News'* sources, specified that the woman, a member of the SS, had been a radio operator under the commandant of the camp in July 1944. Heinz Döllel, a spokesman for the prosecutor's office, said it did not appear that the woman was unfit to stand trial, although the court would not decide whether to proceed with the case until next year. It is most likely that the court, considering being a radio operator to be an abominable crime, will eventually try her.

CHAPTER XIII

THE FIRST BIG LIE OF THE 21ST CENTURY: THE ATTACKS OF 11 SEPTEMBER 2001

Few moderately informed people today hold the official version of the attacks of 11 September 2001. Movements have sprung up all over the world demanding the truth, as the evidence that a big lie has been fabricated is irrefutable. The main problem in finding out exactly what really happened is, as usual, the subjugation of the mass media, which sustains a false interpretation of what happened and conceals the evidence with its treatment of the information, amounting to criminal cooperation in the form of a cover-up. In the United States, numerous associations for the truth about 9/11: pilots, architects and engineers, scientists, firemen, military, actors and artists, medical professionals, lawyers, athletes... are demanding that the facts be clarified. Most of these organisations have joined the so-called "9/11 Truth Movement", formed in 2004. The main problem with the 9/11 truth movement today is that it is highly infiltrated. Those working to fragment and undermine its credibility use the technique known as "muddying the water", which consists of mixing information of all kinds, from the most fantastic to the most real, in order to create confusion and break the cohesion and strength of the movement.

The twin towers in New York did not fall because of the impact of planes or paraffin fires, but collapsed because of controlled demolitions prepared in advance. American Airlines Flight 77 did not crash into the Pentagon. It is absolutely incredible that anyone can still maintain this falsehood: the impact was caused by a missile and there is more than enough graphic evidence of this: videos and photographs show the round holes in each of the rings of the building that were penetrated by the device. Moreover, the wreckage of the plane was never found, but pieces of the missile were. United Ailines Flight 93 did not crash at Shanksville, but was shot down. The official story that heroic passengers sacrificed themselves to save other lives is a fabrication. We will provide sufficient arguments and evidence for all this in the following pages.

Within days of the criminal attacks, George W. Bush declared that the United States was launching a war on terrorism that would last fourteen years. That was the time the 9/11 strategists had calculated that it would take to restructure the Middle East through the wars they planned to launch. In 2016, fifteen years later, the nightmare for the peoples of the region seems endless. Destabilisation is widespread: the wars unleashed by the United States in Afghanistan and Iraq have been followed by disastrous civil wars in both countries and in others in the region provoked from outside. Particularly serious is the case of the total destruction of Syria, carried out by terrorist groups financed and armed by the West, Israel and the Arab monarchies in the region. A civil war is also being waged in Yemen with the direct intervention of Saudi Arabia. Only Iran, Israel's main target, keeps its territorial integrity intact. Today, the intervention of Russia, Iran and Hezbollah in Syria, Turkey's role in the war, the eruptive situation in Bahrain, Lebanon, Egypt and Libya constitute an explosive cocktail that could end in a generalised conflict unseen since the Second World War. All this had its origins in the attacks of 11 September 2001.

A new Pearl Harbour or the lie needed to start the war

In the November/December 1998 issue of *Foreign Affairs* magazine, an article appeared entitled 'Catastrophic Terrorism: Tackling the New Danger'. The article, authored by a Zionist Jew named Philip Zelikow, announced a catastrophic attack that "could entail unprecedented loss of life and property in peacetime and undermine America's fundamental sense of security, as did the Soviet atomic test in 1949. The United States, Zelikow continued, should respond with draconian measures, curtailing civil liberties, allowing greater surveillance of citizens, detention of suspects and lethal use of force. More violence could follow, or more terrorist attacks or counter-attacks by the United States....". This modern prophet was heralding not only the 9/11 attacks and other substitutes, but also the Patriot Act.

After the attacks, this Zionist was appointed executive director of the 9/11 Commission, which published the fairy tale known as the *9/11 Commission Report*. This text, an insult to intelligence, did not answer any of the pertinent questions asked by the public and the 9-11 Truth Movement. The Commission led by Zelikow was aided in its mission to cover up the truth by the invaluable assistance of NIST (National Institute of Standards and Technology), whose lead investigator was another Zionist named Stephen Cauffman. This Jew was the main author of a nonsensical report with humiliating and shameful reasoning that attributed the fall of the three buildings (WTC 1, WTC 2 and WTC 7) to the fires. But let's take it step by step.

Central to the plotters' plans was PNAC (Project for New American Century), formed in 1997 by two extremist Zionists, William Kristol and Robert Kagan, which quickly became an influential and aggressive think tank that set the tone for US foreign policy. Before the attacks, PNAC had called for "some catastrophic and catalytic event, such as a new Pearl Harbour". We know that Pearl Harbour was the attack that Roosevelt, who sacrificed three thousand servicemen in order to get the US into World War

II, had brought about. The PNAC was composed of members of the so-called "neocons", whose intellectual guru or ideologue was the Jewish philosopher Leo Strauss, who before his death in 1973 had directed the doctorate of his protégé Abram Shulsky.

Along with Paul Wolfowitz, Deputy Secretary of Defense and future president of the World Bank, Shulsky was the director of the Office of Special Plans, which in 2003 prepared the invasion of Iraq. Shulsky and Wolfowitz, both Jews, co-wrote a research paper entitled *Leo Strauss and the World of Intelligence*, which promoted the idea that 'a certain amount of deception is essential when governing'. Strauss argued for the efficacy of manipulation in politics, the usefulness of lying and its suitability for leading the masses. Another Jewish disciple of Leo Strauss was Samuel Huntington, author of the famous *The Clash of Civilisations and the Reshaping of the World Order*, in which he articulated his theory of a world in which civilisations clash. Huntington obviously pointed to the new Muslim enemy and predicted an age of confrontation.

Significantly, the leading members of the neocon/PNAC clique were Zionist Jews. They included: Richard Perle, Paul Wolfowitz, Elliot Cohen, Douglas Feith, Kenneth Adelman, Dov Zakheim, Elliot Abrams, Lewis "Scooter" Libby, David Wurmser, Daniel Pipes and Stephen Bryen. Above them all, three goyim had been placed as fronts: George Bush, the puppet put into the US presidency in November 2000 after rigging the election in Florida, where his brother Jeb Bush was governor, Vice President Dick Cheney and Secretary of Defense Donald Rumsfeld, who although not Jewish were also Zionists, in the sense that they shared a defence policy aligned with Israel's interests and were in favour of pushing the US into a protracted war in the Middle East. The draft plan for US global hegemony drawn up by the PNAC was entitled "Rebuilding America's Defenses" and its main author was Dov Zakheim.

In May 2001 Donald Rumsfeld appointed as Pentagon auditor one of these Zionists, perhaps the most fanatical, Rabbi Dov Zakheim, who not only had US citizenship but also Israeli citizenship. In other words, a position of the highest importance was in the hands of a Zionist who held an Israeli passport. An individual whose grandfather was a Russian rabbi married to a woman from Karl's family Marx. The reference book to delve into the manoeuvres of this cabal of conspirators is Michael Collins Piper's *The High Priests of War*[23]. Zakheim's father was a member of the Irgun-related Betar

---

[23] Michael Collins Piper's book reveals that although they are called "neoconservatives", they are hardcore communists and Trotskyites. According to Collins Piper, these "neocons" are a secret cabal of Zionist Jews working behind the scenes. Supported and propelled to power by the bankers, on 11 September 2001 they controlled the White House, the CIA and the Pentagon. Collins Piper provides a wealth of essential information, which demonstrates that the conspirators' ultimate goal is to use the United

terrorist organisation. Dov Zakheim, educated in the teachings of the *Talmud*, a columnist for the *Jerusalem Post* and a member of the editorial board of *Israeli Affairs*, managed to break into the Department of Defence in 1981 under President Ronald Reagan. From then on, this insider moved like a fish in water, infiltrating the Department's National Security agencies. In addition to being a member of PNAC, Dov Zakheim, Bush's advisor while he was governor of Texas and his chief foreign policy advisor during the 2000 presidential campaign, is a member of other think tanks such as the CFR (Council on Foreign Relations), the Heritage Foundation and the Center for International and Strategic Studies.

As early as June 2003, a book was published in Germany that made it abundantly clear that 9/11 was the result of a gigantic conspiracy. We have the Spanish edition, published in 2006 under the title *La CIA y el 11 de septiembre. El terrorismo internacional y el papel de los servicios secretos*. Its author, Andreas von Büllow, an expert on the criminal machinations of the secret services, was for twenty-five years a member of the Bundestag, where he participated in commissions of enquiry into the "services". After serving as Secretary General to the Minister of Defence in the Bundestag, he was Minister of Research and Technology from 1980 to 1982.

This work by von Büllow was groundbreaking in 2003, but today there are hundreds of books claiming that 9/11 was an "inside job". Many of them have been written by paid lackeys to "muddy the waters" and stir things up. In this way, they are intended to discredit "conspiracy theories", , a pejorative way of referring to allegations by "warmed-over minds" that question the official version of certain events or history in general. Significantly, two months after the attacks, on 10 November 2001, George Bush said, and I quote: "We will not tolerate outrageous conspiracy theories about the 9/11 attacks, malignant lies intended to clear the terrorists, the real culprits". Shortly afterwards he formulated another strategic idea: "Either you are with us or you are with the terrorists". Later he followed up with the "axis of evil" to point to the countries he was targeting in his "war on terror".

It is therefore of interest to know how the new Pearl Harbour was prepared, who could have organised the 9/11 attacks and who carried them out. The main agencies involved include the National Security Agency (NSA), the CIA and the Mossad, but there were more. It is clear that the real culprits were able to control the Pentagon, where the official version is that American Airlines Flight 77 hit. As for the lack of control in American airspace, theoretically the most closely guarded in the world and therefore the most secure, it is impossible that the planes were not intercepted by the air force. To avoid this interception, it was necessary to deactivate the

---

States as the pawn to do the globalists' dirty work in their aim to build an international empire with a central government controlled by them.

ordinary protocols of action. It was Donald Rumsfeld who passed the J-3 CJCSI 3610.01A instruction to the Chairman of the Joint Chiefs of Staff, General Richard Myers. Victor Thorn explains in *9-11 Exposed* that, according to DOD 3025.15 (DOD stands for Department of Defense), the instruction was tantamount to dismissal. As for the White House, which was evacuated, it was Vice President Dick Cheney who was left in command of the Presidential Emergency Operations Center (PEOC).

Relevant events prior to the attacks

The World Trade Center (WTC) complex was the brainchild of the Rockefeller brothers, David and Nelson. The latter, who died in 1979, was for fifteen years governor of New York and later vice-president of the United States with Gerald Ford. Both are known to be prominent New World Order (NWO) boosters and Zionists. On 24 July 2001, Larry Silverstein, former president of the United Jewish Appeal of New York, leased the World Trade Center complex to the Port Authority for ninety-nine years. The lease price was 100 million dollars a year. This Jew, who had chaired the UJA (United Jewish Agency), a supposedly philanthropic Zionist organisation, was one of the criminals involved in the New York bombings who made the biggest profits. Instead of being investigated and brought to justice, he is still at large without any problems after having enriched himself through compensation payments.

Politically linked to Likud, Silverstein was a close friend of Ariel Sharon and Benjamin Netanyahu. His friendship with the latter was and is close: before 9/11 they spoke on the phone every Sunday afternoon. It is worth remembering that it was Netanyahu who coined the phrase "war on terror", a slogan that has been in vogue ever since. Multiple reports link Larry Silvertstein to heroin trafficking and money laundering. The negotiator of the operation with the Port Authority was another Zionist Jew, Saul Eisenberg, who was a member of the UJA and the United Jewish Federation. Eisenberg was also vice-president of AIPAC (American Israel Public Affairs Committee), the most powerful Jewish lobby in the United States, whose support is essential to be president of the United States.

With the World Trade Center in the hands of Larry Silverstein, the issue of security at the complex could be controlled with some ease, especially considering that it was in the hands of President Bush's own younger brother, Marvin Bush, who had senior responsibilities at Securacom, the company that oversaw security at the WTC, United Airlines and Dulles International Airport, located some 40 kilometres from Washington. American Airlines Flight 77, which according to the official version crashed into the Pentagon, took off from Dulles Airport. Marvin Bush was also a member of the board of directors of KuwAm (Kuwait-American Coporation), a company that was a major shareholder in

Securacom. Another member of the Bush family, Wirt D. Walker III, a cousin of the Bush brothers, was the CEO of Securacom from 1999 to 2002.

But there is more. A private security company, "International Consultants on Targeted Security" (ICTS) provided security for each of the terminals where the hijackings took place. ICTS is an Israeli company founded in 1982 by members of the Shin Bet. The Israeli agency's security system for passengers consists of assessing their degree of risk based on a series of criteria such as age, name, origin, etc. The method developed by ICTS is called Advanced Passenger Screening (APS). Ezra Harel and Menachem Atzmon are its chairmen and many of its employees were and are former members of the Israeli Defence Force (IDF), i.e. Shin Bet. Therefore, this Israeli company had inside access to vital airports on the morning of 9/11. It is very likely that the US employees included "sayanim", Jews living abroad who take advantage of their nationality to provide information to the Mossad or the Israeli government.

We can now return to the activities of Larry Silverstein and his colleagues in the days before 9/11. After a ninety-nine-year lease on the WTC, the ineffable Silverstein took out a $3.2 billion insurance policy, covering for the first time the terrorist attacks. Of course, Silverstein, Netanyahu's close friend, was a long-time insider, but he was not alone: many more insiders were, as the stock market speculation in the weeks leading up to 9/11 shows. Merryl Lynch, Goldman Sachs and Morgan Stanley, investment firms that occupied twenty-two floors in each of the twin towers, held shares in the two airlines and sold them before the attacks.

Andreas von Bülow explains in the above-mentioned book that the "Israeli Herzliya International Policy Institute for Counterterrorism" had compiled ten days after the attack a number of deals linked to 9/11 infiltrators. The number of United Airlines shares for sale each day, for example, was 4,744 shares, compared to the usual average of 396 shares; American Airlines shares offered for sale each day were 4,515, compared to an average of 748. Both transactions," writes von Bülow, "were therefore eleven and six times larger in volume than usual". Merryll Linch, for example, sold 12,215 shares four days before 9/11 compared to 252 a day previously. The Zim American Israeli Company had leased space on the sixteenth and seventeenth floors of WTC Tower 1. In order to quickly break the lease, which was due to expire at the end of the year, it had to pay a $50,000 fine. A week before 11 September, it vacated its offices. The parent company of the company is "Zim Israel Navigation Company", half of which is owned by the State of Israel and half by "Israel Corporation", owned by Israeli businessman Frank Lowy.

Scott Forbes, a computer expert who worked as a computer analyst for the WTC Fiduciary Trust, testified that on the weekend before 11 September, there was an unprecedented series of power outages and the electricity completely collapsed. Consequently, there were no cameras, lockdowns or other security protocols. In the video *9-11 Marvin Bush head of Securacom at WTCS*, Forbes' statements are echoed in an interview with Victor Thorn in *9-11 Exposed*: "Access was free unless you locked the doors with manual keys. Seeing so many strangers who didn't work at the WTC was unusual. There were men in head-to-toe white jumpsuits with plastic eye visors who pulled rolls of wire from boxes and walked through the buildings that weekend." No one knew who the men were and what they were doing. Scott Forbes' statements were also corroborated by William Rodriguez, one of the best-known witnesses to 9/11. Both suspected what had happened when they witnessed the collapse of the towers. Scott Forbes informed numerous authorities, including the 9/11 Commission, but was ignored. Ben Fountain, a financial analyst, recalls in the video the repeated unusual evacuations that took place in the towers before the attack. In his denunciation of the inexplicable neglect of security measures, some comment that even the explosive-sniffing dogs were missing.

Both Victor Thorn in *9-11 Evil* and Andreas von Bülow in *The CIA and 9/11* highlight the surprising fact that four Israeli-based telecommunications companies have almost complete access to US telecommunications. These companies are: Amdocs, Converse Infosys, Odigo and Checkpoint Systems. The former was chaired until 6 September 2011 by Dov Baharav, when he was replaced by Eli Gelman. Amdocs controls the records of virtually all calls made by the twenty-five largest companies in the United States and is also responsible for billing and telephone support for 90% of the companies. Its main computer system is located in Israel. Andreas von Bülow wisely explains it in these words:

> "90% of the internal telephone calls and probably also a large part of the transatlantic calls between the different telephone companies and their respective networks run through a single settlement company that collects the data to be settled and makes it available. This company, Amdocs, is in Israeli hands. The software comes from Israeli software houses. The company's main computer is not located in the USA, but in Israel.
> Just as it is quite natural that within the framework of the international division of labour an Israeli company, in the award to the best bidder, should be awarded the contract for the collection and settlement of almost the entire telephone service in a country as large as the USA, it is also obvious that the secret services use this very channel to gain access to a large part of the national and international telephone calls, faxes, e-mails and computer connections. This organisation chart is anything but casual. If these channels have been used, the Mossad's wiretappers are to be congratulated. This procedure needs to be made clear to the public and to US politics. But since both US politics and the US media are completely silent on the matter, those responsible can also keep quiet about it".

It couldn't be clearer. This company can analyse and determine telecommunications and through it the Mossad has access to sensitive information in the United States, yet no one opens their mouths to denounce it. Consequently, in the months and weeks before 9/11, the Israelis were able to learn about communications related to the attacks, but not only through Amdocs, but also through the other companies.

The second Israeli telecommunications company is Converse Infosys, which sells wiretapping technology to the secret services and the police. Converse Infosys was also the supplier of computer equipment to the Federal Reserve. This Israeli company is responsible for the installation of the automatic wiretapping equipment. Under the pretext that it is necessary only for the maintenance of the facilities, Converse is connected through direct service lines to all the tapping facilities of the confederation and most of the states. It is through this company, then, that the wiretapping and wiretapping is done. The sexual conversations between Bill Clinton and Monica Lewinsky, used to blackmail the president, were recorded by Converse. Von Bülow explains that US officials suspect that "they have aborted criminal investigations in espionage and drug trafficking matters by following up on wiretapped phone calls". In fact, both Amdocs and Converse Infosys have been accused of stealthily selling their phone records. In relation to the attacks, once again Israel therefore had the ability to tap, at its discretion, any telephone conversation in the US and the eavesdropping could not be detected because it was automatically integrated into the telecommunications system itself.

The Israeli daily *H'aaretz* published a revealing story concerning Odigo, the third Israeli-owned company. According to the newspaper, two hours before American Airlines Flight 11 crashed into the WTC North Tower, Herzliya-based Odigo, which specialises in SMS data transmission, alerted employees at its New York headquarters, located two blocks away from the twin towers, of the impending attack. The company is a leader in the monitoring of instant messaging on home computers. Finally, Checkpoint Systems, also headquartered in Israel, was responsible for a very high percentage of the computer access control bars of the Federal Government and major US corporations.

In short, four Israeli companies controlled almost the entire US communications network. They could therefore act as "Big Brother". Naturally, they were able to create the legend of the nineteen Arab hijackers by tapping only their telephone conversations. So it was these Israeli companies that collected the conversations between the alleged terrorists, who were under constant surveillance. The whole issue of the alleged phone calls of the hijackers' relatives or voices inside the planes must also be understood in terms of the mechanisms of the Israeli companies.

The attacks

That the alleged hijackers could not even fly a light aircraft is a fact that has been confirmed by their flight instructors. Bruno Cardeñosa, journalist and author of *9/11: Historia de una infamia* and *11-M Claves de una conspiración*, in his investigation of the pilots, reports that he interviewed the person who spent the most time with Mohamed Atta, his flight instructor, the Spaniard Iván Chirivella, who also taught Marwan Al-Shehhi, the other alleged suicide pilot, to fly. Chirivella explained to Cardeñosa that during the months of September and October 2000 he spent hours every morning in the plane with the two Arabs: "Although the school's rules forbade it," Chirivella said, "they always flew together. It was an exception, but whoever pays is right, as we all know". Here is a brief excerpt from the interview:

> "If you had to do an estimate, how many pupils were you in charge of at school?
> - About fifty.
> - If you were to rank them according to their category as drivers, where would Al-Shehhi and Atta rank among the fifty students you had?
> - The 49th and the 50th," Ivan answered without a second thought.

The Spanish instructor of Canarian origin, who has been banned from returning to work in the United States after having been there for fourteen years, confirmed that Mohamed Atta was the worst pupil he ever had. It is therefore absolutely impossible that these two students from Chirivella could have performed the very complicated manoeuvres attributed to them. Other flight instructors confirmed the incompetence of the suicide pilots, whose command of English was poor. Hani Hanjour, the bomber who allegedly flew at ground level to hit the Pentagon, was not prepared to take the pilot's exam after 600 hours of flying. In August 2001, he was not allowed to rent a Cessna light aircraft at Bowie airport in Maryland because instructors felt he was not competent enough to fly it.

On the hijacking of planes with plastic knives, von Büllow explains that if the existence of dangerous weapons had been overlooked during baggage and passenger checks, it would have triggered "an avalanche of claims for damages of an astronomical amount under US law". Another fact is that the airlines do not mention any of the hijackers' names on their passenger lists. According to the airlines, none of them checked in. Investigations by British journalists showed that seven of the nineteen named suicide bombers were still alive after the attack. Two newspapers, *The Independent* and *The Daily Mirror*, as well as the BBC managed to find and interview them and the images are on the Internet.

There can be little doubt that the story of the nineteen suicide pilots is a red herring, but neither the FBI nor the American or European media, so demanding when it suits their bosses, were the least bit concerned about the dubious credibility of the list of the perpetrators of the attack, which was offered up within hours as if by magic. The culminating proof, worthy of the worst Hollywood movies, came days later, when Mohamed Atta's passport was found intact in the rubble. In other words, everything was reduced to dust except the passport of one of the suicide pilots, the ultimate proof that he was piloting American Airlines Flight 11. The stupid credulity of the press and public opinion is to weep or to burst out laughing. As we shall see in the following pages, the planes were almost certainly remotely piloted from building No. 7, which was demolished in the afternoon. As for the collapse of the twin towers, there is no doubt that it took place through controlled demolitions.

One could write at length about the inaction of the air defence and the role of General Richard Myers, who headed the General Staff. Andreas von Bülow explains that the air traffic controller detected that the Boeing AA 11 had switched off the automatic transponder at 8:14 and still had time to hear the hijackers report at 8:23 that they had a few planes in their possession and were about to return to Boston-Logan airport. Von Bülow writes: "After switching off the transponder, air traffic control on the ground still had 31 minutes left, and after listening to the conversation on board they had 22 minutes to act before the collision in the north tower. They could follow the aircraft's course and were obliged to inform military airspace control immediately". On 13 September 2001, General Richard Myers testified before the Senate Armed Services Committee that the fighters took off only after the collision at the Pentagon, i.e. one hour after the attack on the North Tower. This was an unacceptable and dangerous explanation, which stunned senators and congressmen. It was replaced shortly afterwards by a NORAD (North American Aerospace Defense Command) version, according to which the fighters had taken off but had arrived too late.

As for the collapse of the twin towers, it is unquestionable that they fell by controlled demolitions. The technical studies of numerous engineers and architects on the steel structures are conclusive. The maximum temperature that burning paraffin can reach is around 375°. Steel only melts at temperatures above 1,300° and loses its stability at 800°. The heat conductivity of a steel structure immediately deflects the point heat in all directions and thus the temperature at the source of the fire drops without delay. The theory that the high temperature was the cause of the collapse of the towers is untenable.

The buildings collapsed because explosive charges were installed at strategic points in the structure. More than a hundred first responders reported hearing the explosions. The name of the explosive used is thermite or nano-thermite. The explosive charges were placed on the steel pillars and at strategic points in the building. The explosion would have been triggered from a computer. The electronic commands were probably programmed and transmitted in successive fractions of seconds by remote ignition. The masses of debris fell in free fall. The speed at which they fell is exactly the speed at which the force of gravity falls, whereby the speed of the falling masses increases from 9.81 metres in the first second to a further 9.81 metres in each subsequent second. Hence they collapsed in 9 and 11 seconds respectively, in an unprecedented collapse in steel-structured skyscrapers. The destruction was extremely rapid. Tons of molten steel were found under the rubble, although some pieces were thrown 200 metres away. 80,000 tonnes of concrete, girders and metal plates were pulverised in the air and massive volumes of expansive pyroclastic clouds were produced. Traces of thermite were found in molten steel and in the dust of the WTC.

Building no. 7 deserves a special mention. It was owned since 1987 by Larry Silverstein. The mortgage was in the hands of the Blackstone Group, whose CEO was a Zionist Jew named Stephen A. Schwartzman. The chairman of the company was another Jew, Peter G. Peterson, who until 2004 was at the same time chairman of the Federal Reserve Bank of New York and was also, together with his partner Schwartzman, a member of the Board of Directors of the CFR. Peterson had been chairman of Lehman Brothers from 1973 to 1977. The building housed offices of the CIA, the Department of Defense, the Securities and Exchange Commission, the U.S. Secret Service, the Office of Emergency Management, four or five banks and as many insurance companies. There were millions of records of ongoing investigations against the Mafia, banks, international drug trafficking, money laundering and terrorism.

World Trade Center Building 7 (WTC 7), located about 100 metres from the North Tower, was not hit by any aircraft, yet its 47 steel-framed floors collapsed at 17:20 on the afternoon of 11 September. The collapse, as in the case of the towers, occurred symmetrically in 6.5 seconds. The collapse of this building was announced 23 minutes before it occurred by BBC News. During the TV broadcast, journalist Jane Standley says that the Salomon building Brothers (WTC 7) has collapsed without knowing that it is visible behind it. It was therefore known in advance that the building was going to fall. The fire brigade was busy moving people away from the vicinity between 16:00 and 17:00. The images show that it is a conventional demolition, as the building collapses from the ground floor. It collapsed from the inside and the external structure folded inwards. Unlike the towers, the dust clouds originated at ground level and not at the height of the upper floors.

Incredibly, the report of the 9-11 Commission Report, made public on 22 July 2004, does not even mention building number 7. In a television interview in 2004, Larry Silverstein stated the following: "I remember a call from the chief of the fire service. He told me they weren't sure they could contain the fire, and I said, 'We've had such a terrible loss of life, maybe the smartest thing to do is to knock it down'. And they made the decision to throw it out and then we watched the building collapse." With the usual brazenness (Chutzpah), Silverstein lies without even considering that the demolition implies that the explosive charges had previously been set. Despite this public acknowledgement by Silverstein, in 2007, the NIST ("National Institute of Standards and Technology") was still studying why it fell. In a report discrediting and discrediting NIST, they ruled out the possibility of explosives and insisted that it collapsed because of the fires.

It was in this building that the remote control centre was necessarily installed, which made it possible to direct the planes against the twin towers. Between 9:00 and 10:00 a.m., before the collapse of the twin towers, WTC 7 was vacated. With no employees left, the real perpetrators of 9/11 had the entire building at their disposal. By 16:00 the dust generated by the collapse of the towers had settled and the criminal team that had operated the remote control was able to leave. At around 16:10 CNN reported that WTC 7 was on fire. At this time, although there were only fires on floors seven and twelve, firefighters were already pulling people out of the surrounding area on the pretext that the building could collapse because of the fires.

As early as the 1950s, the British had developed the technology to fly military aircraft without pilots. In the 1970s this technique, called the "flight control system", was perfected by the DARPA (Defense Advanced Projects Agency), a Pentagon defence agency in charge of adapting military technology for civilian use in order to be able to land hijacked aircraft remotely. The remote control can even deprive the pilot of control of his plane and land it automatically in poor visibility conditions. Andres von Bülow writes the following on the subject of the electronic piloting system:

> "On 11 September, the 19 hijackers allegedly seized the four Boeing 757 and 767 passenger planes and confronted the crew and pilots, some of whom were military trained, with only a few crude knives. The pilots and crews of the four planes were trained and prepared for hijackings. According to the rules, they should have keyed in the 7700 numbers both in the cockpit and elsewhere in the aircraft, thereby alerting air traffic control on the ground of what was happening on board. However, none of the four aircraft gave the signal. The four aircraft flew for more than half an hour without establishing any connection with the ground before they were flown to their targets."

Victor Thorn complements this information in *9-11 Evil*. Thorn explains that Rabbi Dov Zakheim, with his dual citizenship, had been lurking in the corridors of government for more than twenty years. Between 1981 and 1985 he worked in the Department of Defence. From 1985 to 1987 he was Deputy Assistant Secretary of Defence for Planning and Resources. In 1997 he joined the Defence Reform Task Force. As we know, in 2001

Donald Rumsfeld appointed him as Pentagon auditor. Thorn points to him as a high-level agent of the Zionist bankers' cabal of which the Rothschild dynasty is the leading exponent. According to this author, as Pentagon auditor, Zakheim orchestrated the awarding of more than two trillion dollars. But what is most relevant to the aircraft remote control issue is that Zakheim was a former CEO and corporate vice president of Systems Planning Corporation, a defence contracting agency specialising in electronic warfare technologies and aircraft remote control systems. The Radar Physics Group, one of the Corporation's branches, produced the advanced technology called the Flight Termination System, which could remotely control all types of aircraft, including passenger jets. This system had the ability to handle up to ten different flights at the same time and could also terminate their missions. This is exactly what was needed for an operation like that of 11 September 2001, which had been years in the making. We now give the floor to Victor Thorn (the brackets in the quotation are his own):

> "This argument gains even more weight when we see that during his tenure as Pentagon auditor, the military 'lost' 56 fighter jets, 32 tanks and 36 Javelin missile launch units. Finally, Zackheim negotiated a contract whereby 32 Boeing planes were sent to MacDill Air Force Base in Florida as part of a lease agreement. Could these planes, the missing funds and the missing military equipment have been part of an operation to retrofit some airliners with remote control technology for use on the morning of 9/11? If anyone was in a position to do so, it was Rabbi Dov Zakheim.
> His role as the mastermind of 9/11, however, is not yet complete. One of the subsidiaries of his company - Systems Planning Corporation - was an entity known as Tridata Corporation Why is this relevant? Well, after the 1993 WTC bombing (organised by infiltrated elements in the FBI among others), guess who was given the task of investigating the crime? Tridata Corporation. Therefore, Dov Zakheim had access to all the plans of the World Trade Center, and was familiar with its structural stability. Why do you think the 'failed' 1993 bombing took place? Precisely to begin the process leading up to 9/11."

Eric Hufschmid, author of *Painful Questions: An Analysis on the September 11th Attack* and a video supplement to the book entitled *Painful Deceptions*, claims that the bunker that served as the command centre for the destruction of the WTC was located on the 23rd floor of Building No. 7. Andreas von Bülow provides further interesting information. This building," he writes, "contained a hollow space of more than five storeys which housed two transformer substations with ten transformers, each of which was ten metres high and twelve metres wide". The building was erected on top of these transformers. In addition, there were 20-megawatt emergency generators and diesel tanks. Above the generators and the tanks for the emergency generators, "there was," this author continues, "the CIA's counter-terrorism headquarters, but also the espionage section against delegations from all the UN countries in New York". The excerpt below deserves the full quote:

> "In the late 1990s, at the behest of Jerry Hauer, manager of the World Trade Center, an alternative emergency bunker was built between the 23rd and 25th floors of Building 7 for the first mayor of New York to be available as a command centre in the event of a terrorist attack. During the 1990s, fears had already spread that Saddam Hussein intended to attack the USA with the chemical weapon anthrax. For this reason, the emergency headquarters was designed not only for conventional weapons attacks, but also for biological weapons. The command headquarters, with its 4,640 square metres of office space, had its own air supply and a water reserve of more than 40,000 litres. The building could withstand storms of more than 260 kilometres per hour. The emergency generators ran on 22,000 litres of diesel fuel, which was also stored near the ground floor."

As usual, when we find out who Jerome (Jerry) Hauer is, we discover that he is another Zionist Jew, supposedly an expert in bioterrorism. Why this emergency centre for the Mayor's office is installed over five-storey high transformers with 130,000 volts and diesel tanks with a capacity of 159,000 litres is an enigma. In any case, this bunker was probably the operations centre from which the aircraft were guided by remote control. It was also where the entire device for setting off the explosive clockwork charges that caused the towers to fall must have been concentrated.

As for the attack on the Pentagon, there is no trace of the plane. It must be considered that an empty Boeing 757 contains 60 tons of metal, plastic and glass. Then there would be the people and luggage. What happened to American Airlines Flight 77 and the sixty-four people who were supposedly on board is another enigma, yet another one. The only thing that is certain is that no plane hit the building. Suffice it to think that images of the towers were played almost uninterruptedly, over and over again, ad nauseam, but there is not a single footage from the Pentagon. Security cameras at the Pentagon itself, the CITGO gas station, the Sheraton Hotel and the Virginia Department Transportation reportedly filmed spectacular footage of a plane flying low to the ground. The footage recorded by the cameras at these locations was confiscated. Few investigators now dispute that it was a cruise missile that blew a round hole in a recently refurbished side of the Pentagon. It was not yet being worked on routinely, which is why very few people were affected by the explosion. The few pieces of debris that were found were the fuselage of a missile. Images of the impact can be seen on the Internet, since in response to a request from the association "Judicial Watch", the Department of Defence provided two videos showing the missile's wake moments before the explosion.

However, American Airlines Flight 77 did take off. Both military and civilian ground radar tracked the plane on its journey and therefore it must have ended up somewhere. This Boeing was flying from Washington Dulles International Airport to Ohio. Above Ohio, radio communication was interrupted and the transponder stopped transmitting signals to the ground radar. The last conversation with air traffic controllers took place at 8:50. Six minutes later there was another unsuccessful attempt by the air traffic controllers. It is assumed that this aircraft abandoned its route and turned to return hundreds of miles back to Washington. Since the ground controllers already knew what had happened in New York, they tried again and again in vain to establish the connection. According to the official version, it headed towards the White House, then flew over the Pentagon and then crashed into it. Since this is not true, the question is where did flight 77 end up?

The suicide pilot was Hani Hanjour, who a month earlier had been refused permission to take off one of the planes at Bowie airport in Maryland. This aviation ace, if we accept the official version, descended from an altitude of 2,100 metres at a speed of 800 kilometres per hour. To do so, he made a 270-degree turn that allowed him to place the plane just a few metres above the ground. After dismantling telephone wires and passing close to a gas station, he drove the Boeing 757 into the southwest wing of the Pentagon without damaging the grass at all. It was a mind-boggling manoeuvre attributed to an inexperienced pilot incapable of flying a Cessna light aircraft on his own. Air force professionals around the world agree that it would take a pilot of extraordinary skill to pull off such a manoeuvre. Hani Hanjour clearly could not be such a pilot.

Much has been written about United Airlines Flight 93, which flew from Nevark (New Jersey) to San Francisco with forty-six people on board, and, of course, it was used by Hollywood in 2006 to present *Flight 93*, the statutory propaganda film in support of the official version of 9/11. Everything invited to fabricate a media story of American heroes, according to which the passengers learned from their mobile phones that three other planes had been hijacked, so they decided to act selflessly and sacrificed themselves to save unknown people who were going to be targeted by the suicide bombers. So they stormed the cockpit, struggled with the bomber piloting the plane and caused the plane to crash. In reality, it is unlikely that mobile phones with a power of three to five watts could establish and maintain a connection on a plane flying at 800 km/h over a rural area. On the other hand, it is known that mobile phones fail to establish a connection above a flight altitude of 700 metres and usually fail without exception above 2,000 metres. Finally, among the many calls aired by the press, one established that the hijackers could be of Iranian origin, wearing red headbands and red sashes around their waists (as they appear in the film). One of them was carrying a bag in which, theoretically, the bomb was placed on the plane after passing all the controls. Since we have already discussed which companies had telecommunications in their hands and to whom they belonged, we will leave the issue of mobile phones here.

As for what actually happened, Lisa Guliani and Victor Thorn published their joint research in *Phantom Flight 93*. According to these authors, Flight 93 did not crash in Shanksville, Pennsylvania, but was shot down by the military and ended up near a village in New Baltimore, seven miles from where the government intended. In addition, to divert attention from the actual location of the wreckage, a diversionary operation was created: a missile was fired at an abandoned strip in Shanksville, creating a large mushroom cloud and leaving a large crater. Thus, while media attention was directed towards this site, the wreckage of flight 93 was clandestinely removed from the New Baltimore site, which was immediately cordoned off by FBI agents and local state police.

Significant events after the attacks

The removal of evidence was blatant. The metal structures were immediately removed and melted down for recycling before the experts had time to do anything. This was later complained about by some members of the House of Representatives Committee of Inquiry. On 6 March 2002, at a meeting convened to hear the experts' opinion, Professor Astaneh-Asl of the University of Berkeley complained that the pieces had been melted down before he could study the structure and gather more metal parts. In the report, the Commission concluded that the on-site investigation had been hampered and that "some critical pieces of metal had disappeared before the first investigator had arrived on site". The report noted that investigators were not even allowed to keep pieces of metal before they were taken for recycling, so that "key evidence had been lost". Professor Corbett, of the John Jay College of Criminal Justice, complained to the Commission that the engineers conducting the enquiry were part-time and poorly paid.

The mayor's office refused for three days to answer oral and written questions about who had made the decision to send the metal from the towers for recycling. The mayor of New York was Michael Bloomberg, an avowed Zionist who is a close friend of Benjamin Netanyahu. Bloomberg was a partner of the bankers Salomon Brothers and made his fortune through a financial information company: "Bloomberg Limited Partnership". In February 2009, *Forbes* magazine ranked him among the twenty most powerful people in the world. In 2013 he received the Genesis Prize, considered the "Jewish Nobel". The refusal to explain the illegal and irresponsible removal of evidence outraged the families of the victims, supported by the engineers, who believed that a study of the metal supports would have made it possible to determine what had caused the collapse. Bloomberg declared a few months later that there were better ways to explain the 9/11 tragedy. If you want to get a sense of construction methods and design," he said, "then today and in this day and age you should turn to the computer.... Looking closely at just a piece of metal usually doesn't tell you anything. In the weeks following the attacks, the experts were not allowed access to the building plans.

Regarding the salaries of the engineers who worked part-time, Andreas von Bülow explains that they had been so minimal that scientists had worked on their weekends off without being paid. He mentions that critics complained that the "astronomical" figure of $600,000 had been spent on investigating the attacks. For comparison, one need only consider that the Republican majority in Congress at the time allocated $40 million to investigate the Monica Lewinsky case and her sexual relationship with Bill Clinton. While the FBI lab analysed the traces of the president's semen on the intern's dress, NIST was not even interested in analysing the remains of WTC 7. When asked why building No. 7 collapsed, the FEMA (Federal Emergency Management Agency) report shamefully replied that the specifics of the fire in WTC 7 and how the building collapsed were unknown.

More than sixty Israelis were arrested after 9/11. Evidence linking some of them to the attacks is considered classified information. Particularly scandalous is the case of the so-called "Israeli art students", in reality Mossad agents who were always close to Mohamed Atta and the other terrorists. In fact, they lived in the same cities where the nineteen alleged suicide bombers moved. Many of them even lived in the same Florida flat block where Mohamed Atta and some of the alleged hijackers were staying. As early as the spring of 2001, they had been spotted by the Drug Enforcement Administration's (DEA) security department and the FBI, which alerted other agencies to these individuals. The DEA office in Orlando proved the connection of this group of Israelis to drug trafficking. The phone numbers of one of the 'students' linked him to ongoing 'ecstasy' investigations in Florida, California, Texas and New York.

It emerged from an investigation by journalist Carl Cameron that in the weeks before the attacks more than 200 Israelis had been arrested on suspicion of working for foreign intelligence services. After 9/11, US investigators said they assumed the detainees had gathered information about the attacks and had not shared it. "The evidence linking the Israelis to 9/11 is secret," a senior official said when interviewed by Cameron. One such arrest had taken place in early March 2001, that of Peer Segalovitz, who was subjected to interrogation. According to a DEA report released by Justin Raimondo in his article "9/11: What did Israel know?", published in October 2002, Segalovitz admitted that he was one of thirty Israeli art students living in Florida at the time. He would not disclose the reason for their stay, but had admitted that they were pursuing non-legitimate objectives. The 27-year-old "student" admitted that he was an officer (ensign) in an Israeli unit stationed in the Golan Heights with the identity number 5087989 and specialised in blasting.

Following the attacks, five of these Israelis, the so-called "dancing Israelis", were the first persons arrested. Several law enforcement agencies received calls reporting individuals who had not only recorded the events, but were celebrating with glee. The men had been spotted in New Jersey's Liberty Park, near New York, and were in a truck belonging to the moving company "Urban Moving Systems". Here are some of the statements of the people who reported them: "They were recording the disaster with shouts of joy and mockery". "They were jumping for joy after the initial impact. "It looked like they were filming a movie. They were happy, you know... They didn't look shocked to me. I thought it was strange. "It looked like they were related to this. It looked like they knew what was going to happen when they were in the park." There are more, but all the witnesses are in the same vein: the members of the group were celebrating, clapping, excited about the destruction.

During interrogations, they claimed that they were enrolled at the Bezalel Academy of Art and Design. When contacted, Pina Calpen, a representative of the Bezalel Academy in Israel, denied that any of them had studied there during the last decade. They had in fact worked for the Shin Bet and their speciality was the interception of electronic signals. These Israelis were held for two months and interrogated by several FBI counterintelligence agents, who concluded that their activities were part of an Israeli intelligence operation. There were more "students" who moved around with Urban Moving Systems trucks: two others were arrested near the George Washington Bridge in New York. The vehicle was apparently rigged with explosives, as it was blown up after the suspects were arrested. This bizarre event has remained a mystery, as there was no investigation and all that is known are these initial reports.

As for the moving company Urban Moving Systems, it was owned by an Israeli named Dominik Otto Suter. Most investigators avoid this name and are reluctant to pursue it further because they know it leads to direct implications with the Mossad. The Jewish agents arrested were Silvan Kurzberg, Paul Kurzberg, Yaron Shmuel, Oded Ellner and Omer Marmari. All five knew what had to happen and moved around in a large Mossad van, in which Arab clothing, explosives residue and cutters were found. Dominik Otto Suter was on a list of FBI suspects and had even been interrogated on one occasion. When they tried to visit him again, the place had been cleared and Suter had already flown to Israel. In March 2002, the Jewish newspaper *The Forward* reported that American intelligence services had discovered that Urban Moving Systems was acting as a front for the Mossad.

To the surprise of the DEA and the FBI, a judge authorised the deportation of the Israelis two weeks after their arrest. There was outrage and many protests, which eventually had an effect. The Jewish agents were thus held for a further ten weeks, six of which were spent in solitary confinement. Finally, a big shot in the Justice Department who was a deputy attorney general, Michael Chertoff, an Israeli citizen with dual citizenship, came to their aid. His mother had been a founding agent of the Mossad and both his father and grandfather were Talmudic rabbis. Chertoff, an exalted Zionist who was later appointed Secretary of State for National Security, sent Mossad agents back to Israel in November 2001. This Talmudic Jew would later become the principal author of the Patriot Act, which curtailed the rights and freedoms of Americans in the name of fighting terrorism.

Michael Chertoff and Michael Mukasey, another Talmudic Jew who in 2007 was appointed by Bush as US Attorney General, were the two main people responsible for the non-investigation of the 9/11 massacre. Obviously, neither of them had the slightest loyalty to the United States. They are in fact two traitors who should be in jail. There is more to say about Mukasey, who was responsible for ensuring that his colleague Silverstein collected 4.6 billion dollars from the insurance companies. Michael Mukasey and Alvin Hellerstein, another Talmudic Jew, are the judges who have handled the major 9/11-related litigation. A son of Hellerstein's, Joseph Z. Hellerstein, emigrated in 2001 to Israel and lives in a Jewish settlement in the occupied West Bank, where he is a member of one of Israel's leading law firms. Despite the fact that Silverstein had taken out a $3.2 billion policy, Mukasey accepted Silverstein's claims and considered the towers to be two separate targets and not a single attack.

Insatiable, Larry Silverstein, nicknamed "Lucky Larry", in a display of extreme shamelessness, sued American Airlines and United Airlines in 2004, demanding 8 billion dollars in damages. Silverstein accused the airlines of being responsible for the safety violations that allowed the destruction of the WTC. The brazenness was now so blatant that not even Judge Alvin Hellerstein dared to rule against the airlines this time. In 2013, Hellerstein finally ruled that "Lucky Larry" had already been compensated for the loss of its property. Hellerstein justified the verdict by arguing that Silverstein could not be compensated twice for the same damages, as this is prohibited under New York law. However, a spokesperson for Silverstein said in August 2013 that they would appeal Hellerstein's decision.

On Osama bin Laden, Al Qaeda and the fake Arab-Muslim trail

While hundreds of millions of people around the world were still glued to their television screens, images from Palestine unexpectedly appeared: an Arab woman and a group of children surrounding her were presented as if they were celebrating what was happening in New York. In contrast to the pain and fear of the people in front of the scenes of people fleeing in terror, this live footage from Jerusalem was shown repeatedly on all television news broadcasts. Days later, it emerged that the Palestinians in the footage were happy and the children were jumping for joy because they had been given lots of sweets. An article in the *Jerusalem Times* on 14 September 2001 acknowledged that the Israeli Defence Ministry was in charge of the filming. They apparently bought 200 shekels worth of sweets and candies and handed them out to passers-by and children in East Jerusalem.

Once the images had been recorded, they were passed on to CNN via Reuters in London. It is clear that the tape was then deliberately passed on to television newsrooms and news agencies in order to bias international public opinion against the Palestinian people. Von Bülow denounces the malice and servitude of the media in his country: "The German media reproduced in their headlines the pictures of the collapsed towers together with those of the Palestinians shouting for joy". Days later Ariel Sharon took it upon himself to directly link President Arafat and all his people to what happened in America. Sharon declared that Yasser Arafat and the Palestinians were the main terrorists in the Middle East and accomplices of Osama bin Laden.

The attribution of the attacks to Osama bin Laden was almost instantaneous: at 4 p.m. on the afternoon of 9/11, CNN was already pointing to him as the possible perpetrator of the attacks against the United States. This manipulation media quoted official sources and attributed the 1998 attacks on the US embassies in Kenya and Tanzania and also the MSS Cole battleship in 2000 to the Saudi-born terrorist. The next day the media were already linking bin Laden to Al Qaeda and pointing to him as the leader of an international network of Muslim terrorists. The first attack on the World Trade Center in 1993 was also attributed to him. Two days later, the Ministry of Justice published the names of the nineteen hijackers and the State Department threatened all countries that gave support or shelter to terrorists. Both Vice President Cheney and Defence Secretary Rumsfeld referred to some sixty countries and announced a war that was going to be a long one.

The official version based on a false trail was already established within a few days and had to be consolidated. In other words, the thesis that nineteen Muslim terrorists under the orders of the super-terrorist Osama bin Laden had been able to evade the civilian and military surveillance of the most powerful country in the world had to be propagated repeatedly throughout the world. These men, flouting all defence measures, had unimpededly seized four passenger planes with plastic knives and, with no more than superficial notions of light aircraft piloting, had magically directed them with mathematical precision at vital targets in the most protected cities on the planet. Moreover, to further demonstrate their competence as terrorists, they left fingerprints everywhere: luggage in cars, wills, passports, hotel bills.... The official explanations were met with scepticism at first, but as the days, weeks and months went by, the repeated messages became effective and the war against international terrorism was fully justified.

An important part of the propaganda and manipulation campaign were the tapes of bin Laden on horseback; pointing a Kalashnikov; sitting with a rifle on his back; talking to his son; hiding in his mountain hideout in Tora Bora; walking in the company of the Egyptian doctor Aymán al-Zawahirí, his second and successor at the head of Al Qaeda.... Although a Pakistani newspaper initially published an interview with bin Laden in which he denied his involvement in the attacks, the mass media around the world soon spread a new version in which the Al Qaeda leader was proud of the attacks in New York and Washington and applauded them. After expressing his hatred of Americans, he announced further terrorist attacks against the United States and its Western friends. Al-Jazeera, spun out of a BBC station in Qatar, played a key role in giving the videos an aura of authenticity in the Arab-Muslim world. In a recording broadcast by Al-Jazeera, Bin Laden utters these words:

> "God Almighty has reached America in its most vulnerable place. He destroyed its most iconic buildings. Thank Allah. Here we have the United States. From north to south and east to west they are terrified. Praise be to Allah... But when now, after eighty years, the sword falls on the United States, hypocrisy is aroused by lamenting the death of these murderers who stained the blood, honour and holy places of Muslims.... When God Almighty willed that the mission of a group of Muslims, the avengers of Islam, was going to succeed, He allowed them to destroy America. I ask God Almighty to glorify them and make them partakers of Paradise".

This was the bin Laden that propaganda popularised, the public enemy number one, the terrorist whose image was printed on rolls of toilet paper that sold like hot cakes in the United States. However, the reality was different. Osama bin Laden was a double or triple agent. His services to the CIA and the ISI (Pakistan Intelligence Service) were essential. Bin Laden recruited for the CIA fundamentalist Muslim mercenaries in more than forty countries to fight against the Soviet troops that had invaded Afghanistan in the early 1980s. These "freedom fighters", as they were defined by President Reagan, were listed in a CIA database, which spent millions of dollars to pay them. Al Qaeda means precisely "the base". Bin Laden probably also worked for Saudi Arabia, as he was a close friend of the head of its Secret Service. These Muslim mercenaries, known as the "Afghanis", were trained in camps built in the mountains of Afghanistan by Osama bin Laden's construction company, set up with the help of the Americans, but some were also trained in US military facilities. These "Afghanis" were covertly armed by the CIA and the instructors came from Britain, Pakistan and the United States. It is known that the chimerical 9/11 organiser two months before the attacks, in July, underwent more than a week of treatment in a US hospital in Dubai for a kidney ailment. Various media, including *Le Figaro* in its 11 October 2001 edition and *Global Free Press*, reported that on 12 July, CIA delegate Larry Mitchel visited him in the company of a Saudi prince who was the head of the secret services. Everything indicates, therefore, that shortly before 9/11 the relations between the terrorist chief and the CIA were still stable.

Osama bin Laden has been killed and resurrected several times. The last time he was killed was on 2 May 2011 in Abbottabad (Pakistan). In December 2012, less than two years after the "brilliant operation" by the "Navy Seals", the Navy's best special operations corps, the film *Zero Dark Thirty* was released. It is well known that Hollywood wastes no time and takes every opportunity to make money with propaganda films that are sold on all five continents. However, in August 2015, an exclusive interview with Edward Snowden was released to the *Moscow Tribune*, in which the former contractor for the National Security Agency (NSA) claimed that Osama Bin Laden was still alive and residing in the Bahamas.

The fact that media outlets around the world have gone out of their way to discredit Snowden's information is almost certainly a sign that he is telling the truth. Snowden is perhaps one of the most valuable fighters to emerge in a long time. His courage and intelligence are to be admired. Here are his words: "I have documents," he said, "that show that bin Laden is receiving money from the CIA. He receives more than $100,000 a month that is transferred to his personal bank account in Nassau. Snowden said the CIA spread the false news of his death so that the world's security and counter-terrorism agencies would stop looking for him and he could live in peace. It seems that the possibility of killing him had been considered, but Snowden said: "Osama bin Laden was one of the CIA's best agents... What kind of impression would the US leave? What kind of impression would the US leave on its other operatives if it sent in the SEALs to kill bin Laden. Snowden said the Pakistani ISI cooperated with the CIA to make the world believe that the former Al Qaeda leader died in Abbottabad and announced that in his forthcoming new book he would provide documents confirming that bin Laden is still alive.

The truth is known, but all remain silent and obey

The attacks of 11 September 2001 were what in the United States has been called an "inside job", an intricate plan of state terrorism hatched by traitors infiltrating the State Department, the Pentagon and the White House, many of whom were dual nationals. They made use of a host of computer and electronics experts, contractors and explosives technicians who acted under their orders. In deceiving international public opinion, the role of the Jewish capitalist-controlled media was, as usual, essential. The masses are programmed to accept what is presented before their eyes and are unable to see behind the thick smokescreen that hides reality. The New World Order already in place, based on falsification and lies, requires people to be unable to discern between the true and the false.

The immediate purpose of the attacks was to justify a war for control of the Middle East, which from its inception has always been directed against states considered enemies of Israel. During George Bush's two terms in office, a large group of neocons at the service of Zionism and the Occult Power that sustains it took over the Department of Defense, and especially the Defense Policy Board Advisory Committee (DPBAC), a Defense Board that on the morning of 9/11 and during the first years of the Bush Administration was chaired by Richard Perle, nicknamed "the Prince of Darkness", a Zionist who in 1986 had already been considered by the *Washington Post* as "the most powerful man in the Pentagon". It was this Board of Defence Advisors that launched the wars. Ari Shavit, a Jewish journalist for *The Forward*, published a report on 9 April 2003 in which he said: "The Iraq war was conceived by twenty-five neo-conservative intellectuals, most of them Jews".

The main architect of the war against Iraq was Paul Wolfowitz, who created the OSP ("Office of Special Plans"), which was chaired by the aforementioned Abram Shulsky, Leo Strauss's disciple. This Office of Special Plans was so powerful that for two years it even displaced the Defence Intelligence Board (DIA). After Operation Enduring Freedom in Afghanistan, Wolfowitz and Shulsky launched Operation Iraqi Freedom on 20 March 2003. As a reward for services rendered, in 2005 Paul Wolfowitz was appointed president of the World Bank, a position he held until 2007.

On 30 November 2007, former Italian President Francesco Cossiga made explosive statements to the prestigious *Corriere della Sera*. Cossiga said that all Western rulers and all secret services know that the attacks of 11 September 2001 were perpetrated by US and Israeli intelligence services. Francesco Cossiga, President of the Senate from 1983 until his election as President of the Republic, was considered an honest and incorruptible politician who was highly respected by the Italian people. After denouncing "Operation Gladio" and the role of the US and NATO secret services, hidden behind "false flag" operations that resulted in numerous civilian casualties, he had to resign. Cossiga said exactly: "We were led to believe that Osama bin Laden had confessed to being the author of the attack of 11 September 2001 against the two towers in New York, when in fact the American and European secret services know perfectly well that this disastrous attack was planned by the CIA and Mossad to accuse Arab countries of terrorism so that they could attack Iraq and Afghanistan".

That is the most painful truth. Western and international leaders and rulers know the truth, but they dare not reveal it publicly as Cossiga did. Despite knowing the perversion of the Hidden Power that has subjugated peoples and nations all over the world, they prefer to submit to it, for they are not unaware that those who have opposed it have been unfailingly destroyed. The media, partitocracy, co-opted politicians, economic blackmail, bribery, murder, are the fundamental means used to impose fear.

As in the case of the Holocaust, everyone, including the Catholic Church, prefers to go along with the story to avoid painful blows like the one we Spaniards suffered on 11 March 2004. Yes, the Spanish secret services and rulers know today that the carnage in Madrid was, like 9/11, a false flag operation attributed to Al Qaeda and organised by foreign secret services, a heinous crime with political ends that took the lives of almost two hundred innocent people on their way to work. They know, but they can only remain silent. We could write extensively about 11 March 2004 in Madrid, but it is time to stop now.

BIBLIOGRAPHY

ADLER, Cyrus, *Jacob H. Schiff: His Life and Letters*, ed. William Heinemann, London, 1929.

ALGER, John Goldworth, *Paris in 1789 to 1794*, ed. AMS Press, New York, 1970.

ALLISON PEERS, Edgar, *The Spanish Tragedy 1930-1936*, ed. Methuen & Co. London, 1936.

ALLISON PEERS, Edgar, *Catalonia Infelix*, ed. Methuen & Co., London 1937.

ALLEN, Gary and ABRAHAM, Larry, *Nadie se atreve a llamarlo conspiración*, Ojeda, Barcelona, 1998.

ANTELMAN, S. Marvin, *To Eliminate the Opiate* (vol.1), ed. Zahavia Ltd. New York-Tel Aviv, 1974.

ANTELMAN, S. Marvin, *To Eliminate the Opiate* (vol 2), Rabbi Marvin S. Antelman, printed in Israel, 2002.

ANTI-KOMINTERN, *Das Rotbuch über Spanien*, ed. Nibelungen Verlag GmbH, Berlin-Leipzig, 1937.

ARAD, Yitzhak, *Belzec, Sobibor, Treblinka: The Operation Reinhard Death Camps*, ed. Indiana University Press. USA, 1999.

ARMSTRONG, George, *Rothschild Money Trust*, ed. Bridger House Publishers, USA.

ARMSTRONG, Hamilton Fish, *Titus and Goliath*, ed. Victor Gollancz Ltd., London, 1951.

AVTORKHANOV, Adburahman, *Staline Assassiné. Le complot de Béria*, ed. Presses de la Renaissance, Paris, 1980.

AZAÑA, Manuel, *Memorias políticas y de guerra*, ed. Oasis, Mexico DF, 1968.

BACQUE, James, *Other Losses*, ed. Macdonald and Co., London, 1990.

BAKONY, Itsvan, *El comunismo chino y los judíos chinos*, ed. Udecan, Mexico, 1968.

BARNES, Harry Elmer, *In Quest of Truth and Justice*, ed. National Historical Society, Chicago, 1928.

BAR-ZOHAR, Michel, *Les vengeurs*, ed. J'ai Lu, Paris, 1968.

BERBEROVA, Nina, *Histoire de la baronne Boudberg*, ed. Actes Sud, Arles, 1988.

BETHELL, Nicholas, *The Last Secret*, Basic Books, Inc., Publishers, New York, 1974.

BIEBERSTEIN, Johannes Rogalla von, *Antisemitismo, bolchevismo y Judaísmo*, La Editorial Virtual (electronic edition), Argentina, 2011.

BIRD, Kai and LIFSCHULTZ, Lawrence, *Hiroshima's Shadow*, ed. The Pamphleteer's Press, Stony Creek, Connecticut, 1998.

BLACK, Edwin, *The Transfer Agreement: The Untold Story of the Secret Pact Between the Third Reich & Jewish Palestine*, ed. Macmillan Publishing Co., New York, 1984.

BLANC, Olivier, *Les hommes de Londres, histoire secrète de la terreur*, ed. Albin Michel, Paris, 1989.

BLUMENSON, Martin, *The Patton Papers*, ed. Houghton Mifflin Co., Boston, 1972.

BOCHACA, Joaquín, *Los crímenes de los "buenos"*, ed. Ojeda, Barcelona, 2005.

BOLLOTEN, Burnett, *La Guerra Civil española: Revolución y contrarrevolución*, ed. Alianza, Madrid, 1989.

BOLLOTEN, Burnett, *El gran engaño. Las izquierdas y su lucha por el poder en la zona republicana*, ed. Luis Caralt, Barcelona 1975.

BORKENAU, Franz, *El reñidero español*, ed. Ruedo ibérico, Paris, 1971.

BRASOL, Boris, *The World at the Cross Roads*, ed. Christian Book Club of America, Palmdale, California, 1970.

BRASOL, Boris, *The Balance Sheet of Sovietism*, ed. Duffield and Co., New York, 1922.

BRENAN, Gerald, *El laberinto español*, ed. Círculo de Lectores, Barcelona, 1988.

BRENNER, Lenni, *51 Documents: Zionist Collaboration with the Nazis*, ed. Barricade Books, Fort Lee (New Jersey), 2002.

BRITON, Frank L., *Behind Communism*, ed. Criminal Politics Book Club, Cincinnati, 2003.

BRONDER, Dietrich, *Bevor Hitler kam*, ed. Hans Pfeiffer Verlag, Hannover, 1964.

BROUÉ, Pierre, *Les Procès de Moscou*, ed. René Juliard, France, 1964.

BROUÉ, Pierre, *Trotsky y la guerra civil española*, ed. Jorge Álvarez, Buenos Aires, 1966.

BROUÉ, P. and TÉMINE, E., *La revolución y la guerra en España* (2 vols.), ed. Fondo de Cultura Económica, Madrid, 1977.

BUBER-NEUMANN, Margarete, *Under two dictators: Prisoner of Stalin and Hitler*, ed. Pimlico, London, 2008.

BUCHAN John, *Oliver Cromwell*, ed. Reprint Society, London, 1941.

BUECHNER, Howard A., *Dachau: The Hour of the Avenger*, ed. Thunderbird Press, Metairie, Louisiana, 1986.

BULLÓN DE MENDOZA, Alfonso, *José Calvo Sotelo*, ed. Ariel, Barcelona, 2004.

BÜLLOW, Andreas von, *La CIA y el 11 de septiembre.* Ellago, ed. Ellago, Castellón, 2006.

BUTZ, Arthur Robert, *The Hoax of the Twentieth Century*, ed. Theses & Dissertations Press, Chicago, 2003.

CAMPOAMOR, Clara, *La revolución española vista por una republicana*, ed. Espuela de Plata, Seville, 2005.

CARDEÑOSA, Bruno, *11-M Claves de una conspiración*, ed. Espejo de Tinta, Madrid, 2004.

CARDEÑOSA, Bruno *11-S: Historia de una infamia*, ed. Corona Borealis, Málaga, 2003.

CARDOZO, Harold, *The March of a Nation*, ed. The "Right" Book Club, London, 1937.

CARR, E. H., *La Revolución Bolchevique 1917-1923*, ed. Alianza, Madrid, 1979.

CASADO, Segismundo, *Así cayó Madrid*, ed. Guadiana, Madrid, 1968.

CERESOLE, Norberto, *La falsificación de la realidad*, Ediciones Libertarias, Madrid, 1998.

CHEREP-SPIRIDOVICH, Arthur, *The Secret World Government or "The Hidden Hand"*, ed. The Book Tree, Escondido (California), 2000.

CHOMSKY, Noam, *El triángulo fatal: Estados Unidos, Israel y Palestina*, Popular, Madrid, 2004.

COCHRAN, M. H., *Germany Not Guilty in 1914*, ed. Ralph Myles, publisher, Colorado Springs, 1972.

COHEN, Avner, *Israel and the Bomb*, ed. Columbia University Press, New York, 1998.

COLEMAN, John, *The Conspirator's Hierarchy: The Committee of 300*, ed. Global Review Publications Inc. Las Vegas (Nevada),

COLEMAN, John, *The Rothschil Dynasty*, ed. Global Review Publications Inc., Las Vegas (Nevada), 2006.

COLLINS PIPER, Michael, *The New Babylon. Those Who Reign Supreme*, ed. American Free Press, Washington D.C., 2009.

COLLINS PIPER, Michael, *The High Priests of War*, ed. American Free Press, Washington, DC, 2003.

COLLINS PIPER, Michael, *The Golem*, ed. American Free Press, Washington, DC, 2007.

CONQUEST, Robert, *Stalin and the Kirov Murder*, ed. Hutchinson, London, 1989.

CONQUEST, Robert, *Stalin -Breaker of Nations*, ed. Penguin Books USA Inc., 1991.

CONQUEST, Robert, *The Great Terror. A Reassessment*, ed. Hutchinson, London, 1990.

CONQUEST, Robert, *The Harvest of Sorrow Soviet Collectivization and the Terror Famine*, ed. Oxford University Press, New York, 1986.

CORTI, Egon Caesar, *The Rise of the House of Rothschild*, ed. Victor Gollancz Ltd. London, 1928.

CORTI, Egon Caesar, *The Reign of the House of Rothschild*, ed. Cosmopolitan Book Corporation, New York, 1928.

COSTON, Henri, *Les causes cachées de la Deuxième Guerre mondiale*, ed. Lectures Françaises, Paris, 1975.

COSTON, Henri, *L'Europe des banquiers*, ed. Documents et témoignages, Paris, 1963.

COURTOIS, Stéphane, WERTH, Nicolas, PANNÉ, Jean-Louis and others, *El libro negro del comunismo*, ediciones B, Barcelona, 2010.

CUFFI, Canadell José -Oriol, *The Shadow of Bela Kun*, ed. Cat. Casals, Barcelona, 1950.

CUNNINGHAM, Cushman, *The Secret Empire*, ed. Leela Publishing, North Fort Myers (Florida), 2001.

DAVIDSON Eugene, *The Making of Adolf Hitler*, ed. Macdonald and Jane's Publishers Ltd, London, 1978.

DAVIES, Joseph E., *Mission to Moscow*, ed. Victor Gollancz Limited, London, 1942.

DAVIES, Raymond Arthur, *Odyssey Through Hell*, ed. L. B. Fischer, New York, 1946.

DEUTSCHE INFORMATIONSSTELLE, *Dokumente polnischer Grausamkeit*, ed. Volk und Reich , Berlin, 1940.

DILLON, George F., *The War of Antichrist with the Church and Christian Civilization: Lectures delivered in Edinburg in October 1884*, ed. BiblioLife, United States, 2009.

DISRAELI, Benjamin , *Coningsby*, ed. Everyman's Library, London 1911.

DJILAS, Milovan, *Conversations with Stalin*, ed. Harcourt, Brace and World, New York, 1962.

DOLLINGER, Hans, *The Last Hundred Days*, ed. Plaza & Janes, Barcelona, 1967.

DOUSSINAGUE, José María , *España tenía razón 1939-1945*, ed. Espasa-Calpe, Madrid, 1950.

DWINGER, Edwin Erich, *Der Tod in Polen: Die volksdeustsche Passion*, ed. Eugen-Diederichs, Jena, 1940.

DZIAK, John J., *Chekisty: A History of the KGB*, Lexington Books, Lexington, 1987.

ECKEHART, Dietrich, *Cuatro años de gobierno de Hitler*, ed. Zig-Zag, Santiago de Chile, 1937.

ENAULT, Louis, *Paris brulé par la Comunne*, ed. Plon Henri, Paris 1871.

ESSER, Heinz, *Die Hölle von Lamsdorf. Dokumentation über ein polnisches Vernichtungslager*, ed. A. Laumannsche, Dülmen, 1973.

EVANS, M. Stanton, *Blacklisted by History. The Untold Story of Senator Joe McCarthy*, ed. Crown Forum, New York, 2007.

FAY, Bernard, *La guerra de los tres locos*, ed. Organización Sala, Madrid, 1974.

FAHEY, Denis, *The Rulers of Russia*, ed. Browne & Nolan, Dublin, 1939.

FAURISSON, Robert, *Las Victorias del revisionismo*, ed. Ojeda, Barcelona, 2008.

FAURISSON, Robert, *Écrits révisionnistes (1974-1998)*, PDF Sax.overblog.com

FERGUSON, Niall, *The House of Rothschild Money's Prophets 1798-1848* (vol. 1), ed. Penguin Books, New York, 1999.

FERGUSON, Niall, *The House of Rothschild The World's Banker 1849-1999* (vol. 2), ed. Penguin Books, New York, 2000.

FERRER, Benimeli J. A., *La Masonería en la españa del Siglo XX*, ed. Universidad de Castilla la Mancha, 1996.

FERRER, Joan, *History of the Yiddish language*, Universitat de Girona, 2005.

FINK, Carole, *Marc Bloch. Una vida para la Historia*, ed. Universitat de València, Valencia, 2004.

FINKELSTEIN, Israel, *The Archaeology of the Israelite Settlement*, ed. Israel Exploration Society, Jerualem, 1988.

FINKELSTEIN, Israel, *From Nomadism to Monarchy: Archaeological and Historical Aspects of Early Israel*, ed. Biblical Archaeological Society, Washington D.C., 1994.

FLYNN, John T., *El mito de Roosevelt*, ed. Mateu, Barcelona, 1962.

FORD, Henry, *The International Jew. Un problema del mundo*, ed. Orbis, Barcelona, 1942.

FORRESTAL, James, *The Forrestal Diaries*, ed. The Viking Press, New York, 1951.

FOSS, William and GERAHTY, Cecil, *The Spanish Arena*, The Right Book Club, London, 1938.

FRANKEL, Jonathan, *The Damascus Affair. "Ritual Murder", Politics and the Jewis in 1840*, ed. Cambridge University Press, New York, 1997.

FREEDMAN, Benjamin, *Facts are Facts*, (Letter to Dr, David Goldstein), New York,1954.

FREEDMAN, Benjamin, *The Hidden Tyranny*, ed. Liberty Bell Publications.

FRY, Leslie, *Waters Flowing Eastward: The War Against The Kingship of Christ*, ed. Britons Publishing House, London, 1953.

GARAUDY, Roger, *Los mitos fundacionales del Estado de Israel*, Ed. Ojeda, Barcelona, 2008.

GARAUDY, Roger, *Mi vuelta al siglo en solitario*, ed. Plaza & Janés, Barcelona, 1996.

GEORGE, Konstantin, *The U.S.-Russian Entente that Saved the Union. The Campaigner*, July 1978, ed. Campaigenr Publications, New York.

GIBSON, Ian, *Paracuellos: cómo fue*, ed. Arcos Vergara, Barcelona, 1983.

GIBSON, Ian, *Granada, 1936. El asesinato de García Lorca*, Círculo de Lectores, Barcelona, 1986.

GIL-WHITE, Francisco, *The Collapse of the West: The Next Holocaust and its Consequences* (10 vols.), ed. F.A.C.C.E. S, Mexico, 2013.

GILBERT, Martin, *Churchill and the Jews. A Lifelong friendship*, ed. Henry Holt and Company, New York, 2007.

GILLIARD, Pierre, *Le tragique destin de Nicolas II et de sa famille*, ed. Payot, Paris, 1928.

GOLLANCZ, Victor, *In Darkest Germany*, ed. Victor Gollancz Ltd., London, 1947.

GOLDSTEIN, Paul, *B'nai B'rith, British Weapon Against America. The Campaigner* (Vol. 11 no. 10), December 1978, ed. Campaigner Publications, New York.

GOODRICH, Thomas, *Hellstorm: The Death of Nazi Germany, 1944-1947*, ed. Aberdeen Books, Sheridan, 2010.

GOULÉVITCH, Arsene de, *Tsarisme et Révolution*, ed. Alexis Redier (Editions de la Revue Française), Paris, 1931.

GRAF, Jürgen, *El Holocausto bajo la lupa*, ed. Ojeda, Barcelona, 2007.

GRAF, Jürgen, KUES Thomas and MATTOGNO Carlo, *Sobibor: Holocaust Propaganda and Reality*, ed. The Barnes Review, Washington D. C., 2010.

GRAF, Kessler Harry, *Walter Rathenau. Sein Leben und sein Werk*, ed. Rheinische Verlags-Anstalt, Wiesbaden, 1962.

GRENFELL, Russell, *Unconditional Hatred. Culpabilidad de guerra alemana y el futuro de Europa*, ed. Espasa-Calpe, Madrid, 1955.

GRIFFIN, Des, *Fourth Reich of the Rich*, ed. Emissary Publications, South Pasadena, 1981.

GRUSD, Edward E., *B'nai B'rith The story of a covenant*, ed. Appleton Century, New York, 1966.

GUNTHER, John, *Behind Europe's Curtain*, ed. Hamish Hamilton, London, 1949.

GUY CARR, William, *Pawns in the Game*, St. George Press, Glendale, California, 1979.

GUY CARR, William, *Satan, Prince of this World*, ed. Omini Publications, Palmadale, 1997.

HAGEN, Walter, *Le Front Secret*, ed. Les Iles d'Or, Paris, 1952.

HALLETT, Greg, *Hitler was a British Agent*, ed. FNZ Inc, Auckland, New Zealand, 2006.

HALLIDAY, E. M., *Russia in Revolution*, ed. American Heritage Publishing Co., New York, 1967.

HART, Alan, *Arafat. Biografía política*, ed. Iepala, Madrid, 1989.

HARWOOD, Richard, *¿Murieron realmente seis millones?*, edition sponsored by CEDADE, Barcelona, 1986.

HERMANN, Greife, *Jewish-Run Concentration Camps in the Soviet Union*, ed. Truth at Last, Marietta (Georgia), 1999.

HERNÁNDEZ, Jesús, *Yo fui un ministro de Stalin*, ed. Gregorio del Toro, Madrid, 1974.

HERREN, Ricardo, *La Biblia, sólo leyenda y religión*, in La aventura de la Historia, no. 36, ed. Arlanza, Madrid, 2001.

HERZEN, Alexander, *My Past and Thoughts*, ed. University of California Press, Berkeley, 1982.

HESS, Moses, *Rome and Jerusalem*, ed. Philosophical Library, New York, 1958.

HILBERG, Raúl, *La destrucción de los judíos europeos*, ed. Akal, Madrid, 2005.

HITLER, Bridget, *The Memoirs of Bridget Hitler*, ed. Duckworth, London, 1979.

HOBSON, John Atkinson, *Imperialism: A Study*, ed. Cosimo Classics, New York, 2005.

HOGGAN, David L., *The Myth of the Six Million: Examining the Nazi Extermination Plot*, ed. The Barnes Review, Washington, D. C., 2006.

HOGGAN, David L., *Der Erzwungene Krieg*, ed. Verlag der deutschen Hochschullehrer-Zeitung, Tübingen, 1963.

HOGGAN, David L., *The Forced War: When Peaceful Revision Failed*, ed. Institute for Historical Review, Los Angeles, 1989.

HOGGAN, David L., *The Myth of the 'New History': Technics and Tactics of the New Mythologists of American History*, ed. Institute for Historical Review, Torrance, California, 1985.

HONSIK, Gerd, *A Solution for Hitler*, ed. Bright-Rainbow, Barcelona, 1993.

HOWSON, Gerald, *Weapons for Spain: The Untold Story of the Spanish Civil War*, Península, Barcelona, 2000.

HUFSCHMID, Eric, *Painful Questions: An Analysis of the September 11th Attack*, ed. Endpoint Softward, Goleta (California), 2002.

HUGHES, Emrys, *Winston Churchill: British Bulldog*, ed. Exposition Press, New York, 1955.

IRVING, David, *The Destruction of Dresden*, ed. Ojeda, Barcelona, 2009.

IRVING, David, *La guerra de Hitler*, ed. Planeta, Barcelona, 1988.

JACKSON, Gabriel, *Juan Negrín*, ed. Crítica, Barcelona, 2008.

JASNY, Naum, *The Socialized Agriculture of the USSR. Plans and Performance*, ed. Standford University Press, Standford, 1949.

JEFFRIES, J. M. N., *Palestine: The Reality*, ed. Longmans, Green & Co., London, 1939.

JENSEN, B., *The Palestine Plot*, ed. Omni Publications, Hawthorne (California) 1987.

JORDAN, George Racey, *From Major Jordan's Diaries*, ed. Harcourt, Brace & Co, New York, 1952.

JOSEPHSON, Emanuel M., *Roosevelt's Communist Manifesto*, ed. Chedney Press, New York, 1955.

KAHAN, Stuart, *The Wolf of the Kremlin*, ed. Datanet, S. A., Barcelona, 1988.

KAPLAN, Fred, *The Wizards of Armageddon*, ed. Simon & Schuster, New York, 1984-

KARDEL, Hennecke, *Adolf Hitler, Founder of Israel. Israel in War with the Jews*, ed. Marva, Switzerland, 1974.

KARL, Mauricio, *Yalta* (2 vols.), ed. AHR, Barcelona, 1955.

KARL, Mauricio, *Técnica del Komintern en España*, ed. Gráfica Corporativa, Badajoz, 1937.

KARL, Mauricio, *Pearl Harbour, traición de Roosevelt*, NOS, Madrid, 1954.

KARL, Mauricio, *Malenkov*, NOS, Madrid, 1954.

KASTEIN, Josef, *History and Destiny of the Jews*, Simon Publications, New York, 2001.

KAUFMAN, Theodore N., *Germany must perish*, ed. Liberty Bell Publications, West Virginia, 1980.

KENNAN, George F., *Memoirs of a Diplomat*, ed. Luis de Caralt, Barcelona, 1972.

KHADER, Bichara, *Los hijos de Agenor*, ed. Bellaterra, Barcelona, 1998.

KNOBLAUGH, Edward, *Corresponsal en España*, ed. Fermín Uriarte, Madrid, 1967.

KOCH, Paul H. *Illuminati*, ed. Planeta, Barcelona, 2004.

KOESTLER, Arthur, *The Thirteenth Tribe*, Random House, New York, 1976.

KOGON, Eugen, *Sociología de los campos de concentración*, ed. Taurus, Madrid, 1965.

KOLENDIC, Anton, *Les derniers jours. De la mort de Staline à celle de Béria (mars-decembre 1953)*, Fayard, Paris, 1982.

KOLTSOV, Mikhail, *Diary of the Spanish War*, Ruedo Ibérico, Paris, 1963.

KRIVITSKY, Walter, *Yo, jefe del Servicio Secreto Militar Soviético*, NOS, Madrid, 1945.

KÜHNL, Reinhard, *La República de Weimar*, ed. Alfons el Magnàmim, IVEI, Valencia, 1991.

KULISHER, Eugene M., *The Displacement of Population in Europe*, ed. Inland Press Ltd., Montreal, 1943.

LAMM, Hans, *Walter Rathenau. Denker und Staatmann*, ed. Landeszentrale für politische Bildung, Hannover, 1968.

LANDOWSKY, José, *Sinfonía en rojo mayor*, ed. Latino Americana S. A., Mexico, 1971.

LASKE, Karl, *Le banquier noir François Genoud*, ed. Du Seuil, Paris, 1996.

LAUGHLIN, John C. *La arqueología y la Biblia*, ed. Crítica, Barcelona, 2001.

LAZARE, Bernard, *L'antisemitisme, son histoire et ses causes*, Kareline, 2010.

LEESE, Arnold Spencer, *My Irrelevant Defence: Meditations inside Gaol and Out on Jewish Ritual Murder*, ed. The Patriot Press, Henderson (Nevada), 2004.

LENOE, Matthew E. *The Kirov Murder and Soviet History*, Yale University Press, 2010.

LEUCHTER, Alfred, *Leuchter Report*, edition sponsored by CEDADE, Barcelona, 1989.

LEUCHTER, Fred A., FAURISSON, Robert, RUDOLF, Germar, *The Leuchter Reports*, ed. Theses & Dissertations Press, Chicago, 2005.

LIDDELL, HART B. H., *The Other Side of the Hill*, ed. Pan Books, London, 1999.

LIDDELL, HART B. H., *The Revolution in Warfare*, ed. Faber & Faber, London, 1946.

LILIENTHAL, Alfred, *What Price Israel?*, H. Regnery Co., Chicago, 1953.

LINA, Jüri, *Under the Sign of the Scopion*, ed. Referent Publishing, Stockholm, 2002.

LIVINGSTONE, David, *Terrorism and the Illuminati*, ed. BookSurge LLC, USA 2007.

LOCKHART, R. H. Bruce, *Memoirs of a British Agent*, ed. Pan Books, London, 2002.

LOCKHART, Robin Bruce, *Reilly Ace of Spies*, ed. Futura Publications, London, 1983.

LOMBARD, Jean, *La cara oculta de la Historia Moderna* (Four vols.), ed. Fuerza Nueva, Madrid, 1976-1980.

LOOMIS, Stanley, *Paris in the Terror June 1793 - July 1794*, ed. J. B. Lippincott Company, Philadelphia, 1964.

LUTTIKHUIZEN, Gerard P., *La pluriformidad del cristianismo primitivo*, ed. El Almendro, Córdoba, 2007.

MACDONOGH, Giles, *After the Reich*, ed. Galaxia Gutenberg, Barcelona, 2010.

MADELIN, Louis, *Fouché*, ed. Espasa-Calpe, Madrid, 1972.

MADARIAGA, Salvador de, *España. Ensayo de historia contenporánea*, ed. Espasa Calpe, Madrid, 1978.

MANDEL, Arthur, *Le Messie Militant ou La Fuite du Ghetto*, Archè, Milan, 1989.

MANDELL HOUSE, Edward, *Philip Dru: Administrator*, ed. Robert Welch University Press, Appleton (Wisconsin), 1998.

MARGIOTTA, Domenico, *Souvenirs d'un trente-troisième: Adriano Lemmi, chef suprême des francs-maçons*, ed. Facsimile Publisher, London, 2013.

MARSCHALKO, Louis, *The World Conquerors*, ed. Joseph Sueli Publications, London, 1958.

MARX, Karl, *Las luchas de clases en Francia (1848 a 1850)*, ed. Ayuso, Madrid, 1975.

MATA, Santiago, *El tren de la muerte*, ed. La Esfera de los Libros, Madrid, 2011.

MATTOGNO, Carlo, *Belzec in Propaganda, Testimonies, Archeological Research and History*, ed. The Barnes Review, Washington D. C., 2011.

MATTOGNO, Carlo and GRAF, Jürgen, *Treblinka: Extermination Camp or Transit Camp?*, ed. The Barnes Review, Washington D. C., 2010.

McCORMICK, Donald, *The Mask of Merlin: A Critical Study of David Lloyd George*, ed. MacDonald and Co., London, 1963.

McFADDEN, Louis T., *Federal Reserve Exposed. Collective Speeches of Congressman Louis T. McFadden*, ed. Omni Publications, 1970.

McMEEKIN, Sean, *History's Greatest Heist. The Looting of Russia by the Bolshevics*, Yale University Press, New Haven and London, 2009.

MELGUNOV, Sergei P., *The Red Terror in Russia*, ed. Hyperion Press, Connecticut, 1975.

MELGUNOV, Sergei P., *The Bolshevik Seizure of Power*, ed. ABC-Clio Inc. Santa Barbara (California), 1972.

MILES, Jonathan, *The Nine Lives of Otto Katz*, ed. Bantam Books, London, 2010.

MOCH, Jules, *Yougoslavie terre d'expérience*, ed. Du Rocher, Monaco, 1953.

MOCK, James R. LARSON, Cedric, *Words that Won the War: The Story of the Committee on Public Information 1917-1919*, ed. Cobden Press, Meriden (Connecticut), 1984.

MOLA, Emilio, *Memorias de mi paso por mi paso por la Dirección General de Seguridad* (3 vols.), ed. Librería Bergua, Madrid, 1932.

MULLINS, Eustace, *This Difficult Individual, Ezra Pound*, ed. Angriff Press, Hollywood, California, 1961.

MULLINS, Eustace, *The Secrets of the Federal Reserve*, ed. Bridger House Publishers, Carson City (Nevada) 1991.

MULLINS, Eustace, *The Curse of Canaan*, ed. Revelation Books, Staunton, Virginia, 1987.

MULLINS, Eustace, *Mullins' New History of the Jews*, ed. The International Institute of Jewish Studies, Staunton (Virginia), 1968.

MULLINS, Eustace, *The Secret History of the Atomic Bomb*, 1998.

NEILSON, Francis, *The Makers of War*, ed. C. C. Neelson Publishing Co., Appleton, Visconsin, 1950.

NETCHVOLODOW, Alexandre, *L'empereur Nicolas II et les Juifs*, ed. Etienne Chiron, Paris, 1924.

NOSSACK, Hans Erich, *The Sinking. Hamburgo, 1943*, ed. La Uña Rota, Segovia, 2010.

NUNBERG, Ralph, *The Fighting Jew*, ed. Creative Age Press, New York, 1945.

ORDÓÑEZ MÁRQUEZ, Juan, *La apostasía de las masas y la persecución religiosa en la provincia de Huelva 1931-1936*, C.S.I.C., Madrid, 1968.

ORLOV, Alexander, *Historia secreta de los crímenes de Stalin* ed. Destino, Barcelona, 1955.

OSIPOVA, Irina, *Si el mundo os odia*, ed. Encuentro, Madrid, 1998.

OSTROVSKY, Victor and HOY, Claire, *By Way of Deception*, ed. St. Martin's Press, New York, 1990.

PAPPÉ, Ilan, *La limpieza étnica de Palestina*, ed. Crítica, Barcelona, 2008.

PATKIN, A. L. *The Origins of the Russian Jewish-Labour Movement*, F. W. Cheshire, Melbourne, 1947.

PAYNE, Stanley G., *Falange. Historia del fascismo español*, ed. Sarpe, Madrid, 1985.

PEREA CAPULINO, Juan, *Los culpables: Recuerdos de la guerra/1936-1939*, ed. Flor de Viento, Barcelona, 2007.

PERRY, Roland, *The Fifth Man*, ed. Pan Books, London, 1995.

PINAY, Maurice, *Complot contra la Iglesia* (three vols.), Mundo Libre, Mexico, 1985.

PIPES, Richard, *A Concise History of the Russian Revolution*, ed. Harvill Press, London, 1995.

PONCINS, Léon de *Histoire secrète de la révolution espagnole*, ed. Gabriel Beauchesne et ses fils, Paris, 1938.

PONCINS, Léon de, *State Secrets*, ed. Britons Publishing Company, Devon, 1975.

PONCINS, Léon de, *Freemasonry and Judasism Secret Powers Behind Revolution*, A&B Publishers Group, Brooklyn, New York, 2002.

PONCINS, Léon de, *Société des Nations, super-état maçonnique*, ed. Gabriel Beauchesne et ses fils, Paris, 1936.

POOL, Ithiel de Sola, *Satellite Generals: Study of Military Elites in the Soviet Sphere*, ed. Greenwood Press, London, 1976.

POUGET de SAINT-ANDRÉ, Henri, *Les auteurs cachés de la Révolution Française*, ed. Perrin & Cie Libraires-Éditeurs, Paris, 1923.

POUND, Ezra, *Here the voice of Europe. Alocuciones desde Radio Roma*, ed. Nueva República, Barcelona, 2006.

PUNTILA, L. A., *Histoire politique de la Finlande de 1809 à 1955*, Éditions de la Baconnière, Neuchâtel, 1966.

QUIGLEY, Carroll, *Tragedy & Hope*, The Macmillan Company, New York, 1974.

RADOSH, Ronald, HABECK, Mary R and SEVOSTIANOV, Grigory, *Spain Betrayed. The Soviet Union in the Spanish Civil War*, ed. Yale University Press, New Haven and London, 2001.

RAPHAEL, Marc Lee, *Jews and Judaism in the United States: A Documentary History*, ed. Behrman House, INC., New York, 1983.

RASSINIER, Paul, *Las mentira de Ulises*, ed. Ojeda, Barcelona, 2006.

RASSINIER, Paul, *Les responsables de la Seconde Guerre Mondiale*, ed. Nouvelles Editions Latines, Paris, 1967.

RAYFIELD, Donald, *Stalin y los verdugos*, ed. Taurus, Madrid, 2003.

REED, Douglas, *The Controversy of Zion*, Durban, Dolphin Press, 1978.

REED, Douglas, *Insanity Fair*, ed. Jonathan Cape Ltd., London, 1938.

REED, John, *Diez días que estremecieron al mundo*, ed. Akal, Madrid, 1974.

REEVES, John, *The Rothschilds: The Financials Rulers of Nations*, ed. Gordon Press, New York, 1975.

REITLINGER, Gerald, *La solución final*, ed. Grijalbo, Barcelona, 1973.

RENIER, G. J., *Robespierre*, ed. Peter Davies, London, 1936.

RICCIOTTI, Giuseppe, *Historia de Israel. De los orígenes a la cautividad* (vol. 1), ed. Luis Miracle, Barcelona, 1945.

RICCIOTTI, Giuseppe, *Historia de Israel. Desde la cautividad hasta el año 135 después de Jesucristo* (vol. 2), ed. Luis Miracle, Barcelona, 1947.

ROBISON, John, *Proofs of a Conspiracy Against All Religions and Governments of Europe Carried on in the Secret Meetings of Freemasons, Illuminati and Reading Societies*, ed. Forgotten Books, London, 2008.

ROMERSTEIN, Herbert and BREINDEL, Eric, *The Venona Secrets*, ed. Regnery Publishing, Inc., Washington, D.C., 2000.

ROSENSTEIN, Neil, *The Unbroken Chain: Biographical Sketches and the Genealogy of Illustratious Jewish Families from the 15th-20th Century*, ed. Shengold Publishers, Inc., New York, 1976.

ROSS, Marjorie, *El secreto encanto de la KGB: Las cinco vidas de Iosif Grigulievich*, ed. Grupo Editorial Norma, USA, 2006.

ROTH, Cecil, *Los judíos secretos. Historia de los marranos*, Altalena editores, Madrid, 1979.

ROTHMAN, Stanley, LICHTER, S. Robert, *Roots of Radicalism*, ed. Oxford University Press, New York, 1982.

RUDOLF, Germar, *Dissecting the Holocaust*, ed. Theses & Dissertations Press, Illinois (Chicago), 2003.

RUDOLF, Germar, *Resistance is Obligatory*, ed. Castle Hill Publishers, Uckfield (UK) 2012.

RUDOLF, Germar, *Lectures on the Holocaust*, ed. Theses & Dissertations Press, Illinois (Chicago), 2004.

RUMMEL, Jack, *Robert Oppenheimer Dark Prince*, ed. Facts On File, New York, 1992.

SACHAR, Howard, *Israel and Europe: An Appraisal in history*, Random House, Inc. New York, 1999.

SACK, John, *An Eye for an Eye*, ed. Basic Books, New York, 1993.

SAINT-AULAIRE, Count de, *La Renaissance de l'Espagne*, Plon, Paris, 1938.

SALLUSTE, *Les origines secrètes du bolchevisme Henri Heine et Karl Marx*, ed. Jules Tallandier, Paris, 1930.

SÁNCHEZ ALBORNOZ, Claudio, *Origenes de la Nacion Española. El Reino de Asturias*, Madrid, Ed. Sarpe, 1985.

SAROLEA, Charles, *Impressions of Soviet Russia*, ed. Eveleigh Nash & Grayson, Ltd., London, 1924.

SAYERS, Michael and KAHN, Albert E., *The Great Conspiracy Against Russia*, ed. Current Books Distributors, Sydney, 1949.

SCHACHT, Hjalmar, *Memoirs*, ed. AHR, Barcelona, 1954.

SCHLAYER, Félix, *Diplomático en el Madrid rojo*, ed. Espuela de Plata, Seville, 2008.

SCHOLEM, Gershom, *Le messianisme juif*, Calman-Lévy, 1974.

SCHOLEM, Gershom, *Las grandes tendencias de la mística judía*, ed. Fondo de Cultura Económica, Mexico 1996.

SCHÖNMAN, Ralph, *The Hidden History of Zionism*, ed. Veritas Press, Santa Barbara, 1988.

SERGE, Víctor, *Memorias de mundos desaparecidos (1901-1941)*, ed. Siglo XXI, Mexico, 2003.

SETON-WATSON, Robert William, *German, Slav, and Magyar: a Study in the Origins of the Great War*, ed. Williams and Norgate, London, 1916.

SEYMOUR, Charles, *The Intimate Papers of Colonel House* (2 vols.), Ed. Ernest Benn, London, 1926.

SHAHAK, Israel, *Historia judía, religión judía*, Madrid, Antonio Machado Libros, 2003.

SHAHAK, Israel, *Open Secrets: Israel Nuclear and Foreign Policies*, ed. Pluto Press, London, 1997.

SHERWOOD, Robert E., *Roosevelt and Hopkins. An intimate history* (2 vols.) ed. Los Libros de Nuestro Tiempo, Barcelona, 1950.

SKOUSEN, W. Cleon, *The Naked Capitalist*, ed. W. Cleon Skousen, Salt Lake City, Utah, 1971.

SLEZKINE, Yuri, *The Jewish Century*, ed. Princeton University Press, New Jersey, 2004.

SOLOMON, Georg, *Unter den Roten Machthabern*, ed. Verlag für Kulturpolitik, Berlin, 1930.

SOLZHENITSYN, Alexandr, *Archipiélago Gulag* (three vols.), ed. Tusquets (Tiempo de Memoria), Barcelona, 2005 (vols. I and II), 2007 (vol III).

SOMBART, Werner, *The Jews and Modern Capitalism*, ed. Transaction Publishers, United States, 1982.

SPRINGMEIER, Fritz, *Bloodlines of the Illuminati*, ed. Ambassador House, Westminster, 1999.

STARR MILLER, Edith (Lady Queenborough), *Occult Theocracy*, ed. Christian Book Club of America, Palmdale (California), 1980.

STEINHAUSER, Karl, *EG -Die Super-UdSSR von Morgen*, ed. Gruber, Vienna, 1992.

STOLYPINE, Alexandra, *L'homme du dernier tsar*. Alexis Redier (Editions de la Revue Française), Paris, 1931.

SUTTON, Antony C., *Wall Street an the Rise of Hitler*, ed. GSG& Associates, San Pedro (California), 2002.

SUTTON, Antony C., *Wall Street and the Bolshevik Revolution*, ed. Veritas Publishing Co., Morley (Australia), 1981.

SUTTON, Antony C., *Wall Street and FDR*, ed. Arlington House Publishers, New York, 1975.

SZEMBEK, Jean, *Journal, 1933-1939*, Plon, Paris 1952.

TANSILL, Charles Callan, *America Goes to War*, ed. Little, Brown and Co. Boston, 1938.

TAYLOR, Alan J. P., *The Origins of the Second World War*, Penguin Books, London, 1964.

THOMPSON, Thomas L., *The Mythic Past: Biblical Archaeology and Myth of Israel*, ed. The Perseus Books Group, USA, 2000.

THORN, Victor, *9-11 Exposed*, ed. Sisyphus Press, State College, Pennsylvania, 2004.

THORN, Victor, *9-11 Evil*, ed. Sisyphus Press, State College, Pennsylvania, 2006.

TROTSKY, León, *Mi vida. Ensayo autobiográfico*, ed. Cénit, Madrid, 1930.

UTLEY, Freda, *The China Story*, ed. Henry Regnery Co., Chicago, 1951.

VALTIN, Jan, *La noche quedó atrás*, ed. Luis de Caralt, Barcelona 1966.

VEALE, F. J. P., *Advance to Barbarism*, ed. C. C. Nelson Publishing Co., Appleton, Wisconsin, 1953.

VEGA, Lope de, *El niño inocente de la Guardia*, edited by Marcelino Menéndez Pelayo in Atlas, Madrid, 1965.

VELARDE FUERTES, Juan, *Política económica de la Dictadura*, ed. Guadiana de Publicaciones, Madrid, 1968.

VIDARTE, Juan-Simeón, *No queríamos al Rey: testimonio de un socialista español*, ed. Grijalbo, Barcelona, 1977.

VIDARTE, Juan-Simeón, *Todos fuimos culpables: testimonio de un socialista español*, ed. Grijalbo, Barcelona, 1978.

VORA, Erika, *Silent No More*, ed. Xlibris Corporation, United States, 2012.

VRIES DE HEEKELINGEN, Herman de, *Israël. Son Passé. Son avenir*, ed. Librairie Académique Perrin, Paris, 1937.

WALSH, William Thomas, *Isabella of Spain*, ed. Sheed & Ward, New York, 1931.

WARBURG, Sidney , *El dinero de Hitler*, ed. NOS, Madrid, 1955.

WARD, John, *With the "Die-Hards" in Siberia*, London, Cassell, 1920.

WASSERSTEIN, Bernard, *The Secret Lives of Trebitsch Lincoln*, ed. Yale University Press, New Haven, 1988.

WEBSTER, Nesta, *Revolución mundial*, ediciones de "El libro bueno", Mexico, 1935

WECKERT, Ingrid, *Flashpoint: Kristallnacht 1938: Instigators, Victims and Beneficiaries*, Institute for Historical Review, California, 1991.

WEDEMEYER, Albert, *Wedemeyer Reports*, Henry Holt & Co, New York, 1958.

WEINTRAUB, Ben, *The Holocaust Dogma of Judaism: Keystone of the New World Order*, ed. Robert L. Brook, Washington, D. C. 1995.

WEIZMANN, Chaim, *Trial and Error. The Autobiography of Chaim Weizmann*, ed. Hamish Hamilton, London, 1949.

WEXLER, Paul, *Two-Tiered relexification in Yiddish. Jews, Sorbs, Khazars and the Kiev-Polessian Dialect*, Berlin, Mouton de Gruyter, 2002.

WHALEN, William J., *Christianity and American Freemasonry*, ed. The Bruce Publishing Company, Milwaukee, 1961.

WILCOX, Robert T., *Target Patton: The Plot to Assassinate General George S. Patton*, ed. Regnery Publishing, Washington D. C., 2008.

WILTON, Robert, *The Last Days of the Romanov*, ed. Christian Book Club of America, Hawthorne (California), 1969.

WITTLIN, Thaddeus, *Commissar Beria*, Euros, Barcelona, 1975.

ZAYAS, Alfred M. de, *Nemesis at Potsdam. The Expulsion of the Germans from the East*, ed. University of Nebraska Press, Lincoln, 1989.

ZENTNER, Christian, *Las guerras de la posguerra*, ed. Bruguera, Barcelona, 1975.

ZETTERBERG, Seppo, *La Finlande apres 1917*, Editions Otava S.A. Helsinki, 1991.

ZWEIG, Stefan, *Joseph Fouché: The Portrait of a Politician*, ed. Cassell, London 1934.

OTHER BOOKS

OMNIA VERITAS

Jewish and Zionist organisations throughout the world are experiencing a tragedy. A myth, from which they have sought to profit, is being exposed: the myth of the so-called 'Holocaust of the Jews during the Second World War'.

OMNIA VERITAS LTD PRESENTS:

ROBERT FAURISSON

REVISIONIST WRITINGS II

1984-1989

Revisionists have never denied the existence of the camps

OMNIA VERITAS

"By its very nature, revisionism can only disturb public order; where tranquil certainties reign, the spirit of free examination is an intruder and causes a scandal."

OMNIA VERITAS LTD PRESENTS:

ROBERT FAURISSON

REVISIONIST WRITINGS III

1990-1992

Every Frenchman has the right to say that gas chambers did not exist

OMNIA VERITAS

"The question of the existence of Nazi gas chambers is of considerable historical importance, for if they did not exist, we no longer have any proof that the Germans undertook the physical extermination of the Jews..."

OMNIA VERITAS LTD PRESENTS:

ROBERT FAURISSON

REVISIONIST WRITINGS IV

1993-1998

Hence the legal sanctions imposed on those who dispute its existence...

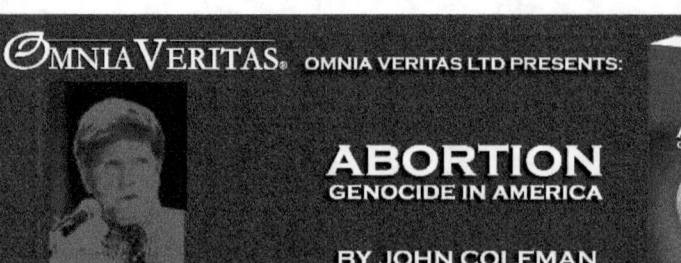

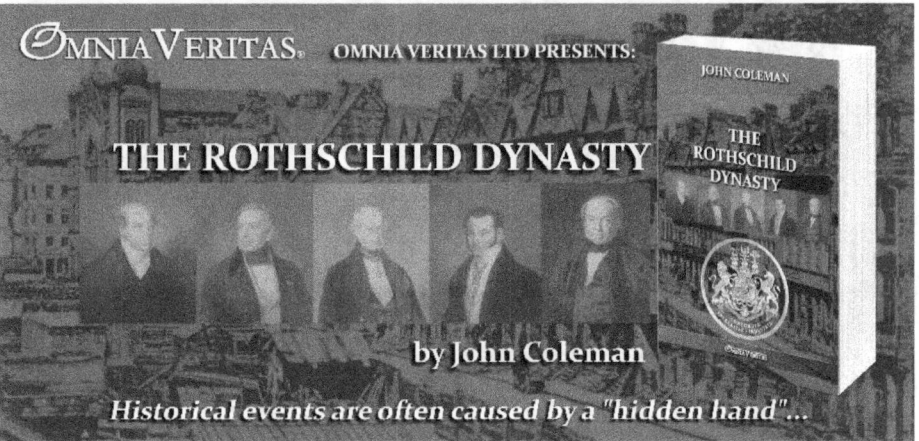

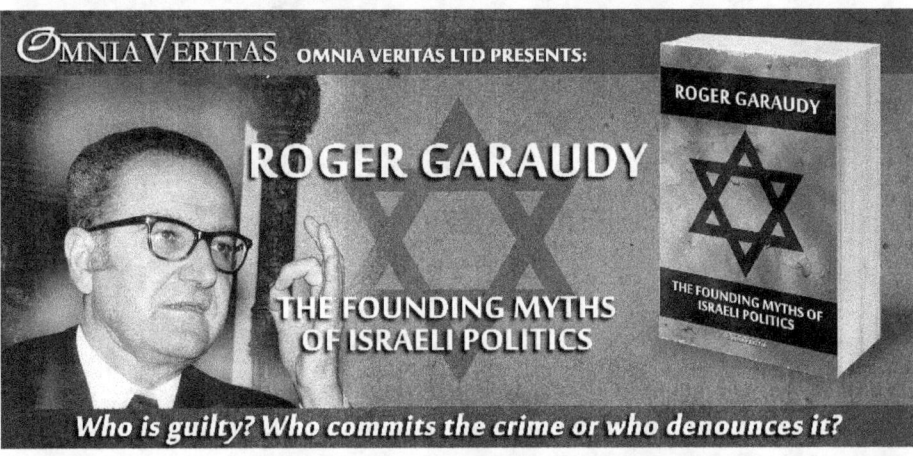

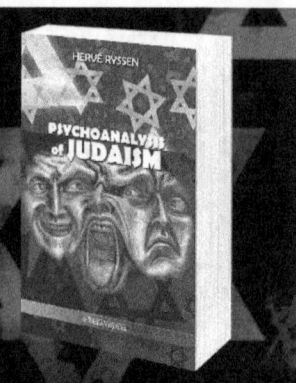

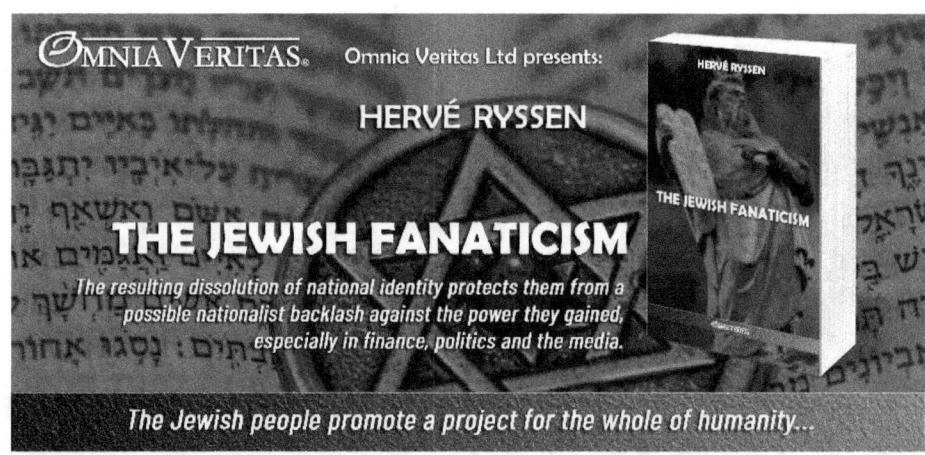

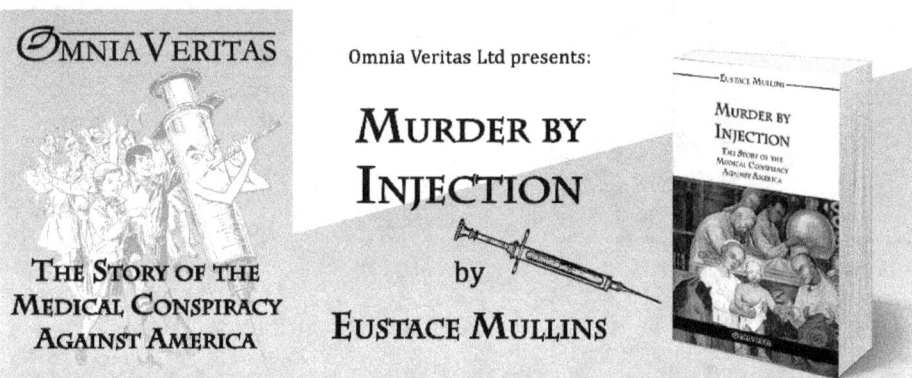

Omnia Veritas Ltd presents:

NEW HISTORY OF THE JEWS

by

EUSTACE MULLINS

Throughout the history of civilization, one particular problem of mankind has remained constant.

Only one people has irritated its host nations in every part of the civilized world

Omnia Veritas Ltd presents:

THE CURSE OF CANAAN

A demonology of history

by

EUSTACE MULLINS

Liberalism, more popularly known as secular humanism, can be traced in an unbroken line all the way back to the Biblical "Curse of Canaan."

Humanism is the logical result of the demonology of history

Omnia Veritas Ltd presents:

THE RAPE OF JUSTICE

AMERICA'S TRIBUNALS EXPOSED

by

EUSTACE MULLINS

American should know just what is going on in our courts

OMNIA VERITAS

Omnia Veritas Ltd presents:

THE SECRETS OF THE FEDERAL RESERVE

by

EUSTACE MULLINS

HERE ARE THE SIMPLE FACTS OF THE GREAT BETRAYAL

Will we continue to be enslaved by the Babylonian debt money system?

OMNIA VERITAS

Omnia Veritas Ltd presents:

THE WORLD ORDER

OUR SECRET RULERS

A Study in the Hegemony of Parasitism

by

EUSTACE MULLINS

The peoples of the world not only will never love Big Brother, but they will soon dispose of him forever.

The program of the World Order remains the same; Divide and Conquer

---

OMNIA VERITAS

Omnia Veritas Ltd presents:

"KILL THE BEST GENTILES!"
"Tob Shebbe Goyim Harog!"
(THE TALMUD: Sanhedrin 59)

JAMES VON BRUNN

WE ARE WITNESSING today on the world stage a tragedy of enormous proportions: the calculated destruction of the White Race and the incomparable culture it represents

The most concentrated attacks on the White Race are occurring in the United States of America

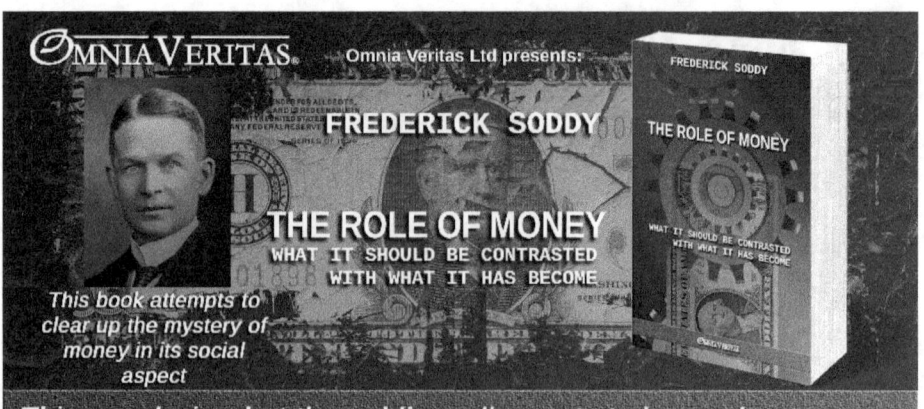

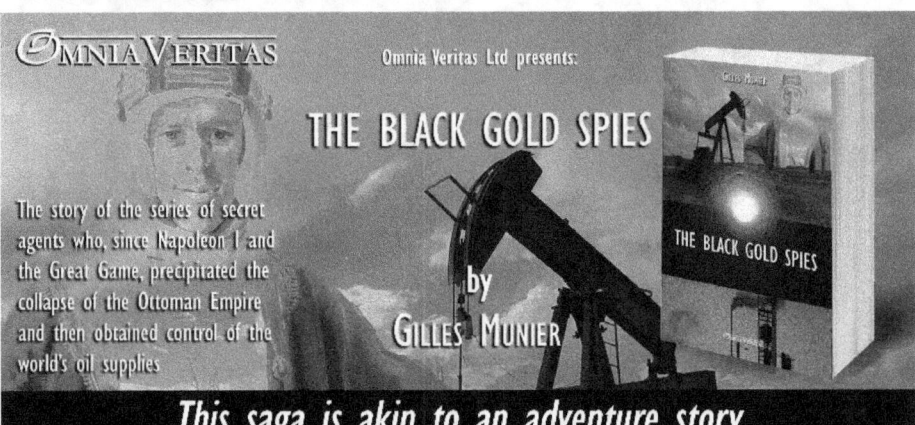

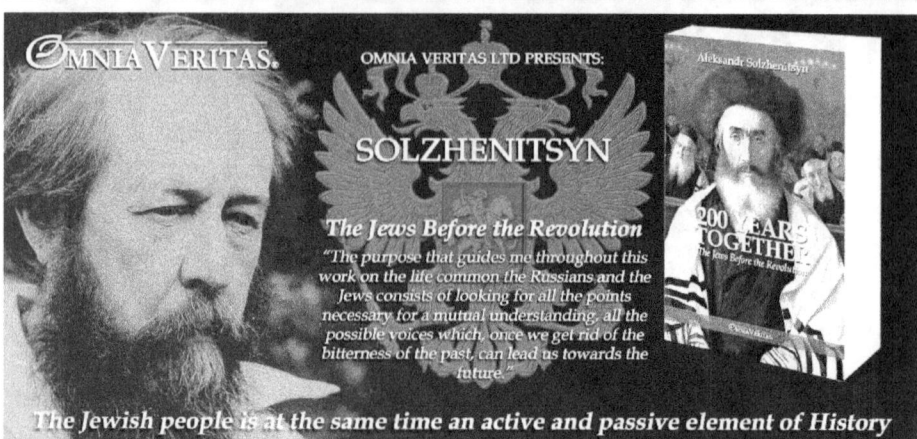

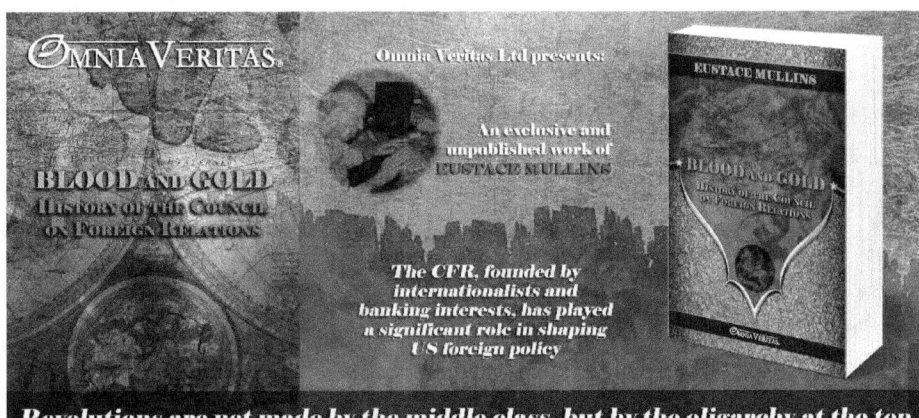
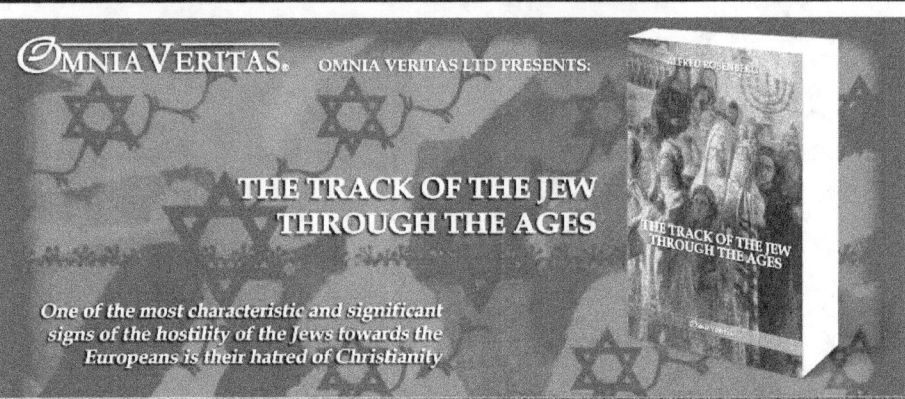

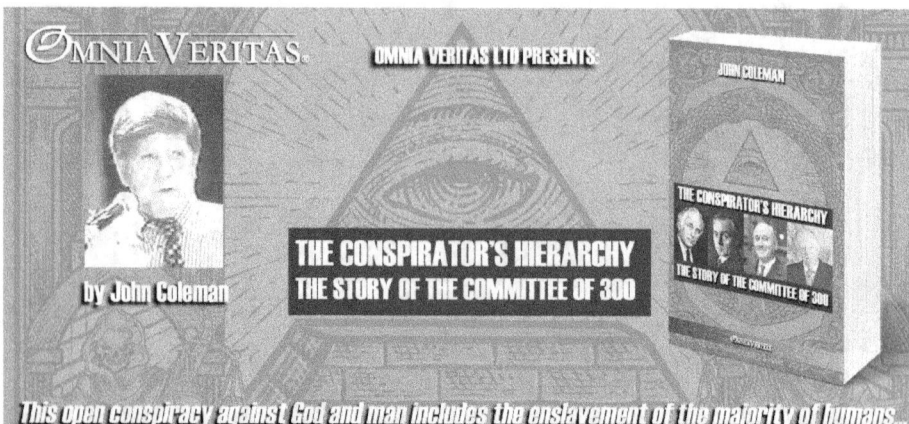

www.ingramcontent.com/pod-product-compliance
Lightning Source LLC
Chambersburg PA
CBHW071947220426
43662CB00009B/1024